ENGAGE, DEBATE, PARTICIPATE

UNITED STATES GOVERNMENT

First Edition

Edited by Jennifer Byrne
James Madison University

cognella®
academic publishing

Bassim Hamadeh, CEO and Publisher
Michael Simpson, Vice President of Acquisitions
Jamie Giganti, Managing Editor
Jess Busch, Senior Graphic Designer
Amy Stone, Acquisitions Editor
Sarah Wheeler, Senior Project Editor/Interior Designer
Natalie Lakosil, Licensing Associate

First published in the United States of America in 2015 by Cognella, Inc.

Printed in the United States of America

ISBN: 978-1-62661-734-6 (pbk)/ 978-1-62661-735-3 (br)

www.cognella.com   800-200-3908

Contents

Introduction

By Jennifer Byrne

Do you ever wonder why it takes so long to pass immigration reform, or what the big deal is over whether suspected terrorists receive trials in New York or Guantanamo Bay? Or, maybe you have absolutely no idea why the new health care reform bill has been so controversial. I mean, what exactly is the broccoli test? And, just maybe, you are wondering why any of this matters anyway! Why do I really need to take a political science class? The truth is that whether you are a politics "junkie" that watches cable news 24 hours a day, 7 days a week or someone who would rather watch paint dry than a political debate, you are affected by politics every day.

So, what is politics and how does it affect my everyday life? Politics is the process of deciding who gets what, when, where, and how; it is essentially a distribution of resources. Politics is the job of government, the vehicle through which policies are made and the affairs of state are conducted. The actions of government are binding on its citizens and residents within its jurisdiction. This means that every time government takes an action, its citizens are directly impacted, and whether it is realized or not, government impacts every aspect of its citizens daily life from rights, security, and health to the workplace, environment, and even relationships. For example, in the United States, government helps to safeguard equality. This does not necessarily mean equality of outcome; the government cannot guarantee that everyone will have a certain job or a certain amount of material wealth, but the government does guarantee that U.S. citizens have an equal opportunity to pursue these goals. Perhaps most importantly, the government guarantees political equality, which has been interpreted by the U.S. Supreme Court to mean: "one person, one vote." That is, all citizens must have equal access to the government and an equal opportunity to influence the decisions that government makes. This also means that all U.S. citizens have the same rights, including the right to complain if their rights are not being respected. Equality can also mean equal protection under the laws and equal accessibility to public goods. For example, the law mandates handicapped access to buildings and requires employers to provide reasonable accommodations to those with disabilities.

Have you ever thought about golfing as a hobby? The sport of golf can illustrate the role of the government in providing equal access. In 2000, professional golfer, Casey Martin, sought to use a golf cart to ride between shots at tour events. Martin has a Klippel-Trenaunay-Weber Syndrome, a circulatory disorder that makes it very painful to walk long distances, which prohibited him from walking the course at the Professional Golfers' Association (PGA) Tour. When Martin requested the use of a golf cart for the duration of the qualification tour, the PGA refused. Martin then sued under Title III of the Americans with Disabilities Act, which mandates an entity operating public accommodations to make reasonable modifications or "accommodations" to individuals with disabilities so long as they do not fundamentally alter the nature of the activity. The PGA asserted that the purpose of walking in between shots is to produce fatigue, which Martin would not endure with the use of such a cart. However, the federal courts found that Martin would already experience substantial fatigue due to his disability, even with the use of a cart, and would not receive any marked advantages over the other players. The PGA also asserted that the players were "entertainers" and not customers that attended the tour and that the PGA was not a public forum subject to the requirements of the law. The courts, once again, disagreed with the PGA, and Martin was able to compete in the tournament, despite his disability; this is an example of politics in action. The requirements of reasonable accommodations extend beyond the golf course and into the workplace. Below are some examples of the way that government affects the everyday lives of its citizens:

Safety and Security: Politicians affect citizens' everyday safety; they make decisions about how many police officers are on the streets and how many streetlights are in each neighborhood, and ensure road and traffic safety. The Environmental Protection Agency ensures that the air is clean, and the Food and Drug Administration ensures that food and medicine are safe for human consumption. The military is also part of the government, and government makes decisions about whether the country is at war or peace.

Work: Not only are employers prohibited from discriminating on the basis of disability, but they cannot discriminate in hiring or promotional policies on the basis of gender or race. In some localities, it is unlawful to discriminate on the basis of sexual orientation.

Health Care: In the U.S., government is not the main provider of health care for most citizens; aside from individuals who are elderly and poor, most residents participate in a privatized system that is predominantly employer-based. However, the government places regulations on these insurance companies. Under the Affordable Care Act, insurance companies are subject to requirements and restrictions. For example, insurance companies cannot drop someone when they become sick or deny them coverage for a pre-existing condition. Insurance companies also must provide routine check-ups and place a cap on out-of-pocket expenses. Thus, the government can affect the quality and cost of the health care that is received from the market.

While you may expect that the government will be involved in issues that guarantee basic health and security, you might not realize the extent to which your everyday life overlaps with politics. What do you plan to do this weekend? Perhaps you plan to do some shopping, try a new restaurant, or even go to a night club? If you go shopping, you will most likely find that you will have to pay a tax on what you buy; this tax money is collected by the government to provide resources, such as roads and schools, to its citizens. If you decide to eat out, the restaurant you dine at must work with the government to pass a health and safety inspection and be given a license to operate and serve food to the public. Finally, if you choose to go to a night club, the government may regulate how late at night the club is allowed to stay open, whether it can serve alcohol, and the noise level it produces. As you can see, the government is ubiquitous, and since the power of the government is derived from the people in a democracy, this does not have to be a negative reality. You will find that, based on ideology, citizens may debate the scope of government involvement in daily activities, affairs abroad, and the free market. But nearly all citizens agree, even many Libertarians who want to limit the scope of government involvement the most, that government has a role to play and basic functions to provide for its people.

This textbook is designed to provide an overview of the history, institutions, and current political debates of the U.S. In addition, you will learn to become an informed citizen and evaluate arguments presented on both sides of the political spectrum. I have divided the presentation of the course material into three sections; in the first section, we will examine the question, "Who are we?" by taking a critical look at American values, exceptionalism, and political culture. We will then turn our attention to the U.S. Constitution and survey the institutions of our government, with an emphasis on the three branches. Finally, we will engage ideas and behavior in American politics by examining topics such as civil liberties and rights, voting behavior, civic engagement, and public opinion.

CHAPTER 1

Why Do We Need Government?

Chapter 1 Vignette

By Jennifer Byrne

In 2001, a U.S.-led effort called Operation Enduring Freedom sought to dismantle the Taliban in Afghanistan in the wake of the September 11, 2011, terrorist attacks in New York City and implement a democratic-style of government in place of the existing totalitarian regime. In a totalitarian regime, the ability to rule and make the decisions of government is restricted to a few individuals who rule in their own interest. The power of the state is centralized and the people of a totalitarian country are controlled in a strict manner under the complete power of the regime with little to no authority to exercise power. Totalitarian regimes are often called "undemocratic" because of this concentration of power and the absence of a meaningful role for the people to play. In contrast, a democracy allows many to participate in its government and make decisions that distribute resources and benefits to as many people as possible. In 2004, Afghanistan had open elections to allow its people to decide who would govern the country, and dreams of building an American-style democracy were beginning to be realized. However, corruption in Afghanistan is now rampant, and the people's trust in the government has been corroded. For example, if one needs to settle a dispute about house ownership, one must pay $25,000. If one is arrested, one must pay a bribe to the police to be released, or should one want to be a police chief, the going rate is $100,000! In fact, most public transactions and positions of power require a bribe. The government itself has ties to the country's opium trade, reputed to be the largest in the world. In short, corruption is widespread and this interferes with the ability for a democracy to flourish in Afghanistan.

Why? In a democracy, the government is responsive to the people. Under the notion of the social contract theory, a democracy's citizens give up some of their rights in the state of nature (a state before the existence of societies where there are no limits except for one's own conscience) in order to receive some benefits from the government in return. The government is supposed to provide its citizens with a uniform rule of law, public goods, a common defense, and the protection of civil liberties. For example, on a deserted island, someone could take your property through physical force; however, with a government in place, rights to property are protected, and those who infringe upon these rights are penalized. The government provides its citizens with public goods, such as police protection, a judicial system, and roads and other infrastructure. In a democracy, it is expected that all citizens have access to these things equally, but in Afghanistan, this is not the case. Only the very wealthy or those with political connections have access to the basic services and products that government is supposed to provide for its people. In a democratic system, the government is sanctioned by the people, meaning that it must always be accountable to the people. In a totalitarian regime, the government derives its power by force and coercion; however, in a democracy, the government derives its power from an agreement with its citizens. Corruption can disturb this very important connection, because it employs the use of a political office for one's own benefit. Rather than distributing benefits uniformly to citizens, benefits are concentrated to a very limited group of individuals. This can cause citizens' trust in government to weaken, and results in a lack of political efficacy. Citizens may begin to think that the government does not care about them and that they are powerless to affect the government's actions.

Critics may believe that Afghanistan's problems stem from the fact that they have not been a democracy for very long, but even in the United States, corruption remains a significant problem. Aside from investigations into terrorism and cybercrime, the FBI spends most of its resources on corruption charges in the U.S. Furthermore, there have been many prominent politicians who acted for their own personal gain rather than in the interest of the people they represented. William Jefferson, a congressman from Louisiana, was indicted for 11 different bribe schemes after large sums of cash were found in his freezer. Rod Blagojevich, the governor of Illinois, was charged with conspiracy, including the alleged solicitation of a personal benefit in exchange for appointment in the U.S. Senate, as one of the state's two seats became open when Barack Obama became President in 2008. He was subsequently found guilty on 17 charges of corruption. In addition to isolated incidents, democratic activist Bryan Weaver declared, "when it comes to Washington, D.C., there's a culture of corruption that really exists. What gets passed off as politics as usual are huge ethical lapses." Examples of this ingrained corruption in the Washington, D.C., are accusations of bank fraud and campaign-finance violations among councilmen, and the resignation

of Harry Thomas, Jr., to serve jail time for embezzling $353,500 in taxpayer funds for programs intended for children.[1]

And the faith in the institutions of government reflect the toll that corruption has taken on the American public—in some instances, congressional approval ratings are less than 10 percent. The fact that the government has struggled at times to function ideally has led to a widespread use of satire to expose its failings. Satire is the use of irony, humor, exaggeration, and/or sarcasm to expose deficiencies and make serious points, most often in the context of contemporary politics and current events. One such example of sarcasm is a nightly "news" broadcast called *The Daily Show* with John Stewart. The host, John Stewart, makes use of the art of satire to discuss politics. One such clip is called, "The Congressional Approver," in which a news correspondent takes to the streets of New York City to find someone who actually approves of the Congress is doing, in light of its very low approval ratings in public opinion polls. After many scathing diatribes about the inadequacies of the current government, the newscaster finds a citizen, Howard Schmool, who says that he approves of Congress. After her initial shock at finding someone so "rare" and "exotic," she turns on her investigative reporting skills to determine what the world must look like to a "14 Percenter," or one of the few Americans who approve of the current Congress. What she finds is that Schmool is an easy-going guy who doesn't mind traffic, portable toilets, greasy pizza, or the Spiderman show on Broadway. The correspondent even takes him to the hospital to get a brain scan; the wit of it all, to suggest that someone must not be right in the head if they actually approve of Congress! Through the use of exaggeration and near ridicule of Schmool, she demonstrates that Congress has alienated many Americans, thereby decreasing political efficacy and trust in government. Through the use of humor, they have exposed how corruption and inefficiency within the government destroys the link between the people and their representatives.

Corruption is particularly problematic in a democracy, because it undermines the citizens' trust in the rule of law, which is one of the most critical functions that a government provides. Because democracies are based on the principle of majority rule, benefits that are concentrated to a select few or directed to one individual diminish the governmental access of the rest of the people. Equality of access and the opportunity for equal influence over the government is the lynchpin of political equality, a very important concept to democratic rule. In the case of rampant corruption, a democracy can quickly degenerate into an oligarchy, a system of government in which many people can rule, but do so only in the interest of a few. Oligarchies are often characterized by large wealth disparities in the population.

One solution to combat corruption is to involve more people in the political process. Citizens may donate their time or their money to political campaigns, and use their voting power to remove politicians that have not upheld the social contract. However, some citizens may have more money to donate to politicians or to organizations that support them than others. In an attempt to regulate "big money" campaign contributions, the Bipartisan Reform Act sought to restrict the timing of "electioneering communications," and it prevented corporations and labor unions from funding such communications from their general treasuries. In *Citizens United v. Federal Election Commission*, an injunction was placed against the showing of *Hillary: The Movie* sponsored by the Conservative lobbying organization Citizens United, which some argued amounted to an electioneering broadcast, because it expressed opinions about whether Hillary Rodham Clinton would make a good president. Upon hearing the case, the Supreme Court decided that since political contributions were akin to free speech, that corporations and unions should not be restricted from raising money and independently producing such broadcasts. In order to mitigate the amount of influence that they could have on the political process, the Court prohibited these organizations from coordinating directly with political parties or candidates. Thus, the organizations should be entirely independent and can raise unlimited amounts of money and produce unlimited advertising campaigns in support or opposition of candidates. One of the criticisms of this case is

that corporations and unions have been given the same rights to free speech as individuals. While this may be controversial in itself, it also has been argued that these entities may drown out the voices of individuals in the political process. How many people are able to spend hundreds of thousands of dollars, and possibly millions or more, to produce ads each election cycle? Yet, these ads have the power to reach millions of Americans. The mixed reception of the Supreme Court's decision can be seen by the statements made in its aftermath by prominent political players:

Citizens United, the group filing the lawsuit said, "Today's U.S. Supreme Court decision allowing Citizens United to air its documentary films and advertisements is a tremendous victory, not only for Citizens United but for every American who desires to participate in the political process."[2] Heritage Foundation fellow Hans A. von Spakovsky, a former Republican member of the Federal Election Commission, said, "The Supreme Court has restored a part of the First Amendment that had been unfortunately stolen by Congress and a previously wrongly-decided ruling of the court."[3]

President Barack Obama stated that the decision "gives the special interests and their lobbyists even more power in Washington—while undermining the influence of average Americans who make small contributions to support their preferred candidates."[4] Obama later elaborated in his weekly radio address saying, "this ruling strikes at our democracy itself" and "I can't think of anything more devastating to the public interest"[5]

A follow-up of the Citizens United decision has come before the Supreme Court this current term. In this case, the caps that are on individual contributions are challenged as a violation of Freedom of Speech.[6] While individuals are capped at donating $2,600 to any given candidate in an election (which is not an issue in the Supreme Court), they are also capped at donating a total of $48,600 every two years for all individual candidate donations. They argue that the law is restricting them from "too much First Amendment" activity. Emily Bazelon, a senior fellow at Yale Law School, argues that the caps were put in place by Congress to prevent corruption and preserve the link between all people and the government. If one individual donates more money, he or she may gain more attention and substantive benefits from the politicians that they support; this is something that an individual with little or no money to donate may not be able to do. In this case, one could conceive of a potential oligarchy, whereby many can govern, but do so in the interest of a select few. In such a system, the gap between the rich and the poor will become very wide, and political influence may be affected by one's wealth. However, one of the charges of government, its most basic function, is to protect liberties. So, should wealthy individuals be able to exercise this liberty without such restrictions?

Endnotes

1. http://articles.washingtonpost.com/2012-06-09/local/35459133_1_william-p-lightfoot-political-corruption-barry, last accessed on November 22, 2013.

2. http://www.politico.com/blogs/bensmith/0110/Citizens_United_on_Citizens_United.html, last accessed on November 22, 2013.

3. http://www.washingtontimes.com/news/2010/jan/21/divided-court-strikes-down-campaign-money-restrict/?page=all, last accessed on November 22, 2013.

4. http://www.whitehouse.gov/the-press-office/statement-president-todays-supreme-court-decision-0, last accessed on November 22, 2013.

5. http://www.whitehouse.gov/the-press-office/weekly-address-president-obama-vows-continue-standing-special-interests-behalf-amer, last accessed on November 22, 2013.

6. http://www.nytimes.com/2013/10/09/us/politics/supreme-court-weighs-campaign-contribution-limits.html?_r=1&, last accessed on November 18, 2013.

Preface

By Matthew Kerbel

Understanding and Using This Book

Unifying Themes: Accessibility, Relevance, and Choice

For many of us, government seems distant and irrelevant—in part because it's so big, in part because it's hard to draw the connection between what political figures do and the things that have meaning in our lives. I constantly talk to students who don't care about the political world, don't see how it affects them, or don't wish to find out. Maybe you feel that way, too. If you do, it certainly doesn't help to have an American government text that portrays government as a far-away abstraction. Too often, I've heard my students complain about government texts being too plodding and inaccessible. I've heard similar complaints from professors.

Here, you'll be presented with an entirely different version of American government. Think of it as an up-close version, where abstractions give way to gritty fundamentals, revealing a government composed of all-too-ordinary people who share our daily concerns and priorities. Members of

Congress struggle to fit in and find ways to get their homework done. Lobbyists struggle to beat out other lobbyists and make the case that will win over members of Congress. Supreme Court justices play high-stakes poker with their colleagues in an effort to shape their decisions on a case without realizing they've been influenced. The political system is filled with situations like these and with people trying to do their jobs under conditions of uncertainty and in the face of great time pressures.

If this sounds familiar, that's the point. Government cannot be relevant to our lives until we're able to see it in terms that make sense to us. This book will encourage you to experience American government in a way to which you can relate, because the truth is that when you strip away the generalizations and remove the distance, the people and situations you encounter in Washington or in your state capital are remarkably like those you encounter in any institution or social situation—including college.

Making government less mysterious and more real should make it easier for you to wrestle with the central question of the book: What do you want your relationship to government and politics to be? We all have a choice to participate in the political system or to opt out, and if we choose to participate, we also can decide how much and in what form we want to get involved. There are a lot of options, starting with voting and branching out to include reading about politics, posting a diary to an online political weblog, giving money to a political cause or candidate, sending email to an elected representative, engaging in protest demonstrations, and much more.

Because the choice of whether and how to participate is deeply personal, only you can make it, and by the time you've finished with this book, I sincerely hope you are interested in doing just that: deciding what you want your political role to be. I could spend sixteen chapters telling you why I believe it's important for you to participate—and I do believe it's important, or I wouldn't have bothered writing this book—but what's the point of that? It's far more important for you to decide for yourself what, if anything, you're going to do, to have ownership of your decision, and to feel comfortable with it. You may conclude that you don't want to have a role in politics or that it doesn't matter whether or not you get involved. With this book, I'll help you make an informed decision, whatever that decision may be.

How This Book Is Organized

Think of this book as a round-trip journey on which you are the navigator. It's a round-trip journey because if you were to read the book straight through, you'd find that in the last four chapters of the book, we're back to talking about some of the same issues we discuss in the first two, reconsidering them in light of everything we've learned along the way. In five parts encompassing sixteen chapters, American Government: Your Voice, Your Future 4e maps out a route designed to take you from understanding your place in the political system to how people connect with government, how the political system works and what it does, and finally—to come full circle—how responsive it is to your demands and desires.

Part 1 Why Should We Care about American Democracy?

We'll start with background on the fundamental concepts you'll need to understand if you're going to be able to make an intelligent decision about what you want your political role, if any, to be. Although this is the most abstract portion of the book, the concepts are illustrated with concrete examples. Think of this part as a presentation of the building blocks you'll need for the rest of the book and the place where you'll encounter foundational questions about the role and purpose of government that will set the tone for the discussions that follow.

Chapter 1 Should We Care about Politics? The question posed by the chapter title is one you will be able to answer for yourself by the time you've finished reading this book. It's a personal question with no correct answer, but an informed response necessitates understanding how government fits into everyday life—whether we care about politics or not. Chapter 1 addresses how societies come together to make choices about governing themselves, discussing the fundamentals of such things as authority, legitimacy, power, equality, and liberty.

Chapter 2 The Constitution and Federalism: Setting the Ground Rules for Politics The Constitution establishes the broad outlines for how American government operates, and federalism is one of the most important and distinctive features of the American system. Together, the Constitution and federalism shape the rules for American politics. We'll look at the origin, makeup, and evolution of both, keeping an eye on how the ground rules influence who is favored and who is disadvantaged in the political process.

Part 2 Citizenship and Democracy

Moving from a discussion of concepts to a discussion of their application, this section explores the parallel issues of how the United States developed as a nation and how individual Americans develop—or don't develop—into political creatures. We'll examine public opinion about politics and politicians, the elements of political culture that lead people to identify as Americans, aspects of political socialization that acquaint us with that culture while teaching the basics of civic involvement, and the kinds of political participation in which, once socialized, we may choose to engage.

Chapter 3 What Is Public Opinion, and What Does It Have to Do with Me? To answer the question posed in the chapter title, we'll look at three important components of public opinion: political knowledge, attitudes, and beliefs. Political knowledge is our factual understanding of politics, and we'll find that it tends to be not particularly extensive. Political attitudes encompass how we feel about politics, such as whether we feel distant from political figures and what they do. Political beliefs involve what we think is true about politics. Together, these elements of public opinion influence the way we relate to what politicians do.

Chapter 4 Who Are We, and What Do We Do? By broadening the discussion of public opinion to include issues of national and individual identity, we consider ways that Americans unite as a nation, come of age as political individuals, and engage in political action. National self-identification is rooted in something we call political culture. The process of political socialization explores how important people in our lives shape our adult perspectives on politics and government. The political activities we might consider doing encompass a variety of forms of political participation—from voting to attending protest rallies.

Part 3 Connections between Citizens and Government

Once we have explored the nature of public opinion and the origins of political involvement, we'll look at three institutions that link us to the people who represent us in government: the mass media, political parties, and interest groups. When working properly, each of these institutions functions like the connective tissue of government by channeling citizen demands and concerns to political figures and information about political figures to citizens. As we'll see, sometimes these connections aren't as clear or as simple as you might expect.

Chapter 5 Mass Media: Influencing What We Think About The media comprise the first of the three linking institutions that we'll examine. Most everyone is familiar with media like television, radio, newspapers, and the Internet, but we may have thought of these media only as sources of entertainment. They also play a central role in politics by providing us directly and indirectly with information that can shape the way we think about our government and the people in it. We'll look at how they do it and evaluate how effectively the media keep us informed about politics and government.

Chapter 6 Political Parties: Connecting Us to the Electoral Process Political parties may be less familiar to us than the media, even though they help to organize a lot of political activity, particularly in terms of how candidates for office are recruited, funded, and ultimately elected. This is the case despite the fact that the Constitution does not provide for parties. We'll look at why the United States has only two major parties (most nations have more), explore how political parties have evolved through American history, and examine how parties are organized and what they do.

Chapter 7 Campaigns and Elections: Vehicles for Democratic Expression One of the most important functions of political parties is structuring the way we choose elected officials. We'll devote a chapter to examining this essential role of parties in connecting candidates and voters. We'll spend some time in the cutthroat world of political campaigns, where the stakes are high and the winner takes all, examining the process for selecting candidates, the strategies candidates use to try to win elections, and the vital role of money in the campaign process.

Chapter 8 Interest Groups: Accessing Government through Common Membership Probably the least familiar of our three linking organizations, interest groups are nonetheless vital to determining important national policies, as people who organize around common interests are the ones who are best positioned to be heard by elected leaders. We will consider what interest groups are, where they come from, why people belong to them, the resources they have to get the ear of government officials, and the way they use those resources to advance their agendas.

Part 4   Institutions of Democracy

The discussion of institutions that connect us with government will lead directly to Part 4, where we address the operation of the institutions that constitute government: Congress, the presidency, the federal bureaucracy, and the judiciary. Rather than regarding them as abstractions, we will treat these institutions as organizations run by people just like us, who (also just like us) have goals and objectives and a lot of work to do, and who try to advance their objectives as best they can with limited resources. We'll look at the world of Washington as a place where lots of people press to get all sorts of things done, looking for allies to help them, while trying to dodge the equally determined efforts of those who oppose them.

Chapter 9 Congress We will begin Part 4 by looking at Congress. Like any institution, including your college or university, Congress operates under a set of unspoken rules that attempt to promote civility and encourage compromise. We'll look at these rules and how Congress is organized to facilitate legislative work—a rather messy process in which it's far easier to frustrate someone else's initiative than it is to get something accomplished. **Chapter 10 The Presidency** The presidency is probably the most visible office in the world, yet it can be surprisingly mysterious—and complex. There is a highly institutionalized side to the presidency composed of a web of offices and presidential advisors operating within the White House. At the same time, the presidency is the most personal of government institutions, responding more to the character of its chief occupant than any other political office. We'll look at how strong presidents have shaped the office and at the many—often contradictory— roles we ask the president to assume.

Chapter 11 The Federal Bureaucracy The president is the chief executive, and the branch of government he ostensibly heads is the executive branch, or the federal bureaucracy. Even though it may be less well known than the president himself, the federal bureaucracy has an important place in the functioning of Washington. Hierarchical and specialized, it is a sometimes explosive mix of lifelong civil servants and political appointees who serve at the president's pleasure. With the president as the head of the executive branch, you might think that bureaucrats would be responsive to him, but the reality is far more complicated. We'll explore why as we examine the functions bureaucrats perform.

Chapter 12 The Judiciary Perhaps the most mysterious branch of government, the judiciary can be just as political as any other institution—despite its dark-robed justices and secretive deliberations. From state courts to the federal courts, up to and including the United States Supreme Court, the judiciary faces a dilemma: It is charged with making judgments it has no power to enforce. As we look at how the court system is constituted, we will explore the informal mechanisms available to judges and justices that give them standing to confront others in the political system.

Part 5 What Government Does and How It Works

We ask our government officials to do two important things: (1) to protect the rights and liberties discussed in Part 1 and (2) to make policy on behalf of the country. We'll see how some policies are more controversial than others and how even the least controversial policies can have their detractors. Does discord mean government isn't responding well to our needs—or is it just a characteristic of being human that we're going to have disagreements about the policies government produces? We'll consider these issues by looking at policy from the standpoint of government responsiveness. We'll examine how effectively the officials we discussed in Part 4 listen to the voices expressed through the institutions we discussed in Part 3—voices reflecting opinions and participation styles of people like us, as we discussed in Part 2.

Chapter 13 Establishing Civil Rights Civil rights policies ensure that the law treats everyone equally and protects individuals from discrimination. We will explore the history and development of civil rights law as it pertains to the struggle for equal treatment fought for by groups that have historically experienced discrimination in America: African

Americans, Native Americans, Latinos, women, Asian Americans, disabled individuals, gays and lesbians, and senior citizens.

Chapter 14 Protecting Civil Liberties Civil liberties are constitutional and legal protections against government infringement on personal freedoms. This encompasses a wide range of freedoms, almost all of which are universally accepted in principle but may be controversial in practice. For instance, the Constitution prohibits the government from restricting religious freedom, but does this right extend to permitting prayer in public places? The Constitution establishes the right of Americans to bear arms, but is this a relatively unrestricted personal right to own firearms or a collective right to form militias? We will explore questions like these, which illustrate the complexity of civil liberties.

Chapter 15 Domestic Policy and Policy Making Domestic policies include budgetary decisions, regulations, and legislation pertaining to how Americans resolve domestic problems. Regulatory policies give government a role in adjusting the marketplace in ways that would not otherwise occur, in order to minimize hazards created by a free market or to maximize its benefits. Domestic legislation comes in several forms, most notably distributive policies, which claim tax dollars for projects or programs that could potentially benefit anyone, and redistributive policies, which transfer resources from one group to another. Because domestic policy decisions have "losers" who bear the cost and "winners" who benefit, they can be controversial. We'll explore this controversy in detail.

Chapter 16 Foreign and Defense Policies Foreign policy is about how the United States conducts itself as a nation among other nations. It encompasses a host of economic, diplomatic, and military concerns, ranging from questions about global trade to relationships with other nations and how much to invest in maintaining a military. An extensive network of political advisors, diplomats, military personnel, and international leaders shape the direction of foreign policy and influence foreign policy decisions, which because of their life-and-death implications are among the most crucial decisions a nation has to make.

A Word on Critical Thinking

You'll find that the more you learn about how American government operates and affects your life, the more important it will be to have the skills to assess the many claims that politicians and elected officials make. Critical thinking skills make navigating the political process possible. With them, you can evaluate the content of news stories, determine if a policy proposal is in your best interest, assess whether claims made by your senator about her performance in office accurately represent her record—all things you'll need to do to have a meaningful political voice.

That's why this book approaches the American political system as a forum for developing critical thinking skills. From the outset, when we talk about the origins and foundation of the political system, through the closing chapters that connect those foundations with policies that affect our daily lives, we'll never stop asking questions about how theory is connected to practice, or why citizens, politicians, reporters, lobbyists, and judges act the way they do, or whether an observation about government is rooted in opinion or fact. Questions like these will develop and sharpen the analytical tools that will make us better citizens—and students—and help us make intelligent decisions about whether and how to participate in politics.

Before You Start:

How to Use This Book

Five things set *American Government: Your Voice, Your Future* 4e apart from conventional textbooks. They are:

· Student Options: Print and Online Versions
· Natural and relaxed writing style
· Modular presentation
· Ease of navigation and repetition
· Interactive study tool: StudyUpGrade

Here's a quick overview of each one.

Student Options: Print and Online Versions

American Government: Your Voice, Your Future 4e is available in multiple versions, offered online, in PDF, and in print. The content of each version is identical. The most affordable version is the online book, with upgrade options including the online version bundled with printable PDF or paperback. What's nice about the print version is it offers you the freedom of being unplugged—away from your computer. The people at Textbook Media recognize that it's difficult to read from a screen at length and that most of us read much faster from a piece of paper. The print options are particularly useful when you have extended print passages like this one to read. Then, you can turn to the Online Edition to take full advantage of the digital version, including search, notes and chat. Use the Search feature to locate and jump to discussions anywhere in the book. You can move out of the book to follow web links. You can navigate within and between chapters using a clickable Table of Contents. These features allow you to work at your own pace and in your own style, as you read and surf your way through the material. (See below for more tips on working with the online version.)

Whether you're working in print or online, each chapter concludes with a set of features designed to reinforce and expand what you've learned, including a concise chapter review, a list of key terms, an annotated bibliography that lists readings you could consult for research projects, and a list of notes with follow-up information.

Natural and Relaxed Writing Style

Conventional textbooks supply you with information. *American Government: Your Voice, Your Future* 4e is a book that can teach. It's not a substitute for the learning you do in class—no book can be—but it is a core learning tool in a way that traditional books cannot be. The difference lies in the way the material is presented to you. Some of this comes from the interactive capability of working online, but an important component of teaching is how information is presented. That's where the style of the book comes into play.

I'm sure you've already noticed that this book has an informal, open quality. That's by design. The intent is to have a conversation between author and reader, much like you would find in a first-person novel or an in-class lecture. The philosophy that guided the writing of this book is that learning is a dynamic process and that we learn best when we interact with the material—when we feel engaged in the story a book tells. In this regard, both the online and print versions are designed to be interactive learning devices. Both present a detailed and thoughtful account of the people, processes, systems, and institutions that comprise American government in an engaging, challenging, personalized, true-to-life manner that talks to you rather than down to you or past you.

Modular Presentation

Most of us are used to learning one chunk of information at a time. So *American Government: Your Voice, Your Future* 4e reduces information to its component parts for easier digestion. You may have noticed how this preface is broken into small, modular sections; in the online version, it's on several brief screens that you can move through quickly and easily. The entire book follows this format.

Moreover, the construction of this book permits some deviation from the traditional linear textbook model, where material is presented through a running text narrative offset with secondary material in boxes. In this book, the set-aside information is not secondary at all, but core text that appears in pedagogical boxes. These features may illuminate or elaborate on a point in the text, or they may use something in the text as a point of departure for a related discussion. They should be regarded as core material, not peripheral content you can ignore.

This is important to remember because it defies convention. You may have seen textbooks that are dotted with little bordered "boxes" that scream, "This is secondary material—don't read me!" Such is not the case with the boxes in this text. Far from it. As you navigate the book, you will find color-coded boxes that supplement the core text by explaining complicated processes in simple terms, placing material about American government in a global context, and challenging you to think about issues and political events. In particular, you will encounter:

- *Demystifying Government* boxes, which clarify things about American Government which might otherwise seem cloudy or complex (light blue boxes);
- *Global Topics* boxes, which invite you to think comparatively about American government in an increasingly interconnected world (red boxes);
- *Biography* boxes, which illustrate the lives of key political figures, helping you to figure out how they fit into the American political system (green boxes);
- *Issue* boxes, which invite you to think about political issues and decide for yourself how you feel about difficult and controversial matters (dark blue boxes).

You'll find glossary terms and footnotes in this material, just like you'll find in the body of a chapter. The only difference is in the way you navigate through them. Having material set aside like this permits you to read ahead and come back if you so choose. It's another way this book presents you with a nonlinear approach to the material. You just have to remember not to ignore it.

Ease of Navigation and Repetition

Whether you're working online or with print, you'll find that the design of the book allows you to move quickly and easily within and between chapters, jumping ahead to explore an essay or game that applies to what you're reading, bouncing back to a place you've already been to review something you haven't seen in awhile. Because repetition is an important part of learning, key terms introduced early in the book are emphasized again when they appear in later chapters, and because we often forget some of what we learned weeks and months ago, key segments of early chapters are repeated for quick review when they are relevant to understanding material in later chapters. It's all part of the philosophy of having a book that teaches rather than simply presents information.

StudyUpGrade—an interactive study tool

You can turbo-charge your online version of *American Government: Your Voice, Your Future* 4e with a unique study tool designed to "up your grade." StudyUpgrade is a software package that layers self-scoring quizzes and flash cards into your online versions. This inexpensive upgrade help you improve your grades through the use of interactive content that's built into each chapter. Features include self-scoring multiple choice quizzes, key concept reviews with fill-in-the-blank prompts, and e-flash cards comprised of key term definitions. For more on this helpful study tool, check out the flash demo at the Textbook Media site.

Harnessing the Online Versions

American Government: Your Voice, Your Future 4e contains the following online features to facilitate

learning and to make using the book an easy, enjoyable experience:

- *Clickable Table of Contents* You can surf through the book quickly by clicking on chapter headings, or first- or second-level section headings. And the Table of Contents can be accessed from anywhere in the book.
- *Key concepts search* Type in a term, and a search engine will return every instance of that term in the book; then jump directly to the selection of your choice with a click of your mouse.
- *Flash-card glossary and self-scoring quizzes* The StudyUpGrade content at the end of each chapter contains self-scoring quizzes, fill-in-he-blank key concepts reviews and e-flash cards using key terms and glossary items.
- *Notes, Highlighting and Chat* Online versions include study apps such as notes, highlighting, and chat. Each of these apps can be found in the tools icon embedded in Textbook Media's online reading platform.

Supplementing the Book

In addition to containing unique online features, *American Government: Your Voice, Your Future* 4e comes with the following supplements on an instructor's CD:

- *Test Item File* A customized test bank available in ExamView Pro containing 100 short-answer questions per chapter for creating original quizzes and exams.
- *Instructor's Manual* An enhanced version of the book offering assistance in preparing lectures, identifying learning objectives, developing essay exams and assignments, and constructing course syllabi.
- *PowerPoint Presentations* Key points in each chapter are illustrated in a set of PowerPoint files designed to assist with instruction.

Should We Care About Politics?

By Matthew Kerbel

Introduction

During your lifetime, when you may or may not have been paying attention to politics, the United States experienced in rapid succession a string of unprecedented shocks to its political system.

Conservatives, led by Republican Newt Gingrich, swept away forty years of Democratic control of the House of Representatives in a massive upset that installed a new order in Congress that ruled at will—for a little less than a year. The Gingrich group soon overplayed its hand and was repudiated by a crafty Bill Clinton, who used his platform as president to turn public opinion against his political adversaries.

Yet, just as Clinton appeared to ascend politically, events surrounding his extracurricular activities with a White House intern named Monica Lewinsky snowballed into impeachment proceedings against him. It was only the second time in history that a president was brought to the brink of political extinction by a Senate impeachment trial. Clinton survived, only to see his handpicked successor, Vice President Al Gore, lose the next presidential election, despite winning more votes than his opponent—only the fourth time in history that happened—and only after the election went

into a seven-week overtime period of ballot challenges that culminated in an unprecedented 5–4 Supreme Court decision that effectively installed George W. Bush in the White House. No one had ever witnessed anything quite like it.

The Republican Bush took office with razor-thin Republican majorities in the House and Senate, only to see the Senate flip to Democratic control within months of his inauguration when one moderate Republican, feeling ignored by the conservative White House, left his party to become an independent. Nothing like this had ever happened before.

If afternoon soap operas had a political theme, this one would have had enough intrigue, sex, and ego to run a long, long time.

But if you didn't notice much of this, or didn't hear your parents talk too much about it—join the club. For all of its great story elements, during times of peace and prosperity, many of us pay little attention to politics, and even if we do pay attention, we often have vague impressions of what's going on rather than fully formed opinions. That's just the way politics works in our lives.

Then came the horrific events of September 11, 2001: the terrorist attacks on the World Trade Center and the Pentagon, and a virtual declaration of war by Washington on terrorism. For many of us, politics was instantly thrust into the center of our daily lives. As anthrax-coated letters began appearing in the mail, Americans of all generations began turning to our elected leaders for reassurance and to government agencies for help. Such is the way of life in a crisis, when public decisions supersede private actions. This, too, is the way politics works in our lives.

In the days following the attack, Americans experienced a wave of unity and national purpose, and political differences were briefly put aside. But, good feelings soon gave way to an era of partisan rancor greater than anything we saw in the 1990s. The invasion of Iraq, initially supported by members of both major political parties and large majorities of Americans, became bogged down in the wake of an insurgency that could not be tamed or overcome. American casualties grew as more people started to regard Iraq as a war of choice justified by questionable claims about the security threat posed by the regime of Saddam Hussein, rather than as a war of necessity fought to protect us from terrorism.

In 2004, a divided nation re-elected President Bush after a high-decibel campaign marked by shrill rhetoric. By 2005, anti-war sentiment entered the mainstream in response to the actions of Cindy Sheehan (see picture, below), the mother of a fallen soldier, who camped out at Bush's Texas ranch during the president's August vacation, demanding that he answer her questions about why America was in Iraq. Her simple act of defiance gave voice to growing anti-war feelings and spawned an anti-Sheehan counter-movement that vocally defended the president and his policy. With no end to the war in sight, public support for the war dissipated, leaving George W. Bush a deeply unpopular president and many Americans with a sour feeling about the direction of the country.

Then came a deep recession and, in 2008, a financial crisis that rocked confidence in global markets and had some economists speculating about whether we were on the verge of a second Great Depression. Against this backdrop, promising to bridge partisan divisions and re-shape America's direction, Barack Obama was elected the first African American President of the United States—a feat so remarkable that, until it happened, mainstream political commentators wondered whether it was possible despite polling evidence that suggested it was inevitable.

In can be draining to come of age in the midst of such tumultuous political activity—but it can be energizing as well, depending on how we react to it. And our reactions can be critical to determining how political events will play out. Whether we pay a lot of attention to politics or ignore it completely, whether in times of comfort or times of anxiety, we live in a country where you can draw a straight line between your choice of whether or not to get involved and the kind of government we get. No one will make you vote if you don't want to, and no one will make you watch the news (well, your professor might, but you'll be back to having free choice over your news-viewing habits in a few months). You can make your own choices about what you know and whether or how much to get involved. Some combination of these individual decisions—and the choice to be apolitical is a decision—determines what happens in Washington, in your state capital, in your community, and to you.

So, should we care about what happens in politics? Does it really matter? Does it only matter in times of crisis? Wait—don't answer yet. Let's talk first about where you fit in—about the big and small ways your American citizenship invites you to interact with democracy—before deciding whether it's worth your time and energy to give politics and government a second thought once you're done with this course. Let's use the quiz in Table 1.1 as a starting point.

Table 1.1. Is It Relevant?

Here's a list of activities that may or may not constitute ways we can interact with democracy. Select the ones you believe have something to do with your relationship with government or politics.

1. Voting in a congressional election
2. Watching the Daily Show on Comedy Central
3. Joining AAA (American Automobile Association) for towing services
4. Trying to drive 10 miles over the speed limit to avoid getting a ticket
5. Making a $10 contribution to a candidate for mayor
6. Attending a private college or university
7. Camping out at Yosemite
8. Buying a Diet Coke
9. Buying a lottery ticket
10. Flushing the toilet

They're all "Yes" answers. Surprised? Here are the reasons why:

1. Easy question: voting is the most obvious way we participate in politics.
2. Political and social satire get us to think about what government is doing.
3. Even though it may not be why we join, organizations like AAA lobby elected officials over legislation.
4. Government officials write a lot of rules we live under, like speed limit laws, and enforce them with agents like police officers who determine whether 10 miles over the limit is bending the law too much.
5. Another easy one: money plays a big role in politics.
6. Whether it's adhering to national antidiscrimination policy on admission or hiring decisions, or administering federally subsidized student loans, even private schools find it hard to escape the influence of government.
7. National parks like Yosemite are preserved through government actions.
8. Almost every state imposes a sales tax on food items. If you live in Delaware or New Hampshire and you answered "no," go ahead and give yourself credit because they have no sales tax.
9. Lotteries are established and supported by state governments, and the proceeds are often used to pay for government programs.
10. You can't even find privacy from government actions here. Most places have a sewer system that wouldn't be there if not for the government.

Score Yourself: If you got 8–10 correct, you pay more attention than most people to politics and government. Odds are you know what C-SPAN is (and if you don't, go to www.cspan.org). If you got 5–7 correct, you have a pretty good feel for the role of government in our lives. If you got fewer than 5 correct, you may be in for some interesting surprises!

Democracy and Everyday Life

Ever since grade school, we've had a pretty basic sense of what it means to live in a democracy. At the same time, we don't always know what democracy means in everyday life, except maybe for some of the obvious things like voting and making contributions to political candidates. These are the most direct and visible ways we interact with government. Think, though, about some of the choices in the "Is it relevant?" quiz. We can also interact indirectly, passively, or without direct knowledge that we're in a political situation at all. We may even interact against our will, like if the dues we pay the American Automobile Association (AAA) for that convenient towing service end up being spent on efforts to get elected officials to support policies we don't agree with.

That's because a democracy as big and complex as ours has great reach in our lives—greater than we probably realize.

In any form, democracy entails a few basic things: participation by the people, the willing consent of the people to accept and live by the actions of government, and the recognition that we all have basic rights that government can't take away from us. These are the things Abraham Lincoln was talking about in the passage from the Gettysburg Address that mentions "government of the people, by the people, and for the people."

It's easy to imagine how these prerequisites for democracy might not always hold. We often choose not to participate—or may end up unknowingly participating without giving consent. At various times in our history, those who did not own property, people of color, women, and young people were denied the most basic political freedoms. Even today there are indications that poor individuals and minorities are more likely to have their voices dismissed through such inequities as living in communities that use cheaper and less reliable methods of counting votes (see Demystifying Government: Ballots that Disenfranchise). We saw evidence of this as recently as the 2000 election

DEMYSTIFYING GOVERNMENT

BALLOTS THAT DISENFRANCHISE

Months after the conclusion of the disputed 2000 election, the question of ballot inequity was still a big topic of discussion. George W. Bush had won the presidency following a pitched battle over the official vote count in the state of Florida—a battle that included questions about confusing and irregular ballots, and machines that made a significant number of mistakes reading ballots.

On the surface, counting votes seems straightforward. We've all voted in class elections—you write your choice on a piece of paper, someone reads the votes and adds them up to get a winner. Easy. But when you start to count votes in large numbers, more sources of error are introduced to what seems like such a simple process. In 2000, one of the problems was with punch-card ballots that worked by using a stylus pen to push little perforated squares called chads out of a piece of cardboard. A machine designed to scan the holes created by the vacated chads counted the votes automatically. The only problem was that it didn't always work well. Chads that didn't fully detach or that weren't punched through could confuse the scanner, a mechanical device that couldn't discern the intent of the voter. Votes that confused the scanner would be set aside without being counted. The voter, in essence, would be **disenfranchised**—denied the right to cast a vote—by virtue of his or her ballot not being included in the final tally.

Any mechanical method of vote counting is going to have its problems, and if these problems were spread evenly throughout the country, we might be able to write it off as an unfortunate but necessary side effect of trying to count a lot of votes quickly and efficiently. Even though some individual votes would be lost, the outcome of the election wouldn't change. But what if there is reason to believe that some groups of people are disproportionately affected by counting errors?

That's the charge leveled by a congressional report released several months after the 2000 election. It found that voting systems like the punch-card method, which tend to make more errors than expensive systems using more advanced technology, were more likely to be used in districts containing low income and minority voters. Consequently, it found a higher rate of uncounted ballots in those districts. If these results are substantiated, they suggest that the inevitable problems caused by vote counting methods fall more heavily on low income and minority voters. In relation to affluent voters, individuals in these groups are disenfranchised at a higher rate.

The seriousness of this charge should be understood in the political environment in which the investigation was undertaken. Congressional Democrats conducted the study, and the groups they allege are being disenfranchised are groups that tend to vote for Democrats. That adds a partisan slant to the issue of disenfranchised voters. At the same time, it's an issue that goes to the core of what it means to have rights in a democracy. So, as we consider the possibility that a balloting method systematically disenfranchises groups of voters with shared characteristics, we might ask another question about finding truth in the political process: Can a group with a partisan stake in the outcome conduct a fair investigation? On the other hand, if a group with a stake in the outcome didn't take the initiative to investigate possible wrongdoing, how would potential problems with the political system ever emerge?

Making Democracy Practical

Does this mean that the democratic ideals that our politicians like to praise at Memorial Day parades don't really work in America? Does it mean that they work, but unevenly? How much does government act poorly or inappropriately, simply because the principles it's based on don't fully translate to real world conditions? No system is perfect, but which imperfections are you willing to live with, and which ones, if any, are intolerable? These are hard questions that don't invite a single answer. And they go to the heart of how we function as a people.

Democracy is both an imperfect system and a complex idea. In fact, the broad principles we're talking about can take on different forms depending on the circumstances—with different results. In the small towns of colonial New England, a form of **direct democracy** took hold that enabled everyone to have a personal say in what government did. On this small scale, it was possible for every citizen of a town to gather in a meeting place and directly influence the way the community governed itself. When you stop to consider the lines in the parking lot if a nation of 310,542,835 people[1] tried to do something like this, you realize why even when we were a much smaller country we decided to take a different course. Instead of direct democracy, we opted to choose people to represent our wishes in government decision making through the indirect mechanisms of **representative democracy**. This system—also called a republican system (you may have heard the United States referred to as a **republic** for this reason)—depends heavily on some familiar things, like holding free elections and keeping elected officials accountable to the voters. It's far more practical than direct democracy, but the trade-off is that it's also more complex.

Buying in to Authority

For a democracy—or any political system—to function effectively, we have to buy in to the basic principles it's based on. That's not always so automatic, especially in a large and diverse country like ours where we often disagree on what government should do and even on what society should look like. Some people want government to tax less, while others want it to spend more on social services; some people oppose the death penalty or legal abortion, while others feel differently. Some of these differences take on a moral dimension, where people hold views that they feel reflect the correct way to live, or the way a just society should act. When feelings about these things become intense, people often don't want to give in. At the same time, governing ourselves in a democracy is all about finding room for compromise.

Against this backdrop of different values and objectives, there has to be some agreement on the rules of the game—on the way we're going to set up our democracy—or else the entire system could topple under the weight of our vast disagreements.

Let's say your candidate for president loses the election. What are you going to do about it? You may stage protests against the winner, speak out against his actions, or work against him in the next election. But even if you think the winner is an incompetent swine, you're probably going to accept what he does as representing the official actions of the president of the United States.

That's because Americans generally respect the **authority** of a victorious candidate—his or her right to assume office and to carry out the responsibilities pertaining to that office. It's one of the rules of the game the vast majority of us accept, even if we sometimes don't like it, and it makes democracy possible. There is nothing automatic about this response; many nations—even democratic ones—struggle to resolve contested claims to authority, sometimes to the point where a military coup results in the overthrow of a legitimately elected government.

Americans have a long history of avoiding violent conflicts over authority disputes. As a society, we've shown a preference for investing authority in officials we may not like on the understanding that there will be other elections that may produce outcomes more to our liking. Even the most outspoken opponents of President Bush and his policies worked within the system for his political defeat in 2004, rather than advocating the violent overthrow of the government. During the summer of 2009, some demonstrators fearful that President Obama's call for health care reform would lead to a government takeover of medical care stormed meetings with their congressional representatives and angrily called for succession, but they continued to protest within the system rather than actually attempt to leave it. Similarly, maybe you don't like the way one of your professors exercises authority—maybe you feel he or she grades arbitrarily—but you probably try to deal with it by remembering it's only for a semester or a quarter, and there'll be other classes.

So, even a candidate elected by the slimmest margin assumes the jurisdiction to act with the authority of the office to which he was elected.

In 1998, former WWF wrestler Jesse "The Body" Ventura narrowly won a three-way race for Minnesota governor. Almost two-thirds of those voting had chosen someone else. But Ventura became governor and assumed the authority of the office—the jurisdiction to propose legislation, negotiate the state's budget, grant clemency to prisoners, and a host of other serious functions. Some cringed when he continued to referee World Wrestling Federation matches, but it didn't interfere with the authority he had from having been duly elected governor of a state.

Inheriting Legitimacy

Now, some people would say that Jesse Ventura was making a mockery of his office when as governor he dressed in the flamboyant outfits of his wrestling days. (Of course, you might just think it was a pretty cool thing to do—but like we said before, people hold all kinds of opinions about things.) If you're the type of person who thinks governors should wear suits (or at least shirts), then seeing Ventura in feathers might make you respect him less as governor. Although that does nothing to undermine his formal authority to act as governor, it could diminish his **legitimacy**, the widespread acceptance of his actions. Diminished legitimacy, in turn, could make it harder for him to maneuver politically because of the resistance he would face from people who doubted him.[2]

Legitimacy is a funny thing because, unlike authority, which is granted by virtue of holding an office, legitimacy is partly inherited and partly earned. One source of legitimacy evolves over time and is rooted in the way we come to accept an office and by extension its occupant as being rightful and appropriate. The German sociologist Max Weber suggested this kind of legitimacy is rooted in tradition and law—that after hundreds of years, for instance, we have come to accept the presidential winner as the legitimate occupant of that office for a period of four years, under a plan set up long ago in the Constitution. This is why most Americans who voted for someone else accept a new president who attains office through normal, legal, time-tested channels. Even his strongest opponents do not call for tanks in the streets.

The legitimacy an official inherits is usually at its peak at the start of a term of office and is often the reason for the "honeymoon" or grace period we tend to give new officials. This was the case with President Obama, who began his administration with strong job approval ratings of 70% or higher. But the initial glow from his inauguration faded after a tumultuous first several months spent advocating for an expensive stimulus package targeted at jump-starting a depressed economy, escalating the American presence in Afghanistan, and initiating a controversial effort to overhaul the health care system. By the end of the summer, only a little more than half the country approved his performance, close to the percentage that had voted for him the previous fall.

Obama's honeymoon experience was more typical than his predecessor's. The postelection period that resulted in President Bush taking office was highly unorthodox and infused with partisanship on both sides. There was the unsavory spectacle of lawyers for the Bush and Gore teams working to count every ballot in areas where large numbers of their likely supporters lived while trying to disqualify as many ballots as they could in the other guy's strongholds. The governor of the disputed state of Florida was the brother of the Republican candidate. The question of whether to continue recounting ballots was ultimately decided by the United States Supreme Court in a split decision that broke along ideological lines, with the most conservative justices voting successfully to stop the recount in an action that essentially handed the election to President Bush.

Aspects of legitimacy based in tradition and law were tested and, to a degree, undermined by what happened in November and December 2000. In fact, the circumstances surrounding this postelection period were so unconventional and irregular that some people were led to the unusual position of questioning the legitimacy of the outcome. With lawyers and Supreme Court justices having had a decisive say in Bush's election, some partisan Democrats and even some reporters talked about whether George W. Bush should be regarded as

the legitimate presidential winner. This sentiment was particularly pronounced in the African American community because of the sense that African Americans had been disproportionately disenfranchised by the balloting irregularities discussed in the Demystifying Government box.

There is another side to the story, and it speaks to the strength of American political traditions even in the face of actions that question those traditions. Even under the irregular circumstances of Election 2000, a majority of Americans accepted the legitimacy of the Bush administration—even some who did not approve of the way he won the office. This speaks to the depth of the American tradition of accepting the declared winner and moving on. It suggests just how strong American traditions are, and how important Americans feel it is as a nation to legitimize elected officials.

In one important respect, the question of President Bush's legitimacy was put to rest for many Americans on September 11, 2001, when the terrorist attacks on the World Trade Center and the Pentagon created an emergency atmosphere in which Americans sorely needed leadership. Bush used his authority as president to speak out against the attacks and lead the American response against al-Qaeda, earning him a level of acceptance originally denied him by virtue of how the election was decided. Even Al Gore publicly stated that George W. Bush was his commander-in-chief.

Earning Legitimacy

In order for our elected officials to act effectively— whether it be in addressing terrorist threats or trying to get Congress to approve a budget—we have to accept their actions as appropriate, even if we don't always approve of them. An official can squander or enhance his well of legitimacy through his behavior in office. That's why those of you who think a public official shouldn't be involved in professional wrestling activities might see Governor Ventura as a less legitimate public servant because of his continued wrestling connections (not to mention the fact that some people even say those wrestling events are fixed). Those of you who think it's a pretty cool thing to do might see Ventura as charismatic and honest, and that could elevate his legitimacy in your eyes. Similarly, Ronald Reagan used his communication skills as president to project an image of strength that enhanced his legitimacy. Bill Clinton's involvement with Monica Lewinsky and his subsequent impeachment diminished his legitimacy in the eyes of some.

Authority and legitimacy may seem like distant abstractions, but we deal with them almost every day. You're dealing with them in your classroom right now, as you navigate your response to the way your professor has decided to structure this class. Before you enrolled, your professor chose to assign this text, and made decisions about the work you would be required to do, the way grades would be calculated, how course material would be presented, whether you would have the opportunity to earn extra credit, how much emphasis to place on attendance and class participation, and a host of related items.

Other professors who teach this course probably would have made different choices because each professor has the authority to define the parameters of instruction—and you're left to contend with those choices. You may find you like that style of instruction, appreciate the course, and end up recommending it to your friends. Or you may take issue with anything from the reading load to how you're evaluated to the way lectures are delivered. In turn, you may find yourself acquiescing to things you dislike, or you may react by daydreaming during lectures, cutting classes, not reading the material fully, or engaging in any number of time-tested ways to rebel against academic authority figures. Regardless of your reaction, though, chances are you never question your professor's right to teach the course as he or she chooses. In other words, you accept your professor's authority to determine the contours of the course.

That is, unless your professor does something that you feel defies the boundaries of his or her authority. Let's look at a hypothetical example of this. Imagine that your professor randomly assigned everyone in your class to one of two groups and permitted everyone in the other group to skip this week's lectures, declaring that they would not be held accountable for the work they missed. You'd probably agree that your professor has the authority to determine if someone is entitled to an excused absence from class. To do so in an arbitrary manner, though, without explanation, feels wrong.

This capricious quality could well undermine your professor's legitimacy by making it seem as if he or she is acting unfairly. Randomly dismissing some classmates but not others is a heavy-handed thing to do, even if it's technically within your professor's authority to do it, which brings the legitimacy of the act into question. To be legitimate, you might expect everyone to be offered the option to miss the lectures, or at least to be provided with a rationale for why some people will be exempt from attending.

When the legitimacy of authority figures is brought into question, it's natural to raise doubts about their right to act as they did, and your choice of how to respond may take on greater urgency than if you simply took issue with their methods of evaluation or one of the many things a professor plainly has the authority to do. Do you accept it and move on, with their legitimacy permanently diminished in your eyes? Do you take action by confronting your professor, or by lodging a complaint with the dean? When you make your decision, how much do you take into account that you're dealing with someone who for the next few months has some leverage over your future—someone who will grade you at the end of the semester?

Power Surge

If you find yourself thinking you would probably not want to risk your grade in a confrontation with your professor, you would be giving up doing something you wanted to do in order to protect your GPA. In this case, you would be reacting to the **power** your professor has over you in your class. Someone has power when they can prevent you from doing something you want to do or make you do something you might not want to do. They can do it by coercing you through implied or overt threats or by influencing you with the promise of something you want or need. In the case of our fictional random dismissal from class, your behavior would be in response to a

DEMYSTIFYING GOVERNMENT

INFORMATION AND POWER IN THE 21ST CENTURY

It's been widely said that knowledge is power. It's been just as widely said that we're living in the information age and that what we know defines our place in society. These may be overworked sayings, but they're overworked for a reason. The fact is that our world is so technical and so specialized that what we know really does go a long way to determining how powerful we are. That's just another way of saying that information is one of the most important resources we'll encounter in our exploration of politics and government.

It shouldn't take too much thought to find places where information matters. Computers are obviously about information, and as we'll find out in a few weeks, the signature media of the twenty-first century like the Internet and twenty-four-hour cable television play a huge role in how we understand political issues, how candidates get elected, and a host of other situations where power is at stake.

We'll also find information popping up (literally and figuratively) in less expected places. Members of Congress can't survive without it. Neither can bureaucrats. Next to money, it's the lifeblood of many interest groups. The president relies on all sorts of information about public preferences before making decisions that could affect his political career. So, when you think about power, think about information as one of the foremost tools of power.

calculation about the likely cost of a confrontation with the professor. No words have to be spoken because the threat of a lower grade would be implied by the situation.

In a raw, basic sense, power is about might rather than right. You could even say that, initially, the people who get to decide the right way of doing things—who determine how authority is constituted—are the ones who wield power most successfully. Power isn't simply the use of force, though. It's subtler than that. It's about convincing other people of mutually shared interests, or threatening them with the loss of something they want, or actually denying them something they want, or providing them with a favor, or any number of other things that might move someone to act the way the person with power wants them to. In this regard, the person with power has tools in his or her arsenal—resources that may be used to change another person's behavior.

When the president says he'll veto an act of Congress in an effort to prevent its passage, he is exercising power over Congress, and the resource he's using is the threat of the veto. But the president can also exercise power by using personal charm or sharing the glow of his popularity—if he happens to have these resources at his disposal because he's charming or popular. Computer firms that make contributions to congressional candidates in an effort to influence their positions on high-tech matters exercise power with the use of money. Lawyers with expertise, lobbyists with information (see Demystifying Government: Information and Power in the New Millennium), you with your ability to vote in elections—all have resources that are desired by others in the political process. Power is exercised when resources are used to achieve a desired outcome.

When you stop to think about it, we're involved in power relationships with other people all the time.

Sometimes we are in the powerful position of being able to offer or withhold resources others want. Sometimes people have power over us because they control resources—like grades—that matter to us. Any individual or group with resources can engage in a power relationship, and power relationships are among the most fundamental at every level of politics from the White House to school boards. Quite often, maybe surprisingly, a mutually beneficial exchange of resources gets others to act in a way they might not have intended. In the American political system, the exercise of power is about mutual benefit a lot more than we might suspect.

When we start to think of power in terms of relationships, we're getting to the heart of what **politics** means. We all have things we want to accomplish and things we want to avoid. And we're always involved in relationships with other people. When you bring human desire and human relationships together, you have the essentials of a process that ultimately determines who gets what. When this process happens in a public sphere so that everyone in the country is potentially affected by what happens, we have politics of the sort that matters in government. Almost seventy years ago, a student of the process, Harold Lasswell, called politics "the study of who gets what, when and how."[3]

Some of us may be more powerful by virtue of having more resources (see Demystifying Government: Do I Have Resources That Matter?); some of us may get heavily involved by virtue of our interest in what government does. But regardless of our level of power or interest in this process, we

are all affected by it—even if you never had a single thought about politics before you registered for this course. That's because politics produces winners and losers on everything from whether we'll be sent to war to how much we'll have to pay in taxes to who gets to operate your favorite TV station to whether embryonic stem cells can be used for scientific research to whether you may legally drink beer. Think of something you encounter in your daily life, and the chances are that in some way it's influenced by politics.

Facts and Judgments

Before we go forward, let's determine how facts are distinguished from judgments. Throughout this course, we're going to be making observations based on analysis of information and observations based on our judgments or evaluations of circumstances. These are different kinds of observations. When we evaluate data or information, we make **empirical** or factual observations about the world around us. No value judgments are involved when we do this. When we say something like, "The president can use his veto power to prevent an act of Congress from becoming law," we're making an empirical observation based on our understanding of the president's powers under the Constitution.

But when we say something like, "It's a good thing for the president to veto an act of Congress," we're making a **normative** observation or value judgment that involves assessing a standard or making an evaluation. We could easily apply different norms

Table 1.2. Normative or Empirical?

The painting contains three shades of blue oil paint	**Empirical:** the artist or art expert can factually distinguish paint shades
The painting would be more dramatic if it contained nine shades of blue paint	**Normative:** this is an opinion, not a statement of fact
The painting would be more effective if it were displayed in a brighter light	**Normative:** this is an opinion, not a statement of fact
The United States may be classified as a republic rather than as a direct democracy because elected representatives make decisions on behalf of the public	**Empirical:** this is based on facts as opposed to value judgments
The United States is better suited to being a republic than a direct democracy because of the vast size of the country	**Normative:** this is an opinion, not a statement of fact

DEMYSTIFYING GOVERNMENT

DO I HAVE THE RESOURCES THAT MATTER?

Everyone has resources, but you can argue—to borrow from George Orwell—that some resources are more equal than others. Some people believe that the resources that most influence political officials are concentrated in the hands of a few, giving this small group disproportionate power to determine political outcomes. Others point to the way Americans like to join groups and feel that the resources held by groups with broad memberships greatly influence the decisions that come out of the political process. Whether you believe the resources that move the political system are held by a few people or many people determines whether you believe political power is wielded by the few or the many.

You may know people who say there's no reason to vote because your vote really doesn't matter, since voting doesn't overrule the actions of powerful, unelected people with wealth, prestige, or access to sophisticated information who make decisions that affect our lives. People who think like this have a lot in common with people who say the political system is characterized by **elitism**, or the belief that government is in practice controlled by a small, centralized hierarchy of people with a wealth of resources at their disposal. Advocates of elitism believe that a stable, resource-rich, permanent elite drives political decisions in the United States, rendering the vast majority of Americans effectively powerless.

On the other hand, many Americans join groups like service organizations; mosques, churches, or synagogues; and other community groups—all sorts of organizations where we expend time (a resource) pursuing matters of interest to us. These groups operate in public, allowing us to voice our interests and concerns in a manner in which they'll be heard. As these groups compete with each other for public attention, it's possible that they shape the way government officials listen and respond. If you agree with this assessment, you're in line with those who say the political system is characterized by **pluralism**, or the belief that government in practice responds to the many (plural) voices expressed through group membership. One advocate of this position is political theorist Robert Dahl, who once wrote of the central role of "all the active and legitimate groups in the population," who "can make themselves heard at the same crucial state in the process of decision."

Obviously, pluralism and elitism present divergent and mutually exclusive ways of understanding who holds power, and sorting through the two approaches is not that simple because it's easy to see where each has merit. It may even be tempting to say that they both describe our political system, but you shouldn't lose sight of the fact that pluralism and elitism assume the system is structured in entirely different ways. Figure 1 (immediately below) illustrates the different ways elitists and pluralists describe the structure of the political system.

or standards and argue that it's not a good thing for the president to issue a veto.

Let's do a quick check. Cover the right-hand column of Table 1.2 and see if you can figure out which of the statements in the left column are normative and which ones are empirical. If some of the statements appear to fit into both categories, it's because the line between a factual evaluation and a value judgment is not always as clean as you might think—which can be a source of misunderstanding in a political discussion if someone makes a value judgment that you take to be a statement of fact!

It's Not Fair!

Let's return one more time to the hypothetical example of your professor randomly dismissing part of your class. Whether you thought it was ridiculous that a professor would dismiss some of the class at random, or whether you thought it was wrong that someone else would get to be excused from work for what appeared to be no good reason, your reaction to the example was based on an assumption about how people should be treated. It must seem fairly obvious that if you're going to make an exception for someone, there had better be a good reason for it.

What may seem less obvious is that sentiment like this doesn't have to be automatic or universal. It's a value judgment, and we're going to find that people make all kinds of judgments about what seems right and fair—judgments that, in their scope and range, contribute to the complexity of political debate. If this sounds normative to you, then you were paying attention when you read "Facts and Judgments" (and if this doesn't make sense, you might want to take a minute and review Table 1.2). Either way, before moving on, take a few minutes to look at Global Topics: Different Countries, Different Choices, where you'll learn an important distinction about normative judgments like this, which are based on values, and empirical observations based on fact.

Once you're clear about what constitutes a normative judgment, we can return to the matter at had—fairness. Would it have been different if you and everyone else had been given the choice to stay or go? Perhaps that would seem less arbitrary and, accordingly, more acceptable. If it feels this way, you're tuned into a prominent way many Americans understand the notion of equality. It's called **equality of opportunity**, and it's about everyone having the same chance for advancement, free from obstacles that might limit some people from realizing their potential. This is essentially what Thomas Jefferson had in mind when he wrote in the Declaration of Independence that "all men are created equal," although his eighteenth-century perspective excluded women, African American slaves, and Native Americans from consideration.

Over time, efforts have been made to incorporate groups Jefferson left out, but the basic idea that people are "created equal" still applies to where we start out in life, not where we end up—to the chances life affords us rather than to the results we achieve.

Valuing equality of opportunity is consistent with supporting government efforts to make the "starting line" more equal. That's why Americans usually support government programs to help underprivileged kids have access to higher education, because education is considered the gateway to opportunity. It's also why Americans generally value **political equality** and believe that everyone should have the same political and legal rights as everyone else. If all votes count the same and if everyone has the same rights in a court of law, the theory goes, then the playing field isn't tilted toward some groups and away from others. Everyone has the same opportunity to make the most of themselves without the political or legal system getting in the way. When you think about it this way, you can apply the language of equal opportunity to the question we were discussing earlier about whether some individuals or groups were disenfranchised during the 2000 election.

To value opportunity is a choice, and it's a different choice than some other countries make. In places like Norway and Sweden, for instance, people place more emphasis than Americans do on **equality of outcome**, on diminishing economic and social disparities among people through government actions that try to level off differences between rich and poor by redistributing resources from top to bottom. If Americans as a group were as interested as Scandinavians in equality of outcome, then our government might provide cradle-to-grave health care, long stretches of paid maternity leave, and generous retirement benefits like they do in Norway and Sweden. Of course, we'd have to pay a lot more in taxes to support programs like these, and that would result in a lot of resources shifting around so that rich and poor alike would benefit equally. A country makes choices like that when it primarily values **economic equality** and **social equality**—both forms of equal outcomes—in which economic and

GLOBAL TOPICS

Different Countries, Different Choices

Why do Scandinavian countries provide far more extensive social services to their citizens the United States? Why do their citizens agree to pay far more in taxes than most Americans would ever accept? Or, to put it another way, why do Scandinavians value equality of outcome so much more than Americans?

Political Scientist John Kingdon has a theory. He speculates that the immigrants who settled the United States and influenced the development of its political system—groups we will discuss in detail in Chapter 4—were fundamentally different from the groups that determined the political rules in other nations. Starting with the original settlers from Great Britain who colonized North America, the United States has long attracted immigrants from other countries who were motivated by religious, economic, or political freedom to take up a new life in an unfamiliar place. These immigrants shared a mistrust of government, either because it stood in the way of worshiping as they pleased or posed an obstacle to self-betterment. They valued self-reliance and were risk-takers, willing to depart familiar surroundings to take a chance on a new life with unknown hazards. And, the choices they made based on the values they held were influential to the development of the United States. In contrast, Native Americans and African Americans who also populated North America and may have made different choices were denied political rights and therefore were shut out of decision-making.

As a group, white immigrants to America were more likely than their counterparts who remained in Europe to believe that individuals can make better decisions for themselves than government can make on their behalf. They were more likely to regard government as a force that blocks individual initiative. In a land that lacked the rigid class structures prevalent in Europe, they were more likely to value opportunity and regard government as a potential obstacle to achieving it. These were not people who would look kindly on paying as much as Norwegians do in taxes (see Figure 15.3 for a comparison of tax revenues in the United States and Scandinavia), or would want government to provide the wide array of social services that Norwegians receive in exchange for their hefty tax payments.

The decisions made by these earliest of settlers structured the choices available to future generations and set the United States on a course that differs significantly from nations, like the countries of Scandinavia, where government is viewed as a source of lifelong social services and as a mechanism for correcting economic and social disparities.[T6]

social distinctions are minimized as a matter of policy and choice.

Just take a quick look at social and economic patterns in the United States, and you'll probably begin to realize how much equality of outcome takes a back seat to equality of opportunity. We're aware of the existence of social classes, of the great distance there is between the wealth of someone like software magnate Bill Gates and people who have to work for a living, to say nothing of people who can't find work at all or who live in poverty. But the size of the disparity might be even greater than you imagine. In 1998, the wealthiest 1 percent of American households had more than 190 times the net worth of the bottom 40 percent combined, and that disparity has increased in recent years. Fifteen years earlier, the top 1 percent had "only" 37 times more than the bottom 40 percent,

Figure 1.1. Economic Equality and Inequality[T4]. If wealth were equally distributed across the population, then there would be no economic classes. Everyone would have the same net worth—that is, each one-fifth of the population would have one-fifth of the wealth. In reality, we're very far from equal outcomes in the United States. The upper one-fifth of the population controls over four-fifths of the wealth. In contrast, the bottom one-fifth accounts for less than .02 percent of the wealth, or less than 1/400 the net worth of the top group.

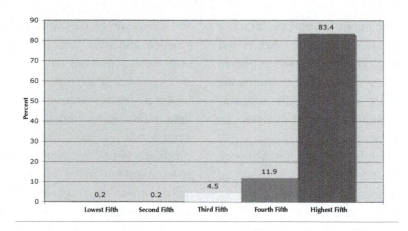

so if anything our recent policies have exaggerated economic inequality. Figure 1.1 illustrates how these differences contrast with pure economic equality. Although we'll find that some efforts are made to address these inequalities, as a matter of policy—and as a matter of choice—Americans tend to make the normative judgment that providing opportunity is generally preferred over equalizing outcomes.

Because we tend not to value equality of outcome, groups that have historically met with discrimination lag behind in their share of economic resources. The earning power of African Americans, Hispanics, and other minority groups falls below the earning power of whites—sometimes well below. For instance, according to the U.S. Census Bureau, in 1999 one in ten whites lived in poverty, compared with better than one in four African Americans and Hispanics. Figure 1.2 explains.

Similarly, the earning power of women is less than the earning power of men who do comparable work. In 2007, women were paid only 77 percent of what men in comparable jobs were paid—a difference that amounts to over $700,000 dollars for the average full-time woman worker over the course of her working life.[4] The federal government is quite aware of these disparities—there's even a Women's Bureau at the U.S. Department of Labor that in past administrations provided a checklist you could use if you were a working woman and you thought you were being unfairly compensated for what you do.[5] Still the inequalities remain, as the statistics show, in violation of a primary assumption about how equality of opportunity should work.

Unequal and Different

The tendency in the United States to emphasize opportunity over outcomes raises important questions about the relationship between the condition of being unequal and simply being different.

Think of someone you know—perhaps a friend, significant other, or classmate. Start thinking of some of the outward differences between you. Maybe there are gender differences, or differences in eye, skin, or hair color. You could be different heights or weigh different amounts. The more you think about it, the longer the list of differences should become because so many factors contribute to the unique way we look.

You would no sooner want these physical differences to determine how others treat you than you would for your professor to randomly determine who

Figure 1.2. Minority Income Levels[T5]. African American and Hispanic households are each roughly two and one-half times as likely as white households to be among households with annual incomes under $15,000. But white households are almost twice as likely as African American and Hispanic households to be among households with annual incomes of $50,000 or more.

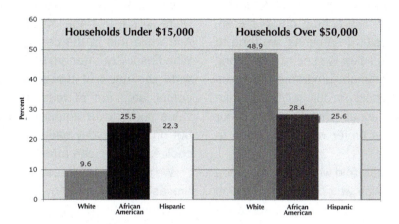

gets to be excused from your next class. Neither, in a normative sense, is fair. Both undermine the central idea of equality of opportunity, which is that all people should be in a roughly comparable situation that permits them to express their talents and abilities.

In theory, we should have the same chance to succeed despite these many differences. Rather, our capabilities and interests should determine what we achieve. Some of us will become shopkeepers, while others become bookkeepers; there will be lawyers and landscapers and teachers and daycare providers and salespeople and waiters and chief operating officers. If we have an even shot at all these outcomes and reach the one we choose because of where we decide to direct our energy, you could say equality of opportunity is working well. There should be no relationship between the outcomes we choose and our surface differences, which have no bearing on our talents and interests.

The fact that we see disparities in outcome based on gender, racial, and ethnic characteristics is a sign that equality of opportunity does not work in practice the way it does in theory. Remember, the dilemma isn't that people end up in different places—that's to be expected—it's that people end up in different places for surface reasons that have no bearing on their talents or ability. It suggests

that some groups face obstacles to achievement simply because they are different.

If an inner-city Hispanic teen scores lower on the SAT than does a white suburban kid, she will likely be denied admission to the best state and private schools and will face a more limited set of college options. Is her score lower because she isn't as bright as her suburban counterpart, or is it because she attended an overcrowded high school and didn't have access to good academic counselors or SAT prep classes? Is it possible that if she had had the advantages of a wealthier school system, her SAT scores would have been higher, and she would have had the same educational opportunities as someone from an affluent suburb?

Like the inner-city teen, other groups—like African Americans facing hiring discrimination and women who are paid less money to do the same work as men—find the playing field tilted against them because of surface differences. At times in our history, these obstacles have become political issues, in that they became the focus of public debate. But the fact that the debate over advancing equality of opportunity needs to consider group differences says a lot about the tricky nature of how our society handles diversity and how diversity poses a challenge to the fundamental American idea that individuals should be provided opportunity free from arbitrary obstacles.

Equal and Free?

How much of your income would you be willing to pay in taxes if you received government benefits in return? Twenty percent? Thirty? Fifty? Eighty? At some point, it'll feel like a drag on your earning power and you'll resist. In America, we tend to reach that point pretty quickly. We see taxes—along with some of the government programs the taxes pay for—as an imposition on our ability to make choices for ourselves about what to do with our money. Many Americans prefer voluntary action to government mandates.

This resistance to being told what to do has deep roots in our country, which was born in a rebellion against a strong central government. It's about **liberty**, about having the freedom to act without others interfering with what we do, and it's at the center of so many of the choices we make when we govern ourselves. Americans place a premium on preserving liberty. It was the rationale for fighting two world wars and the cold war with the former Soviet Union, and it's the thing Americans most fear losing to terrorists. Hours after the World Trade Center was destroyed, President Bush told the nation, "Our way of life, our very freedom came under attack."[6]

In an absolute sense, if we had total liberty, there would be chaos because everyone would do whatever he or she wanted. So, we make choices. One of the biggest trade-offs we make is between liberty and equality. We've already seen how there are several ways to understand what it means for people to be equal. Certain types of equality are more compatible with having liberty, while others may only be attained by placing restrictions on liberty.

Let's see if you can identify the trade-offs between liberty and the five types of equality we've talked about: equality of opportunity, equality of outcome, political equality, social equality, and economic equality. Take a look at Figure 1.3 to gain a sense of the balancing act that has to be maintained in order to preserve both liberty and equality.

Whose Choice?

We've been saying that society makes choices between liberty and equality, normative choices that involve judgments about what we value and what we're willing to trade off to achieve those values. And while this is the case, it's also very abstract. Who is society, after all, but you and me? We didn't write the rules of the game—other people for a complicated set of reasons made the choice to value liberty over equality of outcome long ago—but on an everyday basis, we're faced with lots of choices that we can affect.

We're constantly faced with situations where we are asked voluntarily by others or involuntarily by government to give up some of our liberty to act in order to benefit others. Sometimes, we do this with no problem; other times, it's inconvenient, and we gripe about it or perhaps take things into our own hands and resist the restrictions placed on us.

Take, for instance, the simple act of listening to music. Maybe you live in a dorm or apartment and have a roommate or two. If your roommate isn't around in the middle of the afternoon and you can't find your iPod, you can probably feel pretty good about blasting a CD if you want to without having to think about how it affects anyone else. Your liberty to act is absolute. But if your roommate is there and you have different musical tastes, you've got a choice to make between doing what you want—exercising your liberty to listen to music—and imposing a restriction on your wishes in order to take your roommate's feelings into account. Some of us might factor our roommate's wishes heavily into our decision, whereas some of us might not consider them at all.

If our decision caused conflict, we may or may not be able to manage it privately and peacefully without an RA (a resident advisor in a dorm) or the campus police intervening. If our decision entailed curtailing what we would have done if we were left alone, like listening to a different CD or turning down the volume, we might grumble at our loss of liberty but accept it as a condition of having a roommate.

On a larger scale, conflicts like this between personal liberty and the rights of others are the very things government tries to resolve every day. These conflicts involve trade-offs between liberty and **social responsibility**, or the concern for the rights of others in society. Because our actions constantly affect other people, and because it's human nature to want to pursue our desires and objectives despite this, we are continually asking government to resolve disputes between personal liberty and social responsibility. Essentially, we turn to government to draw the boundaries that determine where individual liberty stops and the needs of society start.

Obviously, not everyone will draw that line in the same place. Not everyone believes that government is always the appropriate arbiter, either, believing instead that individuals should work out their conflicts without government getting involved. A lot of political debate turns on these two facts.

Drinking laws are among those that you may have strong feelings about. As a society, as you're no doubt quite aware, we've decided that it is illegal to purchase or consume alcohol until you turn twenty-one. You probably know the rationale for this, which has to do with the desire to cut down on alcohol-related driving accidents. Essentially, if you are under twenty-one, your liberty (some would call it a right) to drink has been curtailed by government action in favor of the socially responsible position that it is more important to protect the lives of everyone on the roads. That's a choice that stems from a value judgment. You may agree with it or not. But it's the law.

So, what do you do about it? One option is to do nothing—to plan a big celebration on your twenty-first birthday and to do nothing before then. You might take this course of action if you agree with the law or even if you disagree with it but recognize its legitimacy. Another option is to violate the law and try not to get caught. You might do this if you disagree with the trade-offs behind the law, or if you feel drinking alcohol should be a matter of personal choice and not a matter for government to consider. There would be sanctions if you were caught because you would be breaking the law, not changing it. But that would be a consequence you would have to face.

The dual questions of when to give up liberty to protect the rights of others and whether government or private individuals should make the decision have a long history in our country's political debates. As you can probably see, when your liberty is at issue, feelings can get pretty intense. Also, as with all interesting political questions, there are winners and losers, which can make the result of what government does hard for some to swallow.

Compounding the issue is the great range of reactions we have to the tension between liberty and responsibility as well as other questions regularly placed before our political system. The great diversity of America that we were talking about before is both a strength and a complicating factor for our politics. It's a strength inasmuch as the expression of a wide range of viewpoints tends to enhance the decisions we make for ourselves, because a variety of voices coming from different vantage points can make for intelligent and gratifying solutions to problems, much like the blending of many ingredients can make food tastier and more satisfying.

At the same time, diverse perspectives can make it harder to reach a conclusion, complicating the process by which decisions are made. A system designed over two centuries ago to hear primarily the voices of white land-owning males has been required to expand to accommodate the views and desires of people with a wide range of backgrounds, perspectives, and beliefs. How it has managed to do this, and what it means in real terms for you and me, is part of the story you'll read in the next chapter.

So—Should I Care about Politics?

Whether you should personally care about politics is a normative judgment. It's also a personal matter that you'll probably approach differently from your friends. You'll make a judgment that depends in part on how much you think politics matters in your life. No one else can make that judgment for you.

We started out by asking whether it makes sense to care about the political system enough to engage in it because the question goes right to the heart of why you're in this course. If there's absolutely no reason to care about politics, then it's going to

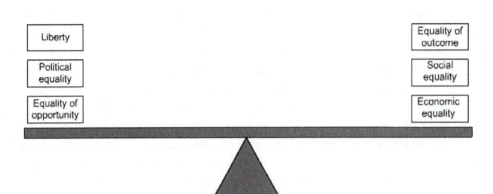

Figure 1.3. Balancing Liberty and Equality

be a long semester or quarter! There are certainly reasons to get involved, but you may feel they don't apply to you. In the end, you may decide like many people that you're just not a political person. At that point, you'll be able to draw your conclusions with your eyes open to the evidence.

But before we can make an informed decision about whether and how much we should care about the public side of life, we should grow to understand it much better. There may already be things you know now that you didn't realize before you started reading this chapter, like how you're involved in power relationships at times when you're totally unaware of them—whether it's in the classroom with your professor or with a membership you may have in the American Automobile Association.

We've already seen that we can be involved in politics even if we don't care about it and even if we're not paying attention. We've talked about how the republican form of democracy we practice in this country reaches into things we may take for granted in our daily life, like having other people elected by us (or by our neighbors if we don't take part) make decisions on our behalf. We've talked about how we tend to act around authority figures, whether they're our professor or our president, and how their ability to wield resources can influence our lives—especially if we see their actions as legitimate.

We identified ways we're involved in power relationships with people every day—directly with people we work and live with, indirectly through the actions of political figures that make decisions on our behalf. We even looked at equity issues—matters of fairness—and how they balance the freedoms that a lot of us feel are extremely important in our lives. We talked about how liberty and equality are much more than abstractions. They're values, and as such, the extent to which we enjoy them, as well as the form they take, are the product of choices and trade-offs made by our society and shaped by government action. Whether we feel it's important to try to contribute to the political dialogue that shapes those trade-offs may be one part of the answer to our question about whether interacting with government matters to us.

We've hinted at the idea that in order to make choices about who gets what, when, and how, we set up rules and then play by them (to a greater or lesser extent). In fact, a specific set of rules is in place that determines how politics works in this country. Some of the rules are legal in nature; a lot of them are set out in the Constitution. But even the Constitution has its roots in a struggle between different ways to define the political ground rules. As we understand those rules, we'll probably come to recognize a little more about where we come from as a nation, and how the resolution of some of our earliest political struggles shaped the political options before us today, some two centuries later. How can the struggles of people long gone be relevant to how we live our lives in the twenty-first century? Chapter 2 has some answers to that question.

Chapter Review

Even though people often speak of America as a democracy, it is best understood as a republic because we elect representatives to make decisions on our behalf. In that respect, our country is a representative democracy rather than a direct democracy, where people would make decisions on their own behalf. A representative democracy is far more practical for a nation as large as the United States, but it is also more complex and can be controversial inasmuch as there can be strong differences of opinion about what representatives should do in our name.

For a republic to function effectively, there has to be agreement on the principles on which it's based. Americans typically respect the authority of elected representatives to act in an official capacity by virtue of holding an office, and for the most part, grant legitimacy to elected officials even when they disagree with them. However, political figures can undermine their legitimacy through their actions because, unlike authority, legitimacy is partly earned.

Elected officials can use their authority and legitimacy to exercise power, although their ability to do so is hardly automatic. Power is about getting others to act the way you want them to, even if they prefer to act otherwise, in order to determine who gets what, when, and how. The tools of power are resources, which can encompass a wide range of things, such as a politician's personal charm, the information supplied to members of Congress by a lobbyist, or the promise of campaign money.

Who gets to exercise power is an important—and open—question. Those who subscribe to the theory of elitism believe that a permanent, unelected elite of corporate and academic leaders, military chiefs, media operators, and bureaucrats holds the resources that matter in government

decision making. Those who subscribe to the theory of pluralism believe that ordinary individuals can exercise power in a republic because the resources that matter to people in government are widely distributed in society.

Many Americans value equality of opportunity, or trying to give people a fair start in life, knowing that people of different interests and abilities will end up in different places. Equality of opportunity comes at the expense of equality of outcome and produces economic and social disparities in the name of protecting individual initiative. Many value political equality on the assumption that ensuring everyone the same right to vote and equal rights under the law promotes equal opportunity.

In truth, we have neither equality of opportunity nor equality of outcome in America, although we are much more likely to support government actions that promote the former. One place where equal opportunity breaks down is in the unequal economic and social outcomes of women and historically disadvantaged racial and ethnic groups because unequal outcomes are supposed to be a product of our different talents, interests, and abilities, not our physical or ethnic differences.

There are also important trade-offs to be made between equality of opportunity and liberty, which is the ability to pursue our objectives, tempered by socially defined boundaries and limited government impediments. Liberty is consistent with equal opportunity because it supplies the freedom to make individual choices. Absolute liberty would generate chaos, so liberty is bounded by social responsibility, or the concern for the rights of others in society. We turn to government to draw the boundaries that determine where individual liberty stops and the needs of society start. But we won't all draw that boundary in the same place, which can lead to political disputes over whether government should create boundaries or leave matters of social responsibility to individuals.

Key Terms

authority The right to act in an official capacity by virtue of holding an office like president or member of Congress.

democracy A government created by the people over whom it rules.

direct democracy Democracy without representation, where each eligible individual participates in decision making.

disenfranchised Losing or being denied the legal right to vote by intentional or unintentional means.

economic equality A form of equality of outcome that values using government policy to minimize the economic disparities found in society.

elitism The theory that government responds to a small, stable, centralized hierarchy of corporate and academic leaders, military chiefs, people who own big media outlets, and members of a permanent government bureaucracy. People who subscribe to this position believe the actions of regular citizens, like voting and joining groups, simply mask the real power exercised by elites.

empirical Any statement based on the assessment of data or the analysis of information, without regard to value judgments.

equality of opportunity One of several ways of understanding equality. This way values giving people comparable advantages for succeeding in life, regardless of the unequal outcomes that may result.

equality of outcome One of several ways of understanding equality. This way values leveling the social and economic inequities among people, rather than attempting to give people comparable advantages for succeeding in life.

legitimacy Widespread public acceptance of the official standing of a political figure or institution.

liberty The ability to pursue your ends and objectives, tempered by socially defined boundaries and limited government impediments.

normative Any statement that invokes a judgment or evaluation. Think of the word norm, which implies a standard for evaluating something.

pluralism The theory that government responds to individuals through their memberships in groups, assuring that government is responsive to a wide range of voices. People who subscribe to this position believe that the wide distribution of resources in society drives the decisions government officials make.

political equality Establishing political and legal rights on the basis of the individual, so that everyone has the same right to vote and is equal under the law. An alternative would be to grant political rights to elite individuals based on wealth or social standing.

politics The process of determining who gets what, when, and how.

power The ability to make others act in a way that they otherwise might not have done.

representative democracy A form of democracy in which eligible individuals choose others to make decisions on their behalf.

republic Any nation with provisions for the selection of representatives who make decisions on behalf of those who select them. James Madison said a republic was "a government in which the scheme of representation takes place," as compared to direct democracy.

resources Anything of value to others that can be used to sway another individual.

social equality A form of equality of outcome that values using government policy to minimize social class distinctions found in society.

social responsibility Concern for the protection of the rights of individuals in a community or society, at the expense of some degree of personal liberty.

Resources

You might be interested in examining some of what the following authors have said about the topics we've been discussing:

Dahl, Robert. *Preface to Democratic Theory*. Chicago: University of Chicago Press, 1956. Different approaches to American democratic theory, with special attention paid to majority and minority rule—things we're going to talk more about in Chapter 2.

Lasswell, Harold D. *Politics: Who Gets What, When, How*. New York: Meridian Books, 1958. A classic discussion of the meaning of power.

Machiavelli, Niccolò. *The Prince*. New York: Penguin Books, 1999. Written 500 years ago, it contains observations about power that still ring true.

You may also be interested in looking at these resource sites:

You can find a good starting place for information on the US government and the people who work in it by going to http://www.usa.gov.

What was government like during its formative years? Frenchman Alexis de Tocqueville traveled America from one end to the other in search of true democracy, and you can find his observations at http://xroads.virginia.edu/~Hyper/detoc.

Notes

1. Population estimate as of December 28, 2010 from the U.S. Census Bureau U.S. Population Clock, at: http:// www.census.gov/main/www/popclock.html.

2. In fact, toward the end of his single term as governor, Ventura found that a large number of Minnesotans had soured on his persona or were unhappy with his official performance. This made it difficult for him to maneuver politically.

3. Harold D. Lasswell, *Who Gets What, When, How* (New York: Meridian Books, 1958).

4. See the AFL-CIO website at: http://www.aflcio.org/issues/jobseconomy/women/equalpay/index.cfm.

5. You may access the Women's Bureau at the U.S. Department of Labor website, at http://www.dol.gov/wb/.

6. "Day of Infamy," *Time*, September 12, 2001.

Table, Figure and Box Notes

T1 Photo Montage: Israeli Prime Minister Yitzhak Rabin, U.S. president Bill Clinton, and PLO chairman Yasser Arafat; property of U.S. Government. The Hubble Space Telescope as seen from the departing Space Shuttle Atlantis, flying Servicing Mission 4 (STS-125), the fifth and final human spaceflight to visit the observatory; photo property of U.S. Government, compliments of NASA. Marquee for The Oprah Winfrey Show, at Harpo Studios in Near West Side, Chicago; photo licensed under the Creative Commons. The PlayStation was released in the mid 1990s and became the best-selling gaming console of its time; photo compliments of Nicholas Wang from Tokyo, Japan; photo licensed under the Creative Commons.

T2 Photo Montage: Left: Cindy Sheehan and supporters at an anti-war demonstration in Arlington, VA in October 2004. Photo licensed under the GNU Free Documentation License. Right: President Bush talks a at his Crawford, Texas Ranch, May 2003. White House photo released in the public domain.

T3 Former Governor of Minnesota Jesse Ventura (real name James Janos); photo compliments of Corey Barnes, licensed under the Creative Commons.

T4 Edward N. Wolff, "Recent Trends in Wealth Ownership, 1983–1998," Working Paper #300, Jerome Levy Economics Institute, Table 2; http://www.levy.org/docs/wrkpap/papers/300.html.

T5 U.S. Census Bureau, Statistical Abstract of the U.S. 2000: The National Data Book, 43, 46.

T6 John W. Kingdon, *America the Unusual*. New York: Worth Publishers, 1999.

CHAPTER 2

 American Culture and
Exceptionalism

Chapter 2 Vignette

By Jennifer Byrne

Syrian president Bashar Al-Assad found himself in the ire of the international community as a team of United Nations inspectors found that the nerve agent sarin was used in an attack in the Ghouta agricultural belt around Damascus on August 21, 2013. Members of the UN Security Council quickly declared the incident a war crime and stated that this was the most significant use of confirmed chemical weapons since Sadam Hussein's use of them in Halabja in 1988.

President Obama almost immediately publicly announced America's role in preventing more widespread attacks with chemical weapons:

"Terrible things happen across the globe, and it is beyond our means to right every wrong. But when, with modest effort and risk, we can stop children from being gassed to death, and thereby make our own children safer over the long run, I believe we should act. That's what makes America different. That's what makes us exceptional.

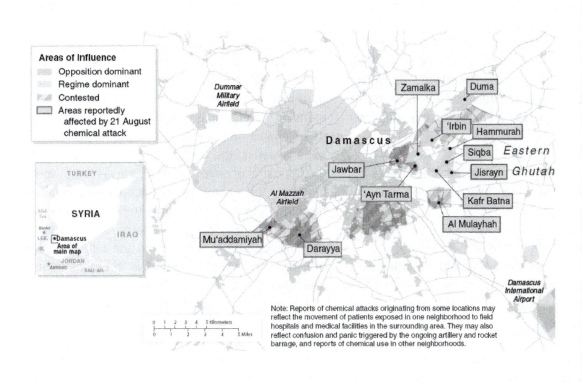

Areas of Influence
- Opposition dominant
- Regime dominant
- Contested
- Areas reportedly affected by 21 August chemical attack

Note: Reports of chemical attacks originating from some locations may reflect the movement of patients exposed in one neighborhood to field hospitals and medical facilities in the surrounding area. They may also reflect confusion and panic triggered by the ongoing artillery and rocket barrage, and reports of chemical use in other neighborhoods.

With humility, but with resolve, let us never lose sight of that essential truth."[1]

This drew criticism for Vladimir Putin, the President of Russia who publicly challenged Obama's statements about American exceptionalism:

"My working and personal relationship with President Obama is marked by growing trust. I appreciate this. I carefully studied his address to the nation on Tuesday. And I would rather disagree with a case he made on American exceptionalism, stating that the United States' policy is 'what makes America different. It's what makes us exceptional.' It is extremely dangerous to encourage people to see themselves as exceptional, whatever the motivation. There are big countries and small countries, rich and poor, those with long democratic traditions and those still finding their way to democracy. Their policies differ, too. We are all different, but when we ask for the Lord's blessings, we must not forget that God created us equal."

Although Mr. Putin said there was nothing anti-American about the article, it drew sharp criticism from the American public and politicians alike. What is American exceptionalism, and how does it affect foreign policy? The main idea behind American exceptionalism is that America is "qualitatively" different from other countries. The idea was first coined by Alexis De Tocqueville when he came to America to make observations on its democracy. He identified five core characteristics that collectively make America unique: individualism, populism, egalitarianism, liberty, and laissez-faire. All of these characteristics are jointly known as the American Creed:

- Liberty—the protection of individual rights
- Egalitarianism—the guarantee of political equality
- Individualism—the freedom of action for individuals over collective or state control
- Populism—ultimate power and authority rests with the people
- Laissez-faire—little to no regulation of the free market

America has a unique history of development, as the ability to rule was opened up to a broad class of citizens rather than monarchs, despots, or religious leaders. While every other industrialized nation has had a socialist or labor movement, America has not. Additionally, America's values and ideology are thought to be "middle of the road." There are no extreme conservative or leftist parties (despite their differences, Democrats and Republicans are both quite moderate in the overall context of ideology), and the connection between other Americans is ideological. If you accept the American Creed, anyone can become an American, regardless of ancestry.

The American Creed gives rise to American cultural values, which are reflected in institutions and to varying degrees among individuals. For example, Americans are thought to be very hard-working and often put in more hours at work and take fewer breaks and vacations than people from other nations. In France, many people will receive up to 8 weeks of paid vacation, while the standard for Americans is a mere 2 weeks. Americans have been noted as being more philanthropic, and many Americans give very generously to charitable organizations. Americans are also some of the most patriotic people in the world and are very proud of their accomplishments in art, literature, science, and the military. Americans view themselves as embodying ideals such as hard work and self-reliance and believe that those who possess these characteristics will be able to make themselves successful despite socio-economic status and background. The idea that one can move up in social and economic standing is known as social mobility. Because of its emphasis on hard work, America has become a superpower on the world stage and boasts one of the largest economies—and military—in the world. In short, the values of American exceptionalism have led America as a country to become very successful in many ways. In its early days, America was characterized as a "beacon on the hill;" a model of democracy where citizens live in prosperity and freedom.

However, American exceptionalism is also known as a "double-edged sword," an idiom that suggests that something can result in both advantages and disadvantages. Americans have some of the highest crime rates and divorce rates in the world. And, while Americans are very patriotic, they have some of the lowest levels of voter turnouts among democracies. In this chapter, you will read about voting laws and how these institutional rules can encourage or hinder participation from voters. There are also drawbacks to American exceptionalism when it comes to foreign policy. In his statement, President Obama implied that Americans have a special power or duty to right the wrong of the use of chemical weapons in Syria. Though he also cautioned that America cannot "right every wrong," the idea that America should police the world because of its unique position is a prominent idea in American foreign policy.[2] This has given rise to the engineering approach to foreign policy, which is characterized by a can-do attitude, the idea that there exists a quick and permanent solution to any problem, and the heavy reliance on technology in the problem-solving process. Putin's critique rested on the principle that no nation has a special position in the world to become unilaterally and uniquely involved in the affairs of other countries.[3]

What message do you think this political cartoon depicts about American exceptionalism?

Endnotes

1. http://www.washingtonpost.com/blogs/post-politics/wp/2013/09/24/obama-tells-other-world-leaders-i-believe-america-is-exceptional/, last accessed on November 18, 2013.
2. http://www.examiner.com/article/american-exceptionalism-and-obama-s-world-police, last accessed on November 18, 2013.
3. http://www.nytimes.com/2013/09/12/opinion/putin-plea-for-caution-from-russia-on-syria.html?pagewanted=all&_r=1&, last accessed on November 18, 2013.

Political Culture, Socialization and Participation

By Matthew Kerbel

Introduction

Are you an American?

Easy question, right? If you were born in or live legally in this country your answer is probably "sure" (otherwise, it's probably "no"). Still, if you are an American, when you think about your identity, is "American" qualified with something else?

Irish American?

African American?

Italian American?

Chinese American?

Cuban American?

German American?

Native American?

Vietnamese American?

Mexican American?

Those qualifiers tell us about where we came from. Many people think of themselves as Americans while simultaneously seeing themselves in terms of their heritage. This says a lot about the richness of the American identity, and helps explain why American politics can be so complex.

On one hand, Americans are many different people with deep roots in a variety of diverse, sometimes conflicting traditions. On the other, Americans share a common set of values, attitudes and beliefs, which together form an American **political culture**. Those values tend to be about "buying in" to the idea of America and how it operates, which is essential in order for the United States to function as a nation.

[There is] much disagreement in America on specific issues of policy. At the same time, there's a lot of agreement on how to set up the political rules of the game. A basic accord supplies the framework for American political culture. It encompasses things like:

- Acceptance of representative democracy and capitalism as superior political and economic arrangements
- Acceptance of the rule of law for resolving disputes and determining political winners and losers
- Belief in compromise with others as a way of achieving objectives
- Agreement on the rules for electing representatives
- Approval of the fundamental choice of liberty and opportunity over equal outcomes

These bedrock qualities of the American political culture help to maintain the legitimacy of the system. If they seem obvious to you, to the point where you find yourself

47

GLOBAL TOPICS

Political Culture in Comparative Perspective

The American political culture is so universally accepted that when we talk about it, you may just think we're stating the obvious. That's not uncommon for something that's part of a core identity—it seems obvious because it's so deeply ingrained. This tends to make it difficult to imagine that the political cultures of other nations may look quite different because of the human tendency to believe that others fundamentally think like we do and want what we want. Because of this, American political culture may be best understood in a comparative perspective, in which we're open to the possibility that people in other nations have a different relationship to their government and to what constitutes acceptable political action.

Have you ever heard someone say that something is "un-American," like "it's un-American not to reward someone for hard work"? Now try to imagine someone saying something is "un-Canadian" or "un-Vietnamese." Most likely, you'll never hear anything like that because thinking about one's nation in terms apart from others is not a part of all political cultures. That's not to say that people of other nations do not notice cultural differences, but they don't necessarily define and describe themselves in terms of those differences. In the United States, though, it's probably not necessary to explain what it means for something to be un-American because, as vague as that phrase is, for many Americans, it encompasses a set of ideas associated with what it means to be an American. In that respect, it is both a part of the political culture and a way of reflecting that culture to others.

Political culture may be understood as the product of a nation's formative political experiences—whether a nation has a long history of democracy or repression or corruption or incompetent leadership. In the early 1960s, researchers Gabriel Almond and Sidney Verba wrote a pioneering study comparing political cultures of different nations, taking into account these historical differences. In *The Civic Culture,* they attempt to explain differences in the levels of political attachment by people in different nations, and identify the characteristics that motivate people to political action.

They found mid-twentieth century Italy to be an alienated political culture, where people had low levels of national pride and lacked confidence in their ability to influence what government did. Almond and Verba attribute these tendencies to a history fraught with tyranny and ineffective efforts at democratic self-governance. In Mexico, they found a sense of isolation from politics and mistrust of authority mixed with great national pride and aspirations toward democracy. They characterize the German political culture, one generation removed from the trauma of World War II, as one where people are knowledgeable about politics and actively engaged in formal political activity like voting, while feeling detached and cynical about politics. And they see the political culture of England as being highly developed, with engaged, interested citizens who take emotional satisfaction from political participation.

These patterns differ from the political culture of the United States, which Almond and Verba regard as a participant civic culture where, in contrast to the other four nations, people are frequently exposed to political messages, feel obligated to participate in their communities and feel competent to do so, tend to voluntarily join groups in large numbers, get emotionally involved in political campaigns, and take great pride in the political system.[T1]

Does this description conform to the way you see America? Would describing it any other way seem—un-American?

thinking, "Who wouldn't agree with these things?," then you are deeply enmeshed in American political culture. In practice, there is no reason to believe people will automatically accept these positions, and individuals in many other cultures do not. That most Americans would accept these points without thinking about it addresses how political culture works: It is composed of principles that are so fundamental as to be almost invisible.

Accepting this broad framework doesn't imply that everyone agrees with the specific choices made in America on matters of policy—far from it, as we saw in Chapter 3. But it does mean that there's a sense of acceptance and even pride in the American system that is a basic part of the identity of many Americans, regardless of their origin. You might even say that without that acceptance, Americans wouldn't have the means for working through the many political differences that arise. It's the same way in other countries, too, even if the particulars of other political cultures are different (see Global Topics: Political Culture in Comparative Perspective).

In this chapter, we're going to explore American political culture in order to get a sense of who Americans are and how American political culture affects politics. Then, we'll move from the collective portrait of a diverse nation to political socialization, the processes that shape our individual awareness of and relationship to politics. Finally, we'll put these general observations together with the individual ones when we look at how political culture and political socialization relate to participation in the political arena in ways large and small.

Political Culture: Who Are We?

A few years ago, the Institute for Advanced Studies in Culture at the University of Virginia attempted to identify some of the constants in American political culture. They discovered nearly unanimous buy-in among Americans for what they call the "American creed"—ideals about the public life of America. Take a second to see how much you subscribe to the "American creed" by answering the five brief questions in Figure 2.1.

Pretty clearly Americans overwhelmingly are proud of their country believe in its goodness and the goodness of its citizens, and even feel that America has a mission to serve as an example for the rest of the world. These elements of political culture may seem abstract, and in one important sense, they are: The nearly universal acceptance of others in theory does not translate into universal tolerance for the practice of people expressing unpopular ideas, as we saw in Section 3.3d, "Tolerance," in Chapter 3. Political culture is manifested through abstract perceptions about self and nation, rather than through specific attitudes, beliefs, and actions that may be at odds with how many Americans view themselves. This infuses political culture with a generous portion of mythology.

We saw the connection many Americans have to their political culture at work in the public reaction to the terror attacks of September 2001. American flags and American flag stickers blossomed overnight on homes, office buildings, and cars. The near-universal sentiment that we had been attacked was

Percent Agreeing

87%	America from the beginning has had a destiny to set an example for other nations
94%	America's contribution is one of expanding freedom for more and more people
95%	America is the world's great melting pot, in which people from different countries are united into one nation
96%	With hard work and perseverance, anyone can succeed in America
95%	Democracy is only as strong as the virtue of its citizens

Source: Survey of American Political Culture[T2]

Figure 2.1. Shared American Ideals?

an expression of an attitude about identifying as an American. At that moment, being conservative or liberal didn't matter, nor did the national origin of one's ancestors. (One unfortunate and important exception to this involved Americans of the Muslim faith and of Middle Eastern origin, who experienced increased discrimination that reflected the worst elements of the hybrid American culture.)

We saw the contours of our political culture during the Cold War as well, even during times of great unrest as a result of strong differences of opinion about such things as the civil rights movement and the Vietnam War. For a while in the 1960s, the American flag became a symbol adopted by those who supported American policy in Vietnam. Some on the other side of this issue burned the American flag as a way of expressing their views, a manifestation of our cultural acceptance of dissent. We know from Chapter 3 that dissent is something people don't embrace quite as strongly as the "American creed." In this regard, everyone may not always accept all cultural values.

Still, even at a moment of great divisions over policy, Americans expressed attitudes and beliefs rooted deep in the political culture. Although at times vocal minorities have advocated the overthrow of the American system, an overwhelming number of Americans—including many who opposed the Vietnam War—continued to feel a patriotic attachment to the American system and rejected the Communist system of the Soviet Union as an inferior alternative.

Group Membership and Tolerance

The tendency for Americans to join organizations is one characteristic of American political culture that separates it from the political cultures of other nations. Observers of American culture have noted this characteristic for centuries. In 1831, the French nobleman Alexis de Tocqueville spent the better part of a year touring the United States, an experience that culminated in publishing his observations in the two-volume work, *Democracy in America*, in 1835 and 1840. In it, he made the observation that America is a nation of joiners,

and that through participating in groups with fellow citizens, Americans learned the fundamentals of compromise necessary to a functioning democracy.[1] Tocqueville noted how, "Americans of all ages, all stations in life, and all types of disposition are forever forming associations. There are not only commercial and industrial associations in which all take part, but others of a thousand different types—religious, moral, serious, futile, very general and very limited, immensely large and very minute."[2] Today, we would call these voluntary groups: civic and religious organizations, political clubs, sports leagues, neighborhood associations, charitable and service organizations, and educational and cultural groups. They need not be expressly political in order to teach how to tolerate and work with others; in fact, most of these groups are not political, and may be devoted to pursuits as recreational and ordinary as intramural sports or playing trumpet in the band or working on the school newspaper.

Recent research confirms what Tocqueville saw over 170 years ago: Americans tend to join groups more frequently and more widely than people in other nations.[3] The more groups we join, the more experience we get in the give-and-take with other people that teaches us how to be tolerant. Therefore, people who join more groups tend to be more tolerant of the rights of others. It is the isolated individual who is likely to be the least tolerant of all.[4]

However, there are indications that over the course of your lifetime, civic engagement has diminished. Historically, there have been peaks and valleys in the degree to which Americans engage in group activities, and evidence suggests that for the past several decades we have been living through one of the valleys. Political scientist Robert D. Putnam writes that over that period, Americans have become increasingly isolated from one another by joining fewer organizations and spending less time with neighbors and friends. As a consequence, Putnam argues that Americans have become detached from the relationships that reinforce basic democratic and civic values. The title of his book, *Bowling Alone*, refers to the disappearance of bowling leagues that once provided a social connection for many people, while providing a visual metaphor for the isolation that characterizes the leisure and work lives of so many people who spend their days living in places where they don't know their neighbors, working alone in cubicles, commuting alone in cars, and recreating alone in front of the television.[5]

Putnam sees in these trends the loss of social capital—the connections we make with each other when we spend our time in association with others. The value of social capital is in its ability to nurture trusting relationships, through which we learn how to compromise and reciprocate with others. These values are associated with having a rich civic life and stand in sharp contrast to the isolation from one another that, according to Putnam, characterizes our time and makes us feel detached and alienated from each other, our communities, and our government.[6]

To reverse these trends, Putnam advocates the daunting task of creating social capital through renewed civic engagement in all facets of life: promoting family-friendly workplaces; designing communities with common areas that promote socializing with neighbors; encouraging clergy to spark a spiritual awakening that will promote religious tolerance; developing Internet activities that engage people in communities; and participating in social and political activities.[7] For many, this would require changing some of the fundamental patterns of our lives—from turning off the TV to joining groups to spending less time in the car. The benefit to individuals could be greater personal fulfillment. The benefit to the political culture would be a deeper investment in the bonds that help a republic endure. Demystifying Government: Virtual Civic Engagement considers whether social media might make something like this possible.

Immigration

Because one component of political culture is the belief that America is an open place accepting of others in need—the idea symbolized by the welcoming torch of the Statue of Liberty—America has been able to incorporate numerous subcultures that immigrant groups have brought with them to this country. This simultaneously makes American

government more interesting—and more complicated. It brings texture to the American tapestry while assembling a much wider set of values than those subscribed to by the Anglican males who wrote the Constitution, making governing the country a challenge.

Changes in political culture—and politics—may be anticipated through the changing face of diversity in America. Cultural changes have also been driven in recent years by shifting migration patterns and the growing number of senior citizens in America. Let's look a little closer at these factors. We'll examine America's long history of immigration and the nature of American cultural diversity, recent patterns of geographic mobility, and the aging of America.

It's probably not overstating things to say that America is a place where just about everybody comes from someplace else. Even the Native American civilizations that European settlers encountered when they came to North America were likely populated by individuals whose origins may be traced to Asia, and to a long walk over what thousands of years ago was a land bridge across the Bering Straits between Alaska and Russia.

Between 1820 and 2000, a total of 66 million immigrants came to the United States, changing the tenor of American life. Of these, better than half (58 percent or 38,460,000) came from Europe. Much of the immigration from Europe came in waves, starting with British and Irish immigrants in the early to mid-nineteenth century, German immigrants following the Civil War, and immigrants from Eastern Europe in the first decades of the twentieth century.

One of the first waves of immigration came from the British Isles, especially Ireland. Between 1830 and 1860, almost 2 million Irish immigrants came to America, representing 40 percent of all immigrants to the United States during that period. Almost another 1.5 million arrived between 1860 and 1890. Many Irish immigrants were Catholic, adding a religious mix to what had been an overwhelmingly Protestant nation.

Germany was the next big departure point. Between 1850 and 1900, following the initial wave of Irish immigrants, a large group of German immigrants came to the United States. The peak

DEMYSTIFYING GOVERNMENT

VIRTUAL CIVIC ENGAGEMENT

There is intriguing evidence that one impetus for renewed civic engagement may be found on the Internet, as people turn to websites that actually encourage them to turn off the computer and meet in person.

A premier example of this is meetup.com, a service designed to allow people to find others online who share their interests and arrange in-person get-togethers. People looking to reach out to others can go to meetup.com and search the database of topics until they find what they're looking for. Topics cover the range of civic and personal interests that Putnam identified as central to community life: books, films, games, health, music, pets, hobbies, work and politics—everything from Audi owners to ferret lovers. You can scan today's list of groups by going to http://www.meetup.com/find/.

Site users can join an existing group or suggest a topic for the purpose of attracting others with the same interest. When a topic attracts enough people in the same geographic area, members vote on a time and a place for a meeting and get together in person, typically in an informal location like a bar, café—or bowling alley. Meetup.com brings together people with the same interests who otherwise might not find each other, but the interaction takes place off line, in the community.

Meetup.com was created with social activities in mind, but it unexpectedly developed an important political function in 2003, as supporters of Democratic presidential hopeful Governor Howard Dean began using the website to organize on behalf of their candidate. The official campaign rapidly recognized the value of meetup.com for national grass roots organizing, and in early 2003, placed a direct link to meetup.com on the candidate's website. Shortly thereafter, Dean's meetup numbers started to soar, growing from several hundred in January to over 65,000 in July, to better than 180,000 before Dean ended his presidential bid the following February.

The first Wednesday of every month became the designated day for Dean meetups, at which thousands of volunteers at hundreds of locations across America would gather in small groups to plan strategy for the Dean campaign. The Dean website trumpeted this activity as the first true grassroots presidential campaign of the Internet era, and attributed the sharp rise in Dean's profile during 2003 to the high degree of interest the candidate generated through meetup.com. As a civic matter, meetup.com became the vehicle by which people who were previously detached from or passive about politics could get involved in a presidential campaign—many for the first time in their lives. It foreshadowed the online-driven civic engagement that would become the hallmark of Barack Obama's 2008 presidential campaign, offering a tantalizing glimpse of how the Internet could can bring people together in the real world to work for a political cause—a far cry from the couch-potato politics of passive observation and detachment offered by television.

was in the 1880s, when 1,450,000 German immigrants represented more than 25 percent of all immigrants during that time. A large influx of immigrants from the Scandinavian countries overlapped the wave of German immigrants. Over 1.5 million Scandinavians, many of them Norwegians and Swedes, came to America between 1870 and 1910.

The turn of the twentieth century witnessed a large influx of Italian immigrants—over 3 million between 1900 and 1920—representing 20 percent of all immigrants during that time. The same period was a peak time for Eastern European immigrants. Three million Russians arrived between 1890 and 1920, 1.2 million Hungarians arrived between 1900 and 1920, and 250,000 Poles arrived during the 1920s. This wave of immigration included a large number of Jews, Russian Orthodox, and other non-Protestants. Notice how as time passed, European immigration moved clockwise, from western to central to eastern Europe.

European immigration tells only part of the story, though. More recently, America has become home to large numbers of new immigrants from different parts of the globe. Specifically:

- Almost three-quarters (72 percent) of the total immigration to the United States from Mexico and the Caribbean has happened since 1970.
- Sixty-two percent of the total immigration to the United States from Asia has happened since 1980.
- Slightly more than three-quarters (77 percent) of the total immigration to the United States from Africa has happened since 1980.
- Slightly more than one-third (34 percent) of the total immigration to the United States

from Central and South America has happened since 1990.

Figure 2.2 illustrates the waves of immigration to America has come in waves from different parts of the world over the course of two centuries.

After each great wave of immigration, Americans' tolerance has been tested, starting with the first influx of Irish immigrants in the 1840s. Nativist Protestants opposed to the foreign, "contaminating" influences of Roman Catholics formed secret societies with names like "The Order of the Star-Spangled Banner" in an effort to combat citizenship for Irish immigrants. Because these organizations operated in secrecy, with their members never claiming to know anything about its leadership, the anti-Catholic crusade was dubbed the **"Know-Nothing" movement.** It survived as a national movement for almost 20 years, until it dissolved over differences about slavery just prior to the Civil War.

The "Know-Nothing" movement showed how tolerance can be sorely tested when some people feel threatened by large-scale changes to their way of life. This regrettable chapter in American history has been repeated several times, as people with different religious practices, skin colors, and native languages came to America

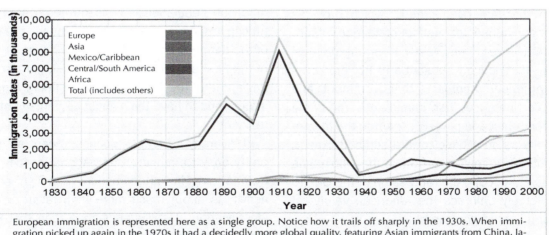

European immigration is represented here as a single group. Notice how it trails off sharply in the 1930s. When immigration picked up again in the 1970s it had a decidedly more global quality, featuring Asian immigrants from China, Japan and Vietnam; Latino immigrants from Mexico, the Caribbean, Central and South America; and African immigrants, whose numbers have doubled every decade since the 1970s.

Figure 2.2. Patterns of Immigration to the United States, 1820–2000[T4]

and, by virtue of their numbers, modified the cultural and political landscape. Jews arrived in large numbers in the early twentieth century to widespread anti-Semitism. The wave of German immigrants was subsiding around World War I, but American involvement in the war generated public hostility to immigrants of German descent. During the 1990s, the most recent wave of American immigrants produced a "close-the-borders" backlash aimed at Latinos, an attitude that's still present in some corners of our immigration debate.

Apart from the psychological component of adjusting to people who may look different or speak and act in an unfamiliar way, periods of widespread immigration invariably put a strain on the resources that government must provide to its swelling population. This poses a material problem for the government and a political problem for elected officials. It's why anti-immigration dictates found a sympathetic audience among those Californians who felt their pocketbooks were being stretched to provide for the needs of a flood of immigrants, many of whom had snuck into California through the Mexican border.

Turn over this picture, however, and you'll find the beneficial side of immigration. People from different cultures bring variety to everything from the arts to politics, adding richness to the things people consider uniquely American. Individuals willingly coming to the United States tend to embrace the "American creed," which provides a common sense of self-identification. Many immigrants—even from vastly different political cultures—instinctively subscribe to key elements of the American approach to government and society. For instance, Irish immigrants who came to America to escape poverty accepted the idea of opportunity as an avenue toward self-betterment. Contemporary immigrants from Cuba who came to America to escape the repression of the Castro regime fiercely embrace the American values of liberty and limited government.

Every generation of immigrants brought with them the myth of the American dream, that their children would find a better life despite the hardships and discrimination that might await them. However glorified this myth may be, to a certain extent, Americans have eventually accepted groups that in their day were derided as dangerously threatening to the established social order. History suggests this may eventually be the fate of the groups some contemporary Americans find threatening.

Diversity

With immigration comes variety. Just look at the 2000 Census. The Constitution requires that a **census** be taken every ten years, in which everyone in the country is supposed to be counted. The census says a lot about the composition of the United States, and tells us how it has changed since the last census was taken a decade ago. Demysifying Government: Slipping through the Cracks tells why an accurate census is so important.

Figures from the 2000 Census confirm the story of America's immigrant past and present. Although about seven in ten Americans is a non-Hispanic white, roughly one in eight is African American, slightly less than one in eight is of Hispanic origin, and one in 25 is Asian American. Also, just as immigrant groups have traditionally settled in specific states or regions, the Census reveals that the South, Southwest, and portions of the Northeast are the most diverse regions of the country. The Latino population is largest in California, Texas, Florida, New York, and New Jersey. The Asian American population is concentrated in California. African Americans are most numerous in the states of the deep South and in the large industrial states of the East and Midwest. In contrast, northern New England and the Great Plains and Rocky Mountain states tend to have the highest percentage of white residents.

If diversity influences politics, then it should be pretty easy to imagine that national politics is far from a singular phenomenon. Although political activity is about much more than racial or ethnic identification, it still stands to reason that states and regions with greater diversity are likely to voice different concerns and interests than states and regions with less diversity. The politics of New York is different than the politics of Idaho in part because of the different groups that settled there.

DEMYSTIFYING GOVERNMENT

SLIPPING THROUGH THE CRACKS

As you can probably imagine, it's impossible to count *everybody* in a nation as vast as the United States. Some people live in remote areas; others are homeless; many others simply elude the reach of census takers. In fact, the Census Bureau estimates that in 1990, about four million people were missed—amounting to 1.6 percent of the population.

This probably doesn't sound like a big deal unless you're really compulsive about record keeping, but from a political perspective, it's huge. Real resources ride on the outcome of the census—big dollars and real power. Some policies provide for federal money to be allocated to states based on population, so states where a disproportionate percentage of the population was undercounted will lose funds they would otherwise be eligible for, while still having to provide for the undercounted people. When we talk about Congress in Chapter 9, we'll see that the census is used to determine which states will gain or lose seats in the House of Representatives, so states where a disproportionate percentage of the population was undercounted will lose representation to which they're entitled.

Compounding the political tension is the fact that all population groups are not undercounted equally, with minority group members far more likely to be overlooked. The Census Bureau estimates that in 1990, 0.9 percent of the white population eluded census takers, compared with 4.4 percent of African Americans and 5 percent of Hispanics. So, members of these groups—not just states—lost out on federal funds and representation in Congress because they were not fully counted.

It turns out that there's a remedy for this disparity, but it's highly controversial. The Census Bureau can estimate the true population using statistical methods, correcting the errors produced by the actual head count.

This possibility generated a huge political battle in the days leading up to the 2000 Census. Because the underrepresented minority groups tend to disproportionately support candidates of the Democratic Party, any statistical adjustment to the census would favor Democrats, probably resulting in the creation of more congressional districts favorable to Democratic candidates. Not surprisingly, Republicans ferociously opposed the statistical estimate, claiming it would amount to a mere guess at the true population—a far cry from the hard numbers required by the Constitution. They argued that even a flawed head count was better than an estimated count, and closer to what the nation's founders had in mind. In 1999, the Supreme Court put its stamp on this reasoning, claiming that using estimated figures for determining congressional representation was unconstitutional.[T5]

But the matter of sampling did not go away. In 2009, President Obama appointed Robert Groves, a statistical sampling expert, to head the census bureau. Groves had been an advocate of sampling during the 2000 census, and some congressional Republicans feared he would rekindle the sampling conflict in advance of the 2010 census, a concern Groves put to rest at his confirmation hearing by asserting he would not use the methodology.[T6]

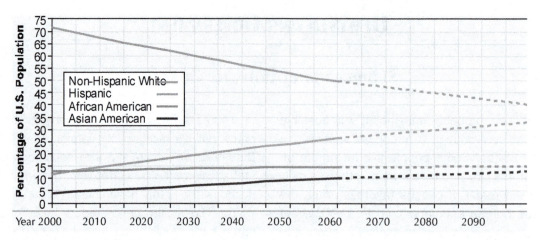

Figure 2.3. Projected Ethnic Group Demographics for the Twenty-first Century[17]. As the white population steadily shrinks in size and the African American population holds steady, the Hispanic population is projected to double between 2045 and 2050, while the Asian American population doubles by 2040. Projecting to the turn of the next century, only four in ten Americans will be white. One-third of the population will be Hispanic.

Some of these differences go back to the distinctions between liberals and conservatives, although this too can be oversimplified. You can review the concepts of liberalism and conservatism in the Demystifying Government box below.

For instance, we mentioned that African Americans are more likely to express the liberal position supporting government activity in economic and social matters—adding a liberal bent to politics in regions with large African American communities. Not every minority group has liberal inclinations, though. Older Cuban Americans, for instance, can be quite conservative politically, lending a conservative quality to regions with large Cuban American communities, like southern Florida.

Probably the biggest story in the 2000 and 2010 Census is the emerging majority of minority groups, so to speak. Those figures we were just talking about from the year 2000 are simply a snapshot of America at a given time. It's also possible to look at trends in immigration patterns and birth rates, and try to estimate what America will look like in the years ahead. The Census Bureau has developed a projection like this, and you can see the results in Figure 2.3.

Keep in mind that this is an estimate based on current trends, and that if immigration or birth rates should change, the estimates could be off. Nonetheless, the most notable thing about the projection is that during your lifetime, the white majority that has always characterized this country will become a numerical minority. By the year 2060, non-Hispanic whites are projected to dip below the 50 percent mark in total population, remaining the largest group in America but shrinking from a majority to a plurality of the population, as His-panics, African Americans, and Asian Americans will together constitute a numerical majority of Americans.

For a nation that's always seen itself as primarily Anglican, these changes promise to create an entirely different identity—one with potentially profound political implications. The questions are speculative, but interesting, even if the answers are unknowable. What would it mean for whites to be just another minority under these new circumstances? Would whites see themselves as a minority? As the largest minority? Or still as a majority? Would they continue to control a disproportionate amount of economic resources by virtue of having been a majority group for so long? Would greater diversity in the population translate into greater diversity among elected representatives, and if so, what might that mean for the direction of our politics?

DEMYSTIFYING GOVERNMENT

REVIEW: LIBERALISM AND CONSERVATISM

Liberalism in its broadest sense endorses an active role for government in addressing social and economic problems, and a more limited role for government in refereeing matters involving personal or moral values.

Liberals advocate government activism (which in a practical sense translates into spending money on government programs) for such social issues as environmental protection, health and child care, urban decay, education and drug addiction, and for such economic issues as welfare and Social Security. In this regard, liberals seek to use the power of government to assist those in need (for instance, through welfare and drug programs) and to compensate for the inequities (like unequal access to health care) or consequences (like air and water pollution) of the economic marketplace.

At the same time, liberals typically believe government should stay out of matters that they consider to be of a moral nature. Consequently, liberals may oppose using government power to limit abortion rights, impose the death penalty, or require prayer in public schools (however, they may be quite comfortable engaging the government to protect abortion rights and defend against school prayer). Liberals may also favor gun control laws, limits on military spending, and tax laws that benefit lower-income people.

Conservatism applies different principles to arrive at mirror-image positions. In its broadest sense, conservatism values the power of the marketplace to address economic concerns and individual initiative to confront social problems, therefore advocating a limited role for government power in economic and social matters. Contemporary conservatism for many years has accepted the reality of America's social welfare programs (although some of today's conservatives have spoken about the need to privatize or eliminate social programs), but conservatives tend to be suspicious of government programs that are not subjected to what they regard as the beneficial self-correcting forces of the marketplace, and that therefore take money out of taxpayer's pockets that could be put toward free enterprise.

Consequently, conservatives advocate less involvement in (and less money for) government programs on environmental protection, health and childcare, urban issues, education, and drug addiction. They regard welfare as a program that can undermine individual initiative, and have been successful in recent years in restructuring government welfare benefits to orient the program toward getting people to find jobs. Conservatives, like liberals, embrace Social Security, but are more likely to be interested in making it a market-oriented program.

Migration

In addition to being an immigrant nation, America has always been a mobile nation. As large numbers of people move around within the United States, politics is inevitably affected. Once an agrarian country centered on rural concerns, America was redefined by industrialization, which brought about massive movement toward urban centers in the late nineteenth and early twentieth centuries. With urban development, political attention turned to urban issues like transportation, sanitation, labor laws, and a host of matters that were irrelevant in an earlier time.

In recent decades, there have been two politically meaningful population shifts: regionally from the old industrial cities of the Midwest and Northeast to the South and Southwest, and nationally from cities to suburbs.

The regional shift is evident when you compare where people lived in 1920 with where they lived in 1960 and 2000. Ninety-odd years ago, the most populous states were in the industrial centers of the Midwest and Northeast that in recent years have been dubbed the "Rust Belt" region, after the aging industries of twentieth-century America that were once their crowning jewels. By 1960, the move to warmer "Sun Belt" states had already begun, and by 2000, America's center of gravity had shifted to the South and West.

The ascendancy of conservative national politics coincided with this migration. Through the 1960s, heavily populated industrial centers were the engine of liberal politics, a key base of political support for presidents like Franklin Roosevelt and Lyndon Johnson who presided over a large expansion in the role of the federal government. These regions lost political clout as they lost population to the Sun Belt states, which traditionally have been more socially and economically conservative.

Now it's easy to overstate the relationship between population shifts and changes in political currents—there's a lot more to it than where people move, as we'll see as we go along. For instance, liberal presidents like Roosevelt and Johnson drew support from outside their base in the Rust Belt. And, in recent years, immigration patterns have started to eclipse the effects of domestic migration, as an influx of more liberal Latino voters has softened the conservative leanings of the Sun Belt and made several Western and Southwestern states fertile ground for Democrats. Still, as people move, congressional districts move with them, and national officials take notice of where the votes are.

The other meaningful migration in recent years has been the steady nationwide exodus of city dwellers to ever-expanding rings of suburbs. The urban exodus began after World War II, and by 2000, a country that originated as a rural nation and experienced urban migration in the twentieth century had become suburbanized. A glimpse of the nation at night, with lights radiating out from core cities, communicates a sense of how America's population spreads out for miles from downtown.

When we think of suburbs, we tend to think of affluence, and it is true that part of the motivation for the post-war migration from inner cities by people with resources was to escape growing urban decay. Today's suburbs are more complex than this; some older suburbs have predominantly working class neighborhoods, and in some places, suburbs are starting to become ethnically diverse.

Traditionally more conservative than residents of urban areas, suburbanites today are a politically complex lot. In the 1996 election, for instance, political analysts made a lot out of the phenomenon of "soccer moms"—suburban women with young kids (whom they shuttled to soccer games, hence the name). These voters tended to be social moderates who were attracted in large numbers to the policies of President Clinton, permitting the Democratic president to make inroads through conservative suburban areas. In 2004, those same analysts labeled these voters "security moms" concerned with terrorism, who were more likely to support President Bush. By 2008, the suburbs had become a rich source of votes for Barack Obama and his message of inclusive "post-partisan" politics.

The politics of affluence does play a role in some urban-suburban issues, however, like education. Public schools in many states are supported with property taxes, meaning affluent suburban communities of private dwellings are able to collect more money to spend on education. This can create wide disparities in the educational opportunities available to urban and suburban schoolchildren, an arrangement that challenges the American notion of equality of opportunity but that, nonetheless, will be defended by suburbanites who benefit from it. As we will see in the section "Black and White, Rich and Poor," with more resources at their disposal than residents of poorer urban neighborhoods, affluent suburbanites have an advantage should they wish to defend the status quo against efforts to fund public schools more equitably.

Age

If you had been born 50 years earlier, the sight of someone over 100 years old would have been highly unusual. Today, it isn't surprising if you know or are related to someone who reached the century mark, and U.S. Census Bureau projections indicate the longevity trend should continue. Add to this the huge number of people in the aging baby boom generation—all those people who were born in the twenty years following the end of World War II—and you have the makings for age to be a key political divide in the years ahead.

In 2000, the U.S. Census Bureau reported that people 65 years or older composed 12.4 percent of the population. Among these, 1.5 percent or 4.2 million were 85 years or older. As these figures increase, the swelling ranks of seniors is bound to put pressure on a Social Security system that was not designed to handle the burden it will face when you're approaching middle age and will have to support it.[8]

As the large Baby Boom generation ages, we're seeing increased political attention paid to health care matters, both routine and extraordinary. Skepticism about proposed changes in health care policy among older voters was one of the largest roadblocks to President Obama's efforts to overhaul the health care system in 2009. With Baby Boomers reaching the point where they face the need for expanded medical resources, more Americans require medical assistance in their advanced years, a heated political debate has emerged over the question of how much government will be asked to do to defray the those costs, especially for those who cannot afford medical services or prescription drugs. And, we're witnessing an intense ethical debate over emerging medical technologies like cloning and performing research using stem cells from human embryos—research that has the potential to advance treatments for diseases like Alzheimer's that affect people later in life but that, by its very nature, raises controversial questions about what constitutes life itself.

Political Socialization: How We Become Political Creatures

How do we become political creatures? The fact is, though, that while we are often not very political by choice, we're still exposed to a multitude of political influences, starting from the time we're very young, through the process of **political socialization.**

Take a minute and think back. Try to identify your earliest political memory—the first time in your life that you can remember being aware of a politician or a political event. It can be about an election, a national event—anything where a political figure was involved.

Chances are, the event you remembered took place when you were between six and ten years old, around the time kids begin to open up to the larger world. And chances are also that it involved the president. For most kids, the president is the first political figure we're aware of, our gateway to appreciating politics. Of course, when kids become aware of the president, it's in the simple way you would expect kids to process information. They really don't understand what the president does, even as they recognize that he is someone important. In other words, young kids will have a limited **cognitive** or factual understanding of the president. Instead, their relationship to the president will be highly **affective** or emotional.[9]

Initial impressions of the president are that he is powerful and good. This was the case in 1958, when presidential scholar Fred Greenstein examined the impressions of President Eisenhower held by fourth through eighth graders,[10] and it was the case in 2000 when Greenstein's study was replicated on the same age groups with respect to impressions of President Clinton.[11] With the exception of eighth graders in the 2000 study, kids in 1958 and 2000 ranked the president as more important than a host of authority figures they knew firsthand, including teachers, principals, doctors, police officers, and religious leaders.[12] In both years, kids were inclined to view the president in positive terms as well, although the 2000 study reveals a tendency for today's generation to hold less positive views overall than kids did in the late 1950s.

This could be the result of greater negative media coverage of the president, or of kids having access to the Internet at a young age, where they are exposed to a wider variety of political messages. The 2000 study revealed that 81 percent of fourth through eighth graders use the Internet, changing patterns of socialization by accelerating exposure to adult political messages.[13] It has long been the case that as kids age, they abandon the generally positive affect toward political leaders that characterizes early socialization, precisely because age exposes us to a more adult appreciation of the political world and, with it, a less childlike view of politicians. Attitudes like **cynicism** traditionally develop during adolescence when a more complex understanding of politics sets in.

Political socialization doesn't just happen passively as we age, though. There are forces that act on us, shaping the way we become political as we venture beyond our childhood homes. These **agents of socialization** are many and varied, and they work on us from birth through early adulthood because political socialization is a process that plays out over a long period of time. There are several important agents of socialization, starting with our parents and siblings in our home as we grow up, continuing with our friends as we get older, our teachers in school, our coworkers when we get a job, and the media throughout our lives.

Family and Friends

Maybe you heard your parents talking about Bill Clinton's involvement with Monica Lewinsky, or about whether they thought the president should be impeached for his actions. Perhaps you have older sisters or brothers who were involved in a cause and liked to talk about it. If your parents voted, maybe they took you to the polls when you were very young. Or you may remember them talking about the price of gas or food or how high taxes are, and blaming it on one politician or another.

It doesn't take much for kids to learn about politics from parents and siblings. The home can be a laboratory for young kids, who absorb an awful lot of information just from the tone of their parents'

voices and from what their parents say about political figures and issues. Kids don't even have to be involved in the conversation; they're pretty good at putting together what they hear to figure out how the world works—or, at least, how the world works based on the way it looks at home. Because kids interact heavily with their families, and because families are where kids figure out who they are by the way others relate to them, parents and siblings are considered a **primary agent of socialization.**[14]

One's childhood home is the place where people experience early life socialization. It's where we internalize a set of values about how the world works that will structure our relationship to politics as we age. From their parents and families, young children learn messages about authority, order, trust, tolerance, cooperation, and obedience. If you grew up in a home with strict parents, you likely internalized different values than if you grew up in a permissive home.

Such early learning is very important as it sets the stage for the continuing socialization of our later years, when we develop a mature sense of our political selves. By no means does this suggest that we become a carbon copy of our parents—far from it. In fact, for all the power of the family to socialize us to politics, you can probably think of many ways you're different from your parents politically. At the very least, you probably hold different positions on many political issues.

Instead, the strongest relationship between parents and kids tends to be on the general level of **party identification,** or the political party you identify yourself with. You could think of party identification as being socialized much like religious identification. In other words, chances are you identify with the same religious group as your parents. At the same time, you may hold different attitudes about the nature or importance of religious worship, or about some of the specific positions of your religious group. This is analogous to holding the same party identification as your parents but disagreeing on particular political issues.

One major study on how effectively party identification is socialized showed that six in ten children had the same partisanship as their parents when both parents had the same partisanship—both were Republicans or both were Democrats.[15] While this is a large percentage—much larger than anything else that's socialized from parent to child—consider that it also means that four in ten children whose parents share a partisan attachment end up identifying with a different party or not identifying with any party. Furthermore, not every child comes from a home where the parents share partisanship. You can pretty much flip a coin to determine the partisanship of kids who come from homes where their parents do not have the same party identification because they are equally likely to be Democrats or Republicans.[16]

From childhood through college and beyond, friendship groups rival the family as an important socializing agent, taking on a central role in political socialization during adolescence. Because peer groups are interpersonal, they are a primary agent of political socialization. But, unlike our families, we get to choose our friends. As teens and even now, we may look for friends who help us fit in at school. If we do, we look for friends who are a lot like us. This means that for many people, peers reinforce rather than challenge existing political beliefs—to the extent that politics enters into friendships at all.

As we get older and the initial influence of family socialization fades, we may be more open to a broader spectrum of opinion in our friendships. If this happens, peers can actually challenge our earlier political learning and serve as an agent for change.[17] This typically does not happen while we're still young, though.

Schools and the Media

It's pretty obvious that a lot of formal learning about politics happens in school. After all, it's happening right now. And it starts in preschool, where we begin to learn about the president and about holidays commemorating political figures. In this regard, schools are an excellent source of political information and a fairly direct agent of political socialization.

Perhaps the strongest contribution of schools to political socialization is a bit less obvious. If you

grew up in the United States, do you remember what your kindergarten classroom looked l ike? Was there a flag over the chalkboard? Did you pledge allegiance every morning, to one nation, "invisible?" Was the room decorated in paper cutouts of turkeys and Pilgrims in November, Lincoln and Washington in February, or were there paper ballots with the names of real candidates on Election Day? Exposure to political symbols and engaging in patriotic rituals works to develop a national identity, making the classroom a subtle but important source of political socialization.

How thoroughly do the schools act as an agent of socialization? Not as thoroughly as family and friends, with whom we are engaged in close interpersonal relationships. Although schooling can give us a basic civic education, for many kids the amount of political learning that occurs in secondary school is limited—you probably remember from Chapter 3 that levels of political knowledge tend to be low among adults. Also, while kindergartners may be taken by stories of how George Washington could not tell a lie, adults are more cynical about politicians, meaning that attitudes learned in school eventually change, beginning in adolescence when we start to see the political world as a complex place.

For these reasons, we may think of school as a **secondary agent of socialization.** Schools matter to our political development, but not as much as parents, siblings, and peers, with whom we have strong and regular interpersonal relationships.

The same may be said of the media, even though common sense may tell us that the media exert a strong influence on our development by virtue of how pervasive the Internet, television, radio, and newspapers are in our daily life. Like schools, the media can be a source of political learning. We live in an information environment so cluttered with noise that it's often hard to make good judgments about what's factual and what's simply opinion. This limits the ability of the mass media to serve as a reliable source of political information.

The media are also surprisingly limited in their ability to shape our political attitudes. The primary reason for this is media messages are impersonal, and have trouble competing with family and friends.

We're more likely to pay attention to or believe media messages that reinforce our existing attitudes, while ignoring others—a phenomenon called **selective exposure.** We may even unconsciously filter out messages that don't conform to our prevailing attitudes, through a process called **selective perception.** Between consciously being uninterested in messages that conflict with our attitudes and unconsciously filtering messages that conflict with our attitudes, the way we use the media puts the brakes on its effectiveness as a socializing agent.

The media are not without effect, however. They may have a socializing influence through their ability to set the boundaries of what we're aware of politically, determining the issues and people we think about. This process is called **agenda setting.** It can be a powerful effect in the sense that things that are not on our agenda will have no place in public political discussion, making them less likely to be considered for political action. The power of agenda setting is limited, though, to influencing what's on our mind. Remember, agenda setting is different from generating opinions—we're not saying that the media have the kind of reach into our lives necessary to formulate opinions on our behalf.

Agenda setting influences what we think about, rather than the attitudes and opinions we hold about the things on our mind.[18] If you find yourself talking to your friends about terrorism or global warming or other topics you know about because they're in the news, you could say that the media helped place those topics on your personal agenda. Your attitudes and opinions about these topics are less likely to be shaped by the media—although we will see that when television commentators consistently portray a politician or an issue in a particular light, our thinking tends to follow from what they say.

Other Influences on Political Socialization

Not everyone is socialized under the same circumstances, which means there may be sharp differences among us in the way we come to understand the political world, even though we will all be exposed to the same agents of socialization. African Americans and women, for instance, have for a long time been socialized differently than whites and men.

Generations of African Americans have had to contend with a political system that produced obstacles to participation, and have had to face the dilemma of how to become socialized to a system that was in some important respects unwelcoming.[19]

Studies indicate that as early as grade school young girls begin to react to messages that suggest they should be less interested in political life than young boys, despite demonstrating greater proficiency with language and greater maturity than boys of the same age.[20]

These varying experiences with political socialization help explain why some African Americans may feel conflicted about embracing the shared experiences of American political culture that we talked about earlier, or why, despite recent gains, women remain disproportionately underrepresented in elected offices with respect to their numbers in the population. They may also help explain why it is possible for us to talk about patterns of public opinion that are distinct to African Americans and women. In the aggregate, African Americans are much more likely to support government solutions to social problems and Democratic candidates for public office than the population as a whole. The tendency for women to hold more liberal positions on social issues than men may also have its origins in the different ways men and women are socialized.

The things that happen when you're young and as you reach adulthood can also shape the way you're socialized to politics. Imagine that you were born into a home that was hit hard by the Great Depression, where food and money were scarce and you had to live from day to day with what little you could find. Perhaps your grandparents or your great-grandparents came of age in an environment like this. It's not too difficult to imagine that the development of their political attitudes could have been driven by issues of scarcity, and perhaps an attachment to government assistance to help mitigate the painful effects of poverty.

Maybe your parents had to contend with the Vietnam War when they were younger. Perhaps they had to confront a decision about whether to go to Vietnam or to resist the draft—a common experience for young people in the middle and late 1960s and early 1970s. Perhaps they were influenced by counterculture demonstrations against the war, which were politically and socially anti-establishment in nature. Intense social experiences like these can have as great an impact as the Depression on shaping the relationship an entire generation develops toward politics. Such **generational effects** on political socialization help explain why large groups of people, like the "Baby Boomers" born in the twenty years after World War II, move through life with a commonly held set of political and social attitudes developed from their formative experiences.[21]

At the same time, where you are in life can interact with how you respond to the formative political events of your generation and alter the way you relate to politics as you age. Baby Boomers like Bill Clinton, who protested the system when in their twenties, were hardly radical in their approach to government when their turn came to run things twenty years later. Maybe you have strong ideals right now about what you hope to do with your life, or how you can contribute to society. That wouldn't be unusual because many people have strong ideals when they're in college, and are really open to the idea of social change.

That's not to suggest you won't have strong ideals twenty years from now—the last thing you need is someone twenty-five years older than you telling you that you're going to outgrow idealism—far from it! You may instead find your idealism living side by side with a growing sense of pragmatism. **Life cycle effects** studied in older people point to the emergence of a kind of practical outlook on things when people acquire jobs, families, and the other trappings of middle age. As you might expect, the older we get, the less open we become to political and social changes. Still, it will be interesting to see how life cycle effects compete with generational effects as the Baby Boom generation ages, to see if generational influences remain strong into old age. How hard is it to imagine grandparent Boomers taking their kids and grandkids to see an octogenarian Mick Jagger in concert?

Political Participation: Getting Involved

Fresh from the process of childhood political socialization, armed with a sense of our political selves, we can go forward into the adult world of politics and participate in a variety of political activities.

Or not.

Truth is, while some people are heavily engaged in politics, it's not all that unusual to find people whose participation is limited to voting—or less. Just like the civic activities we discussed in the section "Group Membership and Tolerance," involvement in political activities is less than it was a generation ago, with particularly sharp declines in the percentage of people who engage in the most widespread political activity, voting.

To many people, **political participation** only means voting. However, it can be a lot more than going to the polls. If you take a look at Figure 2.6, you'll find a list of eight different ways we can participate in politics. Take a second and think about which of these activities you've done in the last year. This should begin to give you a sense of just how much—or how little—Americans get involved politically beyond the voting booth.

Conventional Participation

According to the United States Elections Project, almost 57% of eligible voters cast a ballot in the high-profile, hotly contested 2008 election, in which both major political parties offered a fresh alternative for president, and in which one-third of the Senate and the entire House of Representatives was up for grabs. During "midterm" elections—the elections that fall during the middle of a presidential term in which congressional and gubernatorial seats are the biggest draw—turnout is typically much lower. In 2010, it was under 38%.[22]

That's roughly comparable to the percentage of Americans who claim they talk about politics from time to time, perhaps with the intent of influencing others. Talk may not be cheap, but it is relatively inexpensive compared to other forms of participation, and as the amount of effort involved in an activity

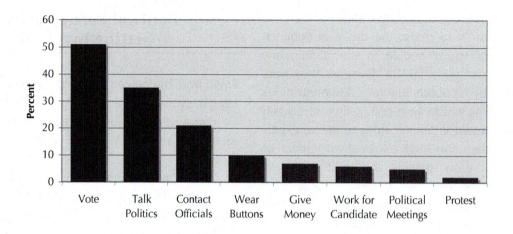

Figure 2.4. Percentage of People Who Claim to Participate in Eight Types of Political Activities[T9]

increases, the number of people engaged in that activity predictably declines. So it is that only about one in five of Americans will call or send a letter or email to an elected official on an issue they feel strongly about.

Only one in ten will wear a campaign button, put a bumper sticker on their car, or display a sign in front of their house in support of a political candidate. Fewer will contribute money to a political candidate or volunteer time to work for a candidate or a political party. Only one in twenty will attend political meetings or campaign rallies.

Unconventional Participation

Even fewer will get involved in less conventional forms of political participation, like engaging in a protest or demonstration, even though American history is replete with examples of protest activity. From the Boston Tea Party prior to the Revolution to Shays's Rebellion during the period of the Articles of Confederation, small but intensely committed groups of dissenters have sought to bring about political change through acts of defiance. In the spring of 2009, individuals opposed to the spending policies of the new Obama administration organized a protest inspired by the Boston Tea Party. Playing on the historical symbolism of colonial-era rebellion, they organized on the Internet to mail tea bags to their elected representatives and the president along with notes explaining the nature of

their concerns. Then, on April 15—tax day—they held rallies in cities across the country to protest what they viewed as the intrusive nature of big government.

Within months, they had shaped their own identity as the "Tea Party," and they continued to assert their influence during the 2010 elections, albeit through a more conventional form of protest. In a number of Republican Senate primaries in states as far-ranging as Delaware, Florida, Kentucky, Nevada, and Alaska, so-called "Tea Party" insurgents upended candidates with institutional party support. A similar phenomenon occurred in a number of Republican primaries for House seats.

Sometimes, protest activities are peaceful but dramatic acts of **civil disobedience**, like those led by the Reverend Dr. Martin Luther King Jr. against segregationist policies in the South in the 1950s and 1960s. Simple but defiant and courageous acts, like Rosa Parks' refusal to give up her seat on a bus to a white man in Montgomery, Alabama, in 1955, drew attention to and helped to change unjust laws.

At times, protest activity turns violent. In stark contrast to Dr. King's peaceful demonstrations, African American neighborhoods in cities across the United States were the site of bloody rioting in the 1960s. In the highly charged atmosphere of the Vietnam War, college campuses across the country became centers of sometimes violent protests. At Kent State University in 1970, police killed four students and wounded nine others during a protest against President Nixon's decision to escalate the war. The 1960s also witnessed political assassination as a tool of protest, including the murders of President John F. Kennedy, his brother Senator Robert F. Kennedy, and Dr. King.

Public reaction to protest activity is not always supportive, particularly if a protest is noisy or disruptive, and especially if it is violent. Sometimes, protests tap competing values—such as when someone agrees with the cause promoted by the protesters but not their methods. We'll look at a case where dueling protests created a collision of values in Issue: Vaccine? Animal Rights? You Decide.

Young and Old, Men and Women

OK, so maybe you looked at the list of activities in Figure 2.4 and thought, "I don't wear campaign buttons. I don't give money to political candidates.

I'm not into meetings and rallies, and I don't know anyone who is." That wouldn't be very surprising. Not only are these types of political activities not widespread, they're especially uncommon among young adults. All forms of political participation are—and with good reason.

Think of the things that are on your mind right now or that have been on your mind at one time or another since you started school. Maybe you're worried about your grades, or how you're going to pay for your education. Friendships and relationships might take up a lot of your time. You could be preoccupied with where you're going to live next semester, or maybe you've got an issue with a roommate that's taking a lot of your energy. Perhaps you have some unresolved matters with your family. You could just be thinking about the plans you have for this weekend or for after you stop reading about political participation.

Grades, money, friends, dating, housing, roommates, family, social plans—some or all of these things are typical of what we spend our time thinking

ISSUE

Vaccine? Animal Rights? You Decide

In June 1999, hundreds of gay and lesbian demonstrators belonging to the group ACT UP (AIDS Coalition to Unleash Power) disrupted a Philadelphia fund-raiser by presidential candidate Al Gore. The group, which practices civil disobedience to draw attention to the plight of AIDS sufferers, carried a life-sized marionette of Gore with big drug companies pulling the strings.

Their complaint was that Gore supported legislation backed by pharmaceutical firms making it difficult for impoverished African nations to purchase generic AIDS drugs that were far less expensive than the brand-name drugs produced by American drug companies. This policy, said the protesters, sealed the fate of

countless numbers of people with AIDS in order for large sums of money to flow to the drug companies—and from the drug companies to the Gore campaign war chest.

The protesters were not supporting Gore's opponent. In fact, they were clear that they did not want George W. Bush to become president. But they did want to bring attention to their plight and felt that without dramatic action, the entire issue, to say nothing of the large matter of finding a cure for AIDS, would go unnoticed. In its manual on civil disobedience, ACT UP instructs would-be participants in nonviolence training, how to stage a demonstration, and how to act when you're arrested and sent to jail.[T10]

It's hard to know how many ACT UP members are also sympathetic to the rights of animals. But another organization, People for the Ethical Treatment of Animals (PETA), has a problem with AIDS activists. PETA objects to the use of animals in AIDS research and stages protests in the attempt to put an end to research that harms or kills animals. In their manual for activists, they make the point that animals, like humans, have rights, and that human use of animals for the purpose of experimentation (or for consumption or clothing) violates those rights.[T11]

Like many protest groups, their activities can be passionate and extreme. The *Wall Street Journal* reported that PETA had engaged in attacks on laboratory facilities at Stanford University where AIDS research with live animals was taking place and had used legal means to slow and at times stop similar research at other sites.[T12] They see their work as a matter of life and death.

So do the AIDS activists.

So, the two groups are in conflict. PETA activists would happily leave AIDS research alone if researchers would stop using animals in their experiments. But an AIDS cure is not possible without animal research. For their part, AIDS activists might be sympathetic to PETA objectives if they didn't feel that people would die in the name of protecting animal rights.

And what of people who voice support for animal rights and an AIDS cure? It's possible to be sympathetic to both, and it's not uncommon for celebrities and public figures to endorse both causes. The work of protest groups makes it plain that beneath such verbal proclamations of support lies a disagreement that is deadly in its intensity.

Think about whether you are more sympathetic to the position of the AIDS activists or the animal right's activists.

AIDS Activists' Perspective

- The plight of people with AIDS needs to be dramatized so that politicians will take action to save them.
- AIDS victims face a life-or-death struggle.
- AIDS research cannot advance without animal experimentation.
- People should not die in the interest of protecting animal rights.

Animal Rights Activists' Perspective

- The plight of animals used for research needs to be dramatized so that politicians will take action to save them.
- Animals used for research face a life-or-death struggle.
- AIDS research is not a problem as long as live animals are not sacrificed to the process.
- Animals should not die in the process of researching cures for human diseases.

My Opinion

In practice, do you agree more with the AIDS activists' perspective or the animal rights activists' perspective? You should decide how to balance:

- The plight of people with AIDS and the plight of animals used for research.
- The need for animal experimentation in AIDS research and the need to protect the lives of research animals.
- The value that people should not die to protect animal rights and the value that animals should not die to cure human diseases.

about as young adults. That doesn't leave a lot of time for joining political campaigns, especially if politics feels so much more remote than these other immediate things. For this reason, political analysts questioned whether Barack Obama would suffer during the 2008 presidential campaign, because some of his strongest support came from young people.

After a while, this starts to change for many of us. We graduate from college and find work. Many people find a long-term partner and settle down in an apartment or house that they rent or own. Life takes on a new rhythm, a more settled rhythm conducive to greater political involvement. For some, this newfound appreciation of political engagement is interrupted briefly as the responsibilities of having young children encroach on time available for civic activity. Otherwise, the tendency to participate in politics builds through middle age, as having the time to get involved coincides with having interests to protect—like a family, a job, or a house—and growing responsibilities like loans and an ever-increasing tax bill. We still have a lot going on like when we were younger, but the things we're doing are more likely to be the sorts of things that lend themselves to political action.

Political participation begins to tail off as we get older and begin to slow down, although senior citizens are among the most politically active of any group when it comes to voting. Even though there is a drop-off in voting after people reach retirement age, the decline is gradual. People in their eighties are still far more likely to vote than people in their twenties!

It has also been the case historically that women have tended to participate less than men. Some of this is no doubt because women were denied the right to vote until 1920. In recent years, women have demonstrated greater political involvement, particularly in the areas of voting and running for elective office. The women's vote has been especially important in recent years—in fact, if only men voted, Bill Clinton would have lost the 1992 and 1996 elections. Additionally, women are starting to serve in elected office at a higher rate than ever before. See Demystifying Government: The Rise of Women in Elected Office.

Even in places where women appear to participate less than men, some of the disparity can be understood in terms of differences in education. In fact, how much education you have has a lot to do with how likely it is for you to get involved politically.

If you look at Figure 2.5, you'll find the percentage of men and women who told the General Social Survey that they engaged in several types of political participation—attending political events, contributing to candidates, and contacting government officials. In each category, you can see that men are slightly more likely to get involved than women, which might lead you to conclude that men participate more than women.

DEMYSTIFYING GOVERNMENT

THE RISE OF WOMEN IN ELECTED OFFICE

One way to gauge the level of political activity by women is to look at how many women have run for and served as governors and senators. The first two women governors followed their husbands in office—Miriam Ferguson in Texas and Nellie Ross in Wyoming, both elected in 1925. After them, fifty years passed before Connecticut's Ella Grasso became the first woman elected to a governorship without following a spouse. By 2002, women were serious contenders in half of that year's thirty-six gubernatorial contests. In 2011, six states had female governors, or 12 percent of the total.[T13]

A similar picture emerges when you look at the Senate, where thirty-nine eight women have served between 1922 and 2011. Initially, a number of these women, too, were appointed to fill seats left vacant by their husbands. Hattie Wyatt Caraway of Arkansas was the rare exception: She was the first woman to be elected to the Senate without benefit of an appointment, in 1931. But, it took until the 1990s for women to become a regular presence in the Senate. In 2011, there were seventeen female senators representing fourteen states (California, Maine, and Washington have two female senators).[T14] These figures, although well below the percentage of women in the population, suggest a change in the political climate in which female candidates are regarded as serious political contenders.

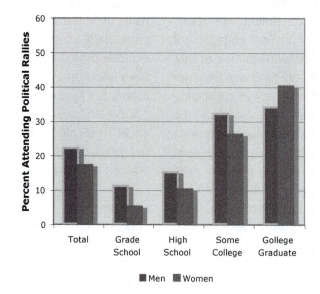

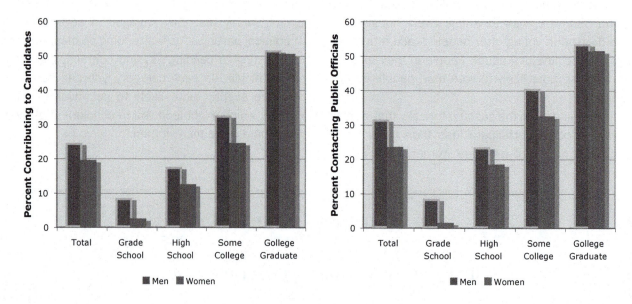

Figure 2.5. Gender, Education, and Participation[T9]. Gender differences in participation depend heavily on education. As education levels increase, gender differences disappear in rates of attending political rallies, contributing to political candidates, and contacting public officials.

But watch what happens to the differences between men and women when you look at their levels of participation in terms of how much education they have. Participation rates rise steadily for men and women as they amass more years of schooling, really shooting up for college grads. As participation rates go up, gender differences shrink or disappear. College-educated women are just as likely as college-educated men to contribute to political campaigns, almost as likely to contact government officials, and somewhat more likely to attend political rallies.

Black and White, Rich and Poor

If President Obama's electoral prospects were dependent in part on support from young people, who traditionally participate at lower levels than middle aged and older people, it was equally problematic that he also depended on the engagement of African Americans, who participate in some—but not all— political activities at lower rates than white. There are multiple reasons for this discrepancy, including a legacy of institutional restrictions against African American voting, and a complex relationship among participation, social and economic resources, and psychological factors that adversely affects African Americans. Just as differences in political participation rates between men and women can be explained by education rather than gender differences, participation differences between African Americans and whites defy simple racial explanations.

In 1972, political scientists Sidney Verba and Norman Nie published a ground-breaking study of American political participation, in which they found that a greater share of African Americans are entirely uninvolved politically than their numbers in the population would suggest. At the same time, Verba and Nie found that African Americans vote at about the same rate as whites and are about even with the rest of the population among the small group of people who are highly active politically. In other words, blacks opt out of the political process at a higher rate than whites, but those that are highly involved are about as active and engaged politically as whites.[23]

The fact that we don't find significant racial differences in voting patterns is noteworthy when you consider the obstacles to voting that African Americans faced in the South until very late in the twentieth century. Although granted the legal right to vote following the Civil War, it took a century before those rights were more than words on a piece of paper.

The years immediately following the Civil War gave few hints that it would take a century before one-time slaves would be free to embrace the political rights promised to them during Reconstruction.[24] A string of federal acts promised to immediately enfranchise African Americans. In rapid succession:

- **The Military Reconstruction Act of 1867** required all southern states to give former slaves the right to vote as a condition of being readmitted to the Union.

- **The Fourteenth Amendment**, ratified in 1868, extended citizenship to former slaves.
- **The Fifteenth Amendment**, ratified in 1870, specifically forbade states to deny the vote to someone on the basis of race, color, or the fact that they were once a slave.
- **The Enforcement Act of 1870** imposed criminal penalties on anyone who would try to deny blacks the right to vote.
- **The Force Act of 1871** shifted the right to oversee elections from the states (some of which vehemently resisted black voting rights) to the federal government.

Initially, hundreds of thousands of former slaves flocked to the political process. African Americans voted in large numbers and were elected to offices at all levels of government. However, as Reconstruction ended and federal troops withdrew from the South in the late 1870s, whites who vehemently opposed black involvement in politics did everything they could to lock them out of the process. Using a combination of violence and political tactics, white southerners ruthlessly put an end to black participation. As northern troops departed the region, southern whites employed violent attacks against African Americans as an intimidation tactic designed to keep them from voting. By the 1890s, with whites back in control of state legislatures, many southern states passed a series of laws designed to make it impossible for blacks to vote. These included:

- **Literacy tests**, which required voters to demonstrate knowledge of the Constitution that might be advanced for you, even if you've already read Chapter 2 of this book. Because many African Americans lacked formal education, literacy tests were an effective way to disenfranchise them. (see Demystifying Government: How Well Would You Do on a Literacy Test?)
- **Poll taxes**, which required voters to pay a tax in order to exercise their right to vote. Although the tax was generally nominal, it had the practical effect of disenfranchising countless black voters who were too poor to pay it.

DEMYSTIFYING GOVERNMENT

HOW WELL WOULD YOU DO ON A LITERACY TEST?

For decades, African Americans had to endure hardship and humiliation in order to register to vote. It was not uncommon for voter registration offices to be open only a few days a month, during work hours. White employers who permitted black workers to take time off to register were subjected to organized economic retaliation designed to threaten the jobs of African Americans who registered. At the Registrars Office, it was common for local deputies to harass, threaten, and intimidate blacks who tried to register. Information on African American applicants would likely find its way from the registrar to the Ku Klux Klan, which would use violence or the threat of violence against blacks who dared to try to register.[T16]

If would-be voters actually made it to the literacy test, they faced an exam designed for them to fail. A case in point is the Alabama Literacy Test, which consisted of three parts: a reading of a portion of the Constitution, which the applicant had to interpret orally to the registrar, and two written sections on constitutional, federal, and state law that were evaluated in secrecy by a Board of Registrars. Here are some questions from that test. See if you can answer them:

- If a person charged with treason denies his guilt, how many persons must testify against him before he can be convicted?
- At what time of day on January 20 each four years does the term of the president of the United States end?

- If the United States wishes to purchase land for an arsenal and have exclusive legislative authority over it, consent is required from _____.
- Name one area of authority over state militia reserved exclusively to the states.
- The power of granting patents, that is, of securing to investors the exclusive right to their discoveries, is given to the Congress for the purpose of _____.
- In what year did Congress gain the right to prohibit the migration of persons to the states?[T17]

As you can see, these questions are challenging (or trivial) even for people with a formal education. They would only humiliate and discourage someone with no education. The combination of legal roadblocks, physical threats, and violence was effective; in many southern counties, the African American registration rate was zero, and it remained this way for decades.

By the way, the answers are: Two persons must testify against someone charged with treason; the president's term ends at noon on January 20; consent for purchasing land for an arsenal has to come from the legislature; the states have exclusive authority over the appointment of officers to militia; Congress grants patents for the purpose of promoting progress; Congress gained the right to prohibit the migration of persons to the states in 1808. Be honest—how many of these did you get right?

- **Grandfather clauses,** which exempted whites—many of whom were as uneducated as African Americans—from having to take literacy tests or pay poll taxes because they were eligible to vote or were descended from someone who

was eligible to vote in 1867—before passage of the Fourteenth Amendment.
- **"White primaries,"** which circumvented the Fifteenth Amendment by keeping African Americans from voting in Democratic Party primaries by declaring the Democratic Party

to be a private organization exempt from laws requiring equal participation. In southern states dominated by the Democratic Party, primary winners invariably won elections, and exclusion from primary voting was an effective way to disenfranchise blacks.

These discriminatory laws remained on the books for decades. Although the Supreme Court ruled grandfather clauses unconstitutional in 1915[25] and "white primaries" unconstitutional in 1944,[26] southern states continued to disenfranchise African Americans until the Supreme Court and Congress actively intervened in the 1960s. By then, African Americans had to overcome the effects of having been locked out of the political process in the South for four generations.

For African Americans who choose not to participate in politics, the underlying causes start with the relationship between race and class. Verba and Nie found that people with higher **socioeconomic status (SES)**—well-educated people with high incomes and high-status jobs—are more likely to have resources that facilitate political participation, and that African Americans are less likely to be represented in the high-SES group. These resources include time, money, and information about politics.

Verba and Nie speculate that there is an intricate relationship between having resources, having the motivation to use them, and getting results. They contend that this relationship explains who is likely to participate and why African Americans are less likely to be represented among political participants.[27]

The economic disparity that distinguishes high-SES individuals from low-SES individuals is associated with a psychological divide. People with more resources to use in the political process, a group in which African Americans are less well represented than whites, are more likely to be oriented toward the political process. They're more likely to be aware of and concerned about the political process, and have a high sense of political **efficacy**, which you may recall from Chapter 3 is the feeling that you can get results if you enter the political arena. This should make sense: If you start out with the necessary tools, you're more likely to feel

you can get the job done. You feel motivated. You participate.

We've already talked about how participation is linked to getting results when we said in Chapter 1 that not participating is always a choice but that people who participate are more likely to get results from government. This works to reinforce the psychological drive to participate because when you actually accomplish something by participating, it's natural to feel like you can get the system to respond to your wishes. You've already done it! To the degree that what people get through participating is tangible, which it often is, participating also works to bolster their supply of political resources that were the catalyst for participating in the first place.

You can probably see how the tangible and psychological rewards that come from participating work to reinforce the tangible and psychological advantages that high-SES individuals start with. So, if African Americans are underrepresented in the high-SES group, they will ultimately be less likely to participate and less likely to believe that participating will make a difference. That's because the process can work in reverse to keep low-SES individuals from wanting to engage in political activity. Low SES means having fewer resources that are useful for participating in politics, which can reinforce the psychological orientation that political participation is a waste of time because the system will not be responsive. This low sense of efficacy discourages participation—and is self-fulfilling.

You can probably also see how participation can reinforce social status, independent of race. With people from higher socioeconomic groups participating more, the political system is going to be more responsive to their interests, which you can probably imagine are different from the interests of people with lower socioeconomic status. For instance, the political interests of unemployed people for job training or unemployment insurance are worlds apart from the concerns of high SES individuals, but the unemployed are not oriented to participate in large numbers in the political process, so they are in a weakened position to make demands on the system.[28] Political officials will be more sensitive to the needs of high-SES

DEMYSTIFYING GOVERNMENT

REVISITING RESOURCES THAT MATTER

Remember when we talked about **pluralism** and **elitism** as different ways to understand who gets what, when, and how? (If not, take a quick trip back to the section "Power Surge.") In a way, when we talk about the connection between having resources and having the motivation to participate in politics, we're revisiting the question of whether political power is held by many or few.

Let's look a little more closely at the case of the long-term unemployed population, typically low-SES individuals who lack the resources and therefore the motivation to participate politically. If political officials are more sensitive to the needs of people who participate, and unemployed individuals tend not to participate, you could make the case that the political system will not be responsive to their interests, choosing instead to respond to the interests of a smaller group of resource-rich, high-SES individuals. You'd be making an argument in support of an elitist perspective of American government, in which few people with a lot of resources exercise power. This conclusion seems to be supported by the claim that people without many resources and who lack efficacy are unlikely to be able to get political figures to respond to their needs.

On the other hand, we might also observe that government does not ignore the needs of the unemployed. There are unemployment insurance policies, job-training programs, and economic plans during periods of high unemployment designed to lower the unemployment rate. Presidents like to boast about how many new jobs were created under their administration. Why does any of this happen when unemployed people are not likely to participate in the political process in large numbers?

Political scientists who have studied this question[T18] claim that other groups will speak for the unemployed in the political system. For instance, unions and civil rights groups, out of self-interest or social justice concerns, may advocate policies that benefit unemployed people. Is this consistent with the pluralist perspective that resources are distributed widely enough for many to wield political power? Is it simply a modification of an elitist argument because unemployed people inadvertently benefit from the convergence of their interests and the interests of a powerful elite? Is it possible that government would respond more quickly or lavish more attention on the needs of the unemployed if they participated in the political process?

individuals, who will be well positioned to reap the rewards of government. For more on the relationship between resources and motivation, see Reinventing Government: Revisiting Resources That Matter.

I Couldn't Care Less!

Maybe you couldn't care less about who participates and what happens to them. There's a word for that. It's called **apathy.** It's a word that is widely used in

the media and in conversation to describe the way many people relate—or fail to relate—to politics. Americans are widely perceived to be apathetic as a result of having low levels of political knowledge and involvement. People who are apathetic avoid political participation because they genuinely don't care about it. (They might want to avoid reading about it, too.)

Or do they? Some research on the topic points to a different conclusion, based on observations of people in social settings who avoided talking about politics. This line of thought suggests that people seem apathetic not so much because they don't care about what's going on but because they feel powerless to do anything about it. Big political problems, even those that could affect us directly, are just that—big—and they can leave us feeling overwhelmed.[29]

In the face of this, and to avoid the social embarrassment that could come from making it appear that we actually believe our opinion might matter or that we could exercise some control over the situation, a lot of people resort to saying "I'm not interested" or "I'm just not paying attention." They strike an apathetic pose, and they resist political involvement, even on issues that hit home, like rapidly increasing tuition costs, where they're quite aware that what happens does matter to them.

Doing this takes work. We have to try hard to be apathetic because it's so natural to care about what happens to us and to those around us. And apathetic periods come in cycles. Maybe your parents grew up during a time when it was cool to be "involved." There was a great deal of interest in the 2008 election, and record crowds estimated at close to two million people gathered in Washington in January 2009 for President Obama's inaugural. Under these social circumstances, you might also find that it can be cool to talk about political problems with friends and neighbors, too.

You may have noticed that this section on apathy is a lot shorter than others in the book. Do you care?

Why Vote?

Bad jokes about apathy aside, when you look at the most commonly engaged form of participation—voting—it's reasonable to ask why anyone would take the time to do it at all. When you look at what you have to do in order to vote in an election in this country, you might reasonably ask how our turnout can be as *high* as 57 percent in a presidential election year. Some countries, like Australia, have close to perfect turnout. In these countries, voting is compulsory because it is regarded as an obligation rather than a right. There's actually a fine for not voting. Under those circumstances, plenty of people manage to find their way to the polls. It doesn't

happen that way in the United States, though, where the process is much more complex and there is no monetary cost to not participating.

First, you have to register to vote. This typically involves satisfying age and residency requirements, although the specifics vary by state. Alabama, for instance, makes you affirm your allegiance to the Constitution and swear that you have no plans to overthrow the legally elected government of the state.

If you live in North Dakota, you have it easy because there's no registration requirement there—you can just skip to the part where you show up at the polls on Election Day. If you live in any other state, you have to be aware of the need to register, know the registration deadline in order to register in time to vote in the next election (it's typically a couple of weeks or so before Election Day), and know how to register.[30]

Until recently, registering to vote in most states involved locating and visiting a state office, like your County Board of Elections. Things got easier with the passage of the **National Voter Registration Act** of 1993. It's commonly called the "Motor Voter Act," because of a provision that makes it possible for you to register to vote when you apply for or renew your driver's license.

The Motor Voter Act has other provisions, also designed to make registration more convenient. All states except for Minnesota, Wyoming, Wisconsin (and, of course, North Dakota) must accept mail-in registration forms, including a national mail-in voter registration form made available by the Federal Election Commission. Agencies that provide public assistance, like Medicaid and food stamps, or services to people with disabilities, are also required to provide voter registration services. Some states, like California, let you register online, while others let you download application forms off the Internet.

The Motor Voter Act makes registration easier than it used to be—if you know about it. If you're like many people, though, you didn't know about it until about a minute ago, unless you stumbled across it when you got your driver's license. It still requires the expenditure of a valuable resource—time—to complete the registration form, and turnout figures

DEMYSTIFYING GOVERNMENT

WHY PEOPLE VOTE

Why do you vote? Some people say:

- Because it's my obligation to vote
- Because it makes me feel good
- Because I feel that I can influence what's happening

If you say, "I vote because I feel it's my obligation to vote," then you're expressing a sentiment about **civic responsibility**, the sense that there are certain things we're obligated to do as citizens of a democracy. Some people feel that the inconvenience of voting is part of the price we pay to maintain privileges like the freedom to speak our mind or to complain when we don't like something.

If you say, "I vote because it makes me feel good," then you know that you don't have to make the difference in an election to feel like you've made a difference. It's efficacy again, in a specific form that relates to voting. Some people get a sense of efficacy from voting because they feel like their voice will be included in the mix of voices expressed on Election Day. Also, it can be gratifying to speak up.

If you say, "I vote because it gives me the feeling that I can influence what's happening," then you are trying to shape your world. Influence is a different type of feeling than efficacy. Some people feel that voting equals influence, regardless of the outcome of an election. They see voting as a way to shape the future course of politics, either by contributing to a candidate's winning margin or by making a show of support for the loser.

suggest it has not significantly boosted voter turnout.

Also, don't forget that registering to vote is only the first step in the process. You then need to find and get directions to your polling place—information that will take time to get—and arrange to take time out of your day to vote. Polls open early in the morning in most states, and typically remain open until seven, eight, or nine in the evening, giving people who work the opportunity to vote without taking time away from their jobs. However, this can mean the added inconvenience of having to get up a little earlier or delay an evening activity, and possibly wait in line during these "prime time" hours.

In recent years, some states have made voting a bit easier by keeping the polls open for several days to permit people to vote on their schedule. In 2008, 32 states permitted some form of early voting, where votes were cast (but not counted) before Election Day.[31] Oregon may have the most convenient system of all, as everybody votes by mail. If you live in Oregon, you can mark your ballot in the comfort of home and mail it to the county elections office or place it in a drop box. As long as it's received by 8 p.m. on Election Day, it counts.[32]

Early voting doesn't minimize the time involved in voting, but it makes it possible to avoid long lines and work around a busy schedule. Voting by mail alleviates the need to know where your polling place is located. But it still takes resources to vote, and in states that still do it the traditional way, voting can be a pain. It requires work and time, and the sacrifice of something else you might want to be doing, like sleeping or going out or being with your family. It may seem particularly burdensome if you're one of those low-efficacy Americans who feel the political system is not going to respond to your wishes and interests anyhow. If you believe your vote does not matter, or politicians are all just a bunch of hypocrites, you're not likely to invest your resources in registering and voting.

So, if voting is such a hassle, why does anyone want to do it? You'll find a few explanations in Demystifying Government: Why People Vote.

Because the mathematics of voting makes the likelihood of casting the deciding vote in an election remote, many people vote because of the attitudes they have about living in a democracy. People vote because they feel they should, or because it makes them feel good, or because it gives them the sense that they have a voice in public affairs.

How Can I Decide?

Chances are some people in your class have voted in a real election, others are eligible but have never voted, and still others may be ineligible to vote in the United States because they're not 18 years old or American citizens. So, to make sure everyone has had a voting experience (or something close to it) before we move on, let's take a minute and cast a vote in a hypothetical congressional election. Imagine you're in a voting booth, staring at the ballot that appears in Figure 2.6. You're trying to decide how to vote in a congressional race between Republican Leonard Fitzsimmons and Democrat Marjorie Carp. Because you know their names and their party affiliations, you have exactly the same information you would have in a real voting booth.

Imagine there are other people in line behind you, so try not to linger too long over your decision.

So, what was your decision? Did you make a choice? Or did you go for the "no vote" option? Maybe you were thinking, "I don't know any of these people. How can I vote?" And, of course, you don't know anything about them—which precisely mirrors the situation of many people who cast ballots in real elections. They still manage to vote. Perhaps you did too. Let's look at how they do it.

Party I.D. Voting

One of the few clues you had to guide you was party affiliation, so if you identify as a Republican, you may have voted for Leonard Fitzsimmons, or if you identify as a Democrat, you may have voted for Marjorie Carp. Even without knowing anything else about these candidates, this is a reasonable thing to do because a simple party label can convey a lot of information. Perhaps you assumed that the Republican candidate is the more conservative of the two. Often, you would be correct. Perhaps you reasoned that you don't know what Carp's positions are on issues that matter to you, but if you're a Democrat, the chances are that she's closer to your beliefs than Fitzsimmons. That seems like a pretty reasonable assumption as well.

You may even have voted for the candidate who shares your partisanship without even wondering what the candidate stands for, simply because you're a strong partisan. Remember, party identification

OFFICIAL BALLOT, U.S. CONGRESS

INSTRUCTIONS: To vote for a candidate, mark an X in the oval beside the candidate you prefer.		
U.S. Congress (vote for **ONE** candidate)	**Leonard Fitzsimmons** (Republican)	⬭
	Marjorie Carp (Democrat)	⬭
	(No vote)	⬭

Figure 2.6. Sample Ballot

is socialized more strongly than political attitudes and beliefs, and if we're predisposed to thinking of ourselves as Republicans or Democrats, it's natural to gravitate to a candidate who shares our identification.

So, party identification can help strip away the confusion of an unfamiliar ballot and provide a reasonable guideline for how to vote. It wouldn't be surprising if many of your classmates voted this way, just as it wouldn't be surprising to find many Americans voting this way in real elections. In recent years, party identification has been a good way to predict how people will vote.

At the same time, party identification may not be quite as strong as it was many years ago. In 1952, 47 percent of Americans claimed to be Democrats and 28 percent identified themselves as Republicans, according to the American National Election Studies. Half of these called themselves strong partisans. That left one-quarter of the electorate as either independent or apolitical.

Compare that to 2009, when Gallup reported only 35 percent identified themselves as Democrats and 27 percent as Republicans, leaving 38 percent of us as independents or apolitical.[33] Although about one-third of the independents said they "lean" toward the Democratic Party and an equal number "lean" toward the Republican Party, we find that people who identify loosely with a political party are a bit more likely than strong supporters to shop around when they vote.[34]

More independents and fewer strong partisans in the electorate can produce **ticket splitting** among voters, where people vote for, say, a Democratic candidate for president and a Republican candidate for Congress. This type of voting pattern can generate divided government, where one party controls the White House and the other controls at least one house of Congress, like we saw during twenty-two of the thirty years between 1980 and 2010, and again following the 2010 elections.

Candidate Characteristics

Did you think about voting for Leonard Fitzsimmons because he has an Irish-sounding name? Maybe you cast your vote for Marjorie Carp because she is the only woman on the ballot.[35] Ethnic and gender identification can be other useful voting shortcuts. In fact, candidates with ethnic sounding names may count on votes from people who will identify with their background. A particularly unusual case of identity voting is discussed in Demystifying Government: The Surprising Success of Victor Morales.

Candidate character, as well as characteristics, may also play a role in voting. Sometimes the character of the candidate—their integrity, or the way they handle their personal or public life—can factor into whether people will vote for them. Bill Clinton is an excellent example of a political figure who conducted his personal life in a way that lost him the respect—and in some cases, the votes—of people who otherwise approved of his performance in office. Another example is South Carolina Governor Mark Sanford. Once considered a possible contender for the 2012 Republican presidential nomination, Sanford's career ran aground in 2009 when he disappeared for five days without explanation, telling his staff that he was taking personal time to hike the Appalachian Trail. But when he was spotted by a reporter getting off a flight from Argentina, the married governor admitted that he had gone to Buenos Aires to end an affair he was having with a woman he called his "soul mate". As details of their relationship emerged, and calls for Sanford's resignation or impeachment grew, he fought hard to retain his office. But Sanford's national ambitions were effectively destroyed, knowing he could not face a national electorate that would use this incident to evaluate his character.

Of course, these are high-profile cases of politicians in the news. Voting for or against a candidate because of their personal characteristics requires having more information about them than their last name or their party identification, and information can be costly to acquire. This limits the circumstances under which people will find themselves in a position to vote on a candidate's character.

DEMYSTIFYING GOVERNMENT

THE SURPRISING SUCCESS OF VICTOR MORALES

It's not every day that someone with no political experience, hardly any money, and no backing from the political establishment can make a credible run for a Senate seat from a major state. However, that's exactly what high school geography teacher Victor Morales did in Texas—twice—as the nominee of the Democratic Party for the Senate in 1996 and as the runner-up in a three-way race for the same nomination in 2000.

To the political establishment, Morales came out of nowhere in 1996, riding around Texas on a shoestring budget in an old pickup truck, to defeat two members of the U.S. Congress for the Senate nomination in a race he lost to incumbent Republican Senator Phil Gramm. Four years later, using the same low-budget strategy, he came in second in a field of three candidates, only to lose a head-to-head runoff with Ron Kirk, the well-funded, party-endorsed former mayor of Dallas.

Part of Morales' success no doubt stemmed from the fact that he was a maverick outsider in a state that likes anti-politicians, and an underdog who achieved a kind of celebrity status through news coverage of his seemingly impossible quest. But Texas Democratic Party leaders promoting Kirk were sensitive to the fact that Morales could count on a large turnout among Latino Democrats, a force in Texas politics, because of his roots in the Latino community. They feared Latino support would not be enough for Morales to be elected to the Senate, but it might just be enough to defeat Kirk for the Democratic nomination.

Eager to avoid a second Morales nomination, Democrats supporting Kirk's candidacy arranged for high-profile endorsements from gubernatorial nominee Tony Sanchez and former San Antonio mayor and U.S. Secretary of Housing and Urban Development Henry Cisneros. The extent to which these endorsements from high-profile Latino figures helped Kirk win the Democratic nomination may never be known, but it illustrates how much political leaders believe voters will support candidates with backgrounds similar to their own.

Issue Voting

More limited still may be the opportunity to vote on the positions a candidate takes on issues. **Issue voting** requires satisfying several conditions, which involve having fairly specific information about the candidates running for an office and the motivation to use it to determine how you'll vote. To cast a vote on an issue, you must:

- Have enough awareness of an issue to have a position on it.
- Be aware of where the candidates stand on the issue.

- Differentiate the candidates' positions on the issues.
- Vote for the candidate whose position is closest to yours.

Take a second and try it. Imagine that our two congressional candidates have announced their position on a hypothetical second stimulus bill similar to the one Congress passed in 2009 providing close to $800 billion to stimulate the economy through a mixture of government spending and tax cuts. Most of the plan entailed spending measures in areas such as education, green energy technology, and highway construction, with about one-third of the spending reserved for individual and business tax

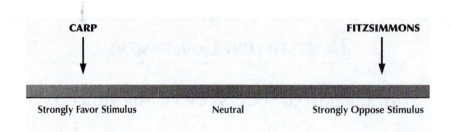

Figure 2.7. Issue Voting: Positions of Two Hypothetical Congressional Candidates on $800 Billion Stimulus Package

cuts. Supporters argued the stimulus was needed to jump-start an economy facing its deepest downturn since the Great Depression. Opponents claimed that the program was an inappropriate use of tax dollars—a wasteful give-away to special interests that would dramatically expand the federal budget deficit. In the upcoming election, let's assume that supporters and opponents are making the same arguments.

Figure 2.7 displays the positions of our two hypothetical congressional candidates. Leonard Fitzsimmons opposes the initiative, saying it's a huge mistake to believe we can "spend our way out of recession." Marjorie Carp strongly supports it with some minor reservations, saying "bold action is needed to get the economy on track" while urging more tax breaks and fewer spending projects.

To cast an issue vote, you would vote for a candidate based on this issue, regardless of where he or she stands on all other issues, and regardless of his or her party identification.

Clearly, you'd have to feel pretty strongly about the issue to do this, and some people do feel that strongly about some issues. Perhaps caring deeply would then motivate you to be informed about the issue, but information can be difficult to come by or complicated to wade through for even the most dedicated voter.

When a team of political scientists investigated voters' decision-making processes in 1956, they found that no more than one-fifth to one-third of voters could satisfy the informational requirements for issue voting.[36] A more recent study of this question found that, in 1992 and 1984, more people—on average, better than half—were able to navigate the informational requirements necessary for issue voting on a host of issues including government spending, crime, job policies, the environment, aid to minorities, and women's rights.[37]

However, the figure was lower in 1988, 1980, and 1976, jumping around a bit from election to election. This could reflect how the information environment isn't always the same from issue to issue or from year to year. Some issues are more complex than others and sometimes it's just harder to differentiate where the candidates stand. In fact, political candidates eager to reach as many voters as possible may intentionally take broad or vague positions, complicating our ability to place ourselves clearly in one camp.

Retrospective Voting

Issue voting is prospective in nature because we're looking ahead and making judgments about what candidates are likely to do after they're elected. Some people make decisions about candidates by looking at the past. When an incumbent is running for reelection, it's fairly typical for voters to view the election as a referendum on his job performance. **Retrospective voting** provides an opportunity for people to look back and evaluate how the official has performed in office to determine whether the incumbent should be retained or replaced.[38]

We might take any number of things into account when making a retrospective evaluation about an official. The candidate's actions on a particular issue or set of issues could be prominent in our thinking, particularly if it's an issue that affects us personally like the economy, or something the candidate made a big deal about when running for office the last time. We might take character into account when making a retrospective evaluation and ask if the official is worthy of our continued support.

It's hard to know exactly what people will look for, but incumbents assume that voters will be judging their actions and record and try to be prepared as best they can. They can never control the timing of events, though. President Obama no doubt believes voters in 2012 will evaluate his economic record and the actions he took to reform the health care system, two of the biggest issues in the 2008 election. But there is no way to know for certain what else might intervene before he faces the voters again.

In Chapter 3, we saw how in 1991, following the swift and decisive American victory in the Persian Gulf War, President Bush (senior) probably believed he would be judged—and rewarded—for his efforts at putting together an effective war coalition. When a recession hit a year later, he found himself vulnerable to assessments that he wasn't sympathetic enough to people who were hurt by the downturn or proactive enough to do something to combat it. This type of reaction is not surprising: Historically, presidents are punished if they have the misfortune to preside over bad economic times during an election year.

George W. Bush faced reelection during a time of economic and international uncertainty, when a majority of Americans said they felt the country was going in the wrong direction. Normally, this spells difficulty for an incumbent, and throughout 2004, President Bush ran even with his challenger, Massachusetts senator John Kerry. Although President Bush was reelected, the country remained divided on his performance to the end, handing the president a narrow three-point victory with a slim majority in the Electoral College.

When Al Gore sought the presidency in 2000, he ran as a *de facto* incumbent. As Bill Clinton's vice president, Gore was in a position to take credit for the prosperity of the Clinton years. Of course, he was also in line to take the blame for the scandals of the Clinton years. Fearful of being seen as too close to Clinton's shortcomings, Gore ran away from

his administration's record, never asking voters to give him credit for good economic times. Whether or not this was an error in political judgment will never be known, but it did neutralize a powerful tool that fortunate incumbents have at their disposal when inviting voters to make a retrospective evaluation of their term of office.

A Look Ahead:
Apathy, Efficacy, and the Media

Remember a little while back, in Section 4.7, "I Couldn't Care Less!," when we were saying that apathy might be about powerlessness? That people may come across as uncaring because problems seem so overwhelming that we might actually feel uneasy suggesting that we believe we can do something about them? It's possible that the media contribute to this situation.

That's because the choice to participate in politics is made in a prevailing climate of public opinion, which is influenced by the media. In the 1960s, when getting involved was cool, the prevailing climate of public opinion supported political participation, even activism and protest—some of the less conventional forms of participation we talked about earlier.

The climate was quite different in the 1980s and 1990s, and this was reflected in the way society is was mirrored back to us on television and in newspapers. If those messages preach conformity, it's possible that we'll feel reluctance to express ourselves, especially if our opinions differ from the norm. We may be discouraged from talking about politics, from participating in political campaigns, possibly even from voting. We'll seem and act apathetic, not just because we may feel overwhelmed by the magnitude of the problems we face, but because we're reacting to a social climate perpetuated by media messages that are unsympathetic to political participation.[39] We're apathetic because we want to fit in.

Media coverage of political events may have an impact on feelings of efficacy as well. From news shows to tabloid talk shows to MTV to Internet websites, we're bombarded with lots of information about politics and government, but we don't have a clear way to make sense of it all. It's easy to get lost or confused in the free market of messages, where everyone seems to have a point of view and it can be hard to figure out whom to believe. As we'll see in Chapter 5, even "credible" media sources like network and local news programs play on our fears and doubts, inviting us to anticipate the worst possible outcomes from events or to accept that our political leaders are motivated by the basest instincts. There's evidence that as television replaced newspapers as our primary source of information, feelings of efficacy began to decline—a pattern that began taking shape more than a generation ago.[40]

The tone of our political discussion just makes things worse. To call it "discourse" or "debate" risks putting a refined label on political coverage that's often harsh and shrill. In an environment where there are so many channels that everyone has to yell to get our attention, how can we know what's truthful, what's partially truthful, what's rumor, and what's totally fabricated? The answer is, very often we don't have a reliable way of navigating through the noise.

Sometimes, we end up believing things about our public officials that aren't entirely true. Sometimes, we just turn the noise off altogether. These are both reasonable responses to our twenty-first-century media environment. Neither does much to facilitate feelings of efficacy.

Of course, it's easy to blame the media for everything from political apathy and inefficacy to why there was no hot water in the shower this morning. The media are so pervasive that they make an easy target, and even though there are places where the media play a critical role in the way the political system operates, it is possible to exaggerate the extent of that role. We'll be sure to aim carefully as we begin to explore the role the media play in connecting us to—or distancing us from—the political world. That's the matter we'll take up next, in Chapter 5.

Chapter Review

American political culture comprises a widely held set of values, attitudes, and beliefs that people have about the United States. It unifies America as a nation despite its great diversity by giving people a sense of an "American creed" that most Americans subscribe to, despite differences about how America should be governed.

Holding these shared values can ease the strain caused by diversity. Throughout history, periods of heavy immigration have typically produced an intolerant reaction, like the anti-Catholic "Know-Nothing" movement of the mid-1800s and, more recently, anti-Latino sentiments. New groups put a strain on resources and bring different customs and traditions that may seem alien and threatening to those who were here before them, although immigrant groups typically embrace American political culture, and over time contribute to the diversity that is one hallmark of that culture.

Changes in our political culture—and our politics—may be anticipated through the changing face of diversity, migration patterns, and the growing number of senior citizens in America. As Asians and Hispanics replace Europeans as the largest immigrant groups, whites are steadily becoming a smaller percentage of the population, and census projections estimate that whites will be a minority by the middle of the twenty-first century.

Political socialization is the process by which we acquire knowledge about politics, along with the attitudes and beliefs that we carry into adulthood. Socialization is a lifelong process facilitated by a series of agents, primary among them our parents, siblings, and friends. Although parents are the most important single agent of political socialization, many parental attitudes and beliefs are not socialized between generations, with party identification the most widely acquired parental characteristic. Secondary agents of socialization include schools and the mass media, which influence political discourse through agenda setting. Political socialization is also affected by the circumstances of our upbringing, with African Americans and women confronting a political environment that has not always embraced their participation; by large-scale events that shape our generation; and by where we are in the life cycle.

There are many ways beyond voting that people participate in politics, like working for a candidate, contacting public officials, contributing money to a campaign, talking about politics, or participating in a protest or an act of civil disobedience. Of these, voting is the most common political activity, although only slightly more than half the eligible voters have participated in recent presidential elections. The likelihood of participating in politics is influenced by age, education, socioeconomic status, and efficacy.

Participation takes effort, and given time and information costs, you can make the case that it's sensible not to vote. Still, people find the motivation to vote because they feel it is their civic responsibility, they get a sense of efficacy from voting, or they believe that voting gives them some influence over politics. Voting decisions may be based on party identification, attributes of the candidate, issues, or retrospective evaluations of candidate performance.

Key Terms

affective Existing in the realm of emotion or feeling.

agenda setting The tendency for topics given great weight by the media to be given equally great weight by those who use the media, such that the people and events considered important by those who determine media coverage will become the people and events that the public considers important.

agents of socialization External influences that shape the way we are socialized to politics, including parents and siblings in the home, friends and coworkers outside the home, and institutions like schools and the media.

apathy A sense of indifference to or lack of interest in politics.

census An accounting or, as Article I Section 2 of the Constitution puts it, an "actual Enumeration" of the residents of the United States, taken every ten years by constitutional decree to assess population growth and population shifts. Census figures are used to determine representation in Congress, as states that lose population between censuses stand to lose House seats to states that gain population.

civic responsibility A sense of duty or obligation to society that some people believe comes along with citizenship.

civil disobedience A peaceful means of protest whereby individuals draw attention to laws they consider unjust by disobeying them and being arrested for their actions.

cognitive A factual awareness or appreciation of someone or something. Cognition implies knowledge and the ability to exercise judgment. This is why we would say that a young child's understanding of the president is not cognitive because kids' awareness of the president as an important figure lacks appreciation of what the president does and why he is important.

conservatism An ideology that advocates limits on government power to address economic and social problems, relying instead on economic markets and individual initiative to address problems like health care and education, while promoting government involvement in moral matters to, for instance, minimize or eliminate abortions or permit prayer in public schools.

cynicism A pervasive attitude of mistrust about politics that may lead people to withdraw from political participation.

efficacy The attitude that you can be effectual and effective in your dealings with government.

elitism The theory that government responds to a small, stable, centralized hierarchy of corporate and academic leaders, military chiefs, people who own big media outlets, and members of a permanent government bureaucracy. People who subscribe to this position believe the actions of regular citizens, like voting and joining groups, simply mask the real power exercised by elites.

generational effects Historical influences felt by an entire generation during their formative years, which shape the way they are socialized to politics.

issue voting Choosing a candidate in an election on the basis of his or her proximity to your position on an issue or issues you consider important.

"Know-Nothing" movement An anti-Catholic movement that formed in the 1840s as a reaction to the first large wave of Irish immigration.

liberalism An ideology that advocates the use of government power to address economic and social problems, like unemployment and environmental protection, while limiting government involvement in moral matters like abortion rights and prayer in public schools.

life cycle effects Changes to the way we relate to politics and society that naturally occur during the course of aging, which typically leave us less open to political and social change as we get older.

National Voter Registration Act Passed in 1993 to simplify and standardize voter registration requirements, the "Motor Voter Act" allows residents of most states to register to vote at the same time as they apply for or renew their driver's license. It also provides for a standardized, national registration form that can be downloaded from the Internet.

party identification An individual's association with a political party. The most common parties Americans identify with are the two major parties, Republican and Democrat. Party identification—also called party I.D.—varies in intensity such that it may be strong or weak. Those who do not identify with any party are typically called independents.

pluralism The theory that government responds to individuals through their memberships in groups, assuring that government is responsive to a wide range of voices. People who subscribe to this position believe that the wide distribution of resources in society drives the decisions government officials make.

political culture The common set of attitudes, beliefs, and values that provide the foundation of support for a political system.

political participation The range of activities people can engage in to influence the political process. While voting is the most commonly performed political act, participation encompasses a host of things—from writing letters to public officials to contributing time or money to a campaign or protesting the actions of government.

political socialization The process by which we acquire political knowledge, attitudes, and beliefs.

primary agent of socialization Parents and siblings exert disproportional influence on the political development of children by virtue of the initial influence they have on kids, giving the family a primary role in the process of political socialization.

retrospective voting Evaluating the past performance of an incumbent to make a judgment about the future—whether the incumbent should be retained or replaced.

secondary agent of socialization Schools and the media have an effect on political socialization, but the effect is less than from primary agents like the family because we do not form close interpersonal bonds with either institution.

selective exposure The tendency to pay attention to messages that are consistent with existing attitudes or beliefs, while overlooking messages that conflict with them.

selective perception An unconscious process by which we filter information that we deem irrelevant, uninteresting, or inconsistent with our attitudes and beliefs, while absorbing information that conforms to our self-perception.

socioeconomic status (SES) A measure of an individual's social position based primarily on education, income, and occupation. High socioeconomic status individuals are more likely to have advanced education, high incomes, and occupations that award high status and demand great responsibility, like professional or managerial work. The abbreviation for socioeconomic status is SES.

ticket splitting Voting for candidates of different parties for different offices, rather than voting a "party line" for all Republicans or all Democrats. Ticket splitting, which has increased in recent years, is a sign of how Americans have been growing independent from political parties.

Resources

You might be interested in examining some of what the following authors have said about the topics we've been discussing:

Almond, Gabriel A., and Sidney Verba. *The Civic Culture: Political Attitudes and Democracy in Five Nations.* Newbury Park, CA: Sage Publications, 1989. This study of several countries lends a comparative perspective to political culture.

Clark, Terry Nichols, and Vincent Hoffmann-Martinot, eds. *The New Political Culture.* Boulder, CO: Westview Press, 1998. This edited volume of essays on comparative political culture reflects contemporary thinking on the subject.

Dawson, Richard E., and Kenneth Prewitt. *Political Socialization: An Analytic Study.* Boston: Little, Brown, 1969. As the name suggests, this volume is a good overview of political socialization, containing a particularly good discussion of the agents of socialization.

Eliasoph, Nina. Avoiding Politics: *How Americans Produce Apathy in Everyday Life.* New York: Cambridge University Press, 1998. An interesting and surprising take on the widely held belief that Americans do not participate in politics because they are apathetic.

Fiorina, Morris P. *Retrospective Voting in American National Elections.* New Haven, CT: Yale University Press, 1988. For those who want to learn more about the evaluations people make about incumbents running for reelection and how those evaluations factor into how people vote.

Putnam, Robert D. *Bowling Alone: The Collapse and Revival of American Community.* New York: Simon and Schuster, 2000. This influential book presents an impressive array of data to support the argument that Americans have become increasingly detached from each other, weakening the civic bonds on which a vital democracy depends.

Tocquevi lie, Alexis de. *Democracy in America.* New York: Vintage Books, 1945. One of the first and most perceptive observers of American civic life, Tocqueville comments on the American tendency to join groups—a characteristic of American political culture that still holds true.

You may also be interested in looking at this resource site:

If you would like a copy of the national voter registration form, you can find it at http://www.fec.gov/votregis/vr.shtml

Notes

1. Alexis de Tocquevilie, *Democracy in America* (New York: Vintage Books, 1945).
2. Cited in Robert D. Putnam, *Bowling Alone: The Collapse and Revival of American Community* (New York: Simon and Schuster, 2000), 48.
3. Gabriel A. Almond and Sidney Verba, *The Civic Culture* (Newbury Park, CA: Sage Publications, 1989).
4. Allan Cigler and Mark R. Joslyn, "The Extensiveness of Group Membership and Social Capital: The Impact on Political Tolerance Attitudes," *Political Research Quarterly* 55:1 (March 2002), 7–25.
5. Putnam, Bowling Alone, 15–28.
6. Ibid., 18–24.
7. Ibid., 402–414.
8. If you work or have worked, you've already started to support the Social Security system. As you age, there will simply be fewer workers contributing to the system and more retirees claiming benefits, so your share of the burden will increase.
9. Fred I. Greenstein, "Children and Politics," in Greenberg, Edward S. (ed.), *Political Socialization* (New York: Atherton Press, 1970), 56–63.

10. Fred I. Greenstein, "The Benevolent Leader: Children's Images of Political Authority," *American Political Science Review* 54 (1960): 934–943.

11. Amy Carter and Ryan L. Teten, "Assessing Changing Views of the President: Revisiting Greenstein's Children and Politics," *Presidential Studies Quarterly* 32: 3 (September 2002): 453^62.

12. Eighth-graders in the 2000 group ranked doctors ahead of the president as the most important authority figures.

13. Carter and Teten, "Assessing Changing Views of the President."

14. Richard E. Dawson and Kenneth Prewitt, *Political Socialization: An Analytic Study* (Boston: Little, Brown, 1969), 105–126.

15. Frank Sorauf, *Party Politics in America,* 2nd ed. (Boston: Little, Brown, 1972), 144.

16. Ibid.

17. Dawson and Prewitt, Political Socialization, 127–142.

18. Maxwell McCombs and Donald Shaw, "The Agenda-Setting Function of the Mass Media," *Public Opinion Quarterly* 36 (Summer 1972): 176–187.

19. Dwaine Marvick, "The Political Socialization of the American Negro," in Dawson and Prewitt, *Political Socialization,* 151–177.

20. Greenstein, "Children and Politics," 59.

21. The term "baby boomers" applies to the generation born during the years 1945–1965, the older members of which came of age during the Vietnam War. See M. Kent Jennings and Richard G. Neimi, *Generational Politics* (Princeton, NJ: Princeton University Press, 1982).

22. United States Elections Project, at http://elections.gmu.edu/index.html.

23. Sidney Verba and Norman Nye, *Participation in America: Political Democracy and Social Equality* (New York: Harper and Row Publishers, 1972), 125–137.

24. Material discussed here may be found in greater detail in "Introduction to Federal Voting Rights Laws," United States Department of Justice, Civil Rights Division, Voting section website. To learn more, go to http://www.justice.gov/crt/.

25. *Guinn v. United States,* 238 US 347 (1915).

26. *Smith v. Allwright,* 321 US 649 (1944).

27. *Verba and Nye, Participation in America,* 125–173 and 334–343.

28. Kay Lehman Scholzman and Sidney Verba, *Injury to Insult: Unemployment, Class, and Political Response* (Cambridge, MA: Harvard University Press, 1979).

29. Nina Eliasoph, Avoiding Politics: *How Americans Produce Apathy in Everyday Life* (New York: Cambridge University Press, 1998).

30. You can find registration deadlines for your state from electionline.org, at http://www.pewcenteronthestates. org/initiatives_detail.aspx?initiativeID=34044.

31. National Conference of State Legislatures http://www.ncsl.org/LegislaturesElections/ElectionsCampaigns/AbsenteeandEarlyVoting/tabid/16604/Default.aspx.

32. http://www.co.multnomah.or.us/dbcs/elections/election_information/voting_in_oregon.shtml.

33. Gallup Poll. "More Independents Lean GOP; Party Gap Smallest Since '05." September 30, 2009. http://www.gallup.com/poll/123362/Independents-Lean-GOP-Party-Gap-Smallest-Since-05.aspx.

34. The NES Guide to Public Opinion and Election Behavior, which may be accessed at http://www.electionstudies.org/. Figures do not sum to 100 percent because of rounding error.

35. Or maybe because you like fish?

36. Angus Campbell, Philip E. Converse, Warren E. Miller, and Donald E. Stokes, *The American Voter* (New York: John Wiley and Sons, 1960), 168–187.

37. Paul R. Abramson, John H. Aldrich, and David W. Rhode, *Change and Continuity in the 1996 and 1998 Elections* (Washington, D.C.: Congressional Quarterly Press, 1999).

38. Morris P. Fiorina, *Retrospective Voting in American National Elections* (New Haven: Yale University Press, 1988).

39. Elisabeth Noelle-Neumann, *The Spiral of Silence* (Chicago: University of Chicago Press, 1984).

40. Michael J. Robinson, "Public Affairs Television and the Growth of Public Malaise: The Case of the Selling of the Pentagon," *American Political Science Review* 70 (June 1976): 409–432.

Table, Figure and Box Notes

T1 Gabriel A. Almond and Sidney Verba, *The Civic Culture: Political Attributes and Democracy in Five Nations* (Newbury Park, CA: Sage Publications, 1980).

T2 1996 Survey of American Political Culture, University of Virginia Institute for Advanced Studies in Culture (IASC).

T3 Immigration and Naturalization Service Fiscal Year 2000 Statistical Yearbook.

T4 Ibid.

T5 The case was *Department of Commerce et al v. United States House of Representatives et al.,* 98–404 (1999).

T6 Timothy J. Alberta, "Census Nominee Rules out Statistical Sampling in 2010." *The Wall Street Journal,* May 15, 2009, at http://online.wsj.com/article/SB124241977657124963.ht.

T7 Source: U.S. Census Bureau.

T8 Ibid.

T9 Data from 2000 National Election Study. The National Election Studies, Center for Political Studies, University of Michigan. Electronic resources from the NES World Wide Website (www.umich.edu/~nes). Ann Arbor, MI: University of Michigan, Center for Political Studies [producer and distributor], 1995–2000. These materials are based on work supported by the National Science Foundation under Grant Nos.: SBR-9707741, SBR-9317631, SES-9209410, SES-9009379, SES-8808361, SES-8341310, SES-8207580, and SOC77-08885. Any opinions, findings, and conclusions or recommendations expressed in these materials are those of the author(s) and do not necessarily reflect those of the National Science Foundation. Data for percentage who voted from official turnout figures from the 2000 election.

T10 You can access the ACT UP Civil Disobedience Manual at http://www.actupny.org/documents/CDdocu-ments/CDindex.html.

T11 You can access the PETA website at http://www.peta.org/about/.

T12 *Wall Street Journal,* June 13, 1996.

T13 National Governors Association website at http://www.nga.org/portal/site/nga/menuitem.42b929b1a5b9e4eac3363d10501010a0/?vgnextoid=d54c8aaa2ebbff00VgnVCM1000001a01010aRCRD&vgnextfmt=curgov.

T14 U.S. Senate website at http://www.senate.gov/artandhistory/history/common/briefing/women_senators.htm.

T15 Data from 2000 General Social Survey.

T16 See "Voting Rights," from the Civil Rights Movement Veterans, at http://www.crmvet.org/info/lithome.htm. T17 To see the complete literacy test, go to http://www.crmvet.org/info/litques.htm.

T18 Kay Lehman Scholzman and Sidney Verba, *Injury to Insult: Unemployment, Class, and Political Response* (Cambridge, MA: Harvard University Press, 1979), 333–356.

American Exceptionalism

A Transcript of David Gergen and Seymour Martin Lipset

David Gergen engages Seymour Martin Lipset, professor of public policy at George Mason University and author of American Exceptionalism: A Double-Edged Sword, *about the dynamics of the American national character.*

DAVID GERGEN: Marty, you've written a book about how and why America is different from many other industrialized countries, and you had an example that helped illustrate that I thought very well about the American experience, the Canadian experience. Twenty-five years ago, both governments announced to the people of their countries that they were going to move to the metric system. What happened, and what does that tell us about America?

SEYMOUR MARTIN LIPSET: Oh, it's a wonderful example, I think. The, both countries, as you say, were told to go metric, to drop miles and inches and go to meters and kilograms and the like, and after 15 years, both countries were supposed to be only metric. Well, you know, if you go to Canada, you see you can drive 100 an hour, that means kilometers, not miles. Canadians— and it's very simple—Canadians were told to go metric, and they did. Americans were

told to go metric, and they didn't, you know, under identical, almost identical, conditions. And you know, Canadians respect the state, are obedient. They're the country in a counterrevolution, the country which preserved the monarchy. The United States is the country which overthrew the state and which is anti-statist and disobedient and, and much more lawless.

DAVID GERGEN: That's part of the American creed, that the values that came out of the American Revolutionary Period.

SEYMOUR MARTIN LIPSET: Right.

DAVID GERGEN: And those values, essentially, as you describe them in the book, were those of liberty, egalitarianism, equality of opportunity, individualism, populism, laissez-faire—I think you identify the five values—

SEYMOUR MARTIN LIPSET: Right. Those are the values.

DAVID GERGEN: That's right. But what I was struck by, I think a lot of us are familiar with the fact that these values grew out of the American Revolution but you, you argue in your book that it's more than the American Revolution, it's also the Protestant experience.

SEYMOUR MARTIN LIPSET: Yeah. Well, the two, I think, key things that affect our values are the Revolution and the institutions that flowed from it, the Constitution and Bill of Rights, but also something which we rarely think about or realize. We are the only Protestant sectarian country in the world, i.e., the overwhelming majority of Americans belong to the Protestant sects, the Methodists, the Baptists, and the hundreds of others. European—Christianity in Europe, what religious sociologists call churches, as distinct from sects—the Catholics, the Anglicans, the Lutherans, the Orthodox—the churches are state-related. They were all state churches. They're hierarchical, and the relationship of the parishioner to the church is that he's supposed to be obedient. He's supposed to listen to the bishop and the priest and so on. American sectarians are congregational. The minister is an employee of the members, and the sectarianism requires that the members read the Bible, study the Bible, make their own decisions, and, and whatever they come to the conclusion is moral, they're morally obligated to, to do it. So we're a much more moralistic country.

DAVID GERGEN: More individualistic in the sense you make your own decisions—

SEYMOUR MARTIN LIPSET: Right.

DAVID GERGEN: —of what your own beliefs are. But once you've reached those, it, it also makes us more moralistic as well.

SEYMOUR MARTIN LIPSET: Right.

DAVID GERGEN: I was interested in that. You know, if you see that in our politics, the flak we went through over the allegations about President Clinton and Jennifer Flowers back in his campaign, and you compare that to the picture of President Mitterrand's funeral in France—

SEYMOUR MARTIN LIPSET: Where his mistress was present with his illegitimate daughter.

DAVID GERGEN: Right. Standing there next to his widow.

SEYMOUR MARTIN LIPSET: Right.

DAVID GERGEN: And, and his children by his widow. And that was just part of what French culture was accepting.

SEYMOUR MARTIN LIPSET: And it also flows, you know, continue in a sex-related area, abortion is a terrible issue with the United States, and it's moralistic and people on both sides feel it is a death issue, life and death issue, and we burn down abortion clinics, or some people do. Now, you can go to Rome, where the Pope sits, and get an abortion. Have you ever heard an abortion clinic being burnt in Rome or in Spain? Italy has one of the lowest birth rates in the world. Quebec has the lowest birth rate in North America. These are all Catholic areas, and you—and they—many—most of these people are Catholics, go to church, but they don't—they don't get moralistic about the whole thing.

DAVID GERGEN: Because they, they have this system in which there's more obedience but there's also sense of perfectibility.

SEYMOUR MARTIN LIPSET: Right. The Church believes and the Christian churches in, in original sin, that human institutions and human beings are inherently imperfect.

DAVID GERGEN: And therefore, when they—and therefore when they sin, you shouldn't take it that seriously, because that's the way they are.

SEYMOUR MARTIN LIPSET: Right.

DAVID GERGEN: Whereas the Protestant sects—

SEYMOUR MARTIN LIPSET: Insist on perfection, on perfectibility, that you don't, that you don't sin, and, and, of course, the United States as a country has reflected this in all sorts of ways in its foreign policy. You know, we, we have—we don't recognize evil countries. We didn't recognize the Soviet Union for a long time, China. We still don't recognize Cuba, which is obvious. We just recognized Vietnam. Well, Franco recognized Cuba six months after Castro came to power, and he was hardly a Com Symp. DeGaulle and Churchill, both of whom come out of church religions, dealt with the Communists, dealt with the Russians, didn't have the same kind of feeling, because sure Russia was an evil country, but no country's good.

DAVID GERGEN: One of your central arguments, I wonder if you could explain it a bit more, is about the double sword quality of our values, that on one hand, our values seem to produce all this dynamism and the innovation and creativity that comes from an individualistic country, but you say there's a double-edge to that sword.

SEYMOUR MARTIN LIPSET: Yeah, because, you know, we're outliers. If you compare all the countries, developed countries, behavior, or the behavior attitude, we're at the extreme. But we're at the extreme in, in many good ways, and we're at the extreme in many bad ways. For example, crime rates, violence rates, whether we have—we have the largest crime rate. We have more people incarcerated. You know, we're a very large divorce rate, and I think the—we have the lowest rate of people voting, and I think these negative aspects are inter-linked with the positive ones. You know, I develop the argument in the book that they come out of the same kinds of things. For example, if you take crime, we place this great emphasis on opportunity, on getting ahead, and getting ahead regardless of social origin, regardless of family background. Well, that means if you don't get ahead, it's your fault, because we assume that this is an open society. Societies which come out of a feudal tradition, where there's more emphasis on inherited stratification family don't place the same feeling of failure, don't put the same onus of failure on individuals who don't get ahead. Hence, in a certain sense, one, the American society tells you to get ahead by hook or by crook and if you can't do it by hook, then do it—then you do it by crook.

DAVID GERGEN: Yeah. I understand the argument about why some of the bad trends we see in the society, the high divorce rates, the high crime rates and so forth, are inherently linked to the same values that produce all the dynamism in the country. What that doesn't explain for me is why some of these rates are getting so much worse.

SEYMOUR MARTIN LIPSET: Well, there I think one has to note that, and I think in almost all of them it's happening all over the Western world. It's not just—it's—and, and America has changed in all sorts of ways the way other countries have changed, where we've all moved from having once been overwhelmingly rural, small town societies, to metropolitan, complex societies, and high-tech societies. We all have increased immigration rates, and we all have—we're going through a technological revolution, which forces many people to change their jobs and social relations. All of these produce increased disruption, and since in our case, as in the Canadian case, or the German case, these negative features defeats the quality of a more—less stable society—are going on, so that—but these are not—I think there are very few of these which are uniquely American.

DAVID GERGEN: In looking for solutions, it was interesting to me what you seemed to be arguing was we should look for solutions that are consistent with our values, we should not try to go to become a communitarian sort of nation, a nation that tries to serve some of these things through group efforts, but, rather, you spoke of moral individualism.

SEYMOUR MARTIN LIPSET: Yeah. I think this is true, i.e., I think efforts to change us in directions which go against our—you know, the American creed— just won't work.

DAVID GERGEN: Yeah. So change is important, but don't try the metric system?

SEYMOUR MARTIN LIPSET: Right.

DAVID GERGEN: Okay. Fine. Thank you very much.

SEYMOUR MARTIN LIPSET: Thank you.

CHAPTER 3

The Philosophy of the Constitution

Chapter 3 Vignette

By Jennifer Byrne

The Notion of a Living Constitution

In 1987, the bicentennial of the Constitution was celebrated; the celebration spanned three years and was dedicated to the memory of the founders of the document that was in Philadelphia. Motifs in the celebration were the knowledge and inspiration of the Framers (the men who drafted the US Constitution) that led to their achievements; the government's nature, origins, and character; and the privileges and responsibilities of citizenship. This proposed celebration was met with marked criticism by Thurgood Marshall, the first African-American justice to the U.S. Supreme Court:

"I cannot accept this invitation, for I do not believe that the meaning of the Constitution was forever 'fixed' at the Philadelphia Convention. Nor do I find the wisdom, foresight, and sense of justice exhibited by the Framers particularly profound. To the contrary, the government they devised was defective from the start, requiring several amendments, a civil war, and momentous social transformation to attain the system of constitutional government, and its respect for the individual freedoms and human rights, we hold as fundamental today. When contemporary Americans cite 'The Constitution,' they invoke a concept that is vastly different from what the Framers barely began to construct two centuries ago.[1]

In his speech, Marshall goes on to discuss the concept of a "living constitution," one that changes over time. Proponents of viewing the Constitution as a "living" document believe that contemporary societal standards should be taken into account when interpreting the Constitution. Marshall cautioned that it would be overly simplistic to celebrate the Constitution in its original form. Among the deficiencies is the fact that the "We the people" preamble did not include everyone; African-Americans were barred from voting, even though they were counted as 3/5 of a person for representational purposes. Furthermore, women did not gain the right to vote for another 130 years. Marshall argues that moral principles against slavery were compromised even in light of the principles that the Revolutionary War was fought for—human equality and "life, liberty and the pursuit of happiness." The words "slaves" and "slavery" were absent from the Constitution, but citizens were divided into "free persons" and "other persons," while slavery ensured that the country would continue to profit from its institution.[2]

There were subsequent laws passed by Congress and interpretations of the Constitution that perpetuated its inequalities on the basis of ethnicity, skin color, and independent, or "free" status. The Naturalization Act of 1790 stated that only "free white persons" were eligible to naturalize. This raised many questions about what constitutes being "white" and whether African-Americans, Indians, Asians, and Hispanics could become American citizens. In *Cherokee Nation v. Georgia*, the Supreme Court ruled that the Framers of the Constitution did not intend for Native Americans to be citizens. In 1922, the Supreme Court ruled in *Ozawa v. United States* that a Japanese man was not eligible for naturalization as he was considered Mongolian—not Caucasian. Bagat-Thind, a Southeast Asian man argued that he was, in fact, Caucasian, but the Supreme Court ruled that most white Americans would not recognize such "heterogeneous elements" among them, meaning that the law dictated who was white based on popular opinion, and not scientific evidence. Thus, they sought to look at what the common man would interpret as "white." Women continued to derive status only through their husbands, and laws stated that women could lose their citizenship if they married a foreigner who was not eligible for citizenship. Without citizenship, these groups were unable to vote and were limited in their political participation; though they were still subject to the laws of the land, including those that placed limitations on their freedom.

One can easily argue that the original constitution was defective, and as Marshall contends, it is the ability to change and adapt to contemporary societal standards that makes the Constitution great. It was the end of slavery, Black codes, and Jim Crow laws that allowed African Americans to begin to have greater political equality. Amendments to the Constitution later ensured women and African-Americans the right to vote, while acts of Congress gave Native Americans citizenship rights. The Voting Rights Act, passed by Congress in 1965, gave the federal government unprecedented authority to monitor state elections, pursuant to the 15th Amendment. Even today, the federal government still recognizes Native Americans, Hispanics, African-Americans, Asians, and women as having a special status and as being eligible for certain benefits in light of their identification as members of historically disadvantaged minority groups.

It is important to note, however, that the United States was not the only country that denied voting rights to women and minorities at the time the Constitution was drafted. The institution of slavery was still prominent in Great Britain and was for several more decades. Voting rights for women went unrecognized by many nations—including industrialized democracies—until many decades, and even a century later. The U.S. was not alone in excluding these groups from the political process, but the system of government that the Framers implemented was revolutionary, as it allowed a uniquely broad class of citizens the right to vote. No religious tests or titles of nobility were required for political office, and property requirements to vote were abandoned or reduced. This was novel at the time, as was the established system of federalism, defined as the sharing of power between two sovereign government entities, the states, and the federal governments. One could also argue that the Framers made compromises that were necessary to gain the votes of individual states to ratify the Constitution, or consequently, today the U.S. might look more like Europe with individual countries. Yet, in the end, it is difficult to find fault with Marshall's contention that our Constitution is stronger and more inclusive currently than in the past, and this should be cause to celebrate.

Endnotes

1. United States Constitution
2. Thurgood Marshall, "Remarks of Thurgood Marshall at Annual Seminar of the San Franciso Patent and Trademark Association" (speech, Maui, HI, May 6, 1987), The Bicentennial Speech, http://www.thurgoodmarshall.com/speeches/constitutional_speech.htm.

The Constitution and Federalism

Setting the Ground Rules for Democracy

By Matthew Kerbel

Introduction

Think back for a second to grade school. Try to remember what your classroom and playground felt like. For many, these places provided our first encounter with rules and structures in social situations. The restrictions generated by those rules may have been unpleasant. At the same time, it's not hard to imagine how chaotic things would have been without them.

This essentially describes the trade-off we face when we consider how to establish the ground rules for politics. Rules place limits on our liberty. But the total lack of rules is a recipe for chaos. A functional government rests somewhere between the extremes of no liberty and chaos—but precisely where is an open question that can cause some intense political disputes.

In the early days of the republic, political disputes over how to write the rules of the game were commonplace because there were different points of view about how deeply government should reach into everyday life. The differences were rooted in the experiences people had with government prior to and during the American Revolution. Some people were influenced by what felt to them like government repression under the British and were determined to avoid establishing a strong central government here. Others feared that if the central government were too weak, it would be impossible for the new nation to function. Out of this debate came America's first halting attempts at self-government.

The results weren't very pretty, at least initially. Many early decisions did not withstand the test of time, and there were ongoing, heated political debates as people on both sides of the strong government question jockeyed for political advantage. Because setting the rules is never a neutral exercise—some groups are inevitably favored at the expense of others—the question of how government should operate was a central issue that consumed American politics for years after the Revolution ended. It's a lively story with implications for how Americans live today because the rules that were settled on still favor some at the expense of others, more than 220 years after they were written. So, as we go back in time to revisit these events, we're really looking at the roots of how we make choices for ourselves in the twenty-first century.

Ground Rules for Revolution

The multiethnic, industrial America of the twenty-first century still operates under rules created by European male settlers in response to circumstances long forgotten by most of us. To understand what America is now we should understand what it was then—who settled this country, what they were looking for, how they were different from some of the people they left behind, and what they experienced in colonial America.

European settlers were risk takers, people willing to leave their homes and everything familiar in search of religious freedom or economic opportunity. If you imagine for a second what it would take for someone to cross a dangerous ocean in a small, precarious vessel on a journey of great uncertainty, you can probably get a sense of how those who came to America differed from those who decided not to make the trip. Notwithstanding the sense of community found in some of the religious groups that came here, there was certainly enough individualism to go around.

Risk-taking and self-reliance are consistent with the desire for government to do less so individuals can maintain more liberty and seek opportunities. From the start, America's white settlers were inclined to favor placing restrictions on government so they could preserve the freedom to go it alone—a freedom they found wanting in the old world.

Their perspective mattered most to America's political development. In the eighteenth century, America's nonwhite settlers and natives were composed primarily of African American slaves and Native Americans, both of whom were **disenfranchised** by Europeans by being kept out of the decision making that produced our constitutional and legal system.[1]

The inclination toward individualism exhibited by white settlers—which goes a long way toward explaining how the rules were written in America—was compounded by events in the decade leading up to the American Revolution, a time when many colonial settlers experienced British policy as heavy-handed and burdensome. Not surprisingly, a string of British legislative acts passed during this time were widely regarded as impositions on liberty.

Table 4.1 on the next page illustrates some of the more salient actions.

The series of events depicted in the timeline, starting with the imposition of the Stamp Act and concluding with the First Continental Congress, represented a British crackdown on colonial life. True, the colonies had never been autonomous, but the vast ocean separating London and Boston effectively afforded the colonies a certain amount of self-rule. The King and Parliament were simply too far away and too preoccupied with other matters to maintain tight control on colonial life. So, for the better part of 150 years prior to the Boston Massacre, colonial settlers drafted constitutions to govern the colonies, created representative assemblies with the authority to draft laws, and held free elections. They had to share this authority with royal governors, but they had a taste of self-government, and they liked it. Against this backdrop, and considering their personal inclination toward preserving liberty, it's no wonder why so many of them found the Coercive Acts to be intolerable.

Within months of the First Continental Congress, the tense, cold standoff turned violent. Clashes between colonists and British soldiers at Lexington and Concord, Massachusetts on April 19, 1775, marked the start of the American Revolution. One month later, the **Second Continental Congress** convened in Philadelphia to coordinate the war effort. One year later, it would declare American independence from Great Britain.

From the outset, the American Revolution differed from other revolutions in the sense that the objective was not to overthrow the existing order and replace it with something new. There was no talk of overthrowing the British monarchy, and the government of Great Britain continued to exist outside the former colonies after conceding defeat to the Americans. Instead, the American Revolution was more of a separation—perhaps the way some of us as teenagers move away from our parents and establish autonomy when we begin to see ourselves as adults and question parental authority. To Americans supporting the war, the purpose was to rebel against the existing order. The British crackdown in America had led some to begin to question British authority, and even though the idea

Table 4.1. British Policy Prior to the American Revolution

Early 1760s: In the early 1760s, American colonists fought along side the British in the French and Indian War. It was a long and expensive war, and the British turned to the colonies to help pay for the war through a series of Parliamentary acts.

1764: The American Revenue Act was passed in 1764. It was widely called the **Sugar Act** because of the tariff it placed on sugar, along with other goods. The Sugar Act was followed in short order by the **Quartering Act**, which forced colonists to shelter British troops, and the **Stamp Act**, which taxed everyday legal documents like marriage licenses and newspapers.

1765: The Stamd Act of 1765 created uproar in the colonies, leading some colonies to refuse to import British goods and to the outcry, "no taxation without representation." The protest led to the repeal of the Stamp Act, but in 1767 Parliament imposed a new round of taxes on goods imported from Great Britain, which led to a new boycott and growing tensions.

1770: The British sent troops to Boston to maintain order, but their presence inflamed tensions. On March 5, 1770, tensions erupted into a skirmish; shots were fired and five colonists were killed in what history remembers as the **Boston Massacre.**

1773: When Great Britain imposed the Tea Act of 1773, giving the East India Tea Company a monopoly over the tea trade in North America, tensions rose again. In the protest known as the **Boston Tea Party,** a group of colonists masquerading as Native Americans boarded ships loaded with tea and dumped the contents into Boston Harbor.

1773: Parliament moved swiftly and severely in response to the Boston Tea Party, initiating what became known as the **Coercive Acts** (in the colonies, the Intolerable Acts). Loading and unloading ships in Boston Harbor was prohibited and the Quartering Act was revitalized.

1774: In response, representatives from most of the colonies gathered in 1774 at the **First Continental Congress** to protest the action, voting to boycott British goods. The Continental Congress lacked **authority,** but it represented a major step forward in forging among the Colonists a sense of collective purpose and the ability for collective action.

Sugar Act: The first in a string of taxes levied by Great Britain on the American colonies. Formally called the American Revenue Act of 1764, it taxed a number of colonial imports, including sugar.

Quartering Act: An act of the British Parliament requiring colonists to house British troops; first imposed in 1765 and then again in 1774 as part of the Coercive Acts.

Stamp Act: A particularly vexing tax levied by the British on scores of legal documents, which led to a colonial boycott of British goods.

Boston Massacre: A precursor to the war that was still five years away, it was the first mortal conflict between colonists and British troops in Boston and resulted in the deaths of five colonists in 1770.

Boston Tea Party: A protest against the Tea Act of 1773 in which fifty colonists dressed as Native Americans boarded British trade ships loaded with tea and threw the contents into the water.

Coercive Acts: Called the Intolerable Acts in the colonies, the Coercive Acts represented the British attempt to clamp down on the colonies following the Boston Tea Party.

First Continental Congress: A gathering of representatives from twelve of the thirteen colonies in Philadelphia in 1774 to protest the Coercive Acts and chart a unified colonial response.

---

authority: The right to act in an official capacity by virtue of holding an office like president or member of Congress.

---

of going it alone was far from universally popular in the colonies (many opposed revolution and hoped to reconcile their differences with the British), by 1775, it had become a viable option.[2]

Ground Rules for Independence

What gave Americans the right to separate from Great Britain? Law and tradition bound them to the British, who saw the Revolution as a profound act of treason. Supporters of the Revolution, though, believed the British had forfeited their right to govern the colonies when they began to deny colonists their liberty. In this idea, they had support from theorists who had written in the abstract about why governments form and under what circumstances they may be overturned.

The founders read widely and were influenced by theorists dating back to antiquity. You could turn to the theoretical influences of three Enlightenment thinkers in particular to find the origins of one of the key philosophical justifications for the Revolutionary

War. The seventeenth-century British philosophers Thomas Hobbes and John Locke and the eighteenth-century Franco-Swiss philosopher Jean-Jacques Rousseau differed in their view of human nature and their prescriptions for how government should operate, but they spoke of government as being the product of a **social contract** among individuals.

Thomas Hobbes wrote that without governments, people existed in what he called the **state of nature**—a ruthless place with absolute liberty where people can easily deny others their liberty and their lives by simple force. Hobbes had a negative view of human nature and painted a brutal picture of what life would be like if we permitted ourselves to exist in the state of nature. In a passage from his book *Leviathan*, Hobbes claims that life in the state of nature is "solitary, poor, nasty, brutish, and short."[3]

The only way to protect people from this ugly situation is for them to give up liberty in exchange for the security of a strong government (a "leviathan," representing government to Hobbes, is a big, powerful monster), essentially to form a social contract with others in which liberty is the price of protection. Hobbes believed that people had to give up most of their liberty—far more than colonial settlers would have been happy with—in exchange for the right to live, which is why he was a supporter of a strong and forceful monarchy.

Although he had a somewhat more upbeat view of mankind, John Locke also advocated for a social contract as the basis of civil society. Locke believed that in the state of nature people possess **natural rights**—to life, liberty, and property—which they enter into a social contract to protect. Since the purpose of government in this contract is to do more than provide physical safety, the reins of government shouldn't be as tight as in Hobbes' vision. To Locke, liberty is something for government to protect as much as it is what you give up to have government protect you. In other words, government needs to be strong enough to protect individual rights but not so strong that it becomes a threat to liberty, so there have to be limits on government that monarchy cannot provide.

Locke went much further than Hobbes, asserting that people form governments and people can dissolve them, through revolution if necessary, should they become too strong and violate individual rights. This was fairly radical thinking in an era of monarchy, when you consider that monarchs claimed their authority came from God. Locke rejected this "divine right of kings," arguing that governments receive their authority from the consent of the governed.

Locke's fingerprints are all over the **Declaration of Independence**, whose author, Thomas Jefferson, was heavily influenced by Locke. The idea that everyone is equal in the state of nature; that people are born with natural rights; that governments are formed to protect these rights; that individuals and not deities form governments; that governments must derive their authority from the people they govern; that people have the right to overthrow a government that fails to protect individual liberty—it's all there, and it all has its roots in Locke's writing.

Perhaps because of what was at stake in the Declaration of Independence, Jefferson can be forgiven for not footnoting Locke. And educated people in 1776 understood where Jefferson's ideas came from. The full text of the Declaration of Independence can be found in Appendix A.

For much of this country's history, Americans have subscribed to Locke's generally positive view of humanity. Having two great oceans to shelter us from the conflicts of the rest of the world surely contributed to American optimism. But, at times of great stress, it may be easier to subscribe to Hobbes' view of the state of nature than to Locke's, and to ask government to step in and provide greater fundamental protection. There are indications that some people reacted this way in the aftermath of the September 11, 2001, terror attacks on the United States, turning to government for protection against a world that appeared to become dramatically more dangerous overnight. See Issue: Hobbes, Locke, and Terror.

For his part, Jean-Jacques Rousseau held a view of individuals that more resembled Locke's positive vision than Hobbes' dismal one. Rousseau was concerned with the relationship between rulers and those they rule, writing in The Social Contract that people submit to the rule of others only because their rights will be better protected by government than if left to the random brutality of the state of nature. But,Rousseau insisted that rulers are bound to protect everyone's rights, not simply the rights of the wealthy and powerful. In his view, rulers who failed to provide these fundamental protections have broken the social contract they have with the ruled.[4] This contractual view of rights is reflected in the list of offenses alleged against King George in the Declaration of Independence.

As with Hobbes and Locke, the theory of government espoused by Rosseau contributed to the rationale for independence and provided the theoretical underpinning for the republic that would arise from it. In this important respect, the ideas guiding the revolution and the republic that grew from it were not original. But the idea of founding a nation on them was a bold and ambitious experiment. The founder's work was radical because they dared to put theoretical abstractions into practice.

Self-Governance—First Attempt

Almost immediately after declaring independence from Great Britain, the Continental Congress went to work to create a framework for collective government. It was a difficult job because the practical need for the new United States to act in concert was balanced by strong concerns about the individual states giving up too much authority to a distant national government that might not be responsive to local concerns. Fears were widespread that a strong national government would be an obstacle to liberty, especially in light of colonial experiences with British rule over the past generation. Furthermore, even though the Declaration of Independence announced a new United States of America, most citizens of this new country identified with their respective state rather than with the collection of states. People would refer to themselves as New

ISSUE

HOBBES, LOCKE AND TERROR

For two decades, political debate in the United States revolved around the question of whether government had grown so large as to be intrusive. After a period in the 1950s, 1960s, and 1970s in which the national government addressed problems of segregation, poverty, crime, women's rights, and a host of other social and economic dilemmas, debate turned to whether in the course of addressing these issues government had grown so strong as to infringe on personal liberties. Through the 1980s, the Reagan and George H.W. Bush (senior) administrations advocated the position that government is a problem more than a solution to problems. In the 1990s, Congress picked up this line of reasoning. You could draw a straight line from Jefferson and Locke to the contemporary argument that big government is a threat to personal liberty.

Then terrorists destroyed the World Trade Center and heavily damaged the Pentagon. Anthrax began showing up in the mail. American troops were dispatched to Afghanistan, and America shifted to a war footing. People stopped talking about government as an intrusion. The state of nature suddenly resembled Hobbes' dark views more than Locke's hopeful ones. People looked to government for aid and assistance in numbers not seen for decades. In keeping with Hobbes' prescription that a strong government is needed to keep us safe and alive, many Americans even began saying they would be willing to give up liberty in return for protection.

An article that ran in The Philadelphia *Inquirer* toward the end of 2001 discussed how "a new view of freedom" had settled into the national psyche, a view far more restrictive than what had been the norm for generations.[T1] It told of how trust in government shot up after the attacks because Americans had become "newly appreciative of safety" and therefore "willing to give [government] unusually broad powers to fight terrorists." Americans expressed willingness to "put up with more government" and give the president "a little more latitude to do what he thinks is right."

Immediately after the attacks, three in four Americans had reservations about immigration and wanted to make it harder for people of other nations to enter the United States, essentially limiting the free passage to America that has been one of the hallmarks of American liberty. Unease about foreigners settled into this nation of immigrants, with the call going out to government to do what was necessary to keep America safe.

Large numbers of people supported a Bush administration directive to try alleged terrorists in secret military tribunals, out of view of the public and apart from the normal judicial system—essentially denying these suspects the ordinary rights allowed others charged with crimes. One individual quoted in the article acknowledged, "That is kind of scary, taking away one of the freedoms Americans believe in." But, he added, "We are at war. I'm more tolerant of that at the moment."

By late 2005, the question of whether government had grown too intrusive seemed to have come full circle. That's when it became known that President Bush—who ran for office as a limited government conservative—had authorized eavesdropping on domestic telephone and e-mail communications without a court order. In other words, the government was monitoring the private conversations and e-mail messages of American citizens without their knowledge and without a warrant.[T2] Bush acknowledged the program, and defiantly said it would continue, justifying his actions on national security grounds. Opponents said it amounted to an illegal and possibly unconstitutional infringement

on personal rights. Either way, it was clear that a conservative administration was directing the government to engage in the most intrusive of activities.

How tolerant should Americans be of this type of government activity? How tolerant are you? Is a strong government necessary when we're faced with potentially devastating threats, and if so, what types of actions should the government take in order to keep us safe and secure? Is it appropriate to restrict immigration? Limit the rights of suspected terrorists? Engage in secret domestic surveillance without the consent of the courts? If you support a strong government for the purposes of protection from terrorist threats, do you also support government activity for the purpose of protection from other naturally arising social ills and injustices, like poverty and crime, or is physical protection different from these things? Your answer to these questions likely rests with whether you accept Hobbes' or Locke's view of human nature and their remedies for maintaining security.

Certainly, the devastation caused by Hurricane Katrina in 2005 and the government's flat-footed response to the crisis echoed the sense of danger Americans felt in September 2001 and underscored the importance of having a competent government that's strong enough to protect us. But, how far should the government go? How well can a nation that declared its independence on Locke's principles fare under Hobbes' perspective of human nature? In the long run, how much liberty will Americans be willing to give up in order to feel safe?

Americans felt in September 2001 and underscored the importance of having a competent government that's strong enough to protect us. But, how far should the government go? How well can a nation that declared its independence on Locke's principles fare under Hobbes' perspective of human nature? In the long run, how much liberty will Americans be willing to give up in order to feel safe?

Yorkers, Virginians, or Rhode Islanders—not as Americans. Why, then, would they accept a strong government of the United States?

At the same time, members of the Continental Congress knew that without a central government, they would not be able to maintain an army, negotiate treaties with other nations, or coordinate commerce among the states. The rules of the game would have to be written carefully.

When a framework did materialize in the form of the **Articles of Confederation,** which were adopted by Congress in 1777 and ratified by all thirteen states in 1781, the results were problematic. The Articles addressed the fear of a strong centralized government by creating a loose federation or "league of friendship" among the states in which "each state retains its sovereignty, freedom, and independence, and every power, jurisdiction, and right, which is not by this Confederation expressly delegated to the United States." In other words, the laws and actions of the individual states were supreme to the actions of the United States. The national government took its cues from the thirteen state governments.[5]

The Articles further protected the states by requiring that national action of any kind would have to win the approval of nine states. The national government was composed of a Congress in which each state had one vote, but any five states could keep the national government from acting. Because of concerns about centralized authority, there was no independent chief executive like the modern-day president. There was no national court system for resolving disputes. The Articles were inflexible: All thirteen states had to agree to amend the Articles; one lone dissenter could put an end to change.

These features conspired to create a national government that was weak and ineffective. The Articles of Confederation created a national government that would not undermine individual liberty, but it also created a national government that could barely act. It couldn't keep states from putting up barriers to trade with other states or resolve trade wars between them. It couldn't raise taxes. It could pass laws, but it couldn't make the states follow them. It was severely limited in its ability to conduct foreign affairs. Because changes had to be approved unanimously, it couldn't do much to fix these weaknesses, especially when groups in some states benefited from the rules as they were written in the Articles.

Small farmers and debtors, of whom there were many in the years following the Revolutionary War, appreciated the fact that the Articles kept politics close to home and receptive to local needs and were among the Articles' strongest supporters. But the industrial revolution was about to hit the new country with the force of a tidal wave, and anyone involved in banking or the trade or manufacture of merchandise was frustrated by the inability of the Articles to regulate commerce among the states and maintain stable international ties. From the standpoint of conducting normal relations with other countries, the Articles of Confederation was a disaster.

If that wasn't enough, hard economic times fell upon the new country following the Revolutionary War. Things were particularly bad in Massachusetts, where heavy taxes and an economic depression placed a disproportionate burden on small farmers, many of whom lost their land and landed in debtor's prison.

Suffering farmers in western Massachusetts blamed their plight on Boston merchants, who pressed for taxes so the state could repay the money it had borrowed from them during the war. In a case of borrowers rising up against unfair conditions they attributed to lenders, a group of debtor farmers took up arms to prevent Massachusetts courts from convening and sentencing debtors.

The insurrection was led by Revolutionary War officer Daniel Shays, and **Shays' Rebellion** started in August 1786 and lasted half a year until the Massachusetts militia put an end to it. It was typical of the type of rebellion that characterized this unsettled time. The national Congress had been powerless to deal with either the complaints or the actions of the debtors, and business groups who had previously been frustrated with the Articles of Confederation now worried that their fundamental interests were threatened.

It was 1787, and the ruling elite had seen enough. It was time to change the ground rules.

Self-Governance—Second Attempt

The rules of the game under the Articles of Confederation turned out to be bulky and unworkable. They were also unusual rules. Most nations do not establish a **confederal system.** They are not a confederation of essentially independent states that band together to create a weak central union. Of course, there were special circumstances involved in trying to bring together thirteen largely autonomous colonies into a single nation, so the type of structure most common in the world—the **unitary system**—was never really an option. And when the framers of the government tried a second time, they again opted for an atypical structure in a **federal system,** still trying to find a way to balance the needs of the states with the need to function as a nation. This time, after a tough political debate, they fared much better.

Although by the spring of 1787 there was widespread sentiment that the Articles of Confederation had to be revised, there were different opinions about what that meant. Those benefiting from the rules of the game would fight hard to maintain their advantages. Others wanted a stronger and more functional central government that would dramatically change the rules. Most everyone was fearful of creating a system that could suppress liberty in the effort to make government more effective. Even if life under the Articles was chaotic, memory of British rule tempered the temptation to overreach in the other direction.

So, a delicate political challenge confronted the fifty-five men who gathered in Philadelphia in May 1787, ostensibly to revise the Articles. In what became known as the **Constitutional Convention,** delegates from every state but Rhode Island[6] assembled for the stated purpose of strengthening the confederation. (See Demystifying Government: Delegates to the Constitutional Convention.) It was clear from the start, though, that the convention was going to abandon the confederal system and replace it with something that might protect against chaos without burying individual liberties. The recognition of that goal was the easy part. Getting there—and getting political support for something new—would pose immense hurdles.

Despite widespread support for a federal system to replace the confederation, the convention nearly fell apart over two central issues: large versus small state representation in the new federal government and the legality of slavery.

Large, populous states like Virginia and Pennsylvania, mindful of their ability to dominate the new national government, advocated a method of representation based on population. Early in the convention, Edmund Randolph introduced what would be known as the **Virginia Plan,** which called for representation in the legislature based on population and a strong national government that would reign supreme over the states. Small states strenuously objected, and in turn, offered an alternative, the **New Jersey Plan.** Far less ambitious, it was essentially a stronger version of the Articles of Confederation, with representation based on states where each state would have one vote in the legislature.

In politics, it helps tremendously to set the agenda, and the Virginia group, by virtue of the fact that they were prepared with a plan, had the advantage of going first and structuring the course of the debate. The New Jersey Plan was offered in reaction to it, but it was voted down by the convention, as was a proposal by Alexander Hamilton that would have provided for an extremely strong central government with a powerful executive who served for life. With the rejection of the New Jersey Plan for a state-centered government and the Hamilton plan for what looked to many like a monarchy, it became clear that the Virginia Plan—soundly positioned between the two—would be the foundation for the new Constitution.

It was equally clear, however, that nothing was going to happen unless the small states were on board, and as structured, the Virginia Plan would never come close to winning broad-based support. The convention deadlocked over the issue, and as May turned into June, tension was as thick as the Philadelphia humidity. Delegates from states large and small didn't want to sacrifice their essential interests, although most everyone wanted to return home with something better than the Articles. In the long run, this created an environment where compromise was possible.

DEMYSTIFYING GOVERNMENT

DELEGATES TO THE CONSTITUTIONAL CONVENTION

The 55 delegates to the Constitutional Convention were an elite group of educated and privileged men. About half had had the rare opportunity to attend college. More than half were lawyers or had legal training, and almost one-quarter were businessmen or merchants. Several, like George Washington, were among the wealthiest people in the new nation, and many of the nation's most prominent families were represented. In keeping with their wealth and status, the delegate list read like a "who's who" of colonial and American politics. Although only eight delegates had signed the Declaration of Independence and only six had signed the Articles of Confederation, eighty percent had been members of the Continental Congress. Not surprisingly, the delegates would be a strong presence in the government they created. The convention boasted two future presidents (Washington and Madison), one future vice-president, four cabinet secretaries, five Supreme Court justices, 19 senators, and 13 House members.

A few delegates had an important influence on the proceedings. By presiding over the meeting, Virginia's George Washington supplied the gathering with an important element of **legitimacy**. As leader of the Continental Army during the Revolutionary War, Washington was easily the most heroic figure in America. Old and frail, the 81-year-old inventor, writer, publisher and diplomat Benjamin Franklin said little at the convention, but his presence made an important public statement about the significance of the proceedings. His democratic sentiments were well known, but the elder statesman from Pennsylvania could work behind the scenes to facilitate compromise among the divergent perspectives held by the delegates.

One of the more critical voices was Virginia's George Mason, who, despite being a vocal and influential delegate, refused to sign the Constitution. His reservations centered on the concern that the government created by the Constitution would be too strong and might trample on the freedoms of those who created it. He feared the lack of a bill of rights (which was subsequently added by constitutional amendment) and the potential for abuses of power by Congress and the judiciary would hurt those without many resources and take power from the states.

The other end of the spectrum was represented by delegates who feared the new government wouldn't be strong enough. New York's Alexander Hamilton, who had married into an aristocratic family, was more concerned about creating a strong central government that could pay its debts and function on the world stage than he was with establishing democratic mechanisms or protecting individual rights. He unsuccessfully proposed to the convention something resembling the British monarchy.

Virginia's James Madison occupied the middle ground between these two perspectives, which helped to make him the most influential member of the convention. Although not an imposing figure or speaker, and despite being one of the younger delegates at age 36, Madison had the greatest influence on the Constitution. An advocate of a stronger central government than what the Articles provided, Madison was a tireless campaigner and natural politician who was able to fashion compromise while successfully advocating his ideas.

The logjam was broken by the **Connecticut Compromise,** which provided a bicameral or two-house legislature. Representation in the lower house—the House of Representatives—would be determined by population, and states would be equally represented in the upper house, or Senate. Voters would directly elect members of the House of Representatives, while state legislators would appoint senators. In this arrangement, the configuration of the House of Representatives would address the concerns of the large states, and the configuration of the Senate would address the concerns of the small states. Apart from the fact that senators are now also directly elected, the Connecticut Compromise established the structure for Congress that exists to this day.

With the Connecticut Compromise came the hope that the convention would bear fruit, but one serious problem remained. If representation in the House of Representatives was to be based on population, should slaves be among those counted? Delegates from southern states, where slavery was concentrated, argued they should be, even though slaves were denied all rights granted to free persons. Of course, counting slaves for purposes of representation would have enhanced the power of southern states in the new Congress.

Some delegates from outside the South would have been happy to outlaw slavery entirely in the Constitution. It wasn't difficult to see the ironic contrast between the language of the Declaration of Independence, justifying separation from Great Britain, and the practice of slavery. As a pragmatic matter, though, slavery was essential to the southern economy, and there would be no union of the states if the convention insisted on pursuing the matter. So, slavery would be left to fester like a raw wound in the body politic for generations as the price of establishing a federal system.

Northern delegates did strenuously object to the southern proposal to count slaves for representation purposes, but this matter was addressed in the **Three-fifths Compromise**—a purely pragmatic attempt to split the difference between the two camps by counting each slave as three-fifths of a person for the purpose of determining representation in the House. As a reflection of the odious nature of the compromise, the final draft of the Constitution never mentions slaves, distinguishing instead between "free persons" (who would be counted fully) and "all other persons."

The summer of 1787 was coming to a close, and compromise was making possible a blueprint for a new federal government.

Ground Rules in Theory and Practice

If the Virginia Plan set the agenda for the Constitutional Convention, Virginia's James Madison developed the blueprint for some of the new government's most important features. Madison was an advocate of a strong central government, but he recognized that if it were to survive, it couldn't be so strong as to threaten individual liberties. Returning to the rationale for independence, Madison reasoned that the new government could be no more threatening to natural rights than American colonists believed the British government had been. That was a tall order to fill. It was one thing to declare independence on the basis of Locke's theoretical principles about the nature of government. It was quite another to design a functioning government that would uphold those principles.

For guidance, Madison turned to the writings of John Locke and eighteenth-century French political theorist Baron de Montesquieu. A supporter of democracy, Montesquieu believed that the best way to protect individual liberty was to make sure that power wasn't concentrated in any one place. He advocated separating powers into three distinct branches of government—an executive, a legislature, and a judiciary—each dependent on the others and therefore able to limit the powers of the others.

These ideas were incorporated into the design of the federal government. The Constitution provides for a system of **separation of powers**, whereby the executive (president), legislature (Congress), and judiciary (Supreme Court) are independent of one another. They represent different constituencies, are chosen by different means, perform distinct functions, and serve for terms varying from two years to life. Because nothing can get done unless they agree to work together, any one can frustrate

Table 4.2. The Three Branches

	Executive Branch	Legislative Branch		Judicial Branch
		House	Senate	
Represents	Entire nation	Small districts	States	The Constitution
Chosen by	Electoral College	The people	The people (originally state legislatures)	The president, confirmed by the Senate
Term	4 years, renewable once	2 years	6 years	Life
Function	Carrying out laws	Writing laws	Writing laws	Judging laws

the initiatives of the other two, a process known as **checks and balances.** You can find a quick overview of the workings of separation of powers in Table 4.2.

It's human nature to want to get things done, but, as we've seen, separation of powers and checks and balances purposely make it difficult for the federal government to accomplish things. One way to think about this frustrating situation is that it's actually a feature of the Constitution designed to protect individual liberty. Here's how it works: Because Congress, the president, and the Supreme Court each can check the initiatives of the other two branches, things can only get done when they work together. Often, their interests won't line up, and one branch will put a check on everyone else—such as when the Supreme Court declares an act of Congress unconstitutional, the president vetoes a bill, or the Senate refuses to confirm a presidential appointee.

It's an inefficient way of trying to do business. Things happen much more slowly than they would if everyone worked together. When the branches continue to disagree, nothing gets done at all. In these situations, the whole process stalls. Everything grinds to a halt. No bill is passed, or the law is struck down, or the appointment doesn't happen.

At the same time, the process makes it hard for any one group or interest to achieve its goals at the expense of everyone else. It forces deliberation and compromise. That helps protect the wishes of those who otherwise might be overwhelmed by the quick actions of like-minded government officials. So, while it may be frustrating, the inefficiency of a decentralized system is also a safeguard. The

Constitution's framers chose to create frustration as part of the price of protecting personal liberty.

Along with separation of powers and checks and balances, the Constitution contained other safeguards designed to protect citizens from the new government it created. The Constitution called for a **republic** or **representative democracy** in which the House of Representatives would consist of people selected by and accountable to voters. Representatives have to face the voters again after a fixed term of two years, and can be tossed out of office if their actions defy the wishes of the people they represent. Originally selected by state legislators, senators are now chosen in the same manner and serve a fixed term of six years.

Other safeguards followed from the ideas of John Locke. Representative democracy implies a government based on **popular sovereignty,** where the government is run by the people it is designed to serve based on the free expression of their will to be governed. Recall that Locke argued against the divine right of kings to rule, asserting that government gets its authority from individuals and must protect the natural rights of those it serves. By implication, if the new government had failed in this endeavor, it would have been appropriate for Americans to reject it and try again.

The Constitution also established a **limited government** by placing specific restrictions on what government can do. This, too, is consistent with Locke's thinking because it is based on the principle that the people rightly decide the appropriate role for government, and that Americans can restrict the government from acting in ways that they feel might jeopardize their liberty. So, for instance, Congress is prohibited—by constitutional amendment—from restricting religious freedom. Contrast this way of thinking with the traditional rationale for monarchy, in which a king's broad authority doesn't take into account restrictions on individual liberty.

A final safeguard—**federalism**—was more a product of necessity than design, but it serves the purpose of placing a check on the actions of government that can be just as strong as separation of powers, checks and balances, representative democracy, popular sovereignty, or limited government. We've already seen how a federal government contrasts with a confederal government, like the one created by the Articles of Confederation, and a unitary government, which is the model for most governments in the world. Federalism regards the bulky architecture of shared authority between the national (federal) government and the states as a feature of the republic. By assigning some functions to the federal government, others to the states, and still others to both, the framers of the Constitution ensured that there would be multiple centers of power.

Throughout our history, federalism has been the source of intense political disputes the likes of which you won't find in too many countries. We'll take a closer look at these disputes in the section "Federalism: Only in America."

For something so important, the Constitution is a simple document. It consists of seven articles and twenty-seven amendments, the first ten of which constitute the Bill of Rights. Take a look at Table 4.3 to see what was in the original, unamended document.

"If Men Were Angels"

The clearest rationale for why the new nation might benefit from all these institutional safeguards appeared in a series of essays written after the Constitutional Convention by Alexander Hamilton, James Madison, and John Jay. First published anonymously between October 1787 and May 1788 in several New York newspapers under the name "Publius," which is Latin for "public man," the eighty-five essays that came to be known as *The Federalist* (to many

today, *The Federalist Papers*) were meant to persuade a reluctant New York State of the advantages of the Constitution. Notwithstanding their political purpose, *The Federalist* remains one of the clearest expressions of how the Constitution was designed to work, not to mention the best surviving glimpse into the thinking of the Constitution's authors.

As a body of work, *The Federalist* addressed the "defects" in the Articles of Confederation (in a series of essays believed to have been written by Alexander Hamilton) and detailed how the new Constitution would correct them without costing citizens their liberty (in an argument made by Madison). Additionally, John Jay, who had experience in foreign affairs, authored a few essays dealing with constitutional structure and foreign relations.

Madison made the argument that the new government had to have numerous power centers in order to protect people from the worst motives of their neighbors, both in and out of government. "If men were angels, no government would be necessary," he wrote. "If angels were to govern men, neither external nor internal controls on government would be necessary." But common sense and knowledge of human nature tells us that we need to be cautious in social endeavors, especially when power is involved.

We've all at times questioned the motivation of people we've met. Maybe they were trying to sell us something, or trying to befriend us, and for whatever reason, the way they acted didn't feel right to us. Madison acknowledged these types of experiences happen all the time, and when you're trying to govern yourself as a nation, you run the risk that a group of people with malevolent motives will band together as a **faction** and work to impose their will on everyone. Even if they are small in number, a faction of highly motivated people can threaten the rest. Madison's fear was that if they were not controlled, factions could impose their will on others and produce **tyranny**, denying liberty to those who did not share the wishes of the faction.

Madison lays out the problem in detail and assesses the possible solutions to it in Federalist #10, ultimately explaining why the new Constitution provided the surest and safest way to address the dangers of faction. In Federalist #51, he goes on

Table 4.3. What Was in the Original Constitution?

Article I	Establishes the legislative branch of government, with instructions for electing representatives and senators, and gives basic guidelines for how Congress should run and what it should do.	
Article II	Establishes the executive branch or presidency. It says that the president shall be commander-in-chief of the armed forces, grants the president the power to make treaties, mandates that the president report to Congress from time to time on the state of the nation, and devotes a lot of attention to presidential selection.	
Article III	Establishes the judiciary. It mandates the establishment of a Supreme Court, stipulating the matters over which it should have jurisdiction, and gives Congress the authority to set up lower courts.	
Article IV	Addresses the relationship between the federal government and the states, including procedures for admitting new states to the union, and defines the relationship of each state to the others.	
Article V	Sets up the mechanism for amending the Constitution.	
Article VI	Transfers to the new government all outstanding debts acquired by the United States under the Articles of Confederation and establishes the Constitution as the supreme law of the land.	
Article VII	Sets up the procedures for ratifying the Constitution.	

to detail how separation of powers and checks and balances work to protect against the danger of tyranny from the government.

In Federalist #10, Madison addresses alternative ways to deal with the dangers posed by factions. Here's a simple way of thinking about what he said. Let's say you wanted the liberty to dress in whatever style appealed to you. Further assume that there is a group of people—a faction—that wanted to impose a national dress code that would forbid the wearing of shorts and nose rings. They could be small in number but highly motivated, plotting to find ways to get you to dress like they do while you're busy going about your life, not giving a second thought to what you wear. Or, they could be large enough in number to overwhelm you. Either way, they could pose a threat to your free expression.

Madison looks at ways to prevent that from happening and considers two options: removing the causes of faction—the things that motivate others to gang up on you—or controlling their effects. Removing the causes of faction would require either removing liberty or giving everyone the same preferences and desires. Neither is a particularly attractive option. In the first case, what's the point

of removing liberty if the objective is to preserve liberty? Madison says this remedy would be "worse than the disease" of faction itself. He likens liberty to air: We need it to breathe, and fire needs it to burn, but if you eliminated air just to put out fires, you'd be extinguishing life in the process. So, this solution is effective, but way too expensive.

What about giving everyone the same preferences and desires? That would result in a society where everyone would look, act, feel, and believe the same things—a place where, say, everyone wore shorts and nose rings. If you're having trouble imagining how this might come about, it's because this is not a practical solution. As long as people have liberty, different opinions will form, and with them, the risk that factions will form. "The latent causes of faction," Madison says, "are thus sown in the nature of man." It's a condition we simply have to deal with.

Madison concludes that if we can't regulate the causes of faction, we need to control their effects so that liberty can be protected. This is where the safety features of the Constitution come into play, starting with the establishment of a republican form of government. As we know, unlike direct democracy, a republic is characterized by elected representatives who are accountable to the people through popular sovereignty. In this depiction of events, our dress-code advocates can vote along with everyone else for representatives to Congress. Their intensely expressed wish for everyone to dress in a particular manner may result in the election of some representatives who share their views, which, in turn, will be expressed in Congress to other representatives who speak for different people who do not share their views. Because they are a faction, it will be hard for them to attain enough support in Congress to impose their wishes on others, although Congress will give them a forum for having their views heard. In a country as large as the United States, Madison speculated that there would be many factions concerned with a host of issues, none of which would be able to dominate the government.

To make things more secure, the Constitution makes it difficult for any one group to dominate the workings of government by separating powers into different branches and through checks and balances. Add staggered terms for elected representatives, different constituencies for elected representatives, and federalism—all the safeguards we talked about earlier—and it becomes difficult for a single faction to manipulate the machinery of government.

At the same time, Madison was sensitive to the need to protect the public from the government. In Federalist #51, he describes the benefits derived from separation of powers and checks and balances, which make it difficult for government to overwhelm individual liberty. By creating different institutions with separate and distinct roles, representing different groups in society, the three branches are likely to adhere to distinct agendas, which they cannot advance alone. As a consequence, each branch will have to moderate its wishes through compromise with the others or submit to the reality that nothing will get done. Either outcome protects the public from the threat of centralized power. "Ambition must be made to counteract ambition," Madison writes. "The interest of the man must be connected with the constitutional rights of the place."

Essays in *The Federalist* are not long, but they were written in the language of eighteenth-century America and should be read slowly.

Selling the Constitution

It may be strange to think of politicians writing essays in an effort to win a political battle, but that's essentially what The Federalist was about. Today, Hamilton and Madison would set up an organization to collect contributions from wealthy like-minded donors and use that money to buy thirty-second television ads in states where ratification of the Constitution seemed shaky. At the same time, even if their methods seem quaint by comparison, the bitter struggle over ratification was as partisan and nasty as anything in politics today.

Those who favored ratification cleverly called themselves "Federalists," leaving their opponents with the negative tag "Anti-Federalists." Since the way you characterize your political opponent goes a long way to structuring the debate (see Demystifying Government: The Politics of Language), this choice of label gave the Federalists the upper hand in the discussion because it's always better to be for something than to want to obstruct something. And if the Anti-Federalists were opposed to the Constitution, and people at large were widely opposed to the Articles of Confederation, then it was reasonable to wonder exactly what the Anti-Federalists were for.

In fact, the Federalists did have the advantage of being more organized than the Anti-Federalists, and of having a cohesive argument for ratification. They had the stature of national figures like Washington and Franklin behind them. They had frustration over the Articles to help their cause. What they didn't have was enough votes.

It was clear to the Federalists that ratification was in serious jeopardy in a number of states. Because state legislatures (rightly) feared losing power under the new constitutional arrangement, they were among the Constitution's strongest critics, and the Constitutional Convention shrewdly maneuvered to have ratification considered in state conventions rather than in the legislatures. But ratification still had to take place at the state level, where officials

DEMYSTIFYING GOVERNMENT

THE POLITICS OF LANGUAGE

Couching the ratification debate in the language of "Federalists" and "Anti-Federalists" is akin to how language is used in present-day debates over contentious policy issues. Think about the way each side in the abortion debate implicitly characterizes the other through the selection of the labels they claim for themselves. Abortion rights supporters call themselves "pro-choice," suggesting that their opponents—implicitly "antichoice"—stand in opposition to liberty. Those on the other side of the question label themselves "pro-life," with clear implications for what that makes the other side. Would anyone willingly claim to be "pro-death"?

stood to lose a lot of power and could be counted on to lead the charge against change.

To confront this difficulty, the Constitution's supporters opted to require ratification from only nine of thirteen states before the new constitutional arrangement would take effect—even though unanimity had been required to revise the Articles. They recognized that unanimity was an unrealistic objective, and were savvy enough to realize that if faced with the reality of the new government taking effect elsewhere on the continent, reluctant states would find themselves with no alternative but to go along.

There were other huge obstacles as well. Anti-Federalists made much of the apparent class bias at the Constitutional Convention, claiming that a group of lawyers and merchants had created a new government that would undermine the interests of farmers and debtors. Considering the conflicts between debtors and creditors that helped fuel the Constitutional Convention, it's not at all surprising that this argument carried a lot of weight. Add this to the sentiment that the country had just finished fighting a war to get away from a strong central government and the Anti-Federalists had a strong case.

In what would become typical of politics in America, the battle was spirited, impassioned—and dirty. Rumors flew in the newspapers. Pagans would control the government. Federal crimes would be punished by torture. The Pope would be elected president.[7]

The claims about punishment and torture stuck, and the Federalists found that they had to respond to charges that the Constitution did not protect people from fundamental abuses of liberty by the federal government. Their answer was a promise to amend the Constitution immediately in a way that would protect individuals from abuses by government. The result of this promise was the first ten amendments to the Constitution—the Bill of Rights—passed as promised by the First Congress and ratified by the states within two years.

The First Congress quickly took up the matter of a Bill of Rights as promised by the Federalists in their campaign to win ratification of the Constitution. On September 25, 1789, Congress passed and sent to the states twelve amendments designed to protect people from abuses of their liberty by the new government. The first amendment, which addressed the number of constituents each House member would represent, was not ratified. The second amendment, which set restrictions on congressional compensation, took 203 years to ratify and became the Twenty-seventh Amendment to the Constitution on May 7, 1992. The remaining ten were ratified December 15, 1791 and became known as the Bill of Rights. Table 4.4 describes each amendment included in the Bill of Rights.

The promise of a Bill of Rights turned out to be a particularly important maneuver by the Federalists. By January 1788, Delaware, Pennsylvania, New Jersey, Georgia, and Connecticut had ratified

Table 4.4. The Bill of Rights

First Amendment	The First Amendment prevents government from interfering with several key personal freedoms, including the freedom to worship, speak, and assemble peacefully. It also prevents the government from restricting freedom of the press and the freedom to petition government.
Second Amendment	The Second Amendment protects the right to bear arms.
Third and Fourth Amendments	The Third and Fourth Amendments provide a right to privacy from government interference. The Third Amendment prevents government from forcing citizens to house soldiers during peacetime—addressing one of the complaints the colonists had against the British. The Fourth Amendment protects against unreasonable searches and seizures of property or personal effects.
Fifth through Eighth Amendments	The Fifth through Eighth Amendments establish a host of protections for individuals accused of a crime. These include the right not to be tried twice for the same crime, the right to be indicted by a grand jury before being tried for a capital crime, the right not to be forced to testify against yourself, the right to due process of law, and the right not to have property confiscated by government without compensation (all in the Fifth Amendment); and the right to a speedy and impartial trial, the right to be informed of charges against you, the right to call and confront witnesses, and the right to a lawyer (all in the Sixth Amendment); and the right to a jury in civil trials (Seventh Amendment); the right to be free from excessive bail and from the infliction of cruel and unusual punishments (Eighth Amendment).
Ninth and Tenth Amendments	The Ninth Amendment is a safety net establishing that any rights not specifically mentioned in the first eight amendments are not necessarily denied. The Tenth Amendment establishes that any powers not granted to the federal government or prohibited to the states are reserved for the states.

the Constitution, but the remaining states were either strongly opposed or too close to call. The outcome in Massachusetts was in question when its convention met in February, and the Bill of Rights concession is credited with making the difference in a narrow vote to approve. It would help make the difference in other narrow votes to come.

Things remained tenuous, though. New Hampshire was leaning against ratification, and in March, Rhode Island held a referendum that rejected the Constitution by a large margin. It was up to Maryland to regain the momentum for the Federalists, which it did in April with a vote to ratify. South Carolina soon fell in line, and when New Hampshire became the ninth state to ratify on June 21, 1788, the Constitution had been officially adopted.

Nonetheless, the battle continued. As a practical matter, the constitutional plan could not have been implemented without the blessing of two of the largest states, New York and Virginia. This was hardly forthcoming. Owing in part to the hard work and political skills of James Madison in Virginia and Alexander Hamilton in New York—of which the publication of *The Federalist* was a part—and in part to the relative disarray of the Anti-Federalists, these two populous states eventually ratified the Constitution, even though the vote in each case was harrowingly close (the margin in the New York convention was three votes of fifty-seven cast). It's quite likely that a majority of New Yorkers and Virginians opposed the Constitution at the time their states ratified it. Hamilton assumed a majority of Americans opposed it, but the Federalists had outmaneuvered their opponents. North Carolina would ratify the Constitution following Washington's inauguration as president. Rhode Island, the final holdout, would sign on almost two years after the document had become official, and there would be a federal republic in the United States. Table 4.5 details how the new government unfolded.

Changing the Constitution

The rules of the game set out in the Constitution have evolved over time, and much of that change has been gradual and evolutionary, rather than sudden and dramatic. Although there are formal mechanisms for amending the Constitution, the

Table 4.5. Constitutional Timeline

It took time before the machinery created by the Constitution came on line. Some of it was being put into place while the ratification process was still playing out. Here's how the new government unfolded between June 1788 and June 1789.

June 21, 1788	The Constitution is adopted when New Hampshire becomes the ninth state to ratify.
September 1788	Congress sets dates for voting for president.
January 1789	Presidential electors are chosen in states that ratified the Constitution.
February 1789	Presidential electors meet and select George Washington as the first president.
March 3, 1789	The government established by the Articles of Confederation ceases to exist.
April 6, 1789	The first Congress of the United States meets to begin organizing.
April 8, 1789	Members of the House of Representatives take the oath of office.
April 30, 1789	George Washington is sworn in as the first president of the United States. The executive branch becomes operational.
June 1, 1789	The first act of Congress provides for senators to take an oath of office and recognizes the oath that House members took on April 8th as official.
June 3, 1789	Senators take the oath of office, and John Adams is sworn in as vice president. Congress becomes fully operational.
February 2, 1790	The Supreme Court meets in first full session. All three branches of the new government are now operational.

Source: National Archives at http://www.archives.gov

greatest change has come through differences in the way the Constitution is interpreted. This has afforded the Constitution the flexibility to respond to two centuries of dramatic social, economic, and political change.

The Constitution's authors were determined not to repeat the mistakes of the Articles of Confederation, which were impossible to amend. At the same time, they wanted it to be difficult to change the supreme law of the land. They decided on two methods for proposing and ratifying amendments to the Constitution, which are described on the next page in Demystifying Government: Amendment Ratification.

Formally changing the Constitution has proved difficult. Since 1789, only twenty-seven amendments have been ratified—ten of which were the Bill of Rights. Many of the ratified amendments broadened the grant of constitutional rights or strengthened the power of the federal government. Table 4.6 provides an overview.

Because so many parties have to agree to amend the Constitution, a large number of efforts have failed. Some of the more significant proposals that never made it include:

- A proposed Equal Rights Amendment that would have made sex discrimination unconstitutional. It was proposed in 1972 with a time limit for ratification. Three-fourths of the state legislatures failed to ratify it by 1982, and it expired.
- Full congressional representation for the District of Columbia. This amendment was proposed in 1978 and expired, unratified, seven years later. To this day, residents of the nation's capital have no representation in the Senate and are represented in the House by a delegate who cannot vote.[8]
- A proposal to allow Congress to limit child labor. Proposed in 1926, it remains ten states short of ratification and has no time limit. But no state has acted on the amendment since 1937.

Many more proposals of lesser note have been unsuccessful, typically unable to muster the congressional support necessary to send them to the states for ratification. Some of the failed attempts over the past few years would have established:

DEMYSTIFYING GOVERNMENT

AMENDMENT RATIFICATION

Amendments need to be proposed, then ratified. The Constitution allows the process to begin at either the federal or state level. At the federal level, an amendment is proposed if it is approved by a two-thirds vote of both the House of Representatives and the Senate. Every amendment to the Constitution has originated this way. It then follows one of two paths. The most typical path is for the amendment to be considered by the legislatures of the fifty states. The amendment is ratified if it is approved by three-fourths of the state legislatures. All but one amendment was ratified this way.

The lone exception was the Twenty-first Amendment, which repealed the Eighteenth Amendment outlawing the sale or manufacture of alcohol. The Twenty-first Amendment followed the other ratification path permitted by the Constitution: it was approved by special ratifying conventions in three-fourths of the states. These were like the state ratifying conventions that approved the original Constitution.

For an amendment to be proposed at the state level, two-thirds of the state legislatures would have to ask Congress to call a national convention, similar to the Constitutional Convention that produced the Constitution. Whatever amendment or amendments the national convention approved would then require the approval of three-fourths of either the state legislatures or state conventions for ratification. This method has never been used.

To review, amendments need to be proposed, then ratified. The Constitution provides two ways to propose amendments and two ways to ratify them. Every amendment in our history has been proposed by a two-thirds vote of both houses of Congress, and all but one has been ratified by a vote of three-fourths of the sate legislatures. The one exception was approved by ratifying conventions in three-fourths of the states. Amendments may also be proposed if two-thirds of the state legislatures request a national constitutional convention. This method has never been used.

- A constitutional right to health care.
- A constitutional restriction against the early release of convicted criminals.
- A constitutional right to own a home.

It's pretty easy to see how difficult it would be to get all the necessary parties to come together to modify the Constitution around these relatively specific issues. It may be less obvious to see how profound changes have occurred through judicial interpretation and political circumstance. Rather than alter the physical document, changes of this nature alter the way we understand the physical document.

The courts have had to deal with countless disputes over constitutional interpretation, and in the process, they have shaped the way the Constitution is applied and understood, sometimes in ways its authors never could have imagined. The Supreme

Court is the arbiter of constitutional disputes, but in a good example of how judicial interpretation has modified the Constitution, nothing in the Constitution itself actually grants this authority to the Supreme Court. As we will see in Chapter 12, early in its history, the Supreme Court interpreted the Constitution to say that the Court's power to review the Constitution was intended by the document's framers.

Changes in political circumstances have similarly shaped the Constitution in unintended ways. For instance, political parties are never mentioned in the Constitution, and with good reason—the Federalists equated parties with factions and saw them as a threat to liberty. Yet, the years immediately following the ratification of the Constitution saw the emergence of political parties, and they have been a central part of our political process

Table 4.6. Amendments to the Constitution

Apart from the Bill of Rights, the amendments to the Constitution—in order of appearance—did the following:	
Eleventh (1795)	Limited federal court jurisdiction in suits against the states
Twelfth (1804)	Modified the method of selecting the president
Thirteenth (1865)	Abolished slavery
Fourteenth (1868)	Expanded the federal guarantees of equal protection of the law and due process of the law to the states
Fifteenth (1870)	Extended voting rights to African Americans
Sixteenth (1913)	Authorized a federal income tax
Seventeenth (1913)	Changed the method of choosing senators from selection by state legislatures to direct popular vote
Eighteenth (1919)	Abolished the sale and production of alcohol; repealed by the Twenty-first Amendment (1933)
Nineteenth (1920)	Extended voting rights to women
Twentieth (1933)	Established that presidential terms expire on January 20th and that congressional terms expire on January 3rd
Twenty-first (1933)	Repealed the Eighteenth Amendment (1919)
Twenty-second (1951)	Established presidential term limits
Twenty-third (1961)	Extended the right to vote in presidential elections to residents of the District of Columbia
Twenty-fourth (1964)	Abolished the poll tax in federal elections
Twenty-fifth (1967)	Provided procedures for handling presidential disability and for filling a vacancy in the vice presidency
Twenty-sixth (1971)	Extended voting rights to eighteen-year-olds
Twenty-seventh (1992)	Prohibited midterm congressional pay increases
The Thirteenth, Fourteenth, and Twenty-fourth Amendments expanded civil rights. The Fifteenth, Seventeenth, Nineteenth, Twenty-third and Twenty-sixth Amendments expanded the right to vote.	

ever since. The Constitution has been flexible enough to adapt to this change.

Soon we'll learn about the complex constitutional mechanism for presidential selection, called the Electoral College. It originally provided for an elite group of individuals, called electors, to debate the merits of the candidates and vote for the one they felt most qualified. Through natural evolution, political parties acquired that function. But the electors still exist, even though they only go through the motions of voting for president. The Constitution was flexible enough to adjust to a situation its authors simply couldn't anticipate.

Federalism: Only in America

Well—almost only in America. Apart from a handful of countries like Canada, Germany, and Switzerland, federal systems are unusual in the world. There has also been movement towards a federated Europe, although as Global Topics: American Federalism versus European Federalism explains, the joint decision-making and collective politics practiced in Europe is a different thing entirely from American federalism. In the United States, federalism is one of the defining characteristics of political debate.

Having states and a federal government as independent power centers is an effective feature of the Constitution designed to keep power from being concentrated in a single set of hands. It is also an awkward design that has caused conflict throughout American history.

The dilemma centers around which power center—the states or Washington, D.C.—gets to have the final word in American politics. There's no doubt that Madison intended the national government to be supreme to the state governments. But this was a point of contention at the Constitutional Convention that wasn't put to rest until the Civil War settled the matter some seventy years later by establishing that the South did not have a right to depart from the Union to form a new confederation.

The Constitution does contain wording that appears to support Madison's position. Article VI states, "This Constitution, and the laws of the United States which shall be made in Pursuance thereof ... shall be the supreme Law of the Land." This seems to suggest that actions of the federal government should override actions of the states, but not everyone saw it this way at first. Only over time, through precedent and judicial interpretation, did this **supremacy clause** cement the position of the federal government as superior to the states. Even today, 150 years after the Civil War, the relationship between the states and the federal government reverberates through our politics. In 2009, with Congress assuming an activist posture in the first year of the Obama administration, Texas Governor Rick Perry even raised the prospect of secession from the union if Washington refused to rein in what he called its "oppression" of the states through what he regarded as the national government's failure to respect the states' Tenth Amendment right to all powers not granted to the federal government.[9] Governor Perry's words raised eyebrows across the country, as they echoed arguments from the Civil War era, although the sentiment he expressed is deeply rooted in the earliest and most fundamental Constitutional battles between the states and the national government.

There are other hints that the Constitution's framers intended for the states to be subservient to the federal government. In Article I, Section 8, Congress is given the authority "To make all laws which shall be necessary and proper for carrying into Execution ... all other Powers vested by this Constitution in the Government of the United States." Implicit in this statement is a large grant of power to the national government that, when broadly interpreted, gives Congress the ability to make laws that states would be obligated to follow.

The key word here is *interpreted*—and there are several different ways of understanding the intent of the Constitution's framers with respect to federalism that could be conveniently applied by people on both sides of the strong federal government question. Beyond giving the federal government the upper hand in its relationship with the states, the Constitution provides little guidance on how federalism is to operate in practice. Consequently, the specific relationship between the federal and state governments has varied at different points in our national history and has evolved over time.

Madison's vision was what might best be termed **nation-centered federalism**, whereby the Constitution was the supreme law of the land, the federal government was a creation of the Constitution, and the states—despite their broad grant of authority—were subservient to both. But those favoring greater state and local control of politics advocated a form of **state-centered federalism**, which turned Madison's perspective on its head with the claim that the Constitutional Convention itself was a meeting of the states intended to revise the Articles of Confederation. Therefore, the Constitution it produced and the federal government it established were essentially a creation of the states, which should have the final say in disagreements over which level of government had the ultimate authority to act.

This might seem like an academic argument, but the implications were tremendous. When southern states seceded from the union during the period leading up to the Civil War, they justified their actions on the basis of state-centered federalism—that the federal union was created by the states, who maintained the right to opt out. In turn, northern states opposed secession—and justified military action—on the basis of nation-centered federalism, that the union of the states was greater than the sum of its parts.

During the decades following the drafting of the Constitution, many took a middle perspective that worked as long as the states and the federal government didn't have to confront irreconcilable differences—the perspective of **dual federalism**, which

GLOBAL TOPICS

AMERICAN FEDERALISM VERSUS EUROPEAN FEDERALISM

Federal systems are rare because federations typically form when a nation is forged from units with a history of political autonomy, like the thirteen American colonies. Few nations can claim a history like this. Switzerland is a centuries-old federation of small states called cantons, some of which date back to a time before Switzerland was a nation. German federalism united several previously independent states in the mid-nineteenth century. The Canadian federation permits the coexistence of English and French-speaking provinces in one nation.

Surrendering sovereign authority to a larger entity can be a complex and complicated affair. For instance, compare federalism in the United States with the movement to create a federated Europe, which has existed in some form since the end of World War II. The European Movement, an international organization that originated in 1947, is committed to the creation of a federal Europe through political, social and cultural integration of European nations. Following a century of devastating European wars, founders of the European Movement believed that the integration of Europe around common political and economic interests was the only path to lasting peace and security on the European continent.[T3]

In 1948, delegates from across Europe participated in the Congress of Europe, where prospects for European integration were discussed by some of the continent's most prominent and powerful leaders.[T4] Two years later, the first steps toward economic integration took place when several European nations agreed to integrate their steel and coal industries. Integration of the nuclear power industry followed, and by 1967 a European Parliament was formed. In 1992, a formal European Union (EU) was created by the Treaty of Maastricht, and

with it a greater degree of formal cooperation among the governments of member nations.[T5]

These steps produced common policies and led to joint decision-making on a host of trade and economic matters and facilitated the development of a common European market through the relaxation of trade barriers. In the 1990s it became possible to travel between European countries without a passport, and today a common currency—the Euro—has replaced the national currency of sixteen EU member nations.[T6]

These developments have produced a host of policies and governing institutions that are binding on member nations. But, cooperation and integration are not the same as federalism. The political relationship among EU member states is quite different from the political relationship among the American states, and the relationship between member states and the EU is different from the relationship between the American states and the American federal government. Despite having coordinated economic policies and a common currency, the nations of Europe remain individually sovereign.

Even as EU membership grew to include Eastern European nations of the former Soviet bloc, steps toward greater integration—and possibly a single European nation—were resisted by those who view them as a threat to national sovereignty. A concerted effort by supporters of a united Europe to win approval of a European Constitution faced a serious setback in 2005 when the people of France and the Netherlands rejected it, leading Great Britain and several other nations to postpone their ratification votes indefinitely. Among the objections voiced by opponents was that calling the document a Constitution rather than a treaty or agreement, and the creation of what they viewed as national institutions for Europe, suggested a degree of unification on par with a federal republic like the United States. In an argument reminiscent of claims made by early opponents of American federalism, European anti-federalists question whether the EU exceeded its authority by, in their view, imposing changes through an illegitimate document that did not express the wishes of the European people.[17] Instead in 2007, leaders of the 27 member nations signed the Treaty of Lisbon, which streamlined and strengthened the institutions and procedures of the European Union without creating a constitutional government.

contended the Constitution had given both the states and the federal government distinct authority over a broad range of matters. In other words, the grant of authority to the federal government could coexist with a different but equally broad grant of authority to the states, sidestepping the matter of which would win a battle of wills.

Dual federalism provided a reasonable way to manage the natural tension arising between the federal government and the states because, during the period stretching from the Constitutional Convention to the Civil War, the federal government and the states for the most part did operate in distinct spheres. Government at both levels was small by today's standards and didn't participate in a wide range of activities, so disputes could be minimized.

When the two clashed, though, they made a loud noise. The most notable conflict during this period came to a head in 1819, when the U.S. Supreme Court had to determine whether the federal government had the right to charter a federal bank and locate it, free of taxes, in one of the states. The decision, in the case **McCulloch v. Maryland,** was the first to clearly enumerate **national supremacy,** or the dominance of the federal government over the states. It's an important case, and it's discussed in Demystifying Government: *McCulloch v. Maryland* (1819).

If the Civil War established that states could not leave the federal union, it also ushered in a period of rapid growth in the United States, which posed new challenges for federal/state relations. As waves of immigrants flocked to American cities during a period of rapid industrialization, government at both the federal and state levels had to address a host of new social and economic concerns. By the start of the twentieth century, a new intergovernmental relationship was forged that lasted for the better part of seventy years. Dubbed **cooperative federalism,** it was characterized by federal-state partnerships, where federal funds were used to help states administer federal priorities at the state level.

The story of American government in the twentieth century is a tale of increasing demands on government through the first two-thirds of the century, followed by a reaction against central government activity in the latter one-third. It's a story with all kinds of implications for how government developed and how it works today, so we'll be coming back to it a lot. The discussion in Demystifying Government: Big Government, Fighting Words, describes how the debate over big government that defines so much of our contemporary politics has its roots in federalism.

With the start of the Great Depression at the dawn of the 1930s, state governments were unable to handle the demands created by massive unemployment. With the election of President Franklin D. Roosevelt in 1932, the relationship between the federal and state governments changed dramatically. The programs of Roosevelt's **"New Deal"** produced an unprecedented expansion in the size and role of the federal government. For the first time, the federal government was involved in such things as unemployment compensation and social security. The federal government also took a bigger role in regulating the economy, and spent money on construction projects to get people back to work. With the New Deal, the federal government became a presence in the lives of American citizens like it never had before.

This active federal role reached its peak in the 1960s during the administration of President

DEMYSTIFYING GOVERNMENT

McCULLOCH v. MARYLAND (1819)

The dispute before the U.S. Supreme Court in *McCulloch v. Maryland* centered on two questions about the scope and reach of the federal government: Could the federal government engage in activities that were not expressly delegated to it in the Constitution, and does the federal government supersede the states when a conflict arises between them? In both cases, the verdict was a resounding yes, setting the stage for the future growth of national power and the eventual repudiation of state-centered federalism.

The particulars center on the establishment by the federal government of a Bank of the United States. First chartered by Congress in 1791 as a means for coining currency, making loans, and centralizing the financial affairs of the United States, the first Bank of the United States was controversial. Not surprisingly, supporters of nation-centered federalism, like Treasury Secretary Alexander Hamilton—always an advocate of a strong central government—were behind the idea. Hamilton justified the creation of the bank on the grounds that the Constitution gave Congress a broad grant of power that extended to just about anything not expressly denied to it. Just as predictable were the Bank's opponents: debtor farmers (who still didn't trust the actions of lenders) and advocates of state-centered federalism, who felt Congress had grossly overreached its authority because the Constitution did not specifically give Congress the power to charter a national bank.

The charter on the bank expired in 1811, but the financial demands of the War of 1812 were justification for President Madison—the same James Madison who guided the development of the Constitution—to recommend that Congress revisit the charter. A second Bank of the United States was subsequently established, and it met with a heightened level of opposition. The state of Maryland imposed a tax on the Baltimore branch of the Bank in 1818, which the Bank's cashier, James McCulloch, refused to pay on the grounds that a state did not have the power to tax a federal entity. Shortly afterwards, the dispute landed in the U.S. Supreme Court.

The decision, written by Chief Justice John Marshall, backed both the power of Congress to establish the bank and the right of the federal government to do so without having to submit to taxes levied by a state. In so doing, Marshall invoked both the **"necessary and proper" clause** and the supremacy clause of the Constitution.

In ruling to support the right of the federal government to charter a bank, Marshall took a broad interpretation of the "necessary and proper" clause, arguing that the language of Article I, Section 8, gave Congress powers that were not specifically delegated to it in the Constitution—powers that were implied but not stated. This interpretation allowed Congress to act with great flexibility in future years, permitting the federal government to grow in authority in relation to the states.

In ruling against Maryland on the tax issue, Marshall invoked the reasoning of nation-centered federalism and a broad reading of the supremacy clause. He argued that as long as the federal government acted constitutionally, its actions were binding on the states. Since Marshall had already established that the bank charter was a "necessary and proper" move for Congress in its constitutionally enumerated capacity to regulate commerce, it followed that the states had no choice but to permit Congress to establish branches of the Bank, tax free, wherever it wished.[18]

Demystifying Government

Big Government: Fighting Words

It's said that the more things change, the more they stay the same. So it is with the debate over the size and role of the federal government. If you listen to some of the arguments for a smaller federal government that have been made over the past thirty years, you might think you were back at the Constitutional Convention. When President Reagan said in his inaugural address, "the federal government did not create the states, the states created the federal government," he was echoing the philosophy of state-centered federalism that had been advocated by those who feared strong federal control some two hundred years earlier—a philosophy that had been rebuffed by Chief Justice Marshall in *McCulloch v. Maryland,* discredited by the outcome of the Civil War, and forgotten in the activism of the New Deal and the Great Society.

When no less a spokesman than the president of the United States makes the case for a smaller, state-centered government, an argument long dead can come roaring back. By the time President Reagan made his pronouncement in 1980, the United States had already taken a few steps back from the activism that was the hallmark of the previous half-century. Subsequently, Reagan took the case much farther than most people imagined he could. Ever since the Reagan years, where you stand on the question of federal versus state power has been a defining question in political debate.

The issue has both practical and philosophical significance. As a practical matter, the more the federal government does, the more it costs—a price that must ultimately be paid in taxes. And, as a practical matter, how effectively government spends those tax dollars can have a bearing on how much people want government to do. A large, strong federal government was popular when it put people to work during the

Great Depression, but less popular when it failed to cure social ills as Great Society programs promised it would.

As a philosophical matter, the big government debate raises the normative question of what government should do. Ronald Reagan was philosophically opposed to the federal government trying to cure social problems, and felt that government is most effective at the local level, where it is closer to the people. He saw a large federal government as the problem, not as the solution to other problems.

When George W. Bush took office in 2001, the large government/small government debate continued to define American politics. Bush cast himself in the Reagan mold, and advanced policies designed to limit what government could do. In his first months in office, during a time of federal surpluses, he successfully advocated the largest tax cut in twenty years, which he argued was a matter of returning excess federal money to the public. Two years later, during a period of mushrooming deficits, he followed up with another substantial tax cut, arguing that it was necessary to get the economy moving again. Opponents argued that the Bush tax cuts would hamstring the ability of government to provide a wide range of programs and services. Supporters did not disagree—and did not complain.

President Obama has articulated a different view of federalism, built around the idea that the federal government is and should be a positive force in American life. He expressed his belief in the value of a strong national government during a September 2009 address to a joint session of Congress, as he made the case for why the federal government should reform the American health care system:

Our predecessors understood that government could not, and should not, solve every problem. They understood that there are instances when the gains in security from government action are not worth the added constraints on our freedom. But they also understood that the danger of too much government is matched by the perils of too little; that without the leavening hand of wise policy, markets can crash, monopolies can stifle competition, the vulnerable can be exploited. And they knew that when any government measure, no matter how carefully crafted or beneficial, is subject to scorn; when any efforts to help people in need are attacked as un-American; when facts and reason are thrown overboard and only timidity passes for wisdom, and we can no longer even engage in a civil conversation with each other over the things that truly matter—that at that point we don't merely lose our capacity to solve big challenges. We lose something essential about ourselves.[19]

President Obama made his case at a moment when many Americans were feeling vulnerable, but his advocacy on behalf of a national health care policy met stiff resistance from congressional Republicans, who stood united in opposition to any reform measures that imagined an expanded federal role. Far from a dull academic exercise, the debate over federalism involves a host of questions about what government will and should do, with real implications for who gets what, when, and how.

Lyndon B. Johnson. The **"Great Society"** initiatives of the Johnson administration took the philosophy of the New Deal one step further, seeking to use the federal government to solve broad social problems, like eliminating poverty and hunger in America. State governments became agents of a federal agenda, carrying out a large number of new social programs that were funded and regulated by Washington. The Great Society created a complex web of programs and regulations, some of which fell short of their goals. As a consequence, the latter one-third of the twentieth century witnessed a gradual reaction against the strong role of the federal government characterized by the New Deal and the Great Society.

In the late 1960s, President Richard M. Nixon attempted to simplify the federal government while shifting the balance of power in running government programs toward the states. He called the initiative **New Federalism.** One characteristic of Nixon's New Federalism was less federal regulation of federal money so that states could have more freedom to decide how to address social problems.

With the election of Ronald Reagan in 1980, the movement toward less federal involvement in everyday life begun in the Nixon administration took a dramatic turn with an effort to shift responsibility for social programs from Washington to the states. Though largely unsuccessful, it represented a bold departure from the New Deal and Great Society. The rhetoric and actions of the Reagan administration reflected the philosophy of those who advocated a limited role for the federal government some 200 years earlier, as Reagan sought to vastly limit the size and scope of the federal government.

President Bill Clinton took office in the wake of the smaller government debate of the Reagan years. Despite a natural inclination for a large, active federal government along the lines of Roosevelt and Johnson, Clinton found himself swimming against the strong Reagan tide. His response to New Federalism was to make the federal government smaller by making it more efficient. Clinton's **"Reinventing Government"** initiative met with modest success.

The small government argument remained popular through the start of the millennium, with George W. Bush as its most visible advocate. In the wake of the September 11, 2001 terrorist attacks on the United States, though, President Bush found himself in the position of advancing a larger role for the federal government in military matters and homeland security, as public sentiment took a turn toward renewed acceptance of a stronger role for Washington in security matters. At the same time, his tax cutting policies have raised speculation among critics that President Bush sought to starve the federal government of its funding in an attempt to return federal-state relations to what they were before the growth of the federal government during the New Deal.

The election of Barack Obama ushered in a sea change in the federalism question, but did not put to rest questions about the appropriate size and scope of the federal government. In Obama, Americans have a president who advocates for an active federal role in solving major problems, departing from the philosophy that guided most of his recent predecessors.

Who Would Create a System Like This?

If you had set out to design a constitutional system, you probably never would have come close to creating the complicated mechanism in place in the United States. The combination of factors leading to the adoption of the Constitution was unparalleled, contributing to the development of a political system the likes of which had never been attempted.

Look at what the authors of the Constitution had to contend with. Any central government they created had to enter into a relationship with the states. For their creation to be viable, they had to produce a government that was strong enough to deal with the social unrest that the Articles of Confederation couldn't handle. If there was going to be any hope for constitutional ratification, they had to address the fears of small states that they would be dominated in the federal government by the commercial interests of the larger states.

They had to face the fact that slavery ran the southern economy. They couldn't create a strong, centralized government or detractors would fear

they were reproducing the type of system they had just fought to leave. And they had to do this knowing they were going to ask the states to ratify a document that diminished their power. Above all, they set about creating a system that would produce a new set of winners and losers from the power structure that was in place, and people are often reluctant to buy into new rules when they're not sure how or if they'll benefit.

To this effort, the Constitution's framers brought a keen understanding of key political writers and a willingness to put political theory into practice. The fact that *The Federalist* could articulate a constitutional *philosophy* is a good benchmark of how much abstract thought guided the writing of the Constitution. The safeguards to liberty built into the Constitution were a consequence of the belief that abstractions could be brought to life. You could call it a crazy belief because, throughout history, violence and not reason had been the hallmark of great changes in governments, where new rules meant new winners and losers. As experimental as the Constitution was in its day, the United States is still using the bulky, complex mechanism designed around the ideas of Locke and Montesquieu.

If the Constitution's authors created the playing field on which to go about the business of politics and government, it remains up to us how and how much we want to get into the game, if at all. We didn't create the rules of American democracy, but these rules shape the decisions we face about everything political, from the options available for political participation, to how we express our views about our leaders, to how we can have a role in deciding what government does or does not get done.

The political world may be all around us, and it may affect our everyday world in ways we may not readily recognize, but that doesn't mean our everyday world has a lot of room for the political world. The process of becoming politically aware and knowledgeable takes time and effort; having opinions about elected officials takes a certain level of interest that not everybody has. Let's take a look at public opinion—what we know, think, and believe about politics, and how it influences the way we relate to what politicians do.

Chapter Review

Years before the American Revolution, conditions were building in the colonies for an eventual separation from Great Britain. The British imposed a series of acts that the colonists found restrictive, including taxes on tea and other goods through the Sugar Act and the Stamp Act, and a requirement that colonists house British soldiers through the Quartering Act. These actions clashed with a long colonial tradition of limited self-rule, including the free election of representative assemblies, and contributed to a growing feeling that something needed to be done—even though separation from Great Britain was far from universally popular.

The colonists were reluctant to give up too much liberty in exchange for security, so when they won their independence they established a weak confederal system of government under the Articles of Confederation, in which the national government was a creation of the states. The Articles turned out to be ineffective, and the new United States had difficulty conducting foreign policy, regulating commerce, and even settling disputes among the states.

The Articles were far from easy to revise, however, because concerns remained about the harmful effects of a strong central government, and because changing the structure of government would create a new—sometimes uncertain—set of winners and losers. Disputes centered on the competing interests of large and small states, and of free and slave states. Eventually, these differences were ironed out through compromise. The Constitution's framers also built a series of institutional safeguards into the new government, including separation of powers, checks and balances, popular sovereignty, limited government, and federalism. These addressed concerns that a strong central government would overwhelm personal liberty.

Because of the political controversy caused by changing the rules of the game, the Constitution was not easily ratified. Those who supported ratification called themselves Federalists. They engaged in a long and sometimes nasty debate with Anti-Federalists in an attempt to get the requisite nine states to endorse the Constitution. Federalists Alexander Hamilton, James Madison, and John Jay authored eighty-five essays known as *The Federalist,* which detailed how the Constitution would address the weaknesses of the Articles while protecting the public from tyranny at the expense of factions. One of the strongest arguments against ratification was that the new Constitution did not contain a Bill of Rights. A Federalist promise to add one as soon as the new government was established tipped the balance in favor of ratification.

Although federalism is an institutional safeguard designed to disperse authority, it has also been a source of great controversy. Prior to the Civil War, the relationship between the federal and state governments was a matter of great controversy. In 1819, the Supreme Court supported national supremacy in *McCulloch v. Maryland,* ruling that the interests of the federal government are supreme when they conflict with the interests of the states. Many still subscribed to the concept of state-centered federalism—the belief that the Constitution and the federal government it established are creations of the states, which maintain ultimate authority. Because the two levels of government typically addressed different matters, regular conflict could be avoided through the principle of dual federalism, which contended that the federal government and the states had their own distinct grants of authority. Dual federalism, however, was insufficient to avoid large conflicts like the one created by slavery.

The nature of federalism changed as government at both levels became more involved in everyday life in response to the growing complexity of America in the twentieth century. Joint endeavors between the federal government and the states, called cooperative federalism, characterized the relationship during the first two-thirds of the last century. In the 1960s, President Nixon introduced an initiative called New Federalism, the first step in an effort to limit the federal role in daily life that was accelerated in the Reagan administration and embraced by the Bush administration. Even though federalism was established over two centuries ago, dramatic changes since then in the relationship between the federal government and the states show how the rules of the political game are always evolving—with consequences for who gets what, when, and how.

Key Terms

Articles of Confederation   The first constitution of the United States, which created a loosely function-ing national government to which the individual states were supreme. It addressed concerns about a strong national government undermining indi-vidual liberty, but it created a national government that was unable to regulate commerce or conduct foreign policy and was abandoned in favor of the United States Constitution just eight years after it was ratified.

authority   The right to act in an official capacity by virtue of holding an office like president or member of Congress.

Boston Massacre   A precursor to the war that was still five years away, it was the first mortal conflict between colonists and British troops in Boston and resulted in the deaths of five colonists in 1770.

Boston Tea Party   A protest against the Tea Act of 1773 in which fifty colonists dressed as Native Americans boarded British trade ships loaded with tea and threw the contents into the water.

checks and balances   The ability of any one of several equal and independent branches of govern-ment to keep the others from acting, designed to prevent power from being consolidated in any one branch. Because any branch can put a check on the others, government can only act when there is cooperation between the branches, a situation that necessitates compromise.

Coercive Acts   Called the Intolerable Acts in the colonies, the Coercive Acts represented the British attempt to clamp down on the colonies following the Boston Tea Party.

confederal system   An arrangement for establish-ing a government out _of a set of component states, in which the national government is the creation of the states and subservient to them. The Articles of Confederation established a system like this in the United States. In today's world, the United Nations may be the most prominent example of a confederation.

Connecticut Compromise   A compromise between the Virginia and New Jersey Plans that broke the deadlock over representation at the Constitutional Convention by providing for a bicameral legislature. Large states would get their demand for repre-sentation based on population in the House of Representatives, while every state, regardless of size, would have two senators, which pleased small states.

Constitutional Convention   A meeting of represen-tatives from twelve of the thirteen states held in Philadelphia in 1787, which produced the federal system of government outlined in the United States Constitution.

cooperative federalism   One of several perspec-tives on federalism, popular during the first two-thirds of the twentieth century, which was defined by joint endeavors between the federal and state governments. Typically, state governments would carry out federal initiatives, using federal money and federal guidelines.

Declaration of Independence   The document drafted by Thomas Jefferson and approved by the Continental Congress in July 1776, stating the reasons for the Revolutionary War and declaring a formal break with Great Britain.

disenfranchised   Losing or being denied the legal right to vote by intentional or unintentional means.

dual federalism   One of several perspectives on federalism, popular during the early years of the republic, which stated that the federal and state governments operated concurrently in separate arenas, and that each had the final say in those areas where it had a clear grant of authority.

faction   A group of individuals who are united by a desire that, if realized, would threaten the liberty of the larger community—in James Madison's words, individuals who are "united and actuated by some common impulse of passion, or of interest, adverse to the rights of other citizens, or to the permanent and aggregate interests of the community." A faction may be defined by size, such as when a majority of citizens threatens the liberty of the minority, or by intensity, such as when a minority of citizens with intensely held preferences threatens the liberty of a disinterested majority.

federalism The division of power between a sovereign federal government and sovereign state governments, which provides that some functions will be performed by the national government, some by the state governments, and some by both the national and state governments. As a feature designed to limit the strength of government, federalism works to decentralize power by creating dual levels of authority.

The Federalist A collection of essays written by Alexander Hamilton, James Madison, and John Jay in an effort to persuade a reluctant public to support the Constitution.

federal system The arrangement created by the United States Constitution, in which the national government and the states share authority over citizens. States may act autonomously to do such things as create school districts, levy taxes, or assemble a police force; at the same time, powers are reserved for the national government, which is supreme to state laws. In addition to the United States, only Canada, Germany, India, and a small group of other nations have federal systems.

First Continental Congress A gathering of representatives from twelve of the thirteen colonies in Philadelphia in 1774 to protest the Coercive Acts and chart a unified colonial response.

Great Society The name given to the programs of President Lyndon B. Johnson, which elevated the federal government to the most prominent role it would play in the twentieth century. The philosophy of the Great Society was that government should try to solve large social problems like hunger and poverty.

legitimacy Widespread public acceptance of the official standing of a political figure or institution.

limited government The idea that power can be denied to government and the people who serve in it, in order to restrict those in positions of authority from infringing upon individual liberty.

McCulloch v. Maryland The 1819 Supreme Court case that established federal supremacy over the state governments.

nation-centered federalism One of several perspectives on federalism, which argues for the supremacy of the Constitution and federal law over state actions.

national supremacy The doctrine that the federal government has the final word in disputes with the states. National supremacy was established through court rulings, precedent, and the victory of the North in the Civil War, eventually resolving the conflict between nation-centered federalism and state-centered federalism in favor of the former.

natural rights Inalienable rights inherent to every individual that cannot be taken away by individuals or government, and that government should be designed to protect.

"necessary and proper" clause A constitutional provision (Article I, Section 8) giving Congress a broad grant of authority to make laws that are binding on the states.

New Deal The name given to the programs of President Franklin D. Roosevelt, which vastly expanded the role of the federal government in an effort to deal with the debilitating effects of the Great Depression on American society.

New Deal coalition The political coalition composed of urbanites, ethnic and racial minorities, unions, liberals, and southerners that made the Democratic Party the majority party during the fifth party system.

New Federalism The name given to the programs of Presidents Richard M. Nixon and Ronald Reagan, which started as an effort to streamline the federal government produced by the Great Society and ended up as a movement to reverse fifty years of federal growth by returning authority to the states.

New Jersey Plan A proposal for the new Constitution, supported by small states, that would have provided for equal representation of large and small states in the national legislature, while limiting the power of the national government over the states.

popular sovereignty Rule by the people based on the consent of the governed.

Quartering Act An act of the British Parliament requiring colonists to house British troops; first imposed in 1765 and then again in 1774 as part of the Coercive Acts.

Reinventing Government The name given to President Bill Clinton's initiative to make the federal government smaller by making it more efficient.

representative democracy A form of democracy in which eligible individuals choose others to make decisions on their behalf.

republic Any nation with provisions for the selection of representatives who make decisions on behalf of those who select them. James Madison said a republic was "a government in which the scheme of representation takes place," as compared to direct democracy.

Second Continental Congress A gathering of representatives from the colonies in Philadelphia in 1775, necessitated by the need to coordinate planning during the Revolutionary War, that functioned as the first central government in colonial America.

separation of powers The division of political power among several equal and independent branches of government to prevent power from being consolidated in any one branch.

Shays' Rebellion A rebellion by debtor farmers in western Massachusetts, led by Revolutionary War Captain Daniel Shays, against Boston creditors. It began in 1786 and lasted half a year, threatening the economic interests of the business elite and contributing to the demise of the Articles of Confederation.

social contract The arrangement in which people agree to give up some of their liberty to establish a government that will protect basic rights that are threatened in the state of nature.

Stamp Act A particularly vexing tax levied by the British on scores of legal documents, which led to a colonial boycott of British goods.

state-centered federalism One of several perspectives on federalism, which argues that the Constitution and the federal government are creations of the states and therefore can be overruled by the states.

state of nature The condition of total liberty in which people are free to act on their impulses, but where individual rights are afforded no protection.

Sugar Act The first in a string of taxes levied by Great Britain on the American colonies. Formally called the American Revenue Act of 1764, it taxed a number of colonial imports, including sugar.

supremacy clause A constitutional provision (Article VI) establishing the relationship between the federal and state governments. The supremacy clause asserts that any conflict between the federal government and the states will be decided in favor of the federal government.

Three-Fifths Compromise A compromise between northern and southern states that broke the deadlock over how slaves should be counted for purposes of representation. Three-fifths of slaves would be included in population totals, benefiting southern states that had the largest concentration of slaves by inflating their representation in the House of Representatives.

tyranny The denial of liberty to individuals through the actions of a faction or through the actions of government itself.

unitary system The inverse of a confederal system, in which a centralized national government creates subnational units like states, provinces, and counties, which derive their authority from the national government. Most nations are unitary systems. In the United States, the relationship between each individual state and its counties, townships, and cities is a unitary relationship, with the states creating and empowering the local governments.

Virginia Plan A proposal for the new Constitution, supported by large states, that would have based representation on population and provided for a centralized national government that could overrule the states.

Resources

You might be interested in examining some of what the following authors have said about the topics we've been discussing:

Hobbes, Thomas. *Leviathan.* New York: Oxford University Press, 1996. This version contains the original text and notes explaining Hobbes' reasoning.

Locke, John. *Two Treatises of Government.* New York: Cambridge University Press, 1994. This is a student version of the text of one of Locke's most influential works, including background on the author and his times.

McWilliams, Wilson C., ed. *Tederalists, the Antifederalists, and the American Political Tradition.* New York: Greenwood Press, 1992. Seven essays explore the thinking and motivation of the people who fought on both sides of the constitutional ratification question, and examine the relevance of their observations to today's politics.

Millican, Edward. *One United People: The Tederalist Papers and the National Idea.* Lexington, KY: University Press of Kentucky, 1990. If you're interested in The Federalist, this book explores the arguments of Hamilton, Madison, and Jay, and the many ways they have been interpreted over the years.

Rossiter, Clinton L. *1787: The Grand Convention.* New York: W.W. Norton, 1987. A richly detailed, illuminating account of the people, politics, and events that shaped the Constitution.

You may also be interested in looking at these resource sites:

You can find The Articles of Confederation at: http://www.usconstitution.net/articles. html.

The Library of Congress offers all of The Federalist Papers online at http://thomas. loc.gov/home/histdox/fedpapers.html.

Notes

1. See John W. Kingdon, *America the Unusual* (New York: Worth Publishers, 1999).
2. For an overview of the events of the Revolutionary War, courtesy of the History Channel, go to http://www.historychannel.com and type "American Revolution" at the search bar.
3. Thomas Hobbes, *Leviathan* (New York: Oxford University Press, 1996), 84. This edition contains the original text and notes explaining Hobbes' reasoning.
4. Jean-Jacques Rousseau, *The Social Contract.* New York: Oxford University Press, 1994.
5. You may access the text of the Articles of Confederation at http://www.usconstitution.net/articles.html#Preamble.
6. Rhode Island refused to send delegates because small farmers with large debts who feared the actions of a convention filled with wealthy creditors controlled the state politically.
7. You can read about these false allegations and the whole story of constitutional development in the article, "A More Perfect Union: The Creation of the New Constitution," at the National Archives website at http://www.archives.gov/nationaLarchives_experience/charters/constitution_history.html.
8. The politics of full representation for the District of Columbia makes it unlikely that this situation will change any time soon, even though it may seem strange that people living in the nation's capital do not have the same rights to representation as everyone else. Because the District of Columbia is a heavily Democratic city, it would certainly send Democrats to the House and Senate—ensuring that Republicans will work to prevent this from happening.
9. Hilary Hylton, "What's All That Succession Rukus in Texas?" *Time,* April 18, 2009.

Table, Figure and Box Notes

T1 *Philadelphia Inquirer,* December 26, 2001.

T2 For a discussion of the Bush program, see James Risen, *State of War: The Secret History of the CIA and the Bush Administration.* New York: The Free Press, 2006.

T3 See the European Movement website at http://www.europeanmovement.eu/index.php?id=5154.

T4 Ibid.

T5 See the European Union website at www.europa.eu.

T6 Ibid.

T7 See the European "No" Campaign website, at www.europeannocampaign.com/293.html.

T8 You can find the text of Marshall's ruling at http://supreme.justia.eom/us/17/316/case.html.

T9 http://www.whitehouse.gov/the_press_office/Remarks-by-the-President-to-a-Joint-Session-of-Congress-on-Health-Care/.

The Nation, State, Regime, and Federalism in the United States

By Raymond Smith

To initiate a discussion of U.S. politics and government in comparative perspective, it is useful to start with three of the broadest concepts used in comparative politics to describe and categorize the political systems of different countries: *nation, state,* and *regime*.

The *nation* can be thought of as a form collective identity among a group of people, generally rooted in a particular geographic location and based on a set of shared cultural attributes such as religion, language, customs, and historical experience. Some nations, such as Japan and Ethiopia, have deep, even ancient, roots; others such as Australia and Costa Rica are comparatively recent creations. Likewise, many nations possess very robust and distinctive identities and a clear sense of their place in the world; China would fit into this category, long calling itself the "Middle Kingdom" because it viewed the Chinese nation as forming the very center of the world. By contrast, some other nations have a sense of nationhood that is more fragile or indistinct, such as Ukraine which has long been overshadowed by its much larger neighbor Russia, with which it has innumerable historical and cultural links. The term "ethnicity" or "ethnic group" is sometimes used more or less interchangeably with "nationality" or "nation." (Note that in everyday use, the term nation is sometimes used synonymously with the word "country," but the usage of the term here is a more technical and academic one.)

The second concept is the *state*, the term used to describe any of approximately 190 sovereign, independent countries in the world. Perhaps the simplest indicator of whether a political entity is regarded as a sovereign state within the international system is whether it has membership in the United Nations which, despite its name, is an organization composed of states (for a listing see: www.un.org/members). By definition, sovereign states have no higher political authority above them, and possess such characteristics as a specified land area, a permanent population, a monopoly on the legitimate use of violence within its borders, and the ability to enter into diplomatic relations with other states; this international system of states is often traced back to a pair of European treaties signed in 1648 called the Peace of Westphalia. The American "states of the Union," for example Vermont or Arizona, share sovereignty within the U.S. but they are *not* states in the international sense. They are, however, important levels of government, as discussed further below.

127

When one particular national or ethnic group forms the large majority of a state, as is often but not always the case, it is termed a *nation-state*. Some nations, such as the Kurds of the Middle East and the Roma (Gypsies) of Europe, do not have their own state; some nations, most notably Arabs, are divided among multiple states. Further, some states, such as Malaysia and Afghanistan, are composed of multiple distinct ethnic groups.

The third concept is that of the *regime*, or the particular configuration of governing principles and institutions that prevail within any particular state. This term became widely familiar in the U.S. with regard to the 2003 invasion of Iraq, which had as its stated goal "regime change" in that country. Notably, when the regime led by the dictator Saddam Hussein and his Baathist Party was toppled by U.S. invasion, Iraq's status as a sovereign *state* remained unchanged, although it was temporarily placed under U.S. occupation. Most regimes are legitimized by a written constitution that spells out how power is organized and allocated within the country. But even the most detailed constitutions rarely capture all the dimensions of how power is actually exercised, and many regimes distort or even disregard their constitutions when it is convenient to do so.

The incumbents of any particular regime— that is to say those currently in public office or otherwise exercising power—are often referred to as the "government." Thus, for instance, the ten-year term of British Prime Minister Tony Blair is often called the "Blair government." In the United States, the term government refers to the entire multi-part structure established under the Constitution; to specify the term of any one president Americans are more likely to speak of presidential "administrations," say the Reagan Administration. Generally, however, the nation, state and usually also the regime predates the individuals in power at any particular moment, and also will outlast them.

The American Nation

Given the comparatively short history of the U.S., the interrelationships among the American nation, state, regime, and government are not quite as clear as they are in many older countries in Europe and Asia. Indeed, the United States has been termed the first "new nation" because it achieved independence from its "mother country" before any other major colony did so and because its national identity was largely self-invented.

This new American nation, of necessity, had to draw upon different markers of identity than that of many older nations such as Denmark or Korea with long histories, distinct languages, and well established national identities. First off, the more than 99% of Americans who are not Native Americans clearly cannot make a claim that their ancestors have inhabited the land since pre-historic times. This is true of a number of countries in the western hemisphere, although some such as Guatemala and Bolivia, forged national identities with a strong component from their much larger population of indigenous peoples.

Cultural attributes also do not provide a clear path to a distinctively American national identity. Although the English language does help to unify the country, English is obviously not unique to the U.S. and many Americans speak English poorly or not at all. Americans also do not share a single religious tradition; indeed religious diversity and non-conformity is an American hallmark. American art, architecture and high culture—whether the neo-classical dome and monumental sculptures of the U.S. Capitol Building or the gothic spires and stained glass windows of the National Cathedral—likewise have many of their roots elsewhere. And the great ethnic and racial mixture that make up Americans renders moot any notion of shared ancestry, except perhaps in the broadest sense of a sense of shared humanity.

Thus the usual cultural, religious, and linguistic markers that might help to distinguish, say, the Polish nation or the Hungarian nation, from its neighbors, are mostly not in place in the United States. Nonetheless, the United States does have a robust civic identity of its own, forged often in the crucible of conflict and violence. Major historical events, especially the Revolution and the Civil War, have provided the country with a pantheon of national heroes such as George Washington, Thomas Jefferson, and Abraham Lincoln. Other developments such as the struggle against slavery and segregation, the westward expansion, the experience of immigration, recovery from the Great Depression, and victory in World War II and the Cold War have contributed to a national sense of purpose and progress, led again by towering figures as Franklin Delano Roosevelt, Martin Luther King, Jr., and, increasingly in popular opinion, Ronald Reagan. Through all of these phases, a panoply of images, symbols and ideas have formed the basis for a common national identity, including: founding documents such as the Declaration of Independence and the Constitution; the American flag and the national anthem and pledge of allegiance that honor it; and iconic buildings and monuments such as the Statue of Liberty, Mount Rushmore, and the Vietnam War Memorial. Thus, although Americans lack the "ancient" roots of many nations in Europe, Asia, or the Middle East, they nonetheless have a very clear sense of who they are as a people—a distinctive sense of "nationhood."

Much of this national identity has always been based upon a specific set of principles and ideas, sometimes collectively called the "American Creed." In a feat that was at the time unique in world history, the founding generation in the United States drew upon political philosophy and their own practical experience in colonial and state government, to first lay out and then to implement sweeping principles by which the U.S. would be governed. These principles revolve around the concepts of individual liberty and freedom from tyranny: as a goal established in the Declaration of Independence, as the motivating force behind the design of the Constitution, as the recurrent concern, even obsession, that animates the *Federalist Papers*.

The subsequent history of the U.S. served to reinforce the centrality of individual liberty and freedom from tyranny, especially when compared to the perceived corruption of the "Old World." The first settlers had had to cultivate a philosophy of total self-reliance in the absence of pre-existing governmental or social structures, an ethos reinforced throughout the westward expansion of the early to mid-19th century which was viewed as the "manifest destiny" of the American nation. Then again throughout the late 19th and early 20th centuries, the U.S. welcomed millions of self-motivated immigrants who arrived in the U.S. to make their own way in the world. These new arrivals were welcomed as full-fledged new Americans as long as they pledged fealty to the Constitution and the principles it embodied. In such an environment, capitalism, democracy, and egalitarianism, and the U.S. viewed itself as a model for the world, "the last best hope of mankind." That the U.S. was a society which abused the rights of African Americans, Native Americans and others is, today at least, usually viewed as a great shortcoming rather than a contradiction of the principles of liberty. And since 1865, the arc of U.S. history has been towards greater participation and individual freedom of the entire citizenry, slowly as that arc may move at times.

Among the other "new nations" of the western hemisphere, some have also have a strong sense of nationhood, while others do not. Like the U.S., Mexico has a unique and distinctive culture and national identity, and a clear sense of its place in history and in the world. Drawing upon the historical memory of such traumatic experiences as the conquest—yet endurance—of the indigenous population, the struggle for independence from Spain, and the revolution against the established elites in the early 20th century, Mexico has forged a strong civic identity that draws upon both native and European roots. With one-quarter of the world's Spanish-speaking population, Mexico also plays a leading cultural role among Latin American nations without submerging its identity into this broader community.

Canada, on the other hand, offers one of the clearest examples of a country where a history of evolutionary rather than revolutionary change has helped to make the question of national identity a perennial preoccupation. Spared the experience of bloody revolution, civil war, or even major internal strife, English-speaking Canadians have had to rely on the slow development of an independent identity from Great Britain, whose Queen remains the

Canadian head of state. Although their territory is vast, Canadians are so hemmed in by inhospitable climate and terrain that about 80% of the population lives in a thin strip of land within 100 miles of the U.S. border, further diluting the development of a distinctive national identity. As one Canadian prime minister famously commented, "Canada has too much geography and not enough history." Today, Canadians (outside Quebec) are wracked by questions about who they are as a people, and about how they are distinct from the British and, especially, from Americans.

In Australia and New Zealand, comparable evolutionary historical processes have led to similar questions. Neither country ever experienced a revolution or a civil war, and both also retain the British Queen as their head of state. With only small indigenous minority populations, both countries traditionally viewed themselves as outposts of the British Empire, maintaining the English language and European culture; some remark that New Zealanders particularly are "more British than the British." Over the past fifty years, however, the collapse of the British Empire, an influx of non-European immigrants, and the economic rise of Asian countries have forced these two nations into an identity crisis over whether they are still essentially "transplanted" European societies or distinctive Oceanic countries with strong linkages to neighboring cultures.

It should be noted that a revolutionary tradition is not essential to the development of a strong sense of nationhood among new nations. The French-speaking, largely Roman Catholic Quebecois of Canada have no revolutionary tradition per se—indeed, Quebec absorbed many highly counterrevolutionary influences when conservative nobility and clergymen fled there after the French Revolution. Still, Quebec enjoys a robust sense of its own nationhood sharpened by centuries of domination by English-speaking Protestants. One of the distinctive features of modern Canadian politics is the perennial question of whether Quebec should become an independent state—through, of course, peaceful and incremental means.

Conversely, Argentina has a revolutionary tradition and powerful patriotic symbolism, such as its much-revered sky blue and white flag, but remains paralyzed in part by confusion over its fundamental identity. Located on the South American continent but with a tiny indigenous population, is it a Latin country like Peru or Brazil or is it fundamentally a nation of Italian, German, Spanish, and other European immigrants? With an educated populace, a developed infrastructure, and bountiful natural resources but recurrent and severe political and economic instability, is it part of the developed world or the developing world? Some have argued that Argentina's 20th century experience of rule by charismatic figures such as President Juan Peron and his wife Evita, and also by a string of military dictators, is caused in part by a national desire for clear direction and decisive leadership.

The American State and Regime

An unusual characteristic of the United States is that its *state* and its *regime* are very closely linked, indeed almost synonymous. In most countries, the state has existed for longer than any particular regime, and many states have seen a number of different regimes over time. Americans, however, have lived under the same regime now since 1789, the year that the U.S. Constitution took effect just seven years after the 13 American colonies achieved full independence from Great Britain. Although it has been formally amended more than two dozen times and also significantly reinterpreted during crises such as the Civil War, the Great Depression, and the Civil Rights Movement, the essential elements of the Constitutional framework have endured for more than two centuries.

To a degree that is quite anomalous, then, the U.S. as a state is largely defined by its Constitution. For instance, the presidential oath of office includes a promise to "preserve, protect, and defend" the Constitution, and naturalizing citizens must swear to take up arms, if needed, to "defend the Constitution." This fusion of the state and the regime can best be seen in the single term "The Republic" as used in the Pledge of Allegiance. When school children, new citizens, attendees at sporting events, and others pledge allegiance "to the flag, and to the Republic for which it stands" they are affirming their support simultaneously for both the U.S. as a sovereign state and for the regime that was established by the Constitution in 1789.

In contrast, some countries have had so many different regimes that they have adopted a numbering system. France, for instance, currently counts itself as in its "fifth republic" since its monarchy was overthrown by the revolution of 1789, a year in which France as a state and as a nation was already centuries old. Yet this enumeration does not even include other non-republican regimes that have ruled France, such as under the Emperor Napoleon and under a military government during World War II. Perhaps the most notorious example of a numbering system of regimes would be that the Nazis use of the term the "Third Reich" to denote the third German empire. By that reckoning, the current Federal Republic of Germany would be that country's fourth regime (or its fifth if the inter-war Weimar Republic is counted).

As the example of Germany demonstrates, any one state may have been under the control of multiple different types of regimes. One key element in defining a type of regime is what it draws upon as the source of its authority and legitimacy—what gives it the right to govern its people? The First and Second Reichs in Germany are examples of *traditional* regimes in that the wellspring of their authority was a hereditary monarchy and aristocracy. In such traditional regimes, rulers have the right to rule because they have always had that right (or have at least had it for a very long period of time). Today, many of the monarchies of the Middle East, such as in Jordan, Morocco, and Saudi Arabia, retain powerful kings who exert a right to rule because they inherited it from their fathers and sometimes also because of their descent from the Prophet Mohammed or their role as protectors of holy sites.

The Nazi's Third Reich in Germany offers a quintessential example of a *totalitarian* regime. As the name suggests, these regimes seek (even if they cannot always actually achieve) total control over all aspects of the lives of their people, whose principal role is to work for and support the goals of the state. In seeking to regulating all aspects of their citizen's lives, totalitarian regimes try to destroy, or at least to completely subordinate, any institutions that might intermediate between individuals and the power of the state, such as political parties, trade unions, churches, even families. To seek such absolute control, totalitarian regimes often root their claims of authority in all-encompassing ideologies, such as the sweeping Nazi vision of Aryan racial supremacy.

Other major examples of totalitarian regimes have drawn not on racial identity but on class struggle as their unifying ideology in the form of Communism. The Soviet Union under Stalin and the People's Republic of China under Mao were strongly totalitarian regimes, and North Korea under the Kim dynasty is as totalitarian as any country in history. Some other non-Communist regimes also fall into the totalitarian category by virtue of their claims to rule based on religion, particularly Islam; the former Taliban regime in Afghanistan and, at times, post-revolutionary Iran come to mind.

Milder but somewhat similar to totalitarian regimes are *authoritarian* regimes that usually lack a totalizing ideology but instead root their right to rule in some more pragmatic claims to authority. These regimes will usually not attempt to regulate and direct all aspects of the personal and professional lives of their citizenry, but will expect them to defer to the regime on political questions. Such regimes may draw on many different sources of authority. One might be a claim to having brought order and/or prosperity to the society, as in the case of contemporary China and Russia under President Vladimir Putin. Often authoritarian regimes draw upon simple brute force wrapped in patriotic language, as has been the case in countless military-backed regimes Latin America, Asia, and Africa.

With regard to the U.S., totalitarianism is an alien concept, although a case could be made that under slavery and segregation, African-Americans were subjected to a form of near-totalitarian control under a totalizing ideology of white supremacy. As for authoritarianism, the U.S. government has occasionally exerted an extraordinary degree of authority during times of crisis, civil strife, or foreign war. During the U.S. Civil War, for instance, Abraham Lincoln suspended some civil liberties and during World War II, Franklin D. Roosevelt ordered the internment of Japanese Americans and largely took command of the economy in order to focus it on military production. But such exercises of authoritarianism have occurred only in exceptional, and very limited, periods within the U.S. experience. Indeed, one of the most enduring features of U.S. politics has been a recurrent fear of excessive concentration of power, from the preoccupation of the Founders with separating, checking, and balancing power to the recent resistance from the courts, Congress and public opinion to George W. Bush's attempts to expand the scope of executive authority.

More representative of the U.S. experience are *democratic* regimes, which draw their authority from the people. The mandate of the people generally is provided in the form of free, fair, and competitive elections, but also from other types of citizen input such as public opinion, social movements, and interest group activity. While democratic regimes may share a common source of authority, often called "popular sovereignty" or the "consent of the governed," there are many different forms that democratic political systems can take. Indeed, a major theme of this volume is that the U.S. model of government and politics is no more or less inherently democratic than many other systems. (For one organization's analysis of which states are democratic, visit www.freedomhouse.org and click on "Map of Freedom.")

Subnational Government

Virtually all countries have two levels of government in common. The *national-level* government, which was discussed above, generally deals with foreign affairs, defense, managing currency, and the regulation of commerce, although often much more. *Local-level* government tends to focus on more mundane and smaller-scale issues, managing day-to-day concerns in areas such as police departments, sanitation, and land-use zoning. Where countries differ significantly is between the national and the local, at the level most commonly termed "provinces," but also known by such terms as "departments," "states," "cantons," or "prefectures." Three principal models exist to describe the inter-relationship between governments

at the national and provincial levels: confederations, federations, and unitary states.

Confederations or confederal states are those in which there exists an identifiable national level government but in which most or all final decision-making remains vested at the provincial level. Although far from a confederal state today, the first, short-lived regime in the U.S. was not that of the Constitution but the Articles of Confederation. The Articles presided over an eight-year period of ruinous instability, with the national government unable to carry out even basic functions, the states engaging in economic conflict that threatened to turn into actual warfare, and each state wielding an effective veto over the national government. It was in specific response to the weaknesses of the Articles of Confederation that the Constitution was enacted in 1789 "in order to form a more perfect union." Of course, the idea of confederation would not disappear in American history, resurfacing during the U.S. Civil War under the banner of "states rights."

Reviewing the world today, it is difficult to find an example of a true confederation. Switzerland was a confederation for over 500 years, and today remains the functioning state with perhaps the greatest devolution of power to its provinces (called "cantons"); still it is regarded as a federation because its national government does retain some key areas of distinct authority. The term used for the founding of Canada is "confederation," but is nonetheless now better described as a fairly decentralized federation, with a great deal of authority exercised both in Ottawa and in the ten provincial capitals. The European Union today, although not a state, perhaps most closely reflects some of the key characteristics of a confederation, with sovereign power retained by member countries that voluntarily cede significant decision-making authority to the EU capital in Brussels. Despite their high degree of economic coordination, the EU national governments retain far greater latitude than the provinces of any country could maintain. Moreover, the EU has found it difficult to coordinating its foreign and military policies, once again underscoring the limitations of the confederal model.

At the other extreme, in *unitary states*, governing authority is clearly vested at the national level, with all or most important decisions made in the capital city and then merely delegated for enactment and administration at the provincial level. Before the American Revolution, the thirteen colonies were subject to the unitary authority of the British king, who appointed and directed the work of powerful colonial governors. Such strong central government was the norm not only in the American colonies, but also among many monarchies in which centralized power had been concentrated in the hands of a single sovereign, the king. Indeed, one of the major breakthroughs of American constitutional theory was the idea that sovereignty could be divisible, *shared* at both the national and state governments.

Today, the unitary model of government remains the most common form of government in the world, used by nearly seven-eighths of the world's national governments. The unitary model is particularly well-suited to small countries in which it is relatively easy for the entire country to be administered from the capital city. But there are also a number of larger states that are unitary states. One prominent example would be Japan, which is subdivided into 47 prefectures (or "provinces"). Although each prefecture has its own elected government, their roles are largely administrative. Tokyo defines political structures and laws that are binding on the prefectures (and also on the country's many municipalities below the prefecture level). Municipal and prefecture governments may be delegated the task of figuring out how best to apply a centrally made decision, such as in the construction of schools or the organization of hospital systems, bur final say—and all revenue raising power—remain in Tokyo.

The third model, that of the *federation* or *federal state*, strikes a middle path between confederal and unitary approaches, with decision-making authority carefully divided between and shared by the national and provincial levels. The United States is an example of a robust federal system, in which the 50 states of the union (the "provincial" level of government in the U.S.) have distinct areas of authority within which the national government may not freely encroach or interfere.

Only about 25 countries, just over one-eighth the world's total, have *federal* political systems. But because federal systems are particularly well suited to diverse, populous countries, these 25 countries represent some 40% of the world's population, most notably India, Brazil, Germany, Mexico, Nigeria, Russia and the United States. Federalism is also well suited to sparsely populated states with large territories to govern, such as the largely under-populated continental landmasses of Canada, Australia, and Argentina. Even in relatively small countries, federalism can be helpful when the population is deeply divided along ethnic, religious, linguistic or other lines, as in Belgium and Switzerland.

One of the most robust systems of federalism can be found in Germany— deliberately imposed by the victors in World War II to deter potentially dangerous centralizing tendencies in that country. The 16 German Länder, or states, continue to enjoy an exceptionally degree of influence, all part of the enduring plan to prevent a return to tyranny in Germany. Indeed, the central government has relatively few powers entirely to itself, mostly issues relating to military, border, and diplomatic questions. Some powers are reserved to the Länder, such as those pertaining to police, public order, and education, but most areas of legislation are subject to the "concurrent" jurisdiction of both. Similarly, the power to tax and allocate revenues is exercised by both the federal and Länder governments. The German system even goes so far as to allow the governors of the Länder to appoint and direct the work of members of the upper house of parliament, the Bundesrat, which has a veto on any legislation directly affecting the Länder.

Why create such a complex system as federalism, particularly when the unitary state approach offers such simplicity? Because the larger and more diverse the territory and population of a country, the harder it is to find "one size fits all" solutions. The relevant political science concept here is that of "subsidiarity," or the idea that as many decisions as possible should be made as close as possible to the people. Hence, the state government in Bismarck, North Dakota is seen as better able to decide on the distribution of public health resources within their thinly populated state than a model designed in Washington, which might be weighted towards states with larger and denser populations. The same basic logic of subsidiarity also helps lead the state of North Dakota to provide its largest cities, such as Fargo and Grand Forks, with local latitude to run their own health departments geared towards those more urban settings.

This distribution of authority can help to tailor programs and maximize the effectiveness of services. It also relieves the burden from national government of managing such a huge array of varied concerns, allowing it to focus on its own major responsibilities, such as foreign policy and national defense. A federal system also allows for flexibility and innovation from which the entire system may benefit. This led U.S. Supreme Court Justice Louis Brandeis to call the states "laboratories of democracy" in which different approaches to governance and public policy can be tried out and evaluated for their effectiveness.

True federalism, however, involves more than merely operational latitude in implementing priorities set at the national level. In this regard, federal systems fall along a spectrum, with some provincial-level leaders clearly able to refuse or resist orders from the national leadership while others can only protest or perhaps delay such orders. The governors of U.S. states or the premiers of Canadian provinces would fall at the stronger end of that spectrum; their counterparts in Mexico and India at the weaker end.

Despite the generally democracy-promoting aspects of federalism, there are also potentially troublesome features. Overlapping and intertwined areas of jurisdiction, as in education and health care policy may lead to a lack of clarity and accountability about which level of government has ultimate responsibility. In times of crisis, tangled lines of authority can also lead to problems, such as when the national government, the Louisiana state government, and the New Orleans city government failed to properly coordinate their efforts during the 2005 Hurricane Katrina crisis. Beyond problems of coordination, there are also serious dangers in federalism that has gone too far, or in which the balance of power between the national and "provincial" government is unclear or unstable. Indeed, the great Constitutional failure in the

American experience, the catastrophic American Civil War, was directly rooted in differing interpretations of "states' rights." Many of the same issues resurfaced in the 1950s and 60s during the Civil Rights Movement, when the national government finally moved to protect its African-American citizens from state-level segregation policies.

Discussion Questions

1. This [article] presents several ways in which the American nation, state and regime are quite different from other countries. What is the analytic value of such comparisons? Why and to what extent do you think the U.S. political system should seek to change itself to more closely resemble other political systems? To what degree do you think significant changes are even possible or desirable?

2. As a federal country, the U.S. has a complex and multi-layered system of government. What advantages would you see to re-organizing political power in the U.S. to be more along the lines of a unitary state? What might be lost if the U.S. were to do so? Can you see any arguments for moving towards a more confederal model?

Further Reading

The First New Nation: The United States in Historical and Comparative Perspective. Seymour Martin Lipset. Transaction Publishers, New York: 2003.

On Democracy. Robert Dahl. Yale University Press, 2001.

America the Unusual. John Kingdon. Bedford/St. Martin's, New York: 1999.

Constitutional Origins, Structure, and Change in Federal Countries (1996) Edited by John Kincaid and G. Alan Tarr. McGill-Queen's University Press, Montreal, Quebec and Kingston, Ontario, Canada.

Comparing Federal Systems in the 1990s (1996) Ronald Watts, Institute of Intergovernmental Relations, Queen's University, Kingston, Ontario, Canada.

CHAPTER 4

Congress

Chapter 4 Vignette

By Jennifer Byrne

President Obama and Speaker of the House of Representatives John Boehner have both drawn sharp criticism for their handling of the budget; on October 1, 2013, the U.S. government shut down over disagreements between the President, House Republicans, and Senate Democrats over the 2014 budget. Under Article I of the U.S. Constitution, Congress is charged with passing spending bills to fund government operations; in the absence of such a bill, most functions of the government, from issuing passports to paying out small business loans, are temporarily suspended. National parks are also closed, and it is estimated that local economies lose approximately 76 million dollars due to the closing of these parks. The parks lost about $450,000 in entrance fees and activities in the first 2 weeks of October. Some services categorized as "essential" such as social security, the military, air traffic control, and the National Weather Service continued to operate while other areas, such as Immigration and Customs Enforcement, required officers to report to work without pay. While millions of government workers continued to work and get paid as usual, it is estimated that over 800,000 workers were furloughed as a result of the shutdown. In terms of percentages, about 41 percent of non-defense government workers were furloughed while the remaining 59 percent continue to work as usual. This has led some to view this as a "slim down," or partial government shutdown. But, while many services continue to run, the failure to produce a timely budget is impacting the U.S. financially as it may cause trepidation in the markets, and the U.S. must be careful not to default to its creditors. Moreover, while the actual financial impact is dependent on the length of time of a shutdown, there are always intangible costs in terms of worker morale and public confidence in government, which we have already discussed as crucial to a well-functioning democracy. No matter how the costs are divided and whether they are viewed to be large or small in scale, shutting down the government and not delivering a budget has consequences. So, then why does it happen?

The most recent shutdown occurred because of differences between the Democrats and Republicans over the Patient Protection and Affordable Care Act, a law concerning health care and insurance in the U.S. that was passed by Congress and later evaluated by the U.S. Supreme Court. The logic behind the Affordable Care Act is to provide more Americans with health insurance while lowering the costs of health insurance for existing customers. The law keeps health care in America privatized, with the exception of the government-run Medicare and Medicaid programs that were already in existence. The Affordable Care Act creates a marketplace exchange, whereby insurance companies will compete for new customers who will have an added incentive to purchase health insurance due to lower rates, and the "individual mandate," which is essentially a penalty on individuals that refuse to purchase health care, imposed in the form of a yearly tax by the federal government. For those individuals that are still too poor to purchase health insurance, the federal government will provide funds for increased Medicaid coverage to the states to cover these individuals. The Affordable Care Act may be beneficial for insurance companies as they might find new customers, but these companies must also abide by federal regulations that forbid them to decline customers with preexisting conditions, drop customers with severe illnesses, and honor a cap placed on the

out-of-pocket expenses that can be charged to patients. They must also provide their customers with coverage for routine check-ups. All of these regulations could impose a serious financial burden on insurance companies, but the mandates requiring both individuals and employers to purchase health insurance should lead to an increase in payment of healthcare premiums, which may offset the cost to insurance companies. The individual mandate introduces a pool of "low-cost" customers whose premiums will help to offset the costlier benefits that must be paid out to very ill individuals. While most of the money for the Affordable Care Act will come from cost-saving measures from the current Medicaid program and the taxes from the individual mandate, there will be some money required to implement the program and some transfer of funds from the federal government to the states.

President Obama and the Democratic party support the implementation of this law in 2014, but many Republicans, particularly in the House, are opposed to the law and do not want to fund it. On September 20, 2013, House Republicans approved a temporary spending measure known as a continuing resolution (CR) that would have

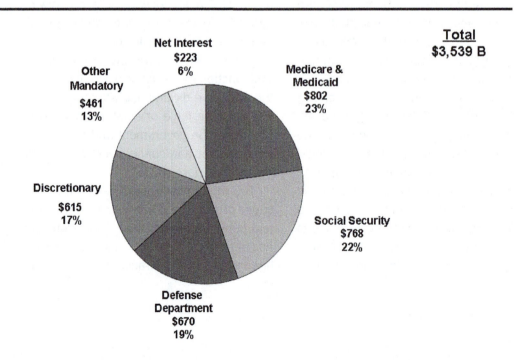

U.S. Federal Spending – Fiscal Year 2012 ($ Billions)

Total
$3,539 B

Net Interest
$223
6%

Other
Mandatory
$461
13%

Medicare &
Medicaid
$802
23%

Discretionary
$615
17%

Social Security
$768
22%

Defense
Department
$670
19%

Source Data: CBO Historical Tables

kept the government running until mid-December, but would have substantially decreased funding for the Affordable Care Act. The Senate rejected the House resolution, claiming that it was designed to essentially gut the Affordable Care Act, and passed its own CR that kept the funding for health care in place. House Republicans, particularly a more conservative group of Republicans known as the Tea Partiers, have argued that the Affordable Care Act will have a negative impact on employers, will cost the federal and state governments too much money, and is an overreach of government authority as it requires individuals to purchase health insurance. The Tea Partiers have refused to consider any budget resolutions that continue to provide funding for the Affordable Care Act, and the Senate majority leader, Harry Reid, has refused to consider any spending resolutions that defund the implementation of the law. Thus, the House and Senate have two different versions of the budget and are at an impasse, as neither side has agreed to a compromise. The government shutdown has served as a negotiating tactic, in order for both sides to try to force concessions from the other. The fight is symbolic, as most of the funding for the Affordable Care Act is not directly tied to the budget, and the cuts would likely not kill the bill.

A second issue pending with the shutdown is that of the debt ceiling. In addition to using tax money obtained from its citizens, the United States government also borrows money to pay its bills, and it is very close to maxing out its current credit, which is somewhere in the neighborhood of nearly 16 trillion dollars. This means that President Obama must borrow more money and must ask Congress to raise the debt ceiling, essentially giving the U.S. a higher credit limit. Failure to do so would mean that the U.S. may default on some of its payments to creditors and be unable to pay for existing programs. However, many House Republicans, who campaigned on the platform of fiscal responsibility, will not consider raising the debt ceiling without substantial cuts to the budget. Though the President suggested a budget, Republicans and Democrats in Congress are at odds with each other about whether to raise the debt ceiling, and where to make cuts in the existing budget.

Take a look at the distribution of the current United States budget. Where is most of the money spent annually? Where do you think that cuts could be made?

Congress

By Matthew Kerbel

Introduction

You don't spend a lot of time thinking about Congress, do you? You're not alone. Many people are capable of having a great day without giving any thought to the workings of Congress, the presidency, the bureaucracy, or the court system. You may well be one of them. However, because we tend not to pay too much attention to our political institutions, it's easy to misinterpret what they do and how they do it.

A place like Congress can seem totally unrelated to our everyday experiences, when, in fact, in many important ways, it's a lot like places that are very familiar to us—your university, for instance—filled with people doing their best to find a way to fit in, manage their time amidst great pressure to do way too much, and avoid making mistakes that could hurt their future careers. If this sounds a little bit like some of what you face in school, it's because you have a lot more in common with members of Congress than you probably think.

In the pages ahead, we'll explore some of those similarities. We'll look at who gets to serve in Congress—the people who choose to run in elections and the characteristics of those who win. We'll examine how new members (called freshmen, just like in school) adjust to unfamiliar surroundings. We'll take some time to figure out what members of Congress do: what it means to serve in Congress, to be part of the congressional leadership, and to handle an unbelievable amount of work—way more than anyone can do at any one time (this may sound familiar to you, too). For some members, the work is just too much, and they decide to drop out, despite the thrill and privilege of serving in Washington. We'll figure out why.

When people do take the time to think about Congress—or when pollsters ask them to think about it—responses are typically negative, at least when they think about Congress as a large, disorganized group of 435 representatives and 100 senators. In a 2009 survey, only 34 percent of those responding wanted to see most congressional representatives re-elected in the 2010 election.[1] However, 52 percent said they wanted to see their own representative re-elected.[2] So, when we put a single human face on the institution, we're much more likely to react positively. As we'll see, Congress is a complex and chaotic institution, but it can be appreciated as the scene of hundreds of individual human dramas.

Getting to Congress: Who Wins and Why?

Many things determine the composition of that relatively small group of people who represent us in Congress. Candidates have to be motivated to run. They need to be willing to put everything in their lives on hold for up to a year so they can knock on doors, make phone calls, plead for money, give speeches, eat large quantities of mediocre chicken, and engage in all the campaigning activities we talked about in Chapter 7. Even if potential candidates have the passion to serve, they still may not run if they're not a good match to their district—say, if the candidate is a Democrat in a heavily Republican area.

Drawing the Lines

The first step in determining who gets to Congress happens before a single candidate decides to run, when lines are drawn on a map that determine the partisan composition of each district that will send someone to Congress. Congressional districts are drawn every ten years following the release of the decennial census. The Constitution requires that each state have at least one House district, with each district represented by a single member (each state, of course, also has two senators). In states with more than one House district, each district has to include roughly the same number of people.

This sounds pretty uninteresting and straightforward, but in fact, the way district lines are drawn can go a long way to determining who gets elected, so the process of **redistricting** is the basis of some pretty intense political battles. For starters, states that gain or lose large numbers of residents in the ten years since the previous census may gain or lose congressional seats.[3] Other states may see significant shifts in their populations, like from cities to suburbs. New lines need to be drawn to reflect these changes, a process that can lead to redrawing the boundaries of many or all previous districts.

If computers did redistricting, it would be pretty dull, but people do it—often elected officials with an interest in stacking the deck in favor of their party. District lines can be drawn in lots of ways to satisfy the population requirement, and the governors and legislators who are responsible for redistricting may look for the best ways to divide the opposition while maximizing their electoral prospects. For a particularly extreme example of a partisan redistricting battle, see Demystifying Government: Texas Republicans versus the "Killer D's."

Redistricting is a complex process that takes place in several rounds and draws a lot of attention from interested parties. Because of federalism, each state has its own procedures for redistricting. A few rely on nonpartisan boards to draw the lines, but most commonly, the governor and state legislators draw district boundaries. Because of the stakes, it's not uncommon for interest groups to get into the act and lobby for boundaries that will help sympathetic candidates. Often, the courts have the final say, either because the governor and legislators couldn't arrive at a plan or because there's a question about the legality of the new districts. It's not uncommon for the courts to completely overturn the work of the legislature. It's also not impossible for a group challenging a redistricting plan to seek relief in a court that's historically supportive of their position.[4]

In 2002—the first congressional election year following the 2000 census—Republicans were well positioned to take advantage of the opportunity to draw new district lines. By controlling the governorships of twenty-seven states and holding majorities in at least one legislative house in thirty-four states, Republicans believed they could strongly influence many redistricted maps. Their political superiority turned out to be balanced by demographic factors, though, like increases in the numbers of Hispanic and African American voters, who tend to favor Democrats.[5] In the end, Republicans were able to turn the playing field to their advantage in some states, like Pennsylvania and Michigan, but nationally, the 2002 redistricting battles ended up largely as a partisan wash. A national census was conducted again in 2010, with Republicans again holding a commanding number of governorships and state legislatures at the start of the redistricting process, but facing the same demographic factors that worked against them ten years earlier.

When states lose House seats, unless an incumbent retires, it's inevitable that two incumbents are going to be thrown together in a newly redrawn district, forced to fight against each other for their political lives. Depending on which party has the political advantage in drawing the new districts, incumbents of the same party could be forced to battle it out in a primary, or incumbents of different parties could be pitted against each other in the general election. In 2002, we saw both types of spectacles, and it got ugly. Because (as we'll see) incumbents can generally depend on an easy ride back to Congress, redistricting can cause a sudden and unexpected end to a House career.

In Michigan, the longest-serving House member, seventy-six-year-old Democrat John Dingell, was forced into a primary against a more liberal four-term incumbent, Lynn Rivers. The two ran neck and neck, as unions, environmentalists, and women's groups that normally unite behind Democrats took sides and battled it out in an intense race that Dingell narrowly won. In Connecticut, Nancy Johnson, a powerful Republican incumbent, was forced by redistricting into a general election battle with James Maloney, a popular Democratic incumbent. In a normal year, both would be expected to win reelection easily. In the redistricting year of 2002, Johnson defeated Maloney after a bitterly fought race.[6]

It Looks Like Some Kind of Serpent

Sometimes partisan state legislators go out of their way to construct districts like this in order to give one party a distinct edge, pulling voters from small enclaves of partisan supporters and allowing district lines to meander over a wide range of territory in the most unlikely fashion. It's called **gerrymandering**, and it's an age-old political practice whose origins predate the actions of nineteenth-century Massachusetts Governor Elbridge Gerry, who in 1811 signed off on a salamander-shaped district (hence the name gerrymander) designed to be a safe haven for Jeffersonian Democrats. Does it work? The evidence is mixed, although a case can be made that strong candidates from the

DEMYSTIFYING GOVERNMENT

TEXAS REPUBLICANS VERSUS THE "KILLER D'S"

With the nation deeply divided along partisan lines, and with a handful of closely divided congressional districts determining which party gets to run Congress, any plan to tinker with congressional boundaries can lead to open political warfare. Nowhere was this more evident than in Texas, where Republicans sought to redraw congressional district lines in the summer of 2003—two years after the issue had been revisited at the scheduled time following the decennial national census.

Republicans were in control of the Texas governorship and legislature for the first time in generations, leaving them in a strong position to have their way with the boundaries for their thirty-two congressional districts that favored Democrats by a narrow 17–15 margin. With direction and encouragement from national Republican leaders, Texas Republicans flexed their muscles. They proposed legislation to redraw district lines in such a way as to secure as many as five additional Republican seats in the U.S. Congress.

Democrats saw this as a power play and cried foul, saying it was unprecedented for a political party to alter district lines except in response to a new census. Republicans countered that they weren't doing anything that Democrats wouldn't have done when they ran the state—they were simply exercising their right as the majority party to draw the congressional map. The Republicans were in a perfect position to play hardball politics because with the governorship, state Senate, and state House under their control, they held all the cards. Except one.

Texas Democrats couldn't block passage of the redistricting plan, but if enough of them failed to report for work, they would deny the legislature the quorum (or minimum number of members) it needs to conduct business. So, in May 2003, fifty-one Democratic members of the Texas House fled to Oklahoma, where they stayed until the end of the regular session of the legislature. Now it was the Republicans' turn to cry foul, but there was nothing they could do, as Oklahoma's Democratic governor welcomed and protected the Texas Democrats. The fifty-one refugees became partisan folk heroes to opponents of the redistricting plan, who dubbed them the "Killer D's" (for Democrats).

The battle wasn't over, though. That summer, Texas Governor Rick Perry called a special session of the legislature for the purpose of considering the re-districting bill. This time, eleven Democrats in the Texas Senate exiled themselves to New Mexico, again preventing a quorum and bringing the special session to a halt. Said one state senator, speaking from a hotel in Albuquerque, "We're availing ourselves of a tool given to us by our Texas constitution to break a quorum. It's not about Democrats, it's about democracy."[T1]

Perhaps, but in the end, the Democrats' tool turned out to be a delaying tactic that only worked as long as everyone stayed together. As beautiful as New Mexico may be, Texas Republicans knew that the opposition couldn't remain there forever, and Republicans eventually won the redistricting war when the Democrats' unity cracked. In the 2004 election, their efforts bore fruit, as five additional Republicans were elected to Congress from Texas, sending four incumbent Democrats to early retirement.

disadvantaged party are discouraged from running in gerrymandered districts.[7] Certainly, partisans from both sides of the aisle continue the practice because they believe it gives them an edge.

Since 1990, some states have engaged in the controversial practice of **racial gerrymandering**, drawing district lines that group together far-flung populations of African American or Hispanic voters for the purpose of assuring representation for these groups. The effort began in response to language added to the Voting Rights Act in 1982 prohibiting states from diluting the voting power of racial minorities, which was interpreted broadly in some states as a green light to gerrymander in order to bolster the influence of minorities.

The effects of racial gerrymandering cut two ways. Although the districts it created sent generally liberal African American and Hispanic representatives to Congress, neighboring districts that lost these voters became more conservative. In 1992, seven districts represented by Democrats lost at least 10 percent of their African American constituents to racial gerrymandering. By 1996, all seven were represented by Republicans—enough to help Republicans hold the majority in Congress.[8] Ironically, a procedure designed to enhance minority representation in Congress had the effect of diluting minority influence because, as we will see, influence in Congress flows to those in the majority.

Because it's so controversial, racial gerrymandering has been the subject of court challenges. A sharply divided Supreme Court has voted to curtail the process on multiple occasions, overturning some of the more far-reaching districts on the grounds that they represented an effort to segregate voters.[9] By the end of the 1990s, a number of states reacted to the Court's position by redrawing the boundaries of racially gerrymandered districts to reduce the concentration of minority voters.

Who Runs for Congress— And Who Makes It?

Against this backdrop of partisan maneuvering over district boundaries, a potential candidate needs to take a good, long look in the mirror before embarking on an expensive and time-consuming public campaign that could easily come to nothing. If you were thinking of running, you'd want to take a look at who lives in the district and assess how closely your background and political views match your would-be **constituents**. You would also need to make sure the timing is right for a run, especially if you have to abandon a lower office where you could probably win reelection.

A big part of this calculation involves whether or not you will have to face an **incumbent**. Challengers don't like to face incumbents, and for a good reason. With the contacts they have and with their ability to raise large sums of money, incumbents are hard to topple. Since World War II, better than nine in ten incumbent representatives and almost eight in ten incumbent senators seeking reelection have been victorious—a figure that (as we'll see later on) has only been increasing in recent years. Incumbents may play to their strength by raising large sums of money in an effort to scare off strong competition,[10] and the strategy is likely to work, unless the nation is going through an economic downturn or experiencing a moment when voters are unhappy with the status quo, like they were in 2006, 2008 and 2010.

Some candidates are self-starters who make the judgment to run on their own, although to have a chance at success it helps if they have a high level of **name recognition** from a previous job. This favors amateurs who've previously worked as television commentators, actors, athletes, or at other high-visibility jobs. Many candidates are encouraged to run by political party operatives, who engage in candidate recruitment as one of the formal functions of political parties.

Candidates with strong personal qualities that attract voters are always in demand. In 2005, a special election was held when a vacancy arose in Ohio's second congressional district near Cincinnati. The district is highly conservative, and Democratic candidates typically are not competitive. However, this particular election was different, because Democrats nominated outspoken Marine Major Paul Hackett, a political novice who had volunteered for active duty in Iraq. Hackett's candor and his willingness to criticize President Bush's conduct

of the war—in a district where Bush won a lopsided share of the vote just months earlier—garnered national attention for the race and enabled Hackett to create a strong base of support. Hackett lost, but he finished within four points of Republican Jean Schmidt—the best showing for a Democrat in that district in thirty years.

Lately, given the high cost of campaigning and the central role of money in winning elections, Democrats and Republicans are looking more frequently toward wealthy candidates who can self-finance campaigns. As the Demystifying Government feature indicates (Today's Candidates: Fortune and Fame), candidates with these qualities are in great demand because of the prospect what they could deliver on Election Day.

As a constitutional requirement, you have to be at least twenty-five to serve in the House of Representatives, a resident of the state from which you're seeking election, and an American citizen for seven years. You don't have to live in the district you represent as long as you live in the same state, although as a practical matter, it's bad politics to ask people to vote for you when you live somewhere else. To be a senator, you have to be at least thirty and an American citizen for nine years.

On paper, this appears to open membership in Congress to most of us (at least in a few years). However, with the emphasis on wealth and popularity in candidate recruitment, it shouldn't be too surprising that Congress is far from a mirror of American society. (See Demystifying Government: Changes to the All-Male Club.) What may be surprising is how different it is from the country as a whole on such things as occupation, education, religion, race, and gender. Remember our earlier discussion about **pluralism** and **elitism**? When it comes to the characteristics of congressional members, background similarities favor some groups over others, even though Congress is a less homogeneous place than it was when you were born. Check out Figure 6.1 for some demographics on the 112th Congress that convened in 2011.

So, what of these apparent inequities between congressional members and the populations they represent? If Congress is largely an educated, professional, white, male and Protestant bastion, can it

DEMYSTIFYING GOVERNMENT

TODAY'S CANDIDATES: FORTUNE AND FAME

When you're the one-time chairman of the investment firm Goldman Sachs, you can afford to pump $60 million of your personal fortune into your quest for a U.S. Senate seat. That's exactly what Jon Corzine did in his successful 2000 attempt to become Senator Jon Corzine of New Jersey. Though a political novice, Corzine's personal fortune made him an attractive candidate to the Democratic Party as it attempted to hold the Senate seat being vacated by Senator Frank Lautenberg. For his part, Corzine said the money was necessary to level a political playing field that included opposition from a former governor and a well-known member of Congress, each of whom had far greater name recognition. In 2005, Corzine built on his political success when he was elected Governor of New Jersey (although his luck ran out in 2009 when he lost his re-election bid).

In 2002, Republican Party officials helped pave the way for former Red Cross President Elizabeth Dole to run for the North Carolina Senate seat left vacant by the retirement of Republican Senator Jesse Helms. In Dole's case, name recognition rather than personal wealth was the reason for Republican enthusiasm. The former transportation secretary, presidential candidate, and spouse to 1996 Republican presidential nominee Bob Dole is a highly visible and widely well-regarded public figure (despite her unsuccessful attempt to win the 2000 Republican presidential nomination), and something of a celebrity in her own right. Having a candidate of that stature and visibility helped Republicans hold on to Helms' seat for six years, although Dole, like Corzine, lost her re-election bid.

However, fortune and fame do not guarantee electoral success. Multi-millionaire and former Massachusetts Governor Mitt Romney spent over $42 million of his own money in his quest for the 2008 Republican presidential nomination. One of his opponents, former Tennessee Senator Fred Thompson, had Hollywood and network television credentials to his name—including a recurring role in the television drama *Law and Order*. Neither one got very far in a race that went to Senator John McCain.

Figure 6.1. Who Gets to Serve[T4]

Gender	Once a nearly exclusive male club, Congress has seen an influx of women in recent years. Still, at about one-sixth of the membership of Congress, women are well under-represented with respect to the population.
Race	Even with advances by minority groups in recent years, the 112th Congress is still overwhelmingly white. Only 8 percent of members are African American and 5 percent are Hispanic, roughly half the percentage of their numbers in the population. Out of 535 representatives and senators, there are 10 Asian Americans and one Native American.
Occupation	Not too many organizations can claim that almost 40 percent of its members are lawyers (apart from law firms, of course), but that's the case in Congress, where lawyers far outnumber all other professionals. Business people come in second, followed by educators. Remember when we said celebrities make good candidates? Recent Congresses have included several astronauts, including former Senator John Glenn; former football players like Representative Steve Largent; former baseball players like Jim Bunning, who once pitched a perfect game in the major leagues; and comedian Al Franken, best known for his work on "Saturday Night Live."
Education	Unlike the population at large, almost everyone in Congress is college educated. Three-quarters have graduate or professional degrees.
Religion	Almost everyone in Congress has a religious affiliation, compared with about 70 percent of Americans. Most are Protestant, although 29 percent of the membership is Catholic (slightly more than the nation as a whole) and 7 percent are Jewish (about three times the national figure). The 112th Congress has only two Muslims.

DEMYSTIFYING GOVERNMENT

CHANGES TO THE ALL-MALE CLUB

In 1992, an unprecedented number of women were elected to Congress in what the press dubbed the "Year of the Woman." Ever since, although the vast majority of members are male, there has been a notable female presence in an institution that previously functioned as something of an all-boys club.

The presence of female lawmakers has made some differences in the ways of Congress. Legislative matters considered to be "women's issues," like family leave during pregnancy and illness, funding for breast cancer research, and workplace discrimination, have found their way onto the agenda.[T2] Some have made it into law.

It takes time to accumulate power in Congress, and more than a decade later, some women are beginning to do just that. In 2001, Representative Nancy Pelosi became the first woman elected to a leadership position in Congress when she was chosen to be the House Democratic Whip; one year later, she became House Democratic leader. And in 2007, she became the first female Speaker of the House, a job she held for four years.

As in any institution, though, change can be slow and those who are there at the start can find it frustrating. Marjorie Margolies-Mezvinsky, a member of the Class of 1992, has stated that she and her female colleagues suffered indignities from congressional workers and some male members who treated them as second-class citizens. She recalls an experience she had during a presidential State of the Union Address to a joint session of Congress, which she felt provided a good measure of how far women in Congress had come—and how far they still had to go:

I remember sitting with my colleagues, looking around at all 435 of us. The women stood out in a truly dramatic fashion, and I thought, my gosh, people are going to turn on the tube tonight and see us and they're going to realize that the rest of the nation has begun to inch itself into this body. I was sitting next to North Carolina Democrat Martin Lancaster, who was trying to point out somebody on the other side of the aisle, and he said, "He's the guy with the receding hairline, gray hair." And I said, laughing, "You've eliminated nobody!" My point is that the people who have always been outside of the system are now beginning to infiltrate it. There aren't enough of us, but we're working on it—all the time.[T3]

function as a representative institution? The answer depends on how we look at the idea of representation. As a descriptive matter, the answer would have to be no because the congressional class picture doesn't look very much like the portrait of America. As a substantive matter, the answer could still be yes. To engage in **substantive representation**, a member of Congress has to be able to act in the interests of groups to which he or she does not belong. If you believe that a white representative can promote the interests of African Americans or Hispanics, that a male representative can advance the agenda of women's groups, or that a college-educated lawyer can advocate the concerns of blue-collar workers, then you may be able to make the case for Congress as a representative institution, despite the fact that it draws its members from a nonrepresentative elite group of Americans.[11]

Adjusting to Congress

Think back for a minute to freshman orientation, to what it felt like to be in a new place surrounded by new people. Maybe you traveled far from home, and everything looked new. Maybe you're a commuter, or going to a local school, and you had to confront new ways of doing things and new people as you made the transition from high school to college. Remember how you felt? Many people experience moments of frustration or confusion, even sadness or homesickness, during those first crazy days of college. You want to fit in, but everything is new, and you're not always sure how to do it.

As distant and remote as Congress may seem, new members are human and experience many of the same feelings. No place can compare with Congress (just like nothing exactly compares with college), so arriving there several months after experiencing the thrill of being elected (much like arriving at school several months after the excitement of getting that acceptance letter) can leave a person bewildered.

One member relates the story of getting to her new office to find it unfurnished. She was advised by a senior member to roam through the office building corridors looking for discarded furniture. So, she did, furnishing her office with stuff other people had cast off, not unlike the way some people furnish an off-campus apartment.[12]

One way we try to fit into a new place, be it college or Congress, is by learning the ways of the institution, the **norms** people live by as they try to get along with each other. Norms are unspoken and unwritten rules of behavior. No one has to teach us about them—we observe norms and internalize them, and if we violate them, we'll probably hear about it from a friend or from someone in a position of authority. For instance, it may be okay for you to get a visit from a friend at midnight while you're living at school. The norm for late-night visits when you're back at home with your parents over the summer could be something quite different. No one

Table 6.1. Congressional Norms

Norm	Definition	Example	Benefit
Specialization	specialization: The legislative norm that members of Congress should become experts in a legislative field.	Becoming an expert on global warming	Congress addresses a range of complex issues and needs members' expertise to handle them intelligently
Legislative Work	legislative work: The legislative norm that members of Congress should stay on top of the work required by the committee that deals with their area of specialization.	A subcommittee chairman being prepared for a hearing	If some members are not prepared, the burden of their negligence is passed to other members
Courtesy	courtesy: The legislative norm that members of Congress should treat each other with respect and avoid personal attacks, regardless of how much they may disagree.	Referring to a member you may personally dislike as "honorable" or "distinguished" during floor debate	Kind words cool the heat of conflict and keep debate moving forward.
Institutional Patriotism	institutional patriotism: The legislative norm that precludes members of Congress from acting or speaking in ways that would discredit the institution.	Avoiding getting entangled in a bribery scheme	Discredit brought upon the institution undermines every member's base of power
Reciprocity	reciprocity: The legislative norm that encourages members of Congress to support each other's initiatives, even if there is no direct political benefit in doing so.	An urban senator voting for crop subsidies in return for a rural senator supporting mass transit aid	When everyone reciprocates, everybody benefits; if no one reciprocated, no one would benefit

has to tell you this—you know what's going on—although your parents probably will say something if you violate the norm.

Norms help people ease into a new institution, but they also serve the institution by helping it run more smoothly. Many people don't get to choose their freshman roommate, and sometimes, things don't work out too smoothly, but by observing the norms for good roommate behavior, you can make the best of a bad situation. In much the same way, members of Congress do not get to choose their colleagues—voters in other districts do—but they have to find a way to work together. Norms help smooth the way for members who might not choose each other as colleagues if they had the option.

The five norms in Table 6.1 have existed in Congress for decades. Take a look at the table for a definition of each norm and an explanation of how it benefits members of Congress.

The last norm you looked at—reciprocity—can assume a couple of specific forms. The example in the table, where members trade support for each other's pet projects, is called **logrolling**, evoking the kind of cooperation people exhibit when they stand on a log and try to roll it down a river.[13] Logrolling helps members get the kind of projects for their home districts that constituents love—and that can only help their reelection prospects—although as Demystifying Government: The Golden Fleece points out, it's often the case that one member's beneficial project is a case of wasteful spending to those in other districts who do not benefit.

Reciprocity can also be expressed through **compromise**, or flexibility, over an issue that a member may feel strongly about—like the wording of legislation. Since what goes around comes around, members have an investment in compromising with each other, with the expectation that at some later time, others will offer the same courtesy to them. The same is true with **integrity**, which is a critical component of reciprocity. You probably know from personal experience how you feel about a friend who promises something and doesn't deliver. As one member put it, "you don't have to make these

DEMYSTIFYING GOVERNMENT

THE GOLDEN FLEECE

One commonly expressed knock against Congress is its tendency to waste money. You can probably see how logrolling could encourage spending on dubious projects because to win the support of colleagues for a pet venture, members only have to signal that they want support for a particular item (and show their willingness to support the pet projects of others). They don't have to justify the importance of the undertaking, and other members who want their projects supported aren't in a position to raise questions.

Although you can always find someone ready to defend the merits of any congressional action, some things seem on the surface to be just a bit more dubious than others—projects that are criticized as being **pork-barrel** items because of

their apparent wastefulness. In 1975, former Wisconsin Senator William Proxmire began issuing a monthly "Golden Fleece" award to those projects funded by Congress that in his view seemed particularly wasteful. His purpose was to bring logrolling out of the shadows of congressional deal making and to shine light on pork-barrel spending in order to curtail it.

What kinds of things did Proxmire single out over the years? How about $1.2 million to preserve a Trenton, New Jersey, sewer as an historical site; $20,000 to build a limestone replica of the Great Wall of China in Bedford, Indiana; and $6,000 for a report instructing the Army on how to buy a bottle of Worcestershire sauce!

commitments [to other members], ... but if you do make them, you had better live up to them."[14]

Remember, norms are enforced by the people in the institution, and stay in effect because the institution benefits along with its members. So, specialization is held in place by virtue of the tremendous amount of detailed work that Congress has to handle and the fact that it's in everybody's interest for the work to get done, which can best be accomplished if every member contributes. Likewise, the norm of doing legislative work is held in place by the fact that everyone benefits if everyone does a small share of the heavy lifting. If you've ever been in a group project where not everyone contributed equally (but everyone was in the same boat when it came to getting graded), you can probably appreciate how easily resentment could be generated toward those who did less work. Since congressional legislative work is like a big group project, specialization keeps the institution moving forward while minimizing those resentful feelings.

Of course, if norms no longer benefit those involved, they can evolve out of existence. One norm that's not in Table 6.1 is **apprenticeship**, even though it was a hallmark of how Congress did business for the better part of the twentieth century. Freshmen members were expected to refrain from voicing their opinions in committees, introducing legislation, or drawing attention to themselves as they learned the ropes from senior members and acclimated to the ways of Congress. Apprenticeship maintained institutional stability and was a great way for new members to learn other norms.

If you happen to be a freshman, you probably don't think much of a norm that has you speaking only when you're spoken to and holding back on what you came to Congress to accomplish. If you had a large enough group of like-minded peers, you might want to do something about it.

That's essentially what happened to apprenticeship in Congress. In 1974, in the wake of the Watergate scandal that rocked the Nixon administration, a huge freshman class of 103 young, reform-minded newcomers was elected to Congress. They felt they had a mandate to change things in Washington, and they weren't about to be quiet or wait their turn. Backed by the strength of their large

numbers, they fashioned themselves as a new type of member, more entrepreneurial and outspoken, as they brushed aside apprenticeship as an antiquated norm.[15]

Today, the effects of their independent spirit continue to change the ways of Congress and strain some of the other norms. Members have become more media-savvy and self-promotional; some (especially in the Senate) devote great energy to positioning themselves to run for president. In the process, they may be absent from Congress more than in the past, and fail to keep up with their legislative work the way you may at times let extracurricular activities cut into the time you devote to your homework.[16] Likewise, when Republicans took control of the House of Representatives in 1994, testy moments followed between the two parties as Democrats, not used to being in the minority, chafed at what they considered heavy-handed tactics employed by the new Republican majority who were rewriting the informal rules of the institution. Courtesy was severely tested in the process, as it has been during the highly partisan years since then, but perhaps because in the end everyone benefits more from cooperation than conflict, the norms that had developed over the decades were bent but not broken. Even as partisanship produces tension in Congress, members continue to rely on existing norms to find their place in a complex institution.

Serving in Congress: How Congress Works

New members of Congress arrive at an institution that's been shaped by centuries of history, but the broad contours of what Congress does—and what members are expected to do in Congress—can be traced to the parameters established in the Constitution.

Article I of the Constitution establishes a **bicameral** legislature with a House of Representatives (created in Section 2) and a Senate (created in Section 3) as the two branches. As constitutional articles go, it's pretty long because it takes great pains to spell out exactly what the Congress would do. The powers specifically granted to the House and Senate are called **enumerated powers**, and they go well beyond what the national legislature could do under the Articles of Confederation.

Enumerated powers include the power to tax, with all revenue bills required to originate in the House of Representatives, the body designed to be closer to the people. Other important enumerated powers include the ability to regulate commerce among the states and with other nations, coin money, raise a military, declare war, establish post offices and roads, and create a court system below the Supreme Court (which is itself established by the Constitution).

Then Article I gives Congress the ability "To make all Laws which shall be necessary and proper for carrying into Execution the foregoing Powers, and all other Powers vested by this Constitution in the Government of the United States, or in any Department or Officer thereof." This "necessary and proper" clause has been interpreted over the years as a broad grant of **implied powers**, which has allowed Congress to consider matters that could not have been anticipated by the Constitution's authors.

Despite going into detail on a range of congressional responsibilities, the Constitution leaves it up to each house to determine how it's going to put into place the procedures to do its job. The Constitution dictates that a majority of members of a house is required to form a quorum (which, as we noted in the Demystifying Government box "Texas Republicans versus the "Killer D's"), is the number of members required for a legislative body to meet and do business) and that each house has to keep a record of its public votes and proceedings, but it leaves to each house the ability to determine how to do business. As a consequence, the two houses operate under different sets of rules.

How the House Works

In a simpler time, the first Congresses (see Demystifying Government: How Congresses Get Their Numbers) debated important matters as a group, and if legislation was deemed appropriate, a committee was established to discuss the nuts and bolts. However, it didn't take long before the need to process a growing workload led to the establishment of permanent or **standing committees**,

---

DEMYSTIFYING GOVERNMENT

HOW CONGRESSES GET THEIR NUMBERS

Maybe the phrase "the first Congresses" in the first paragraph of Section 9.4a sounded a little funny to you. If it did, it's because you're probably used to thinking of Congress as a singular (albeit bicameral) entity. It is, of course, but when we talk historically about Congress, we classify each group that serves together as "a Congress," and we give it a number.

So, the First Congress served from 1789–1791, with the first year constituting the first "session" of the First Congress and the second year constituting the second session. Why two years? That's the stretch between congressional elections. The entire House of Representatives is up for election every two years (a short period designed to keep representatives responsive to public opinion). One-third of the Senate is also up for election every two years (a full Senate term is six years). When they reconvene in January following the election, the new collection of members—the "new Congress"—gets a new number.

The 112th Congress was elected in November 2010 and sworn in January 2011, to serve until January 2013.

Table 6.2. House Committees and Subcommittees, 2010[T5]

Committee	Members	Subcommittees
Agriculture	46	6
Appropriations	66	13
Armed Services	66	7
Budget	39	0
Education and Labor	49	5
Energy and Commerce	58	5
Financial Services	72	6
Foreign Affairs	49	7
Homeland Security	34	6
House Administration	9	2
Judiciary	40	5
Natural Resources	52	5
Oversight and Government Reform	39	5
Rules	13	2
Science and Technology	44	5
Small Business	36	5
Standards of Official Conduct	10	0
Transportation and Infrastructure	75	6
Veterans' Affairs	28	4
Ways and Means	41	6

which were organized to deal with ongoing matters like budgetary or military concerns. By the 1820s, standing committees would debate legislation before it was brought before the full House.

Because most legislation needs to go through the committee process to make it to the floor for a vote, many of the thousands of proposals introduced each session for consideration never get a hearing and simply die on the vine. The few proposals that make it to committee are typically sent to one or more **subcommittees** of the standing committee. The detail work of legislating takes place in subcommittees, which are specialized units suited to ongoing relationships with interest groups of the sort we talked about in Chapter 8 when we discussed **iron triangles**. Together, twenty standing House committees support 100 subcommittees, each with its own chairperson and agenda (the Senate's sixteen standing committees support seventy-four subcommittees). Table 6.2 lists the names of the standing committees of the House, along with the number of House members serving on the committee and the number of subcommittees each committee had

in 2010 (the names and sizes of committees and subcommittees will vary slightly from Congress to Congress). Notice how some of these committees have more people in them than an upper-division political science class!

If a bill fails to clear a subcommittee, it dies; otherwise, it's sent back to the full committee where it can again die if it fails to win passage. Even if it wins full committee approval, it's not out of the woods yet. That's because the House places restrictions on the terms of debate and on what bills get to move to the floor for final consideration. As with the development of standing committees, House rules on debate evolved over the years. Initially, House debate was fluid and unlimited. As the House grew in size and legislation grew in complexity, the House began placing limits on how long members could speak, and procedures were instituted to control the flow of legislation.

In the late nineteenth century, the House established a process by which legislation would be channeled from standing committees through a **Rules Committee** before it could come to the floor for debate and a vote. Despite the fact that a standing committee may have worked for months or longer on legislation, if it failed to be assigned a "rule" from the Rules Committee, it would simply disappear from legislative consideration. If the Rules Committee decides to assign a rule and bring a measure to the floor, it can set the terms of the debate, including whether amendments can be offered that would change the bill. If a bill is brought to the floor with a rule that prohibits amendments, then members have only the choice to vote the bill up or down as it's written. This gives the Rules Committee—and the political party controlling it—enormous power to set the terms of the House agenda.[17]

If an issue lends itself to short-term review, the House may establish a **select committee** (also called a special committee) to investigate. Senate rules permit the establishment of select committees as well. Select committees are established for one congressional session and then expire. Instead of reporting bills like a standing committee, they usually review a matter and make recommendations for action. For instance, prior to the start of the millennium, the Senate established a select committee to investigate the much-talked-about (but ultimately inconsequential) Y2K computer problem, which threatened to shut down computer systems on January 1, 2000 if software mistakenly read the date as January 1, 1900.[18]

A member introduces legislation in the House by literally dropping it in a wooden box at the front of the chamber. Any member can do it for any reason—to advance a personal priority or the priorities of constituents or interest groups. At that point, the bill is referred to a committee or, in some cases, multiple committees that have jurisdiction over the content of the proposal. For most bills, that's the end of the line. A select few undergo the generally slow process of moving through subcommittee, where hearings are held that shape the content of the emerging bill or determine whether it will ever come to a committee vote.

These are the textbook procedures for moving legislation through Congress and, well, this is a textbook, so what better place than here to describe it? Not every bill travels that route, however. There

are House procedures that allow the leadership to circumvent the committee process entirely, which they may do in politically sensitive situations. It happened in 1996, when House Republican leaders moved a last-minute budget resolution directly to a floor vote following an unsuccessful confrontation with President Clinton over spending priorities. There's also a procedure called a **discharge petition**, which, if signed by half the membership (218 representatives), plucks a bill from committee and brings it to the House floor for a vote. It's usually very difficult to get half the House to go along with a discharge petition, although it can happen—like it did in 2001, when supporters of campaign finance reform forced a vote on the campaign reform bill that would eventually become the McCain-Feingold Act.[19]

How the Senate Works

The early Senate operated like the early House, first as a deliberative body then through the work of standing committees. Owing to its smaller size, it never faced quite the same pressures as the House to limit debate or control the flow of legislation. So, the Senate doesn't channel legislation through a Rules Committee, and senators maintain the privilege of unlimited debate time. This gives senators a legislative weapon not available to their colleagues in the House: the **filibuster**, or the ability to talk a bill to death on the Senate floor. If one or more senators simply refuse to stop talking about a matter under discussion, they can bring the Senate to a halt. A filibuster can only be ended by a vote of cloture, which requires a supermajority of three-fifths, or 60 percent of the Senate to enact. This means a minority of 41 senators can block a bill if they stick together and refuse to support **cloture** (see Figure 6.2). Before the cloture provision was enacted in 1917, it was even harder to silence a senator because a unanimous vote was required to make a determined senator sit down. The filibuster can be a powerful procedure in the hands of a determined Senate minority—and a tool of last resort for outnumbered senators.

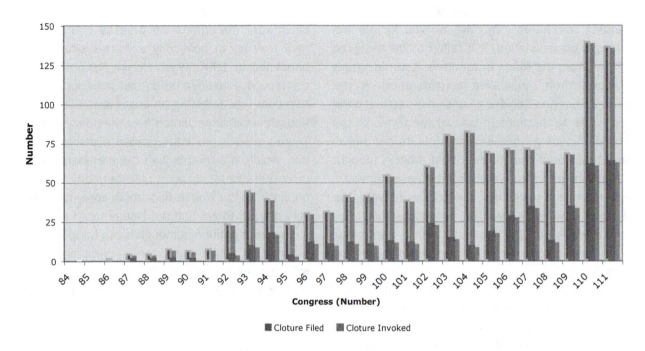

Figure 6.2. Explosion of the Filibuster, 84th Congress (1955) through 111th Congress (2011)[T6]

When a senator has the floor during debate, he or she can talk about anything for as long as he or she wants. Although the picture of a senator reading listings from the phone book or talking about his or her grandchildren may seem funny (and, yes, it's really happened), a filibuster is serious business because it gives a minority of the Senate the opportunity to delay or prevent legislation they oppose despite the presence of majority support. And, in recent years, filibusters have been sustained simply through the failure of cloture votes, without the minority holding the floor and bringing Senate business to a halt. This has coincided with an explosion of filibusters as a tool of the minority to block legislation, as Figure 6.3 attests. The blue bars indicate the number of cloture motions filed to end filibusters, and the red bars indicate the number of those motions that succeeded.

Through the 1950s and 1960s, the filibuster was used strategically and selectively. It was a favorite tool of conservative senators opposed to civil rights legislation. A seventy-four day filibuster delayed the landmark Civil Rights Act of 1964 from coming to a vote, and South Carolina Senator Strom Thurmond personally held the Senate floor for over twenty-four hours (a Senate record) in an unsuccessful effort to

block the earlier Civil Rights Act of 1957.[20] In recent years, use of the filibuster has become a routine procedure, reflecting entrenched partisan sentiment in the Senate. Notice the two outsized blue bars on the right of Figure 6.2. They correspond to the 110th and 111th congresses (2007–2011), where legislation routinely faced blocking tactics by a Republican minority that saw the filibuster as an effective way to slow or stop the Obama administration's agenda. In fact, 22% of all cloture votes taken in the 91 years between 1919 and 2010 took place during the 110th and 111th congresses.[21] That's why when President Obama and Senate Democratic leaders plotted strategy to reform the health care system in 2009, their working assumption was that they would need 60 votes to pass anything in the Senate, because the Republican minority was almost unanimous in its opposition to Democratic proposals and planned to use the filibuster to stop them.

Filibusters have also come into play during the judicial confirmation process. When Democrats controlled the Senate for the majority of the first two years of the Bush administration, they could keep President Bush's judicial nominations bottled up in committee if they were so inclined, as we'll see in "Confirming Presidential Appointments." When Republicans regained Senate control after the 2002 election, Democrats turned to the filibuster as the only tool available to them to block court appointments. However, it was a tool they used selectively. Recognizing the danger of being painted as obstructionists by the majority, Democrats filibustered only a few Bush appointees. As a counterstrategy, Republicans repeatedly called for cloture votes, forcing Democrats to go on record numerous times against the president's appointees while attempting to chisel away at the opposition. Perhaps because only a few judges were targeted, Senate Democrats repeatedly held together to sustain their filibusters. As Demystifying Government: Going Nuclear indicates, tensions over judicial filibusters threatened to boil over in 2005, at the cost of potentially paralyzing the Senate.

The standing committee, subcommittee, and select committee structure is much the same as it is in the House, although with fewer members, there are more committee and subcommittee leadership opportunities. Virtually every senator has a leadership role somewhere, even newly elected senators. Table 6.3 lists the names of the standing committees of the Senate, the number of senators serving on each committee, and the

number of subcommittees associated with each committee, in 2010. Notice how much overlap there is between House and Senate committees, even though each house organizes its standing committees independently.

In some cases, the House and Senate establish **joint committees** to commonly investigate or study a matter that concerns both houses. Much of what joint committees do is routine and detailed. For instance, the Joint Taxation Committee pools House and Senate staff to help with the technical details of writing tax legislation.[24]

In an entirely different context, the two houses of Congress will form conference committees when they pass different versions of the same legislation. The Constitution requires that the House and Senate pass identical legislation before it's sent to the president for consideration, but it's probably easy to see how that's not likely to happen when legislation has to pass separately through the network of rules and committees in each house. So, when both houses pass their own version of a bill, they form a **conference committee** made of up of representatives and senators that tries to hammer out differences between the two versions of the legislation, writing compromise language that committee members believe will be acceptable to

Table 6.3. Senate Committees and Subcommittees, 2010[T8]

Committee	Members	Subcommittees
Agriculture, Nutrition and Forestry	20	5
Appropriations	28	12
Armed Services	24	6
Banking, Housing, and Urban Affairs	20	5
Budget	22	0
Commerce, Science, and Transportation	22	7
Energy and Natural Resources	22	4
Environment and Public Works	18	7
Finance	20	5
Foreign Relations	18	7
Health, Education, Labor, and Pensions	20	3
Homeland Security and Governmental Affairs	16	6
Judiciary	18	7
Rules and Administration	18	0
Small Business	18	0
Veterans' Affairs	14	0

Demystifying Government

Going Nuclear

After padding its majority after the 2004 session, there was talk among the Republican leadership about implementing a so-called "nuclear option" of prohibiting filibusters of judicial nominees, and in May 2005 the Senate came close to pulling the trigger. Ostensibly, the controversy was triggered by Democratic threats to filibuster seven of President Bush's federal judicial nominees. But, with Chief Justice Rehnquist ailing and a battle for his replacement looming, Senate Republicans were looking to clear the way for whomever President Bush appointed, in what promised to be a bruising partisan battle.[17]

Eliminating the filibuster would have required a parliamentary maneuver whereby then Vice President Cheney, in his capacity as president of the Senate, would rule that judicial filibusters are unconstitutional (a controversial action, as typically such decisions are made by the Supreme Court), on the grounds that the Constitution does not stipulate that a supermajority is necessary for cloture. His ruling would have had the effect of changing Senate rules, which requires the support of a majority of senators, but not the supermajority required for cloture. Democrats, of course, would object, and perhaps threaten to block the rule change with a filibuster. But, Republicans said they would set aside the objection and back it up with a simple majority vote. So, if fifty Republicans joined Vice President Cheney, Senate rules would have been amended to permit a simple majority to end judicial filibusters, paving the way for Republicans, with their 55-seat majority, to approve all of the president's appointees.

Such a change would have been a jarring departure from traditional methods of doing business in the normally staid Senate—hence the "nuclear" label. Democrats threatened retaliation. If the power to filibuster judicial nominees were stripped away, they promised to use other parliamentary maneuvers to bring the business of the Senate to a grinding halt, plunging the Senate into a metaphorical "nuclear winter." The threat was designed in part to mobilize business interests with legislation pending in Congress to pressure the Republican leadership to pull back, but it could not stop the march toward confrontation.

As the battle approached, the Senate became a tense place. The leadership of both parties dug in for a fight, and it looked like a nuclear battle would be unavoidable.

Then, at the last minute: compromise. Seven Republicans and seven Democrats struck an agreement that kept the rules in place. The Democrats agreed not to filibuster three of President Bush's nominees, and to support future filibusters only in unspecified extraordinary circumstances. In exchange, the Republicans agreed to vote against efforts to change Senate rules. Strong partisans on both sides of the aisle condemned the agreement, but there was nothing they could do, because enough Democrats signed on to end the filibuster of the three Bush nominees, and enough Republicans signed on to kill the nuclear option. Armageddon was avoided as the institutional tendency toward compromise prevailed.

majorities in both chambers. If they fail to do so, the legislation dies. If they succeed, the bill they produce still has to be approved by both houses.

Introducing a bill in the Senate works pretty much the way it does in the House. However, because the Senate is less formal and "clubbier" than the House, individual senators have more range to influence the path of legislation. In contrast to the formal discharge petition required by the House to bypass the committee process and bring a bill to a floor vote, any senator can request that a bill go directly to the floor (in reality, though, a senator would need the support of the Senate leadership to be successful). Because the Senate doesn't use a Rules Committee to prohibit a bill from being modified during floor debate, any senator can introduce an amendment to a bill being debated on the floor—forcing the Senate to act on the amendment even if it has nothing to do with the legislation being discussed. This privilege effectively circumvents the committee process. If a senator wishes to introduce a civil rights amendment to a bill on veteran's benefits, the rules allow it.[25]

Figure 6.4 provides an overview of the whole process of how a bill becomes law. Despite procedural differences between the two houses, notice the parallel structures in place between the House and the Senate for considering legislation. Notice, also, how each step in the process provides opponents with an opportunity to derail legislation. When you think for a second about all the places where proposals can die, it's not surprising that thousands of proposals flood into Congress but only a handful become law.

Serving in Congress: What Congress Does

As the legislative branch of government, Congress has its hands in the development of both domestic and foreign policy. Of course, because power is separated among the branches of the federal government, Congress is continually engaged in a push-pull relationship with the president, sometimes spearheading the national agenda and sometimes following the president's lead.

Generally speaking, Congress is more assertive in domestic issues and follows presidential leadership in foreign affairs. Every president comes to office with a domestic policy agenda—President Bush, for instance, wanted to cut taxes and partially privatize Social Security—but members of Congress can be fairly vocal about putting their imprint on the president's ideas, rejecting the president's agenda, or advancing an agenda that's entirely different than the president's.

The two branches may act together, particularly if the president's party also runs Congress, as was the case when President Bush won approval for his tax cut proposal in 2001. As we noted in Chapter 6, though, even shared party affiliation is not a guarantee of mutual objectives. President Clinton failed to marshal support for the largest initiative of his first term—an overhaul of the health care system—even though his party controlled both houses of Congress. It was sixteen years before another president would try again, and even though President Obama's Democrats also controlled both houses of Congress, he, too, found it difficult to broker agreement around any one approach to health care reform.

When Congress and the president are of different parties, congressional leaders can be in a position to steer the national agenda. When Democrats briefly regained control of the Senate in 2001 after Vermont Senator Jim Jeffords bolted the Republican Party, the Senate immediately discarded President Bush's agenda to consider items that the president had no interest in pursuing, like campaign finance reform.

Foreign affairs are another matter. Although the Constitution gives Congress important tools for the conduct of foreign policy, it also gives a broad grant of authority to the president, and over time, the president has emerged as the premier voice in international matters. Congress has the power to declare war (something it has not done since World War II), and the Senate has the power to confirm ambassadors and ratify treaties. In turn, the president is commander-in-chief of the armed forces, and, as we'll see in Chapter 10, best positioned to move public opinion in times of international tension. As a consequence, Congress typically defers to presidential leadership on foreign and defense issues. As you will see in the Issue feature, Iraq: Weighing the Pros and Cons, Congress often has very little choice but to go along with the president.

On the other hand, Congress plays a central role in several important government activities: making budgets, overseeing the actions of the bureaucracy, confirming a wide range of presidential appointments, and removing other officials from office. Let's look at each one in turn.

Figure 6.4. The Legislative Process

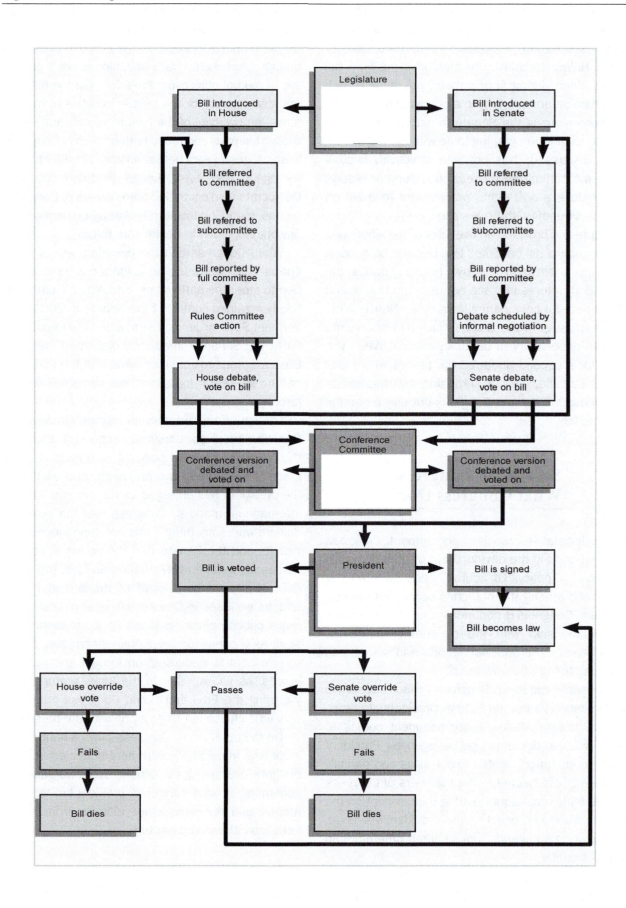

Making Budgets

If you've ever tried to save for something or figure out how you're going to spend limited funds on a bunch of needs, then you know how tricky it can be to write a budget. Add the individual wishes of hundreds of members of Congress and the president into the mix, and it shouldn't be hard to see how writing a budget is one of the most complex, sensitive, and important things Congress has to do. Members who sit on committees with a hand in budget writing find that they are rarely lonely.

Budget writing is an annual affair that typically takes an entire year to complete. A number of committees get into the act, in keeping with the decentralized way the House and Senate function. The process has been more coordinated, though, ever since the passage of the **Congressional Budget and Impoundment Control Act of 1974**.[22] A lot of the action happens in the House and Senate Appropriations Committees, which are charged with reporting bills that determine how much money government agencies and programs will have to spend (appropriations refer to legislation authorizing the government to spend money).

The procedure is complex, but it follows this outline: First, the House and Senate budget committees set guidelines and budgetary priorities. Then the appropriations committees are supposed to allocate money in line with those priorities. They approve spending bills to cover the variety of items in the federal budget. If the sum of these expenditures exceeds the budgetary guidelines, the expenditures are brought into line with the budget targets through a process called **reconciliation.** For both houses to end up with the same budget, differences between them are resolved in a conference committee, after which final approval on a budget can be sought in both houses.[23]

If budget guidelines necessitate changes in tax law, the House Ways and Means Committee and the Senate Finance Committee get into the act. As the tax-writing committees of Congress, they draft legislation specifying which taxes will be raised and by how much.

Because so much money is at stake, and because real policy changes can be made by the act of budgeting, there are always a lot of congressional fingerprints on the final act.

Oversight of the Bureaucracy

Congress may pass laws, but the bureaucracy is responsible for implementing laws, or carrying them out. This gives the bureaucracy a lot of freedom to interpret the intent of Congress, although Congress does have a function that can allow it to retain some control over how the bureaucracy implements legislation. It's called **oversight**, the process by which Congress reviews the actions of the bureaucracy to see that laws are being enacted as Congress intended. Most congressional oversight is carried out through the committees and subcommittees that share jurisdiction over a policy area with agencies and departments in the bureaucracy.

This sounds fairly neutral, but in fact, congressional oversight can be politically charged. The bureaucracy is part of the executive branch, and the president's political opponents in Congress can try to interfere with agencies they feel are implementing the law in accordance with the president's wishes instead of their own. Oversight can be a weapon for members of Congress who seek to diminish what they regard as excessive or unnecessary government programs. During the budgeting process, oversight can have dramatic consequences for government programs, as Congress can reduce (or threaten to reduce) funds to agencies, or put restrictions on how money is spent, all set against the backdrop of competing political and ideological agendas about what government should and should not do. When Republicans were in charge of Congress during the Bush years, for instance, they cut the budgets of programs they felt did not warrant government spending, such as Amtrak and public broadcasting. When Republicans regained control of the House in 2011, they again promised to employ strict oversight methods.

At the other end of the spectrum, oversight can be anything but acrimonious. The cooperative nature of iron-triangle relationships can turn oversight into something of a lovefest between bureaucratic agencies and the congressional committees supposedly overseeing them, fueled by mutual friendships with like-minded interest groups. When this happens, congressional committees work to protect agencies from scrutiny, investigations, and loss of funding.[26]

Sometimes even representatives or senators who in other instances are vocal critics of government spending will work to protect agencies that benefit interest groups with cooperative ties to their office.

ISSUE

IRAQ: WEIGHING THE PROS AND CONS

In late summer 2002, rumors percolated through Washington that the Bush administration had made up its mind to conduct a military strike against Iraq in the not-too-distant future. The president himself fueled these rumors, as he spoke in increasingly belligerent tones about the dangers posed by Iraqi President Saddam Hussein's efforts to stockpile biological, chemical, and nuclear weapons.

The idea of a military campaign against Hussein was controversial. Among America's allies, only Great Britain expressed public support (a position not shared by a large portion of the British public), and some members of Congress expressed concern about the United States moving ahead without the United Nations' involvement. Others in Congress felt an unprovoked attack on Iraq would constitute a serious and potentially dangerous departure from the American position to use military options in selfdefense, possibly giving cover to other nations to use force against their adversaries. Still others raised questions about the risks and costs of an all-out assault, whether the administration had a workable vision for a post-Hussein Iraq, and if war with Iraq would deflect resources and attention away from the campaign against terrorism.

Against this background, the Bush administration began sending signals that it might consider taking action without congressional backing. This possibility generated a firestorm of congressional criticism, and in September, President Bush relented: He would not take action against Iraq without first consulting Congress.

What exactly did that mean? Would he ask Congress for its input and then take action against Iraq regardless of what Congress said? Would he seek a vote of approval from Congress, with the understanding that he would move against Iraq even if congressional approval were not forthcoming? Would he ask Congress for its consent to take action, and change course if it wasn't granted?

As commander-in-chief, Bush was in a strong constitutional position to order an attack on Iraq even without congressional backing. He would be doing it without a formal declaration of war, but there are many precedents for doing that, from the Korean War to Vietnam to the Persian Gulf. He was in a strong political position as well. Many members, regardless of their views on the wisdom of an invasion, would regard a congressional vote as a demonstration of American resolve, which is why history shows that Congress is reluctant to position itself against a president who is about to commit American troops to fight overseas. This situation was no different. In fall 2002, Congress voted to support the war wage early the following year.

Still, the vote was not an easy one for many members, as the decision to support or oppose the Iraqi invasion had a couple of important wrinkles. Typically, members of Congress like to support the president on military matters, in deference to his role as commander-in-chief. This is particularly true for a popular president, which

President Bush was in late 2002. Members also try to avoid being labeled as "soft" on something as important as national security. On the other hand, representatives know that it can be even more devastating to an official's career to support a war that bogs down in heavy fighting, produces a lot of American casualties, emboldens anti-American terrorists, damages the economy, or unleashes unexpected and unwanted side effects—such as the use by Iraq of chemical or biological weapons against American troops.

In 2002, there was no way to predict that the capture of Baghdad would be quick, American casualties would be light, and Saddam Hussein would not use weapons of mass destruction against American troops. Of course, there was also no way to predict that the American occupation of Iraq after the war would be difficult and costly in lives and dollars, and that one of the most compelling justifications offered by the administration for supporting the war—the existence of Iraqi weapons of mass destruction—would be brought into question. In the immediate aftermath of the overthrow of the Hussein government, the war was wildly popular with Americans. In the months following that high point, opinion was more divided. By mid-2005, Americans had become restless with what had become an unpopular war. In 2008, Barack Obama would win the presidency in part on a promise to end it.

If you're in Congress, how do you vote when you can't anticipate events or public reaction to events? You can listen to your constituents, but if they tell you to support the war, you know it won't mean anything if later on they've turned against it. You can take a calculated risk and make the decision that you feel will be the least likely to come back and haunt you later. Or you can listen to your inner voice and vote according to what you feel is best for the country. This would allow you a clear conscience, knowing you voted responsibly on a matter of grave importance, but it could also leave you politically exposed if events turn against your position.

So, think about it—if you were in Congress in 2002, how would you have voted, and why? Consider several different methods of decision-making. First, you will want to take a look at the evidence for war and decide whether you in principle support it. Then, you will want to assess how your constituents feel about going to war and determine whether or not they are sending a clear message about how they would like you to vote. You'll want to consider your institutional place as a member of Congress—whether you feel it is appropriate for Congress to support the president as commander-in-chief, or to provide a check and balance to presidential military action. After that, you should do some political calculations. Think about how popular the president is, and about the political value of supporting him if you are a Republican and the political cost of opposing him if you are a Democrat. Finally, try to estimate what public opinion will be about the war in a few months (remember—it's an election year) and in a few years. Since you do not have the advantage of hindsight, you have to make your best judgment.

Now it's time to make a decision. Consider whether you will base your vote on:

· Principle.
· Constituent opinion.
· Your sense of the proper institutional role of Congress.
· The political value of supporting or opposing the president.
· Your estimate of how popular or unpopular the war will be.

Confirming Presidential Appointments

The Constitution simply gives the Senate the responsibility to offer "advice and consent" when the president nominates people to fill vacancies in the bureaucracy and the court system. In reality, the function of confirming presidential appointees can be an institutional and ideological tug-of-war between the legislative and executive branches, as we saw when we were discussing the filibuster—especially when senators and the president have dramatically different ideas about how conservative or liberal appointees should be.

When a presidential nomination is made, it is referred to the appropriate Senate committee for deliberation, and if approved, to the floor for a final vote. The committee holds hearings on the nominee, which are often smooth and uneventful, although they can be contentious if there is a philosophical rift between the nominee and committee members.

Presidents are most likely to win approval for major cabinet-level appointments made as they come into office, on the grounds that a president has the right to appoint people of his choosing to key positions. However, even this is not guaranteed if an appointment is controversial. For instance, President Bush's appointment of former Undersecretary of State John Bolton to be Ambassador to the United Nations angered Senate Democrats, who contended he lacked the diplomatic skills necessary for the post. Democrats filibustered the nomination, leading President Bush to take the unusual step of circumventing the Senate and appointing Bolton to a temporary term using a constitutional provision enabling the president to make interim "**recess appointments**" while Congress is out of session.

Recess appointments don't require approval, and those appointed can only serve until the end of the congressional session—but they're highly controversial. Recess appointments anger senators, who see the appointments as a way for the president to circumvent the normal legislative process.

Traditionally, Senate hearings center on the nominee's qualifications for office, but in recent years, almost anything goes: moral issues, personal or family background, financial dealings, medical history—any or all of these could be open for discussion. Senators looking for justification to turn down a nominee can turn almost anywhere for a rationale to vote no.[27] This is particularly true for judicial nominations, which tend to be more contentious than other presidential nominations. You'll find a good example of just how contentious things can get in Demystifying Government: "Bork" Becomes a Verb.

Senators can also drag their feet on holding hearings for nominees or place "holds" on nominees they dislike. Until 2011, "holds" could be made anonymously, permitting obstructing senators to shield their identities. Senate Democrats accused Senate Republicans of using these tactics during the Obama and Clinton administrations to block liberal judicial appointees; Senate Republicans accused their Democratic counterparts of dragging their heels on a host of President Bush's bureaucratic and judicial nominees when they controlled the process. When the Senate fails to act on a nomination, unless the president takes the unusual step of making a "recess appointment" or appointing the nominee on an "acting" basis, the position simply remains vacant. After ten months in office, President Obama had won Senate confirmation for only six of his appointees to the lower federal courts, compared to 28 for President George W. Bush and 27 for President Clinton in their respective first years in office.[28]

Impeachment

No political power is greater than the power to throw someone out of office, and the Constitution grants that power exclusively to Congress. **Impeachment** is a two-step process involving both houses. The House of Representatives can impeach any federal official, including the president, vice president, Supreme Court justices, and federal court judges. Impeachment requires a majority vote of the House and is similar to an indictment in court in that it charges the official with one or more counts of misconduct. Once articles of impeachment are approved, a trial is held in the Senate, where evidence is presented to support each accusation. With the chief justice of the Supreme Court presiding, the

DEMYSTIFYING GOVERNMENT

"BORK" BECOMES A VERB

It's hard to find a single reason why the Senate confirmation process has become so ugly—it wasn't always that way—but one place to look is President Reagan's 1987 nomination of Robert Bork to the Supreme Court. Under intense pressure from liberal interest groups who feared Bork's constitutional philosophy was too conservative, and with the ideological direction of the Court hanging in the balance, Democratic senators subjected the nominee to rigorous questioning about his philosophical perspective, pronounced him unfit to sit on the Supreme Court, and voted down his appointment. Many conservatives were livid. They claimed that a nominee's philosophy had never been grounds for Senate action, that the president had the legitimate right to appoint someone who shared his ideological outlook, and that liberal senators had distorted Bork's record. Civility in the nomination process fell by the wayside as an ideological war of sorts was declared; "Bork" entered the language as a verb. To many conservatives, to be "Borked" meant to be ambushed and destroyed politically through misrepresentation and lies, and they vowed to be more media savvy and proactive next time.

Things got worse four years later, when President Bush (senior) nominated Clarence Thomas to the Supreme Court. Thomas, a conservative African American judge, would replace liberal justice Thurgood Marshall—the first African American to sit on the Court—guaranteeing a shift in the Court's ideological center. Again, interest groups on both sides of the ideological spectrum geared up for full-scale battle, determined to win at any cost.

When the hearings began, little appeared to stand in Thomas's way. A southerner who began life in poverty, Thomas's story was a compelling one, and his judicial record, though undistinguished to critics, didn't raise any red flags. Then word leaked to the press of sexual harassment charges leveled against him by a former employee, University of Oklahoma law school professor Anita Hill, and the hearings took a bizarre turn. The Senate Judiciary Committee, run by Democrats, opted to explore the sexual harassment charges as the television cameras rolled. Conservative groups charged that it was a setup; Thomas himself pointedly called it a "high-tech lynching" of an African American nominee by white senators.

Today, sexual harassment is widely discussed and understood (in part, because of the Thomas hearings), but at the time, many Americans were not familiar with the topic, so it hit with tremendous force. Hill leveled her accusations as Thomas defended against them in what was arguably the most thorough exploration of the issue to date. All the while, it was hard to separate partisanship from the discussion, as evidenced by the pattern of Thomas's Democratic detractors grilling the nominee as his Republican supporters put Hill's credibility on trial. Ostensibly, the subject was sexual harassment, but the subtext was clearly politics and power.

Thomas was confirmed, 52–48, in one of the closest Senate votes ever for a Supreme Court nominee, and he took his seat on the Supreme Court under a cloud of controversy. The bitterness of the battle never fully dissipated and is on display whenever Senate Democrats or Republicans try to delay, defeat, or destroy a presidential nomination that threatens to move the judiciary or the bureaucracy in a direction they don't like.

impeached official is permitted to offer a defense against the charges. At the conclusion of the trial, each senator casts one vote on each article of impeachment, with a two-thirds majority required to remove the official from office.

The Constitution is especially vague on what constitutes an impeachable offense, stipulating only "Treason, Bribery, or other high Crimes and misdemeanors." Through the years, it has fallen to others to determine what this means. Invariably, the interpretation is political because, although the impeachment process looks like a trial, the jurors are elected officials responsive to public opinion. Regardless of the merits of the case, it's politically difficult to impeach and convict an official who has a lot of popular support.

It's also the case that impeachment doesn't happen very often. It's a complicated process with a low likelihood of conviction, designed that way so that political adversaries wouldn't routinely employ it. Only seventeen officials have been impeached since the Constitution was ratified, and only seven were convicted—all federal judges.[29]

There have been only two presidential impeachment trials—Andrew Johnson in 1868 and Bill Clinton in 1998—and both took place against the backdrop of partisan politics. Johnson, a southerner who took office upon the assassination of Abraham Lincoln, was strongly at odds with a Congress unsympathetic to the South in the period following the Civil War. When Congress passed the Tenure of Office Act, requiring congressional approval before a presidential appointee could be removed from office, Johnson ignored it, believing it to be unconstitutional. The House rushed to impeach him, eager to see Johnson removed for political reasons. He prevailed in the Senate by one vote.

President Clinton's impeachment grew out of charges that he perjured himself when he lied under oath about his sexual relationship with White House intern Monica Lewinsky. Since the charges did not stem from an issue related to the president's official conduct of his office, reporters, political analysts, and constitutional scholars questioned whether President Clinton's alleged offenses were impeachable. These questions were reinforced by the political nature of the proceedings, as the House voted almost along party lines to impeach. A dramatic Senate trial concluded in Clinton's acquittal on one count of perjury and one count of obstruction of justice. Both counts failed to produce even a simple majority of senators supporting conviction.

Richard Nixon is the one president who likely would have been convicted, on charges related to his conduct during the Watergate scandal, but he circumvented the impeachment process by becoming the first president to resign from office. Nixon faced removal in the wake of evidence pointing to a broad pattern of abuse of power stemming from his participation in and cover-up of events surrounding a break-in at Democratic Party headquarters. When a bipartisan majority of the House Judiciary Committee voted to recommend that the full House impeach the president, it became apparent that Nixon lacked the votes to avoid impeachment in the House or conviction in the Senate. Had the proceedings continued, it would have been the only time in history that the gravity of the charges against a president would have compelled significant numbers of his own partisans to vote to remove him from office.

This is a good time to stop for a second and review the broad outlines of what we've been discussing. Let's do it by briefly comparing a few key elements of the House and Senate—see Table 6.4.

Leading Congress

When the authors of the Constitution left it up to each house to figure out how it was going to function, they didn't imagine a role for political parties because, as we know, they viewed parties as factions and assumed (or hoped) that they would never develop. As it turns out, parties mean everything in Congress. They determine who gets to lead Congress, control congressional committees, set the agenda, and set the rules. Power flows to the majority party; frustration visits the minority. For this reason, congressional leaders are highly motivated to attain and keep majority status.

In both houses, the majority is simply the party with the most seats. However, just like in congressional elections where all the representation goes

Table 6.4. Comparing House and Senate

	House	Senate
Number of Members	435	100
Districts	Congressional Districts	States
Member Terms	2 Years	6 Years
Elections Held	Every 2 Years for Everyone	One-third Every 2 Years
Distinctive Functions	Originate Revenue Bills Write Articles of Impeachment	Ratify Presidential Appointments Hold Impeachment Hearings Ratify Treaties
Most Powerful Committees	Appropriations Budget Commerce Rules Ways and Means	Appropriations Armed Services Commerce Finance

to the winner, all of the leadership benefits go to the majority party. Even a one-seat advantage (like Senate Democrats had in 2001 and 2002) permits the majority party to have a majority of its members on all committees, to have its members chair all committees and subcommittees, and to have its leader set the legislative agenda. That's why when Senator Jeffords defected from the Republican Party during the 2001 legislative session and decided to become an independent who votes with Democrats on leadership issues, the entire chamber was turned on its head. Overnight, (mostly liberal) Democrats replaced (generally conservative) Republicans as leaders and committee chairs, bringing with them an entirely different set of legislative priorities and the power to have them heard.

Leadership Structure

The different traditions and procedures in the House and Senate translate into differences in the degree to which the majority party can clamp down on the minority. The Senate offers more opportunities to members of the minority party to express their will through the filibuster and through courtesies extended individual members. It operates on the principle of **minority rights**, whereby deference is granted to the concerns of those whose party does not control the chamber.

The House, in contrast, functions on a **majoritarian principle** that frustrates dissent. After more than a century of dealing with rules that permitted

legislative minorities to derail legislation, the House, around the turn of the twentieth century, instituted rules that give the leadership of the majority party tight control over all proceedings.

The **Speaker of the House** is the foremost leader in the chamber. Chosen by a caucus of the majority party, then ratified by a party-line vote of the full House, "Mister Speaker" (as he is addressed) is one of the premier leaders in Washington (not to mention second in line for the presidency after the vice president). He has both formal and informal powers, which allow him to advance his priorities and the priorities of his party, regardless of the wishes of the minority. Formally, the Speaker presides over the House, resolves disputes as they arise, decides which committees will consider legislation, and determines who will serve on conference and select committees. Informally, the Speaker can influence the Rules Committee (affecting the scheduling of debate and votes on legislation), reward members for their loyalty (or punish members for their independence), influence assignments to standing committees, and function as the spokesperson for the House of Representatives in the press.[30]

Unlike other congressional leadership offices, the position of Speaker of the House is mandated by the Constitution. Article 1, Section 2 says that "The House of Representatives shall choose their Speaker and other Officers," leaving the rest of the leadership structure to evolve through custom and practice. What the Constitution does not say is that the Speaker has to be a member of a majority party (remember, no parties are mentioned in the Constitution) or even a member of the House. However, every Speaker has been a House member, and every contemporary Speaker has been a majority party member with many years of service in the House.

The Speaker is assisted by the rest of the majority party leadership, which, like the Speaker, is selected by a caucus of the majority party at the start of each congressional session. The key positions are the **majority leader** and the **majority whip**. The majority leader is the floor leader for the majority party, responsible for doing the everyday work of moving the party's legislative agenda through the House: lining up the support of committee chairs, gauging levels of support among House members, and persuading members to vote the party position. The majority leader is assisted in this effort by the majority whip. The name suggests whipping up or rounding up votes, which is a good description of what the whip does. The whip reminds party members of key votes, counts heads to determine if the party position is likely to prevail, and when necessary, leans on members to vote with the leadership.

Because, as we mentioned in Section 6.4a, "How Parties in Government Function," we do not have **responsible parties** in government, members—even powerful committee chairs—cannot be assumed to support the positions of leadership, and legislators will not automatically heed the wishes of a president of their party. This fact has been the cause of a lot of anguish over the years as party leaders have tried—some more successfully than others—to keep their members in line.

For example, in 2003, President Bush and Republican congressional leaders faced a revolt by a few congressional representatives of their own party over the Medicare prescription drug benefit discussed in Chapter 8. Republican leaders kept the final vote on the measure going all night in a frantic effort to convince enough recalcitrant conservatives to give their president a victory. One reporter recalled feverish efforts by House Speaker Dennis Hastert and his lieutenants:

> The House's reigning Caesars were running around in circles, going back once, twice, and three times to conservatives who were clearly hard "no's" and had been that way for days. Tom Feeney, R-Fla.? No thanks. Steve Chabot, R-Ohio? Didn't like the means-testing provision. Todd Akin, R-Mo.? The [Republican] whip, fellow Missourian Roy Blunt, had him out in the Speaker's lobby all alone and was getting nowhere.[31]

It took close to three hours and a few personal phone calls by the president to round up enough votes to secure passage of the measure. In time, however, the victory raised serious questions about the tactics used by the House leadership and the administration—including the prospect that Republican leaders had employed threats to change the votes of reluctant members, and that the White House knowingly withheld the true cost of the measure to keep conservatives on board—in an extreme example of what can happen because congressional representatives are free to go their own way.

The minority party counterparts to these leadership positions are the **minority leader** and **minority whip**. As leaders of the party out of power, their roles parallel their counterparts in the majority but without the ability to shape the legislative agenda. So, the minority leadership advocates the policy alternatives of the minority as they look for opportunities to develop alliances with wayward members of the majority in an effort to frustrate the majority party's agenda.

Leadership in the Senate operates a little differently. There is no counterpart to the Speaker of the House. Instead, the Constitution makes the vice president of the United States the presiding officer of the Senate, where his formal title is president of the Senate, and his one formal power is the ability to cast tie-breaking votes. However, unless it looks like the Senate is heading for a tie vote, you probably won't find the vice president anywhere near the Senate. In his absence, the chore of presiding over the Senate falls to the **president pro tempore**, a mostly honorary position that typically goes to the longest serving member of the majority party. Apart from being third in line for presidential succession behind the vice president and the Speaker of the

House, the president pro tempore has no formal powers and typically finds the job of presiding over the Senate to be as dull as the vice president does. That's why, on any given afternoon, it's not unusual to find junior senators presiding over the proceedings, not as an honor but as an obligation assumed by those with the least standing in the chamber.

In the absence of a powerful figure like the House Speaker, the Senate is led by the majority leader and majority whip. They determine the items on the legislative agenda and work to keep their majority in line. It can be a harder job than what befalls their House counterparts because of the Senate's less hierarchical traditions that permit individual senators to go their own way. The minority leader and minority whip function much like their House counterparts. Figure 6.5 shows the House and Senate leaders after the 2010 election.

Maybe you're getting the sense that political parties have emerged as the organizations that hold Congress together, structure its operations, and help to centralize an institution staffed by hundreds of ambitious people from different regions of the country with varying personal agendas and objectives. Without parties to provide structure, it's quite possible that the legislative branch would be a much harder place to run—particularly in the Senate, where customs and procedures give voice to individual and minority opinions.

The other side of this coin is that during times of intense partisan division like we've experienced over the past few years, the efforts of party leaders can serve to heighten philosophical differences between the two camps, leading to hard fought battles over legislation and, more broadly, the general direction of the country. Even with Democrats holding large majorities in the House and Senate, as they did following the 2008 election, party leaders can find themselves with surprisingly little margin for error in carrying out their legislative plans. With Republicans almost unanimous in their opposition to Democratic plans for a stimulus package aimed at jump-starting the economy in 2009 and legislation to reform health care—the two largest domestic items on President Obama's first year agenda—Democratic leaders could afford to lose few of their members if they hoped to advance their

objectives. This was particularly so in the Senate, where Democrats needed all 60 of their members to end filibusters staged by all 40 Republicans, so there is intense pressure on leadership to keep members in line. Under the circumstances, things can get nasty.

There are a number of things the leadership can do to appeal for party cohesion. Leaders can shower members with rewards for adhering to the party line on key votes. They can listen to members and incorporate their interests as legislation is formulated. They can help them get committee assignments that will promote their career goals—by putting them on committees that afford them power in Congress or that address their personal legislative interests or the interests of their constituents. Leaders can go to member districts and campaign for them, and use their clout to raise money for member reelection efforts.

Any or all of these things can just as easily be withheld from members who cause trouble for the leadership, but only to a limited extent. Remember, it's in the leaders' self-interest to help party members win reelection because holding the majority fulfills the promise of power in Congress, and every reelected member brings an incumbent or would-be majority leader closer to that goal.

Party Structure

For the congressional member who is not part of the leadership, party business is conducted primarily through participation in the **party caucus**. Each party in each house has a caucus, which conducts leadership elections and finalizes committee assignments at the start of each new Congress, and provides a forum for discussion of policy issues and party legislative strategies. The caucus is the place where House Republicans, House Democrats, Senate Republicans, or Senate Democrats can articulate their interests or concerns about the positions the party might take, in an effort to build general agreement for the positions that the leadership will move forward. (Although it's the same term, this use of caucus should not be confused with a caucus that

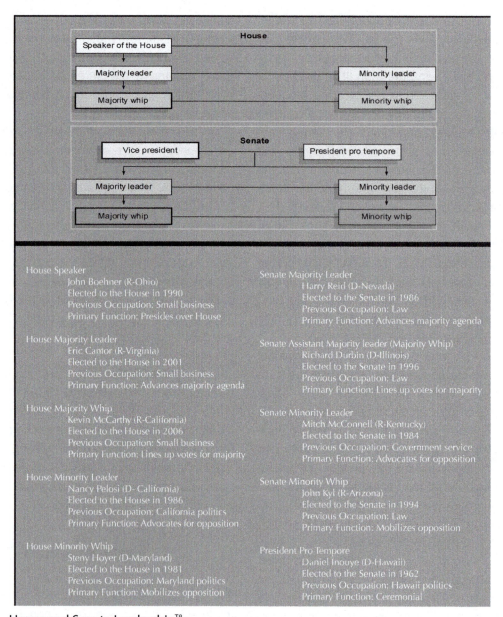

Figure 6.5. House and Senate Leadership[T8]

meets to elect delegates to a political party convention, like the Iowa caucus.)

Caucus can also be used as a verb: When Senator Jeffords left the Republican Party in an evenly divided Senate to become an independent, he altered majority control because of his willingness "to caucus" with Democrats. By attending the Senate Democratic caucus and supporting Democratic leadership candidates, he gave Democrats enough votes to elect their leaders and become the majority party.

Complementing the relatively informal caucus are party committees (see Table 6.5) that help coordinate the political and policy interests of the parties. Because these committees serve partisan purposes rather than institutional purposes, they're different and apart from the standing committees and subcommittees we talked about earlier. These committees give partisan advice on developing legislative strategy, recommend committee assignments by matching members with committees that can help them politically, and help party members with reelection needs.

A quick glance at a couple of these committee websites could give you a richer sense of how they

Table 6.5. Party Committees and Their Purposes[T9]

	Committee	Purpose
House	Republican Policy Committee	Build consensus for party policy positions
	Democratic Policy Committee	Build consensus for party policy positions
Senate	Republican Policy Committee	Research and draft party policy positions
	Democratic Policy Committee	Develop party positions and priorities
House	Republican Steering Committee	Assign Republicans to committees
	Democratic Steering Committee	Communicate/Implement party priorities Assign Democrats to committees
Senate	Republican Committee on Committees	Assign Republicans to committees
	Democratic Steering and Outreach Committee	Coordinate party policy agenda Assign Democrats to committees
House	National Republican Congressional Committee	Elect Republicans to the House
	Democratic Congressional Campaign Committee	Elect Democrats to the House
Senate	National Republican Senatorial Committee	Elect Republicans to the Senate
	Democratic Senatorial Campaign Committee	Elect Democrats to the Senate

operate and what they do. For instance, the Senate Republican Policy Committee (RPC) bills itself as "helping shape the GOP game plan:"

> The Republican Policy Committee (RPC) publishes a variety of policy papers that are used by Republican Senators and their staffs to prepare for committee deliberations, floor debate, and votes. These RPC publications, which are posted on this website, include in-depth policy papers on issues facing Congress, legislative notice summaries for every major bill awaiting Senate floor action, and a variety of shorter papers on timely issues as they arise.

> Every week the Senate is in session, Republican Senators gather in the Capitol for a policy lunch meeting, hosted by Chairman [Sen. John] Thune. At this meeting, Republican Senators discuss issues before the Senate, review the anticipated agenda, and discuss policy options.[32]

The Senate Democratic Steering and Outreach Committee, in addition to its committee assignment function, works to coordinate the Senate Democratic legislative strategy with Democratic allies outside Congress:

> The Senate Democratic Steering and Outreach Committee is dedicated to fostering dialogue between Senate Democrats and community leaders from across the nation. Each year, the Steering Committee hosts several meetings with advocates, policy experts, and elected officials to discuss key priorities and enlist their help in the development of the Democratic agenda in the Senate. We are committed to serving as a liaison between Senate Democratic offices and advocacy groups and intergovernmental organizations.[33]

Beyond these committees, members can find numerous opportunities to gather in less formal or smaller partisan group settings to discuss goals, map strategies, and mediate disputes.

Congressional parties in both houses occasionally hold retreats (typically in a pleasant setting outside Washington) for the purpose of boosting party unity. Like on a college campus, there are plenty of extracurricular groups you can join in Congress, where you'll find other people with similar partisan or ideological interests. For instance, the Republican Study Committee is a House Republican group dedicated to advancing a small-government, socially conservative agenda. The Congressional Black Caucus and the Congressional Hispanic Caucus are organized around identity politics. The Blue Dogs are a group of moderate-to-conservative House Democrats that tries to build bridges between liberal Democrats and Conservative Republicans.

Committee Structure

Congressional leadership and party structures play big roles in the organization of the committee system. There are so many committees—the structure is so decentralized—that parties step in to hold things together. We've already talked about how committees are organized around parties and how leadership plays a critical role in making committee assignments, attempting to match members with committees that will advance their careers.

However, there are a few things we haven't addressed about the committee structure that are important to the way they operate. One is how the ratio of Republicans to Democrats is determined. Another is how member preferences are matched to committees. Then, there's the all-important matter of seniority.

We've said that the majority party receives a majority of seats on all committees, but the magnitude of that advantage will vary, depending on how many seats the majority party occupies. In a closely divided legislature of the sort we saw during the first years of the century, the majority party will command only a small advantage on most committees, but there can be exceptions. For instance, the majority party may demand disproportionate representation on the House Rules Committee, allowing majority leadership to control the flow of legislation to the floor. When one party controls a comfortable majority of seats in the House or Senate, as the Democrats did after the 2008 election, their numerical advantage on each committee grows as well.

At the start of every Congress, new members will seek committees on which they want to serve and will typically lobby their leadership to get them. Members are goal-directed, and see committee service as an opportunity to advance career objectives. Those interested primarily in making laws will gravitate to policy-oriented committees, like the House International Relations Committee or the Senate Health, Education, Labor and Pensions Committee. Those seeking to climb the leadership ladder in Congress will be drawn to committees where they can exert influence on the congressional agenda, like the Ways and Means Committee or the Rules Committee in the House. Members from competitive districts with reelection on their minds will want to join committees where they can benefit from the perks of pork, like the House Transportation and Infrastructure Committee.[34]

Although leaders try to accommodate assignment requests, not everyone gets what they want. Just like in many universities, where seniors have priority over freshmen when enrolling for courses, **seniority** gives long-serving members an edge in having their committee requests fulfilled. Seniority also plays an important role in committee leadership. As a long-standing matter of custom, each **committee chair** is the member of the majority party with the longest continuous service on the committee. The longest-serving member of the minority party is the **ranking minority member.** Although there have been a few cases over the past several decades of a party caucus granting a committee chair to someone other than the longest-serving member, the seniority custom is rarely violated.

Because most legislation first goes to committee for a hearing, a committee chair can have enormous power over the legislative process. A committee chair is no longer the iron-fisted dictator of an earlier time, although he can still influence the committee's agenda, budget and staff, and may have influence over determining subcommittee memberships. He can decide how—or whether—to route legislative proposals to subcommittees. He can decide when—or whether—to schedule a vote to send legislation on for consideration by the full chamber. By delaying action on a bill he doesn't like, a chair can keep the rest of Congress from considering it, even if the bill has widespread support. As a result, chairs are well positioned to fashion committees to suit their interests.[35]

Health care reform was such a complicated legislative task that it fell under the jurisdiction of five separate committees—three in the House and two in the Senate. Each had to approve a reform measure before the entire House or Senate could vote.[36] Four of the five committees completed their work quickly, but the Senate Finance Committee took a lot longer as the committee chair, Sen. Max Baucus, attempted to craft a proposal that Republicans could support. Considering the high degree of opposition among congressional Republicans to any health care reform, this was a monumental task, but it was within the chairman's discretion to pursue it, and the entire process came to a halt for several weeks while the rest of congress waited for Baucus to unveil his committee's measure.

Working in Congress: Washington

Okay, see if this sounds familiar to you. It's final exam week. You have four tests in the next three days, and while you've done your best to keep up with most of the reading, you realize you're facing a few long days and nights.

Now imagine that finals week goes on forever, and you'll have a sense of what the workload is like for members of Congress. There's always more to do than can get done, and just like you're always aware that you'll be getting graded at the end of each term, every member keeps an eye on when their term ends and they have to face the voters again.

Members have to fulfill a number of obligations, all with implications for how well they'll do on Election Day. When they cast a vote on legislation, when they do work on committees, when they address the concerns and complaints of constituents,

they realize they're doing things with the potential to assist—or undermine—their reelection prospects. It's a lot to cover, and it's probably not exaggerating things too much to say that a big misstep, or a lot of small missed steps, could put their future in jeopardy.

On the Job

Representatives can be easily overwhelmed. They need to make judgments about a wide range of issues, many of them detailed and technical. With the exception of perhaps one or two issues, members are limited in their level of expertise. It would be like taking a series of liberal arts courses in everything from biology to art history to sociology to psychology, and feeling a sense of command only in your major subject—except, where you probably take no more than five courses per term, representatives are inundated with many more than five complex issues they need to address.

Members of Congress typically spend more time in committee rooms than you spend in classrooms; just like the job of learning takes place in class, the detail work of Congress takes place in committee. Between committee and subcommittee assignments, members are regularly overbooked and have to make choices about which hearings to attend. It would be as if you registered for seven three-credit courses and some of them met at the same time.

More than committee work pulls members in competing directions. They need to meet with lobbyists and constituents, they're expected to spend time on the floor of Congress debating and voting on legislation, they have to pay attention to their public image by devoting time to the media and by making public speaking engagements, and they are presented with a steady supply of social functions that offer opportunities to "network" and conduct business. It's not unusual for a representative's day to begin early and end late in the evening.

Then there's the commute. Members must return to their districts regularly or they risk losing touch with their constituents at the grass roots. Some members who live close to Washington are able to divide their time between the Capital and their district, spending long weekends at home or even driving or taking the train if they're very close. Others have a much longer way to go: Imagine if you represented California—or Hawaii. Once home, members keep working, often on weekends, taking care to meet with constituents, locally based interest groups, and financial supporters.

Staff to the Rescue

Of course, they don't have to do it alone. The typical House member has a full-time staff of up to eighteen paid employees and nine college interns. The typical senator has a paid staff of between thirty and thirty-five and nine college interns. Typically well educated, young, and willing to trade off higher pay elsewhere for the thrill of working with powerful people and the ability to make important professional contacts, staffers help manage the workload by performing a number of important roles:

- *Administrative assistants (AAs)* help manage the Washington office, provide political advice to the representative or senator, and function as an intermediary in dealings with constituents, lobbyists, and other members.
- *Legislative assistants (LAs)* help manage the member's committee work by writing speeches and bills, analyzing legislative proposals, and following up on committee and subcommittee meetings the member misses.
- *Caseworkers* devote their time to helping constituents with problems and work either out of Washington, D.C., or out of one of the member's home offices. Representatives on average have two or three "branch offices" in their districts; senators average four offices in their state.
- *Press aides* are responsible for the member's media relations, including communicating the member's message to the press and managing communications with constituents through newsletters and, in some cases, surveys of constituent opinion.[37]

Take a look at some of the things a member of Congress might face on a typical day. You'll find them in Demystifying Government: A Typical Day on the Hill. This is a fictional composite, but it's based on the real thing. Imagine you're the representative with the scheduling conflicts shown (in some cases, this will require a lot of imagination): a conservative, pro-business Democrat from a competitive district in the Northeast with an interest in affordable housing, air pollution (particularly the problem of acid rain), and homeland security—all of which are important to the constituents who support you. During much of the day, scheduling conflicts make it impossible for you to be everywhere and do everything you would like. You'll have the chance to decide how you will resolve these conflicts by selecting the events you're going to attend and those you're going to miss from a set of available options. Remember, some of what you miss can be taken care of by your staff—but not everything.

Also, remember that there's a potential cost every time members of Congress fail to show up for an event that a staff member can't cover, either in the form of a lost opportunity, an angry constituent, a violated congressional norm—or the appearance that they are just not doing their job.

Voting on Legislation

If you felt it was an intrusion on your busy schedule to have to vote on legislation creating a "National Asparagus Day," you can probably get a sense of the range of things—big and small—that representatives are called upon to decide. Maybe which way to vote on something like an honorary holiday is a no-brainer (you support it!), but there are a lot of more substantive votes a member has to cast and—let's face it—with so many technical issues to decide, members have to cast plenty of votes on things they know nothing about.

So, they need voting strategies. To simplify what could be confusing decisions on unfamiliar matters, members of Congress engage in **cue taking**, looking to other members for reliable signals on how to vote. There are several commonsense shortcuts that members might take. They could turn to a

DEMYSTIFYING GOVERNMENT

A TYPICAL DAY ON THE HILL

Conflicts in congressional schedules are the rule, rather than the exception. Every decision disappoints some groups. The conflicts listed below are typical of what you would have to face if you served in Congress. Take a look at each one and figure out, in each case, which options you would chose.

Conflict 1

- 7:50 A.M. Breakfast with Chamber of Commerce officials from home district to discuss business interests and the Chamber's political support for your reelection campaign
- 8:00 A.M. Breakfast meeting with fellow Blue Dog Democrats to discuss centrist legislative strategies

Consider: Meeting with lobbyists connected to your district instead of going to a regularly scheduled meeting with other conservative Democrats is the less risky choice. Maintaining good relationships with sympathetic groups will help you earn their money and support for your next reelection effort. You can always meet with the Blue Dogs next week.

Conflict 2

- 8:55 A.M. A long, impromptu meeting with a Republican colleague who wants your vote for a bridge construction project in her district; she is willing to support construction of a military helicopter in your district in return
- 9:00 A.M. Meeting with computer company lobbyists about adding funding to combat cyberterrorism in the homeland security bill

Consider: This is a tough call with no obvious good choice. The tradeoff you're arranging with your colleague will help you bring an important pork-barrel project back to your constituents. However, the computer lobbyist you're neglecting is a potential political supporter who wants to talk about an important legislative matter.

Conflict 3

- 10:15 A.M. Meeting with a postal worker from your district who is retiring after 50 years of service without ever calling in sick
- 10:20 A.M. Floor vote on designating an official "National Asparagus Day"

Consider: The meeting will matter to the postal worker (who may turn out to vote in the next election), it will likely get you favorable coverage in the local papers back home, and you'll build up good will with the postal workers in your district. The vote, on the other hand, is symbolic; missing it would be a problem only for a member from a district that produces asparagus.

Conflict 4

- 10:45 A.M. Hearing on acid rain (Committee on Energy and Commerce Subcommittee on Energy and Air Quality)
- 11:00 A.M. Hearing on possible NASA expedition to Mars (Committee on Science Subcommittee on Space and Aeronautics)

Consider: You can't go to every hearing. Of the two, the hearing on acid rain is probably the more important one to you because your constituents will have a direct interest in the effects of acid rain. Your legislative assistant can keep tabs on the meeting you missed.

Conflict 5

- 1:15 P. M. Floor debate. Prepared remarks (two minutes) on proposed homeland security bill
- 1:20 P. M. Unscheduled visit by elementary school group from home district looking for personalized tour of Congress
- 1:20 P. M. Hearing on affordable housing: Committee on Financial Services Subcommittee on Housing and Community Opportunity, on which you are ranking minority member

Consider: It makes sense that you'd want to deliver your remarks on an important measure like homeland security, but it's difficult to miss a meeting of a subcommittee where you're the ranking member without violating the norm of doing your legislative work. You could always have your remarks entered in the permanent record without actually presenting them. As hard as it is to overlook school kids from home—remember, their parents may be voters—the visit was unannounced and can be handled by your staff workers.

Conflict 6

- 3:00 P. M. CNN Interview on affordable housing
- 3:00 P. M. Floor vote on raising the minimum wage by 20 cents an hour

Consider: This is another tough call. You want the publicity that CNN can give you, but your opponent in the next election could raise questions about why you are not doing your job if you do not vote on an important measure like the minimum wage.

Conflict 7

- 8:00 P. M. Evening reception in Georgetown with lobbyists from Greenpeace
- 8:00 P. M. Evening function at the White House honoring the Canadian prime minister, an opportunity to discuss the topic of acid rain
- 8:00 P. M. Quiet time with family

Consider: The Greenpeace reception would allow you to mix with sympathetic lobbyists who support your environmental concerns. However, the presidential function has the added benefit of allowing you to talk to the Canadian prime minister about one of your pet issues—and it's at the White House. All of this weighs against time with your family, which is always a tough choice to make.

colleague who shares their philosophical outlook and vote the way the colleague is voting. They could seek advice from a member with expertise on the legislation being considered, such as a member of the committee that held hearings on it. If they are junior members, they might look for someone with seniority who has been around long enough to be familiar with the matter at hand. If they are in the House, they could turn to a member of their state delegation, someone from their area who is known and trusted. This sort of cue makes particular sense if the legislation could have an impact back home, like a measure that could affect an industry in the member's state.[38]

If a member's vote on the issue is important to other members but does not concern the member or his or her constituents, it would probably be an appropriate time to engage in logrolling, where the member would exchange his or her vote for future support on something that does matter to the member. Logrolling can be accomplished informally before a final vote on legislation, and it can involve a number of members. One former senator, sounding a whole lot like anyone who has ever called in favors from a friend, explained how he put together majority support for a bill: "Maggie said she talked to Russell, and Tom promised this if I would help him on Ed's amendment, and Mike owes me one for last year's help on Pete's bill."[39]

Cue taking is necessary when a lawmaker doesn't know much about the legislation on the table, and logrolling is effective when the outcome of a vote doesn't matter to the representative. Every so often, though, members have to cast votes that matter to their constituents on things their constituents are aware of and feel intensely about. These are the votes that get noticed, the votes that could influence how constituents react the next time they see the member's name on a ballot. Perhaps it's a vote involving an industry that employs a lot of people back home, like the automobile industry in the Midwest or the tobacco industry in the South. Maybe it's a vote about something that touches people's lives in a direct way, like tax increases, health care costs, Social Security benefits, or education. These votes require extra care.[40]

Likewise, members will take notice when an issue mobilizes elite groups in their districts. Issues of this nature tend to be narrow and don't involve large numbers of constituents, but they can matter strongly to the group with a stake in the outcome—like, for instance, cigarette manufacturers facing a new surcharge on their product. Because elites are politically active, resource-rich groups that can use their clout to help or hinder a member's reelection prospects, they can command a lot of notice despite their size.

On occasion, these votes can be tricky, depending in part on how strongly representatives feel about the matter at hand, whether their position is at odds with the position of their constituents, and if they believe they should vote their mind rather than the preferences of the people who elected them. Demystifying Government: Burke's Dilemma explains.

They do these things because they recognize that while most votes will be inconsequential, there will always be a handful of votes on salient issues that can generate political risk. The riskiest type of vote is on a highly visible and unpredictable matter that the member cannot avoid, like the decision members of Congress had to face in 2002 over whether to support military action against Iraq. Some representatives who were in Congress in 1991 remembered agonizing over whether to support President Bush (senior) on the Persian Gulf War. Some who voted against it were attacked by opponents for being weak on defense issues—a charge that can have devastating political consequences. However, at the time they were asked to vote, members had no way of knowing that the war would produce a swift military success with little cost to the United States. Had the war gone differently, their vote against would have appeared cautious and wise. Members faced the same type of uncertainty in the vote on the second Iraq campaign, as we saw in the previous Issue discussion.

Working in Congress: Back Home

Whether members regard themselves as delegates or as trustees, the folks back home are the ones who will decide whether they get to return to Washington for another term. Legislative voting is, of course, one of the determining factors that constituents might use when they decide whether to reelect an incumbent. There's another side to the job that's more personal and often more mundane than what a member does in Washington. It's about constituent service, and it's a key part of what members of Congress do to keep their voters satisfied with their performance.

Constituent service can help the entire district at once or serve one constituent at a time. Members are always looking out for things to bring back to their districts—tangible items like public projects or federal jobs. These are the fruits of logrolling, and since every member needs them, every other member is sympathetic to the need to trade off favors for favors. Remember the $1.2 million historical sewer in Trenton, New Jersey, that we mentioned in Demystifying Government: The Golden Fleece? That represents a $1.2 million federal outlay to a congressional district. The replica of the Great Wall of China in Bedford, Indiana? That's a $20,000 outlay to a congressional district. Members can point to them at reelection time as concrete evidence of their effectiveness in serving community interests and needs.

DEMYSTIFYING GOVERNMENT

BURKE'S DILEMMA

Before you get the sense that legislators try to make everyone happy all the time, you should consider a couple of things. Legislators have values, and sometimes, they want to cast votes on principles that could contradict constituent wishes. Some legislators believe that they were hired to vote their conscience and experience, to do what they felt was best for the nation even if it contradicts the views of their constituents. These considerations can factor into their voting decisions, depending in part on how they view the notion of representation.

Edmund Burke, eighteenth-century political philosopher and member of the British Parliament, espoused the view of representatives as **trustees** who are elected to exercise their best judgment of the national interest. His perspective conflicts with the more widely held contemporary American view that representatives are **delegates** of the people who put them in office and are thereby obligated to vote their constituents' wishes. Both are legitimate ways to understand representation.

Most of the time, the difference between the trustee and delegate approaches to representation isn't relevant. Because most votes are not controversial, and because the personal philosophy of candidates recruited to run for office typically matches the prevailing views of the district, sharp differences between representative and constituent do not emerge often or can get lost in the shuffle of legislation.

However, should members face a rare, highly visible vote on a matter where their best judgment puts them at odds with their constituent's wishes, they face a dilemma. In fact, they face "Burke's Dilemma," as Burke himself found his view of the national interest in conflict with the wishes of his constituents.

It's probably easy to see how the trustee view of representation can have its political costs. On matters of principle, it's also easy to see how representatives might wish to risk these costs and vote against their constituents' wishes in order to do what they feel is best for the nation.

It's unusual for a single vote to mean the difference between political life and death. Often, members will consider their overall voting record as they look toward the next campaign, rather than worry about any particular vote. They'll try to avoid casting what political scientist John Kingdon calls a "string of votes" against a series of constituent interests that could form the basis for a future campaign against them. They'll also try to be conscious of ways to explain the more controversial parts of their voting record to their constituents, perhaps by pointing to other actions more in line with constituent wishes, or by finding shelter for their vote in the supportive words of the president or other authorities their constituents might respect.[T10]

On a more individual level, members (with an important assist from their staff) regularly perform **casework** for constituents who have problems they would like to see handled by the federal government. Casework is homework in the literal sense of the word because it requires members to use their legislative positions to address requests from people back home that can be serious and important—as well as mundane or tedious. Just like the relationship that so many of us have to doing homework, it's fair to say that most legislators do not find this to be the most fulfilling part of their job. However (just like our homework assignments), it's important to do (your grade—and their reelection prospects—hinge on doing it), and the work never stops pouring in.

Some casework involves problems constituents have with government agencies. For instance, a constituent having trouble getting his Social Security check or veteran's benefits might contact a member of Congress for help. Someone having trouble getting a passport also could turn to his or her member for assistance. So might somebody whose child wants a congressional nomination to attend West Point.

Not all casework is about navigating the bureaucracy. Lots of people contact their member of Congress because they want to receive a flag that was flown over the Capitol (flags are raised and lowered over the dome with great frequency in order to provide this service).Many are interested in arranging a tour of the House, Senate, or White House during their family trip to Washington.

Other requests are just downright odd. Members have been asked for recipes, transportation on military aircraft, help changing a grade in a college course (don't bother trying—it can't be done), and all sorts of unusual, personal items.[41] These requests are granted if possible, or turned down gently, but they're always taken seriously because there's no point in antagonizing a potential voter, even though responding to these requests takes time.

All constituent requests may get a hearing, but members of Congress do not regard all constituents the same way, especially as they think about the next election. Members try to be alert to the groups of constituents they can count on to vote for them, those they can count on to support them intensely, and those whose support they probably can never win. The strong supporters can be pretty easy to identify, but at the margins, many representatives will confess to some fuzziness in their picture of whom they can rely on politically.

Political scientist Richard E. Fenno uses the term **home style** to describe the way members approach these different constituency groups. The way representatives size up the political inclinations of people in their district can affect the way they allocate staff resources in the district, how they fashion their trips home, and how they explain to their constituents what they do in Washington.[42]

Fenno says members—without being fully conscious of it—divide their districts into a set of overlapping constituencies based on perceptions of political support. From this perspective, a relatively small number of people can have a disproportionate influence on the member's approach to the whole district. Figure 6.6 illustrates the different layers of constituents that make up a member's district. Imagine that the circles in the figure represent different constituent groups in a district. Consider that constituents who are closer to the "bull's-eye" have more influence with their representative.

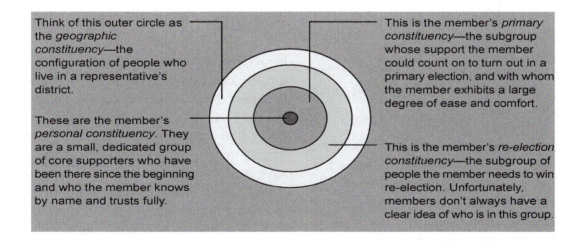

Think of this outer circle as the *geographic constituency*—the configuration of people who live in a representative's district.

These are the member's *personal constituency*. They are a small, dedicated group of core supporters who have been there since the beginning and who the member knows by name and trusts fully.

This is the member's *primary constituency*—the subgroup whose support the member could count on to turn out in a primary election, and with whom the member exhibits a large degree of ease and comfort.

This is the member's *re-election constituency*—the subgroup of people the member needs to win re-election. Unfortunately, members don't always have a clear idea of who is in this group.

Figure 6.6. Constituencies inside Constituencies[T11]

Staying in Congress

It shouldn't be too hard to figure out that when you add up the cost of all those staff members and the price of travel back to the district, members of Congress have a number of perks that ease the burden of their jobs and help grease the way towards reelection. The truth is, we haven't even scratched the surface of the rewards members of Congress get when they serve.

Perks

You can start with the prestige of office (which is greater for senators but not so shabby for representatives). Tack on an annual salary of $174,000.[43] Then, there are the perks, such as:

- Administrative and clerical staff allowance: $875,000 (House); $1.9–3.2 million (Senate).
- Legislative staff allowance (Senate): $2.4–$3,6 million.
- Office expenses: $195,000 (House average); $129,000–$470,000 (Senate average).
- Travel allowance, based on distance home from Washington.
- Government subsidized health and life insurance.
- Franking (postage) allowance (unlimited).
- Long-distance telephone allowance.
- Recording studio.
- Automobile leasing privileges.
- Computer supplies.
- Pension plan (typical lifetime benefit with retirement at age 60 after 20 years: $1,000,000).
- Free office and airport parking.
- Richly furnished offices for senior members and secret Senate "hideaway" offices.
- House and Senate gymnasium, staffed by physical therapists.
- House Child Care Center.
- Subsidized haircuts (Senate only).
- Subsidized House and Senate restaurant privileges.[44]

It's hard to put an exact figure on the salary and benefits a member receives because a lot depends on sliding scales adjusted by the distance a member has to travel from home or by the population of a senator's state. But it should be pretty easy to see that service in Congress can easily return annual salary and benefits in the multi-million dollar range, along with perks that you wouldn't be able to find in most other jobs.

These numbers have been growing steadily over the last quarter century. Take the salary figures as an example. In 1990, congressional salary was $98,400, which means it increased by $75,600 in two decades. That's a steep increase in a relatively short time—and quite a change from the $6 per day members earned in the First Congress!

More importantly, much of what members get in the form of taxpayer-subsidized benefits helps them stay in office. Travel allowances enable members to return to their districts to bolster support among their primary and reelection constituencies. The "franking" privilege, which allows members to substitute their signature for postage, enables them to send newsletters to constituents at no charge—newsletters that keep constituents familiar with their members' name and accomplishments (as told from the perspective of the member, of course). Access to video and audio recording equipment enables media-savvy members to take their positions to constituents in a more visible way.

Media Access

In fact, the media-saturated environment in which all political figures operate gives members of Congress a number of opportunities to keep their images and messages in front of constituents in a way that most political challengers would find hard to match. Your representative and senators have websites where you can go to find the latest "news" about what they've been up to, packaged to present your member in the most favorable light. Websites also facilitate casework by giving constituents an easy way to make frequently asked requests.

It's worth taking a second to check out one of your representative's websites. Go to http://senate.gov and click on "find your senators" to locate the senators form your home state. If you're not from the United States, you could select the state your school is in, or any state you like. Click on their name and you'll be directed right to their website. Take a minute to look around, especially at the way they present themselves. What's your reaction?

A few years ago, congressional websites were new commodities. Around the same time, some members began communicating with their constituents through email. Today, social networking media have also reached Congress. You shouldn't be too surprised if your member has a Facebook page or tweets his or her activities. Some members periodically post diaries on political weblogs that cater to readers who share their philosophical views. These activities permit members to stay in touch with their more politically tuned-in constituents in a way that wasn't possible just a few years ago.

At the same time, Members of Congress still rely heavily on conventional media. By virtue of their position in Congress, members are newsworthy and can command the attention of local radio and television in their districts with little effort. Depending on the news agenda and their seniority, members can have easy access to national media as well, although the national press often gravitates to members based on their seniority and expertise. Committee chairs presiding over an issue in the news will find themselves in demand, as will members of the leadership of both parties and practically any senator regardless of the story. Chairs or leaders who call press conferences to discuss an issue will certainly get coverage.

Everyone in Congress can take advantage of C-SPAN, the cable service that provides coverage of floor debate and key hearings on three channels operating 24/7. If a member wants to make points with the folks back home, a two-minute appearance from the floor of the House or Senate broadcast on C-SPAN offers an opportunity that wasn't available to earlier generations.[45]

The value of all this media attention rests with the ability it gives members to publicize themselves and their actions. Members naturally want to claim credit for doing things they know their constituents will support, and the media (supplemented by member websites and newsletters) provide a natural way to do this. Leaders want to do the same thing for their party and will use the media to communicate whatever messages they feel give them an advantage over their adversaries, even to the point of staging media events to draw attention to their message.

The Incumbency Advantage

Although it's difficult to pin the reelection advantage incumbents have on the fact that they have perks that tilt the electoral playing field strongly in their direction, it's not difficult to see how an incumbent's resources can be used to get the better of potential competition. Members use perks to personalize their office in an attempt to make reelection contests a judgment on them as someone constituents have come to recognize, feel comfortable with, and relate to as their representative in Washington. With people feeling weaker partisan attachments than in the past, it's a strategy that makes sense.

The one thing that is clear is that competitive elections—especially in the House—are going the way of the Tyrannosaurus Rex. Even though two of the last three congressional elections saw a change in the party controlling the House, incumbents are nonetheless being reelected in higher numbers than ever and, in many cases, by higher margins. During the last two decades of the twentieth century, incumbent House members were reelected on average 90 percent of the time, a figure that's notably higher than it was during the previous two decades.[46] In 2002, Democrats needed only to claim seven seats in the 435-seat House to win the majority. It should have been easy to do with every seat in contention. They were unsuccessful, though, in part because close to four hundred of those contests were over before they began, with the incumbent party virtually assured of remaining in power.[47]

In addition to incumbents strategically using the perks of office to personalize elections, other possible explanations for this strong incumbency advantage are the decline of strong challengers and the redrawing of more district lines to keep them safe for the party in power. Looming over everything is money. PAC money flows more freely to those who hold the reigns of power than to those who wish to replace them, and Chapter 8 showed us just how much money now floods the political system.

Incumbents overall are able to far out-raise their challengers—in some cases, acting preemptively to raise so much money well in advance of the election that strong challengers never make the race. Challengers looking at an incumbent with name recognition, access to the perks of office, and a huge wallet are acting rationally if they think they'll never be able to catch up, and in the process, never be able to communicate their message and structure the agenda of the race. (This also explains the reason why both parties have recently looked to wealthy candidates who can self-finance campaigns against incumbents.)

The ability to raise large sums of money has a darker side. Members know they have to raise money to maintain their advantage, and they have to raise it in large quantities as campaign costs are high and continue to soar higher. Imagine serving in the House and having to run for reelection every two years. You'd never be done with your fund-raising. Senators have six years between contests but have to run statewide—a more expensive proposition, except in small states.

Money may be easy to come by, but members still have to ask for it. Some find the process distasteful. If you think about it for a second, no matter how big your ego or how much you feel you're worth it, many people cannot glide easily into a room filled with strangers, give a five- or ten-minute presentation about how important their reelection is to everyone in attendance, and then ask for large sums of cash.

Herein lies a key dilemma of twenty-first century legislative politics. Members of Congress are showered with perks. They have power and visibility. Once elected, the likelihood of keeping their job is greater than at any time in memory.

But the job has become more distasteful than ever before.

Between constant fund-raising, intense partisan bickering, endless casework, and long hours away from home and family, members can be forgiven for wondering whether the demands of such a seemingly glamorous occupation are worth it. In an era when it is more possible than ever to make a long career out of serving in the national legislature, it's not unusual for members to ask themselves whether it pays to serve.

Would you stay? It's a difficult question to answer if you've never put in the effort to run for office, just like it's hard for you to say if you'd go to college again until you've been through it once. It might seem easy to say no to staying in Congress, but if you were elected to one term in the House, you have already spent two years campaigning and raising money before you were sworn in, and another two years in office doing more campaigning and raising more money for your anticipated reelection campaign. That's four years of campaign work in order to serve two years in office. It's hard to walk away from an investment like that.

So, while some walk away, many stay despite the complaints—and some of them strive for higher office. For those who see elected office as a career, an eye is often turned to the next level of the political food chain. House members with long-term ambitions will wait for a Senate seat to become vacant. Many senators look in the mirror at some point in their careers and see a future president.

And why not? Even though the Constitution makes Congress the centerpiece of the political establishment, in the contemporary world no one is more visible than the American president. As an office, the presidency is quite different from Congress—less deliberative, less collaborative, and far more dependent on the actions and even the personality of one individual. It's also hard to make a successful bid for the presidency from Congress, even though so many members have tried. In this regard, Barack Obama is the exception to the rule. Given the huge differences between the two offices, maybe it's not surprising that only Obama, John F. Kennedy and Warren Harding successfully made the move down Pennsylvania Avenue to the White

House. Let's turn to Chapter 10 and see what they found waiting for them when they got there.

Chapter Review

People tend to hold negative opinions of Congress but positive opinions about their representative, which in some ways, is fitting for an institution that in recent years has become much more personalized. Before you can get to Congress, you have to run for election, and the way House district lines are drawn is a political matter that can dramatically influence who wins elections (senators, elected statewide, don't face this issue). Gerrymandering is the process of drawing district lines for political purposes, to bolster the prospects of one party at the expense of the other.

With the high cost of campaigning, wealthy candidates who can finance their own race have become popular in recent years. Although women have been elected to Congress in larger numbers than ever before, members are still overwhelmingly male. Most members of Congress are white, college-educated professionals.

Like any institution, Congress has informal norms of behavior that members learn as they become familiar with the institution. Congressional norms emphasize flexibility, compromise, and civility—qualities that might not arise spontaneously in the often-contentious legislative environment.

The House and the Senate are organized differently, with the House less likely to tolerate minority dissent. Where the House places strict limits on debate, the Senate is respectful of the individual wishes of its members to the point that a single senator can filibuster legislation unless sixty colleagues vote to terminate debate. Both houses are organized around standing committees and subcommittees that hold hearings on legislative matters. Among the important functions Congress performs are writing an annual federal budget and overseeing the actions of the bureaucracy. The Senate confirms presidential appointments, and both houses play a role in the impeachment of federal officials.

A parallel leadership structure is in place in both chambers, with the majority party responsible for determining the legislative agenda and chairing committees. The leader of the majority party in the House is the Speaker, who presides over the chamber. The vice president of the United States presides over the Senate, but this is largely a ceremonial role with the important exception of being able to cast tie-breaking votes. Both parties have leaders and whips. With few exceptions, committee leadership is determined by seniority.

Members of Congress face an intense legislative workload and the responsibility for handling constituent problems. Staff members help manage the work, but members still rely on shortcuts like cue taking from other members to figure out how to vote on a wide range of issues they know nothing about. Voting is a particularly important concern for members, who need to avoid casting a string of votes against different constituent groups, who might oppose them in the next election.

Members tend not to see their district as a uniform entity, instead focusing their energy on maintaining good relationships with voters they believe are most likely to renominate and reelect them. It can be a demanding job. For all the perks of office that give incumbents an electoral advantage over challengers—including access to media resources that help them boost their name recognition and communicate messages to voters—the demands of casework and fund-raising can make the job a taxing one. This leads some members to walk away from public service, although many make a career out of running for and serving in Congress.

Key Terms

apprenticeship The legislative norm that says freshmen members of Congress should limit their activity and defer to senior members as they learn the ways of the institution. Apprenticeship is no longer enforced in Congress.

appropriations Legislation permitting the government to spend money that determines how much will be spent and how it will be spent.

bicameral A legislature composed of two houses.

casework Service performed by members of Congress for constituents with individual problems or complaints that they would like the government to address.

cloture The procedure for ending a filibuster. A cloture vote requires a 60 percent majority of the Senate.

committee chair The member of Congress responsible for running a committee, who can have great influence over the committee agenda and, by extension, the legislative process.

compromise A form of reciprocity in which members of Congress exhibit flexibility over their legislative objectives in exchange for future flexibility from their colleagues.

Conference committees Committees made up of members of both houses of Congress, assembled when the House and Senate pass different versions of the same legislation. If the conference committee can iron out the differences, a compromise version of the legislation is sent back to both houses for final passage. If it cannot arrive at a compromise, the legislation dies.

Congressional Budget and Impoundment Control Act of 1974 An act designed to centralize the congressional budgeting process, which established current procedures and timetables for writing a budget.

constituents Individuals living in a district represented by an elected official.

courtesy The legislative norm that members of Congress should treat each other with respect and avoid personal attacks, regardless of how much they may disagree.

cue taking Looking to other members of Congress for guidelines on how to cast a vote on a technical or unfamiliar matter.

delegate A philosophy of representation that says officials are elected to carry out constituent interests, even when these interests conflict with what the representative believes is the right thing to do.

discharge petition A House procedure that forces a floor vote on legislation stalled in committee. To succeed, a discharge petition must be signed by half the House membership.

elitism The theory that government responds to a small, stable, centralized hierarchy of corporate and academic leaders, military chiefs, people who own big media outlets, and members of a permanent government bureaucracy. People who subscribe to this position believe the actions of regular citizens, like voting and joining groups, simply mask the real power exercised by elites.

enumerated powers Powers directly granted to Congress by the Constitution.

filibuster The strategy available to senators to delay or derail legislation by refusing to relinquish their time on the Senate floor. The filibuster is possible only in the Senate, where rules permit unlimited time for debate.

gerrymandering Drawing district lines in a way that favors the electoral prospects of the party in power.

home style The way legislators approach constituents, determined partly by how they size up their support in the district.

impeachment The power granted to Congress to remove from office the president, vice president, judges, and other federal officials.

implied powers The broad constitutional grant of power to Congress that allows it to make all the laws that are "necessary and proper" to carry out its enumerated functions.

incumbent An official presently serving in office.

institutional patriotism The legislative norm that precludes members of Congress from acting or speaking in ways that would discredit the institution.

integrity A key component of reciprocity in which members of Congress are expected to keep their word with each other and honor their commitments.

iron triangle The ongoing, mutually beneficial relationship among an interest group, members of Congress sharing the interest group's objectives, and bureaucrats in federal agencies responsible for carrying out legislation pertaining to the interest group's field. Iron triangles can develop in any policy area, and many distinct iron-triangle relationships form because the federal government is responsible for a large number of policies.

joint committees Committees composed of members of the House and Senate that consider matters of interest to both houses.

legislative work The legislative norm that members of Congress should stay on top of the work required by the committee that deals with their area of specialization.

logrolling A form of reciprocity in which members of Congress exhibit mutual cooperation for each other's pet projects.

majoritarian principle Procedures, such as those in place in the House of Representatives, that limit the ability of the minority party to influence the shape of legislation or the direction of the legislative agenda.

majority leader The number-two leadership position in the House of Representatives and the number-one leadership position in the Senate. In the House, the majority leader is the chief assistant to the Speaker; in the Senate, the majority leader is the chief leader on a par with the House Speaker.

majority whip The number-three leadership position in the House of Representatives and the number-two leadership position in the Senate. In both instances, the whip is responsible for mobilizing party members to support the leadership on key issues.

minority leader The number-one leadership position for the opposition party in the House of Representatives and Senate, whose responsibilities mirror those of the majority leader but without the ability to set or advance the legislative agenda.

minority rights Procedures, such as those in place in the Senate, that permit members of the minority party the opportunity to resist legislative actions they oppose.

minority whip The number-two leadership position for the opposition party in the House of Representatives and Senate, whose responsibilities mirror those of the majority whip.

name recognition An informal measure of how much the public is aware of a candidate or elected official, based on how widely people are able to identify who the candidate or official is.

newsworthy The conditions under which a story warrants publication or dissemination, based on a set of values applied by newspaper editors and television producers. Newsworthy stories typically have conflict, proximity and relevance to the audience, timeliness, and familiarity.

norms Unspoken rules of behavior that people adhere to in an institution like Congress that allow people to fit in and help the institution run smoothly.

oversight The process of congressional review of the bureaucracy.

party caucus The group of all members of a political party in the House or Senate that meets to discuss and formulate legislative priorities.

pluralism The theory that government responds to individuals through their memberships in groups, assuring that government is responsive to a wide range of voices. People who subscribe to this position believe that the wide distribution of resources in society drives the decisions government officials make.

pork barrel Wasteful or unnecessary spending that can result from logrolling. Whether something is a pork-barrel project or a valuable use of taxpayer dollars may depend on whether you stand to benefit from it.

president pro tempore The senator charged with the honorary duty of presiding over the Senate in the absence of the vice president of the United States.

racial gerrymandering Drawing district lines in a way that combines disparate populations of minority groups in order to guarantee representation by those groups in Congress.

ranking minority member The minority party counterpart to the committee chair, but without the power to influence the direction of the committee.

recess appointments The constitutional power granted to the president to make nominations while Congress is out of session that do not require Senate approval. The appointments stand until the end of the congressional term.

reciprocity The legislative norm that encourages members of Congress to support each other's initiatives, even if there is no direct political benefit in doing so.

reconciliation A procedure in the budget-writing process, whereby appropriations made in a number of congressional committees and subcommittees need to be brought in line with spending targets established early in the process.

redistricting The process by which congressional districts are redrawn every ten years following the release of new census data.

responsible parties Political parties whose legislative members act in concert, taking clear positions on issues and voting as a unit in accordance with their stated positions.

Rules Committee The committee of the House that channels legislation to the floor for debate and a vote on passage.

select committee A House or Senate committee established on a temporary basis to review a specific matter. Typically, select committees make recommendations but do not move legislation.

seniority The custom of awarding committee chairs on the basis of length of service.

Speaker of the House The leader of the majority party in the House of Representatives who exercises control over the operation of that branch through formal and informal means.

specialization The legislative norm that members of Congress should become experts in a legislative field.

standing committees Permanent congressional committees that handle matters related to a specific legislative topic.

subcommittees Subunits of standing committees that do the detail work involved in writing legislation.

substantive representation The ability of a legislator to represent the agenda or interests of a group to which he or she does not personally belong.

trustee A philosophy of representation that says officials are elected for their wisdom and to exercise their judgment of the national interest, even when it is at odds with their constituents' wishes.

Resources

You might be interested in examining some of what the following authors have said about the topics we've been discussing:

Davidson, Roger H., and Walter J. Oleszek. *Congress and Its Members*, 12th ed. Washington, DC: CQ Press, 2009. A comprehensive overview of topics relating to the operation of Congress, including congressional structure, leadership, and decision making.

Dodd, Lawrence C., and Bruce I. Oppenheimer, eds. *Congress Reconsidered*, 9th ed. Washington, DC: CQ Press, 2008. A selection of essays covering a variety of topics related to the operation of Congress.

Fenno, Richard F. *Home Style: House Members in Their Districts*. New York: Longman, 2009. The author traveled with members of Congress to see how they approach their constituents as they work for reelection.

Kingdon, John W. *Congressmen's Voting Decisions*, 3rd ed. Ann Arbor, MI: University of Michigan Press, 1992. A pioneering study of how members of Congress decide to vote.

Margolies-Mezvinsky, Marjorie. *A Woman's Place: The Freshmen Women Who Changed the Face of Congress*. New York: Crown Publishers, 1994. A former member of Congress discusses how the institution was changed by the largest influx of female representatives in its history.

Ornstein, Norman J., Thomas E. Mann, and Michael J. Malbin. *Vital Statistics on Congress, 2008*. Washington, DC: Brookings Institution Press, 2008. A thorough source of data on Congress.

You may also be interested in looking at your senators' websites. Go to www.senate.gov and enter your home state in the "Find Your Senators" window in the upper-right. Check out your home state senators' voting records, personal backgrounds, and other information. You can also view the Senate floor schedule, recent vote results, and Senate news.

Notes

1. "A Year Out, Widespread Anti-Incumbent Sentiment," The Pew Research Center for the People and the Press, November 11, 2009, at: http://people-press.org/report/561/anti-incumbent-sentiment.
2. Ibid.
3. States can even gain population and lose seats if their growth was slower than population growth in other states.
4. Roger H. Davidson and Walter J. Oleszek, *Congress and Its Members*, 7th ed. (Washington, DC: CQ Press, 2000), 48–49.
5. Ibid.
6. Situations like this are rare, even during redistricting periods.
7. Linda L. Fowler, *Candidates, Congress, and the American Democracy* (Ann Arbor, MI: University of Michigan Press, 1993), 84–87.
8. Davidson and Oleszek, *Congress and Its Members*, 53–56.
9. Ibid., 56–59. The central cases were *Shaw v. Reno* 509 US 630 (1993) and *Miller v. Johnson* 515 US 900 (1995).
10. Davidson and Oleszek, *Congress and Its Members*, 64–69.
11. Hannah Pitkin, *The Concept of Representation* (Berkeley, CA: University of California Press, 1967).
12. Marjorie Margolies-Mezvinsky, *A Woman's Place: The Freshmen Women Who Changed the Face of Congress* (New York: Crown Publishers, 1994), 35. The member this happened to is Representative Jennifer Dunn, a Washington State Republican.
13. Sure, people roll logs down rivers. Check out http://uslogrolling.com/. The origin of the term, though, is believed to be in the nineteenth century custom of neighbors cooperatively rolling logs to build a fire.
14. David W. Rhode, Norman J. Ornstein, and Robert L. Peabody, "Political Change and Legislative Norms in the U.S. Senate, 1957–1974," in Glenn R. Parker (ed.), *Studies of Congress* (Washington, DC: CQ Press, 1985), 151; emphasis in original.
15. Burdett Loomis, *The New American Politician* (New York: Basic Books, 1988), 6–19.
16. David W. Rhode, Norman J. Ornstein, and Robert L. Peabody, "Political Change and Legislative Norms in the U.S. Senate, 1957–1974," in Glenn R. Parker (ed.), *Studies of Congress* (Washington, DC: CQ Press, 1985), 181–184.
17. Barbara Sinclair, *Unorthodox Lawmaking: New Legislative Processes in the U.S. Congress* (Washington, DC: CQ Press, 1997), 5–6.
18. Davidson and Oleszek, *Congress and Its Members*, 205.
19. Sinclair, *Unorthodox Lawmaking*, 9–31.
20. U.S. Senate, at http://www.senate.gov/artandhistory/history/common/briefing/Filibuster_Cloture.htm.
21. U.S. Senate, at http://senate.gov/pagelayout/reference/cloture_motions/clotureCounts.htm.
22. Davidson and Oleszek, *Congress and Its Members*, 205–206.
23. Sinclair, *Unorthodox Lawmaking*, 32–50.
24. You can read about the Congressional Budget and Impoundment Control Act of 1974 online at http://budget.senate.gov/democratic/commhist.html.
25. Sinclair, *Unorthodox Lawmaking*, 63–69.

26. Davidson and Oleszek, *Congress and Its Members*, 324–330.

27. Ibid., 314–317.

28. "For Obama Judicial Nominees, Confirmation is Slow Process," LATimes.com, November 16, 2009.

29. Davidson and Oleszek, *Congress and Its Members*, 328.

30. Ibid., 165.

31. Mike Viqueira, "Medicare Vote Got Surreal in House," MSNBC News, November 24, 2003.

32. Senate Republican Policy Committee, at http://rpc.senate.gov/public/.

33. Senate Democratic Steering and OutreachCommittee, at http://democrats.senate.gov/steering/index.cfm?pg=.

34. Richard Fenno, *Congressmen in Committees* (Boston: Little, Brown, 1973).

35. Christopher J. Deering and Steven S. Smith, *Committees in Congress*, 3rd ed. (Washington, DC: CQ Press, 1997), 124–182.

36. The reform measures passed by the three House committees were merged into one bill considered by the entire House, and the measures passed by the two Senate committees were merged into a separate bill considered by the entire Senate.

37. Davidson and Oleszek, *Congress and Its Members*, 153–155.

38. John W. Kingdon, *Congressmen's Voting Decisions*, 3rd ed. (Ann Arbor: University of Michigan Press, 1989), 75–96.

39. Davidson and Oleszek, *Congress and Its Members*, 279.

40. Kingdon, *Congressmen's Voting Decisions*, 29–45.

41. If you're interested in obtaining one, keep in mind that there's a charge and you should allow six weeks for delivery.

42. Fenno, *Congressmen in Committees*, 1–53.

43. As of 2009. Data from the House of Representatives, at http://www.house.gov/daily/.

44. Figures are as of 1999 and are compiled from Davidson and Oleszek, Congress and Its Members, 153–155, and the National Taxpayer's Union.

45. If you're curious about who's on C-SPAN right now, just go to their website at http://www.c-spanvideo.org/schedule.

46. Fowler, Candidates, *Congress, and the American Democracy*, 74–81.

47. The Campaign Finance Institute, at http://www.cfinst.org/.

Table, Figure and Box Notes

T1. "Texas Senate Democrats Flee Session." *Washington Post*, July 29, 2003, Sec. A.

T2. Roger H. Davidson and Walter Oleszek, *Congress and Its Members*, 7th edition (CQ Press, Washington, D.C. 1999), 130–31.

T3. Marjorie Margolies-Mezvinsky, *A Women's Place: The Freshmen Women Who Changed the Face of Congress* (New York: Crown Publishers, 1994) 38–39.

T4. Congressional Research Service, "Membership of the 111th Congress: A Profile;" and Congress.org.

T5. United States House of Representatives, at http://www.house.gov/house/Committee WWW.shtml.

T6. United States Senate, at http://senate.gov/pagelayout/reference/cloture_motions/clotureCounts.htm.

T7. Tom Grieve, "Everything You Wanted to Know About the Nuclear Option." *Salon*, May 12, 2005.

T8. United States Senate, at http://www.senate.gov/pagelayout/committees/d_three_sections_with_teasers/committees_home.htm.

T9. Roger H. Davidson and Walter Oleszek, *Congress and Its Members*, 12th edition (CQ Press, Washington, D.C. 2009).

T10. John W. Kingdon, *Congressmen's Voting Decisions*, 3rd ed. (Ann Arbor: University of Michigan Press, 1989).

T11. Richard F. Fenno, *Home Style: House Members in Their Districts*. New York: Longman, 2009.

CHAPTER 5

 Policy Making

Domestic Policy and Policy Making

By Matthew Kerbel

Introduction

Should the government spend more money to protect the environment? In one recent survey, 52 percent of Americans said yes. What about more money for health care? That was supported by two-thirds of the population. Education? Seventy-four percent said spend more on that. Fifty-six percent want to spend more on law enforcement. About half want to spend more on Social Security.

How about taxes to pay for all these spending increases? Should taxes be raised? Hardly. Sixty-three percent of survey respondents said taxes are *too high* and should be lowered.[1]

Welcome to the world of domestic policy making, where we ask government officials to make choices on our behalf about how to spend our tax money. Collectively, the guidance we give them is a bit confusing. We want our representatives to support popular programs that benefit a lot of people, like Social Security, and spend money dealing with problems that concern a lot of us, like education and the environment. We also tend to feel we're paying *too much* in taxes and that a lot of that money gets wasted on things that government shouldn't be doing. This feeling is compounded by the fact that

we don't have the option of stipulating how we want our tax dollars spent.[2]

Things aren't any less murky when it comes to whether or how government should regulate the way we go about our lives. Many things of value, like clean drinking water, safe workplaces, and cars that don't explode on impact, won't happen without a guiding hand (or a firm shove) from government. Still, many people recoil from the idea of having government place restrictions on their freedom.

You can make the argument that domestic policies should not be the product of a popularity contest. Some programs that assist disadvantaged people, like welfare and Medicaid, are controversial because the taxpayers who support them are not the ones receiving the benefits. That may not be sufficient reason, though, to curtail them. Instead, controversial policies are best developed (or rejected) following protracted political debates about what and how much government should do to assist the needy, or fight crime, or encourage the use of fuel-efficient cars.

We'll focus our attention on those debates because they represent the place where we can have the most influence over the political process. We'll emphasize two controversial types of domestic policy, where the decisions we make define what we're like as a society. The first is regulatory policy, which revolves around issues of how much the government should intervene in the operation of free markets. The second is social welfare policy, which you may be surprised to find is about a lot more than simply helping people in need. We'll also look at the budgetary process and discuss federal taxing and spending policies—two political buzzwords that are often heard in domestic political debates.

Regulatory Policies

If everything the free market produced were beneficial for society, we wouldn't be talking about government managing private affairs, but the quest to maximize self-interest can have undesirable consequences for society as a whole. If you run a manufacturing plant where the cheapest way for you to dispose of industrial waste is to dump it in the river, you're probably going to do it unless someone stops you. If you run an airline and decide you want to fly from Denver to Cleveland, imagine the danger and confusion that would result if you just started flying jets without regard to who else might be sharing the skies.

This is where government steps in with **regulatory policies** designed to maximize benefits or minimize hazards that private enterprise alone will not address.

There are several reasons why government might regulate private activity:

- The market can cause confusion that undermines the public interest.
- The market may not give consumers important, beneficial information that could influence their choices.
- The market may produce undesirable personal outcomes.
- The market may produce undesirable social outcomes.

Let's look at each of these possibilities.

Serving the Public Interest

Let's say you wanted to operate a television station in Salt Lake City. You have the necessary financing, so you proceed to put in place the hardware you'll need to set up your station. To give yourself the best possible market position, you'll of course want to broadcast on the most desirable frequency. No doubt, so will your competition. If you and the others were to go ahead and start broadcasting without regard to one another, the result would be chaotic. You know this, of course, and so do your competitors, but why should you be the one to back off and take a less desirable frequency?

Enter government and the requirement that you have to apply for a license before you operate a television station. The Communications Act of 1934 protected the broadcast spectrum as a public resource and established the Federal Communications Commission (FCC) to issue public licenses to private organizations wishing to operate radio and television frequencies.

With the authority to regulate the airwaves by granting broadcasting licenses, the federal government can hold broadcasters to a set of standards that promote the "public interest." If protection against monopoly control of the media is considered to be in the public interest, as it was through the 1980s, the FCC can place limits on the number of licenses it will grant to a single corporation that wants to operate multiple television and radio stations in a given city. If public affairs programming is considered to be in the public interest, the FCC can require that television and radio stations devote a percentage of their broadcast time to news and information programs as a condition of keeping their license. If increased minority ownership of broadcast outlets is considered to be in the public interest, as it has been in recent years, the FCC can give licensing priority to minority-run organizations.[3]

As with any domestic policy, regulation produces winners and losers. When the government regulates in the effort to serve the public interest by determining who can provide a public service like operating a broadcast outlet, winners and losers are narrowly constrained to those elite groups—for instance, broadcast organizations—that apply for government licenses. This type of regulation is called a **competitive regulatory policy** because not every applicant to operate a television or radio station will be granted a license (of course, a corporation denied a license to broadcast in one city can apply to broadcast in another). As part of its regulatory function, a regulatory agency can assess applicants against established "public interest" standards, and decide which applications will be approved.

Providing Beneficial Information

Do you smoke cigarettes? Even if you don't, you're probably familiar with the warning label that appears on every pack, informing you of the risks of smoking. Warning labels have appeared on cigarettes in some form since the 1960s, when cigarette manufacturers were required to publish the qualified message that "cigarette smoking may be hazardous to your health." The tobacco industry opposed the move to tag their product as a health risk, but Congress authorized the labels under its obligation to notify the public about product hazards

once evidence began to mount that cigarette smoking might be linked to health problems. Their intent was to keep cigarettes on the market but to notify smokers that using them could be risky, in order to give consumers the information they would need to make an informed purchasing decision.[4]

This type of **protective regulatory policy** comes into play when government officials decide the public is best served by being provided with information that would not be supplied voluntarily by manufacturers or service providers. In the case of cigarettes, the requirement to instruct the public about smoking perils falls far short of a policy that would prohibit the sale of cigarettes entirely, resting instead on the principle that consumers can make intelligent purchasing decisions provided they are informed about potential product risks.

Similar logic guides the requirement that food products carry nutrition fact labels, which state how much fat, sodium, cholesterol, and the like is contained in a serving of every packaged item you can find on supermarket shelves. Regulations stipulate that product servings have to be standardized for ease of comparison and dictate the standards a product has to meet before it can be

DEMYSTIFYING GOVERNMENT

GOT MILK?

In 1998, the Food and Drug Administration (FDA) issued new regulatory guidelines to standardize the use of the terms "fat free," "reduced fat," and "low fat" in food products. The move was designed to make it easier for shoppers to know exactly what they were getting when they bought an item, and to compare the fat content of that item with other products.

The change had the effect of replacing some old, familiar terms with new ones. Take the case of milk labeling. The new FDA regulations provided that:

- "Skim milk" would be known as "fat-free milk." It may also be called "nonfat" milk.
- "Two percent fat-free milk" would be known as "reduced fat milk."
- "One percent fat-free milk" would be known as "low-fat milk." It may also be called "light milk."
- "Whole milk" would be known as ... "whole milk."[T1]

Got that?

designated "low fat" or "fat free" (see Demystifying Government: Got Milk?).

Some beneficial information is regulated so that business competition is carried out in an open environment. The Securities and Exchange Commission (SEC) has a long list of requirements for establishing public access to investment information. For instance, if you look for a home loan one day, you'll find that all lending institutions need to make their rates public. That protects you by making sure you've got access to the full range of information you need to find the best terms for your loan.

Preventing Undesirable Personal Outcomes

Some of our most far-reaching labor laws were protective regulatory provisions that emerged out of the sweatshop conditions found in many industrial facilities during the early part of the last century. Child labor, long a fixture in agrarian, nineteenth-century America, took on a gruesome quality as children as young as six years old would perform factory work for up to thirteen hours a day. Adults and children alike had no choice but to work for measly wages in dirty and often unsafe factories. Today, we would consider these circumstances unthinkable, but at the time, they were the natural outgrowth of an industrial market that required a lot of cheap labor.

It wasn't until 1938 that Congress passed the Fair Labor Standards Act, which imposed meaningful regulations on such things as child labor and compensation. Among other things, it established a minimum wage, overtime pay for long hours, and a minimum age of sixteen for entering the nonagricultural labor force.[5] As a consequence of federal regulation, things we take for granted as being fundamental to the structure of the contemporary workplace—like guaranteed minimum pay, overtime, and safe working conditions—have become commonplace.

Preventing Undesirable Social Outcomes

An unregulated market can also produce conditions that are harmful or undesirable to society. The pressure to maximize profits can make cutting corners an attractive option to some companies, provided they don't go too far and undermine public confidence in their products. When producers make decisions about how unsafe to make a product, the temptation remains to push the limits too far, with the consequences being dangerous consumer products, unhealthy food, and unsafe drugs.

The rationale behind imposing government safety standards on everything from kitchens in restaurants to the construction of automobiles is to take safety decisions out of the hands of those who supply goods and services, who must bear the cost of making their products safer, and put them in the hands of government regulators who are positioned to think about the public interest rather than profitability. The next time you hear about a product recall or a restaurant that was shut down for health violations, you'll know it's because of a violation of regulatory guidelines that may not have been picked up if the manufacturer or restaurant had been permitted to self-police.

Regulations also require manufacturers to assume the cost of the unwanted by-products of production that would otherwise be passed along to everyone in the form of pollution. Environmental contamination produced by factory exhaust, toxic waste, and water pollution is a collective problem without a natural market solution. It's rational for producers to forego the often considerable cost and effort of environmental cleanup if they can. Regulatory policies requiring industrial polluters to constrain or repair environmental damage impose a form of social responsibility on industries that otherwise would, out of self-interest, exercise the liberty to avoid or ignore these costs. Essentially, government regulations coerce producers to pay the social costs of doing business rather than permit that cost to be passed on to society.

How Much Regulation?

Regulations can be controversial, and you can probably see why. If you're the cigarette manufacturer who has to post warning labels that encourage people not to buy your product or the industrial plant that has to pick up the cost of antipollution devices, you're likely to balk at government regulations. Even if you're not, you may find yourself averse to the idea of regulation. The public has decidedly mixed attitudes toward regulatory policies. We generally want the benefits of clean air and safe food, but many people experience regulatory restrictions as unwelcome government interference—an attitude rooted in our fundamental embrace of liberty.

So environmental interest groups make a popular case when they argue in support of regulatory policies that would promote clean air and water, while former President Bush also would get applause when he advocated fewer government regulations. You may even be philosophically inclined toward regulation in general but oppose particular regulations that are personally burdensome. A supporter of clean air who rides a bicycle to work is likely to be more supportive of a $2-per-gallon gasoline tax designed to regulate automobile use than is an environmentalist in an SUV. Your position on regulatory matters may well come down to whether you benefit more than you pay.

Some people don't object to the cost or philosophy of regulation so much as they have a problem with the way regulations are made and the sometimes undesirable effects they have. Their complaints have more to do with regulations that misunderstand and therefore fail to treat the problems they're designed to regulate, and with unintended side effects of regulations.

Take the example of a thirty-five-page Environmental Protection Agency regulation that required oil refineries to filter smokestacks for the pollutant benzene. An Amoco refinery in Virginia complied with the regulation at a cost of $31 million, only to find that their investment did virtually nothing to cut down on the benzene being emitted by the plant. That was because the pollution was coming from fumes escaping from gasoline being pumped into barges on the loading docks. The regulation missed this simple point.[6]

There are plenty of other examples available to anyone who wants to make the case that regulations written in Washington run the risk of missing what's going on in the places where they are to be implemented. Critics point to such things as the unanticipated consequences of regulations designed to scrub toxic waste from land to be reused for industrial purposes. To avoid the expense of complying with this requirement, industries rationally seek to locate on clean sites further away from highly developed urban areas. To reach them, workers have to spend more time in their cars. The result: more pollution.[7]

Critics of regulatory policies sometimes object to the process by which regulations are developed and implemented. They see individual initiative being hamstrung by rules written by lawyers, and feel the evils that regulations are designed to address could be fought more successfully by the commonsense insights of those who are close to the problem.[8]

Some regulatory costs and benefits are intangible, leaving decisions about whether to regulate open to nonmonetary considerations. The question of whether to open the Arctic National Wildlife Reserve in Alaska to oil drilling is a sensitive issue that pits regulatory tendencies against free-market interests over a course of action that's filled with intangibles. Read on for a discussion of the matter in Issue: Environment vs. Oil.

Distributive Policies

Regulatory policies are controversial because they create clear winners and losers, and because they invoke the debate over how much government should do to manage private affairs. **Distributive policies** are much less contentious. They entail spending tax dollars on a large host of items that individually benefit specific constituencies but, when taken collectively, offer something for just about everyone. This makes it hard to identify true winners and losers, inasmuch as the costs and benefits of distributive policy are spread around, and easy to make the claim that, in

ISSUE

Environment vs. Oil

In the farthest reaches of northeastern Alaska, beyond the majestic mountains of the Brooks Range, lies 19 million acres of wilderness called the Arctic National Wildlife Refuge (ANWR). Most Americans will never see it, but it's home to over 160 species of birds, 36 types of land mammals, and a wide assortment of marine life sharing what the U.S. Fish and Wildlife Service says is "among the most complete, pristine, and undisturbed ecosystems on earth."[T3] Wandering caribou share the land with musk oxen, grizzly bears, and wolverines; snow geese and golden eagles dot the horizon. Coastal lagoons, tundra, boreal forests, and snow-capped mountains create an unmatched habitat that supports the rich diversity of wildlife. It is home to the Gwich'in people, who sustain themselves with food and clothing provided by the caribou of the Porcupine River and sustain their culture through intricate links to the coastal plain, which is their sacred ground. All have lived under the protection of the U.S. government, which has maintained the refuge under the direction of the Department of the Interior and has protected it from development.

None of this would be controversial if the Arctic National Wildlife Refuge wasn't sitting on top of a large deposit of oil. Americans, of course, depend heavily on oil to sustain themselves and their culture. Each year Americans consume two and one-half times more energy per capita than Europe and Japan[T4]—one-third of the world's oil consumption goes to meet the needs of 5 percent of the world's population. [T5] Although there are productive sources of domestic oil, including Prudhoe Bay in Alaska, America cannot maintain its level of energy consumption without foreign imports, including oil purchased from politically volatile regions like the Middle East. In an era when Americans face the prospect of terrorism from groups that are active in the same parts of the world that supply foreign oil, the prospect of becoming less dependent on overseas oil supplies becomes more pressing and appealing.

In the wake of the attacks of September 11, 2001, President Bush made the argument that the United States would become more energy self-sufficient by drilling for oil in the Arctic Refuge. Legislation to do so was approved by the House of Representatives in 2001 before dying in the Senate,[T6] but the idea never fully disappeared. John McCain made oil drilling a key component of his campaign's energy plan, and his running mate, Alaska Governor Sarah Palin, was supportive of drilling in ANWR. But should we do it? What are the risks? Would it yield the benefits promised by proponents of drilling? How viable are the alternatives?

Environmental groups like the Alaska Wilderness League warn of catastrophic regional and global damage if oil-drilling equipment is permitted in the Arctic Refuge. They assert that oil drilling would destroy the delicate balance of the regional ecosystem by altering the historic migratory patterns of birds and land animals, threatening species that are dependent on them, and destroying the habitat that sustains the Gwich'in people. The potential for damage from oil spills and drilling-induced temperature increases have environmentalists fearing an epic disaster that could lead to the disappearance of wildlife, lakes, and forests as the permafrost melts through the effects of accelerated climate change.[T7]

Oil interests paint a different picture. Chris Kelley, a representative of the American Petroleum Institute, told the British Broadcasting Corporation that oil drilling is now handled in a manner that's safe for the environment, pointing to the smaller size of oil rigs that can drill multiple wells from one location, minimizing the amount of land surface that's affected.[T8] In his view, the environmental risks of drilling are trivial compared to the potential benefit of having the oil.

Still, critics of drilling question whether ANWR would produce enough oil to make a dent in foreign oil dependency. They point to government reports that say there is less recoverable oil in the Arctic Refuge than once believed, like a 1995 study from the U.S. Geological Survey that sharply downgrades the amount of oil previously believed to exist in the Arctic Refuge to the point where the best estimates indicate insignificant production—far less than needed to make the United States energy self-sufficient.[T9] Journalist and environmentalist Mark Lynas writes that all the oil in ANWR would only keep American homes and industries running for half a year.[T10] A far better alternative for environmentalists

would be to encourage energy conservation measures at home. Simply improving car mileage efficiency by 3 mpg would in one year save double the amount of oil that the most optimistic projections say is under ANWR.

Oil interests dispute these claims. They say energy conservation can only be one part of a national strategy that includes looking for new sources of oil and natural gas, and that ANWR is perhaps the most promising untapped domestic source. They emphasize the benefits of additional oil drilling, which produces more jobs in the oil industry and throughout the economy from companies that do business with oil interests. They also make the point that residents of Alaska share the economic benefits of oil drilling through payments made by the state from oil royalty funds. These jobs and revenues extend to the Gwich'in, helping to compensate for whatever disruption drilling may cause in their lives.

the aggregate, everyone benefits to some degree from distributive policies.[9]

To be sure, some of what we call distributive policy is the end result of **pork-barrel** politics, but that's not to say that distributive policies are simply wasteful. Many distributive policies are **public works** projects: infrastructure development that is undertaken exclusively or predominantly by government. Many of these are built and maintained by states and localities, and include such facilities as roads, bridges, schools, hospitals, sewer systems, airports, and municipal water plants. However, the federal government supports a long list of public works projects as well, sometimes operating on its own and sometimes providing federal funds to offset the cost of state projects.

In 2009, President Obama signed a stimulus bill designed to jump-start the sagging economy by, in part, spending federal money on a host of public works projects, including:

- $1.3 billion for highway, bridge and road repairs
- $1.1 billion for airport improvements

- $8 billion for high speed rail development
- $220 million for levee repairs on the Rio Grande
- $650 million for watershed and Forest Service improvements[10]

In one way or another, we all benefit from expenditures on national infrastructure. Even if you don't drive a car, you benefit indirectly from expenditures on highways and roads whenever you buy products at a store that were shipped by truck (see Demystifying Government: Interstate Highways and the Politics of Distribution). You may never fly on a plane, but you benefit from public expenditures on airports every time you send or receive an overnight package. Because most people recognize these benefits, expenditures on distributive policies of this nature are typically easy to accept.

There are places, though, where the question of how much to spend becomes a matter of public debate. One such place is the military budget. National defense is one of the most important services provided by the government, something we all contribute to through our taxes and something

Demystifying Government

Interstate Highways and the Politics of Distribution

One of the more ambitious public works projects this country ever attempted is the Interstate Highway System, which makes it possible for you to drive from New York to San Francisco, or from Canada to Mexico, without stopping for a traffic light. The idea for an integrated system of highways dates back to the Great Depression (the 1939 New York World's Fair had an exhibit touting the "highway of the future"), but preoccupation with World War II kept plans from moving forward until years later.

The Federal-Aid Highway Act of 1944 authorized the development of a national system of interstate highways, setting the stage for future work. Half the cost of the project was to be funded with federal money, but plans were to be developed and implemented by individual state highway departments, pitting urban against rural interests over the issue of whether federal money would be allocated according to population density or the number of miles that had to be covered. Construction began in 1947, but was bogged down as states diverted federal highway money to other pressing local needs, complained that funding was too low to cover costs, or simply found federal construction guidelines to be too onerous.

The project received a major boost in 1954, as President Eisenhower committed his administration to the completion of a national highway network, couching the initiative in terms of economic need (to promote the transportation of goods and recover billions of dollars in labor lost to traffic jams), safety (to reduce highway deaths), and not insignificantly, national security (as a method of evacuating cities in the event of nuclear war). The latter point may seem ridiculous in today's post-Cold War world (or silly to anyone who's been stuck in a highway traffic jam on a holiday weekend). In the political environment of its day, however, Eisenhower's case helped break the political logjam.

It took two years for Congress to work through the contentious issues of how much the federal government would spend, how the funding would be allocated to the states, which taxes would be assessed to pay for the program, and how to calibrate a pay scale for construction workers operating in different parts of the country with widely varying wage rates. Compromises on these matters made possible the Federal-Aid Highway Act of 1956, which produced within a decade the Interstate Highway System that is now a fixture on the American landscape.[T11]

we all benefit from. Because we make it a major national priority, procurement of military items takes up a big portion of the federal budget. In fact, our military budget is the largest on earth, which leads some people to ask how much military spending we need in order to assure our security. We'll take up the issue in Chapter 16, when we talk about defense policy.

Social Welfare Policies

Possibly the most contentious domestic policy issues involve promoting social welfare. This is because social welfare policies are **redistributive policies**, where one group (such as working taxpayers) covers the costs while another group (such as the unemployed or poor) receives the benefits. Table 7.1 provides a quick overview of the major federal social welfare policies, including who's eligible for them and how they're funded.

Table 7.1. Social Welfare Policies

Policy	Who Benefits	Who Pays	How It Works
Temporary Assistance to Needy Families (TANF)	The poor	Federal taxpayers ($20.5 billion in 2008)	Federal money is provided to states through block grants for the purpose of moving welfare recipients into the workforce. Using federal guidelines, states determine eligibility and benefits.
Medicaid	The poor	Federal and state taxpayers ($330.8 billion in 2007)	Jointly funded by the federal and state governments, Medicaid provides medical services to low-income individuals and families, including the elderly and disabled.
Food Stamps	The poor	Federal taxpayers ($34.6 billion in 2008)	Recipients receive coupons that can be redeemed like cash for food in grocery stores in order to provide the means for a healthy diet. The program is run by the Federal Department of Agriculture but administered by the states.
Earned Income Tax Credit	The working poor	Federal taxpayers who do not receive the credit ($33 billion in 2008)	Low-income wage earners are eligible for a payment when they file their federal income tax return. The payment either reduces the amount of income tax owed or provides the taxpayer with a refund check that exceeds the amount of tax owed.
Supplemental Security Income (SSI)	The elderly, blind and disabled	Federal taxpayers ($45.2 billion in 2009)	Money from general tax revenues is provided in the form of monthly cash payments to eligible seniors, the blind, and disabled individuals with limited income. People who get SSI usually also get Medicaid and food stamps.
Social Security	Retired and disabled workers, regardless of income	Workers and employers, through payroll taxes ($675 billion in 2009)	Social Security provides retirement benefits in the form of monthly cash payments to workers over age 62 (full benefits kick in at age 65) who have worked a required number of years and to insured families of deceased workers. Social Security also provides disability payments to people under age 65 who cannot work because of physical or mental impairment.
Medicare	The elderly and disabled, regardless of income	Workers and employers, through payroll taxes; federal taxpayers; and Social Security recipients ($461.1 billion in 2009)	Medicare Part A provides hospital insurance to persons over 65 and the disabled, with benefits paid to participating hospitals, emergency rooms, and nursing facilities. Workers and employers support it through payroll taxes. Medicare Part B provides voluntary supplementary medical insurance, covering up to 80 percent of outpatient medical expenses in exchange for a monthly premium and a small deductible. Medicare Part C offers a subsidized private insurance alternative, and Part D offers a subsidized prescription drug benefit.
Unemployment Insurance	Unemployed people, regardless of income	Employers, through federal and state taxes (34.8 billion in 2008)	Workers who lose their jobs involuntarily and are able to work are entitled to payments to offset part of their lost wages for a temporary period of time, up to a maximum of 26 weeks in most states. Recipients pay income tax on the benefits. Each state, under the direction of the Federal Department of Labor, administers its own version of the program.

Redistributive policies sound like the same thing as distributive policies, but they are entirely different. Remember, with distributive policies, there are no clear "winners" or "losers" because the costs and benefits of distributive policies are spread around. In contrast, redistributive policies redistribute resources from one group (which bears the cost) to another (which receives the benefit).

If redistributive policies sound like an attempt to address outcome disparities, you're right, and that adds another layer to the conflict produced by having one group of "winners" and a different group of "losers." Given our historical choice of equal opportunity over equal outcomes, many Americans are uneasy with the government getting heavily involved in programs that redistribute resources, at least up to a point. Welfare, for instance, is at its most controversial when people view it as a "way of life" rather than as short-term assistance, less so when it's viewed as a way to offer greater opportunity to traditionally disadvantaged groups.

There are exceptions to this controversial quality of redistributive policies. Social Security—perhaps the most popular federal program—is redistributive. It's just that most people don't know it.

Social welfare policies usually involve making **transfer payments** from federal coffers directly to qualifying individuals. Typically, these are direct cash payments to individuals who meet the eligibility requirements for programs like unemployment compensation, veteran's pension and life insurance, Social Security, or welfare benefits. Transfer payments also take the form of food stamps and assistance for medical services offered through Medicare and Medicaid.

Social Welfare for the Poor

The chief rationale for social welfare policies that aid the disadvantaged is found in the large income disparities that exist in the United States—disparities which grew larger in the last two decades of the twentieth century. Income during this period increased for Americans across the board, but the richest group got so much richer that the poorest Americans saw their share of total income decline.

Disparities in wealth—what people own—are even greater.

In order to design government programs to assist the poor, you need a standardized definition of poverty. This is easier said than done because defining an income boundary that separates the poor from everyone else is an arbitrary exercise, no matter how or where that limit is set. The first to attempt it was a social worker named Robert Hunter, who studied the poor in America at the turn of the twentieth century and determined that an average (for those days) family of five lived in poverty if they earned less than $460 annually in industrial regions of the North, or $300 in the rural South. This was the minimum income that Hunter estimated was necessary to provide subsistence food, clothing, and shelter. To earn less than that, he said, was to live by the "same standard that a man would demand for his horses or slaves."[11]

There have been many attempts since Hunter to calculate a **poverty line**. Under a formula in use for the past two generations, the U.S. Department of Health and Human Services placed the poverty line for a family of four at $22,050 in 2009.[12] This figure does not account for people who are living just above the poverty line, who could easily slip below it through an unforeseen reversal of fortune. It also does not indicate how many of these individuals are permanently poor and how many might be able to climb above the poverty line with an improvement in their financial circumstances.

Measured against the poverty line, 43.6 million Americans, or 14.3 percent of the population, lived in poverty in 2009, up from 13.2 percent in 2008. The rate was almost double this figure for African Americans and Hispanics, and considerably higher (21 percent) among people under the age of 18. Poverty especially afflicts female-headed households severely. Regardless of whether they are white, African American, or Hispanic, women raising children without partners are more likely than any group to find themselves without the means to make ends meet.[13]

Determining who qualifies as impoverished is only part of the problem surrounding the design and administration of social welfare programs meant to aid the poor. The way you go about dealing with the effects of poverty has a lot to do with what you believe the causes of poverty to be, and on this point there is a great deal of disagreement. Is poverty the result of the actions of the impoverished or of the situation in which they find themselves? There are several schools of thought, among them:

Individual Explanations

- The poor lack the skills or motivation necessary to climb out of poverty.
- With well-paying jobs out of reach, the poor lack the motivation to get the training that would make them marketable.

Economic Explanations

- Social programs are generous enough to serve as a disincentive to finding work because they make minimum wage jobs look like an unappealing alternative to welfare.
- The economy does not produce enough well-paying jobs to employ everyone.

Cultural Explanations

- The chronically poor develop a "culture of poverty" apart from mainstream culture, in which initiative and hard work are not valued.[14]

These arguments tend to divide along ideological lines. Conservatives traditionally attributed poverty to the personal characteristics of the poor, whose perceived lack of personal skills or motivation is reinforced by social programs that create a "culture of poverty" that discourages initiative. Liberals traditionally believed poverty was rooted in economics and were more likely to shy away from attributing

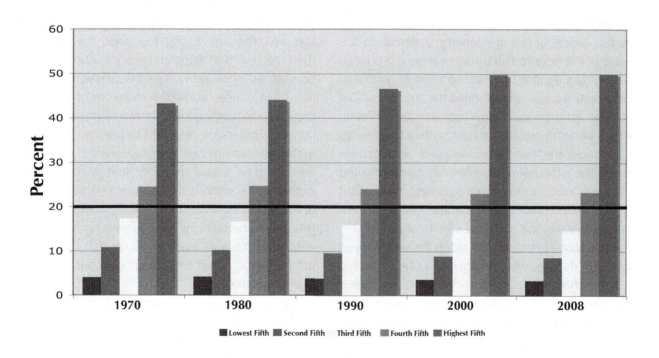

■ Lowest Fifth ■ Second Fifth ■ Third Fifth ■ Fourth Fifth ■ Highest Fifth

Figure 7.1. Income Inequality[T12]. Full income equality would mean that everyone's earnings were the same: The top one-fifth of the population would earn the same as the bottom one-fifth, so all the bars in the figure would read on the horizontal line at the decades. In 1970, the income disparity between the lowest one-fifth and the highest one-fifth of the population was roughly 11:1. This ratio remained unchanged through 1980. By 1990, though, the poorest group fell further behind, and in 2008, the disparity between richest and poorest had grown to over 14.5:1. Monumental income growth of the top five percent is one big reason for the shift. The top five percent earned 21.5% of aggregate income in 2008, up from 16.6% in 1970.

poverty to cultural attributes, while believing motivational obstacles to overcoming poverty are rooted in a lack of opportunity caused by an economy that cannot produce enough jobs for the poor.

This has caused the two groups to talk past each other. One prominent conservative social theorist called the social welfare programs of the 1960s and 1970s a "trap" that "tried to provide more for the poor and produced more poor instead"[15] by substituting handouts for hard work. Liberals responded by accusing conservative critics of trafficking in mythology about cultural, individual, and economic characteristics when they assert that success comes to those with better values and the free market is the best mechanism for creating economic winners and losers.[16]

These traditional positions have shifted a bit in response to changing economic conditions. Liberals, who in the 1960s tended to blame poverty on bad economic times, were more inclined during the boom years of the 1980s and 1990s to say the changing global economy undermined the desire of the poor to find work because it produced well-paying jobs that they had no hope of attaining. Conservatives, who once derided the poor as lacking initiative, later spoke of how increasingly generous welfare benefits provided a disincentive to working. In essence, the two sides swapped perspectives on how the economy and human nature contributed to poverty, with conservatives speaking more about the economic irrationality of welfare policy and liberals emphasizing the personal effects of poverty.[17]

If this looks to you like an inconclusive and even confusing debate, you probably won't be surprised to learn that public opinion has also fluctuated considerably on the issue of how we view the poor. The moral dimension of poverty leads some to believe that the poor are unworthy of assistance. People holding this view tend to equate welfare recipients with laziness because of their perceived dependence on the state, with socially undesirable behaviors like crime and drug use, or with behaviors that disregard family values, like out-of-wedlock childbirth. Yet, these attitudes vary in prominence in the public debate about poverty, tending to receive more attention during periods when public officials talk about "getting tough" on welfare.[18]

The same uneven pattern of public opinion applies to whether people feel we spend too much money on welfare programs. From 1976 to 1996, majorities twice found welfare spending to be too high: in the late 1970s and again in the early 1990s, with a peak near 60 percent in 1994, just before federal welfare programs were overhauled. These peaks in popular opposition to welfare coincide with peaks in the number of people on welfare. So, while it's possible these fluctuations in public opinion reflect shifting attitudes toward the poor, it's also possible that attitudes toward the poor follow attitudes about the cost of public support for the poor.[19]

It's reasonable to assume that people are aware of increases in spending on social programs for the poor because transfer payments to those in need automatically increase as more people qualify for assistance. Social welfare programs are **entitlements**, meaning everyone who fits a benefit category is eligible for support. The government places a **means test** on programs aiding the poor, like Medicaid, food stamps, and Supplementary Security Income, so that as more individuals fall below the poverty line (or a similar statistical measure of eligibility), they automatically qualify for transfer payments. In contrast, programs designed to address temporary setbacks (like unemployment insurance) or support seniors (like Social Security and Medicare) are entitlements without means tests: If you become unemployed or reach the legal age designated for retirement benefits, you're eligible for those benefits regardless of whether you're rich or poor. As entitlements, social welfare policies are expensive and open-ended.

In Issue: Maintaining Welfare Reform, you can read about the history of welfare programs in the twentieth century and the welfare reform debate. The high cost of welfare payments in the early 1990s was one factor that contributed to dramatic changes in the way the federal government approaches assistance for the poor. The ascendancy of conservative arguments about the deleterious effects of welfare and the public belief that welfare programs had become too expensive also contributed to a revolution in the relationship between the government and welfare recipients, in which policy goals

ISSUE

MAINTAINING WELFARE REFORM

Welfare is among the most controversial redistributive policies in America, and in the past few years, it has been the subject of tumultuous debate and change. For the last two-thirds of the twentieth century, a key article of faith in the relationship between the government and the people has been the responsibility of the government to provide a safety net for people at the bottom of the economic ladder. By 1996, the philosophy of individual responsibility had replaced the philosophy of government protection. Proponents of that change say it has been a remarkable success. Opponents are not so sure.

Welfare policy dates back to the Great Depression. As part of the Social Security Act of 1935, the federal government established the Aid to Dependent Children program, which originally provided funds to states that wanted to assist children living in poverty. Over time, the program grew into **Aid to Families with Dependent Children** (**AFDC**), with a fixed set of eligibility rules and benefits extending to families with children living below the poverty line. Because AFDC was means-tested, anyone who met the income standard was eligible. This made AFDC an expensive redistributive program, especially during difficult economic times when more people qualified. It was expanded in the 1960s as part of President Johnson's Great Society efforts to end poverty in America, and began to function in tandem with a handful of other federal benefit programs like **food stamps** (a program to partly defray the cost of food, which was designed to combat malnutrition, not to provide welfare), Medicaid (which extended medical care to AFDC families), and the **Earned Income Tax Credit** (a 1975 addition that offers a cash supplement to low-wage earners who leave welfare for work).[T13]

In the mid-1990s, a pair of political forces emerged to produce profound changes in how the federal government approached the chronically unemployed and the working poor. In 1992, Bill Clinton campaigned for president as a centrist "new" Democrat, someone who would be willing to rethink the welfare entitlement that had been at the core of Democratic Party philosophy since Franklin D. Roosevelt. His campaign promise to "end welfare as we know it" led to a 1993 task force to explore new approaches to welfare policy followed by two years of discussions of partisan and bipartisan proposals aimed at moving welfare recipients into the workforce by modifying welfare eligibility rules.

Then in 1994, when free-market Republicans swept to power in the House for the first time in four decades, action on reforming federal welfare policies took a sharp right turn. Their proposal, detailed in the "Contract with America," emphasized using federal money as a form of transitional support to move people quickly off welfare while eliminating welfare as an entitlement.

Called the "Personal Responsibility Act," it expressed the philosophy that individuals need to take charge of their own lives and could not look for permanent government support. Opponents charged that they wanted to remove the social safety net that had been a part of the federal government's promise to our poorest citizens since the 1930s, but congressional Republicans had the momentum. With President Clinton facing reelection without having acted on welfare reform, he knew he had to accept a program that was philosophically in line with what the Republicans were offering. So, in 1996, President Clinton signed the

Personal Responsibility and Work Opportunity Reconciliation Act.

The 1996 law ended welfare as an entitlement under AFDC and replaced it with a program called **Temporary Assistance for Needy Families (TANF)**. This represented a dramatic shift in the philosophy of welfare assistance. Federal money under TANF is supplied to states in the form of a block grant, which in 2008 amounted to $39.8 billion per year, for administration by the states to welfare families. The assistance is transitional money supplied to welfare recipients for a limited time as they move off the welfare rolls and into the workforce. States have flexibility to determine eligibility for TANF assistance and to decide the conditions recipients have to meet.[T14]

Supporters say welfare reform strengthens families, ends the culture of dependency that developed among long-term welfare recipients, and moves individuals formerly on welfare toward independence and self-reliance. They point to figures showing, since 1996, declining welfare dependency and child poverty, stabilized out-of-wedlock birth rates, and rising employment rates among single mothers—and they attribute this to cultural and economic changes made possible by welfare reform.[T15] In fact, statistics show welfare cases plunged from 4.8 percent of the population when the reform measure was signed in 1996 to 2.6 percent by 1999.[T16]

However, others dispute these figures. They say statistics deflect attention from countless individual cases of hardship and adjustment difficulties. Although many people have moved from welfare to work, critics claim that many of the jobs are low-wage positions that don't offer benefits, sometimes leaving workers worse off financially than they would have been on welfare. The difference is still made up by remaining federal assistance programs like food stamps, Medicaid, and the earned income tax credit. At the same time, one-third of welfare-to-work families reported having less money to buy food, and 40 percent had trouble paying rent, mortgage, and utility bills.[T17]

Because the consequences of major changes in social policy often do not reveal themselves until many years after their inception, the debate over the success and wisdom of welfare reform continues. Welfare policy manifested by AFDC and welfare policy manifested by TANF reflect two sharply different views of America, with different ideas about whether the government should provide a uniform safety net for the poor or encourage those on assistance to find market solutions to poverty.

Arguments in Support

Several arguments are typically offered in support of welfare reform. Proponents might say:

- It represents the best of American values. Hard work and individual initiative are backbone American values that were being undermined by traditional welfare policies.
- It strengthens families. Welfare reform has been responsible for declining child poverty, fewer out-of-wedlock births, and rising employment rates among single mothers.
- It encourages self-reliance. Long-term welfare recipients leave behind a culture of dependence on federal assistance.
- It encourages innovation. Permitting states to function as laboratories for welfare-to-work policies is a creative use of federalism.
- It's recession-proof. Even in difficult economic times, states have successfully moved people off welfare and into jobs.
- It works. The number of people who have moved off welfare and into the marketplace is evidence for the success of welfare reform.

Arguments Against

Opponents of welfare reform policies might argue:

- It represents the worst American instincts. Government has a responsibility to provide at least a minimal safety net for the most needy.
- It hurts families. Many welfare-to-work families find poorly paying jobs and have trouble making ends meet.
- out entitlements like Medicaid and the earned income tax credit, welfare-to-work families would suffer even greater economic hardship.
- It encourages inequity. Permitting states latitude in the implementation of TANF creates a mix of unequal requirements.
- Boom times mask problems. As the fast economy of the late 1990s yielded to the recession of 2001, welfare claims began to rise in most states, putting a drain on strapped budgets.

- It's too soon to know if it works. Many major social changes require years to show unexpected or unintended effects.

My Opinion

When deciding your opinion on welfare reform, ask yourself if welfare reform:

- Represents the best American values or the worst American instincts.
- Strengthens or hurts families.
- Encourages self-reliance or only appears to.
- Encourages policy innovation or inequities.
- Is recession-proof or vulnerable to economic downturns.
- It works—or whether it's too soon to know.

shifted from long-term support to moving people off welfare and into the job market. You'll find that the debate over welfare reform continues to rage, with some people claiming it to be a tremendous success and others finding it merely symbolic, as they seek to return to a policy where the government guaranteed support to the most needy Americans. As you read, think about whether reforms to the welfare system should be maintained.

Social Welfare for Everyone

In an age when many people have little faith in the government to operate successful social programs, **Social Security** stands out as the great exception, as you will see when you read Issue: Privatizing Social Security. It is so popular, in fact, that some people don't realize it's a government program! Many others have no idea that it's a form of social welfare, a redistributive program that transfers resources from young to old. But it is.

Social Security provides a retirement safety net for millions of Americans regardless of need, as well as insurance payments to eligible families of deceased workers and disability payments to people who are kept from working by physical or mental

impairment. Together with the hospital and medical insurance provided to the elderly and disabled through **Medicare**, seniors and the disabled receive a level of government support that protects them from having to worry that age or injury will leave them destitute. As entitlements, Social Security and Medicare are available to all, regardless of income or wealth.

Of course, as entitlements Social Security and Medicare are open-ended government commitments, and that's at the heart of a major political debate. Our aging population and spiraling medical costs make both programs increasingly expensive. This is addressed in Issue: Privatizing Social Security, along with a controversial alternative that has been proposed to keep Social Security solvent into this century. None of the available options for fixing Social Security is particularly attractive, which makes the politics of Social Security especially contentious. As you read, try to evaluate the alternatives available for maintaining the solvency of the Social Security program, and think about the advantages and disadvantages of partial privatization of Social Security—an option that holds the promise of finding new revenues for retirees at the cost of changing the ironclad commitment of a retirement safety net.

"Corporate Welfare"

What would you call a government cash payment to large corporations that protects them from uneven market conditions? Critics call it "corporate welfare"—and those who opposed welfare reform measures made a point of contrasting what they saw as the government's generosity to business interests with its stringent treatment of welfare recipients. Supporters call it a safety net for businesses that otherwise could be unfavorably affected by circumstances they cannot control.

ISSUE

Privatizing Social Security

Social Security has been called the "third rail of politics"—touch it and you die. Created by the Social Security Act of 1935 during the Great Depression to assure a basic level of subsistence to people in their retirement years, it is arguably the most successful federal program in history. It has achieved its stated purpose and provided generations of seniors with a social safety net that has enabled them to anticipate a basic level of economic stability after retirement. Working people have come to expect that they will not have to endure sudden poverty in old age.

The irony is that Social Security is not what it appears to be. Many of us think Social Security works like a pension or retirement account where the money I we pay in to the Social Security system during our working years accumulates in value and is there for us to live on after we retire. That would make Social Security a distributive policy. But it isn't.

Social Security provides cash benefits to people who have reached retirement age, survivor benefits to immediate family members of a covered worker who dies before retirement, and disability benefits to injured workers and their families. It's all funded by a payroll tax on workers and employers, which goes into a trust fund that makes Social Security payments. The tax is automatically deducted from every eligible worker's paycheck. When a worker becomes eligible for benefits, the Social Security Trust Fund pays out. But the dollars paid out today are the dollars collected today, making Social

Security a redistributive program—essentially a welfare program that doesn't disqualify people based on need that transfers resources from the young to the old.[T19]

The fact that Social Security is a redistributive program dressed up to look like a distributive program—the separate trust fund helps recipients feel like they're getting their own money and not a handout from government coffers—makes it palatable to middle-class recipients who might otherwise object to participating in anything resembling welfare (along with Medicare, it's the reason why most social welfare spending goes to the middle class, not the poor). However, the program's structure makes Social Security sensitive to changes in population dynamics. In 1940, the first year the trust fund paid monthly benefits, 222,488 people received a combined $35 million. Since then, an explosion in the population, greater longevity, and cost of living adjustments (COLAs) made annually so payments keep pace with inflation have combined to place a tremendous strain on the system. In 2008, 50.9 million beneficiaries received a combined $615 *billion* in payments.[T20]

That's an awful lot of voters receiving an awful lot of money, hence the "third rail" problem. However, long-term demographics are not kind to Social Security, and everyone across the political spectrum recognizes that at some point modifications will have to be made to this popular program. As baby boomers have begun to retire, demand on the system has only increased, and with fewer workers to replace them, the tax base available to provide for this large batch of retirees will shrink. In 1950, when birth rates were high and life expectancy much lower than it is today, there were 16.5 workers to pay for every Social Security recipient. In 1990, each retiree was supported by 3.4 workers. By 2050, it's projected that there will be less than 2 workers to pay for every retiree—and more than one-third of those retirees is expected to be over age 80.[T21]

It's no wonder why so many people your age believe you'll never see a penny in Social Security benefits. You'll start paying Social Security taxes as soon as you start working—if you work now you already are—but opinion surveys suggest that if you're like 70 percent of eighteen-to thirty-four-year-olds, you're not confident that Social Security will be solvent when you reach retirement.[T22] It's an expression of doubt about the ability of politicians to address the problems that lie ahead.

When the system first faced the prospect of a shortfall as a result of a period of rapid inflation in the 1970s, officials addressed the situation by increasing payroll taxes slightly and cutting benefits at the margins. That was enough to keep the program solvent for a projected fifty years. Now, the fifty-year window is approaching fifteen years, and the principal choices for restoring the program this century are the same as they were in the 1970s—raise taxes, cut benefits, or push back the retirement age, making people ineligible for benefits until they're older. Not too many politicians will want to propose any of these alternatives. However, if the system is not adjusted, at some point it will run into trouble, so the discussion of how to "fix" Social Security remains a salient topic in Congress and the White House in 2011

There is one alternative to tax increases and benefit cuts, but it's controversial. What if Social Security were restructured so that it operated more like a traditional retirement account? In other words, what if some of that payroll tax money were freed up for investment so that it could potentially grow over the course of time, rather than be transferred to today's recipients? There are a number of ways to do this, with the most widely discussed involving partial privatization of the Social Security system.

Under partial privatization plans that have circulated around Washington, a percentage of Social Security taxes would be diverted to private accounts that workers would individually control. Depending on the plan, there might be limits on how it could be invested, but workers would have control over what to do with the money. Unlike the transfer payments that characterize the present program, these funds could be invested, leaving them free to rise and fall with the market. The balance of the payroll tax would continue to be used to cover transfer payments to present-day Social Security beneficiaries, but by necessity at a sharply lower level than what is currently provided.

The benefits of doing this are apparent. Over time, markets generally perform very well, and people would stand to earn more for their retirement if they were allowed to become investors. Many Americans have a natural faith in markets, and, in keeping with a deeply felt love of liberty, are willing to take chances provided they also have control over their money. To many, the risks of putting money in the market are preferable to the burden of additional taxation.

Partial privatization plans had a lot of public support in the late 1990s, when the booming stock market was providing middle-class investors with annual double-digit returns. Some people looked at the taxes they were required to pay to the Social Security Trust Fund and complained loudly that if the government would only let them invest that money, they could really make it grow.[T23] At the time, they were right. Then, when the high-tech bubble burst at the turn of the century, market forces no longer seemed so friendly, and some who had been enthusiastic about partial privatization had second thoughts, feelings only reinforced when the market crashed in 2008.

Opponents doubt that partial privatization will save money, arguing that the transition from a pay-as-you-go system to a partially private investment system would take hundreds of billions of dollars (some say as much as $1 trillion) out of present-day benefits so funds could be shifted for private investment. They fear today's retirees would bear the brunt of that cost. They also doubt that Americans would quickly abandon the psychology of a social safety net for seniors, and would resist permitting grandma and grandpa to live out in the cold because they invested poorly or suffered a market downturn at the wrong time, such as during the financial crisis of 2008. This could mean there would be political pressure for an expensive government bailout of hard-luck investors, just as the financial crisis generated intense pressure for a government bailout of banks.[T24]

Against the backdrop of deeply divided sentiment about the wisdom of partial privatization, President Bush reached for the third rail during the early months of his second term, calling on Congress to take up a measure that would have diverted a portion of Social Security funds to personal accounts. To avoid a battle over the particulars, the president refrained from discussing the details of his proposal, hoping first to line up support from congressional Republicans and a few moderate Democrats to generate momentum for what everyone knew would be a Herculean political task.

But, not one Democrat signed on and—without the promise of bipartisan cooperation—a number of Republicans refrained from committing to any plan that would alter the status quo and anger their constituents. President Bush traveled the country during the first half of 2005 trying to drum up support for partial privatization, but as people began to pay attention to the issue, public support for the president's approach eroded. By summer, the Bush Social Security plan was moribund; by fall, it was quietly shelved. Members of the president's party had decided they would rather position themselves for re-election than face political electrocution by supporting a controversial change to a popular program.

One thing both sides agree on is that partially privatizing Social Security would signal a dramatic change from the intent of the original Social Security Act. Instead of having government provide a guaranteed retirement safety net, it would only require that everyone save something for retirement, leaving everyone's bottom-line retirement package I up to the way they invest and the direction of the market. These are vastly different social commitments. When we think about which direction to take, it's important to think about the underlying promise we want government to make to us and the nature of the obligation we want to make to one another.

Arguments in Support

Multiple arguments have been made to advance the cause of partially privatizing Social Security. These include:

- It's our money. We know much better than anyone else how to invest it, and we can be responsible for what happens to our investments.
- It's better than tax hikes. Demographics indicate that in the not-too-distant future dramatic increases in costs or cuts in benefits will be needed to keep the system working. Partial privatization eliminates this ugly necessity.
- Partial privatization relieves pressure on the young. Without partial privatization, people entering or about to enter the workforce will bear the brunt of paying for the larger number of retirees that will go ahead of them, either through higher taxes or lower benefits at retirement.
- Market risk is better than political risk. People who don't have faith that politicians will effectively correct what's wrong with Social Security are willing to take a chance on

the market as long as they can maintain control over their own money.

- Partial privatization is consistent with liberty. Ours is the largest free-market economy in the world. We should have a retirement program that is consistent with the values of individual initiative and investment choice.

- Look at the stock market. During the 1990s, careful investors would have earned enough to be ahead of the game even during the downturn that followed, and over the long term, the market should outperform the fixed rate of transfer payments currently used by the Social Security system.

Arguments Against

There are as many arguments against partially privatizing Social Security as there are for endorsing it. Opponents might say:

- It's our safety net. Partial privatization would undercut the primary guarantee of retirement security for all, dramatically undermining the program's central promise and purpose.

- Retaining the present system is worth the price. It's not true that there are no alternatives apart from partial privatization that people would be willing to accept. Social Security is so popular that people would embrace a tax increase if that was what it took to keep it solvent.

- Partial privatization hurts the elderly. In order to privatize Social Security, funds presently transferred to retirees would have to be diverted for individual invest-

ment. The amount involved could total in the hundreds of billions of dollars, and that money has to come from somewhere. It's most likely to come out of present-day benefits.

- Social Security carries no risk. As structured, the Social Security system is insulated against the capriciousness of the market, it has never missed a payment, and it is popular with the American public.

- Partial privatization is at odds with social responsibility. If we come to see Social Security as an individual retirement program, we sever the collective bonds that come from providing for the whole community.

- Look at the stock market. Perhaps partial privatization looked appealing during the boom years of the 1990s, but not during the down years that followed and certainly not during the market collapse of 2008.. Sudden economic downturns can undermine the savings of people about to retire, who can't wait for years for the market to recover.

My Opinion

When registering your opinion, ask yourself if partially privatizing Social Security:

- Is about our money or our safety net
- Is better or worse than tax hikes.
- Relieves pressure on the young or hurts the elderly.
- Is or is not worth the risks.
- Is consistent with liberty or at odds with social responsibility.
- Is a good idea only when the market is doing well.

This difference of perspective is at the core of the debate over agricultural subsidies, an issue that you may be more familiar with if you live in a rural area. Agricultural subsidies don't grab national headlines, which means Congress can address them in relative anonymity. This gives interested parties greater freedom to operate behind the scenes to lobby for government support. Consequently, agricultural subsidies do not appear to be going away any time soon.

Is this a desirable thing? The matter isn't clear-cut. After you've had a chance to read about it in

Issue: Farm Aid or Corporate Welfare?, think about your opinion on the desirability of agricultural price supports and whether you believe they amount to corporate welfare.

Taxing and Spending

Apart from decisions about war and peace, writing a budget and deciding how to pay for it are the most important choices Congress and the president make. That's because budgeting drives substantive determinations about who gets what. Choices about how the tax code is structured and how money is

ISSUE

FARM AID OR CORPORATE WELFARE?

Agriculture is a risky and uncertain business. Drought, floods, temperature extremes, and other natural disasters can play havoc with this critical industry—and with the lives of people dependent on it. Government can step in to try to add an element of stability to agriculture, and has been doing so since the Depression. The Agricultural Adjustment Act of 1933 was the New Deal response to an oversupply of crops that was keeping prices low. Farmers voluntarily agreed to decrease production of such staples as corn, wheat, rice, and cotton in exchange for payments from the government. This was followed a year later by establishment of the Commodity Credit Corporation, a government corporation charged with making favorable loans to farmers in exchange for agreements to control crop production. The Agricultural Adjustment Act of 1938 introduced price supports, or payments to farmers to make up the difference for low market prices.[T26]

Farm prices rebounded as a result of these measures, and ever since, farm subsidies have been a part of domestic policy and politics. A subsidy is a government payment for which nothing is expected in return. Such payments have been used to keep farmers from producing a crop that's in abundant supply and to maintain crop price stability. Over time, they've come to

be regarded in the agricultural sector as a safety net for farmers akin to welfare for the poor and Social Security for retirees.

They are also highly controversial. In large part, that's because of the changing nature of agriculture and the way farm subsidies are allocated. In recent years, the small, independent farmer has become increasingly rare, as large corporate farms have come to dominate an industry now known as "agribusiness." Because subsidies are distributed on the type and amount of crop a farm produces, big corporate farms that produce more corn, wheat, rice, cotton, and soybeans (the most heavily subsidized crops) can claim a disproportionate share of the subsidy. Small farmers who produce these crops are only eligible for a tiny subsidy, and small farmers who produce other crops are not eligible for anything.[T27]

The result: 60 percent of farmers do not get a penny of assistance. Among the others, in 2000, 57,500 farms received subsidies of $100,000, while 150 of the largest farms surpassed $1 million.[T28] Among the top recipients were farms owned by the John Hancock Life Insurance Company, Chevron Oil, banker David Rockefeller—even basketball millionaire Scottie Pippen.[T29] You can probably see why critics call it corporate welfare.

In an effort to address this imbalance, Congress in 1996 passed the Federal Agriculture Improvement and Reform Act, which set limits on how much individual farms could receive from the federal government. However, supporters of farm subsidies argued these limits shredded the agricultural safety net—after all, 40 percent of farmers *did* receive something—and they have had enough political clout to get Congress to bypass its own limits by passing annual emergency supplemental bills every year since 1998. In 2001, supplemental farm subsidies exceeded $5.5 billion. The 2002 farm bill committed $180 billion over ten years.[T30]

Still, advocates of farm subsidies point out that the serendipitous nature of the weather is a risk that no other industry faces, making it an economic necessity for the government to regulate agricultural prices. They note that other nations do the same thing, many to a greater extent than the United States,[T31] and contend that without government laid, thousands of farmers would go under. If that happened, advocates argue that land prices would plummet, and businesses that rely on farmers would be pulled down with them. From this perspective, there is too much riding on agriculture subsidies for the government to pull them back.

Opponents counter with the argument that other industries that are just as vital to the economy and just as risky do not receive support. The weather doesn't determine the fortunes of the software industry, but try convincing people who lost everything in the "dot-com" bust that their field doesn't carry extreme risk. From this vantage point, there's no obvious reason to bolster farmers, especially as the one-time reality of the small, independent, hard-working farmer recedes into myth. Even if lifting agricultural subsidies hurts businesses that rely on income from farmers, opponents argue that the extra money in our pockets from not having to pay for agricultural relief would more than compensate for the damage to the economy.

The interesting political wrinkle in the farm-subsidy debate is that supporters cut across geographic as well as ideological and partisan lines. Big-government Democrats from rural states regularly team up with limited-government Republicans from rural states to advocate assistance for farmers. In principle, you might expect some of these supporters—those who see government as an instrument for helping the disadvantaged and those who espouse the virtues of I the free market—to oppose government aid to agribusiness. Instead, the overarching principle in play is more practical than philosophical.

Arguments in Support

Supporters of farm subsidies point to the importance of agriculture to the economy. They say:

- It's a safety net. Other social programs protect urban and suburban workers; farmers also need to protect their livelihood.
- Farming is the backbone of America. Federal dollars help farmers feed America and the world.
- Farming is unusually risky. Subsidies are necessary so that farmers can survive hazards no other industry or business has to face, like extreme weather.
- It's good for the economy. Without subsidies, farms would fail, taking farm-related industries along with them.

Arguments Against

Opponents of agricultural subsidies consider them to be a misuse of money. They claim:

- It's corporate welfare. Public money subsidizes huge corporations that successfully lobby for public money they have no right to get.
- Farming has become agribusiness. The largest outlays go to large businesses, not to small, independent farmers.

- Many businesses are risky. Singling out agriculture for assistance is arbitrary and unnecessary.
- It's bad for the economy. The money transferred to agribusiness would benefit the country far more if taxpayers invested it or spent it.

My Opinion

When considering your opinion on farm subsidies, think about the arguments supporting and opposing it. In particular, ask yourself if farm subsidies:

- Are a safety net for farmers or corporate welfare for big businesses.
- Maintain the "backbone of America" or line already-deep pockets.
- Help offset unusual risks, or arbitrarily help an industry that's no riskier than others.
- Are good or bad for the economy.

appropriated are often made out of public view. They involve a lot of small, technical, and detailed decisions. Nonetheless, they are worth paying attention to because they determine how the burden of supporting the government is distributed across economic groups and how much money is (or is not) available for government to do the things we say we want it to do. In this regard, taxing and spending decisions may be viewed as social welfare choices that determine how and how much government will redistribute wealth.

We discussed how the federal budget is drafted as part of our discussion of Congress in Chapter 9. Before moving on, you may wish to review the process, which is described in Demystifying Government: Making Budgets.

Tax Policy

It's pretty clear that most federal revenue comes from people like you and me. Here's how it breaks down:

- In 2008, the federal government raised $2,524 trillion, slightly less than half of which came from personal income taxes. That's roughly equal to 17.7 percent of **gross domestic product (GDP)**, or the combined value of all the goods and services produced by the United States in 2002.
- Another one-third of revenue ($901 billion) came from Social Insurance payroll taxes, like Social Security and Medicare taxes, unemploy-

ment insurance taxes, and federal employee retirement payments.

- Slightly more than one in ten federal dollars ($304 billion) came from corporate income tax payments. At about 2 percent of GDP, the corporate tax burden has fallen considerably over the years; it was 4.5 percent of GDP in 1955.
- Excise taxes constitute a small portion of the tax pool. These include taxes on specific products and services like alcohol, tobacco, and telephone services. Next time you look at your telephone bill, find the line that lists the federal tax owed—it's a small but regular feature of your bill.
- Other taxes include a miscellaneous group of revenues, like customs duties, estate taxes, and gift taxes.

If you're like most Americans, you probably think that income tax rates are very high. Think again: In comparison to other western nations, the United States Treasury makes relatively few demands on our bank accounts. The United States tax burden ranks second from the bottom in comparison to other industrialized nations, as Figure 7.2 attests.

Not convinced that our taxes are comparatively low? Neither are most Americans. If you were to track attitudes about the appropriate size and scope of government, you'd find that Americans rank at the top of industrialized nations in the belief that private or individual initiative is often preferable to public solutions to social problems. It's a belief with deep roots in the individualistic strains

DEMYSTIFYING GOVERNMENT

MAKING BUDGETS

If you've ever tried to save for something or figure out how you're going to spend limited funds on a bunch of needs, then you know how tricky it can be to write a budget. Add the individual wishes of hundreds of members of Congress and the president into the mix, and it shouldn't be hard to see how writing a budget is one of the most complex, sensitive, and important things Congress has to do. Members who sit on committees with a hand in budget writing find that they are rarely lonely.

Budget writing is an annual affair that typically takes an entire year to complete. A number of committees get into the act, in keeping with the decentralized way the House and Senate function. The process has been more coordinated though, ever since the passage of the **Congressional Budget and Impoundment Control Act of 1974**. A lot of the action happens in the House and Senate Appropriations Committees, which are charged with reporting bills that determine how much money government agencies and programs will have to spend (**appropriations** refer to legislation authorizing the government to spend money).

The procedure is complex, but it follows this outline: First, the House and Senate budget committees set guidelines and budgetary priorities. Then the appropriations committees are supposed to allocate money in line with those priorities. They approve spending bills to cover the variety of items in the federal budget. If the sum of these expenditures exceeds the budgetary guidelines, the expenditures are brought into line with the budget targets through a process called **reconciliation**. For both houses to end up with the same budget, differences between them are resolved in a conference committee, after which final approval on a budget can be sought in both houses.[T25]

If budget guidelines necessitate changes in tax law, the House Ways and Means Committee and the Senate Finance Committee get into the act. As the tax-writing committees of Congress, they draft legislation specifying which taxes will be raised and by how much.

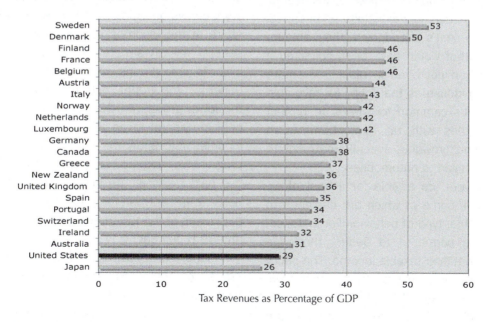

Figure 7.2. Government Tax Revenues as a Percentage of GDP [T33]

of our political culture that we discussed in Chapter 4, and it helps explain why Americans frequently feel that government takes too much of our hard-earned money, when in fact we pay less in taxes than almost anyone else.[20]

Then there's the issue of how the tax code is structured, which compounds questions about the extent of the tax burden with issues of tax equity and fairness. There is no single or obvious way to tax people. In fact, people were once taxed on the number of windows in their home, on the assumption that more windows meant greater wealth, and windows were harder to hide from the tax collector than assets like money or livestock.[21]

The way government defines what forms of wealth and income are taxable is a political matter that determines how much various social groups will have to pay. Typically, groups with more political power are able to protect their interests most effectively. At the turn of the twentieth century, when the influx of immigrants produced enormous demand for new public works projects, upper-income citizens maneuvered to have their wealth declared tax exempt out of fear that they would have to pay the bill. These efforts hit a roadblock as the Progressive movement gained steam and advanced laws taxing wealth.[22]

Even when tax laws are on the books, officials can tinker with them by creating exemptions targeted at particular groups of taxpayers. Tax exemptions are officially called tax expenditures because, from the government's standpoint, they amount to lost revenue that would have been collected if the exemption had not been in place. Corporate tax breaks go to industries that lobby for favorable treatment, and it's common for states to protect dominant industries with tax exemptions, such as North Carolina providing special treatment to tobacco and Michigan to automobiles.

Private taxpayers are eligible for a host of exemptions as well, some of which are designed to promote a particular type of behavior. For instance, homeowners are permitted to deduct mortgage interest costs from their taxable income. The policy rationale behind this tax expenditure is that it encourages home purchases by making home ownership more affordable. This, in turn, stimulates the economy through increased production of lumber and building supplies, as well as washing machines, refrigerators, and other appliances that homeowners need. Of course, it also benefits the interests of realtors and builders (who lobby to protect it), and is skewed to the upper- and middle-income taxpayers who are most likely to own homes.[23]

Some of the most expensive tax expenditures in terms of their cost to the federal treasury in 2008 were:

- Exclusion of employer health care contributions ($131 billion).
- Exclusion of employer pension contributions ($118 billion).
- Home mortgage interest deduction ($89 billion).
- Capital gains deduction ($54 billion).
- State and local tax deduction ($49 billion).
- Deductions for charitable contributions ($47 billion).
- Child credit ($28.4 billion).[24]

Tax rates are also political choices with real consequences for how much people are expected to pay. Ours is a **progressive income tax**, meaning it has a series of graduated rates that increase with one's income. (In contrast, a **regressive tax** imposes a proportionately greater burden on low-income earners. Sales taxes are regressive because a tax everyone pays on food or clothes represents a bigger share of the incomes of low-wage individuals.) In general, the tax structure is redistributive because lower income groups pay proportionately less than upper income groups, and most Americans fall into the lower groups. In 2001, one in four Americans paid no federal taxes at all because their taxable incomes fell below the lowest tax bracket on the progressive income tax scale. Another one in two paid taxes at the lowest marginal rate of 15 percent. In contrast, less than 5 percent combined paid taxes at the top three marginal rates of 31, 36, and 39.6 percent.[25]

Furthermore, although higher levels of income are taxed at higher rates, upper income people also have access to a wider range of deductions and shelters for avoiding tax payments on some of their income. When you take into account adjustments to income, the average taxpayer assessed at the 39.6 percent marginal rate (who averaged $1.1 million in income in 2001) paid 27.4 percent of his or her income in taxes.[26] Adjustments apply to lower wage earners as well. In 1996, a typical person earning between $20,000 and $30,000 paid 7.6 percent of his or her adjusted gross income in taxes. Those earning between $50,000 and $75,000 paid 12.1 percent.[27]

Not everyone is happy with this structure. In recent years, there has been discussion of replacing the progressive income tax with a **flat tax** that would operate on an entirely different set of assumptions. Issue: The Flat Tax discusses this controversial idea with a dedicated following.

ISSUE

THE FLAT TAX

Critics of our complicated tax code joke darkly that if the Internal Revenue System were put in charge of tax simplification, the entire tax form would be reduced to one line that reads, "Enter your income," next to which it would say, "Pay this amount." But advocates of a flat income tax are serious about simplifying the tax code to the point where we would have, as was once advertised on the website flat-tax.gov, "your tax return on a postcard." It sounds appealing. But is it a good idea—and is it fair?

Advocates say yes—and yes. Here's how things would change if flat tax advocates get their way. Our graduated income tax structure would disappear, meaning higher levels of income would no longer be taxed at higher rates. Gone, too, would be the deductions we talked about earlier, including popular deductions for home mortgage interest and charitable contributions, as well as tax credits for the poor and shelters that businesses and wealthy people can take advantage of to protect part of their income from being taxed.

One flat-tax plan promoted by former House Majority Leader Dick Armey would replace the present system with a single, across-the-board rate of 17 percent with almost no deductions. A certain amount of income would be entirely exempt from taxes—the Armey proposal set the floor at $36,800—meaning individuals and families

earning less than that amount would pay no taxes. Everyone else would pay a flat 17 percent on everything above $36,800, minus savings, which would not be taxed. Income derived from dividends, interest, and capital gains would no longer be taxed.

Supporters of the flat tax say it offers a number of advantages over the graduated tax system, the most significant of which are simplicity and fairness. It's remarkably simpler than the present system, which appeals to people who struggle with filling out their tax forms every year, or who have to pay considerable sums to someone to do it for them. Simplicity could benefit the overall economy as well. Without deductions, people will not be motivated to skew their spending behavior toward things that will lower their tax burden. If their choices are more natural, the argument goes, the market can operate more efficiently. Because saving money would be the one way to lower your taxable income, there would be extra incentive to put money away, which is also good for the economy.[134]

The argument about fairness comes from the fact that everyone would pay the same rate. Indeed, this is one way of understanding tax fairness: It's a view based on equality. If everyone is subject to the same tax rate, everyone will shoulder the same share of the tax burden. Some would make the additional argument that a flat tax is the best political measure for protecting individual liberty against encroachment by public officials, by creating one class of taxpayers who would be united against efforts to raise taxes or tinker with the tax code.[T35]

However, there is another way to regard fairness. Flat-tax opponents contend that the only way for the tax code to be fair is for it to consider that people live under vastly different financial circumstances. They believe people are not entirely responsible for their financial station in life, and taxation is a place where some balance can be regained. This perspective argues for a graduated system like the one we have in place, where people are taxed according to their ability to pay. Progressive income-tax structures place a proportionately greater burden on those who can most afford it, on the assumption that with greater means comes a greater share of the burden to help the poor.[T36]

This counterargument about fairness dovetails with a counterargument about simplicity. Although no one likes to pay taxes, it can be seen as a shared burden or common experience that binds us as a democracy and connects us to the political process. Taxes are the means by which we make collective choices. If we assume that the individual choices we make are somehow better or more valuable than these collective choices—an attitude implicit in the effort to minimize taxation—we can easily find ourselves minimizing government and public life. From this perspective, tax simplification puts a strain on democracy by de-emphasizing collective decisionmaking.[T37] In other words, we may not like to eat vegetables, but if we don't, we're going to harm ourselves in the long run.

Of course, there are those who oppose tax simplification because they believe it's just simplistic—that advocates promise too much when they claim the burden will be equally shared. In this regard, opponents may accept the point made by advocates that equal tax burdens are fair, but reject the premise that the flat tax will deliver. They point to the elimination of taxes on capital gains, interest, and dividends as a windfall to be realized by the wealthiest taxpayers, while everyone else simply loses deductions that had benefited them.

A couple of things make deciphering the flat-tax proposal difficult. Both sides make claims based on projections, using figures that the other side disputes. From these claims, they assert that the flat tax either will or will not burden the middle class, will or will not be good for economic growth, will or will not lead to higher wages, and will or will not spur investment. This is characteristic of many policy struggles, where both sides use figures carefully to make claims that can neither be proved nor disproved unless or until the policy is implemented (and perhaps not even then).

Also, both sides have ideological agendas that go beyond the case they make for simplification and fairness. Conservative supporters of the flat tax would like to see government spend less, and would use tax reform as a vehicle for cutting tax revenues as leverage to cut federal spending. That's why the Armey proposal would raise less revenue than what the government takes in under present tax law (he acknowledged this point in his website). Liberal supporters of the present system would like to see the tax code become more progressive, in the belief that the wealthiest Americans should be compelled to contribute disproportionately to the mutual pot. Liberals tend to regard any massive accumulation of wealth as a threat to the opportunities of people with few resources, and would not be unhappy about using tax policy to achieve greater redistribution of wealth.

So there's a lot going on here. Tax law is more than numbers: It's social policy that affects how we behave, how we spend, how we save, and how we regard America as a nation. A lot rides on that little tax-return postcard.

Arguments in Support

Numerous arguments have been made in support of the flat tax. Some of these are:

Spending Policy

If you've ever had to cover your expenses with money you've earned from working, you know what it's like to budget funds in order to make ends meet. In an ideal world, the amount of money you take in would bear some resemblance to the amount you spend. In the real world, you might have to borrow to pay for a major necessity like tuition or a car, or to afford a luxury you really want, like a spring break vacation. You might take out a loan or run up an unpaid balance on your credit card. In either case, you pay for having additional funds now by making interest payments later. The longer you go without

- It's fair. Everyone would pay the same rate, and it doesn't just benefit the wealthy. People earning below a certain amount would pay no taxes at all.
- It's simple. Tax simplification benefits individuals who struggle with the time and cost of filling out annual returns, and benefits the economy by not forcing people into making spending choices to reap the rewards of a tax deduction, allowing the free market to operate more efficiently.
- Charitable contributions will go up. People will have more to spend as they save a larger share of their income, and historically we give more to charity when we have more to give.
- Homeowners will benefit. Lenders will no longer have to pay a tax on the interest they receive from borrowers and would pass the savings along in the form of lower interest rates.
- It will impose fiscal discipline. A flat tax rate of 17 percent would generate less revenue than the current system, forcing politicians to spend less money because they will have less on hand.

Arguments Against

Opponents of the flat tax counter every argument made by its supporters. They say:

- It's unfair. Taxing income at the same rate across the board punishes people at the lower end of the earning scale because a fixed percentage of a small income trans-

lates into a greater burden than a fixed percentage of a large income.
- It's simplistic. For instance, only the wealthiest face taxation of interest, dividends, and capital gains, and not having to do so offsets the tax shelters they'll give up. Ordinary taxpayers won't have this opportunity.
- Charitable contributions will go down. The flat tax will eliminate the existing deduction for charitable contributions, which is designed to give people an incentive for voluntary giving.
- Homeowners will suffer. The present tax law permits a deduction for mortgage interest payments, permitting people to buy homes that might otherwise be out of their reach. The flat tax eliminates that break.
- It will raise the deficit. A flat tax rate of 17 percent would generate less revenue than the current system, and since politicians have a poor record of cutting spending, they will end up passing along the difference as deficit spending.

My Opinion

When registering your opinion on the flat tax, ask yourself if the flat tax:

- Is fair or unfair.
- Is simple or simplistic.
- Will help or hurt charitable giving.
- Will benefit or harm homeowners.
- Will impose fiscal discipline or contribute to deficit spending.

making interest payments, the more you have to pay out over time.

The federal budget works pretty much the same way. Federal budget numbers may be staggeringly large—can you visualize a $2 trillion budget?—but the temptation to spend beyond our means applies just as much to the public sphere as to our private exploits with credit cards, and the issue is compounded by the fact that hundreds of lawmakers with different interests have a say over what goes in the budget. The all-too-human tendency to spend now and worry about how to pay for it later has been at the center of national political debate for a generation.

One point of confusion in this debate is the difference between the federal deficit and the national debt. Many people confound the two, but as Demystifying Government: Deficits and Debts points out, they're different—and recognizing the difference is fundamental to establishing a reasoned opinion on deficit spending.

Except for a few years in the late 1990s, the government has run a deficit every year since 1969. There are a number of reasons for deficit spending, some of them arguably more justifiable than others. Sometimes the government runs a deficit accidentally because expenditures or revenue projections were incorrectly estimated when the budget was written. Emergencies like war, a terrorist strike, or a major natural disaster can cause the government to run a deficit because it has no choice but to spend money that wasn't budgeted to address these unexpected circumstances. Congress and the president may even intentionally run a deficit during economic downturns in order to stimulate the economy through increased spending (this was part of the logic behind the stimulus package passed by Congress during the first weeks of the Obama Administration). Each of these circumstances is short-lived and does not add considerably to the national debt.[28]

Sometimes, though, Congress and the president are unwilling to make difficult choices to keep the budget in balance, resulting in long-term deficit spending. This happened in the 1980s, when President Reagan sought to reduce the size of the federal government through cuts in taxes and domestic expenditures while spending more on national defense. Politically popular tax cuts and added defense money proved easy to institute, but curtailing domestic spending meant confronting constituents who benefited from government programs. The result was a policy that spared many domestic programs and looked the other way as deficits climbed to unprecedented levels that regularly surpassed $200 billion per year, which simply deferred the problem for future generations. The roaring economy of the late 1990s brought the government a windfall of unexpectedly high tax revenues and helped end deficit spending temporarily; by 1998, the government was running a small surplus. This was short-lived, however, as large deficits returned with the economic slowdown that set in at the turn of the twenty-first century, coupled with expensive tax cuts favored by the Bush administration, high defense needs following the September 11 terror attacks, the Iraq War, the cost of recovery after Hurricane Katrina, the price of bailing out large banks that teetered on the edge of bankruptcy following the 2008 financial meltdown, and the cost of President Obama's 2009 stimulus package.

Strong political and ideological forces make deficit spending hard to stop once it gets started. Although many of us support the idea of a balanced budget in theory we are more likely to be moved to political action to keep Congress from cutting programs that benefit us rather than to rise up in protest against red ink on a ledger sheet. Interest groups will keep the pressure on legislators to protect their programs, and as we saw in Chapter 8, they have the resources and relationships they need to be persuasive. Consequently, members of Congress are more likely to feel constrained to maintain or increase spending in the face of large deficits while acknowledging the importance of fiscal responsibility in their public remarks. Their words address the widespread constituent desire for responsible budgeting, but they avoid taking actions that would extract a great political cost. As politicians of both parties realized in the 1980s, it's easy to run against an incumbent who voted to cut back a popular program, but it's hard to run against

DEMYSTIFYING GOVERNMENT

DEFICITS AND DEBTS

When the government takes in less than it spends in a given year, it runs a **deficit**. This is easily confused with the **national debt**, but they are different. The deficit is an imbalance between revenues and expenditures in a given year. After climbing out from under years of deficit spending in the late 1990s, the federal government became heavily indebted again during the second Bush administration; in 2009, the Congressional Budget Office projected a deficit of over $1.6 trillion. When the government runs a deficit, it has to borrow to bridge the gap and to make interest payments on the money it borrows, just like you or I would. The amount the government borrows is its debt, and interest on the debt becomes a budgetary expense. As the government continues

to run a deficit, it has to keep borrowing, which increases both the size of the debt and the portion of the budget that goes to paying interest on the debt.

As of early 2011, the national debt was $14.110 trillion, or $14,110,420,810,062.28[T38] to be exact. The debt is owed mostly to domestic banks and financial institutions, and to holders of treasury bonds and savings bonds, although state, local, and foreign governments hold a portion of the debt.[T39] You can get an exact account of the national debt today from the Treasury Department, at http://www.treasurydirect.gov/NP/BPDLogin?application=np.

an incumbent who helped run up large, abstract deficit numbers.[29]

Philosophically, arriving at a balanced budget pits different conceptions of the appropriate size and role of government against each other. This, too, can hinder action. Liberals who support social welfare spending are more likely to favor tax increases over spending cuts to achieve balance. Conservatives prefer spending cuts, and some favor tax reductions in part to force the issue of reducing the size of government, hoping to leave Congress with no choice but to reduce domestic spending as a result of lower revenues and higher deficits.[30]

This difference reflects a deep philosophical division over what government should be doing, and is a way of using tax policy to legislate social outcomes.

The matter of cutting the budget is complicated by the fact that large portions of it cannot go under the axe. A host of expenditures are mandatory, which means they cannot be touched. These include

Social Security and Medicare payments, unemployment insurance, federal retirement benefits, and means-tested entitlements. Interest on the debt is also a fixed cost. With these expenses removed from consideration, you're left with 35 percent of the total budget for discretionary items, and about half of that is earmarked for defense, which is politically unpopular to cut.

Figure 7.3 shows the major spending categories in the 2010 budget. A look at the chart should show you how much of the budget is beyond the control of the budgeters. As more people retire, the percentage of the budget dedicated to Social Security will grow with it. The same is true of Medicare. Programs that help the needy and unemployed become more costly during economic downturns—precisely when tax revenues drop because fewer people are working. The easiest way to pay these costs is to borrow, but as we continue to run deficits, the portion of the budget dedicated to interest payments grows, too, squeezing out the relatively small set of discretionary expenditures.

Social Security (19%): The largest federal program, providing monthly retirement and disability benefits to 46 million people

Medicare (13%): Provides health-care coverage to 40 million seniors and people with disabilities

Medicaid (8%): Provides health-care coverage to over 34 million poor and disabled Americans

Nondefense Discretionary (20%): The portion of discretionary spending not earmarked for the military, including all programs for education, training, science, technology, transportation, housing and foreign aid

National Defense (19%): The portion of discretionary spending earmarked for the military

Interest Payments (5%): This is the interest paid on the national debt

Other Mandatory Expenditures (16%): Includes unemployment insurance, payments to farmers, federal retirement and insurance programs, and other means-tested entitlements including food stamps, Supplemental Security Income (SSI), veterans' pensions and the child nutrition program

Figure 7.3. Where the Money Goes: Federal Government Expenditures, 2010

These economic limitations constrain the political options available to the elected officials who write the budget, contributing to the high-stakes nature of budgetary politics.

Chapter Review

Regulatory policies depend on government action to minimize hazards or maximize benefits that will not be attended to by the free market. Competitive regulatory policies restrict the provision of a service or good, like operating a television station, to organizations that win federal licensing approval. Protective regulatory policies provide the public with information the government believes is beneficial to disseminate, like health warnings on cigarette packs. Regulation can be controversial because of widely held beliefs about limiting government involvement in the marketplace, even when the results of regulation, like clean air and safe food, are extremely popular.

Distributive policies are typically less controversial because they benefit everyone to some degree. Many distributive policies are public works projects financed by state and local governments, sometimes with federal support like the Interstate Highway System.

In contrast, social welfare policies are redistributive because the beneficiaries are different from the people who pay the bill. Many social welfare policies, like unemployment compensation, veteran's benefits, Social Security, and Temporary Assistance to Needy Families, involve transfer payments of federal dollars to qualifying individuals. Social welfare policies for the poor are controversial among people who believe they contribute to a "culture of poverty." As entitlements, social welfare programs deliver benefits to everyone who meets the eligibility requirements, like being unemployed or retired. Some programs are means-tested, such that eligibility is dependent on meeting a statistical standard, like having an income below the poverty line in order to receive welfare benefits.

Contrary to popular belief, most social welfare dollars do not go to support the poor. Social Security, which benefits retired workers, is the largest social welfare program and arguably the most popular government program. It is redistributive because today's workers provide the money used to support today's retirees.

Substantive decisions about domestic policy are made through budgetary politics involving raising and spending tax money. The structure of the tax code is a political matter that determines how the tax burden will be shared across income groups. The American tax code is progressive, as higher levels of income are taxed at higher rates, although deductions, or tax expenditures, permit individuals with higher incomes to reduce their payments.

Because tax cuts are politically popular and it's hard to cut funds for programs with a constituency, the federal budget has run a deficit, or spent more than it has taken in, almost every year since 1969. Deficit spending contributes to the national debt, which is the accumulated money owed—with interest—on past deficits. A large percentage of mandatory expenditures, like money earmarked for transfer payments and interest on the debt, compounds the difficulty of making spending cuts and contributes to deficit spending.

Key Terms

Aid to Families with Dependent Children (AFDC) The original federal welfare program, developed during the Great Depression as part of the New Deal, which extended subsistence benefits to families with children living below the poverty line.

appropriations Legislation permitting the government to spend money that determines how much will be spent and how it will be spent.

competitive regulatory policy A type of regulatory policy designed to protect the public interest by restricting the provision of a service or good to organizations that win federal licensing approval.

Congressional Budget and Impoundment Control Act of 1974 An act designed to centralize the congressional budgeting process, which established current procedures and timetables for writing a budget.

deficit The gap created in the federal budget when the government takes in less than it spends in a given year.

distributive policies Domestic policies primarily aimed at directing tax money to a range of public works items. Distributive policies tend not to be controversial because benefits are widely shared.

Earned Income Tax Credit A negative income tax for low-income families, who receive rather than make cash payments when they file their income tax returns.

entitlements Social welfare programs targeted to specific groups of individuals, like senior citizens or the unemployed. Benefits are available to all who meet the program requirements, although some entitlements for the poor impose a means test.

flat tax A proportional tax that would set the tax rate equally for all taxpayers, regardless of their income level.

food stamps A federal program designed to fight malnutrition among people in need by defraying the cost of food.

gross domestic product (GDP) A measure of national productivity, the gross domestic product is the total value of goods and services produced by a nation during a fixed period of time.

means test Eligibility requirements placed on social welfare programs aiding the poor, which restrict participation to individuals whose incomes fall below set levels.

Medicaid A social welfare program initiated as part of President Johnson's Great Society efforts to end poverty in America, which extended medical care to families receiving support through Aid to Families with Dependent Children (AFDC). States are permitted to enact their own Medicaid eligibility standards, following federal guidelines.

Medicare The federal social welfare program that provides hospital and supplementary medical insurance to senior citizens and the disabled.

national debt The amount the government borrows to pay for accumulated budget deficits.

pork barrel Wasteful or unnecessary spending that can result from logrolling. Whether something is a pork-barrel project or a valuable use of taxpayer dollars may depend on whether you stand to benefit from it.

poverty line A statistical determination of poverty based on income and family size that is used to establish eligibility for some social welfare programs designed to assist those in need.

progressive income tax A tax structure with graduated income rates designed to increase the tax burden on higher-income earners.

protective regulatory policy Regulations that supply consumers with information needed to make informed purchasing decisions about such things as cigarettes and home loans or that prevent undesirable personal or social conditions like child labor or unsafe food.

public works Civic projects built with tax dollars.

reconciliation A procedure in the budget-writing process, whereby appropriations made in a number of congressional committees and subcommittees need to be brought in line with spending targets established early in the process.

redistributive policies Domestic policies, like those promoting social welfare, that take resources from one group in the form of taxes and provide goods or services for another group, typically those in need.

regressive tax A tax structure that increases the tax burden on lower-income earners. Sales taxes are regressive because as incomes decline, the tax becomes a larger percentage of total income, and therefore, a greater burden.

regulatory policies Domestic policies designed to protect the public from harmful conditions that could result from unrestrained free-market competition or to ensure the benefits of a level playing field for private competition.

Social Security The popular social welfare program that provides benefits to retirees regardless of need. Social Security also offers insurance payments to families of deceased workers and disability payments to impaired workers.

tax expenditures Tax breaks in the form of exemptions targeted at groups of taxpayers or, in the case of corporate taxes, at specific industries.

Temporary Assistance for Needy Families (TANF) The 1996 welfare reform program that replaced Aid to Families with Dependent Children (AFDC) and ended welfare support as a federal entitlement. TANF is designed as a transitional program that supports welfare recipients temporarily as they move into the workforce.

transfer payments The direct payment of public money to individuals who qualify for it under the terms of a social welfare program.

Resources

You might be interested in examining some of what the following authors have said about the topics we've been discussing:

Harris, Richard A., and Sidney M. Milkis. *The Politics of Regulatory Change: A Tale of Two Agencies.* New York: Oxford University Press, 1996. An examination of the politics behind regulation and deregulation.

Hayes, Sharon. *Flat Broke with Children: Women in the Age of Welfare Reform.* New York: Oxford University Press, 2004. A look at welfare policy from the perspective of single mothers dealing with the environment created by welfare reform.

Howard, Philip K. *The Death of Common Sense: How Law Is Suffocating America.* New York: Random House, 1996. The author makes a case against regulatory policy, contending that regulations written in Washington routinely miss their intended mark while stifling local initiatives that could be far more creative and effective.

Kelso, William A. *Poverty and the Underclass: Changing Perceptions of the Poor in America.* New York: New York University Press, 1994. Kelso considers the changing arguments made by liberals and conservatives about the reasons for poverty in America.

Murray, Charles A. *Losing Ground: American Social Policy 1950–1980.* New York: Basic Books, 1994. A controversial and influential conservative critique of the social welfare programs of the 1960s and 1970s.

Rubin, Irene S. *The Politics of Public Budgeting: Getting and Spending, Borrowing and Balancing*, 6th ed. Washington, DC: CQ Press, 2009. Rubin provides an accessible overview of budgetary politics.

Notes

1. All figures come from the 2000 General Social Survey.

2. The one notable exception is a federal income tax checkoff that routes three dollars of your tax return to a fund for publicly financing presidential candidates without increasing your overall tax payment. Some states also have tax checkoffs for a variety of publicly financed causes like wildlife protection, child-abuse protection, and senior-citizen support.

3. For an overview of the history and procedures of broadcast licensing, see the Museum of Broadcast Communications website at http://www.museum.tv/eotvsection.php?entrycode=license.

4. There are questions about the effectiveness of warning labels. Canada goes much further than the United States to draw the connection between smoking and illness, by requiring the placement of pictures of diseased lungs, gums, and hearts over large portions of its cigarette packs.

5. See the Bureau of Labor Statistics, "Child Labor Laws and Enforcement," *Report on the Youth Labor Force* (U.S. Dept. of Labor, November 2000), at http://www.bls.gov/opub/rylf/pdf/chapter2.pdf.

6. Phillip K. Howard, *The Death of Common Sense: How Law Is Suffocating America* (New York: Random House, 1994), 7–8.

7. Ibid., 8

8. Ibid.

9. Theodore Lowi, "American Business, Public Policy, Case Studies and Political Theory," *World Politics* 16: 4 July 1964): 677–715.

10. Proublica.org, at www.propublica.org/special/the-stimulus-plan-a-detailed-list-of-spending.

11. James T. Patterson, *America's Struggle against Poverty, 1900–1994* (Cambridge, MA: Harvard University Press, 1994), 7.

12. The 2004 Health and Human Services Poverty Guidelines, at http://aspe.hhs.gov/poverty/04poverty.shtml.

13. U.S. Census Bureau, at http://wvvw.census.gov/hhes/vvww/poverty/data/incpovhlth/2009/highlights.html and http://www.census.gov/hhes/www/poverty/data/incpovhlth/2009/table4.pdf.

14. William A. Kelso, *Poverty and the Underclass: Changing Perceptions of the Poor in America* (New York: New York University Press, 1994), 31–45.

15. Charles Murray, *Losing Ground: American Social Policy, 1950–1980* (New York: Basic Books, 1984), 9.

16. Arnold Vedlitz, *Conservative Mythology and Public Policy in America* (New York: Praeger, 1988), 1–15.

17. Kelso, *Poverty and the Underclass*, 42–43.

18. Joel F. Handler, *The Poverty of Welfare Reform* (New Haven, CT: Yale University Press, 1995), 1–6.

19. Elaine B. Sharp, *The Sometime Connection: Public Opinion and Social Policy* (Albany, NY: State University of New York Press, 1999), 177–207.

20. John W. Kingdon, *America the Unusual* (New York: Worth Publishers, 1999).

21. Irene S. Rubin, *The Politics of Public Budgeting: Getting and Spending, Borrowing and Balancing*, 3rd ed. (Chatham, NJ: Chatham House Publishers, 1997), 42.

22. Ibid., 42–43.

23. Ibid., 43–53.

24. Budget of the United States Government, Fiscal Year 2008.

25. Citizens for Tax Justice, at http://www.ctj.org/html/margfaq.htm. Citizens for Tax Justice is a nonprofit, nonpartisan interest group that researches and advocates issues of tax fairness.

26. Ibid.

27. Allen Schick, *The Federal Budget: Politics, Policy, Process*, revised ed. (Washington, DC: Brookings Institution Press, 2000), 158–159. When social insurance, corporate and excise taxes are factored in, the effective tax rate for earners in the $20,000-$30,000 range is 17 percent, and for the $50,000–$75,000 range, 23.9 percent. Individuals with incomes of $1,000,000 or more are taxed at an effective rate of 35.3 percent.

28. Rubin, Politics of Public Budgeting, 177–179.

29. Ibid., 182–183.
30. Ibid.

Table, Figure and Box Notes

T1 "Milk Gets a Makeover—New Labels Help Make Shopping a Snap." American Dietetic Association, June, 1999.

T2 Image Source: Steven Chase, U.S. Fish and Wildlife Service. This image or recording is the work of a U.S. Fish and Wildlife Service employee, taken or made during the course of an employee's official duties. As a work of the U.S. federal government, the image is in the public domain.

T3 U.S. Fish and Wildlife Service, at http://arctic.fws.gov/index.htm.

T4 Alaskan Wilderness League, "Oil Drilling and the Arctic National Wildlife Refuge," at http://www.alaskawild.org/our-issues/americas-arctic/.

T5 BBC Reports, "Head to Head: Arctic Oil Drilling," "August 2, 2001, BBC.

T6 Ibid.

T7 Alaskan Wilderness League, "Oil Drilling."

T8 BBC Reports, "Head to Head."

T9 Ibid.

T10 Alaskan Wilderness League, "Oil Drilling."

T11 Richard R. Weingroff, "Creating the Interstate System," U.S. Department of Transportation Federal Highway Administration.

T12 Data from the U.S. Census Bureau, at http://www.census.gov/compendia/statab/2011/tables/11s0693.pdf.

T13 "A Brief History of the AFDC Program," at http://aspe.hhs.gov/hsp/AFDC/baseline/1history.pdf.

T14 Presidential Welfare Reform Fact Sheet, 2002.

T15 Ibid.

T16 Department of Health and Human Services Administration for Children and Families, at http://www.hhs.gov/children/index.html.

T17 "Impact of Recession and September 11 Seen of Welfare Caseloads," Center for Law and Social Policy, March 20, 2002.

T18 This work is in the public domain in the United States because it is a work of the United States Federal Government under the terms of Title 17, Chapter 1, Section 105 of the US Code.

T19 History Page, Social Security Online, at http://www.ssa.gov/history/briefhistory3.html.

T20 Susan A. MacManus, *Young v. Old: Generational Combat in the 21st Century* (Boulder, CO: Westview Press, 1996), 3–9.

T21 Ibid.

T22 "Social Security Politics," *Cato Daily Comment,* May 12, 2000. Data originally cited in May 11 Roll Call.

T23 Ibid.

T24 "Bush and Social Security: The Full Facts," Washington State Democrats online newsroom.

T25 Barbara Sinclair, *Unorthodox Lawmaking: New Legislative Process in the U.S. Congress* (Washington, D.C.: CQ Press, 1997), 63–69.

T26: Senate Agriculture Committee website, at http://ag.senate.gov/site/.

T27 Brian Riedl, "How Farm Subsidies Become American's Largest Corporate Welfare Program," The Heritage Foundation Policy and Research Analysis, February 25, 2002.

T28 Environmental Working Group website, at http://farm.ewg.org/farm/.

T29 Andrew Cassel, "Why U.S. Farm Subsidies are Bad for the World," *Philadelphia Inquirer*, May 6, 2002.

T30 Ibid.

T31 Reported on the American Embassy in Paris website.

T32 Data from Office of Management and Budget.

T33 Data from Organization for Economic Cooperation and Development, 1999.

T34 Robert Shapiro, "Why Fairness Matters: Progress vs. Flat Taxes," Report of Progressive Policy Institute, April 1, 1996.

T35 Hoover Institution, "Questions and Answers about the Flat Tax," at http://media.hoover.org/sites/default/files/documents/0817993115_157.pdf.

T36 Ibid.

T37 Ibid.

T38 As of noon February 9, 2011.

T39 The U.S. Treasury Department has a website for answering frequently asked questions about deficits and the national debt, at http://www.treasurydirect.gov/govt/resources/faq/faq_publicdebt.htm.

T40 Data from Office of Management and Budget.

Immigration on the Public Mind

Immigration Reform in the Obama Administration

By Adalberto Aguirre, Jr.

The mere mention of the word "immigration" in public discourse often results in technical and moral arguments about the presence of Mexican immigrants in U.S. society. Although Mexicans are not the only ones immigrating to the United States, in public discourse immigration is regarded as a "Mexican" problem. Despite a long history of Mexican immigration to the United States, and the contributions Mexican immigrants have made to the social and cultural fabric of American society, Mexican immigrants are portrayed in negative social roles and in threatening images. Fueling negative portrayals and public policy responses to Mexican immigrants is the general societal perception that Mexican immigrants threaten the distribution of valued resources. For example, news stories about undocumented Mexican immigrants seeking medical and educational services have been instrumental in prompting politicians to devise legislation that restricts their access to public-sector services (Marchevsky and Theoharis, 2008; Sanchez, 2007).

The media's portrayal of Mexican immigrants as reluctant to assimilate into U.S. society, or to learn the English language, motivated California voters to approve Propositions 187 and 227 (Aguirre, 2002). Proposition 227 dismantled bilingual education in California so as to force Mexican immigrant children to learn English, while Proposition 187 barred Mexican immigrants from access to public assistance and social services. Unsurprisingly, both propositions fueled volatile nativist sentiments in California over who is entitled to reside in the state. Interestingly, these propositions were a catalyst for attacking diversity in the state's population, resulting in the passage of an anti-affirmative action initiative, Proposition 209.

Transforming the issue of immigration into a moral crisis in U.S. has been a public preoccupation with media depictions of a swarm of Mexican immigrants who are robbing Americans of jobs and housing. The public's perception of Mexican immigrants as a threat to social behavior and civic values motivated the Hazelton, Pennsylvania, city council to pass a law that prevented Mexican immigrants from working and living within the city's limits. City ordinances and state initiatives that target Mexican immigrants represent a public policy designed to protect the quality of life enjoyed by Americans and to shield civil society from the threat of Mexican immigrants. Perhaps the most egregious example of this policy is Congress' decision to authorize the construction of a wall along the U.S.-Mexico border; in effect, the built environment is used to separate Americans and Mexicans.

The news media have undoubtedly been instrumental in constructing images that inform and shape perceptions and meanings in the public mind, and these images are often reflected in public policy responses to immigration. Moreover, the media influence the association between people's perceptions of social issues and their political evaluations of these issues (Domke, McCoy, and Torres, 1999). As a representative of the public's collective sentiments, the political state promotes public policy that reflects the public mind.

Immigration Policy

Barack Obama's election as president of the United States has revitalized the need for social change based on the common good. According to President Obama, "When I ran for president, I did so because I believed that...it was possible for us to bring change to Washington."[1] In response to the president's call for change, advocates for immigration reform hope that he will promote a policy that is more responsive to people's needs, rather than an expression of bureaucratic efficiency in dealing with immigrants. Latino congressional leaders hope that President Obama will honor his campaign promise to put millions of undocumented immigrant workers on a "pathway to citizenship" during his first year in office (Wallsten, 2009a). However, given the rather large and complex problems the Obama administration faces—the banking crisis, escalating wars in the Middle East, global warming, and an emerging battle over health care reform—there may not be room on the president's agenda for immigration reform during his first year in office.

My purpose here is to examine how the Obama administration has developed a strategy for responding to immigration issues. To do so, I identified the members of a policy working group that advised Obama on immigration during the presidential campaign. I then searched the news media and professional publications to identify key statements or comments regarding immigration made by the group's members. Examining these statements and comments may enable the construction of an interpretive framework for discussing the form

immigration policy might take in the Obama-Biden administration.

The Policy Working Groups

During the presidential campaign, Policy Working Groups were created to develop priority policy proposals and plans for action during the Obama-Biden administration.[2] Groups focused on the following areas: the economy, education, energy and environment, health care, immigration, national security, as well as technology, innovation, and government reform. The mission statement for the immigration working group states:

> Our nation's immigrant heritage and its commitment to the rule of law are among its greatest strengths. But in recent years, a broken immigration system has burdened our economy and challenged our values. The Immigration Policy Working Group is working on a plan to implement the President-elect's commitments to fix the immigration system through legislative and executive actions that promote prosperity, enhance our security, strengthen families, and advance the rule of law.

The policy working group on immigration was co-chaired by:

T. Alexander Aleinikoff: Dean of the Georgetown University Law Center and Executive Vice President of Georgetown University; former General Counsel and Executive Associate Commissioner for Programs at the Immigration and Naturalization Service during the Clinton administration; Senior Associate at the Migration Policy Institute (1997 to 2004), where he now serves on the Board of Trustees. He has written widely on immigration, refugee, and citizenship law, as well as on constitutional law.

Mariano-Florentino (Tino) Cuellar: Professor and Deane F. Johnson Faculty Scholar at Stanford Law School. He served in the Treasury Department as senior advisor to the Under Secretary for Enforcement during the Clinton administration;

he was elected to the American Law Institute and served on the boards of numerous organizations, including Asylum Access and the Stanford Center for International Security and Cooperation. He has written on how organizations manage complex regulatory, migration, international security, and criminal justice problems.

The members of the policy working group were:

Preeta Bansal: Partner in an international law firm (Skadden, Arps, Slate, Meagher & Flom LLP); former Solicitor General of the state of New York.[3]

Dennis Burke: Co-Chief of Staff, Arizona Governor's Office; former Chief Deputy Attorney General for the state of Arizona.[4]

Maria Echaveste: Lecturer in Residence, Boalt Hall School of Law, U.C.-Berkeley; former senior White House and U.S. Department of Labor official.[5]

Tara Magner: Director of Policy, National Immigrant Justice Center.[6]

David Martin: Principal Deputy General Counsel of the Department of Homeland Security; Warner-Booker Distinguished Professor of International Law, University of Virginia School of Law.[7]

Esther Olavarria: Senior Fellow at American Progress; former chief immigration counsel to Senator Edward Kennedy on the Senate Judiciary Committee; co-founded the Florida Immigration Advocacy Center.[8]

Shilpa Phadke: Director, Glover-Park Group (strategic communications firm in Washington, D.C.).[9]

Mark Rosenblum: Attorney, private practice.[10]

Immigration Viewpoints

I searched news media sources and professional publications for opinion pieces, political commentary, or academic articles written by members of the policy working group on immigration. My search was limited to items that directly addressed immigration issues. For some committee members, I was unable to identify any items.

T. Alexander Aleinikoff

In a 2001 opinion piece in *The American Prospect* regarding the Gramm proposal for increasing enforcement of immigration laws and surveillance of the U.S.-Mexico border, Aleinikoff writes that "there is little evidence that a massive enforcement build-up at the border has prevented determined migrants from coming to jobs waiting for them in the U.S.—although it has raised the prices charged by smugglers and has contributed to increased numbers of deaths at the border as migrants use more remote crossing points."[11] Aleinikoff argues that increased border enforcement will lock in "an undocumented population that is ineligible for green cards and unlikely to return home because of the high cost of getting back to the U.S."

Instead, Alienikoff suggests that a transformation in the U.S.-Mexico migration relationship requires that the U.S. "move toward legalization of undocumented Mexican immigrants who are established and working in the U.S. Such measures enable employers to enjoy a more stable workforce, families to remain united, individuals to secure social protections, and, over time, immigrants to fully incorporate into and participate in their communities." In the end, U.S.-Mexico immigration policy "should be modern enough to reflect the need for the intelligent regulation of an increasingly integrated labor market, and traditional enough to reflect our long and deeply held values as a country that allows and encourages immigrants to become full members of our nation."

Aleinikoff questioned the placement of the Immigration and Naturalization Service (INS) in the Department of Homeland Security (DHS). By making it a subunit of the DHS, Aleinikoff states that the INS "would inevitably view all immigration issues through the lens of fighting terrorism."[12] Aleinikoff has also argued for the development of a green card policy that allows immigrant workers in the fields to earn wages that provide them with adequate housing and safety. According to Aleinikoff, the implementation of a green card policy that is just for immigrant workers might result in a "slight rise in the price of produce. But it is a fair guess that Americans would be willing to pay a bit more for fruits and vegetables to improve the lives of the hundreds of thousands of farm workers and their families who provide America's bountiful harvest while living below the poverty line."[13]

Tara Magner

In an essay published by the MIT Center for International Studies, Tara Magner argues that immigration reform in the Bush administration failed because the "Bush administration has retreated into an 'enforcement first' or 'enforcement only' approach that ignores the economic and labor needs of the country."[14] According to Magner, Congress failed to pass a package of comprehensive immigration reforms because anti-immigrant advocates portrayed immigrants as "displacing native-born workers, draining social programs, and overtaking American communities."[15] Magner argues that a comprehensive approach to immigration reform that "creates legal avenues for immigrants to live and work in the United States combined with tough but humane border security and law enforcement—including employer sanctions for bad actors who continue to skirt the law or abuse workers—is the most viable solution for security and economic growth. It is also a solution that honors the oft-stated, if not always fulfilled, vision of America as a melting pot that welcomes and protects immigrants."[16]

David Martin

In an article published in the *New York University Journal of Legislation and Public Policy,* Martin discusses the immigration reform controversy by identifying eight myths that are used to counter immigration reform proposals. Martin (2007: 526) states: "The one truly indispensable component of viable immigration reform must be steps that will steadily build a stable, enduring, and functional enforcement system. In my view, only by developing the capacity to enforce the deliberate choices that the nation makes about immigration can we reduce the bitter polarization these issues have produced and thereby calm the wild swings of policy that we

have witnessed for two decades."[17] Martin goes on to note that "I definitely want to see the United States develop an effective, balanced, and well-designed enforcement system ... centered around workplace verification and follow-up, though bolstered by effective border policing. Enforcement ... is a crucial component of reform. No combination of guestworker provisions or legal migration expansion, short of virtual open borders, will obviate or even reduce the enforcement requirement."[18]

An Interpretive Framework

Based on the materials written by members of the immigration policy group, I identified several markers indicating how the Obama administration might promote immigration reform. Alienikoff stressed legalization of undocumented Mexican immigrants; Magner identified tough but humane border security and law enforcement, as well as employer sanctions for those that skirt the law or abuse workers; and Martin highlighted workplace verification and effective border policing. If these are guides for how the group advised President Obama on immigration reform, then the Obama administration might focus on the following key points: (1) providing options and/or opportunities for undocumented immigrants to get on the "pathway to citizenship"; (2) effective methods for border security that do not necessarily criminalize immigrants; and (3) employer sanctions for those that violate the law and/or abuse immigrant workers.

Interestingly, on July 1, 2009, federal officials notified more than 600 businesses in the United States that their work records would be audited in an effort to identify companies that hire undocumented workers. The move to audit these records signals a new direction for the Obama administration regarding immigration reform that focuses on employer violations and moves away from the Bush administration's focus on apprehending undocumented immigrants. As a result, the "Obama administration has made tougher enforcement aimed at employers a cornerstone of its immigration policy. In April, the federal government issued new guidelines to immigration agents instructing them to focus on employers who hire illegal immigrants rather than just to arrest workers. The administration is also working to improve and expand an employment verification program" (Gorman, 2009: AI). So far, two of the markers—employer sanctions and work verification—are guiding the Obama administration's immigration reform efforts.

Concluding Remarks

Four days before meeting with lawmakers in the White House on June 25, 2009, to discuss immigration reform, President Obama stated that his "pathway to citizenship" plan requires new legislation to "clarify the status of millions who are here illegally, many who have put down roots" (Wallsten, 2009b: B1). This "pathway to citizenship" plan implements the marker on legalizing undocumented immigrants. President Obama also stated that: "For those who wish to become citizens, we should require them to pay a penalty and pay taxes, learn English, go to the back of the line behind those who played by the rules" (*Ibid.*). In short, for undocumented immigrants wishing to become U.S. citizens, Obama administration reforms involve sanctions—penalties and taxes, learning English, and waiting behind others who "played by the rules."

Latino leaders and immigration advocates had hoped that President Obama would honor his campaign promise to put millions of undocumented immigrants on the pathway to citizenship (Nowicki, 2009), but the summit meeting failed to produce a definite timetable. Democratic leaders in Congress have indicated that they may not have the votes necessary to pass a comprehensive immigration reform bill in 2009 (Wallsten, 2009c). President Obama's inability to promote immigration reform in 2009, especially his pathway to citizenship plan, could signal that immigration is not the priority issue that he promised it would be. According to Sacramento Bishop Jaime Soto, a member of the U.S. Conference of Catholic Bishop's Committee on Migration, the Obama summit meeting on immigration "will tell us whether the administration is serious about enacting comprehensive immigration reform this year or is perhaps getting timid and abandoning the commitment that it made during the campaign" (Nowicki, 2009: A1). If President Obama does not enact a comprehensive immigration reform bill during his first term in office, Latino leaders and immigration advocates may find it difficult to accept the president's promise that immigration reform will be a priority in his second administration.

Notes

1. See http://news.bbc.co.uk/2/hi/americas_6/22/2009.
2. At http://change.gov/learn/policy_working_groups.
3. At http://redijf.com/cms.
4. At http://twincities.bizjournals.com.
5. At http://infoweb.newsbank.com.
6. At http://news.nationaljournal.com.
7. At www.depauw.edu/news.
8. At www.americanprogress.org/experts/olavarriaEsther.
9. At www.beyondthe11th.org/board.
10. *Op.cit.* at I.
11. T. Alexander Aleinikoff, "A Response: Toward a New U.S.-Mexican Immigration Relationship—Logic and Legality." *The American Prospect* (April 26, 2001). At www.prospect.org//cs/articles.
12. T. Alexander Aleinikoff, "INS Covers More Ground Than Homeland Security." *Los Angeles Times* (July 1): B 1 .
13. T. Alexander Aleinikoff, "The Green Card Solution." *The American Prospect* (November 30, 2002). At www.prospect.org//cs/articles.
14. Tara Magner, "Immigration Reform: Failure and Prospects." MIT Center for International Studies (September 2007): 1.
15. *Ibid.*: 2. See also her "Immigration Reform That Just Might Work" (October 18. 2007).
16. *Op. cit.* at 14. p. 3.
17. Martin (2007).
18. *Ibid.*: 552.

References

Aguirre. Jr., Adalberto. 2002 "Propositions 187 and 227: A Nativist Response to Mexicans." Charles F. Hohm and James A. Glynn (eds.), *California's Social Problems* (second edition). Thousand Oaks, CA: Pine Forge Press: 303–324.

Domke, David, Kelley McCoy, and Marcos Torres. 1999 "News Media, Racial Perceptions, and Political Cognition." *Communication Research* 26: 570–607.

Gorman, Anna. 2009 "L.A. Employers Face Immigration Audits." *Los Angeles Times* (July 2): A1.

Marchevsky, Alejandra and Jeanne Theoharis. 2008 "Dropped from the Rules: Mexican Immigrants, Race, and Rights in the Era of Welfare Reform." *Journal of Sociology and Social Welfare* 35: 71–96.

Martin, David. 2007 Eight Myths About Immigration Enforcement." *New York University Journal of Legislation and Public Policy* 10: 525–553.

Nowicki, Dan. 2009 "Immigration Vies for Spot on Busy Agenda." *The Arizona Republic* (June 25): A1.

Sanchez, Jennifer. 2007 "Senate Rebuff May Mean Utah, Other States Next Immigration Reform Battle-grounds." *The Salt Lake Tribune* (June 29): B1.

Wallsten, Peter. 2009a "Citizen Plea in Danger: Quick Results from the White House Immigration Meeting this Week Deemed Unlikely." *The Baltimore Sun* (June 22): A1.

2009b "Obama to Open Immigrant Debate." *The Press-Enterprise* (Riverside, CA, June 21): B1.

2009c "New Snag on Immigration Reform." *Los Angeles Times* (June 26): A20.

CHAPTER 6

The Presidency

Chapter 6 Vignette

By Jennifer Byrne

Presidency—War on Terror

Yasar Hamdi was born to immigrant parents in the United States in 1980 but grew up in Saudi Arabia. When he was 20, he left home to go to Afghanistan, where he was present at an Al-Qaida training camp. Hamdi's parents argued that he quickly became disillusioned with the camp and remained in Afghanistan to do relief work and could not return home after the start of the War in Afghanistan in 2001. He was later captured in November of 2001 by Northern Alliance Forces (allies of the U.S.) with hundreds of surrendering Taliban forces. He was later caught up in a prison riot, which he survived, and was transferred first to Guantanamo Bay and then to Norfolk Naval Base in Virginia.[1] What is so special about Yasar Hamdi? It turns out that after the September 11, 2001, attacks, President Bush interpreted his executive power as Commander-in-Chief of the U.S. Armed Forces, and under Article II of the U.S. Constitution, issued a military order called Detention, Treatment, and Trial of Non-Citizens in the War Against Terrorism.[2] Those detained under this presidential military order were labeled "enemy combatants." Although the term enemy combatant had been defined

before in *Ex parte Quirin*, the term was applied during the Bush Administration to 1) anyone who was a member of Al-Qaida and or planned, aided, abetted, or engaged in terrorism and 2) anyone deemed to be considered an enemy combatant by the executive branch. So why does any of this matter? Well, it turns out that the term enemy combatant determined whether or not you received due process. If one was labeled an enemy combatant, one could be detained indefinitely without explanation of the charges and without a trial. Enemy combatants also could be subject to coercive interrogation techniques, containing ten "enhanced interrogation" techniques, including water boarding.

Hamdi's father filed a suit on his behalf for a writ of *habeas corpus*, an order that would ask the courts to review whether or not Hamdi's detention was lawful. At that point, Hamdi had been imprisoned for more than 2 years with no charges filed against him and no access to the courts, or an independent decision maker. President Bush argued that the power granted to him as Commander-in-Chief and an authorization by Congress to use military force allowed him to label detainees as enemy combatants and allowed the executive branch to supervise their detention and imprisonment without any oversight. Proponents of using enhanced interrogation techniques on detainees, not filing charges, and not providing attorneys argue that these strategies help in obtaining information that may be very sensitive, classified, and involving national security matters. The Bush administration sought to obtain information about the Al-Qaida network and possible terrorist attacks that might be planned for the future. Due to the sensitive nature of the information between the government and the detainees, the Administration did not want trials to take place in civilian courts, where coerced information was not admitted, and all information would be made public.

The Supreme Court disagreed with the President and argued that a United States citizen has the right to due process and the right to file a writ of *habeas corpus* unless the Congress suspends this right or the courts are no longer functioning. While the Court allowed the President to create the enemy combatant category and to hold separate trials with separate rules for such detainees, Justice Sandra Day O'Connor noted that, "an interrogation by one's captor, however an effective intelligence-gathering tool, hardly constitutes a constitutionally adequate fact-finding before a neutral decision-maker."[3]

As the Court never ruled that the independent decision-maker had to be the federal courts, President Bush established military tribunals to review the cases of enemy combatants. The military tribunals were challenged in a subsequent case, *Hamdan v. Rumsfeld*. The Supreme Court once again found challenges rooted in the separation of powers and inadequate due process safeguards. The Supreme Court found that President Bush needed to first obtain authorization from Congress before creating the tribunals. The Supreme Court also took issue with the fact that the tribunals admitted evidence obtained by coercion and through hearsay. The commissions had to comply with the Uniform Code of Military Justice and with international protections in the Geneva Convention. Since Hamdan was excluded from certain parts of his trail that were deemed classified, the trail was determined to be illegal.

President Barack Obama's administration ceased using the term enemy combatant in 2009 to separate the new administration from the detention policies of the Bush administration. The dropping of the term is largely symbolic, as there are still detainees at Guantanamo Bay. Nevertheless, in a memo entitled New Actions on Guantanamo and Detainee Policy, the Administration continued to advocate a four-part strategy for closing Guantanamo, despite receiving funding from Congress to transfer the remaining detainees. The memo also provided a fact sheet of the current policies regarding the treatment of detainees housed at the Guantanamo Bay facility, including procedures to meet the due process standards set forth by the Supreme Court during the Bush Administration. Among these is the resumption of the military commissions with the help of Congress. Though President Bush had worked with Congress to pass the Military Commissions Act of 2006 in *Boumediene v. Bush*, the Supreme Court ruled that the commissions still lacked adequate safeguards when it came to due process and found the section of the legislation unconstitutional. The Court also struck down a provision that banned detainees from filing writs of habeas corpus in the federal courts. To address the shortcomings of the commissions, the Obama Administration has put in place a ban on using statements against the detainees that were taken in an inhumane way or by coercion. Obama also passed an executive order that requires periodic review of each detainee so that continued and prolonged detention is justified. Finally, the Administration cited a commitment to Geneva Convention standards. However, even with these new policies, detainees are still subject to a separate system of law and access to the federal courts has been limited. This is due to a series of federal court decisions that instruct judges to embrace a presumption that the federal government's evidence from Guantanamo is reliable and to examine the totality of the circumstances, rather than closely analyzing each individual piece of evidence. Since this ruling, the odds of detainees winning their cases has decreased substantially, from 58 percent of cases won by Guantanamo detainees after the *Boumediene v. Bush* ruling to just 8 percent since 2010.

Endnotes

1. http://www.cnn.com/2004/LAW/04/27/detainees/, last accessed on November 14, 2013.

2. http://georgewbush-whitehouse.archives.gov/news/releases/2001/11/20011113-27.html, last accessed on November 14, 2013.

3. Hamdi v. Rumsfeld, 542 U.S. 507 (2004)

The Presidency

By Matthew Kerbel

When we approach the presidency, we enter a place that is fundamentally different from the world of Congress. Five hundred and thirty-five people give way to a single individual with a large supporting cast. The decentralized, institutional feel of the legislative arena disappears in favor of the personal mystique of a powerful man who lives and works in the shadows of the few others who have served before him.

Many of us have emotional reactions to the president that we don't have toward Congress. He can generate strong feelings in us—both positive and negative. We can be quick to comment about the job he's doing. His personal life is on display for us to judge. His quirks and foibles are magnified by television. Comedians make fun of him. We compare him to others who held the job, even presidents long ago that we don't personally remember, and have opinions about how he stacks up. We measure him for greatness, even as we are critical of his actions.

Many of us also have specific ideas about the qualities we want in our presidents (something we probably never think about in relation to members of Congress), personal characteristics we expect them to have. Take a second to think about this. Table 9.1 contains qualities that some people look for in the president.

If you're so inclined (or if you're asked by your professor), compare notes with your classmates about what they want in a president. Chances are, many of them have a long wish list. Are they looking for honesty? Integrity? Intelligence? Decisiveness? Strength? Determination? Flexibility? Experience? The ability to bring people together? Legislative skills? Communication skills? Good looks? These are just a few things people commonly say they expect their presidents to have. Does Barack Obama have all these qualities? Of course not—it's such a demanding set of characteristics that we're much more likely to find them in a comic-book superhero than a person. But demand we will—and we feel disappointed when our presidents let us down.

Political scientist George Edwards sums up the dilemma by noting that "all" we want from our presidents is "leadership yet responsiveness, flexibility yet firmness, statesmanship yet political skill, openness yet control, and empathy for ordinary people yet uniqueness. In other words, the president is expected to be all things to all people."[1]

If in reality presidents don't have all of the personal characteristics we want them to, you might wonder why we maintain such high expectations of them. Maybe it's that

235

Table 9.1. Things I May Want in a President

Here are a number of characteristics people may say they want in a president. Look them over and decide how many of these characteristics are on your list, and whether there are other qualities you would want that are not listed here.

Characteristic
Brave
Can unite people
Curious
Decisive
Determined
Empathetic
Faithful
Firmly held convictions
Flexible
Good communicator
Good legislative skills
Good-looking
Good politician
Honesty
Integrity
Intelligent
Leadership skills
Life experience
Open to ideas
Politically savvy
Responsive
Sensitive
Strong
Thoughtful
Understands people

Comedians regularly made fun of George W. Bush's intelligence. Lots of people—even his friends—felt Bill Clinton flip-flopped on important things and was deceptive when it suited his purposes. And Richard Nixon—during the Watergate scandal—was widely criticized by members of both political parties for disregarding personal liberties and trampling on the Constitution. Maybe you made these connections, maybe not.

What you may not have realized is that these are exactly the things that critics said about some of our more respected presidents, long before their faces were depicted on currency. It may surprise you to know that the things some people say about George W. Bush were also said about George Washington. Thomas Jefferson thought the first George wasn't particularly bright. Alexander Hamilton thought Washington craved power and control. His critics thought Washington paid way too much attention to his image and not enough to substance.

The things people said about Clinton echo what critics said of Thomas Jefferson, who was widely mistrusted, even by his allies, and believed to be someone who would say one thing and then turn around and say something contradictory if it suited his purposes.

Trampling on the Constitution? It was said about Lincoln as well as Nixon, by critics who watched Lincoln shut down opposition newspapers, arbitrarily arrest political dissenters, and deny prisoners who felt they were unlawfully incarcerated the right to petition for their release.

So, how did Washington, Jefferson, and Lincoln end up on Mount Rushmore if in their day they were criticized like our current presidents? The answer partly lies in the difference between myth and reality. Time has a way of making mortals heroic, of glossing over the flaws that make people human, especially if those mortals served at a critical time in our history like during the establishment of the constitutional system

past presidents set our expectations, and we want our recent ones to measure up. As part of our socialization to politics in elementary school, we internalize legends about the giants who held the office long ago, people like Washington, Jefferson, and Lincoln. In contrast, we hear so much criticism of recent presidents. Table 9.2 lists criticisms widely leveled against three recent presidents in the press and in public opinion.

Table 9.2. Criticism of Recent Presidents

President	Popular Criticism	Criticism Also Leveled Against
George W. Bush	Secretive Not substantive Not bright	George Washington
Bill Clinton	Duplicitous Deceptive Inconsistent	Thomas Jefferson
Richard Nixon	Disregards Constitution Ignores personal liberties	Abraham Lincoln

or the Civil War (our recent presidents did not have the opportunity to lead the United States to victory in the Revolutionary War, draft the Declaration of Independence, or emancipate the slaves). As a nation, we crave our heroes, and because of the psychological attachments people have to the presidency, our past presidents naturally fill the role. We know Washington didn't chop down that cherry tree, but deep down, many of us want to believe in leaders who could not tell a lie.

Besides, the presidency is the one office where greatness is the yardstick of performance. For many years, historians led by Arthur M. Schlesinger have been classifying past presidents as great, near great, average, below average, and failures.[2] Table 9.3 shows an updated composite ranking of the presidents, compiled from several sources. Some names remain affixed at the top—Lincoln, Washington, Franklin D. Roosevelt. Others are hopelessly in the cellar—Grant, Buchanan, Harding.

What's interesting is that some presidents move around the rankings over time. Dwight D. Eisenhower was ranked twenty-first in Schlesinger's 1962 survey (low average) but rose to tenth (high average) when his son replicated the exercise in 1996. Recent presidents like Clinton, Bush (senior), Carter and Ford are all bunched in the middle. Will they still be there twenty-five or fifty years from now? Like most everything else, presidential performance looks different when viewed through the prism of time.

Presidents and presidential candidates, of course, are well aware that greatness is the standard by which they will be measured, and they play to it. You never hear presidential candidates promising to be the next Herbert Hoover. If there is a reason for caution in all this, it's that the Mt. Rushmore myth can influence the expectations we have of our presidents, elevating them to a place that's out of proportion to the realistic expectations of a complex and complicated office.

Table 9.3. Ranking the Presidents[T1]

Top		Middle	Bottom
Lincoln	Reagan	Clinton	B. Harrison
F. Roosevelt	Polk	Carter	Arthur
Washington	Jackson	Ford	Grant
T. Roosevelt	Monroe	Taft	Hoover
Truman	McKinley	Nixon	Fillmore
Wilson	J. Adams	Hayes	Tyler
Jefferson	Cleveland	Coolidge	W. H. Harrison
Kennedy	Madison	Taylor	Harding
Eisenhower	J. Q. Adams	Garfield	Pierce
L. Johnson	G. H. W. Bush	Van Buren	A. Johnson
			Buchanan

President Ford recognized this and played against the myth when he was elevated to the presidency upon Richard Nixon's resignation. "I'm a Ford, not a Lincoln," he told the nation, explicitly lowering expectations about his performance. It's only when we're offered the promise of a Lincoln that we can be set up for disappointment, because even Lincoln wasn't the Lincoln of myth when he walked the earth.

The wide-ranging and wildly unrealistic characteristics we look for in our presidents coincide with equally unrealistic and contradictory performance expectations. Just look at some of the things we expect the president to deliver:

- *Policy leadership:* On fundamental issues, we look to the president rather than Congress for leadership and direction. More than anyone else in the political system, we expect the president to keep us prosperous and safe, and we tend to punish presidents who fail to deliver. We hold these expectations despite the fact that the president is subject to forces beyond his control in the conduct of economic and foreign policy.[3]

- *Global leadership:* We expect the president to be the embodiment of America in the world, projecting a strong and compassionate image in line with how many of us like to view our global presence. In relations with other countries, the president is expected to act both wisely, as a statesman, and shrewdly, as a politician, despite the fact that this would require playing a unifying and divisive role simultaneously.

- *Crisis management:* The president is the person we turn to in a crisis, and we expect him to be in command. We expect the president to use his expertise and political skills to end a crisis successfully and in short order, with minimum harm to Americans, even though confusion may reign in the White House, information about what's happening may be incomplete, situations may change swiftly and unexpectedly, and good options may not be available.

- *Symbolic leadership:* We expect the president to be someone we can look up to and identify with, almost like a parent is to a young child. We want to be moved when he speaks. We want him to embody the best of us, and through his words and actions, project those positive characteristics back to us. Symbolically, we want him to be the image on Mount Rushmore, and many of us are sorely disappointed when he projects his human flaws rather than his idealized strengths.

- *Legitimacy for the system:* The president is as close as we get to a monarch, and like a king, we want the president to confer legitimacy on our collective sense of ourselves. We want him to act honorably so that his actions reflect well on American democracy and so that we may regard him as a unifying force. We want this despite the fact that the presidency is a political job, and politics is inherently divisive.

So, the myth of presidential greatness encourages a series of performance expectations that are at best contradictory and at worst impossible to fulfill. Presidents attempt to deal with this by compartmentalizing what they do, acting out different roles at different times, making a rousing speech for public consumption at a summit meeting with other world leaders while working outside the spotlight on the divisive politics of policy making. The compartmental approach can work up to a point, but presidents inevitably run up against their limitations and the many roadblocks built in to the federal system. Some presidents simply play one or two of these roles better than others. President Bush received high marks for providing crisis management following the September 11, 2001 terrorist attacks (although his widely criticized response to Hurricane Katrina undermined his reputation). President Clinton was considered a strong policy leader. President Reagan provided a lot of people with symbolic leadership. It's a lot to expect them to perform all these roles at the same high level. But we do.

Growth of the Presidency

What's more, we have high expectations for performance in a presidential office that, on paper, doesn't have very much substance. The presidency started out as a poorly defined second cousin to Congress. Only time, precedent, and the actions of some of its more aggressive occupants have shaped the presidency into the powerful branch we know today.

Take a look at Article II of the Constitution, which establishes the presidency (you can find the full text in Appendix B and a discussion of the highlights in Demystifying Government: You Want to Be President?). Notice how short it is compared to Article I, which establishes Congress. It's only four sections (compared to the ten sections composing Article I)—and if you take away the material on the president's term of office, presidential elections, eligibility requirements, compensation, the oath of office, the requirement that the president make a State of the Union address to Congress, and **impeachment**, you're left with a grand total of two paragraphs dealing with what the president is supposed to do.

Article II opens with the declaration: "The executive Power shall be vested in a President of the United States," but it doesn't elaborate. The executive power? What's that supposed to be?

The authors of the Constitution were purposely vague about this central point. In colonial America, they had been pretty familiar with strong executives, both in the form of the King of England and the royal governors he appointed to oversee the colonies—who were widely regarded as corrupt officials who abused their power. In contrast, freely elected colonial legislatures served as a democratic check on these executives. The experience led them to conclude that strong legislatures were the best way to protect personal liberties.[4] So, they created a strong legislature in Article I, paying detailed attention to how it would function. Secondarily, they created the office of the president, whose grant of executive power was meant to be more vague than broad.

From these beginnings, the office of the presidency grew erratically, strengthened by precedent and by a few opportunistic presidents inclined to use ambiguous constitutional language to enhance their power. George Washington established expectations for the office by instituting standards for everything from how the president should be addressed (he preferred the constitutional designation of, simply, "the President of the United States" to Vice President John Adams' more regal, "His Highness the President of the United States and protector of their Liberties"), to procedures for how the executive branch would conduct business, to how long the

---

DEMYSTIFYING GOVERNMENT

YOU WANT TO BE PRESIDENT?

You'd better be thirty-five years old. And you must be a natural-born citizen of the United States who's lived here fourteen years. So says the Constitution.

Here are a few other procedural matters pertaining to the presidency that are set down in Article II:

- The presidential term is four years.
- Congress establishes the president's salary but can't change it while he's in office.
- If the president dies or resigns, the powers and duties of the office "devolve on the Vice President." The Twenty-fifth Amendment, ratified in 1967, allows the presi-

dent to temporarily assign his powers to the vice president if he is going to be incapacitated, such as if he's going under general anesthesia during an operation. It also provides for the vice president and a majority of Congress or the president's cabinet to make the vice president "Acting President" if they judge the president to be unable to function; and it permits the president to fill a vacancy in the vice presidency, subject to confirmation by a majority vote of both Houses of Congress.
- The president has to "from time to time" give Congress "Information of the State of the Union," but it doesn't have to be in a formal speech.

- The president and vice president may be removed from office if impeached for and convicted of "Treason, Bribery, or other high Crimes and Misdemeanors." We discussed impeachment in Chapter 9 (Section 9.5d, "Impeachment").
- At his inauguration, the president is required to take the following oath: "I do solemnly swear (or affirm) that I will faithfully execute the Office of President of the United States, and will to the best of my Ability, preserve, protect and defend the constitution of the United States." George Washington added: "So help me God." So has everyone who came after him.

president should serve (two terms, long before it was mandated by constitutional amendment).[5]

Andrew Jackson, who took office in 1829, was the first to assert a direct presidential connection to the people, strengthening the office with respect to Congress, which had previously played that role. Abraham Lincoln claimed unilateral power for the presidency as he led the Union through the Civil War. Following a period of congressional reemergence in the second half of the nineteenth century, a succession of presidents from Grover Cleveland to William McKinley to, most notably, Theodore Roosevelt, contributed to the expansion of presidential power.[6] Echoing Jackson, Roosevelt articulated his philosophy of a presidency limited only by what the Constitution prohibited him from doing (which, admittedly, is not much), calling himself "a steward of the people bound actively and affirmatively to do all he could for the people."[7]

The twentieth century witnessed a line of presidents who exercised aggressive leadership. Woodrow Wilson sought to be a strong party leader who could move public opinion and, with it, command congressional support. Franklin D. Roosevelt, governing during the Great Depression and World War II, was a proactive leader who presided over unprecedented expansion in the size and scope of the executive branch. Lyndon Johnson dominated

Congress, establishing the center of policy making in the White House. Richard Nixon went to war with Congress over his attempts to expand presidential prerogatives, impounding funds for congressional initiatives he disliked and acting unilaterally in his prosecution of the Vietnam War. Ronald Reagan used the force of his personality and strong communication skills to move public opinion and congressional opponents.[8]

Sources of Presidential Power

Over the last century, success in the presidency came to hinge on the ability to articulate a message and establish a bond with voters. The advent of mass media made direct communication with the public more possible—and more necessary. Today, it's unthinkable for a day to go by without the president appearing in, or even dominating, the news agenda. The ubiquitous president is a late twentieth-century phenomenon that's worked to supplement the president's limited formal powers with a wealth of informal powers—for those presidents who know how to use them.

Formal Presidential Powers

Apart from giving the president that vague grant of "executive Power" and the equally vague (or broad) mandate to see to it that "the Laws be faithfully executed," the Constitution gives the president very few formal powers. The only specific powers expressly granted to the president are:

- *Appointments:* The Constitution gives the president the power to appoint ambassadors, Supreme Court justices, and other federal officers, like federal court judges, cabinet secretaries, and agency heads. The Senate has to confirm the president's nominees.
- *Treaties:* The president can negotiate treaties with other nations, subject to ratification by two-thirds of the Senate.
- *Commander-in-chief of the army and navy:* The Constitution makes the president the civilian commander of the military.

- *Veto power:* The president can veto an act of Congress, though Congress can override the veto with a two-thirds vote of both houses.
- *Recess appointments:* Presidential appointments made while the Senate is out of session do not require ratification, and stand until the end of the congressional session.
- *Convene Congress:* The president may call a session of Congress at any time.
- *Receive ambassadors:* The president officially greets representatives of other nations on behalf of the United States.
- *Pardon power:* The president may pardon anyone suspected, accused, or convicted of any crime for any reason without explanation (see Demystifying Government: Pardon Me?). Presidential pardons are final and cannot be overturned.

Time and tradition have supplemented the president's constitutional powers. For instance, the Constitution never mentions **executive privilege,**

DEMYSTIFYING GOVERNMENT

PARDON ME?

The presidential pardon power has its origins in the traditional right of kings to be the final arbiter of disputes, which is why it is an absolute power. In fact, it's something of an anomaly: No other elected federal official can unilaterally grant clemency. This can cause controversy if a president is viewed as issuing pardons for political purposes.

On his last day in office, President Clinton ignited a scandal by issuing 140 pardons, some of them controversial pardons of political supporters, including a pardon of fugitive international financier Marc Rich, who was wanted by the Justice Department on fraud charges, and a pardon of his half-brother Roger, who faced allegations of illegal lobbying.

Perhaps the most famous use of the pardon power was President Ford's full pardon of his

predecessor Richard Nixon for all actions taken by Nixon while he was in office. The pardon eliminated the possibility that the former president would be tried as a private citizen for illegal activities stemming from the Watergate scandal. Ford contended the pardon was necessary because a criminal trial of a former president would prevent the nation from healing. Critics contended the pardon placed Nixon above the law, shielding him from facing responsibility for his actions. There was even speculation at the time that Ford had agreed to pardon Nixon in exchange for the latter's resignation, but if this was so, it exacted a great political cost from Ford, who narrowly lost election to the presidency two years later. Also, it should be remembered that a president has the power to pardon anyone: Before he resigned, Nixon easily could have pardoned himself.

and Congress has never fully accepted it, but presidents have been known to use it freely. It's the power to keep material originating in the executive branch confidential. Although presidents find it helpful—and convenient—to be able to designate material as "privileged," executive privilege is far from an absolute power and can best serve as a defensive maneuver against Congress.

Typically, presidents have claimed executive privilege on matters surrounding national security, on the grounds that public exposure would undermine sensitive government operations—a position that's been upheld by the courts. Presidents have relied on executive privilege to keep members of the executive branch from testifying at congressional hearings and to prevent the release of sensitive documents.

They have also claimed executive privilege in political circumstances to avoid the release of politically damaging information. President Nixon tried unsuccessfully to use executive privilege as a rationale to prevent the release of tapes of Oval Office conversations that implicated him in the Watergate affair.

The Bush administration, arguing an important principle and not politics is involved, claimed executive privilege to prevent the release of information related to meetings between the vice president and energy company officials regarding the development of the administration's national energy policy—even though the vice president isn't the chief executive.

When you add up the president's formal powers, there's not a whole lot a president can use on an everyday basis that will help him politically. Most of the powers are situation-specific and only come into play when the president is faced with treaties he can negotiate, ambassadors he can receive, legislation he can veto, or individuals he can pardon. Recess appointments can only be made during those few weeks when Congress is out of session, and as we said in Chapter 9, the Senate regards them as hostile acts, so many presidents have been reluctant to make them. The appointment power can be formidable and can enable the president to put his mark on the executive branch and the judiciary—but it's only one aspect of the president's job. Likewise, commanding the military is an awesome power, but

much of the president's involvement in domestic and foreign affairs doesn't involve military matters. The constitutional powers granted the president simply do not have a lot of day-in, day-out value.

Informal Presidential Powers

Unlike formal powers, the prerogatives of the presidency can be enormously helpful to a president who wants to put his imprint on politics and policy. Political scientist Richard Neustadt distinguished formal, constitutional powers from informal means of exercising political power, saying the president may not occupy the strongest constitutional position with respect to Congress (which has the final word in overriding vetoes, confirming appointments, and even impeaching the president), but a skillful president can dominate Washington politically through careful use of the informal advantages his office provides. In fact, we will see that most of the president's power comes from informal sources. Neustadt recognized that the doctrine of separation of powers created three branches of government that need to find common ground in order to get anything accomplished. In this environment, a skilled and determined president can emerge a political leader.[9]

He does it by using **persuasion**, by convincing others in Washington whom the president needs to get things done that his interests are their interests. There is no strict formula for doing this, but Neustadt claims the president can have maximum leverage if he enjoys a strong professional reputation in Washington and a high level of public prestige. Maintaining these requires creating favorable impressions of his ability and support.

A president's **professional reputation** is the judgment of him made by others in Washington, based on what he says and what he does. A president who rises above what is expected of him, acts consistently, and stands behind his beliefs is in a solid position to bargain for what he wants.[10] Immediately following the terrorist attack of September 2001, many in Washington who previously doubted whether he was up to the job perceived President Bush as steady, firm, and reassuring. His political stock soared as Bush erased impressions that he was a political lightweight. For several years, President Bush enjoyed the reputation of being a strong, decisive leader. Then, following the administration's halting response to Hurricane Katrina in 2005—which came at a time when the president was experiencing numerous political troubles—that reputation was replaced with far more critical assessments of his managerial and political acumen.

A president's **public prestige** is the impression formed by others in Washington of his standing with the public, and like the president's reputation, high levels of prestige can enhance his persuasiveness by making him a political force to be dealt with. In this regard, the president's public prestige and professional reputation can reinforce each other.[11] When President Bush asked Congress for approval to use military force against Iraq in September 2002, his strong public standing on matters of security and defense made it difficult for some members of Congress to oppose the request, despite their doubts about the advisability of the Iraq mission.

If President Bush had been an unpopular president at the time, congressional opponents of the Iraq War might have found it easier to voice their disapproval without worrying that their constituents would blame them for defying the president. Similarly, low standing with the public can undermine a president's professional reputation. Following the Hurricane Katrina fiasco, the president's popular support fell dramatically, reinforcing the growing perception in Washington that his professional reputation was not what it once had been.

Malleable Public Opinion

Writing over forty years ago, Neustadt saw the president's personality and popularity as secondary factors in determining the president's prestige. Today, anyone who works as a political advisor to the president would pay a great deal of attention to these things. Earlier presidents could take their **mandate** to lead from the election results, but contemporary presidents have to contend with a never-ending barrage of public opinion polls

commissioned by independent research firms, major newspapers and television networks, political parties—even the White House—that measure presidential approval on an ongoing basis.

This gives the president a sliding mandate—a pliable environment for governing that can make him more or less persuasive as his term progresses.[12] Following his re-election victory, with his public support moderately strong, President Bush declared that the judgment of the voters had given him a new well of political capital, which he intended to use to restructure the Social Security system—a massive and politically risky undertaking. However, the president's mandate for change never materialized, owing to the fact that his re-election victory was narrow, generating less political capital than he needed to convince Congress to embark on a gigantic overhaul of a popular program. To complicate matters, the president had said very little about his plans for Social Security during the campaign, making it difficult for him to claim that his re-election victory gave him a direct mandate to make changes to the program.

Because public support is neither steady nor reliable, presidents can have a difficult time mobilizing the public. Even a president with a high standing in public opinion polls can find that it is an effort to rally Congress and the public behind his policies. Much depends on the substance and style of his approach, and on events beyond his control that might independently move public opinion away from him. Starting in late summer 2009, with public support for overhauling the health care system eroding, President Obama embarked on a concerted drive to rally the public behind his reform efforts with a barrage of public appearances, including one before a Joint Session of Congress, that was credited by Washington observers with turning the tide of opinion back in his direction. Sometimes, the best the president can hope to do is move public opinion at the margins, getting some people who were opposed to become indifferent, or some who were indifferent to be supportive. Sometimes, small movements in public opinion are enough to secure the results the president wants—for instance, getting a wavering senator or two to support the president—while at other times, they fall short.[13]

DEMYSTIFYING GOVERNMENT

WHEN DO POLLS GET IN THE WAY OF GOVERNING?

In film and on television, hypothetical presidents make decisions from the heart or the gut without obsessing over the details of polling data. Real presidents are far more likely to keep trusted pollsters as close advisors and rely on their counsel when deciding what positions they should take and how they should act. There are a couple of ways to view this reliance on survey data, which mirror the different legislative roles—the **delegate** and the **trustee**.

When the president keeps his finger on the pulse of public opinion, it could be argued that he's acting like a delegate to govern as the public wishes. However, more than members of Congress, presidents are valued for their wisdom and leadership abilities, characteristics of the trustee role, which include the ability to set a national direction and build support when it's lacking. This is a daunting task for presidents who rely heavily on the safety of public approval.

It's also possible to put polling data ahead of principle. Polls might direct the president to do what's expedient or politically convenient, rather than what he would like to do or what in his judgment is best to do. For instance, it may be responsible but politically unpopular to propose changes to the Social Security program in order to address a projected shortfall in Social Security funding. President Bush campaigned in 2000 on a controversial change that would have permitted limited private investment of Social Security funds—a plan that looked politically appealing when the stock market was booming. Two years later, as stock values fell sharply, pollsters advised Bush to stop talking about the proposal and to stop using the term "privatization" because voters now viewed it negatively—as the president found to his dismay when he

attempted to introduce "personal accounts" (the poll-tested replacement for "privatization") for Social Security in 2005.

At another level, when we see the president changing or shading positions in response to polls, it can work against the desire some people have to view the president as an independent leader. True, part of this desire is rooted in those sometimes unrealistic expectations of the president that we talked about earlier. Unrealistic or not, though, expectations can translate into attitudes. In theory, we might like to see the president move boldly on principle against the tide of public opinion. In practice, the president's political advisors would most likely say it's not worth the risk of alienating the electorate.

Not every president will listen to this advice. Despite the primacy of polling data in White House decision making, presidents have been known to buck the suggestions of their pollsters when facing problems that demanded risky, unpopular solutions. President Bush (senior) violated his most prominent campaign pledge— "read my lips: no new taxes"—and supported a tax increase in order to win congressional support for an economic package he felt on the whole was best for the economy (thus triggering a political backlash that undermined his reelection prospects). Back in the 1950s, when the science of modern polling was emerging, President Truman (who was often beset with weak job approval ratings) was fond of saying, "I wonder how far Moses would have gone if he had taken a poll in Egypt? What would Jesus Christ have preached if he'd taken a poll in Israel? ... It isn't polls or public opinion of the moment that counts. It is right and wrong and leadership."[T2]

The possibility of moving public opinion at the margins factored into President Obama's health care strategy, as it became evident in mid-2009 that Senate Republicans were standing firmly against the president's reform push. Facing potential defections from a few Democrats representing conservative states, the president tried to rally public opinion behind health care reform in the hope of influencing Olympia Snowe and Susan Collins, two Republican senators from the politically moderate state of Maine. But, overall support for Obama's efforts slipped as the complex legislative process played out. Senator Snowe broke with her party and was the only Republican to support the legislation on the Senate Finance Committee, but made it clear that her vote in committee might not reflect her vote on final passage of the bill. "My vote today is my vote today," she said, in a nod to the complexities of public opinion on the matter in her home state. "It doesn't forecast what my vote will be tomorrow."[14] Several months later, despite White House efforts, Snowe announced she would not buck her party and voted against the bill, along with the rest of the Senate Republican caucus.[15]

The summary figure that president-watchers (and presidents) look at to gauge presidential effectiveness is support for the president's performance in office: the percentage of Americans who approve and the percentage who disapprove. However, the polling environment is complex because pollsters ask so many questions—about individual policies, hypothetical approaches to problems, approval of the president as an individual, and much more.[16] Demystifying Government: When Do Polls Get in the Way of Governing?, demonstrates how data on presidential performance are used.

With all the variables involved in opinion polls, there is one constant to the shape of presidential job approval that applies to almost all contemporary presidents: It goes down with time. Flush with the excitement and great expectations produced by a winning campaign, new presidents often come to office with a reservoir of goodwill that translates into a **honeymoon** period with the press and the public.[17] Trading on the unrealistic expectations of the presidential myth, new presidents offer the promise of great things; even people who supported

the losing candidate are typically willing to give the new president a chance.

It doesn't take long for reality to set in. After a few weeks or months, unrealistically high expectations give way to the reality of governing, where hard choices by necessity begin to alienate groups of constituents. This is particularly the case during difficult economic times, which are generally blamed on the person in the White House. Presidential approval falls. The honeymoon becomes a distant memory.[18] President Obama's initial job approval numbers were in the high sixty-percent range immediately after his inauguration. By the fall of 2009—after whirlwind eight months of governing—they were in the low 50s, close to the margin he had been elected with a year before, and for much of 2010 more Americans disapproved than approved of his performance in office. Figure 9.1 shows the unmistakable downward trend in presidential job performance scores in presidents dating back to Lyndon Johnson.

Even though the general trend in presidential approval is downward, events can conspire to bolster a president's public standing. Typically, if a president is reelected, there is a brief "second honeymoon" characterized by an uptick in public approval. Even after his narrow re-election victory, President Bush enjoyed an increase in public approval—although his second honeymoon was very brief, owing to growing public concern over the war in Iraq, economic conditions, and the president's unpopular efforts to reform Social Security.

It is also quite commonplace for traumatic national events to produce a **rally effect**, whereby people turn to the president for leadership, temporarily bolstering his support scores in the process. The interesting thing about a rally effect is that it tends to happen regardless of what the president does, how well he performs, or whether he does anything at all. After President Reagan was shot in a failed assassination attempt in 1981, his job approval went up seven points. Early in his administration, President Kennedy ordered a failed assault on Cuba known as the Bay of Pigs invasion. It was a fiasco, the president admitted it was a mistake—and his job approval ratings went up. Americans were taken hostage in Iran during the Carter administration, the president did nothing, and his approval scores

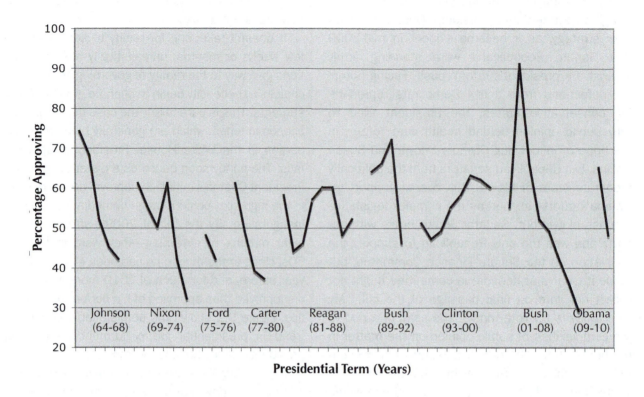

Figure 9.1. Down They Go. The general direction of presidential job performance scores is down. Of the eight presidents to hold office before Barack Obama, only Ronald Reagan left office on the upswing, and only Reagan and Bill Clinton left with a majority of the public approving their performance.[T3]

went up, too.[19] But gravity inevitably takes its toll on rallies. In Carter's case, as the Iranian hostage crisis dragged on for 444 days, his public support took a nosedive.

President Bush experienced an unconventional pattern of public support in the early years of his administration because of the unusual way he came to power and the dramatic impact of the 2001 terror attacks. Instead of coming to Washington awash in good feelings, Bush had a stunted honeymoon following his contested election. Then the tragic events of September 11, 2001, united the public around the president, who saw his job approval top 90 percent—an unprecedented level commensurate with events. Bush's job approval scores remained high one year later, even as large numbers of Americans expressed concern about the direction of the economy. It seems that many people were willing to forgive the president for falling stock prices and a poor job market, either because they blamed the terror attacks for bad economic times

or because their support for Bush's work in foreign affairs weighed more heavily in their overall assessment of his job performance.

In his second and third years, President Bush experienced a more customary pattern of public support. The president continued to realize a decline in popular support into his second year as unemployment mounted. This decline was halted by another rally event—the Iraq War—which briefly produced a surge in presidential approval that dissipated over the summer of Bush's third year, when American troops faced violence in postwar Iraq and the job market remained weak. The capture of Saddam Hussein in late 2003 produced another temporary bump in support for President Bush, but he faced strong political opposition throughout the 2004 presidential campaign as his approval rating sagged into the high 40 percent range.

Then, in his fifth year, President Bush experienced something of the mirror-image to the dynamics in play early in his first term. Although presidential

DEMYSTIFYING GOVERNMENT

PRESIDENTIAL CHARACTER

Political scientist James David Barber suggested that one way to think about presidential character is to assess whether a president has an energetic, active approach to his job or a removed, passive style, and then to determine if the president takes pleasure in his activity or feels burdened by it. By crossing these two characteristics (activity and self-esteem), Barber arrives at four presidential character "types" or patterns into which every president can be classified.

The four types are displayed below: "active-positive;" "active-negative;" "passive-positive;" and "passive-negative."[T4]

Barber was heavily influenced by the behavior of Presidents Johnson and Nixon, whom he considered dangerous because of what he saw as "an energy distorted from within." Both were "active-negative" types who deceived the press and public, Johnson during the Vietnam War and Nixon during the Watergate scandal.

Barber claims that presidents with different character profiles would have behaved less compulsively and self-destructively, and he says we need to be aware of character issues before "hiring" a new president in order to avoid future troubles. However, his work is not without controversy. He admits to a preference for active-positive presidents (a categorization that even *sounds* more appealing than "passive" or "negative"), who display the energy of a Johnson or a Nixon but who are flexible and adaptive. However, this choice could be said to favor a governing model in which the president is an activist, rather than one where the president delegates the particulars of a limited agenda. Furthermore, because Barber's categories are broad, classifying presidents using his framework leaves room for a fair amount of interpretation.

Active-Positive	*Active-Negative*
Examples: Franklin D. Roosevelt John F. Kennedy • Flexible and adaptive • Develops and grows over time • Feels capable of meeting job challenges • Well-grounded • Results-oriented	Examples: Lyndon B. Johnson Richard M. Nixon • Compulsive and insecure • Distorted ambition, which compensates for low self-esteem • Trouble managing aggressive feelings • Unable to correct misguided actions • Dangerous power-seeker
Passive-Positive	*Passive-Negative*
Example: Ronald Reagan • Compliant • Reacts to events rather than assert himself • Nice guy searching for affection • Low self-esteem • Often disappointing in public office	Example: Dwight D. Eisenhower • Does little and enjoys little of what he does • Motivated by duty and service • Inflexible • Withdraws from conflict • Could lead the nation adrift

second terms are customarily marked by an over-time decline in public approval, the Bush presidency lost support more quickly and to a greater degree than most of his recent predecessors. One year after he won re-election, Bush's performance was embraced by less than 40% of Americans, bogged down by the on-going war in Iraq, soaring fuel costs, and the indictments of high-level Republican officials. Such unusually low support, realized so quickly in the president's second term, was the bookend to Bush's unprecedented high approval ratings early in his first, marking for the second time in five years an unusual extreme in presidential approval.

Rally effects aside, presidents labor—often unsuccessfully—to keep their performance ratings up in an effort to marshal their power. Political scientist Theodore Lowi, writing during the Reagan administration, saw a democratic dilemma in what he calls the personal presidency, where presidential power is built on popular support for things the president realistically can't deliver because the constitutional system is designed to frustrate his initiatives, not advance them. Only rarely can a president prevail over institutional checks and balances—like during a national crisis when he can rally Congress to his side. These are the exceptions—but we expect them to be the rule, an expectation that's inflated by our mythical notion of what the president can do and by presidents who play to that myth for political reasons, making promises that are hard to deliver.

Lacking the institutional powers necessary to play to public expectations, Lowi claims presidents engage in sales efforts to convince the public that they've met those expectations. He says that following a sincere effort to keep their promises, presidents spend their terms trying to create the illusion of success. Appearance replaces performance, sending performance expectations further out of whack with reality.[20]

With the personal side of the presidency playing such a large role in how the president governs, the makeup of the president's character can be important. Admittedly, character takes into account a lot of factors—it can be hard to pin down exactly what it is, much less figure out how it relates to presidential performance. One provocative approach

to understanding presidential character is considered in Demystifying Government: Presidential Character.

The Media as a Presidential Resource

It's easier for presidents to sell the idea that they're performing than it is to actually perform because they have greater access to tools that allow them to speak effectively than to act effectively. Belying the chronic drop-off in public support that awaits most presidents is the fact that they have considerable resources at their disposal in their ongoing efforts to keep the public behind them. Most noteworthy is the megaphone the president can use to amplify his voice above the din of official Washington and command the attention of the press: There are 535 members of Congress, and the nine Supreme Court justices operate largely out of public view; the president is the only officer who alone can speak for a branch of government, an administration, or the nation. In this regard, the president can depend on the media to be an important source of informal power that enables him—if he is skillful—to elevate the importance of a constitutionally weak office.

The "Bully Pulpit"

Teddy Roosevelt called the president's elevated vantage point the "bully pulpit" ("bully" in Roosevelt's day meant wonderful), and presidents who have been skillful communicators (or who have had shrewd and skillful communications aides) have been able to command it with some success. Roosevelt served during the height of mass-circulation newspapers and he shrewdly recognized the president's ability to use the mass media to reach out to the public and advance his agenda.[21] Subsequent presidents have mastered radio, television and the Internet as vehicles for reaching the public with their messages. But all contemporary presidents who routinely engage in media strategies can trace their efforts to what Teddy Roosevelt started over one hundred years ago.

One of the more typical ways that presidents use the "bully pulpit" is by appealing directly to Americans through the media to support their agenda. Political scientist Samuel Kernell calls this strategy "**going public**," and although it can be traced back in some fashion to Teddy Roosevelt, it has become the centerpiece of modern presidential governing styles.[22] President Obama "goes public" every time he makes a televised speech, appears at events around the country or the world, or employs **media events** to draw attention to and build support for an initiative. Today, presidents will go so far as to talk about policy initiatives in front of a backdrop bearing a slogan that tersely reinforces his main point—something like "Protecting Worker's Rights" or "Preserving Precious Natural Resources." It may seem cheesy and more suited to a salesperson than a national leader, but when the president goes public, he in effect becomes salesperson-in-chief.

Even casual attention to television or the Internet would reveal that presidents frequently engage in public sales efforts. The point is to put pressure on members of Congress, while circumventing them at the same time. In Neustadt's terms, "going public" involves the president leveraging public prestige by moving voters to his position, rather than bargaining with members of Congress directly. Because these are the same voters who pass judgment on members of Congress, the strategy can be effective.

Media Operations

As objectionable as it may be to some people, public relations and advertising campaigns have become an integral part of White House operations and an essential part of being president. A large number of high-level White House staff members devote their time to developing, managing, and communicating the president's message on a daily basis. In the Bush White House, the key players reside in the **Communications Office**, contributing to the strategic planning of the president's policy agenda by formulating daily messages and planning media events designed to get the press to discuss the president's agenda and to do so in the way the president desires. In effect, the Communications Office tries to set the agenda for the agenda-setters in the press.

As part of this effort, the Communications Office coordinates the following communications functions:

- *Contact with national reporters.* The **press secretary** is the conduit between the president and the press. He or she manages requests for interviews with White House officials and holds regular **press briefings** with national newspaper, television, radio, magazine, and wire-service reporters who cover the White House, answering their questions—or avoiding them if doing so is in the president's interest. In recent administrations, the press secretary has worked to keep tight control over the flow of information.
- *Contact with local reporters and special interest media.* The Media Affairs Office is responsible for handling requests by local television and radio stations, newspapers, and specialized media, such as business, religious, and sports publications, for interviews with White House personnel and official information. The Media Affairs Office also maintains the White House website at http://www.whitehouse.gov.
- *Speechwriting.* The president employs a number of people who put words in his mouth, scripting everything from formal addresses to talking points for presidential appearances.[23]

The point of the effort is to get the White House to speak with one carefully crafted voice, which is often difficult to accomplish. The job of coordinating a single message can be daunting because so many people work with and around the president, all of whom have personal agendas that are not always the same as the president's. Administration officials routinely circumvent the official communications operation by giving news leaks to the press when it serves their purposes, even if it undermines the president's official message. Some White Houses are "leakier" than others. The Obama White House is tightly run, whereas the Clinton White House was known for its lack of discipline. The Bush White

DEMYSTIFYING GOVERNMENT

IS PRESIDENTIAL NEWS MANAGEMENT A PROBLEM?

It may be a normatively good thing for democratic processes when the White House is unable to control the message it wants to communicate on a daily basis. After all, it's critical for information to flow freely if we're going to have the chance to be well informed, and at its core, presidential news management is about restricting information to the press and, by extension, to us. The argument against coordinated presidential news management strategies is that controlling the flow of information to the press will always serve the president's political purposes—presenting him and his policies in the best possible light. It may not simultaneously serve the public interest if, in the process, information is withheld or manipulated.

News management in the George W. Bush White House fell under intense scrutiny in 2003 when it came to light that the president may have intentionally or unintentionally misstated the level of the threat posed by Saddam Hussein prior to the American invasion of Iraq. As part of his effort to win public support for the Iraq War, President Bush made the claim that Hussein possessed weapons of mass destruction and was engaged in developing nuclear weapons. After the invasion, Iraqi weapons of mass destruction were not found, and reports surfaced that claims about Hussein's nuclear capability were based on faulty intelligence that high-level administration officials may have known to be false.

Critics who wanted to know how the White House could successfully exaggerate and misrepresent the Iraqi threat when war hung in the balance blasted a highly efficient White House news management operation that prevented careful press scrutiny of the facts. With the president, vice president, and key advisors speaking in concert about information they tightly controlled, critics charged the administration could not be effectively challenged as it led the nation to war under what they said were false pretenses. The president himself only met with the press once during the prewar period—see the discussion of press conferences that follows—and that was in a controlled setting in which the reporters who would get to ask questions were preselected to minimize the likelihood that they might raise issues the president did not want to address.

To those who felt it was in the national interest for the administration to convince the public to support the Iraq War by any means, careful news management advanced their desired outcome. To those who argued that the best way for citizens of a republic to make informed is for them to be provided with a full rendering of pertinent information, the White House news management strategy was seen as undermining intelligent public decision-making.

House was highly intolerant of **news leaks**, unless they were put out on purpose with the blessing of the Communications Office to test public reaction to a policy move the White House was planning.[24] Their discipline had meaningful consequences for policy, as you'll see when you read Demystifying Government: Is Presidential News Management a Problem?

Presidents also have a couple of other tools to get their message to the public through the press. Presidents skilled in structured question-and-answer formats have relied on **press conferences** with reporters who cover the White House to disseminate the official line on topics of importance to the administration. Press conferences can either be conducted privately or staged as television events. President Kennedy, for instance, was fond of televised press conferences because he could use them to speak directly to the public, in effect turning them into media events where reporters were props.[25]

Presidents generally cannot control what happens at a press conference, of course, but press conferences don't have to be risky ventures for them. They can take questions from reporters known to be friendly to the administration. Presidential advisors can usually anticipate the major questions reporters will ask, and speechwriters can craft responses in advance. Even if a question isn't about something he wants to address, the president can give a quick and general response and move rapidly to something he wants to talk about. Because reporters customarily are limited in their ability to follow up, it can be hard for them to get the president to address something he doesn't want to talk about. All this restricts how informative press conferences can be.[26]

President Clinton held press conferences less frequently than some of his recent predecessors; President Bush rarely held them, opting instead to let his press secretary interact with reporters. In the first months of his administration, President Obama has been inclined to address the press regularly. However often they held formal press events, every president since Franklin D. Roosevelt has held background briefings or "**backgrounders**," where reporters are given information "off the record"—meaning they can use it as long as they don't attribute it to its source. Any administration official may hold a backgrounder, and unlike press conferences, they can be a good source of information for reporters. The administration can use backgrounders to float a policy idea without having the president's fingerprints on it in case it flops with the public (much like the way news leaks can be used), or even to send messages to other nations about possible foreign policy initiatives without yet having to defend them as official policy.[27]

Tensions with Reporters

As presidents have come to view the press as a tool in a public relations campaign, reporters have pushed back by looking critically, even cynically, at the president's motives and by reporting his actions accordingly. Today, presidential news is more likely to be about the motivation underlying what the president said or did than simply about his words or actions. By reporting on the presidential public relations machine, reporters try to dilute its effects by drawing attention to it.

It may be hard to believe that for a period before the Vietnam War, the president was widely regarded by the press as a public servant who spoke for the nation, and reporters would pass his words on uncritically. That was before the Johnson administration lied to reporters about American progress in Vietnam and the Nixon administration lied about the president's involvement in Watergate. Media advisors to Presidents Reagan, Clinton, and George W. Bush relentlessly stage-managed the president's image, leading reporters who felt they had been lied to by Johnson and Nixon to experience the additional burden of feeling controlled by the White House. The cumulative product of these experiences was the creation of an adversarial relationship between reporters and the president, in keeping with the relationship between reporters and political figures.

For a period of several years following the September 11, 2001 terrorist attacks, reporters covering President Bush assumed a more respectful and less critical tone reminiscent of coverage in the early days of television, in keeping with widespread calls for national unity. But, when the administration's slow response to Hurricane Katrina undermined the president's reputation as a decisive leader and capable manager, reporters who witnessed the bungled response first-hand began to revert to the more confrontational position they had taken toward President Bush's immediate predecessors.

Once again, the contours of a complex relationship between reporters and the president came into view. Presidents want to control the timing and content of news stories. So do reporters. Because the president's ability to persuade the public and official Washington depends so heavily on the media, he can't do without the reporters who cover his actions. At the same time, because the prestige and career advancement of those who cover his actions depend on having access to the White House, reporters can't do without the president.[28]

Because it's an ongoing relationship, both parties typically find a way to cooperate, although reporters will find some administrations to be more forthcoming than others, and levels of cooperation change over the course of time. Political scientists Michael Grossman and Martha Kumar identify three distinct phases in the relationship between the president and the press, starting with a period of alliance when an administration is new and reporters are engaged in developing relationships with new people in the president's press operation. It's a time when reporter and administration self-interest calls for cooperation, as both groups benefit from covering the administration in a favorable light.

It usually doesn't last long. Once the administration gets down to the business of governing, conflicts and controversies are inevitable. Reporters, seeing these items as **newsworthy**, diverge from the White House view of how (or whether) the story should be covered. A phase of competition sets in, leading reporters and White House officials to engage in manipulative actions for control of the agenda. The competition phase can endure for a long time before giving way to detachment, when the administration gives up on trying to build support for its agenda, abandoning its most intensive efforts to control the press. During the detachment phase, the president more or less avoids the press, and his schedule is tightly controlled.[29] Detachment is likely to set in during the final years of a president's second term, when reporters find greater newsworthiness in the race to replace the incumbent. In the Bush administration, the phase of competition left reporters griping that the Communications Office controlled information so tightly that, in the words of one reporter—uttered long before the devastation of Hurricane Katrina—"If the National Hurricane Center were as stingy with its information, there would be thousands dead."[30]

Chief Executive

For an officer with a brief constitutional job description, the president performs a wide range of policy and political roles: chief executive, chief legislator, chief of state, commander-in-chief, and chief of party. We'll look at each one in turn. Although we will find in these roles the occasional constitutional power like the ability to make appointments, the veto power, and the power to negotiate treaties, almost every tool the president wields has developed through custom and practice, placing them in the realm of informal powers—like the president's use of the media—that have expanded the capacity of a constitutionally limited branch.

When we talk about the president as the **chief executive**, we mean he's the chief executive officer of the United States, as well as the chief of the executive branch of government, or the bureaucracy. In this capacity, he exercises "the executive Power" in a number of specific ways.

Making Appointments

We said earlier that presidents have the formal power to make appointments to key federal positions, which are subject to Senate confirmation. A big part of his role as chief executive rests with the appointments the president can make to upper-level positions in the bureaucracy. These include top appointments to the departments, agencies, and commissions that comprise the federal bureaucracy—and there are a lot of them, from large departments like Defense, Justice, and Treasury, to more narrowly focused agencies like the Federal Election Commission, the Federal Trade Commission, and the Nuclear Regulatory Commission. The Library of Congress has a complete list, which you may find online at http://www.loc.gov/rr/news/fedgov.html. If you go there, be sure to scroll down to the bottom of the screen to get a sense of the scope of the executive branch.

There are serious limits to the president's appointment power. All in all, over 1.85 million people (not including postal workers) were employed in the executive branch in 2008.[31] Of these, the president appointed only a few thousand. The rest are civil servants, who get and hold their jobs independent of political considerations and are not indebted to the president. Furthermore, there are limits to the president's ability to remove people he appoints. The president cannot remove appointees who have fixed terms of office, like members of the Federal Communications Commission or the Federal Reserve Board, just as he can't remove judicial appointees. He has a lot more latitude over political assistants and cabinet members, whom he can remove at will.

The Constitution does not give the president the power to appoint a **cabinet**. It doesn't even mention one. However, every president has had one. George Washington had four cabinet secretaries: State, War, Treasury, and Justice. Today, there are fifteen (see Table 9.4).

In the Obama administration, seven other people also have cabinet "rank." They are: the vice president, the president's chief of staff (Bill Daley), the United States trade representative (Ronald Kirk), the United States Ambassador to the United Nations (Susan Rice), the chair of the Council of Economic Advisers (Austan Goolsbee), and the directors of the Environmental Protection Agency (Lisa Jackson) and the Office of Management and Budget (Jacob Lew).[32] Cabinet rank is assigned at the president's discretion, so these other individuals will vary from administration

to administration. Several of these other cabinet-level officials in the Obama administration are part of the White House staff, or what is more formally called the **Executive Office of the President (EOP)**—the large, sprawling staff that assists the president in making political and policy decisions on a wide range of matters.

Contrary to widely held popular belief, presidents rarely convene their cabinets to get advice and make decisions because cabinet members function first as the head of their respective departments and only second as presidential advisors.[33] More often, communication in cabinet meetings flows in one direction: from the president to the cabinet secretaries, on whom the president relies to advance administration policies. It would be frustrating for the president to try to do otherwise because cabinet secretaries, as specialists in their own areas of expertise, have little in common with each other. As the heads of large departments, they may also have conflicting interests and agendas—something that doesn't lend itself to a frank and open exchange of ideas and advice.

Table 9.4. The President's Cabinet

Department	Created	2011 Obama Cabinet
State	1789	Secretary of State Hillary Rodham Clinton
Defense	1789	Defense Secretary Robert Gates
Treasury	1789	Treasury Secretary Timothy Geithner
Justice	1789	Attorney General Eric Holder
Interior	1849	Interior Secretary Kenneth Salazar
Agriculture	1862	Agriculture Secretary Thomas Vilsack
Commerce	1903	Commerce Secretary Gary Locke
Labor	1913	Labor Secretary Hilda Solis
Health and Human Services	1953	HHS Secretary Kathleen Sebelius
Housing and Urban Development	1965	HUD Secretary Shaun Donovan
Transportation	1966	Transportation Secretary Ray LaHood
Energy	1977	Energy Secretary Steven Chu
Education	1979	Education Secretary Arne Duncan
Veterans' Affairs	1988	Secretary of Veterans' Affairs Eric Shinseki
Homeland Security	2002	Homeland Security Secretary Janet Napolitano

Preparing Budgets

Congress has the power of the purse, but as chief executive, the president has a hand in formulating the budget. Like the cabinet, this role is not mentioned in the Constitution, but as the federal government took on more responsibilities in the twentieth century, the executive branch grew in size (revisit Table 10.4 to see how many cabinet departments were created after 1900). The president as chief executive naturally assumed a larger role in creating the budgets for these departments.

This role was formalized in the **Budget and Accounting Act of 1921**, which detailed the president's responsibility in the budget process. Among its key provisions are:

- The requirement that the president submit an annual budget proposal to Congress, reflecting his spending priorities and estimating how much money it's going to take to keep the executive branch operational for another year.
- The establishment of the **Office of Management and Budget (OMB)**, formally the Bureau of the Budget, which assists the president in formulating his budget.
- The establishment of a congressional investigative office, the General Accounting Office (GAO), designed to ensure the accountability of the executive branch.

The president's budget proposal is just a recommendation, and in a Congress controlled by the opposition party, it's likely to be "dead on arrival." However, because the president gets to draft a formal proposal, he gets to be a player in the budget debate that takes place in Congress. At a minimum, he has a forum for presenting his priorities. If he's dealing with a sympathetic Congress, he'll find that his recommendations are given serious consideration.

Issuing Executive Orders

The Constitution instructs the president to "take Care that the Laws be faithfully executed," but without a road map showing how to do this, presidents since Washington have used **executive orders** to make directives to the bureaucracy that do not require congressional approval and that carry the force of law. Executive orders are another informal presidential power because they are based on a broad interpretation of the Constitution. They permit the president to act unilaterally on matters that are not itemized in the Constitution, and the courts have generally upheld the president's right to issue them.

Most executive orders are procedural or of little interest, but on occasion, presidents have used executive orders to do an end run around Congress and create policy. President Truman used an executive order to desegregate the armed forces (which are part of the executive branch). President Johnson used an executive order to require that private businesses receiving federal contracts (through executive branch departments) implement affirmative action policies. President Reagan used an executive order to ban abortion counseling in federally supported clinics. President Clinton used an executive order to overturn it.[34]

Chief Legislator

In addition to being chief executive officer and presiding over the executive branch, the president plays a central role in the legislative process by shepherding an agenda through Congress. Or, more accurately, every president tries to get Congress to approve his initiatives. In making the president **chief legislator**, the Constitution gives the president the vantage point from which to lead Congress but offers no guarantee of success. Much of the capital a president accumulates by developing a strong professional reputation and enhancing his public prestige goes to convincing Congress to support his legislative initiatives. Win or lose, presidents know their leadership skills will be evaluated in the next election on the basis of how well they moved their program through Congress.

Proposing an Agenda

The origins of a president's agenda may be found in the election campaign—in the platform drafted at the party convention where the president was nominated and the rhetoric of his campaign speeches—and in the issues the president makes a priority upon taking office. Advancing that agenda can be difficult, as presidents meet with mixed degrees of success in converting their priorities into congressional priorities. Sometimes, this is because what the president wants to accomplish is simply not what the congressional leadership wants to do. President Nixon had to deal with this when he came to office. Sometimes, it's because presidents set out too many priorities for Congress to handle and find that their effort to accomplish a lot of things results in little or nothing getting done. President Clinton met with this fate when he tried to make four huge issues—health care, trade, spending, and taxation—his top priorities in his first term.

It's often hard to predict how effectively a president is going to manage his role as chief legislator. President Nixon faced resistance from an opposition Congress, but so did President Reagan, and Reagan was able to get Congress to accept his agenda, whereas Nixon was not. President Clinton tried unsuccessfully to get a Congress controlled by his own party to do a lot; President Johnson faced the same situation and was largely successful.

The differences? They can be explained in part by the situation surrounding the president's rise to power. President Johnson took office upon John F. Kennedy's assassination, and a year later won a lopsided election victory over a weak opponent. President Reagan won only slightly more than half the popular vote but carried better than 90 percent of electoral votes. Even though Reagan's election was in part a repudiation of incumbent Jimmy Carter, the press interpreted the election as a mandate for Reagan's legislative agenda, and that helped shape the public's response. The same interpretation followed Johnson's election, with similar results. Whether or not either interpretation was warranted, it had the effect of creating a climate in which the new president could place his agenda at center stage. Neither Nixon nor Clinton had this advantage.[35]

Lobbying Congress

Still, a mandate—or the appearance of a mandate—is simply a tool. Presidents need to maximize their resources of persuasion if they're going to put this tool to good use. They and their aides need to quickly identify their top legislative priorities. They need to organize staff members who will be responsible for **legislative liaison**—maintaining ongoing contact with Congress and lobbying for the president's proposals at every step of the legislative process. They need to develop a strategy about how they're going to do this. They need to access and absorb volumes of technical information on their policy priorities so they're ready for the inevitable questions or problems that will arise with Congress. They need to have insight into the ways of the federal government, or be clever enough to surround themselves with others who do. They need to persevere through the long and often frustrating legislative process, despite the emotional or physical toll it may take.[36]

If the administration has its priorities straight, is organized, efficient, strategic, informed, familiar with Washington, and tireless, it can approach Congress from a position of strength. Then, if the president has capital by virtue of his electoral mandate, professional reputation, and public prestige, he has a chance of seeing his legislative priorities move through Congress. At least, that's the way it would work in an ideal world.

Everything could be in place for the president, and circumstances might still work against his best efforts. If an international crisis arises, it's likely that the president's domestic agenda will get sidetracked. If members of Congress are gearing up for reelection, it's possible that little legislating will get done because members will be more interested in drawing partisan distinctions than in making the compromises necessary to advance legislation.

That's why the timing of a president's actions is so important. There's a good reason we've been talking about legislative efforts during the early days of a presidential administration—during the honeymoon—when official Washington is typically most open to listening to what the president has to say. Time is the president's enemy if he wishes to lead Congress. This is why President Obama moved swiftly to get Congress to enact the largest and most difficult component of his domestic agenda—health care reform—in his first months.

One presidential aide put it this way: "You've got to give it all you can that first year. Doesn't matter what kind of majority you come in with. You've got just one year when [members of Congress] treat you right and before they start worrying about themselves."[37] Another presidential assistant picks apart the typical four-year presidential administration like this: "You should subtract one year for the reelection campaign, another six months for the midterm [elections], six months for the start-up, six months for the closing, and another month or two for an occasional vacation. That leaves you with a two-year presidential term."[38]

Vetoing Legislation

Perhaps the president's strongest legislative weapon is negative. The Constitution gives the president the formal power to veto legislation sent to him by Congress, which has to muster a two-thirds vote in both houses to **override** the veto and make the legislation into law without the president's approval. The veto can be a strategic tool that a president can use to try to shape legislation to his liking and can be particularly useful to presidents who face a Congress controlled by the opposing party. If the president threatens to veto legislation while it's being considered by Congress, and the threat is credible—meaning members of Congress believe the president will go through with it—they could decide to reshape elements of the legislation to the president's liking. Considering how hard it is to muster two-thirds majorities in both houses to override a veto, such shifting might make sense to legislators who would at least come out with some of what they want. It also means that a president doesn't always have to use the veto for it to be a potent weapon; the mere threat of action sometimes will suffice. Demystifying Government: Some Constitutional Tricks discusses other options the president has when considering how to act on legislation.

If a president does veto a bill, the odds are great that the veto will hold up. Of 1,496 regular vetoes[39] cast between 1789 and 2010, only 109 have been overridden—about 7 percent. Presidents only have to worry about an override if they veto a bill that has widespread public support or if they're up against a Congress dominated by the other party. The latter situation is rare, although it has happened. President Ford, a Republican, faced overwhelming Democratic House and Senate majorities, which kept passing legislation he did not support. Ford's response was to use the veto pen forty-eight times in two and a half years, only to see twelve of them, or 25 percent, overridden—a rate of override about three and a half times the presidential average.[40] Under the circumstances, the strategy of using the veto as a way to get Congress to bend to the president's wishes was unavailable to President Ford. His only viable strategic option was to use the veto to send a message of disapproval to the legislature. Figure 9.2 shows how many vetoes the presidents since John F. Kennedy have cast.

Through his first six years in office, President Bush vetoed only one bill—legislation that would have lifted funding restrictions on embryonic stem cell research. In total, Bush only vetoed ten bills in eight years. As Figure 9.2 indicates, this figure is historically low for recent administrations. Instead, the president relied to an unprecedented degree on signing statements—written pronouncements by the executive accompanying his signature on legislation. Other presidents have issued signing statements, but not to the same extent as President Bush and largely for the purpose of clarifying their views on the legislation they were signing. By one count, President Bush issued close to 800 signing statements in his first six years, besting by 200 the total number issued by all his predecessors *combined*.

And Bush's use of signing statements was highly controversial, because he employed them to qualify and in some cases nullify the contents of the bills he has signed into law, thereby greatly expanding the power of the executive with respect to the legislature. In 2006, a bipartisan task force convened by the American Bar Association came out strongly against Bush's use of signing statements, and the

DEMYSTIFYING GOVERNMENT

SOME CONSTITUTIONAL TRICKS

The Constitution lets the president pull a nifty maneuver if Congress passes legislation he doesn't want to sign and then adjourns within ten days of acting. It's called a **pocket veto**, and it lets the president veto a bill by doing absolutely nothing. Because Congress is out of town, a presidential veto could not be delivered to Congress for its consideration. So, the Constitution under these circumstances gives the president two options: Sign the bill, or put it in your pocket and forget about it. After the ten-day window is over, if the bill doesn't have the president's signature, it dies. This makes a pocket veto absolute—it cannot be overridden.

On the other hand, if Congress is in session and the president receives legislation he doesn't particularly like but has decided not to veto, he has the option of leaving it on his desk for ten days, at which point, it becomes law without his signature. A president might do this as a way of signaling that he recognizes he doesn't have the support to sustain a veto, but because he dislikes the legislation, he's going to let the bill become law without his name on it.

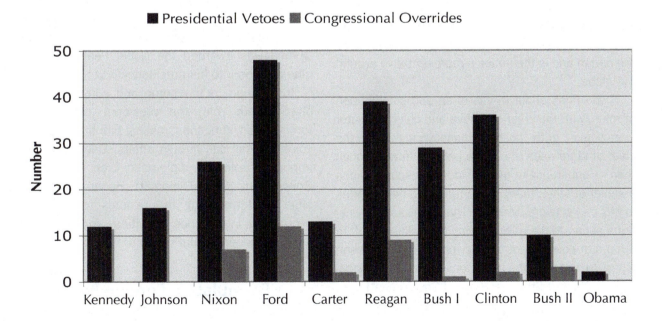

Figure 9.2. Presidents and their Vetoes [T6]

philosophy that suggests a president can interpret laws to his liking and sign—then gut—laws he does not like. The Bar Association flagged this as a serious violation of separation of powers and checks and balances, and urged Congress to prohibit the president from issuing signing statements without making a full report to Congress offering a legal basis for disregarding the law he has signed. They also urged the president to simply use his constitutional veto if he does not agree with an act of Congress.

Chief of Staff and Foreign Policy Leader

If the president's chief executive and chief legislator roles are marked by the strategic allocation of resources in an ongoing, often frustrating tug-of-war with Congress, the president as **chief of state** lives a much more charmed existence. A chief of state is a nation's official envoy to the world, a nation's symbolic and ceremonial head. The chief of state greets foreign dignitaries and has formal state dinners in their honor. The chief of state gets to light the official White House Christmas tree, and grants honorary recognition to celebrities. He speaks for the nation and is the nation's representative around the globe.

If you think about it, this is an odd combination of roles, with the chief executive and chief legislator engaging in gritty political maneuvering while the chief of state rises above the political fray. Although there is substance to the president's responsibilities as chief of state, many of the functions he performs in this capacity are symbolic. That's why so many nations separate the roles, leaving the political stuff to a head of government and permitting a nonpartisan figure to assume the ceremonial role (see Global Topics: Chief of State vs. Head of Government).

Because we roll all these roles into one job, we ask the president to unify us as our symbolic representative and move us forward as our government leader—even though politics is, by definition, a divisive business. This can lead to some interesting wrinkles in the way presidents act and in the way we relate to our presidents. For instance, while

opinion polls repeatedly showed large percentages of Americans approved of Bill Clinton's policy agenda, the litany of finance and sex scandals that pockmarked his administration marred his performance as chief of state. Some who saw Clinton as unprincipled or shady objected to him being the official voice of the United States, preferring instead someone they could relate to or be proud of.

George W. Bush tapped this desire when he campaigned for office as someone who people would be proud to have as their symbolic leader. Following the 2001 terror attack, President Bush continually emphasized his role as chief of state, both to unify the nation and, subsequently, to leverage the support he was receiving for his partisan political battles with Congress. For Bush, being a successful chief of state became a resource in his role as chief legislator.

When Barack Obama ran for the presidency, he emphasized that having a person of color assume the presidency would send an important message to other nations. Attuned to the symbolism of the office, Obama has made reference to his historic election as emblematic of a change in America's posture toward the rest of the world, which had become strained during the Bush years. In what could be interpreted as a symbolic response, President Obama was awarded the Nobel Peace Prize just nine months into his presidency.

In addition to the pomp and ceremony of the chief-of-state role, the president performs key foreign policy functions, making him the paramount voice in American foreign affairs. One of his more important roles is diplomatic (see Demystifying Government: Chief Diplomat). He is also responsible for formulating the nation's foreign policy, overseeing intelligence activities, and functioning as commander-in-chief of the armed forces.

Formulating Foreign Policy

In keeping with the general tendency for the chief-of-state role to be less contentious than the president's domestic policy roles, the president typically finds himself with more leeway in foreign affairs than he does when he engages in the inevitable domestic

GLOBAL TOPICS

CHIEF OF STATE VS. HEAD OF GOVERNMENT

In Great Britain, a partisan prime minister, selected from the majority party in Parliament, performs the functions that are comparable to our chief executive and chief legislator. But Queen Elizabeth is the chief of state, the ceremonial leader who can rise above politics and represent Great Britain to the world. This type of arrangement, where an elected official runs the government while the head of state is a royal figure, is not uncommon around the world. In Denmark, Queen Margrethe reigns as chief of state while Prime Minister Lars Rasmussen runs the government. Belgium's King Albert is head of state, but leaves the governing to Prime Minister Yves Leterme.

Other nations divide the chief of state and head of government functions between a president and prime minister, maintaining a republican form of government in a parliamentary system. [T7] President Anibal Cavaco Silva would greet official visitors to Portugal, while Prime Minister Jose Socrates takes responsibility for running the government. Austria, Italy, Germany, Ireland, the Czech Republic and Hungary are among the nations that also have this arrangement. [T8] China has a separate president and premier but without the constitutional underpinnings of republican government. [T9]

In practice, the range of constitutional models is wide. In some systems, presidents have more than a symbolic role and play a part in governing, potentially posing a challenge to the prime minister. France and some Latin American nations have such "semi-presidential" systems. [T10] The issue of the governing role taken by a chief of state can be a difficult one. On one had, the chief of state needs to offer legitimacy to a nation and serve as a source of political stability. On the other, presidents can clash with prime ministers in parliamentary systems should they claim to have an independent source of legitimacy and political support. [T11] Because of this, systems that separate the chief of state function from the head of government function may find themselves facing difficulties which, while different from those confronting the American president in a system that combines the two functions, are nonetheless problematic.

By the way, if you live in Canada or Australia, you too have prime ministers running the government. But your chief of state? Queen Elizabeth II of England—even today—through an emissary known as a Governor General.

clashes with Congress. This distinction led political scientist Aaron Wildavsky to contend that there are "two presidencies" with distinct patterns of political support—a domestic policy presidency, where presidential initiatives often get bogged down in the thistle of congressional opposition, and a foreign and defense policy presidency, where a determined president can almost always have his way. [41]

The key place Wildavsky looks for evidence of the two presidencies is in the record of success presidents have had in the formulation of policy. Where

presidents have had mixed results moving domestic proposals through Congress, succeeding most thoroughly in the rare instances when they are propelled by a major crisis (like Franklin Roosevelt during the Great Depression) or when their party comprises an overwhelming congressional majority (like Lyndon Johnson in the 1960s or Barack Obama during his first two years), Wildavsky finds that presidents who wanted to pursue a foreign or military course typically succeeded.

DEMYSTIFYING GOVERNMENT

CHIEF DIPLOMAT

The pageantry and pomp that serve as the trappings of the chief of state can mask a substantive role accorded the president. Think of him as the **chief diplomat**—as the person the Constitution makes responsible for receiving "Ambassadors and other public Ministers." Officially, this means that before ambassadors of other countries can set up shop in the United States, they must present their credentials to the president. This apparently ceremonial function gives the president the right to extend American **diplomatic recognition** to other nations—to decide whether the representative of a nation has legitimacy in the eyes of the United States.

Recognition by a major power like the United States can build instant global credibility for a new nation or a regime that takes power following a revolution or uprising. Situations like this don't come around often, but when they do, decisions about whether or when to extend diplomatic recognition can reverberate globally. For instance, in the confusion surrounding the demise of the Soviet Union, the United States faced the prospect of recognizing a host of self-declared independent states that previously had been part of one nation.

Wildavsky finds several reasons for this. Unlike domestic policy, foreign policy is dangerous; events can move quickly and the consequences can be monumental. This tends to focus the public on the president's foreign policy actions and motivate presidents to devote a lot of resources to foreign policy formulation. No one else in Washington can rival the administration's investment in foreign policy expertise or its ability to speak with one voice.[42]

Wildavsky wrote during the heightened tensions of the cold war, leading some to reevaluate his argument with the passage of time.[43] Today, in a world where protection from terrorist threats dominates the foreign policy agenda, we can find some anecdotal evidence that the president again may have a relatively free hand in formulating foreign policy. It took only a few weeks in 2002 for President Bush to convince a reluctant Congress to endorse his plans to invade Iraq if that nation refused to permit open inspection of its weapons programs. Yet, at about the same time, the president remained unable to advance key elements of his domestic agenda, including legislative proposals on tax and Social Security reform.

Negotiating Treaties and Making Executive Agreements

The president's formal constitutional prerogative to negotiate treaties with other nations seems on the surface to contradict that idea that it's smooth sailing for presidents in foreign affairs. Because treaties have to be ratified by a two-thirds vote of the Senate, presidents may find that the negotiating they have to do with the legislative branch is much more difficult than the negotiating they had to do with the other nation or nations involved in the treaty. Historically, the Senate has not been shy about defeating even high-profile treaties with strong presidential backing; probably the most notable twentieth-century example is the defeat of the Versailles Treaty by the Senate following World War I, which kept the United States out of the League of Nations.

However, as is often the case with the president, there is an informal mechanism available to him that circumvents the constitutional complexity of navigating treaties through the Senate. Presidents can avoid a resistant legislature by issuing **executive agreements**, which do not require congressional action. The president can negotiate executive agreements with leaders of other nations, a practice with a long history even though it is not provided for in the Constitution. Once signed, executive agreements have the force of law. This gives the president great latitude in foreign policy negotiations, provided those nations are willing to forego the stature of a

treaty. When President Bush and Russian President Vladimir Putin were negotiating nuclear arms reduction in 2002, one point of discussion was whether any agreement produced by the talks would be subject to congressional approval—a move that would offer Russia the type of respect afforded the Soviet Union during the cold war days of joint superpower arms talks.

ISSUE

DOMESTIC SURVEILLANCE

It's not easy to conduct a widespread domestic search for potential terrorists while maintaining the freedoms and rights we're entitled to under the Constitution. The issue prominently arose on a couple of occasions since the September 11 attacks, surrounding Bush administration anti-terrorism initiatives that supporters felt would keep the country safe from terrorist activities and opponents felt was a violation of personal rights.

One controversial proposal for domestic surveillance entailed establishing a network of domestic informants to root out terrorists at home. The Bush Justice Department lobbied hard for it, but had to scale back plans in the face of criticism from civil liberties groups. Ultimately, the administration failed to get its program included in the 2002 Homeland Security Act, which established the cabinet-level Department of Homeland Security. In fact, language in the Act expressly prohibits the Justice Department from initiating the program. Nonetheless, President Bush continued to advocate for expanding domestic surveillance, and the issue maintained its relevance in the wake of ongoing discussions about how best to locate and isolate potential terrorists.

The domestic surveillance program dubbed "Operation TIPS" (for Terrorism Information and Prevention System) was first introduced by

the Justice Department in January 2002. The objective was to recruit and deputize up to one million Americans to gather information for the government, reporting suspect actions of their neighbors and coworkers. The plan would have recruited postal workers, utility workers, cable installers, transit workers, shippers, and truckers to report "suspicious" activity. Under protest, the government dropped the provision to actively recruit postal and utility workers, while still permitting them to volunteer for the program.

Former Attorney General John Ashcroft offered repeated assurances that the program would not infringe on personal liberty and that it was a necessary step to secure the security of Americans against small terrorist cells that could be operating within our borders. He said law-abiding Americans would not be targeted and that the program would only be a way of alerting the government to suspicious activities. He contended that terrorist cells can be very small—sometimes no more than a few people—but they are capable of doing great damage if they're not stopped. One of the most effective ways to stop them is to bring surveillance to the grassroots level in the form of investigators who would blend in with a neighborhood and get to know residents well. At the same time, the attorney general vigorously objected to characterizing the program as "spying."

Administration officials used a similar argument several years later, after the *New York Times* disclosed that the president had signed a secret order in . 2002 to permit domestic surveillance of American citizens without a warrant. The order enabled the National Security Administration to scan large numbers of private e-mail and telephone conversations without a court order. The administration defended the program as a necessary venture in time of war to quickly identify terrorist activity, claiming that the time it would take to obtain a court order to scan the conversations risked letting valuable information slip away. Opponents of the plan regarded the program as an unnecessary violation of privacy rights.[T13] Former President Jimmy Carter called the plan "illegal."[T14]

The surveillance disclosure also set off a firestorm of criticism from Congress about the issue of separation of powers. Congressional Democrats and some Republicans questioned why the administration hid the program from them—only a handful of congressional leaders were briefed about it—and why the administration didn't ask Congress to modify existing law if the president felt it was too restrictive. These questions arose in early 2006, when the Senate Judiciary Committee held hearings into the surveillance issue. Attorney General Alberto Gonzales faced angry questions from senators who wondered whether the president's position negated the need for Congress to oversee executive activity, essentially neutralizing the role of the legislative branch in foreign policy decision-making. Gonzales vigorously disagreed with that perspective while characterizing the surveillance program as "both necessary and lawful," saying, "The administration has chosen to act now to prevent the next attack with every lawful tool at its disposal, rather than wait until it is too late."[T15]

During the period leading up to the hearings, public opinion remained mixed on whether the Bush initiative was a good idea that helped keep the country safe or a dangerous idea that undermined the basic tenets of American democracy. To be sure, the sense that your personal phone calls or e-mail messages might be subject to surveillance might make you uneasy, just like the prospect of the cable guy being a government snitch didn't sit well with many Americans and some members of Congress. Just as opponents of Operation TIPS called the initiative unnecessary because people can already report suspicious activity on their own, opponents of telephone and e-mail surveillance noted that a procedure already in place permitted the president to get a warrant to scan conversations from a secret court, and to do so after the fact if time necessitated immediate action.

Opponents of both initiatives were concerned about the secretive nature of the programs, and the possibility that such secrecy could lead to abuses. Those opposing Operation TIPS were concerned that the cover of being in a federal program would give untrained ordinary citizens the sense that they can do police work, but inadequate preparation would result in a mountain of blind leads and false charges. They argued that racial profiling would be inevitable, with false accusations creating huge problems for people who would then have to clear their names in an environment where many of us are inclined to assume guilt rather than innocence.

If that happened, opponents said, the liberty of people falsely accused of being terrorists would be severely threatened, the accused would face possible incarceration and deportation, and it would all be done without effective controls. Opponents of telephone and e-mail surveillance echoed these sentiments.

Do domestic surveillance programs flirt too closely with creating a police state in a free society as civil libertarians argue? Or are they reasonable programs designed to offer a greater degree of security in an uncertain time, as Attorneys General Ashcroft and Gonzales claimed?

Arguments in Support

The Bush Justice Department defended its domestic surveillance initiatives by saying:

- It's critical. Without good surveillance, it may be impossible to root out terrorists.
- It's not spying. The programs would simply alert law enforcement officers to individuals who draw attention to themselves by their actions.
- It's constitutional. The president has the authority to take extraordinary security measures in wartime.
- Honest citizens would not be targeted. Americans who mean and do no harm would not be affected.
- Civil rights remain in force. Someone targeted through surveillance would still be innocent until proven otherwise.

Arguments Against

Opponents of domestic surveillance questioned the Bush administration's approach by saying:

- It's creepy. Do you really want your letter carrier working secretly for the government, or government officials listening to your phone calls?
- It's spying. What else do you call it when people are reporting information about their neighbors or listening to your private messages behind your back?
- It's unethical. Domestic surveillance threatens to undermine personal freedom.
- It could result in abuses of power. Who knows who would be targeted by a secret government program operating free of congressional oversight.
- Civil rights are at risk. In a climate of fear, anyone targeted for surveillance could be regarded as a terrorist.

My Opinion

It's difficult to maintain security in an open society. Americans want to feel safe and protect hallmark liberties, but efforts to provide security can quickly bump up against personal rights protections. You should consider whether the Bush administration surveillance initiatives cross the line between liberty and security. When formulating your opinion on domestic surveillance, consider the history of the issue and the arguments supporting and opposing it. In particular, ask yourself if domestic surveillance:

- Is critical or creepy.
- Is or is not spying.
- Is constitutional or unethical.
- Would protect honest citizens or result in abuses of power.
- Would protector undermine civil rights.

Supervising Intelligence Activities

Since September 11, 2001, many of us have become more aware than before of our intelligence operations and the complex business of gathering information about groups or individuals who might pose a threat to national security. The secretive world of intelligence gathering falls under the auspices of the president through the director of central intelligence, whom the president appoints with Senate approval. It's been that way since the National Security Act of 1947 established the Central Intelligence Agency (CIA), the organization responsible for providing the president with information on security threats, under the supervision of the director of central intelligence.[44]

The CIA also reports to the **National Security Council (NSC)**, the primary body for assisting the president with security-related decisions. In addition to the president's national security advisor, the NSC includes select cabinet officials (including the secretaries of state, defense, and treasury) and receives military briefings from the chairman of the **Joint Chiefs of Staff**, the president's primary military advisor.[45]

In response to the attacks on the World Trade Center and the Pentagon, President Bush proposed and established a cabinet-level Department of Homeland Security, which entailed conducting the largest reorganization of the federal government since Franklin D. Roosevelt was president. The new department combined a host of security-related and information-gathering organizations under one administrative umbrella in an effort to create a coordinated agency charged with border security, emergency preparedness, and antiterrorist intelligence gathering.

The creation of the Department of Homeland Security was widely embraced by members of both political parties. This was not the case for other Bush administration anti-terrorism initiatives, which skirted a sensitive line between keeping people safe and violating their personal rights. You can read about these sensitive conflicts in Issue: Domestic Surveillance.

Commander-in-Chief

The Constitution gives Congress the power to declare war, but it gives the president the power to wage war. In the eighteenth-century world of the Constitution's framers, where troops were committed to battle following a formal declaration, the president's military powers were expected to be secondary to Congress. In a twenty-first century world, where the military response to crisis is often swift and troops are sent into battle without formal declarations, the president's power as **commander-in-chief** of the armed forces looms large.

The president has several advantages over Congress in the conduct of military affairs. He has the formal power to move American forces overseas and commit them to battle. As we just noted, he has an intelligence and advisory structure that can keep him abreast of international developments, providing him with information that Congress does not have. He can act unilaterally and swiftly. Informally, he can move public opinion behind him once he acts.

The swelling of the president's military resources follows the growth of the United States as a world power. Until about seventy years ago, presidents had access to very limited advice and data for making military judgments, as there was

little in the way of a defense establishment like we have today.[46] That was before the commander-in-chief was responsible for a nuclear arsenal, and before America's permanent military establishment ballooned in size and reach in response to the country's central place in world affairs. Although presidents have claimed the power to commit troops without congressional authorization since John Adams sent the navy to do battle with France, the scope, magnitude, and extent of American involvement overseas has made presidents serving since the middle of the twentieth century the central figures in military affairs.

In the 1970s, Congress tried to fight back. In the wake of the divisiveness of the Vietnam War, many members of Congress felt Presidents Johnson and Nixon had overstepped the boundaries of their role as commander-in-chief, and they were determined to reassert their constitutional prerogative over military matters. The result was the **War Powers Act of 1973** (which passed over President Nixon's veto), the intent of which was to limit the president's ability to initiate military action without congressional approval. It does this by requiring in the absence of a declaration of war that the president consult with Congress before taking action and periodically while troops are in the field. If Congress does not ratify the president's action within sixty days, the president has to bring the troops home (this may be extended to ninety days if the president claims immediate withdrawal poses a risk to the troops).

The promise of the War Powers Act was that balance in military affairs would be reestablished between Congress and the president, but it hasn't quite worked out that way. Presidents have ignored the War Powers Act, choosing instead to continue to commit troops as they always did—and Congress hasn't tried to reign in the president. There are good political reasons why. As Vietnam faded into memory, passions subsided, and subsequent congresses weren't eager to confront the president. If Congress pressed the point and the president decided to challenge the constitutionality of the War Powers Act, it's not at all clear that the act would hold up to scrutiny if the Supreme Court decided that it provides Congress with a veto over the president's actions (this would be considered a "legislative veto," and the Constitution only grants veto power to the president). As a practical political matter, because the president can typically rely on the public rallying behind him at least briefly when he sends troops abroad, it's difficult for Congress to stand up to the president when he's engaged in the role of commander-in-chief.

Chief of Party

It's nowhere to be found in the Constitution, but by custom, the president is the head of his political party. Political parties are decentralized organizations built from the ground up. Despite this structure, as the highest elected national official, the president is well positioned to give a face and a voice to his party and, if he enjoys popular support, contribute heavily to party campaigning and fund-raising functions. It's an advantage the party out of power simply can't match.

Particularly when it comes to raising money, the president can be a party's biggest weapon. When President Clinton was in office, he routinely barnstormed the country, headlining fund-raisers that brought in record sums of money for the Democratic Party. President Bush exceeded Clinton's fund-raising records to the benefit of the Republican Party, raising over $260 million for his reelection campaign. President Obama has not been shy about attending fundraisers or campaigning for fellow Democrats, such as embattled New Jersey Governor Jon Corzine, who lost a difficult re-election bid during the new president's first year in office.

Being party chief is not without its complications. An unpopular president can leave a party effectively leaderless, and because no one else commands the national stage like the president, no one else can step in as party leader if a president lacks popular support. Candidates for other offices will not want to be seen on the same stage with him for fear that their association will cost them votes. President Bush was so unpopular during the congressional elections held in the middle of his second term that he became a powerful political weapon for the *opposition* party. More than one Republican running for Congress conveniently found himself with something else on his schedule when word came that the president wanted to campaign for him.

Even popular presidents may find that there are limits to their political reach. Two generations ago, when more people voted strictly by party, presidential candidates routinely carried members of Congress into office on their **coattails**. Today people are more likely to split their ticket, voting for Republicans for some offices and Democrats for others. It's not uncommon for congressional candidates to get more votes than their party's presidential candidate receives in their district. This leaves the president—even a popular one—with limited political leverage, as the congressional candidates they campaign for often do not win their office on the strength of the president's campaign. In 2001, at the height of his prestige, President Bush visibly threw his support behind the Republican nominees for the two governorships up for election that year, in Virginia and New Jersey. Despite his efforts, both candidates lost.

The president may also face problems reconciling the blatant partisanship of the party-leader role with the president's other responsibilities. President Bush wrestled with this dilemma right before the 2002 congressional elections as he tried to remain above politics as chief of state while campaigning for Republican candidates as chief of party.[47] The balancing act was particularly delicate: The president tried to look serious and statesmanlike as he moved the nation closer to a conflict with Iraq, while also hopping around the country unleashing partisan rhetoric at political rallies. In his chief-of-state role, he was trying to unify the nation and prepare the world for military action, but the chief-of-party role required the president to get down into dirty, divisive partisan muck in order to rally the faithful and win votes for Republicans. The strategy carried risks for Bush's professional reputation, which would have been undermined had he appeared too partisan or divisive at such a somber moment.

You could say that Bush's problem reflects the crosscutting expectations we place on our presidents. It illustrates the dilemma that presidents face as they juggle contradictory roles.

The Institutional Presidency

It seems as though the more we ask the president to do, the more help he requires—and the more assistance he gets in the form of a large, bureaucratic staff centered around the Oval Office. In Section 10.5a ("Making Appointments"), we briefly made note of this staff in our passing reference to the Executive Office of the President (EOP). When the presidency was a fairly small office prior to the major expansion in federal functions that occurred during Franklin D. Roosevelt's administration, the White House staff was equally small. By way of comparison, Roosevelt left behind a personal staff of fifty-three people, which had swollen to over 350 by the time Bill Clinton took office. During the same period, the president's budget advisors almost doubled in number, and his national security staff more than tripled.[48]

Inside the Executive Office of the President

Every administration organizes the EOP a little differently, but there are a number of constants that have endured from administration to administration. Every recent president has organized the **White House Office** around a **chief of staff**, who coordinates the workings of the White House Office and serves as a key advisor with intimate access to the president. The White House Office typically includes the president's personal secretary, legal advisors, political advisors, and in recent administrations has grown to include the Communications Office and offices that handle contacts between the White House and Congress, interest groups, and the president's political party.[49]

The inner circle of the White House Office contains the president's most trusted and influential confidants. Typically, these people are the president's longtime associates or personal friends, including people who worked with the president when he held lower offices and people who had high-level positions in the president's election campaign.

The rest of the EOP is just as compartmentalized, containing offices that assist the president on things ranging from budgetary to security matters.

The Office of the First Lady

The Executive Office of the President is housed in the West Wing of the White House. Across the way, in the East Wing, you'll find the offices of the first lady. There's no official role for the first lady, but the wife of the president is an important symbolic figure in American life, especially in an era when television cameras make her a public figure (whether or not that's her wish). Jacqueline Kennedy was the first to play the role of national hostess on television, projecting an air of youth and glamour akin to her husband's televised persona.

Traditionally, the first lady has played a social role, hosting guests at the White House. However, a few presidential spouses have seen themselves as more than official greeters. Eleanor Roosevelt, wife of Franklin, played an active role in her husband's administration. Ahead of her time, anticipating the revolution in women's roles that would begin twenty years after she left the White House, Eleanor Roosevelt lobbied her husband on behalf of the social issues she advocated. She wrote a newspaper column and was a media presence, promoting causes like rights for women and minorities.

Nancy Reagan maintained a far more traditional public image, but behind the scenes, she was influential in her husband's administration. People who worked in the Reagan White House understood the importance of being on good terms with the president's wife, and her close relationship with the president made her an important, though informal, advisor. Once, when reporters were shouting questions at President Reagan that he was unable to hear against the din of background noise, television microphones picked up Nancy Reagan whispering an answer in her husband's ear, which promptly came out of his mouth. It was a rare glimpse of how involved she was in the workings of the administration.

Hillary Rodham Clinton took the role of first lady to a place none of her predecessors had been—directly into the West Wing, where she set up shop with a personal staff. An attorney with experience as a congressional aide, she came to the White House with the resume of someone who might have applied for work in the Executive Office of the President. As a candidate, Bill Clinton joked about his wife's ability and influence by saying that they offered voters a "buy one, get one free" option.

In office, it came to pass. Bill Clinton put his wife in charge of a task force exploring proposals for restructuring the way Americans receive health care, a role so out of sync with the traditional work of a first lady that it sparked a national debate. When the Clinton health care proposal tanked, Hillary Clinton shared the blame with her husband and never again took a visible policy role in her husband's administration. Nonetheless, she continued to be an influential advocate in the White House, and in the last year of the Clinton administration, she became the only first lady to be elected to public office when she won a Senate race in her adopted state of New York. In 2001, as President Clinton was moving out of the Oval Office, Senator Clinton was settling into her new workspace on the other end of Pennsylvania Avenue. Seven years later, Senator Clinton parlayed her time at both ends of Pennsylvania Avenue into frontrunner status for the Democratic nomination for her husband's old job. Although she lost a bitterly fought contest with Barack Obama, her rival saw fit to ask her to join his cabinet, where she serves as Secretary of State.

When Hillary Clinton left the White House, she was replaced in the East Wing by Laura Bush, a more traditional first lady who kept a lower and less controversial profile. Like many contemporary first ladies, she became a public advocate for a cause—in this case, literacy and childhood education—which she had promoted since her days as a teacher and librarian in Texas.[50]

Michelle Obama has positioned herself somewhere between her two immediate predecessors. Acutely aware of her symbolic role, she has kept a high profile as the mother of two young daughters—the first thing you will see if you go to her webpage is the statement: "first and foremost, she is Malia and Sasha's mom."[51] But she is also a Princeton and Harvard educated lawyer with an impressive

resume in community service work, and she has paired her professional and family backgrounds to speak out on the importance of community service and balancing work and family responsibilities.

Second in Command

Here's a job description for you to consider: You get to attend the occasional funeral for a head of state, preside over the Senate (where no one will complain that you hardly ever show), and otherwise make yourself available just in case something happens to your boss. For this, you will be well compensated with a good salary and a nice house in a great location.

Perhaps, you find the prospect of a job like this appealing, but many of the people who have served as vice president have commented on the remarkable emptiness of a position that is, after all, the only other nationally elected office in the United States. The first vice president, John Adams, bemoaned, "My country has in its infinite wisdom contrived for me the most insignificant office that ever the invention of man contrived or his imagination conceived." Thomas Marshall, vice president under Woodrow Wilson, compared his situation to "a man in a cataleptic fit: He cannot speak; he cannot move; he suffers no pain; he is perfectly conscious of all that goes on, but has no part in it." John Nance Garner, Franklin D. Roosevelt's first vice president, put it more succinctly: "The vice presidency isn't worth a pitcher of warm spit."[52]

It's probably not surprising that ambitious men could feel hamstrung in the vice presidency, or that the office itself was a late addition to the Constitution, where it was never more than a pencil sketch of an institution. The vice presidency gave the Constitution's authors a method of presidential succession that didn't violate separation of powers by relying on a congressional officer, and it resolved the issue of who would preside over the Senate and cast tie-breaking votes when necessary. It also created a dilemma for its occupants, who are given little authority and no power, and who until recent administrations have been reduced to waiting around in case something happened to the president (Demystifying Government: Moving from Second to First looks at the fate of a couple of recent vice presidents with presidential aspirations).

Throughout the nineteenth century and well into the twentieth, vice presidents were frequently the object of ridicule or neglect. Selected by party leaders to provide geographic or ideological balance to the presidential nominee, qualifications for the number two office rarely advanced beyond the ability to carry a state or a voting group that the presidential candidate could not. As political circumstances evolved from year to year, necessitating a different balance in the next election, vice presidents found themselves highly expendable commodities: No nineteenth-century vice president was renominated for a second term by a major political party. After Martin Van Buren in 1836, none was nominated for president.[53]

Since seeking the office wasn't much of a career move, it didn't draw the interest of big political names. Daniel Webster rejected overtures from Whig Party leaders to be their vice-presidential nominee in 1848, saying facetiously, "I do not wish to be buried until I am dead."[54] The nomination went instead to Millard Fillmore, who apparently didn't mind. So, most vice presidents were second-tier political figures who spent their time looking for something useful to do. Some didn't even bother to stay in Washington. Van Buren's vice president, Richard M. Johnson, left town in 1837 to operate a tavern.[55]

Circumstances changed dramatically in the middle of the twentieth century, making the modern vice presidency a much more desirable office both substantively and politically. When Harry Truman became president upon the sudden death of Franklin D. Roosevelt in 1945, World War II was ending. America and its allies were drawing plans for the shape of the postwar world, and the United States had been secretly developing an atomic bomb, but Truman was uninvolved in and largely unaware of these efforts. When he became president, he had to come up to speed quickly and was left to make life and death decisions that affected the future shape of the world. From that point on, it became clear that the vice president had to be someone who could step into a role that now had global implications.

That didn't mean that vice-presidential candidates didn't still have to give political balance to a ticket. But after 1945, presidential candidates needed to assure the country that they were running with someone who had the capability and

DEMYSTIFYING GOVERNMENT

MOVING FROM SECOND TO FIRST

The revamped, contemporary vice presidency is viewed as a stepping-stone to the presidency, but how successful have recent vice presidents been in achieving that ambition? When George Bush (senior) was elected president immediately after serving eight years as vice president to Ronald Reagan, he became the first vice president to take that step on his own since Martin Van Buren succeeded Andrew Jackson in 1836.

Al Gore tried to replicate the feat in 2000 but fell short. His troubles illustrate how the vice presidency can cut both ways when its occupant seeks the top prize. As a visible national figure, Gore had no trouble raising money and winning the nomination of his party. At the same time, he was saddled with the scandals of the Clinton years, and as a member of the administration, he had trouble distancing himself from them. Journalists wrote of Gore's dilemma trying to emerge from President Clinton's shadow, but the reality of the vice presidency is that it's hard for its occupant to run for president as his own person.

experience to become president at a moment's notice. Their choice would come to be seen as an example of their judgment and leadership ability.

This applied in 1976 when Jimmy Carter selected Senator Walter Mondale to be his running mate. The liberal Mondale, a midwesterner and Washington insider, provided natural political balance to Carter's more conservative southern base. Mondale's four years as vice president turned out to be historic, as Carter offered him more policy responsibility than any vice president in history to that point. He had a West Wing office, access to presidential information, and met regularly with the president, serving as a key advisor. Al Gore played an even larger role in the Clinton administration, as the president made him primarily responsible for making decisions in a range of policy areas, including the environment, technology, and telecommunications.[56] Dick Cheney followed Gore as vice president and played a highly influential role, serving as one of President Bush's most trusted advisors with arguably more input to policy decisions than any vice president in history. Vice President Joe Biden, selected by President Obama to add experience and gravitas to a ticket headed by a young senator, is an important advisor to the president, especially on matters of foreign affairs. But can a vice president capitalize on this experience? Table 9.5 shows just how difficult it is to move up to the top spot from the vice presidency.

The Ebb and Flow of Presidential Influence

As an institutional matter, the president and Congress have long been in a tug-of-war befitting two institutions dependent on each other to get things done. The early presidents who stretched the reach of the presidency through a broad interpretation of the presidential role—presidents like Thomas Jefferson, Andrew Jackson and Abraham Lincoln—did so at the expense of Congress. This is why we've seen strong presidencies followed by periods where Congress grabbed back some of the authority that it felt rightfully belonged to the legislature.

The War Powers Act was passed during such a time, following a string of presidential administrations considered "imperial" for their regal tone and extensive claims of authority. If Franklin D. Roosevelt forever enhanced the role of the president when his administration dramatically increased the sweep of federal authority, the advent of America as a global power and the nuclear tension of the cold war gave late twentieth-century presidents godlike power over life and death. We looked to them to protect civilization and keep us safe from nuclear annihilation, giving them unprecedented opportunities to use their informal powers to strengthen the office. People started calling them the "leader of the free world." That's

Table 9.5. Did They Become President?

Vice President	President Served	Became President through Presidential Death or Resignation	Ran for President, Won	Ran for President, Lost
Nixon[T16]	Eisenhower		YES	YES
Johnson	Kennedy	YES		
Humphrey	Johnson			YES
Agnew[T17]	Nixon			
Ford	Nixon	YES		
Rockefeller[T18]	Ford			
Mondale	Carter			YES
G. Bush	Reagan		YES	
Quayle[19]	G. Bush			YES
Gore	Clinton			YES
Cheney	G.W. Bush			

why the "imperial presidency" reached its height under Presidents Kennedy, Johnson, and Nixon, in the frostiest days of the cold war.[57]

It's not too hard to see how presidents serving under these conditions might take on imperial characteristics. The president has always had personal privileges, but the benefits of the presidency assumed regal characteristics under cold war circumstances. Imagine how you'd feel if you never had to wait in line for anything. You never had to drive a car, and you never got stuck in traffic because roads were closed off when you were coming. Every time you walked into a room, people would stand. Military bands would play "Hail to the Chief" when they spotted you. Airplanes would take off within thirty seconds after you boarded. It would be hard for most people not to let this go to their heads. Now consider what happens when they're also calling you the "leader of the free world." The effect would be to create a sense of privilege befitting an emperor.

As the president took on the characteristics of a monarch, the Executive Office of the President took on the air of a court. George Reedy, who served as press secretary to President Johnson, compared the situation in the White House to one you'd find in a palace, where courtiers cater to the king's ego, fight among themselves for the leader's attention, and engage in petty acts to undermine each other in the larger pursuit of winning the king's favor.

What does not happen in this atmosphere is an honest, hard-hitting exchange of ideas. Aides feel pressed to say yes to the president, regardless of how much they may privately disagree with what he's doing. To disagree was to risk the wrath of the chief executive and to be displaced from power. No one felt they could do what Reedy believed was necessary to reestablish a healthy atmosphere in the White House: Occasionally tell the president to "go soak his head."[58]

Bad ideas can be hatched in such an insular environment, without dissent to sharpen the president's thinking—and they were. The prosecution of the Vietnam War proceeded as President Johnson listened to advisors who assured him that escalating the conflict was the best policy, partly because they feared punishment if they dissented. This

effectively trapped Johnson inside a gilded echo chamber, where the failure to hear dissenting voices kept him from recognizing that he was losing the support of the public. President Nixon's administration was secretive to a fault—the chief of staff tightly controlled all contact with Nixon—and in his imperial seclusion, Nixon believed he could get away with illegally thwarting his political opposition. He was, after all, the "leader of the free world."

That was when Congress fought back—with the War Powers Act and with impeachment proceedings against Richard Nixon, stemming from illegal activities conducted in a climate of White House secrecy. A period of congressional dominance followed, coinciding with the weak presidencies of Gerald Ford and Jimmy Carter.

Recognizing that presidential grandeur had taken the presidency too far away from its political roots, President Gerald Ford followed Richard Nixon in office with a deliberate effort to make the president ordinary. Naturally unaffected and down to earth, Ford fit the role perfectly. In his first days in the White House, he held a media event designed to communicate the message that this president would not be an emperor: There in the kitchen was the new president in a bathrobe, making his breakfast toast. We had entered a period of the anti-imperialist president, the president of the people. Ford did away with the pomp that surrounded his predecessors, even to the point of requesting at times that "Hail to the Chief" be replaced by the fight song of his alma mater, the University of Michigan.

His successor also used populist symbols to communicate the message that his presidency was the antithesis of Johnson's and Nixon's. President Carter broke with tradition by leaving the limousine that carried him to the White House after his inauguration, choosing to walk the parade route, hand-in-hand with his wife. He wore cardigan sweaters instead of suits and ties. He invited people to call him "Jimmy."

Interestingly, the public eventually tired of this folksy presidential style, in no small part because of how it became intertwined with downsized presidential performance. It's impossible to know if Ford would have become a folk hero—the ordinary man in the White House—had he not generated so much ill will by pardoning President Nixon for his Watergate-related crimes or presided over an ailing economy. Likewise, the image of a plainspoken peanut farmer might have become Jimmy Carter's presidential legacy had he been able to tackle the rampant inflation that undermined the nation's standard of living, and crises abroad that left many feeling that America had become a weak nation.

Ironically, despite the wrenching experiences of Vietnam and Watergate, the events of the Ford and Carter administrations left some people yearning for a return to the imperial presidency. Ronald Reagan promised to restore pomp and glitter to the office as part of a broader message of regaining a sense of national strength and pride. For many, it was the right message at the right time, playing to the enduring wish that the president provide a king-like legitimacy to the American system.

Events continued to shape the office after Carter's term, facilitating the conditions for a return to the imperial presidency, punctuated by an interlude defined by more down-to-earth politics. With the cold war still raging, many Americans found security in the regal trappings of the Reagan years. At the same time, the Reagan administration advocated policies that, for the first time since Franklin Roosevelt, assumed government was the source of our problems, not the solution to our problems. There was a profound transformation in the political debate, which for the first time in generations made it acceptable to consider shifting power away from Washington. In the process, President Reagan undermined one of the two pillars on which the imperial presidency had been built: the sense that the president, as the chief executive of the national government, was ultimately responsible for providing a huge range of services that could not be had elsewhere. As power began to flow out of Washington and to the states, the president's royal position was inevitably diminished.

Then the Berlin Wall came down, the Soviet Union crumbled, the cold war ended, and the other pillar supporting the imperial presidents—the fact that each was the "leader of the free world"—lost its currency. Without having to assume the posture of someone faced with decisions of global life and death, Bill Clinton could reach out to voters as a

pop-culture figure rather than as a regal figure. He could appear on a late-night television variety show wearing shades and playing the saxophone, as he did during his presidential campaign. He could turn up on MTV and answer a question about the kind of underwear he prefers. In their day, no one could have imagined Presidents Johnson or Nixon answering a question about whether they liked boxers or briefs. For that matter, no one could have imagined either man being in a situation where the question would have been asked.

During the ten years or so prior to your adolescence, the presidency was experiencing a kind of adolescence of its own. The office had returned to pre-imperial dimensions. Congress reasserted itself to the point where in the first months following the 1994 Republican takeover of the House and Senate, the president briefly became secondary to Congress in political importance. Several years later, an energized Congress impeached but failed to convict President Clinton for his actions stemming from the Monica Lewinsky scandal.

Perhaps, things would have continued on this path had America not been the object of a major terrorist attack. Having elected in George W. Bush a president with admittedly no foreign policy experience, foreign affairs ironically became the focal point of his administration. With this came a return to the serious business of being global leader, and not coincidently, a return to some of the trappings of the cold war administrations: increased secrecy and the reassertion of presidential authority over Congress. The decision to invade Iraq was made in this climate. Years later, as the details of how those decisions were made began to become public, echoes of the Johnson and Nixon administration reverberated through questions raised by administration critics about whether the failure to listen to dissenting voices resulted in critical errors of judgment about the rationale for war.

One of the ironies of the modern presidency is that even at its most imperial, the one branch that the president seemed to have the least influence over was his own. There are interesting reasons why the "leader of the free world" often comes across as the head of the bureaucracy in name only. In reality, things are often different than what you'd expect from an organizational chart of the executive branch that has the president's name at the top.

Chapter Review

Because the presidency is the only federal office that's personified by an individual, it's the only office where performance expectations are elevated to unrealistic heights. It's not uncommon for people to evaluate the president against a mythical ideal derived from the presidency's vast folklore, nor is it unusual for people to feel disillusioned when presidents do not live up to this standard.

The Constitution gives the presidency few formal powers, initially designing it to be secondary in importance to Congress. Over time, through the efforts of strong presidents who mostly served during crises, the office has greatly expanded in size and influence. This permits savvy and skillful presidents to exercise the informal prerogatives of their office and wield power by effectively persuading others in the Washington community to support their interests. Cultivating a strong professional reputation and high levels of public prestige can bolster presidential persuasion.

Contemporary presidents rely heavily on public relations to boost public approval—they have a Communications Office to do the work—though despite their best efforts most presidents lose support over time. Their office gives them a big megaphone for influencing the news agenda, and presidents like to stage media events in order to take their message to the public on their own terms. However, journalists typically struggle against the president's desire to set the agenda, causing friction that's part of the competitive relationship between the White House and reporters.

The multiple and mutually exclusive roles the president must play contribute to the complexity of the office. As chief executive, the president is in charge of the government's executive branch or bureaucracy, and is responsible for executing the laws passed by Congress. As chief legislator, the president can propose a legislative agenda and attempt to persuade Congress to accept it, relying on his legislative liaison staff to lobby Congress. The president also plays the largely symbolic chief-of-state role, whereby he attends official functions and hosts foreign dignitaries. As chief diplomat, the president has the ability to extend diplomatic recognition to leaders of other nations, lending credibility to their regimes.

As commander-in-chief, the president is the civilian head of the armed forces. This gives him the power to commit troops and to wage war. Congress retains the power to declare war, but because contemporary wars are often waged without being declared, the military balance between the two branches has shifted heavily toward the president. In 1973, Congress tried to regain some of its military authority by passing the War Powers Act, requiring the president to get congressional approval to commit troops for more than sixty days, but presidents have largely ignored the measure.

The president's most divisive role is chief of party. Being the most prominent and powerful member of his party gives the president a platform for raising campaign money and stumping for his party's candidates for lower office. Contemporary presidents have rarely had coattails, though, limiting their influence over other races.

Over the past seventy years, the presidency has grown into a multifaceted institution centered in the Executive Office of the President. The White House Office contains the president's closest aides and coordinates the daily workings of the White House. Other offices handle national security issues, domestic policy, trade and budget issues, and environmental matters.

The president and Congress historically duel with each other for dominance in the federal system. The executive branch became ascendant with the New Deal programs of Franklin Roosevelt's presidency and the importance of the president as global leader during the cold war. The end of the cold war and a shift in public support toward a philosophy of less government growth permitted Congress to reassert itself in the 1990s. The shift in national priorities following the 2001 terror attacks has again revitalized the presidency.

Key Terms

backgrounders Off-the-record exchanges between the president or administration officials and reporters. Whatever a reporter learns at a backgrounder can be used in a story, but the source of the information cannot be revealed.

Budget and Accounting Act of 1921 The act providing the legal basis for presidential participation in the budget process, by requiring the president to submit an annual budget to Congress for its consideration.

cabinet The name given to the collection of secretaries of the executive departments. Despite commonly held beliefs to the contrary, the cabinet rarely serves as an advisory body to the president.

chief diplomat A constitutional role of the president, in which he has the power to recognize ambassadors from other nations.

chief executive The role the president plays as head of the executive branch, in which he carries out the constitutional directive to "take Care that the Laws be faithfully executed."

chief legislator The role the president plays when he offers a legislative agenda and attempts to win congressional approval for it.

chief of staff One of the president's top political advisors and the formal head of the White House staff.

chief of state The role the president plays as ceremonial head of the United States.

coattails The ability of a victorious presidential candidate to sweep congressional candidates of the same party into office on the strength of people voting for one political party.

commander-in-chief The president's constitutional role as civilian leader of the armed forces.

Communications Office The White House office responsible for coordinating the president's media operations, including speechwriting and liaison with national and local reporters.

delegate A philosophy of representation that says officials are elected to carry out constituent interests, even when these interests conflict with what the representative believes is the right thing to do.

diplomatic recognition Formal acceptance of the legitimacy of another nation or its representatives.

executive agreements Legally binding presidential agreements with other nations that do not require congressional approval.

Executive Office of the President (EOP) The large staff of advisors to the president that comprises the president's political and policy operation.

executive orders Presidential directives to the bureaucracy that are legally binding and do not require congressional approval.

executive privilege The power of the president, established by custom, to keep Congress, the courts, and the public from having access to presidential documents and communications.

going public The presidential strategy of using the media to appeal directly to the public to support presidential initiatives.

honeymoon The initial weeks of a new presidential administration when enthusiasm and good press typically translate into high public-approval ratings.

Joint Chiefs of Staff The group of military advisors comprised of the heads of the army, air force, navy, and marines.

impeachment The power granted to Congress to remove from office the president, vice president, judges and other federal officials

legislative liaison White House lobbyists who maintain regular contacts with members of Congress and congressional committees, in order to help guide the president's legislative agenda.

mandate A directive by voters to the president to move ahead with the program he promised when he was a candidate. A large mandate produced by a lopsided vote gives the president a strong bargaining position with respect to Congress to set and advance the agenda in Washington.

media events Activities staged by campaigns or political officials that have enough news value to draw press attention to a message the politician wants to communicate.

National Security Council (NSC) The group of senior policy advisors responsible for helping the president shape national security policy.

news leaks The tactic used widely by White House officials of releasing information to the press on an anonymous basis when it serves their interests to have the information publicized. Some leaks are unauthorized and unwanted by the White House.

newsworthy The conditions under which a story warrants publication or dissemination, based on a set of values applied by newspaper editors and television producers. Newsworthy stories typically have conflict, proximity and relevance to the audience, timeliness, and familiarity.

Office of Management and Budget (OMB) The executive office responsible for developing the president's annual budget proposals by evaluating requests for funding among departments and setting the president's spending priorities.

override The congressional power to overturn a presidential veto by a two-thirds vote of both houses of Congress.

pardon power The unilateral power of the president to grant unconditional clemency to anyone for any reason.

persuasion An informal source of presidential power that gives skilled presidents the opportunity to influence the decisions of members of Congress and others in Washington whose support the president needs to accomplish his political objectives.

pocket veto The presidential prerogative to veto a bill without taking action. Presidents may issue pocket vetoes only if Congress has passed

legislation within ten days of adjournment. A pocket veto cannot be overridden.

press briefings Formal exchanges of information between the press secretary and the national press covering the president.

press conferences Scheduled meetings between reporters and political figures like the president, which give the press access to the official and an opportunity to ask him or her questions firsthand.

press secretary The liaison between the White House and the national press covering the president.

professional reputation The sense among Washington officials of the president's political skills and abilities. It is one of the keys to effective persuasion, as it enhances the president's ability to bargain.

public prestige The sense among Washington officials about whether the president is well regarded by the public. It is one of the keys to effective persuasion, as it enhances the president's ability to bargain.

rally effect The tendency for Americans to unite around the president during a crisis, temporarily bolstering his job-approval ratings.

recess appointments The constitutional power granted to the president to make nominations while Congress is out of session that do not require Senate approval. The appointments stand until the end of the congressional term.

trustee A philosophy of representation that says officials are elected for their wisdom and to exercise their judgment of the national interest, even when it is at odds with their constituents' wishes.

veto power The constitutional power granted to the president to block an act of Congress. It takes a two-thirds vote of both houses of Congress to override a presidential veto.

War Powers Act of 1973 A congressional attempt to reassert the role of the legislature with respect to the president in military affairs by restricting the president's ability to wage war.

White House Office That portion of the Executive Office of the President organized to serve the president's immediate needs.

Resources

You might be interested in examining some of what the following authors have said about the topics we've been discussing:

Barber, James David. *The Presidential Character: Predicting Performance in the White House*, 4th ed. Englewood Cliffs, NJ: Prentice Hall, 2008. Barber's effort to understand presidential performance by systematically classifying presidential character is as interesting as it is controversial.

Burke, John P. *The Institutional Presidency: Organizing and Managing the White House from FDR to Clinton*, 2nd ed. Baltimore: Johns Hopkins University Press, 2000. A look at the way the institutional White House is structured.

Edwards, George C. *Presidential Approval: A Sourcebook*. Baltimore: Johns Hopkins University Press, 1990. Edwards examines how popular support influences what the president is able to do.

Jones, Charles O. *The Presidency in a Separated System, 2nd ed*. Washington, DC: Brookings Institution, 2005. Do we expect too much from our presidents, considering the limits the Constitution places on the office?

Lowi, Theodore J. *The Personal President: Power Invested, Promise Unfulfilled*. Ithaca, NY: Cornell University Press, 1985. Lowi explores the president as symbolic figure who fills a complex emotional role with the public.

Milkis, Sidney, and Michael Nelson. *The American Presidency: Origins and Development, 1776–1998*, 5th ed. Washington, DC: CQ Press, 2007. An historical account of growth and change in the presidency.

Nelson, Michael, ed. *The Presidency and the Political System*, 9th ed. Washington, DC: CQ Press, 2009.

A wide-ranging set of essays covering important topics about the presidency.

Neustadt, Richard E. *Presidential Power: The Politics of Leadership*. New York: The Free Press, revised 1991. In a seminal work on presidential power, Neustadt makes the case that personal persuasion, not formal authority, is the key to presidential effectiveness.

You may also be interested in looking at these resource sites:

The White House, at http://www.whitehouse.gov

National Security Council, at http://www.nsa.gov

Office of Management and Budget at http://www.whitehouse.gov/omb

Council on Environmental Quality, at http://www.whitehouse.gov/ceq

Department of Homeland Security, at http://www.dhs.gov/dhspublic

Office of the Vice President, at http://www.whitehouse.gov/vicepresident

Office of Administration, at http://www.whitehouse.gov/oa

Office of National Drug Control Policy, at http://www.whitehousedrugpolicy.gov

Office of Science and Technology Policy, at http://www.ostp.gov

Office of the United States Trade Representative, at http://www.ustr.gov

Council of Economic Advisors, at http://www.whitehouse.gov/cea

Notes

1. George C. Edwards III, *The Public Presidency: The Pursuit of Popular Support* (New York: St. Martin's Press, 1983), 188.

2. Arthur M. Schlesinger, Sr., who published a list of great presidents in 1948, initiated presidential rankings. Lincoln came in first, followed by Washington and FDR. Grant and Harding pulled up the rear.

3. Edwards, *The Public Presidency*, 187–191.

4. Sidney M. Milkis and Michael Nelson, *The American Presidency: Origins and Development: 1776–1998*, 3d ed. (Washington, DC: CQ Press, 1999), 2–3.

5. Ibid., 66–84. Washington might have served a third term if he hadn't wanted to retire so badly. After his successor, John Adams, became the first president

to be voted out of office, Thomas Jefferson honored the two-term tradition, and it stood until Franklin D. Roosevelt sought and won four terms in office starting in 1932. The Twenty-second Amendment (ratified in 1951) makes the two-term limit a constitutional requirement.

6. Ibid., 85–221.

7. Ibid., 196. This was most evident in international affairs, where Roosevelt exercised strong leadership independent of Congress—a model for American presidents of the twentieth century who served during America's emergence as a global power. See also 206–212.

8. Ibid., 222–241, 262–276, 307–327, and 340–353.

9. Richard E. Neustadt, *Presidential Power: The Politics of Leadership* (New York: The Free Press, revised 1991), 42–63.

10. Ibid., 64–87.

11. bid., 88–106.

12. Paul Brace and Barbara Hinckley, *Follow the Leader: Opinion Polls and the Modern Presidents* (New York: Basic Books, 1992), 18–19.

13. George C. Edwards III, *At the Margins: Presidential Leadership of Congress* (New Haven: Yale University Press, 1989), 142–143.

14. Gail Russell Chaddock, "Olympia Snowe Gives Healthcare Reform Its First Republican Vote," *Christian Science Monitor,* October 13, 2009.

15. David H. Herszenhorn and Robert Pear, "Final Votes in Congress Cap Battle on Health Bill," *New York Times*, March 25, 2010.

16. If you want to get a sense of the variety of matters that pollsters get into, take a look at the home page of one polling firm, Gallup, at http://www.gallup.com/Home.aspx/.

17. Not every president gets the benefit of a honeymoon period. George W. Bush didn't have much of a honeymoon because of the raw feelings left by the unprecedented events surrounding how he came to office. Bill Clinton's early difficulties securing approval for key Cabinet appointees and his controversial early steps supporting gays in the military energized Republicans to oppose him immediately.

18. Brace and Hinckley, *Follow the Leader*, 22–27.

19. Ibid., 27–30.

20. Theodore Lowi, *The Personal President: Power Invested, Promise Unfulfilled* (Ithaca, NY: Cornell University Press, 1985), 1–21.

21. Milkis and Nelson, *The American Presidency*, 200–202.

22. Samuel Kernell, *Going Public: New Strategies of Presidential Leadership* (Washington, DC: CQ Press, 1986), 1–4.

23. You can read more about the Communications Office at http://www.whitehouse.gov/government/off-descrp.html.

24. Edwards, *At the Margins*, 141–146. If an administration is considering a policy and wants to see how the press would react to it, they can leak the information anonymously and see if reporters shoot down their "trial balloon" before the president officially announces it.

25. bid., 112–115.

26. Ibid., 115–119.

27. Ibid., 119–121.

28. Michael Baruch Grossman and Martha Joynt Kumar, *Portraying the President: The White House and the News Media* (Baltimore: Johns Hopkins University Press, 1981), 3–13.

29. Ibid., 273–298.

30. Jim Rutenberg, "White House Keeps a Grip on Its News," *New York Times*, October 14, 2002. The *New York Times* discussed the conflict as it played out in the Bush White House, which included press complaints about the lack of presidential press conferences and news leaks.

31. United States Office of Personnel Management, Demographic Profile of the Federal Workforce.

32. If you're interested in what these folks look like, you can find their pictures at http://www.whitehouse.gov/administration/cabinet.

33. George Washington tried to rely on his cabinet for advice, but found it to be ineffective because of sharp differences among its members. Subsequent presidents didn't fare much better.

34. You can find a list of recent presidential executive orders at http://www.whitehouse.gov/briefing-room/presidential-actions/executive-orders/.

35. Charles O. Jones, *The Presidency in a Separated System* (Washington, DC: Brookings Institution, 1994), 147–181.

36. Paul Charles Light, *The President's Agenda: Domestic Policy Choice from Kennedy to Carter* (Baltimore: Johns Hopkins University Press, 1982), 13–25.

37. Ibid., 13. Attributed to Harry McPherson, aide to President Johnson.

38. Ibid., 17.

39. The figure does not include pocket vetoes. If you include all vetoes, the total for the period is 2,563. See http://clerk.house.gov/art_history/house_history/vetoes.html.

40. Ford issued a total of sixty-six vetoes. This total includes eighteen pocket vetoes. See http://clerk.house.gov/art_history/house_history/vetoes.html.

41. Aaron Wildavsky, "The Two Presidencies," *Trans-Action* 4 (December 1966), 7–14.

42. Ibid.

43. See Donald A. Peppers, "The 'Two Presidencies' Thesis: Eight Years Later," in Steven A. Shull, ed., *The Two Presidencies: A Quarter Century Assessment* (Chicago: Nelson-Hall Publishers, 1991), 26–35; and Richard Fleisher and John Bond, "Are There Two Presidencies? Yes, But Only for Republicans," in Shull, *The Two Presidencies*, 119–142.

44. You can read more about the Central Intelligence Agency online at https://www.cia.gov/about-cia/index.html.

45. To read more about the National Security Council, go to http://www.whitehouse.gov/nsc/.

46. Wildavsky, "The Two Presidencies," 7–14.

47. See "Bush Feels Heat of U.N. Debate, U.S. Elections," *Washington Post*, October 27, 2002.

48. John P. Burke, *The Institutional Presidency: Organizing and Managing the White House from FDR to Clinton*, 2nd ed. (Baltimore: Johns Hopkins University Press, 2000), 13–18.

49. Ibid., 14–15.

50. For an overview of all the first ladies, see http://www.whitehouse.gov/about/first-ladies.

51. You can read more about Michelle Obama at http://www.whitehouse.gov/administration/first-lady-michelle-obama.

52. Milkis and Nelson, *The American Presidency*, 401–407. That last quote is commonly circulated but not exactly accurate. Garner, salty Texan that he was, actually compared the office to a different bodily fluid.

53. Ibid., 404.

54. Ibid.

55. Ibid., 405.

56. Ibid., 410–416.

57. Arthur M. Schlesinger Jr., *The Imperial Presidency* (Boston: Houghton Mifflin, 1973).

58. George E. Reedy, *The Twilight of the Presidency: From Johnson to Reagan* (New York: New American Library, 1987).

Table, Figure and Box Notes

T1 Sources: Reuters; Tim H. Murray and Robert K. Blessing, *Greatness in the White House: Rating the Presidents from George Washington through Ronald Reagan* (University Park: Pennsylvania State University Press, 1994); and Harold W. Stanley and Richard G. Niemi, *Vital Statistics on American Politics 1999–2000* (Washington, DC: CQ Press, 2000).

T2 Paul Brace and Barbara Hinckley, *Follow the Leader: Opinion Polls and the Modern Presidents* (New York: Basic Books, 1992), 19.

T3 Lyn Ragsdale, *Vital Statistics on the Presidency*, revised edition (Washington, DC: Congressional Quarterly, 1998) and http://www.gallup.com.

T4 James David Barber, *The Presidential Character: Predicting Performance in the White House*, 4th ed. (Englewood Cliffs, NJ: Prentice Hall, 2008).

T5 All three images in the public domain and property of the U.S. Federal Government.

T6 Source: Office of the Clerk; U.S. House of Representatives, at http://clerk.house.gov/art_history/house_history/vetoes.html.

T7 CIA World Factbook.

T8 Ibid.

T9 John Higley and Rhonda Evans Case, "Australia: The Politics of Becoming a Republic," *Journal of Democracy* 11:3 (2000), 136–150.

T10 CIA World Factbook.

T11 Arend Lijphart, "Constitutional Design for Divided Societies," *Journal of Democracy*, 15:2 (2004).

T12 Image is in the public domain and property of U.S. Federal Government.

T13 Dan Eagan, "Bush Authorized Domestic Spying," *Washington Post*, December 16, 2005, A1.

T14 Kathleen Hennessey, "Ex-President Carter: Eaves-Dropping Illegal," *Associated Press*, February 6, 2006.

T15 Rueters News Services, February 6, 2006.

T16 Nixon ran and lost when he was an incumbent vice president in 1960; he ran again and won eight years later.

T17 Agnew resigned the Vice Presidency under a cloud of scandal and was replaced by Ford.

T18 Rockefeller had been an unsuccessful presidential candidate before Ford selected him to serve as vice president; he did not run for president afterward.

T19 Quayle ran in the Republican primary in 2000, eight years after leaving office. He did not win the nomination.

The Cost of Confusion

Resolving Ambiguities in Detainee Treatment

By Kenneth Anderson and Elisa Massimino

The treatment of detainees—interrogation, detention, and trial—has been among the most controversial policies in the Bush administration's global war on terrorism. Indeed, many of the questions that have arisen in the detainee treatment debate are fundamental to counterterrorism policy, and the next administration will have to provide its own answers as a basis for whatever approach it adopts. What has been the import of declaring a "war on terror"? Is this a wise or sustainable organizing principle for counterterrorism policy? What are the respective roles of the three co-equal branches of government in establishing and enforcing the rules? What is the relationship between national security and respect for human rights? Are security and rights competing interests in a zero-sum game?

We believe that there are some general principles that can be shared across progressive and conservative lines on which national counterterrorism policy should be grounded. We do not aim to examine all aspects of counterterrorism policy, which would require us to address a wide array of issues of national security, civil liberties, and human rights—surveillance, seizure of asserted terrorist assets, use of force short of armed conflict, assassination and targeted kidnapping policies, and many other

matters. We focus instead on three specific and closely related issues— interrogation, detention, and trials of detainees—as sources of the principles that should guide counterterrorism policy. We start here because issues of detainee treatment raise profound questions of American values.

Should Counterterrorism Policy Be a "War" on Terror?

Within days—hours, even—of the Al Qaeda attacks on September 11, 2001, the Bush administration was characterizing it and the US response as a war. While some argued that the attacks simply constituted criminality on a mass scale, bipartisan opinion in the United States largely coalesced around the view that the United States was at war, and at war with a transnational, nonstate actor that had declared war upon the United States. This view gradually was transformed in the rhetoric and policy of the United States into what the Bush administration dubbed the "global war on terror." Although the administration—in an effort to recall the Cold War idea of a long struggle against a persistent enemy—recently sought to rename the effort the "Long War," the original moniker persists.

Why does the terminology matter? At one level, using the war framework helps build public support for confronting terrorism; the images, analogies, and metaphors that are used to justify the national response shape what kind of action the public supports and its perception of how long and how deep the struggle might be. The invocation of war can justify a great many measures that would not otherwise be contemplated in a peaceful constitutional democracy—emergency powers, strictures on civil liberties, the use of force outside of ordinary domestic police powers, a sense of national unity in a time of crisis that transcends politics, and a heightened expression of presidential and commander-in-chief power, potentially at the expense of the other constitutional branches of government. All of these measures were evident in the response following September 11; it would be accurate to say that despite some misgivings of civil libertarians, in the immediate aftermath of the attacks, there was broad sentiment across party lines and across American society that all of these options for a national emergency were appropriately on the table and that *war* was a good way of summing up the situation.

Six years on, unsurprisingly, this unity has evaporated. Questioning government and the policies of the party in power is deeply ingrained in our political DNA. In the case of a war that is today more ideological and metaphorical than "hot"—resembling, in this regard, the Cold War—fundamental questions of policy are bound to arise. Thus the very idea of a "global war on terror" is today seen as the policy of a particular presidential administration in a way that it was not immediately following September 11. At this point, the war on terror no longer serves as simply a synonym for US counterterrorism policy. The very question of whether US counterterrorism policy should be conceived as a *war* is precisely what is at issue; to refer to it as a war on terror is to presume the conclusion to a fundamental and contested issue. Hence, in this paper, when we refer to *counterterrorism policy*, we mean it in a generic sense of the set of issues on the table, and when we refer to the *war on terror*, we mean the specific and actual, contested and contestable policies of the Bush administration.

We agree that in the moment of crisis and its immediate aftermath, the president exercised extraordinary powers appropriate to the executive role, including the power to use force to prevent and disrupt further attacks. Moreover, just as we agree that the moment of crisis occasioned extraordinary executive powers, we also agree that over time, those powers must diminish in a return to ordinary constitutional order. As a democracy, we must fashion a response to the ongoing threat of terror in a constitutionally democratic way. Heightened executive power eventually must give way to democratic, majoritarian procedures. The legislature, as a co-equal branch of government, might understandably be sidelined in the moment of crisis but, we agree, must reassert itself if it is to remain a constitutional co-equal. Likewise, the courts must ensure that individual rights under the Constitution and obligations under international law are observed. Such rights are a constitutional obligation of the legislative and the executive branches to protect (although they may well have their own views as to the content and meaning of such rights), but it is the province of the courts, finally, to determine and enforce them.

The characterization of counterterrorism policy as a war on terror affects how domestic political and constitutional processes come into play and is, therefore, far more than simply a matter of public motivational rhetoric. It is language deeply imbued with legal implications. We believe that over time, the characterization of counterterrorism policy as a war must be limited to its use as a strategic paradigm for dealing with nonstate actors that have arrayed themselves as enemies of the United States, but it must be carefully confined to make clear that this is a strategic, rather than legal, use of the term. Otherwise, the United States risks going down the road of authoritarian anti-Communist states in the Cold War—Chile, for example, or Guatemala—using the threat of communism as a justification for a permanent state of emergency and emergency presidential powers. This is not to say that the threats posed by terrorism are not real and that the strategic conception of war was not useful—only that the responses must be crafted within constitutional democratic processes and that war, within those processes, has a highly specific legal meaning that is not applicable to most matters of counterterrorism policy.

Domestically, the executive branch strengthens its powers insofar as the immediate crisis is characterized as a war because the Constitution gives special powers to the president and commander in chief. More precisely, few question the enhanced powers of the president in a moment of crisis such as September 11; when the crisis is converted into a war, those powers become the powers of a commander in chief for as long as the war goes on. It has long been apparent that the strengthening of those executive powers has been an independent goal of the Bush administration, apart from the war on terror itself and sometimes at considerable cost to it. We disagree about the breadth of the president's powers in war, but there is little doubt that those powers depend on how broadly *war* may validly be defined for legal purposes of the laws and customs of war. But we are in agreement that as a legal matter, the administration's definition of the war is unacceptably broad.

Characterizing counterterrorism efforts as a *war* has quite different implications, however, for actions taken by the United States abroad.[1] The Bush administration has wanted quite inconsistent things from its characterization of these actions as a global war on terror. There is, first of all, an inconsistency in strategic vision in the characterization of war. The administration has wanted to make clear to the American people, as well as to the world at large, that the United States is willing to pursue terrorists wherever they seek to hide—to deprive them, in the language of the 2006 national counterterrorism strategy, of safe havens—and to do so using all the tools of war. Under this view, the entire world is a battlefield. And yet, even as a matter of strategy, the idea of a global war is more metaphor than reality; the world in its entirety is not—not even potentially—a battlefield. The strategic engagement with terrorists is partly in Afghanistan, but it is also even more so in Pakistan—and the United States, for political reasons, at this moment is plainly not willing to make Pakistan a battlefield. It is also, from a strategic standpoint, an engagement with ideologues and radicalized clerics and their

followers in such places as Hamburg, Birmingham, and Paris—but they obviously will not be battlefields except in an entirely metaphorical sense. In our view, insofar as counterterrorism policy requires *all* of the tools of government, most of those tools will *not* in fact be the tools of war in the actual meaning of armed conflict. Instead, they will involve surveillance, interdiction of terrorist financing, intelligence gathering, diplomacy, and other methods. Thus the language of global war is necessarily metaphorical. It should not diminish the national resolve to defeat the enemy to acknowledge that actual war is only one tool in that struggle.

Thus trying to apply the term *war* to the entire effort when it is only intermittently a war *operationally*, and therefore *legally*, in particular times and places creates significant problems. The Cold War was strategically well-considered as a war; yet only occasionally and in certain places around the world did it operationally and legally constitute war. Such is the case with the war on terror. Calling global counterterrorism policy a *war*—not only as a strategic concept but as a global operational fact that invokes a specific legal characterization—has profound legal implications and anomalous legal consequences.

Invoking the Law of War in Global Counterterrorism

Invoking war as the strategic policy frame has the virtue of recognizing the way that our enemies see their actions with respect to us. Likewise, from the viewpoint of the administration, invoking war as the policy frame has the virtue of rhetorically separating the current response to terror from policies of the past that essentially treated terrorism as a matter of organized crime gone global, appropriate for law enforcement and the criminal justice system, not the military and war.

But the *legal* invocation of war against a nonstate, transnational actor or actors creates many anomalies in the application of the law of war, an essentially state-centric legal regime. Counterterrorism is a global struggle against an enemy which, while obviously real, cannot be identified by the usual indicia of victory or defeat—the end of a regime, the occupation and control of territory, the destruction of enemy forces. It is therefore hard to know when, if ever, the war will be won for legal purposes, a question that is critical for prisoners, who have a legal right to be released at the end of fighting. One might as well say spatially that the entire world is a battlefield, and that temporally, the war will be won when the threat of terrorist violence is banished from the world, which will be a long way off indeed. If correct in any sense, it is only useful as a strategic metaphor, a way of saying that our enemies are not limited to any particular place or people and that they take a long view of their struggle, as a guide to strategic analysis and a spur to our own long-term counterterrorism policies.

Other issues arise, however, when our terrorist adversaries are portrayed as warriors—issues on which the coauthors are divided. Such a depiction can have the unintended consequence, Massimino points out, of elevating the stature of the enemy in the eyes of its own potential constituency by boosting Al Qaeda's mythic appeal as the defender of Islam, its own preferred image. Anderson, on the other hand, believes that how our enemies see the struggle must be integrated into how we see it.

However useful war may be as a strategic concept, it cannot stand as a legal definition triggering the rights and duties under the laws of war, which rightly require a more tangible and operational foundation. It would be like saying that the Cold War, at every moment of its 40-year run, was legally an armed conflict with the Soviet Union and the Warsaw Pact. The fact was, instead, that however much the United States conceived the Cold War in strategic terms as a *war*, it did not treat it as a legal state of war governed by the law of armed conflict. Recourse to the law of armed conflict was then, as should be the case now, limited to active hostilities rising to the traditionally accepted definition of an armed conflict. We must not confuse the important insights of a strategic view of counterterrorism as metaphorical war with the legal implications of invoking the formal laws of armed conflict.

The Bush administration's invocation of the laws of war may be strategically useful, but it is simply at odds with the legal requirement of an "armed conflict" triggering of the laws of war. The operational conduct of counterterrorism to date has involved several armed conflicts and might involve more, but the global war on terror does not meet the legal definition of an armed conflict.

We therefore agree that the Bush administration's global claim is incorrect as a matter of law. The administration has dealt with the lack of fit between the nature of the conflict and the laws of war in radically inconsistent ways—but always, it must be said, in ways that benefit its preexisting desire to strengthen the hand of the executive branch. We examine three issues—detention of individuals as enemy combatants, trials by military commissions of detained enemy combatants, and interrogations—in which this disconnect has had the most profound consequences.

Detention

The laws of war permit belligerent powers to detain captured enemy combatants without charge or trial for the duration of the conflict in order to prevent them from rejoining the fight. The Bush administration embraced the laws of war and claimed under them the traditional legal right to hold detainees, for example at Guantanamo Bay, until the end of hostilities. What is at issue here is not the right of a belligerent in wartime to hold combatants—this is undisputed. The dispute is over the very definition of *war* in the "global war on terror." This is a difficulty of legal definition all on its own on which the coauthors are agreed that the administration was wrong.

While claiming the rights of a belligerent to detain captured enemy combatants, however, the Bush administration at the same time, through the office of the White House counsel, made one of the most legally and conceptually ill-considered moves in its entire counterterrorism strategy. It concluded that, although the war on terror was a *war*, the Geneva Conventions—the laws of war—did not apply to those detained in it. Terrorists are not lawful combatants, it argued, and hence fall outside the law altogether. They could thus be dealt with by the commander in chief at his discretion.

The inconsistency produced by this decision was breathtaking. The United States was taking detainees not only on traditionally defined battlefields such as Afghanistan but also at O'Hare airport in Chicago and Bradley University in Peoria. The administration argued first that the constitutional war powers of the president provided the basis for these detentions; later, it argued that the detainees were combatants who could be held for the duration of hostilities. Invoking constitutional war powers, or alternatively, the laws of war, as a basis for holding detainees without charge or trial in the domestic legal system, while simultaneously denying that the laws of war applied to them, created a legal black hole that threatened to subvert the laws of war altogether.

Indeed, this critique was shared by most of the military's own uniformed law of war legal specialists in the military, who have argued that the Geneva Conventions should apply only to battlefield detainees, no matter how one defined the strategic scope of the "war." Al Qaeda flunked the tests of Article 4 of the Third Geneva Convention on POWs, and hence its members were not entitled to the privileges of POW status. Prisoners of war are held to keep from taking up arms again but are not subject to prosecution or punishment, provided that they have complied with the laws of war. For Al Qaeda's part, though, while its members were *combatants* by virtue of taking an "active part in hostilities," the group's systematic violations of the laws of war rendered them unprivileged combatants individually, i.e., unlawful belligerents under the laws of war. They could be detained under the law of war and, as unprivileged combatants, charged with crimes arising from their acts of belligerency, such as murder and destruction of property. Legal procedures for trials of unlawful combatants derive from the terms of Article 75 of the 1977 Additional Protocol I of the Geneva Conventions.[2]

But this international law of war approach went unheeded by the administration. Instead, the administration sought to hedge against legal challenges to its war-without-law approach by holding detainees at Guantanamo which, it hoped, would be beyond the reach of US courts and habeas corpus. It lost on the substance of that argument in the

Rasul case, having rested it on a claim of executive power so overreaching that it failed, on the habeas corpus issue, to gain even Justice Scalia's vote.

We are in agreement that the scope of the administration's global war on terror is legally too broad. There are two wars in which the United States is currently involved: Afghanistan and Iraq. Other armed conflicts may develop, but the world is not a battlefield in its entirety, and the United States may not seize and detain as combatants under the laws of war individuals not directly engaged in these armed conflicts. On this fundamental point we are agreed.

We disagree, however, as to the concept of illegal combatancy. Massimino takes the view that a person who flunks the tests of legal combatancy in Article 4, Third Geneva Convention, becomes thereby a civilian protected by the Fourth Geneva Convention (albeit one who may be charged with violations of the laws of war). The International Committee of the Red Cross (ICRC) also takes this view, along with a significant body of the human rights community. Anderson believes that such an approach effectively rewards combat that violates the laws of war and that a person who fails the tests for legal combatancy is not a civilian, but an illegal combatant, an unlawful belligerent. The disagreement is far from merely academic; it involves fundamental questions of treatment of civilians under the Fourth Geneva Convention (who nonetheless may be detained as security risks, but with considerably greater protections than those afforded unlawful belligerency).

These disagreements between the authors notwithstanding, both agree that the current legal situation is an unsatisfying and unworkable mishmash of bits of highly contested international law combined with Bush administration policy decisions, Supreme Court opinions that are themselves bits of this and that, and narrow legislative fixes designed to satisfy minimum requirements of the case law. The Supreme Court, in successive cases and with various hedges, has allowed certain domestic law remedies at Guantanamo such as habeas corpus which, while arguably defensible holdings under US domestic law, have no historical or textual basis in the law of war, at least regarding foreign combatants. Yet at the same time that the court has grafted essentially domestic law onto the question of detention, it also has found, in *Hamdan*, that the conflict is governed by Common Article Three of the Geneva Conventions. This legal holding thus puts a certain practical floor under the administration's conduct—prohibiting cruel, humiliating, or degrading treatment of detainees and violence to life and person.[3]

The administration, for its part, has responded to this holding by acknowledging the application of the Geneva Conventions as a largely formal matter, asserting that in any case, the United States is in compliance with Common Article Three. In the Military Commissions Act of 2006, the administration sought and obtained legislation to insulate it from habeas corpus, claims by detainees asserting the Geneva Conventions, or other claims to the contrary.

The most important additional issue with respect to detention policy is who has the power to determine that one is a combatant in the first place and not, say, an innocent shepherd or someone sold into our custody for bounty by the Northern Alliance. The administration has asserted that this is a matter of executive branch discretion. Prior to the Supreme Court's decisions in the *Rasul, Hamdi,* and *Hamdan* cases, it based this view on the claim that the Geneva Conventions did not apply to these detainees, hedging its bets by keeping them in Guantanamo, which it hoped would be beyond the reach of the federal courts. After losing, in part, its habeas as well as other claims defended on executive power grounds in *Rasul* and *Hamdi,* it established limited tribunals for detainees, apparently intended to satisfy the requirements of the Third Geneva Convention, Article 5, requiring, in cases of doubt, a tribunal to determine combatant status.

Those tribunals are of a limited nature—and judicial review of them is confined to the question of whether the tribunal followed its own procedures. They have, as a result, been sharply criticized on due process grounds. These combatant status tribunals, however, exist for purposes of establishing the basis for detention, not for the separate question, addressed below, of trials for violations of the laws of war.

Congress has written legislation narrowly designed to meet the requirements of *Hamdan,* and the president has signed it: the Military Commissions Act (MCA). That legislation is an admixture of fundamentally domestic assertions of authority, with one eye defensively fixed upon the requirements of Common Article Three. Among other things, it purports to deprive the courts of jurisdiction with respect to habeas claims by alien unlawful enemy combatants, and deprives them of the ability to allege violations of the Geneva Conventions before any court.[4] It makes the decision to detain someone designated by the president as an enemy combatant—potentially even for life—an executive branch determination, and almost entirely unreviewable by the federal courts.

If one assumes hypothetically that the executive branch is infallible in its judgment as to who is or is not a terrorist, then one might accept such an arrangement. In such an "infallible executive" scenario, Anderson would support such detentions, while Massimino would not. But since neither Anderson nor Massimino regards the executive branch's designations as actually or potentially infallible, we agree strongly that this procedure, as enshrined in the MCA, is unacceptable and not remediated by the provision of limited combatant status review hearings.

Congress has so far agreed that federal court access will not be permitted. Whether the Supreme Court ultimately will defer to the two political branches of government on this legislation's many extraordinary measures is at this point unknown, but no one doubts that litigation will be both lengthy and momentous. Changes in party control of one or both houses, or other political factors, or further court decisions, are highly likely to produce new legislation or significant modifications of existing legislation—already, the new Democratic Congress following the 2006 midterm elections is considering amending the MCA, particularly with respect to habeas corpus.

Yet the pattern of highly reactive legislation is unfortunately likely to continue. Rather than pushing for truly systematic reform (as recommended by the authors of this chapter further below), the US legislature seems content to react either to a specific court decision or to a particular demand of the executive branch.

Trials of Detainees by Military Commission and Combatant Status Review Hearings

Not many months after September 11, the administration announced that it did not intend to submit alleged terrorists to regular trial by the federal courts except in particular circumstances, but would instead submit them to trial by military commission.[5] This procedure is fundamentally different from the combatant status review hearings described in the preceding section. Those combatant status review hearings are not a judgment about guilt or innocence; they are hearings designed to offer a limited review of whether the person being detained should be called an "enemy combatant" at all and whether that person continues to pose a security risk to the United States.[6] The combatant status review hearings are akin to administrative detention hearings, rather than a trial. By contrast, the military commissions, as originally conceived and in the tradition of US military law stretching back to the Civil War, are military trials on charges of violations of the laws and customs of war.

Although possessed of a long history and indisputably part of military law, such commissions have been hotly disputed in their specific application in the global war on terror since they were first promulgated in executive orders following September 11, through to their legislative authorization in the MCA of 2006. The policy objective of the administration following September 11 was stark—to make entirely plain that it was breaking with the criminal law approach to transnational terrorism pursued by earlier administrations. The paradigm would be war and, henceforth, it would operate under the laws of war.

Military commissions were thought to provide a form of justice that is defensible under US law and military custom as well as international law and custom (once the administration had reversed course on the relevance of the Geneva Conventions in establishing unlawful belligerency). The most fundamental objection to military commissions in the global war on terror—one which we share—is that whatever the concept of battlefield detainee arising from either international law or US military law and custom, the invocation of a global war on terror, with the entire world a battlefield encompassing Al Qaeda detainees found in Afghanistan and a US citizen detained in Chicago, is simply too broad to sustain its legal weight.

The *Hamdan* court held that the executive branch exceeded its authority in establishing military commissions that differed from provisions of the Uniform Code of Military Justice, but the court also emphasized that these issues could be resolved through legislation. (It also held, by reason of finding that Common Article Three applied, that the administration had to proceed with trials that fell within the meaning of Common Article Three's language of "regularly constituted courts.")[7] Accordingly, the administration sought legislation designed merely to ratify what it already had designed and put in place. Opposition developed in the Senate, however, with Republican Senators John McCain, John Warner, and Lindsay Graham all insisting on changes to the procedures for military commissions. After rounds of negotiations on the trial issue, as well as the detention and interrogation issues, the White House and the senators reached agreement, and the MCA was signed by the president in October 2006. Democrats largely stayed out of the wrangling between the three Republican senators and administration, although they fiercely attacked the bill as it came to a vote and overwhelmingly voted against it. At this writing, the new Democratic Congress is considering efforts to amend it.

Although we agree, in principle, that military commissions *can* be used to try individuals for violations of the laws of war, and although we further agree that the global war on terror is too broad a definition of *war* to support the *universal* application of military commissions to all detainees that the administration determines to put on trial, we disagree as to the proper "fix." Massimino would require that all those not captured on a traditionally defined battlefield be tried, if suspected of criminal violations, in regular US courts, while limiting military commissions to those captured on battlefields as traditionally defined in US military and international law. Anderson agrees that military commissions should ideally be limited to those captured on traditionally defined battlefields, but does not believe that those otherwise captured should necessarily be tried in regular US courts. He believes, as discussed below, that Congress should create a special, civilian counterterrorism court to try such cases, with limited habeas review by regular US courts; if such reform is (as is likely) unreachable, then he prefers the current MCA approach (modified to include a limited form of regular court review).

With respect to the initial decision to detain and its review through the combatant status review tribunals (CSR tribunals)—as distinguished from any trial that might later follow for alleged crimes by unlawful belligerents—we agree that the CSR tribunals are inadequate as a procedure and put far too much determinative power into executive branch hands—not just in a moment of uncertain security risk, but permanently. To the degree that current legislation gives the executive branch full power to detain a person as an enemy combatant potentially forever (and we disagree about whether the MCA in fact grants such power to the president), it ought to require a far more substantive process of review than reflected by the combatant review status tribunals.

Just as we differed as to the proper fix for the issue of trial venues and procedures, we likewise differ, however, as to the proper remedy regarding the decision to detain and to continue to detain. Massimino believes that individuals who cannot be properly considered combatants in an armed conflict, but who nonetheless are suspected of criminal conduct, should be tried in the regular federal courts. With respect to those who cannot be tried but who pose a serious threat to national security, she believes that in (the unlikely event of) a full-scale reform of counterterrorism policy, there might be limited room for legislative enactment of an administrative detention procedure, outside the laws of war and outside the military altogether, provided that it comported with the strict requirements of international human rights law.

Anderson believes, by contrast, that allowing a backdoor route into the full federal courts through habeas or other mechanisms is neither required for noncitizens nor acceptable from the standpoint of national security. He would prefer the current MCA legislation to full habeas access to federal court. On the other hand, agreeing that the current law lacks sufficient protections, he would prefer comprehensive counterterrorism reform to create a special civilian counterterrorism court with special rules of procedure, evidence, and review that address the special issues of terrorism. While agreeing that the United States needs a procedure for administrative detention in terrorism cases using a special civilian counterterrorism court as its vehicle, Anderson is skeptical that international human rights law can serve except in a general and hortatory way as the standard to be met. Anderson further believes that a special counterterrorism court should be created but limited to two functions—to review administrative security detention decisions by the executive and to try terrorist criminal cases for specified terrorist crimes, taking over from both the regular federal courts and military commissions.

But there is a significant convergence of views here on a crucial issue, despite other disagreements of approach. We think that, apart from whether these cases should be heard by the federal courts or, in Anderson's view, a special counterterrorism court, any comprehensive reform of counterterrorism should take the military out of the business of detention generally in the war on terror—including detention and the holding of detainees, combatant status review hearings, and military commissions. The "armed conflict" part of the war on terror should be confined as a legal matter to armed conflicts as traditionally defined in the law of war.

Yet the legislation passed by Congress to satisfy *Hamdan*, the MCA, underscores the increasing distance between the law of war and the domestic law definitions applicable to detention and military commissions. The MCA effectively twists itself into a pretzel seeking to reconcile a law of war and military law paradigm with something that, even if it is not traditional criminal law, does not bear great resemblance to traditional law of war. The definition of an unlawful enemy combatant in the MCA, for example, bears very little resemblance to the traditional definition of a combatant in the laws of war. On the contrary, the MCA fundamentally reaches to definitions of persons to be detained that are appropriate instead to administrative detention procedures, using such standards as "material support" for terrorism.

That being the case, it is time to call it what it is (administrative detention), cease applying a military law rationale to it that does not really work, and make it a civilian rather than military jurisdiction. The military, we suspect, would agree. Similarly, on the habeas issue: While no one seriously wants to extend habeas protections to ordinary soldiers taken prisoner on the battlefield, the reason the issue is now under such bitter debate is because we *also* understand that seizing an American citizen at O'Hare airport is scarcely the same thing as the capture of German soldiers in Normandy and that it *does* raise questions about habeas corpus. The pretzel twisting and creation of more and more domestic law purporting to be military law or international law of war—while having an ever-smaller substantive connection with it—risks both the integrity of our domestic law and the integrity of our military law and commitment to the international law of war. While we disagree on exactly how to redress this, we are firmly in agreement that the limitless legal extension of the war paradigm exemplified in the MCA does not work. The current jerry-rigged structure makes little sense now and will not function in future administrations, irrespective, frankly, of whether and the extent to which the courts bless it or not.

Interrogation of Detainees and the Definition of Torture

Perhaps no issue in the war on terror has aroused greater passions than the interrogation of detainees. While there is widespread rejection of torture as un-American, citizens of this country are profoundly divided as to the morality of other harsh interrogation techniques, those that constitute cruel, inhuman, or degrading treatment short of torture. Many

believe that we should not be parsing a distinction between torture and other cruelty; many others believe that refusing to use such techniques when they could prevent catastrophic terrorist attacks is itself a breach of morality. The United States is not the first country to grapple with terrorism, and it is not the first to face the moral and legal dilemmas raised by these questions.

The administration's initial approach to interrogations was to assert executive branch power and exploit what it saw as ambiguities in the rules. Where the domestic criminal law prohibited torture, lawyers at the Justice Department produced a memo construing the statute so narrowly that "old-fashioned" torture methods—cigarette burns, breaking fingers—would not qualify as torture, and reassured interrogators that in any event, the president can authorize violations of the law in his power as commander in chief. Where the Geneva Conventions required refraining from torture, cruel treatment, and outrages upon personal dignity, administration lawyers argued that, as unlawful combatants, detainees in US custody were not entitled to those protections. Where treaty obligations required the United States to prevent the use of cruel, inhuman, or degrading treatment, the administration reinterpreted a reservation to the treaty to mean that the United States was not bound by the prohibition on cruelty when it acted abroad. When Congress passed the McCain Amendment and overruled this interpretation, requiring US personnel everywhere in the world to refrain from cruel, inhuman, and degrading treatment of prisoners, reports surfaced that administration lawyers had found a way around that, as well, by interpreting the prohibition as a flexible standard that would allow cruel treatment in circumstances that did not "shock the conscience." When the Supreme Court ruled in *Hamdan* that the humane treatment standards of the Geneva Conventions (found in Common Article Three) were binding on the United States in its treatment of all detainees, the administration sought to replace that standard with its more flexible "shocks the conscience" interpretation. Congress rejected the administration's proposal to redefine Common Article Three, but it narrowed the scope of what constitutes a war crime in ways designed to immunize past conduct. The president nonetheless concluded upon signing the bill into law that the CIA could continue to use a set of "alternative interrogation techniques" beyond those authorized for use by the military.

In the face of these efforts to circumvent the rules, the president's repeated assertions, however sincere and heartfelt, that "we don't torture" ring hollow around the world. And that is not surprising. We have, in fact, tortured detainees in our custody. According to the Pentagon's own figures, at least eight of these were literally tortured to death—beaten, suffocated, frozen, hung. How do we account for this from a country that led the world in drafting the international convention prohibiting torture?

Torture and other forms of cruelty gain a seductive appeal during times of insecurity because of the lure that their use might "work" to protect innocent civilians from catastrophic harm. But what does it mean to say that torture "works"? No systematic study has ever shown that inflicting torture or other such cruelty yields reliable information or actionable intelligence.[8] When the Pentagon released its new Army Field Manual on Intelligence Interrogations last September, rejecting cruel and inhumane tactics, Lieutenant General John Kimmons, deputy chief of staff for Army Intelligence, explained it bluntly: "No good intelligence is going to come from abusive practices. I think history tells us that. I think the empirical evidence of the last five years, hard years, tell us that."[9]

Moreover, even torture that produces accurate information may work against US interests. Longstanding army doctrine cautions that the use of such techniques, if revealed, could undermine public support for the war effort and degrade respect for the standards on which US troops rely for protection. And certainly the abuses at Abu Ghraib were effective only in undermining US moral authority and providing a boon to jihadist recruitment.

But despite all this, the lure of torture—or if not torture, something very close—remains strong. There persists a communal American fantasy that if we are ever faced with a ticking time bomb scenario, we can save the day and avert disaster if only we overcome our squeamishness and "take off the gloves." Indulging in this fantasy has led American

policy far off track and away from the values of life and human dignity for which it claims to be fighting this long war. It is time to put the fantasy aside.[10]

We share the view that intelligence is one, if not the most important, tool in combating terrorism today. We also start from the premise that torture is and should remain illegal. While there is a range of conduct that the United States has agreed to—and should refrain from (and we may disagree about where that line should be drawn)—the conduct on that spectrum for which a person can be held criminally liable (war crimes, torture) must be made crystal clear.

The MCA provides some additional clarity. It defines what it calls "grave breaches of Common Article Three," the violation of which could subject a person such as a CIA official to criminal liability. They are: torture, cruel or inhuman treatment, performing biological experiments, murder, mutilation or maiming, intentionally causing serious bodily injury, rape, sexual assault or abuse, and taking hostages. It recognizes that the executive has the authority to define lesser offenses and the terms of their criminal liability, as well as to "interpret" the meaning of the provisions that do not amount to grave breaches. The act provides protection from legal action for government officials engaged in interrogations prior to the act (by making amendments to the War Crimes Act retroactive to its passage in 1997), and provides that the Geneva Conventions cannot be invoked as a source of rights in any court.

Thus, while the law clarifies some matters, it leaves others open for interpretation. Murder, for example, mutilation, and rape are clear enough. But, strikingly, even something as fundamental as torture is not entirely clear under the new law. During debate about the legislation, Democratic and Republican members of Congress in both houses gave examples of conduct that, while not explicitly listed in the statute, would, in their view, constitute a grave breach—waterboarding; forced nudity; forcing a prisoner to perform sexual acts or pose in sexual positions; beatings; electric shocks, burns, or other physical pain; the use of dogs to terrify; induced hypothermia or heat injury; and mock executions. But none of these techniques, some of which had previously been authorized by the administration, were explicitly listed in the statute.

This is a mistake. Anderson and Massimino disagree about many aspects of interrogation procedures, but we agree that it is the obligation of Congress and the administration to be transparent and specific with respect to what constitutes a crime under US law.[11]

Why is this failure to be specific so problematic? Because the people of the United States are deeply divided as to the substance of these issues—torture, not torture, degrading treatment, not degrading treatment, etc.—and because such terms as *humiliating* or *degrading* are not plainly objective in the way that, say, murder is, the only clear democratic means to establish their meaning is through the process of legislation. But to meet this need, such legislation must be specific, transparent—and above all avoid euphemism, generalities, and vagueness. Granted, no lawmaker willingly votes in a way to make him or herself any more accountable than absolutely necessary—but the importance of these issues is such, and the divisions among the public is such, that only public votes on these issues can give the answers democratic legitimacy. There is, of course, a further question as to whether the courts, in their role as protectors of individual rights, would defer to the legislature's judgments, and we likely disagree as to the extent of deference owed. But we do not disagree on the obligation of Congress to legislate plainly on these questions.

We believe this as a fundamental principle of fairness, not because we think that interrogators should seek to walk right up to that line of criminal conduct. To the contrary, we believe that in order to prevent torture, US policy must build a buffer of additional prohibitions, like a fence around the Torah.[12] As former Navy General Counsel Alberto Mora wrote in a memo critical of interrogation policies that permitted the use of cruelty and other force short of torture: "Once the initial barrier against the use of improper force had been breached, a phenomenon known as 'force drift' would almost certainly begin to come into play. This term describes the observed tendency among interrogators who rely on force. If some force is good, these people come to believe, then the application of more force must be better."

Although agreeing that the prohibitions against torture require a buffer, we nonetheless would likely disagree with the content of what that buffer zone should be.

Many countries that have faced a terrorist threat have imagined themselves immune from the force drift phenomenon. In Israel, Turkey, the UK in Northern Ireland—every democracy that has tried to walk along the edge of this cliff, by authorizing abusive treatment only in emergencies or only with respect to certain types of suspects, has ended up falling off. Once physical cruelty and inhumane treatment is authorized, it is very difficult to contain and control within preset parameters.

Just as the use of force tends to "drift" upward, it likewise migrates between agencies. For this reason, we also agree that both the prohibition against torture, and the "fence" around that prohibition, should apply equally to all US personnel. In other words, there should be a single standard of humane treatment to which all US personnel—military and civilian—adhere.

This does not mean that all detainees must be treated alike. We are not arguing here that Khalid Sheikh Mohammed must be granted the privileges to which prisoners of war are entitled. But there should be no daylight between the baseline humane treatment standards governing military and CIA interrogations.[13] In wartime, those standards are found in Common Article Three of the Geneva Conventions. Outside of armed conflict, they are found in international human rights and domestic law.

The authors disagree, however, as to the application of international human rights law. Anderson takes the view, for example, that the International Covenant on Civil and Political Rights does not, in accordance with its text and longstanding US views, apply extraterritorially. Massimino believes that such treaties bind US actions wherever they are taken. Our view of how widely human rights law would serve as a check on US action thus differs considerably.

Many have argued that while it is fine to have these standards, we would be wise to keep them to ourselves. Before the new Army field manual on intelligence interrogations was issued, the Pentagon

290 ★ Engage, Debate, Participate

seriously considered attaching a secret annex in which techniques permitted for use only on certain detainees would be listed. The argument for this approach was that transparency about which techniques interrogators could use would aid the enemy in resisting. But our biggest problem now is not that the enemy knows what to expect from us, it is that the rest of the world, including our allies, does not. So long as they believe that we are willing to engage in torture and other cruel, inhuman, and degrading treatment—conduct for which we routinely condemn others—we will continue to pay for past mistakes.

Conclusion: The Choice of Paradigms

This chapter has focused on the three most domestically and internationally divisive issues in the war on terror—detention, trial, and interrogation. There are many other issues of grave importance, but these three capture the fundamental questions of value that must be answered by national policy in pursuing counterterrorism. And our answers on such essential matters—even in the face of polarizing controversy—will help build a coherent and sustainable counterterrorism policy. Our recommendation is that there be a return to basics, a return to the question of fundamental paradigms in US counterterrorism policy.

Counterterrorism has been presented since September 11 as the choice between a criminal law model of counterterrorism and a war model of counterterrorism. That binary seems to us wrong. What we describe as the war on terror represents a strategic view of a long struggle in which strategic war concepts are appropriate to frame the conflict. They do not describe, however, the legal requirements for invoking the law of war in a global war on terror. The contradictions and strains that arise from trying to fit counterterrorism policy into the straightjacket of war, while at the same time seeking to use the law of war as a means to insulate the executive branch from established checks and balances, are nearing a breaking point. The MCA is likely to accelerate

political crises as much as defuse them because it is so ill-structured a settlement for the long term—designed, as it was, to meet the narrowest requirements of a Supreme Court decision and make up for mistakes made early in the interrogation and detention process.

The counterterrorism policies of any new administration or new Congress, of whatever party, Republican or Democratic, must start from a view that counter-terrorism operates across a wide range of activities. At one end is law enforcement, particularly domestic law enforcement (the kind that breaks up domestic terrorist plots). At the other end is war—actual war, armed conflict involving armies and troops and the weapons of war. War, we can now begin to see, is more often aimed at government backers of terrorists rather than the terrorists themselves. The real action against terrorists themselves takes place in a zone between those two extremes. The tools in this zone include surveillance, tracking and seizure of terrorist assets, cooperation with foreign intelligence and police services, domestic security measures for key infrastructure, protection of air travel, and so on. It also includes detention, interrogation, and the use of force short of war, such as attacks on terrorist training camps, targeted assassinations of terrorists, and other uses of violence that do not always rise to the legal level of "armed conflict."

It is this ground between the extremes that inevitably will be the focus of most of our counterterrorism efforts in the future, and we badly need legal rules to define that zone of action and its limits. The coauthors may disagree over precisely how those rules should be shaped and, perhaps most deeply, over the role of the courts in monitoring and policing the activities of this category of activity. But we are agreed that developing this center category of activities, which are neither pure criminal justice nor war, will be the key to a counterterrorism policy that moves beyond policy binaries that ill-serve the United States, operationally and legally. Comprehensive counterterrorism policy for a new administration and a new Congress will necessarily look beyond the simple alternatives of law enforcement or war.

Notes

1. Or against non-US citizens. The Military Commissions Act of 2006, for example, distinguishes flatly between citizens and noncitizens. We disagree as to whether this distinction of nationality is appropriate or consistent with domestic or international human rights law.

2. Although the United States has not ratified Protocol I, it has accepted that Article 75 reflects customary law binding on the United States.

3. Yet the court seems not to have considered the possibility that by finding that the conflict with Al Qaeda is a conflict "not of an international character" so as to invoke Common Article Three, it arguably cut out application of nearly all of the rest of the Geneva Conventions, including the grave breaches provisions, for example, and the Article 5 tribunal mechanism for determining combatant status, all of which arguably require that the conflict be an Article 2 international armed conflict precluded by application of Common Article Three. We ourselves disagree (as do military law experts) as to the legal consequences of the court's rather sparsely reasoned holding on this vital question.

4. The MCA purports to do more than deprive detainees of a private action under the GCs. It says that no person can invoke the GCs as a source of rights, even in a habeas or other action.

5. We use *military commission* and *military tribunal* here interchangeably; we reserve the term *court martial* for regular proceedings under the full mechanisms available to US soldiers under the Uniform Code of Military Justice.

6. The issue of habeas corpus is most relevant to the detention question, rather than trials under the military commissions, since habeas pertains in the first place to the legal grounds for holding the detainee.

7. What constitutes a "regularly constituted court" for purposes of Common Article Three promises to be a hotly contested issue, which *Hamdan* failed to quiet, and it is an issue on which we likely disagree but will not pursue here.

8. This is not the same as saying that nothing revealed under torture is ever true. But intelligence must be more than simply true in order to be useful. When US personnel beat an Iraqi Army general, bound him, and stuffed him head first into a sleeping bag, the only information he revealed before he died was information already known to his interrogators.

9. Anderson is frankly skeptical of the assertion that torture does not produce useful information, or at least does not produce useful information distinguishable from intelligence "noise." However, he does not argue for making torture legal under any circumstances. The fundamental issue, for Anderson, is not the illegality of torture, but how it and other terms such as *inhumane treatment* or *cruelty* are to be concretely defined so as to make transparently clear what is legal and illegal.

10. Anderson notes that even if, as he acknowledges, the "ticking time bomb" scenario is largely, though not entirely, a chimera that is tangential to the daily toil of thwarting terrorist plots, it enjoys political support that cannot be dismissed out of hand. A significant range of political figures—including Hillary Clinton, Chuck Schumer, and John McCain—have said they might resort to torture if necessary in such a scenario. It cannot, therefore, be viewed purely as a fixation of the Bush administration.

11. A further issue that deserves a clear policy is whether certain techniques are permissible in certain situations. Can more aggressive interrogation be used on a known terrorist mastermind such as Khalid Sheikh Mohammed, as opposed to a person who may still turn out to be the innocent shepherd? We differ as to this general principle—Anderson in favor, Massimino against—but we agree the matter must be clarified in legislation.

12. According to Jewish law, the precepts of the Torah were to be "fenced around" with additional restrictions in order to prevent violation of the core precepts themselves.

13. Anderson believes that while a comprehensive reform of the existing system should establish a single standard across the US government, there are practical difficulties. He believes that the existing US military manual is too restrictive, for instance, in a case like Khalid Sheikh Mohammed. Since revision of the military manual is in Anderson's view not likely, and probably not wise, he would accept two standards today: one applicable to the military, and one applicable to all civilian agencies. Massimino would hold the civilian agencies to the military standard.

CHAPTER 7

The Courts

Chapter 7 Vignette

By Jennifer Byrne

What's Broccoli Got to Do with It?

Have you heard of something called the "Broccoli Test?" This is also known as the "broccoli question." The idea is that if Congress can force U.S. citizens to buy health insurance, can they force U.S. citizens to buy broccoli, too? Can Congress determine what a person will buy in the market? In such a case, would there be any limits on what Congress can do? If U.S. citizens simply will not accept the idea that Congress can do anything it pleases, then there needs to be a "limiting principle" to explain why Congress can mandate individuals to buy health insurance, but not broccoli. This is the job of the Supreme Court. Not only does the Court interpret the provisions of the Constitution, but also they write opinions to provide guidance to lower courts about how to apply the law. In fact, some would argue that it is the duty of the Supreme Court, and not the Obama Administration or the Congress, to articulate a limiting principle that will allow for the individual mandate to stand while simultaneously limiting the ability of Congress to mandate the purchase of privately made products.

As we have learned, the United States government has shut down over the implementation of the Affordable Care Act. In this short snapshot, we will consider the constitutional grounding for the most controversial part of the Affordable Care Act: the individual mandate. The individual mandate requires that all individuals buy health insurance or pay up to a $695 yearly penalty so that all Americans can have access to affordable health care, including those with pre-existing conditions or other costly illnesses. The individual mandate also helps to ensure that tax payers do not pay for costly emergency room visits made by those that currently do not have health insurance. But the individual mandate has been very controversial and has faced a huge criticism, including in the form of the broccoli test. Can the government force a private consumer to purchase a product in a free market? In a previous case, *Wickard v. Filburn*, the Supreme Court ruled that Congress could stop individuals from growing wheat for private consumption because of the indirect effects this would have on the market. It is also controversial because of the balance of power between the federal government and the states. Typically, states deal with many medical issues under 10th Amendment powers that give them authority over issues of health, morality, public welfare, and safety.

So, does Congress have the power to pass and implement the individual mandate?

Congress has a power listed in Article I over interstate commerce. A majority of Congress argues that health care insurance is a product of interstate commerce since the actions of someone in a particular state, such as the decision not to purchase insurance, could affect the rates for insurance in another state. Thus, the individual mandate is an economic regulation.

- "Individuals who choose to go without health insurance are making an economic decision that affects all of us—when people without insurance obtain health care they cannot pay for, those with insurance and taxpayers are often left to pick up the tab," claimed Stephanie Cutter, a White House adviser on health care policy.[1]

But, some states think that Congress has overstepped its bounds and find that the individual mandate conflicts with their own laws. For example, the State of Virginia has the Health Care Freedom Act, passed in response to the Affordable Care Act, which states that no resident of Virginia shall be required to obtain or maintain an individual health insurance policy. Thirteen states initially filed suit in the federal courts stating the Congress has exceeded its constitutional authority in Article I and was imposing on state policy powers protected in the 10th Amendment. It was also argued that compelling an individual to buy a product in the market violated individual liberty.

- "Neither the Supreme Court nor any federal circuit court of appeals has extended Commerce Clause powers to compel an individual to involuntarily enter the stream of commerce by purchasing a commodity in the private market," according to Judge Henry Hudson of the federal appeals courts in Richmond, Virginia.[2]

While the 4th and 6th Circuit courts dismissed the state lawsuits and allowed the individual mandate to stand, the 11th Circuit court ruled the mandate unconstitutional creating conflict in the federal courts and a confusing interpretation of the law. If an individual is a resident of Virginia, does this mean that the state law is applicable to that individual, and he or she is no longer required to buy health insurance? If an individual is a resident of Michigan, does this mean that he or she must purchase health insurance, as the Circuit courts for that region dismissed the state lawsuits? This is an instance where it is necessary for the Supreme Court to intervene. The Supreme Court hears less than 100 cases per term, usually less than 1 percent of those cases that are appealed to it. The Supreme Court tends to select cases that present conflicts in the lower courts so that it can clarify precedent. All of the cases it hears must involve a federal question, meaning that it must present a question or conflict involving the U.S. Constitution or an act passed by the federal government. Clearly, this case appears to be a dead ringer for the Court to have on its limited docket!

So, do you have to buy broccoli? And what else might you have to do next?

The Supreme Court did uphold the individual mandate as an appropriate exercise of the constitutional powers of Congress. But, rather than throw an entire piece of legislation out, they did find the limiting principle that prevents Congress from compelling individuals to purchase private goods. In a compromise decision, the Supreme Court ruled that the mandate could not be considered constitutional under the commerce clause, but that the law would stand as a tax, which is clearly within the powers of Congress listed under Article I. Just as the Congress taxes products such as tobacco and alcohol, they may tax individuals who fail to buy health insurance.

Endnotes

1. http://usatoday30.usatoday.com/news/washington/2011-08-12-health-care-ruling_n.htm, last accessed on November 15, 2013.
2. http://www.nytimes.com/2010/12/14/health/policy/14health.html?pagewanted=all&_r=0, last accessed on November 15, 2013.

The Judiciary

By Matthew Kerbel

Introduction

Quick: What do you think of when someone says the judiciary? The Supreme Court, perhaps? Justices in long black robes? An imposing marble building? Something totally removed from your everyday experience?

The **judiciary** has always been the branch of government that seems different from the rest of the political system: more secretive and distant, and removed from the body blows of politics. Its devotion to the law distinguishes the judiciary from the other institutions we've been discussing, not in the sense that it doesn't engage in the process of deciding who gets what, when, and how, but in the way it goes about doing this. The judiciary is the place where laws are interpreted and disputes are resolved. It rests at the heart of the **legal system**, which includes members of Congress and the president, who create laws that others may challenge; the bureaucracy, which implements laws in a manner that may cause disputes; individuals or interest groups with grievances; attorneys who argue legal issues on behalf of individuals or interest groups with grievances; and even police officers, who bring conflicts to the attention of the judicial system by enforcing the law on the street.[1]

Its involvement with matters of justice seems to put the judiciary above raw politics, and there are characteristics of the judiciary that you simply won't find anywhere else in the political process. Take the U.S. Supreme Court as an example. Its members are not elected (justices are appointed by the president and confirmed by the Senate). They serve for life, and never have to hire pollsters or media consultants to create a public image or position themselves for the next political campaign. Although they may be strong partisans, they shy away from involvement in partisan gatherings like political party conventions and do not stage media events like elected officials. They deliberate in private and never disclose what is said. This seems nothing like the other two branches of government, where popular participation in regularly scheduled elections is designed to keep officeholders accountable to the electorate.

The trappings of the Court only contribute to this mystique. We'd think it was silly if the president appeared in public in a dark robe, but on a Supreme Court justice, the robe evokes tradition and prestige, suggesting a certain respect for those who walk the imposing marble-laden corridors of the temple-like Supreme Court building.

The Court's symbol of "Lady Justice," blindfolded as she balances scales, depicts objectivity and fairness—characteristics rarely on display when Republicans and Democrats face off in a political or policy debate. In form and content, the Supreme Court appears a world apart from the political system we've come to know.[2]

But is it? If Court actions were only influenced by legal criteria, the answer might be yes, but we will see that this is far from what really happens. As we read on, we'll come to perceive the Court as a highly political institution that may operate differently from other political institutions but that is nonetheless steeped in politics.

There are clues to the Court's political persona, some more obvious than others. For example, the president and senators consider their political agendas when selecting and acting on appointments to the Supreme Court and lower courts in the federal judicial system, and political disputes over appointment confirmations can be ferocious. Nominees themselves may be political figures or individuals with partisan activity in their pasts. Their judgments on the Court are invariably influenced by their political principles, and the decisions they render can put them at the heart of partisan disputes.[3] The Court may be a legal institution, but it exists in a political world.

A Judiciary Without Power

By virtue of its position in this political world, the Court is at something of a disadvantage relative to the legislative and executive branches. The judiciary is, by design, the weakest of the three branches of the federal government. Alexander Hamilton, writing in Federalist #78, called it "the least dangerous to the political rights of the Constitution; because it will be least in a capacity to annoy or injure them." As Hamilton noted, the executive holds the power to enforce the law, and the legislature has the power to tax:

> The judiciary, on the contrary, has no influence over either the sword or the purse; no direction either of the strength or of

the wealth of the society; and can take no active resolution whatever. It may truly be said to have neither FORCE nor WILL, but merely judgment; and must ultimately depend upon the aid of the executive arm even for the efficacy of its judgments.[4]

In other words, the Constitution's authors put the judicial function in an institution that would have to rely on a separate institution—the executive—to enforce its rulings. Simultaneously, the Constitution made the judiciary the branch that was to exercise judgment over the decisions of the executive, potentially putting the two branches at odds with each other while making the judiciary dependent on the executive to carry out rulings that could come at the executive's expense. Demystifying Government: A Weak Judiciary versus No Judiciary, contrasts this weak judiciary with the earlier lack of a judiciary under the Articles of Confederation.

It took very little time after the ratification of the Constitution for Congress to flesh out the new judiciary, although it would be a while before the judicial and executive branches would come into conflict over the enforcement of judicial decisions. That's because it took a while for the nascent court system to find its bearings.

With little in the Constitution to guide them (Article III established the jurisdiction and tenure of justices, but otherwise is silent on the matter of how to organize the court system) and Federalists in command of the debate, Congress established a set of lower courts in the **Judiciary Act of 1789**. It set the number of Supreme Court justices as six (it is now nine), and assigned pairs of Supreme Court justices to each of three new circuit courts (occupying the lower level of the new court system).[5] So, not only would there be lower federal courts, but Supreme Court justices would have a hand in staffing them.

Serving on two courts at once probably sounds like a tall order, but the truth is that for the first decade of its existence, the Supreme Court didn't have much to do. It also didn't have a permanent home or staff, suffered from rapid turnover among justices, and didn't have much of an institutional identity or public prestige.[6] Consider the inaugural

DEMYSTIFYING GOVERNMENT

A WEAK JUDICIARY VERSUS NO JUDICIARY

A weak judicial system designed under the doctrine of separation of powers was an upgrade from the mechanism in place for resolving national disputes under the Articles of Confederation. That's because there was no independent judiciary for resolving national disputes under the **Articles of Confederation**. Recall that the federal government under the Articles centered on a single legislature, which was composed of representatives of the states. The legislature could attempt to resolve conflicts, but the absence of a separate national judiciary left the young nation without an efficient forum for resolving the numerous disputes that arose among the states, and was widely considered a defect in need of correction by the delegates to the Constitutional Convention.

Like so much to emerge from the Convention, the judicial branch is the product of compromise between those who wished to establish strong federal institutions and those concerned about the rights of smaller states. Federalists who supported the **Virginia Plan** would have established a federal Supreme Court and a multitiered system of lower courts. Supporters of the **New Jersey Plan**, which called only for a federal Supreme Court to act as final arbiter in cases arising in state courts, were worried that a federal court system posed a threat to states' rights.[T2] The delegates resolved the issue by punting. In a characteristically vague passage, Article III of the Constitution vests the "judicial power" in the Supreme Court "and in such inferior Courts as the Congress may from time to time ordain and establish." It would be up to the new Congress to determine what, if anything, those "inferior Courts" would look like.

session of the Supreme Court, meeting in the Royal Exchange Building in New York City on February 1, 1790. Three justices were absent, and two of those missed the entire court session—which lasted all often days.[7] During that time, the justices who were present chose a seal for the Court and appointed a clerk. They didn't rule on any cases because no business was before the Court. In fact, they didn't rule on any cases for three years.[8]

As in so many other areas, George Washington supplied a model for his successors in the way he went about appointing justices to the Supreme Court. Faced with the opportunity to fill every slot on the Court, Washington did a few things that presidents still do today:

- *Appoint ideologically compatible judges*. All six Washington appointees were loyal Federalists. Even though the Federalists were not organized as a formal party, Washington nominated judges who shared his ideological penchant for a strong national government. Presidents throughout history have sought philosophically compatible judicial nominees from their political party.

- *Offer representation to key interests.* In the late eighteenth century, this meant providing geographic balance: Three of Washington's appointees were southerners, and three were northerners. As political interests changed, the particulars of offering representation to specific groups changed as well. In the twentieth and twenty-first centuries, religion, race, ethnicity, and gender have replaced regional concerns as factors in court appointments.

- ***Don't expect the best.*** Washington's Supreme Court nominees were uneven in their abilities and reputations. Subsequent presidents have found that they can't always get their top choices to serve on the Court, that political criteria like ideological compatibility or satisfying key interests may necessitate settling for a lesser candidate, and that nominees who seem promising may turn out to be disappointing.
- ***Be especially careful when nominating the chief justice.*** Washington's choice was John Jay, one of the authors of *The Federalist* and a New York lawyer and judge. Washington believed that the chief justice had to be a widely acclaimed jurist whose ethics were beyond reproach.[9]

For Washington, appointing justices was far from the contentious experience it is today, because sleepiness was the rule during the Court's first decade. With little prestige and an insignificant role in the federal government, the Court during this time was marked by high turnover and few responsibilities. It ruled on little more than fifty cases during that time and drew little attention to itself.[10] All of that changed with the dawn of the new century and the entrance on the scene of Chief Justice John Marshall, one of the most influential justices in Court history.

Judicial Review

John Marshall (see biography) was appointed chief justice by President Adams in 1801 and served in this capacity for thirty-four years, during which time he fashioned the Court into an equal partner with the executive and the legislature. Many of the procedures in place today were originated under Marshall's tutelage.[11] For instance, before Marshall, it was customary for every justice to write a separate opinion every time the Court ruled on a case, but Marshall recognized the political value of presenting a unified front for the Court by keeping

differences among justices behind closed doors. He instituted the practice of hammering out disagreements in private deliberations, then handing down single opinions on cases.[12]

Marshall's most important and enduring contribution to the Court was the practice of **judicial review**. Today we take for granted that the Supreme Court has the authority to review the actions of Congress or the president and declare them unconstitutional. In fact, many people think of constitutional interpretation as the essential purpose of the Supreme Court because the most important thing it does is validate or overturn the acts of others in the political system—but such authority is not expressly granted in the Constitution. It derives from a ruling in the 1803 case **Marbury v. Madison**. It's a complex and important case, involving political power plays, conflicts of interest, and a great twist ending. You can find the facts in the Demystifying Government box, *Marbury v. Madison*: The Brief Version.

The logic behind Marshall's ruling in *Marbury v. Madison*—that Congress overreached by expanding the Court's jurisdiction, and so, the Court must strike down an act of Congress—requires a certain leap of faith. The rationale he gave for saying Congress overstepped its authority when it gave the Court the power to issue writs of *mandamus* in the Judiciary Act of 1789 was that the Constitution didn't stipulate that Congress had the authority to expand the Court's jurisdiction in this manner. Maybe so, but the Constitution also didn't stipulate that the Court could review an act of Congress and declare it unconstitutional—at least not directly. Marshall was asking us to accept a broad view of constitutional interpretation in the matter of judicial review while he was asking us to take a narrow view of constitutional interpretation in the matter of the Judiciary Act of 1789. Of course, what was anyone going to do about it? Because the Court could simply refuse the authority to issue writs of *mandamus*, it had the final say in the matter.

During his long tenure as chief justice, Marshall handed down several decisions that shaped the course of our national development by resolving questions about the key political issue of the day, the relationship between the federal government and the states, in favor of the federal government. We

DEMYSTIFYING GOVERNMENT

MARBURY V. MADISON: THE BRIEF VERSION

In 1800, John Adams was defeated for re-election by his political rival Thomas Jefferson.

Before leaving office, Adams attempted to fill the federal judiciary with as many sympathetic Federalists as possible. This is also when he appointed John Marshall to be Chief Justice of the Supreme Court.

John Marshall was also Adam's secretary of state. In that role, it was Marshall's job to deliver Adam's judicial commissions for them to become official.

The commission had to be delivered before Jefferson was sworn in as president. Marshall ran out of time and failed to deliver several commissions, including the appointment of William Marbury, whom Adams had appointed justice of the peace for the District of Columbia. James Madison became secretary of state when Jefferson became president. For partisan reasons, he ignored the appointment of Marbury and his sixteen colleagues, which Marshall had failed to deliver in time. Marbury sued Madison, and the case went to the U.S. Supreme Court.

Marbury asked the court to issue a *writ of mandamus*, a court order commanding an official to act—in this case an order to Secretary of State Madison to deliver Marbury's judicial appointment. The Supreme Court was granted the authority issue writs of mandamus as part of the Judiciary Act of 1789.

Setting aside the conflict of interest Marshall faced by having been the individual responsible for Marbury's dilemma, as chief justice, Marshall faced a dilemma of his own. Circumstances made it clear that Marbury was entitled to his appointment, but if Marshall issued the writ, President Jefferson most certainly would have told Secretary Madison to ignore it. And if he ruled against Marbury, the court would have looked weak.

Marshall fashioned a solution in one of the most ingenious Court decisions in American history. He agreed that Marbury was entitled to his appointment, but that Congress had exceeded its constitutional authority when it gave the Court the ability to issue writs mandamus. He therefore struck down the provision of the Judiciary Act of 1789 that gave the court that authority. It was a self-executing order that didn't require Jefferson's enforcement. Marbury didn't get to be justice of the peace, but Marshall had expanded the Court's reach by claiming the power of judicial review.

previously profiled the case **McCulloch v. Maryland** (1819), which was a turning point in the establishment of federal dominance over state governments and an endorsement of a broad constitutional grant of power to the federal government. In *Gibbons v. Ogden* (1824), the Marshall Court established the supremacy of the federal government over matters of interstate commerce.

Marshall's durability was so great that he was still presiding over the Supreme Court at the start of Andrew Jackson's administration, during the transition to the second party system, and he was still frustrating chief executives who favored states' rights with his Federalist rulings. Marshall's opinion in the 1832 case *Worcester v. Georgia* upholding federal rather than state jurisdiction over Cherokee land rights so angered President Jackson that the president is alleged to have said, "John Marshall has made his decision, now let him enforce it."[13]

The Court System

A system of federal courts began to emerge in the 1790s, when a justice earned his keep by doubling as a judge on a lower "circuit" court since there wasn't much work for the Supreme Court to do. We noted that the Judiciary Act of 1789 created the first lower court system: three circuit courts corresponding to the eastern, middle, and southern sections of the country. The original arrangement called for each circuit to be staffed by two of the six Supreme Court justices, along with a permanent district judge.[14]

The court got its name because the justices would "ride circuit"—they literally covered the territory twice a year on horseback or carriage, hearing cases along the way. And they were miserable. Roads were horrendous, the weather was often bad,

BIOGRAPHY

John Marshall

Timeline:

1755: Born September 24 on the Virginia frontier

1775: Enlisted for service in the Revolutionary War

1779: Studied law at the College of William and Mary

1782: Elected to the Virginia House of Delegates

1788: Selected to Virginia Constitutional ratifying convention

1797: Appointed by President Adams as U.S. envoy to France

1799: Elected to Congress from Virginia

1800: Appointed by President Adams as Secretary of State

1801: Appointed by President Adams as Supreme Court Chief Justice

1803: Wrote the majority opinion in *Marbury v. Madison*

1819: Wrote the majority opinion in *McCulloch v. Maryland*

1835: Died July 6, after serving 34 years as Chief Justice

Overview: John Marshall was forty-five years old when President John Adams appointed him to be chief justice of the Supreme Court in 1801. The oldest of fifteen children, Marshall came from modest roots to distinguish himself in several fields of service. A captain in the Revolutionary War, Marshall studied law at the College of William and Mary and practiced law in his native Virginia. He served as a Federalist representative to the Virginia House of Delegates, as an American envoy to France, and briefly as a member of the U.S. Congress. In 1800, Adams tapped Marshall to be his secretary of state. The following year, as Adams' term was about to expire, he appointed Marshall to the Supreme Court, where Marshall served longer than almost anyone in history—until he died in 1835. Marshall was a bitter political enemy of the man who followed Adams in office, fellow Virginian Thomas Jefferson—who also, by a strange quirk of history, happened to be Marshall's second cousin. Jefferson, who never lacked for the ability to turn a phrase, referred to Marshall as "that gloomy malignity." Adams, in contrast, was more than satisfied with Marshall's long record of service on the Court. Just prior to his death, Adams proclaimed, "My gift of John L Marshall to the people of the United States was the proudest act of my life."[T3] and justices had to be away from their families for long stretches of time. One justice, Levi Woodbury, who served in the 1840s, wrote of the "villaneous sea-sickness" he experienced riding circuit in a stagecoach:

> I think I never again, at this season of the year, will attempt this mode of journeying. Besides the evils before mentioned I have been elbowed by old women—jammed by young ones—suffocated by cigar smoke—sickened by the vapours of bitters and w[h]iskey—my head knocked through the carriage top by careless drivers and my toes trodden to a jelly by unheeding passengers.[15]

Within ten years of their establishment, more circuits were added along with more district judges but the custom of riding circuit persisted through the nineteenth century, even though justices were required to do it less frequently. In the twentieth century, the circuit court system grew enormously. There are now eleven circuits in the United States.

Today, the federal system is a three-tiered system, with the circuit courts functioning as appeals courts. This parallels the structure in place in each of the fifty states, which have their own state court systems to hear cases arising out of violations of state law. Because each state has its own Constitution, the specifics of the court systems vary from state to state. It's reasonable to picture the federal court system existing in tandem with a system of fifty state courts.

One way to think of the differences among these courts is to consider the differences in their **jurisdiction,** or the types of cases each has the authority to hear. In both the federal and state systems, most cases originate at the bottom level and are appealed upwards.

There are exceptions. The Constitution grants the U.S. Supreme Court original jurisdiction over certain types of conflicts, meaning they can originate at the top rather than having to work their way through the system. The Supreme Court's original jurisdiction extends to cases where there is a dispute involving:

- The United States and a state
- Two or more states
- Citizens of different states
- A state and a citizen of another state
- Foreign ambassadors

The Supreme Court has **appellate jurisdiction** for all other cases, meaning the cases have to originate in lower courts and work their way through the judicial system on appeal.

Broadly speaking, state courts have jurisdiction over most criminal law and civil law—ranging from serious offenses like murder and robbery to minor offenses like traffic violations to civil issues like divorce and inheritance disputes—because most criminal and civil laws are state laws. For this reason, most trials are held in state courts, and 95 percent of judges are state judges.[16]

Federalism presents us with fifty state court systems that operate parallel to the federal system we've been discussing. Figure 11.2 demonstrates how the two systems are structured and how they operate. For the most part, each of these systems has three tiers. The trial level is where most cases originate. State trial courts hear cases involving state law, while federal district courts hear cases involving federal law. There are ninety-four federal district courts. Appellate courts hear cases appealed by those who lost at the trial level. In the federal court system, there are eleven circuit courts of appeals covering eleven geographic regions of the country, plus a court of appeals for the District of Columbia and one for the federal circuit. Federal courts also hear appeals of decisions by independent regulatory agencies. Every state has a top-tier court, which is typically the final stop for an appeal. Most—but not all—states call this the supreme court. Of course, the U.S. Supreme Court has the final word on cases appealed through the federal court system. About 65 percent of its cases come through this route.

Although the federal and state court systems have similar structures, their jurisdictions are so different that it's appropriate to think of them as separate entities. Their paths cross only in rare circumstances. If a case heard in state court raises a contested point of constitutional law, it can be

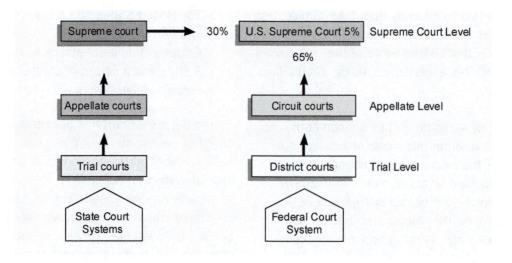

Figure 11.2. The Court System and Appeals Process [T4]

appealed from the state court system to the federal court system, where it is heard directly by the U.S. Supreme Court. Roughly 30 percent of U.S. Supreme Court cases originate this way. Unless a constitutional question is raised in a state trial, there can be no appeal to the federal court system, and the state supreme court has the final word in the matter.

The remaining 5 percent of U.S. Supreme Court cases originate in the Supreme Court itself. These cases fall under the Court's original jurisdiction and involved disputes among or between states, or where the United States or a foreign nation or its representative is a party. Also, some cases involving civil rights or reapportionment claims can be appealed from the trial level directly to the U.S. Supreme Court.

When the Supreme Court refuses to hear a case on appeal, the word of the lower court is final. Because circuit courts operate under a wide range of judicial philosophies and ideological perspectives, the specific circuit court to hear a case can be critical to the outcome. So, blind justice only tells part of the story. The state or circuit in which a case is heard and the judicial philosophies of the individuals hearing a case all have tremendous bearing on judicial outcomes.

Deciding Cases

When a court agrees to hear a case, it typically goes through several steps before issuing a judgment. Judges or justices hear arguments from attorneys representing the two sides of the matter, meet privately in conference to discuss the case, and draft their opinions on the case before the final vote is revealed. We'll look at the Supreme Court to get a sense of how this process works.

Oral Arguments

The first stage of the process is oral argument. Early in its history when the Supreme Court had little work to do, oral arguments could go on for hours or days. Today, unless there's an exception, oral arguments last one hour. They are held in the relatively small courtroom in the Supreme Court building, with the robed justices sitting on an elevated podium, looking down at the attorneys arguing the two sides of the case. You can visit if you like—oral arguments are open to the public. But you may have to wait in a long line for just several minutes of viewing because only about three hundred seats are reserved for the public.[17]

The atmosphere is solemn and the pace quick. Characteristically, justices will cutoff the presenting attorneys in midsentence, challenging a statement they made or raising a related point. Other justices may jump in, taking the questioning in whatever direction they see fit. It's possible for attorneys' time to expire before they get to make the presentation they had prepared. The experience can be overwhelming and breathtaking, much like an intellectual contact sport.

The questions justices ask can supply clues to the way they're likely to rule. If a justice who is typically in the middle of the ideological spectrum on an issue appears to question one side more sternly than the other, it could be an indication of the way that justice is leaning—at least for the moment. Sympathetic justices may ask questions designed to elicit a response from the attorney arguing the side of the case they favor in order to get the record to reflect a point the justice will want to argue later on. Similarly, hostile justices may hammer the attorney arguing the side of the case they oppose in order to expose flaws in the attorney's reasoning.

Some justices find oral arguments decisive; others find them useless Justice Oliver Wendell Holmes, who served during the first three decades of the twentieth century, would write letters or doze off while the attorneys were speaking).[18]

Conferences

Oral arguments are heard on Mondays, Tuesdays, and Wednesdays. Conferences to discuss the week's cases are held on Wednesdays and Fridays. Conferences are private, affording justices a closed setting for the frank exchange of opinions. With the huge workload the Court has to address, there is little time to deliberate at length about any particular case unless it is of exceptional magnitude. Instead, justices gather to see whether there is a consensus opinion. They may reason with each other about the case, or make emotional appeals. They may or may not take a formal vote. If they do, it's understood that their votes may be reversed at any time until the final decision is written and announced.[19]

Even though no one is privileged to the deliberation that occurs among justices, it's not unreasonable to assume that they think and act as strategically as anyone in elected office. This contention is

in keeping with the idea of the Court as a political body, as well as with the idea that justices have a view of government and society that they want to advance. Because they don't have to run for office, they're free from the basic strategic decisions that face members of Congress and the president, like what their constituents desire and whether it's too close to an election to take a controversial position.

Instead, a justice's strategy can center on ways to move the law closer to his or her desired position. That entails assessing the likely actions of the other eight people in the room and deciding on a course of action that appears most likely to lead to the justice's desired outcome—an exercise that invariably takes into account the styles and personalities of the other justices as much as the abstract merits of an argument. From this type of reasoning, justices can decide whether their best choice is to advance the position they most desire or, if their position appears to be in the minority, compromise on something less in the hope of building a coalition with other justices.[20]

Writing Opinions

When justices write opinions, they state their vote on a case and the reasoning behind it. Justices will exchange drafts of opinions before they're made public as a form of negotiation, often making revisions to accommodate other justices they seek to have join them. It's part of a persuasive process in which justices try to get their colleagues to adopt their reasoning. Depending on the mixture of personalities on the Court at any time, this experience can range from collegial to contentious. As in any group of people, justices with a soft touch have often found themselves influential in bringing other justices on board, and have played the role of consensus-builder. In contrast, things can get ugly when dealing with justices who have lesser social skills.[21]

The majority opinion expresses the judgment of the Court, but it may not be the only word on a matter. The legal reasoning behind a decision is as important as the decision itself, and will determine how far reaching a decision will be. Justices who come to the same conclusion may do so for entirely different reasons—and even disagree with each other on the justification for their conclusions. Because of this, a justice may issue a **concurring opinion**, which supports the majority decision but provides a different legal justification for getting there. A justice who disagrees with the majority position explains his or her reasoning in a **dissenting opinion**.

Staff

Considering the enormous workload of the Supreme Court—or any court for that matter—trained staff are brought in to assist with the burden. Much of a court's work falls to law clerks, who serve as assistants to justices and judges. There are over 2,000 law clerks in the federal system, working either for individual justices and judges or for an entire court. Law clerks typically engage in legal research, prepare background notes for oral arguments, and assist in drafting opinions.[22] The position of clerk on a high court is a prestigious and competitive one, and can be a valuable stepping stone for someone beginning a legal career. Perhaps because Supreme Court justices hail disproportionately from the Ivy Leagues, there is a strong tendency to select clerks from Ivy League law schools.

Selecting Cases

When feeling unfairly treated, people sometimes say "I'll take my case all the way to the Supreme Court if I have to!" The assumption, of course, is that that's where we'll finally find justice, and the expectation underlying the claim is that we *could* take any case to the Supreme Court—that everyone who has a grievance is entitled to a hearing.

That's not exactly how it works. In fact, surprisingly few people who petition the Court get a hearing. The Supreme Court has a lot of latitude over its agenda. Sure, others have to bring suit before the Court can hear a case, but the Court can avoid cases in areas of law it doesn't want to address, and select cases in areas of law it wants to decide.

It can turn aside cases that it believes raise a political rather than a constitutional question.

It can turn its head away from cases that it feels are not "ripe" because they were brought too early—for instance, if there are other legal avenues available to the person bringing the complaint—or if it feels a case is "moot" because the law has changed in a way that would settle the controversy. Who determines what's "ripe" and what's "moot"? The Supreme Court—and it can make these judgments broadly, using them to circumvent or delay wading into a controversy that it wants to avoid. It doesn't have to give a reason for rejecting a case, and the party bringing the case is out of luck if the Court refuses to listen.[23] Like Marbury, who never got the judgeship he was entitled to, individual outcomes matter less to the Court than legal judgments.

Sometimes, events force the Court to take a case. In 2003, the Supreme Court met in an unusual special session to rule on the constitutionality of the McCain-Feingold campaign finance law, in order to resolve any controversies about the new legislation before the 2004 primaries were held. Once the Court decided it had standing to intervene in the stalemated 2000 presidential election, it had no choice but to act before electoral votes were delivered to Congress. These salient cases are the exception, though. For the most part, the Court can decide its own agenda.

Reading Tea Leaves

The Court considers only a small number of cases on its **docket**, or list of cases. In a typical year, about 10,000 cases will brought to the Supreme Court, and the Court will hear about 75 of them.[24] When the Court agrees to review a ruling of a lower court, it issues a **writ of certiorari** ordering the lower court to send all records of the case. If the Court denies *certiorari*, the appeal is not heard, and the ruling of the lower court stands.[25]

The choice of cases at the opening of the Court's annual term (on the first Monday of each October) is typically a strong clue as to the controversies the Court is prepared to consider, and "Court watchers" will speculate about what the justices' choices indicate about the direction the Court will take. This can be a little like trying to predict the future by reading tea leaves, but the Court does send signals that at least will make sense after the fact—by the following spring, when all the term's decisions have been handed down.

The selection of a case that challenges a landmark abortion ruling, for instance, would mean that the Court is prepared to revisit the abortion question. What's less clear is whether it would be looking to reinforce established law or to reconsider it. Overlooking a prominent case on abortion rights that was ripe for appeal would send the message that the Court does not wish to engage the issue at this time, although that may mean that the Court is entirely finished hearing cases on this matter, or simply not inclined to do so during the present term.

Members of the Court also send signals to the **solicitor general**, who argues cases on behalf of the administration, that the Court is interested in hearing a case on a particular question. The solicitor general will take these signals to mean that the Court is receptive to deciding a particular question in which the government has an interest and will take action to present an argument to the Court. The solicitor general is responsible for deciding which attorney in his or her office will argue a particular case and will personally argue high-profile cases and cases of particular concern to the administration.

The solicitor general operates out of the Department of Justice, so even though he or she represents "the government," his or her positions will reflect the administration's agenda. This gives the administration influence over the position the government takes before the Court, which in turn can influence the Court's judgment.[26]

Interest Groups and Case Selection

More than ever before, interest groups of the wide variety we addressed in Chapter 8 engage the judicial system to advance or advertise their causes. This is a sensible strategy for a number of reasons. Interest groups have the resources to engage in protracted court fights as a result of their funding

and organization. Legal victories hold the potential to be wide-ranging, broadly advancing the group's goals. Even legal defeats keep the interest group's concerns in the press and therefore on the public agenda. Also, a sympathetic judiciary can prove to be a swifter and more effective route to interest group objectives than working the political side of the federal government, with all its access points designed to slow progress. This was the rationale for the involvement of the National Association for the Advancement of Colored People (NAACP) in the *Brown v. Board of Education* case, which resulted in advancing the cause of desegregation more swiftly than could have been done through the legislative process.[27]

As with the solicitor general, justices sympathetic to a particular cause may send signals to interest groups advancing that cause that the Court is prepared to hear a case on the issue. If the signal is sent to groups advancing one side of a contentious issue, it can be a strong indication of how the Court would like to rule. Because litigation is commonplace among interest groups, it typically takes little time for the group to get its legal team in place and take advantage of the opportunity the Court is giving them.

As part of an overall legal strategy, interest groups commonly file **amicus curiae** briefs with the Court, engaging in litigation as a third party to a suit that interests them. Literally "friend of the court," *amicus curiae* briefs can be solicited by a justice who intends to refer to them when writing an opinion in a case. More frequently, interest groups who have a partisan interest in the outcome of a trial voluntarily submit them—and they can be influential. When justices make reference to the arguments in *amicus curiae* briefs in their written decisions on a case, you can tell which groups had an impact on their reasoning.[28]

Nomination Politics

Because the judicial philosophy of the people in the black robes matters so much to the direction of the Court, political battles can erupt whenever the president has an opportunity to name someone to the Supreme Court or to one of the lower federal courts. This is particularly true during times like the present, when the nation is closely divided politically. It's why conservative Senate Republicans worked hard to delay confirmation hearings on President Obama's more liberal Court appointees, and why Democrats did the same when they controlled the Senate during the latter portion of the Bush administration. More than at any time in memory, confirmation battles over nominees to every level of the federal bench have been marked by divisive, strong-arm tactics.

Just months after his inauguration, President Obama faced a high-profile vacancy on the Supreme Court with the resignation of Justice David Souter, a Republican appointed by the first President Bush who nonetheless tended to side with the Court's more liberal justices. Obama's nominee to replace Souter was Sonia Sotomayor, a federal appellate judge from New York. Conscious of the divisiveness of recent Supreme Court battles, President Obama recognized that his selection of Judge Sotomayor would make identity politics an important element of the confirmation hearings. As the first Hispanic and only the third female Supreme Court nominee, Sotomayor would present herself to the Senate as the embodiment of the American Dream: the daughter of Puerto Rican parents raised in a South Bronx housing project who earned a scholarship to Princeton and then graduated from Yale Law School before becoming a prosecutor and trial judge.[29]

But, identity politics can cut both ways, and some Senate Republicans grilled Sotomayor about remarks she had made suggesting that her upbringing and experience might guide her judicial judgment. The thrust of their criticism was that sympathies derived from her background might make her a partial arbiter of judicial questions. Their objections made for some pointed moments during Sotomayor's confirmation hearings, and in the end thirty-one Republican Senators voted against her, although that number fell far short of denying her a place on the Supreme Court.

Truthfully, the sort of jockeying and positioning that characterized the Sotomayor confirmation hearings isn't all that interesting to ordinary people, and

with the exception of very heated nomination battles (which Sotomayor's was not) that occasionally play out on television, most of us don't pay attention to what goes on when the president sends the Senate a judicial nominee. However, interest groups pay a lot of attention, and if a nominee promises to alter the balance of a court, groups that stand to gain or lose from the shift will organize in a hurry.

The politically charged nominations of Robert Bork and Clarence Thomas to the Supreme Court generated intense resistance from Senate Democrats. They also generated strong lobbying efforts by groups on both sides of the ideological spectrum. In terms of sheer numbers, Bork was actively supported by twenty-one interest groups and actively opposed by seventeen in his unsuccessful bid to join the Supreme Court. Seventeen groups also mobilized to support Thomas, who was opposed by an unprecedented thirty-two interest groups in an unsuccessful effort to keep him off the Court. To put this in historical context, President Eisenhower's 1953 nomination of Earl Warren to be chief justice generated no interest group support and opposition from only two groups, and in the twenty-two years between Warren's nomination and President Ford's lone nomination to the Court (Justice John Paul Stevens) in 1975, a grand total of forty groups mobilized in support and forty-three groups mobilized against seventeen nominees.[30]

Then things heated up in the 1980s, as President Reagan acted on his pledge to appoint conservative justices who would counter the judicial liberals who had controlled the Court's agenda during the preceding three decades. Through the Reagan and first Bush administrations, interest groups battled fiercely over Court nominees. When two vacancies occurred on the Supreme Court in the summer of 2005 through the resignation of Justice Sandra Day O'Connor and the death of Chief Justice William Rehnquist, conservative and liberal interest groups geared up for what everyone expected to be an intense battle over their replacements. Historically, presidents get what they want even when there's a fight—but they don't get everything they want. President Reagan lost the fight over the Bork nomination, and President Nixon had two nominees—Clement Haynsworth, Jr. and G. Harrold Carswell—turned away following widespread

Table 11.1. Supreme Court Nomination Scorecard: Nixon (1969) through Obama (2010)

President	Number of Justices Nominated	Number of Justices Confirmed	Percent Confirmed
Nixon	6	4	66.7%
Ford	1	1	100%
Carter	0	—	—
Reagan	5	4	80%
G.H.W. Bush	2	2	100%
Clinton	2	2	100%
G.W. Bush	2	2	100%
Obama	2	2	100%

questions about their qualifications. Overall, the Supreme Court scorecard favors the president, even if he has to fight hard for his nominee. See Table 11.1.

Presidents can increase the odds of confirmation by considering the prevailing political winds before making a nomination. President Obama had the advantage of a Senate dominated by Democrats to help propel his nominations of Sonia Sotomayor and Elena Kagan. President Bush may have been forced to appoint less conservative nominees to the Supreme Court than John Roberts and Samuel Alito had the vacancies that led to their nominations occurred after Democrats regained control of the Senate in the 2006 election (for more discussion of the Roberts nomination, and for a look at how sometimes presidents are forced by political circumstances to back away from their nominees, see Demystifying Government: The Brief and Unlikely Nomination of Harriet Miers).

Senatorial Courtesy

Regardless of the partisan composition of Congress, presidents as a matter of custom defer to the opinion of senators from the home state of a judicial nominee to one of the lower federal courts before sending the nomination to the full Senate. This custom is called **senatorial courtesy**, and it derives from the Senate's long history of institutional patriotism. Even though the Senate approves most judicial nominees, there's a sense among senators that they do not want to

be a rubber stamp for any president. They take their constitutionally mandated role to offer advice and consent seriously, and the most direct way they can protect this is by permitting senators an informal veto over nominees from their home states.

Typically, a senator will object if the president is about to nominate a political adversary from back home. Senators can be particularly influential in derailing a nomination if they share a political party with the president, although senators of the opposing party have been known to influence presidential appointments. Remember, too, that even when a senator successfully blocks an appointment from his home state, there's no guarantee that the president will come back with another nominee from that state. In that regard, presidents always get to make the last move.[31]

The practice of senatorial courtesy goes back to the first president and the first Congress, when President Washington nominated Benjamin Fishbourn to serve as a naval officer in Savannah, Georgia. Both Georgia senators objected, and the full Senate made it clear that it intended to back its colleagues even though the nominee was qualified to serve. When Washington backpedaled and nominated someone else who was acceptable to the Georgians, he became the first president to engage in the dance of senatorial courtesy that has been repeated many times through history.[32]

Professional Influences

Senatorial courtesy is the most political of the external influences on the president's choice of a nominee, but it is not the only influence. Members of the court and members of the bar also have their say over nominees at every level of the court system. Presidents have been known to contact sitting judges and justices to solicit opinions about people who would become future colleagues, and it's not unheard of for the communication channels to work in the other direction, with members of the judiciary lobbying the president.

The American Bar Association (ABA), the preeminent legal professional association, routinely offers its opinion on whether a presidential choice

Demystifying Government

The Brief and Unlikely Nomination of Harriet Miers

When Justice Sandra Day O'Connor announced her retirement in the summer of 2005, the long-awaited battle over the direction of the Court appeared to have arrived. O'Connor had been a swing vote on a Supreme Court that had not lost a justice in eleven years—a remarkably long stretch without turnover. With the re-election of President Bush months earlier, many conservatives eagerly awaited the opportunity to replace O'Connor's moderate vote with a reliably conservative one.

President Bush initially nominated John G. Roberts to fill O'Connor's position. A Harvard-educated lawyer serving on the U.S. Court of Appeals for the District of Columbia, Roberts came with impeccable conservative credentials and a strong judicial background. Senate Democrats immediately objected to the nominee on grounds that O'Connor's replacement should not be someone who would shift the balance of the Court to the right. But, on the merits, they faced an uphill struggle opposing his confirmation.

Then, circumstances conspired to change everything. Shortly before Roberts' confirmation hearings were to begin, ailing Chief Justice William Rehnquist died, leaving a vacancy at the top of the Court. It would have been impossible for the president to nominate and Congress to confirm a replacement in time for the opening of the Court's new term one month later, especially with the hearings for the O'Connor seat scheduled to occur first. To complicate matters, President Bush was at this moment ensnared in the fallout of the administration's slow response to Hurricane Katrina, limiting both the political capital available to him for a brutal nomination fight and his ability to devote full attention to selecting a nominee.

Bush's solution to this problem was to elevate Roberts to the Rehnquist slot, withdrawing his nomination of Roberts to be O'Connor's replacement and instead nominating him to be Chief Justice. Although some Democrats objected, Roberts was considered to be no more conservative than the man he was replacing, and the long-anticipated fireworks over the Chief Justice appointment failed to materialize. Within one month of the nomination, Roberts took his seat at the head of the Supreme Court, in time for the start of its October session.

Of course, elevating Roberts necessitated a new nominee for the O'Connor seat, and when Bush selected White House Counsel Harriet Miers for the job, his conservative supporters were baffled. A Texas attorney whose ascendancy in Washington was the result of the support of the president she served, Miers was a largely unknown quantity with no judicial experience and—even more disconcerting to some of the president's strongest conservative supporters—a vague record on social issues. Key social conservatives spoke out in opposition to the nomination, while the strongest note of praise for the nominee came from Harry Reid—the Senate *Democratic* leader. The battle over the direction of the Court was finally on, but not in the way anyone anticipated: conservatives were leading the charge against their own president.

And they succeeded. Before her confirmation hearings began, Miers withdrew her name from consideration. President Bush replaced her with Judge Samuel A. Alito, a conservative jurist serving on the U.S. Court of Appeals for the Third Circuit. Although Alito's nomination generated the kind of fireworks from liberals that Miers' nomination had generated from conservatives—and although liberals regarded him as more conservative than O'Connor—the president had the votes in the Senate to confirm him, and Justice Alito took his seat on the U.S. Supreme Court in late January 2006.

is qualified. A favorable nod from the ABA's Federal Judiciary Committee lends a level of professional approval to the political business of judicial nominations. Strategically, it can give a president cover for a controversial nomination by permitting the president to point out that the nominee's peers consider him qualified for service. When President Reagan submitted the nomination of the deeply conservative Antonin Scalia, he knew it would be hard for liberal senators to oppose someone who by reputation was qualified to serve on the Supreme Court (the ABA endorsed him as "well qualified"). Reagan tried a similar strategy with the Bork nomination, but the ABA came back with a mixed verdict, with only 10 of 15 members of the Federal Judiciary Committee giving their approval.[33] This, in turn, gave Bork's opponents an opening to exploit.

A nominee without a strong network of professional allies and without a long legal history can run into trouble during the confirmation process. This contributed to the problem President Bush faced with the nomination of his White House Counsel Harriet Miers, which suffered in part because Miers had few allies in the legal community to come to her defense when opponents questioned her qualifications to sit on the Court. As the president's personal attorney, she found that Bush was her strongest and most enthusiastic supporter, but that it wasn't enough to have the president urging senators and interest group leaders to support Miers because he believed in her.

Table 11.2. Roman Catholic and Jewish Supreme Court Justices through 2011

Roman Catholic Justices		
Justice	Appointed by	Dates of Service
Roger B. Taney	Andrew Jackson	1836–1864
Edward D. White	Grover Cleveland	1894–1921
Joseph McKenna	William McKinley	1898–1925
Pierce Butler	Warren Harding	1922–1939
Frank Murphy	Franklin D. Roosevelt	1940–1949
William J. Brennan	Dwight D. Eisenhower	1956–1990
Antonin Scalia	Ronald Reagan	1986–
Anthony M. Kennedy	Ronald Reagan	1988–
Clarence Thomas	George H. W. Bush	1991–
John G. Roberts	George W. Bush	2005–
Samuel A. Alito, Jr.	George W. Bush	2006–
Sonia Sotomayor	Barack Obama	2009–
Jewish Justices		
Justice	Appointed by	Dates of Service
Louis D. Brandeis	Woodrow Wilson	1916–1939
Benjamin N. Cardozo	Herbert Hoover	1932–1938
Felix Frankfurter	Franklin D. Roosevelt	1939–1962
Arthur J. Goldberg	John F. Kennedy	1962–1965
Abe Fortas	Lyndon B. Johnson	1965–1969
Ruth Bader Ginsburg	Bill Clinton	1993–
Stephen G. Breyer	Bill Clinton	1994–
Elena Kagan	Barack Obama	2010–

Diversity

As presidents attempt to appeal to diverse constituencies, there is political advantage in selecting high-profile nominees who are not white male Protestants (which the overwhelming majority of Supreme Court justices have been). As a consequence, today's Supreme Court is more diversified than in the past with respect to religion, race, and gender.

Barriers to diversity fell slowly. Although President Jackson appointed the first Roman Catholic to the Court in 1836 (Chief Justice Roger B. Taney), it took until 1894 for President Grover Cleveland to appoint the second (Justice Edward D. White). An unprecedented six present justices are Roman Catholic—Roberts, Scalia, Kennedy, Thomas, Alito and Sotomayor—but they also represent half of all Catholic justices who have ever served on the Court.

Louis Brandeis was the first Jewish justice, appointed by President Wilson in 1916, and for many years thereafter, one seat on the Court was informally considered to be a "Jewish seat." This tradition was interrupted by President Nixon and restored by President Clinton, who appointed two the present Court's three Jewish justices, Ginsburg and Breyer.[34]

Of 112 Supreme Court justices who served through 2011, a combined 20 have been Roman Catholic or Jewish (see Table 11.2).

The first African American on the Court was former civil rights attorney Thurgood Marshall, appointed by President Johnson in 1967. When he stepped down in 1991, President Bush (senior) replaced him with Clarence Thomas, who is the Court's second African American justice. Although this appeared to establish a "black seat" on the Court, Thomas' conservative orientation couldn't have been more different from Marshall's liberalism, angering some African American activists who felt the Thomas appointment was a cynical ploy to use race to keep liberal senators from blocking the nomination of a conservative.

When President Reagan ran for office, he promised to nominate the first woman to the Court, and he kept his promise with the appointment of Sandra Day O'Connor in 1981. She is joined by Justice Ginsburg, Justice Sotomayor, and Justice Kagan as the only women to serve on the high court to date. Justice Sotomayor is also the first Hispanic member of the Supreme Court.

Because of this history, the Court in 2011 looked far more diverse than at any other point in its history, with six Catholics, three Jews, three women, and one African American among its membership. For the first time in history, there are no Protestant justices. Viewed another way, however, there is a great degree of homogeneity. Five justices are over sixty. Seven are men; eight are white. Six attended Harvard Law School. The other three went to Yale. Take a second to browse through their profiles in Figure 11.3 to get a sense of who was serving on the Court in 2011.

Diversity on the lower federal courts is a less politically salient matter. These positions get very little public attention, and in some instances, this leads presidents to make different choices than they would for the high-profile Supreme Court. President Reagan, for instance, may have made it a priority to put a woman on the Supreme Court, but less than eight percent of his 368 lower-court appointments were female. Only one-fifth of George W. Bush's lower-court appointees were women.[35]

Among recent past presidents, Bill Clinton did the most to put women and minorities on the federal bench. Despite these efforts, federal judges are overwhelmingly well-to-do middle-aged white male attorneys from elite law schools. The tendency for judges to come from the same elite clique goes a long way toward explaining the other demographics because when the middle-aged appointees of the recent past were in law school, these schools were still largely bastions for well-to-do white men. So, to a large degree the relative lack of diversity on the federal bench can be explained in terms of a long-standing lack of diversity in the elite legal community.[36]

Justice Ruth Bader Ginsburg tells of attending a reception for her class while she was at Harvard Law School in the 1950s. There were over 500 students—and only nine women. She recounts the dean of the law school asking each of the nine "what we were doing at the law school occupying a seat

Figure 11.3. Who Are the Supreme Court Justices?[T5]

that could have been filled by a man."[37] As elite law school graduates have become less overwhelmingly white and male, it's possible that the demographics of the lower federal courts will begin to change, but this will also require a commitment to diversity by future presidents, whose appointments will be made out of public view.

Judicial Surprises

Republicans appoint Republicans and Democrats appoint Democrats, but that doesn't mean that presidents always get the results they expect from the people they place on the federal bench. There are numerous examples of presidents being

surprised (or horrified) at the positions taken by their judicial appointees. Perhaps the most striking example from the twentieth century is President Eisenhower's appointment of Chief Justice Earl Warren, who led the most liberal and activist Court in modern times, particularly in the area of civil rights.

If the moderate Eisenhower had gotten what he was looking for in a chief justice, Earl Warren's activism never would have happened. Eisenhower, a Republican, considered several other moderate Republicans before settling on Warren as his nominee to preside over the Court. Two of these were his Secretary of State John Foster Dulles and New York Governor Thomas E. Dewey.[38] It's highly unlikely that either one would have been an activist chief justice committed to turning the Court into a forum for advancing civil rights the way Warren did.

Then again, few people suspected it of Warren—at least few in the Eisenhower administration suspected it. The president thought he was getting a centrist Republican like himself. Perhaps the broad support Warren had commanded from Republicans and Democrats in his three successful campaigns for California governor should have been a clue to his inherent activism, or the fact that his independent streak so distressed the leadership of the California Republican Party that they promoted Warren's appointment to get him out of the state. In any event, Eisenhower was in Warren's debt for the work the governor had done in moving the California delegation behind him in the 1952 Republican Convention, and it is of such political considerations that monumental decisions at times emerge. So, Eisenhower planted Earl Warren at the helm of the Supreme Court believing he had chosen an experienced administrator with moderate tendencies.[39] He later called it the biggest mistake of his presidency.

There are good reasons for judicial surprises like Warren. A president often makes appointments based on the recommendations of aides (particularly to lower court positions) without personally knowing the nominee. While a dossier on a nominee's history can tell a lot, it can't always predict how he or she will behave on the bench. Perhaps nominees at the ideological extremes can be fairly predictable—Antonin Scalia, for instance, had a record of unfaltering conservatism going back to his youth—but between the extremes, where most nominees are found, it can be much harder to predict the future.

Justice David Souter, who was replaced by Justice Sotomayor, had been a member of the court's liberal bloc. That's not how President Bush (senior) expected things to turn out when he nominated him. The president was looking for a conservative nominee who was likely to be an abortion opponent, but given the certainty that his nominee's record in adjudicating abortion cases would be a major factor in the pending confirmation battle, he preferred someone who hadn't left a lot of tracks on the issue. Bush's chief of staff John Sununu recommended

Souter, a fairly obscure Appeals Court judge from Sununu's home state of New Hampshire. Souter fit the requirements perfectly, leaving little ammunition for congressional supporters of abortion rights to claim that Bush's nominee would tip the delicate Court balance away from the *Roe* decision.

The problem for Bush was that Souter was hard for everyone to judge—including Bush himself. He took it on faith (along with Sununu's judgment) that he had produced a reliably conservative vote for the Court—but Souter turned out to be much more independent than the president had bargained for and frequently voted with the Court's liberal justices. Souter surprised Bush and turned into a disappointment for his conservative supporters, who saw his appointment as one that got away.

Even when the president has a personal history with a nominee, it can be impossible to tell how the nominee will mature on the bench. Judicial philosophies can develop and change over time, and our perspectives on things sometimes alter with age. John Paul Stevens was considered a moderate conservative when President Ford appointed him in 1975, but as the Court became more conservative, he became more liberal.

It's equally impossible to know how a nominee will respond to issues that simply cannot be anticipated at the time of her or his confirmation. Lifetime appointments hold out the possibility, even the probability, that the issues of greatest concern to the president making the appointment will give way to an unexpected set of issues during the nominee's term of service. When Franklin D. Roosevelt named William O. Douglas to the Supreme Court in 1939, it would have been impossible to foresee that he would be at the center of an activist Court that would revolutionize civil rights law before his retirement in 1975. Justices named to the bench fifteen years ago could not have anticipated having to make judgments about privacy on the Internet or human cloning, although these are emerging as important areas of dispute. Knowing a nominee's position on abortion policy doesn't offer a clue as to how he or she might decide cases in other legal areas.

A Political Court

If justices must go through the political system to be nominated and confirmed, if personal background and judicial philosophy influence a justice's approach to the law, and if bargaining strategies shape court judgments, it should be clear that the Supreme Court—for that matter, any court—is hardly the neutral arbiter of conflict that its symbols would suggest. Justices may never have to face the judgment of voters, but they are enmeshed in a political process. Perhaps their biggest political challenge is reflected in the dilemma that presented itself to Chief Justice Marshall and which the Court continues to face centuries after *Marbury v. Madison*: In the end, it must rely on the president to enforce its decisions. Marshall may have established the Court as an equal branch of government and begun the long process of developing prestige and admiration for the Court, but at every point in its history the Court has had to be particularly attuned to the politics of the other branches to maintain its precarious place in the federal constellation.

Justice Felix Frankfurter (who served from 1939 to 1962) was attempting to protect the myth of an apolitical Court when he declared, "When a priest enters a monastery, he must leave—or ought to leave—all sorts of worldly desires behind him. And this Court has no excuse for being unless it's a monastery."[40] Frankfurter knew this was hardly the case. Far from being cloistered, the Court survives by reacting to the hardball pursuits of the elected officials populating government's other branches.

The resources it has to bring this about are intangible, but if properly used they can be extremely effective in protecting the Court's political position. One thing the Court has in its favor is the deep well of respect developed over the centuries with generations of Americans. Such legitimacy can make it difficult for presidents to disobey or disregard the Court, as their constituents would not look kindly on a president defying what would be widely perceived as a legitimate act of a respected institution.

Ironically, the symbols we talked about at the opening of the chapter that make the Court seem so removed from politics—the dark robes, the marble building, the secret deliberations—contribute to the mystique that is so much a part of the Court's legitimacy. Put another way, these "nonpolitical" characteristics serve a highly political purpose in protecting the reverence many people feel for the Supreme Court—an opinion that gives the Court leverage with the more powerfully equipped executive and legislative branches. No doubt, Frankfurter was trying to perpetuate this mystique by comparing the Court to a monastery.

To maintain this high level of legitimacy, justices throughout history have been attentive to political currents, often selecting and ruling on cases they feel the public is ready to accept. Recognizing that the large degree of popular good will invested in the Court could be threatened by rulings that took the country where it did not want to go, justices will often keep an eye on the same political trends that elected officials live by. Sometimes events force the Court to hear a controversial case of such magnitude that the results are likely to be met with disapproval from some quarters. By paying attention to popular opinion, the Court can defend its political position by squaring its legal positions with the politicians who will be called upon to enforce the Court's words.

Public opinion and legitimacy interact in a delicate dance, each one reinforcing the other. We can see strains of this in Franklin Roosevelt's infamous "court packing scheme," where the Court's legitimacy was threatened by the actions of an enormously popular president, and in the harrowing case of *United States v. Nixon*, where a Court ruling directed President Nixon to commit political suicide.

Packing the Court

Although Franklin D. Roosevelt had large numbers of sympathetic Democrats in Congress to pass his New Deal programs during his first term, conservative justices appointed by Roosevelt's Republican predecessors dominated the Supreme Court. They were philosophically opposed to the New Deal, and during FDR's first four years in office, they struck down much of the president's program, often by a 5–4 vote. It was a classic case of how separation of powers works to impede rapid change, even when a landslide election gives one party control of the other two branches.

Roosevelt, of course, was uninterested in a textbook tutorial on separation of powers and was frustrated by how the Court was thwarting his initiatives. Following his landslide 1936 reelection, he decided to do something about it. Roosevelt asked Congress to give him the authority to expand the size of the Court by adding one new member for every sitting member over the age of 70, a proposal that would have allowed Roosevelt to nominate six new justices and theoretically give his New Deal legislation a 10–5 majority on a new fifteen-member Supreme Court.[41] Supporters called it judicial reform. Opponents called it packing the Court.

Roosevelt's proposal failed even though he had a large partisan advantage in Congress. Democrats who embraced New Deal programs nonetheless had difficulty supporting a plan that would have so blatantly undermined the Court's legitimacy, even though it would have assured the legality of their legislation. Years of building the public's trust by appearing above politics worked to protect the Court from political tampering.

There's a postscript to the story, though. As the Senate Judiciary Committee was preparing to hold hearings on Roosevelt's plan in 1937, Justice Owen Roberts broke away from the anti-New Deal coalition and began ruling in favor of Roosevelt's programs. In *West Coast Hotel Co. v. Parrish* he sided with the New Deal forces in support of a minimum wage law. In *National Labor Relations Board v. Jones and Laughlin Steel Corporation* he voted to uphold the National Labor Relations Act.[42] Recognizing the direction the country was moving and tacitly acknowledging the importance of public opinion to preserving the Court's legitimacy, the conservative Roberts helped stave off a direct assault on the Court by aligning his judgments with public sentiment. It was called the "switch in time that saved nine."[43]

Even though his plan to pack the Court fell through, Roosevelt would exercise enormous influence over the Court's judicial direction. He would nominate eight justices during his tenure as president, leaving a judicial legacy that would outlast his administration. His first appointment came

shortly after the Roberts switch. To get back at the Senate for failing to approve his judicial plan, and to make a point with the Court, Roosevelt nominated Senator Hugo Black, who had been at the forefront of the congressional fight in favor of packing the Court. Roosevelt knew that senators would never reject one of their own, and the Supreme Court would have no choice but to welcome one of its more vocal critics.[44]

The Nixon Tapes

On very rare occasions, the Court is called upon to render a judgment that threatens a confrontation with the president in a way that recalls Marshall's dilemma with *Marbury v. Madison*. It happened again in 1974, in ***United States v. Nixon***, when the Supreme Court faced the prospect of issuing a ruling that would jettison President Nixon from office. One key difference between the two cases was the enormous legitimacy the Court could fall back on in making its judgment in the Nixon case. It turns out that it needed all the legitimacy it could muster.

The complex series of events that came to be known as the Watergate scandal originated with a burglary at the Democratic National Committee (DNC) headquarters in Washington's Watergate Hotel. It was 1972, and although President Nixon would win a second term in a landslide later that year, his reelection committee left nothing to chance. Documents had been copied and wiretaps had been placed on telephones at rival Democratic Party offices before a security guard caught five burglars at the DNC headquarters one June evening. They had in their possession telephone numbers for the White House, establishing a connection between the burglars and the administration that would eventually reach to the highest level.

By the next year, congressional and public outcry forced Nixon to appoint a special prosecutor to investigate Watergate. Through that investigation, word surfaced that Nixon had secretly taped all his conversations with aides and visitors to the Oval Office. The audio record could prove vital to the work of the special prosecutor and members of Congress, who by 1973 were holding hearings into whether to impeach the president over his role in Watergate, but they would first have to get Nixon to hand over the tapes.

The scandal was spiraling out of control as it began attaching itself to high-ranking administration officials. Former Attorney General John Mitchell, once head of the Justice Department, was charged with obstruction of justice for his role in trying to block the investigation from reaching the Oval Office. To build his case against Mitchell, Special Prosecutor Leon Jaworski issued a subpoena for Oval Office tape recordings. Nixon refused, claiming his private conversations were protected by executive privilege. This made the matter a constitutional issue that would have to be resolved by the Supreme Court.[45]

Nixon knew the political damage that would result if the tapes were made public because they showed that he was instrumental in planning the cover-up of the Watergate break-in, implicating him in a scheme to obstruct justice. One tape, considered to be a "smoking gun," is a conversation between Nixon and his Chief of Staff H. R. "Bob" Haldeman, recorded just six days after the break-in. It shows that Nixon knew everything that was going on from the start and is chilling in the matter-of-fact way Nixon goes about plotting to obstruct justice in order to make sure the public never found out how much he knew. The plan he considered, as recommended by Attorney General Mitchell, involved getting the FBI's Watergate investigation "under control" to keep it from going in "directions we don't want it to go" by getting FBI Director L. Patrick Gray to "stay the hell out of this."[46]

Nixon's claim of executive privilege raised a constitutional question that would have to be resolved by the Supreme Court. Nixon argued that executive privilege provided the president with confidentiality so that he could speak openly with his confidants about matters of national importance. Jaworski contended that executive privilege did not protect a president from releasing private materials that potentially implicated him in a crime.

As the Supreme Court heard arguments in the case of *United States v. Nixon*, the president's political world was crumbling. Impeachment efforts were moving forward in the House, and the president's support was eroding in the Senate, even among members of his own party. Public opinion stood behind the position that Nixon should release the tapes, as the public widely believed that Nixon had something to hide. The Court would have the public on its side if it ruled against Nixon.

However, it would also have to rely on Nixon to enforce the ruling. There was little doubt that the tapes would incriminate Nixon, since he fought so hard to keep them secret. Would he comply with a court order to release them? What were his options if he did not?

The stakes could not have been higher. Failure to obey the Court would have thrown the nation into an unprecedented constitutional crisis, in which the president put his political survival above the rule of law. What then? Would Nixon use the ensuing crisis to clamp down on the justice system the way the tapes showed he tried to clamp down on the FBI, possibly suspending the Constitution and declaring martial law? That may sound ridiculous to us today, but plenty of people were worried about exactly that scenario. Nixon was under immense political pressure. Those close to him worried that he would see the Court as an enemy and lash out at it.

Under the circumstances, the Court needed to muster all its legitimacy and send the message that the president had no choice but to comply with an order that would lead to his political demise. It did so by ruling unanimously that executive privilege did not apply in this case, and that the president would have to hand over the tapes. Even one dissenting opinion could have given Nixon an opening to make the claim that the Court had ruled in error, but the justices—including four Nixon appointees—did not give him that opportunity.

The nation waited breathlessly for Nixon's response. With popular opinion lined up against him and a Supreme Court that had placed on the line the full measure of public allegiance it had developed over nearly two centuries, the president succumbed to the order. Doing so left him without any more political options. The revelations in the tapes meant certain impeachment by the House and conviction by the Senate. Barely two weeks after the Court's ruling, on August 8, 1974, Nixon announced to the nation that he would become the first president in history to resign the office.

United States v. Nixon demonstrates that judgments can in fact be powerful—that words can have dramatic political repercussions. As with Roosevelt's attempt to pack the Court, it shows how public opinion factors directly into the Court's ability to make controversial rulings (or resist succumbing to the efforts of a popular president), provided that it has been able to build a reservoir of legitimacy with the public. Justices who have been sensitive to keeping the institution in good standing with the public, like Owen Roberts, have been willing to put their judicial philosophy and personal beliefs aside, or at least engage in compromise with other justices, in order to protect the Court's political standing. In rare circumstances where the Court is not able to bridge ideological differences among its members, justices put the Court's legitimacy at risk. We witnessed such an event following the 2000 presidential election.

Squandering Legitimacy?

In December 2000, the Supreme Court walked into the middle of an entirely different tempest—the biggest presidential election controversy in 124 years—when it agreed to hear the Bush campaign's request to put a halt to manual recounts of Florida ballots that did not clearly register a vote for president. George W. Bush and his Democratic rival Al Gore were separated in the final Florida count by several hundred votes out of millions cast, with the eventual winner to receive all of Florida's electoral votes, and with them the presidency. For weeks America was riveted by the recount battle, as several Florida counties manually reviewed unmarked and poorly marked ballots using different standards for determining the intent of the voter.

The election battle ended abruptly when the U.S. Supreme Court terminated all recounts in the controversial case of **Bush v. Gore** (2000). Seven of the justices felt that the inconsistent recount standards employed in different counties were unconstitutional, but only five of them—all Republican appointees and the Court's most conservative members—argued that the calendar permitted no remedy to correct the inconsistencies because the time had come for

electors to report. Four justices with a more liberal voting record strongly disagreed. Unlike the case of *United States v. Nixon*, the Court split into two camps, which were so sharply divided that they were unable to find common ground on which to build consensus. The final vote was 5–4; the recounting would stop, and Bush would become president.

The ruling left the nation as divided as the Court, and it left the Court bitter about what it had done. For a brief time, the Court's veil of secrecy was lifted as justices uncharacteristically displayed their feelings in public, revealing deep disagreements and great resentment. Justice Clarence Thomas, a member of the conservative majority, appeared on C-SPAN within a day of the ruling to deny that partisan considerations had influenced the decision. Chief Justice Rehnquist made the same assertion to reporters.[47]

Meanwhile, the four dissenting justices angrily castigated the majority, writing that the decision "inevitably cast a cloud on the legitimacy of the election."[48] Some openly questioned if the decision would have the same effect on the Court. Justice Ginsburg, who sided with the minority, saw the ruling as a political victory for "the home crowd"—a reference to the conservative majority fashioning what she believed to be a legally questionable ruling in order to put the candidate they preferred in the White House. Justice Breyer, also on the losing side of the case, worried that the partisan overtones of the ruling would undermine the legitimacy of the judicial process, and by extension, the legitimacy of the Court.[49]

Were the dissenters worried for no reason? Although it's true that the Court spoke with two voices on a politically charged, controversial topic while wading into a hotly contested political debate, it isn't clear that it undermined the reverence with which many Americans view the judiciary. In fact, surveys taken shortly after the ruling in *Bush v. Gore* suggest that, overall, the public was no less likely to think well of the Supreme Court than before the ruling.[50] At least in the short term, the Court appears not to have squandered its legitimacy by stepping into the 2000 election firestorm (although certainly many Democrats considered the decision to be suspect and ideologically motivated). Ironically, this could be because while public opinion was divided on who had actually won the election, by the time the Court made its ruling, a consensus was emerging that the recount saga had gone on too long and any resolution would be desirable. Despite the controversy surrounding how they did it, the Court provided the American people with the closure many were seeking.

Consistency and Legitimacy?

To dissenters, one of the more disturbing components of the Court's ruling in *Bush v. Gore* was the requirement that it not be applied to any subsequent case. In other words, the majority made it clear that it was settling a contested election but that it was not establishing a legal precedent. This appeared odd because throughout its history, the Court has operated on the assumption that the collective body of constitutional interpretation contained in the Court's previous rulings provides the basis for making present-day judgments.

This has led the Court to place a premium on consistency. The Court puts a lot of stock in the doctrine of **stare decisis**, or "let the decision stand." *Stare decisis* encourages the Court to use its previous rulings as the basis for making present-day judgments and makes justices generally reluctant to overturn previous decisions, especially judgments that have become part of established law. This can lead justices who disagree with previous Court judgments to uphold them, even as they proclaim their differences with the interpretations of their predecessors.

At the same time, the Court does reverse course, especially in less than monumental matters. By one count, the Court overturned an average of four precedents per year between 1960 and 1999.[51] It's generally easier for the Court to reverse itself on a newly decided matter than on long-standing constitutional interpretation. See Demystifying Government: Abortion Rights and Established Law.

Reliance on precedent provides the Court with stability that contributes to its legitimacy. Reluctance to make dramatic changes to past rulings despite shifts in the Court's ideological composition distinguishes the Court from the other two

federal branches, where swift changes of direction typically characterize partisan shifts. Even when given to ideological motivation, astute justices move slowly to project the appearance of allowing precedent to triumph over self-interest.

Cautious tendencies such as these can paradoxically pose a dilemma when the Court is faced with a previous ruling that was simply a bad judgment. Following *stare decisis* means the Court may take a long time to reverse a burdensome decision, sometimes allowing changes in public opinion to make the outdated ruling untenable. In such cases, the Court eventually protects its legitimacy by changing course or finds its legitimacy tarnished and its judgments discarded by history.

When Events Overturn the Court

Sometimes, events conspire to reverse a bad judgment of the Court. The case of **Dred Scott v. Sanford** (1857) is a profound example. Dred Scott was a slave who had been taken by his owner to Illinois and the Wisconsin territory, where slavery was prohibited under the terms of the Missouri Compromise. When he was returned to the slave state of Missouri, he petitioned the Court to maintain his freedom on the grounds that he had been residing previously in a free state. A judgment in his favor would have undermined the institution of slavery throughout the Union.

Chief Justice Roger Taney had no intention of allowing this to happen. His Court ruled that no person of color, be they free or enslaved, could be considered a citizen of the United States, and therefore Scott had no legal basis to bring suit. Taney's decision referred to Scott (and all black persons) as "an ordinary article of merchandise" that had no rights. Furthermore, in the first direct challenge to Congress since *Marbury v. Madison*, Taney overturned the key provision of the Missouri Compromise that precluded slavery in northern states and territories, effectively making slavery legal nationwide.[52]

Legal scholars widely consider the *Dred Scott* decision to be the Court's lowest moment. Charles Evans Hughes, Chief Justice during the 1930s, called the ruling one of the Court's "self-inflicted

DEMYSTIFYING GOVERNMENT

ABORTION RIGHTS AND ESTABLISHED LAW

Prior to 1973, abortion was prohibited in many states. The landmark ruling in the case of *Roe v. Wade* changed that. The Court found that a constitutional right to privacy prohibited states from restricting the availability of abortions during the first three months of pregnancy, and struck down all laws that did so. Abortions were suddenly legal across the country.

Prior to the ruling, the abortion issue was not at the top of the national political agenda, but that quickly changed. As we know, the best way to influence the political process is to organize, and following *Roe v. Wade*, groups seeking to recriminalize abortions organized rapidly. They focused initially on a political and legal strategy, whereby they worked against the election of candidates for high office who were on record as supporting abortion rights, and challenged abortion laws in an effort to get the Supreme Court to reverse or chip away at its decision in *Roe*. The effort eventually bore fruit, and by the early 1980s a sizable congressional contingent and the president, Ronald Reagan, favored reversing the *Roe* decision.[T7]

This did not lead the Court to make an about-face, however. Advocates of reversal argued before the Court that the reasoning used to reach the *Roe* decision was faulty, but this was initially rejected. In *City of Akron v. Akron Center for Reproductive Health* (1983), the Court overturned restrictions imposed on abortion rights by the city of Akron, and in so doing, acknowledged the importance of precedent. In the majority opinion in the *Akron* case, Justice Powell wrote, "Arguments continue to be made ... that we erred in interpreting the Constitution. Nonetheless, the doctrine of *stare decisis*, while perhaps never entirely persuasive on a constitutional question, is a doctrine that demands respect in a society governed by the rule of law. We respect it today, and reaffirm *Roe v. Wade*."[T8]

As the 1980s progressed, groups pressing to overturn *Roe* benefited from an effective campaign to keep the abortion issue at the forefront of the political agenda. Meanwhile, President Reagan had the opportunity to appoint to the Supreme Court justices who were philosophically opposed to legal abortion. When the Court again considered the issue in *Webster v. Reproductive Health Services* (1989), advocates of a Missouri law restricting abortions attacked the trimester language in *Roe* that decriminalized abortion in the first three months of a pregnancy, contending that it was unworkable, arbitrary, burdensome, and flawed. If their argument held sway in what had become a far more sympathetic Supreme Court, they hoped it would provide the legal rationale for undermining the *Roe* decision. A majority of five justices upheld the Missouri law, but they were divided on the issue of whether their verdict should be used to overturn *Roe*, so the 1973 decision survived what had been its sharpest test to date. With the appointment of two Justices supportive of *Roe* by President Clinton, the status quo continued through the 1990s,[T9] but with the appointment by President Bush of two conservative justices, the Court in the 21st century has been willing to consider limiting the scope of *Roe*.

We can derive several lessons from this history:

- *Precedent matters*: On major decisions, it takes a lot to move the Court to change what it has established. However, even if the Court is unwilling to reverse itself, it may well be open to chipping away at previous decisions.
- *Politics matters*: Who sits on the Supreme Court (a function of who serves as presi-

dent), whether an interest is well organized, and the climate of public opinion all factor into the receptivity of the Court to a line of argument.

• *Argument matters*: Even when justices come down on the same side of a case, they may do so for different reasons. The way a case is presented to the Court can mean the difference between victory and defeat.

wounds."[53] It destroyed the Court's legitimacy in the eyes of abolitionists as it intensified irreparable national divisions over slavery. Within three years, in part because of the effect of the Court's decision, the nation would explode into civil war.

Ultimately, the *Dred Scott* ruling was reversed, not by the action of a future Court, but by constitutional amendments approved in a different political climate. With the passage of the Thirteenth and Fourteenth Amendments following the Civil War, slavery was abolished and blacks were granted full citizenship. Taney's decision was rendered moot and his reasoning discredited, but the *Dred Scott* case remains as a warning about the lasting dangers inherent in any case where the Supreme Court establishes a bad precedent.

When the Court Overturns Itself

It took almost sixty years, but the Supreme Court eventually jettisoned another racially charged ruling, this time by establishing a new precedent in a subsequent case. The original case in question was **Plessy v. Ferguson** (1896), which established the constitutionality of separate public facilities for whites and nonwhites.

Homer Plessy was arrested in 1892 for sitting in the "whites only" car on a Louisiana railroad. Because he had black ancestors, he was considered black under Louisiana law and required to travel in the "coloreds only" car. Plessy went to court to challenge the constitutionality of the segregated railroad, contending it violated the Thirteenth and Fourteenth Amendments. The Court disagreed. Writing for the majority, Justice Henry Billings Brown asserted that the Fourteenth Amendment "could not have been intended to abolish distinctions based on color, or to enforce social, as distinguished from political equality."[54] As long as the facilities available to blacks were on par with those available to whites, segregation was legal.

In a lone dissent that proved to be generations ahead of its time, Justice John Harlan contended, "our Constitution is color-blind, and neither knows nor tolerates classes among citizens. ... In my opinion, the judgment this day rendered will, in time, prove to be quite as pernicious as the decision made by this tribunal in the *Dred Scott* case."[55] Harlan was right on target. However, it would take until 1954 before a majority of the Supreme Court would agree.

The vehicle for overturning its stand on legal segregation was **Brown v. Board of Education** (1954), which revolved around the case of a grade-school girl named Linda Brown, who had to walk to a distant all-black school even though there was an all-white school in her Topeka, Kansas neighborhood. Her father tried to enroll her in the nearby all-white school but was turned down. With legal assistance from the National Association for the Advancement of Colored People (NAACP), the Browns sued the Topeka Board of Education, asking the courts to strike down barriers to integration. Because the ruling in the *Plessy* case clearly made separate educational facilities legal, the lower courts sided with the Board of Education.

It was left to the Supreme Court to stand up to its past, and the politics of the moment made this possible. Earl Warren, just two months into his term as Chief Justice, had an opportunity to correct what the Court had done in 1896 and change the direction of American politics. In a unanimous decision, the Warren Court overturned fifty-eight years of constitutionally sanctioned segregation in a landmark ruling that began breaking down racial barriers in American institutions.

Taking direct aim at *Plessy*, Warren wrote, "Does segregation of children in public schools solely on the basis of race, even though the physical facilities and other 'tangible' factors may be equal, deprive the children of the minority group of equal educational opportunities? We believe that it does. … We conclude that in the field of public education the doctrine of 'separate but equal' has no place. Separate educational facilities are inherently unequal."[56]

With those words, the Court made a rare about-face in the wake of changing political conditions, propelling the groundbreaking work of the civil rights movement of the 1950s and 1960s. See Appendix F for excerpts of key civil rights decisions.

Activism and Restraint

It's probably evident by now that the competing philosophical approaches to the role of the Court that justices hold can make an enormous difference in how much the Court contributes to social change. In this regard, the people wearing the robes matter a lot. John Marshall and Earl Warren were activists who expanded the role of the Court in the political process and in American life. More restrained justices serving during the same periods in history would have done it differently, resulting in less development of federal power in the early nineteenth century and in fewer civil rights advancements in the twentieth century.

Judicial Activism

As a proponent of **judicial activism**, Warren presided over a revolutionary expansion in minority group rights, criminal defendant rights, voting rights, equal representation, and personal expression. Between 1953 and 1969, the Warren Court acted aggressively, among other things, to

- Desegregate schools.
- Draw legislative boundaries so they reflected the "one person, one vote" principle.

- Protect individuals accused of crimes from self-incrimination (the famous "Miranda Rights" that police read to suspects prior to arresting them come from the 1966 case *Miranda v. Arizona*).
- Guarantee legal representation to criminal defendants who could not afford it.
- Forbid mandatory prayer in public schools.
- Expand press freedom by requiring public figures to prove that reporters acted with malice to support a claim of libel.[57]

If you're thinking that all this was controversial, you're right. Critics charge that judicial activists are less interested in interpreting the law than in making it, a role that is constitutionally reserved for Congress. Warren's critics repeatedly charged him with usurping powers that were reserved for others, which—along with the agenda his activism promoted—instigated sales of "impeach Earl Warren" bumper stickers.

If the Court takes a measure of public opinion before acting, though, it should be remembered that the Warren Court served during a period of social upheaval that suited it well. Certainly, the Court's activism contributed to the upheaval, and without a doubt, public opinion was sharply divided over a lot of what it did. Then again, public opinion was sharply divided over everything important happening during the 1960s, when rights for African Americans, women, and young people were at the forefront of the political agenda. It's hard to envision an activist Court taking the positions that the Warren Court did in an era that's more conducive to conservative politics, like what we saw in the decades after Warren left the Court.

Still, it would be a mistake to equate judicial activism with political liberalism. The aforementioned Felix Frankfurter, whose long service included a stint on the Warren Court before his retirement in 1962, was an economic conservative who advanced his preferences by striking down laws that conflicted with his agenda—in other words, through judicial activism.[58] Members of today's conservative Supreme Court who have worked to reverse some of what the Warren Court did could also be seen as conservative activists. It is not uncommon for the Roberts

Table 11.3. The Growth of Judicial Activism through Two Centuries, 1801–2001[T10]

Court	Years	Supreme Court Decisions Overturned	Acts of Congress Overturned	State Laws Overturned
Marshall	1801–1835	3	1	18
Taney	1836–1864	4	1	21
Chase	1865–1873	4	10	33
Waite	1874–1888	13	9	7
Fuller	1889–1910	4	14	73
White	1910–1921	5	12	107
Taft	1921–1930	6	12	131
Hughes	1930–1940	21	14	78
Stone	1941–1946	15	2	25
Vinson	1947–1952	13	1	38
Warren	1953–1969	45	25	150
Burger	1969–1986	52	34	192
Rehnquist	1986–2001	34	25	86

Court to overturn precedent, as they did in 2010 with campaign finance law in the *Citizens United v. Federal Election* Commission case. Often these votes rest on a narrow 5–4 majority, with the Court's most conservative justices voting with the majority.[59]

Judicial Restraint

Today's Court has its share of justices who practice *judicial restraint*, or the philosophy that the judiciary should yield to the actions of the legislature and executive unless they are blatantly unconstitutional. To a justice who practices judicial restraint, a bad policy, an unnecessary policy, even an unfair policy that is permitted under the Constitution should be left alone.[60] Clearly, someone who takes this approach to the judiciary would never think of using the Court as a vehicle for advancing an activist political agenda. This became a point raised ironically by liberals during the Roberts and Alito confirmation hearings, as they sought assurances that these conservative jurists would regard *Roe v. Wade* as established law and not seek to overturn it. Although restraint and conservatism seem to go hand-in-hand, it's possible for conservative judges to make activist rulings.

Some of the justices who practice judicial restraint are also **constructionists** when it comes to interpreting the Constitution. Constructionists believe that the Constitution should be subject to a literal or narrow interpretation, and understood within the context in which it was written.[61] So, for instance, strict constructionists might oppose the reasoning behind the *Roe* decision that legalized abortion on the basis of a constitutional right to privacy on the grounds that the Constitution does not enumerate privacy as a right, and that the framers of the Constitution did not intend for there to be such a right. A constructionist philosophy is conservative in nature and stands in clear opposition to judicial activism. Not surprisingly, recent conservative presidents like Nixon, Reagan, and both Bushes have favored judicial nominees who hold to this philosophy.

Despite the prevalence of Republican justices, the Supreme Court in recent years has been actively engaged in reversing its own decisions, acts of Congress, and state laws. The period since Chief Justice Warren took over the Court in 1953 through the present has been an unparalleled era of judicial activism, in which the Court as a whole has injected itself regularly into the political process. Between 1953 and 2001, the Court reversed 131 of its earlier rulings. In the previous century and a half, it had only done this eighty-eight times. Table 11.3 fills in the details. Despite the conservative direction the Court has taken since Warren's departure, it is now a matter of course that the judiciary is an active, equal—and legitimate—branch of government.

Questions of judicial activism and restraint often play out around divisive social concerns. Same-sex marriage is one such issue. It has been percolating in state courts in recent years, and has become a significant issue on the national political agenda. Ultimately, it is an issue likely to be decided as much in the federal courts as in the legislative process. Take a look at Issue: Same-Sex Marriage, and think about how you would like the courts to act on the question of whether gays and lesbians should be given the right to enter into legal partnerships.

As an equal participant in the political process, the cumulative actions of the courts at every level have tremendous bearing on how we live our lives. The way the courts exercise this influence is itself determined by things beyond the control of the judiciary—like other political actors and the political climate of the times—and by the philosophical leanings of the people in the dark robes. Would the federal government be weaker today if John Marshall had not been Chief Justice for the first three decades of the nineteenth century, when clashes over federalism were being resolved? Would the Civil War have occurred when it did had Chief Justice Taney not tried to codify slavery as the law of the land? Would the civil rights agendas of the 1960s have been different without Earl Warren? Would Al Gore have become president had one justice voted differently?

In the courts as everywhere else in the political system, the rules of the game and the way they're interpreted by people in authority determines who gets what—who wins and who loses. Nowhere is this more evident than in the area of public policy, the outcomes produced by the political process in

ISSUE

SAME-SEX MARRIAGE

When your parents were young, chances are they never heard a discussion about whether people of the same sex should be allowed to marry. That's because homosexuality was in the closet and the only marriages available to gay people were marriages to people of the opposite sex that provided cover for behavior that was considered deplorable and criminal. Then, as part of the sexual revolution of the 1960s, gays became more visible and gradually appeared on the nation's social and political radar. In 1988, Ms. magazine published an anonymous article by a woman entitled, "I Left My Husband for the Woman I Love."[T11] By 2000, openly gay characters were being featured on prime time television programs and same-sex partnered households numbered close to 600,000.[T12] Times had changed dramatically.

As is so often the case with dramatic social shifts, the political system was both the place where gay rights advocates pressed for legal advances and the focus of resistance to the gay rights movement. Initially, political conflicts centered on demands by gay rights groups for civil rights protections and resistance by groups hoping to protect traditional social values. It wasn't until the 1990s that same-sex unions became part of that debate[T13] when a dramatic judgment by a Hawaii Circuit Court judge opened the door to legalized same-sex marriage in that state and brought the issue to national attention. The 1996 case *Baehr v. Miike* established that Hawaii had no constitutional basis for denying a marriage license to a same-sex couple. [T14] With that judgment, Hawaii appeared on the verge of becoming the first state to recognize gay marriages.

The decision sparked a backlash by groups seeking to preserve marriage as a heterosexual institution. By 2001, thirty-five states had passed laws prohibiting the recognition of same-sex unions that might be licensed in other states. These laws were bolstered by federal legislation—the 1996 Defense of Marriage Act—which declared that marriage as a legal matter referred only to heterosexual marriage, and that no state would be obligated to recognize a same-sex marriage from another state. In 1998, Hawaii voters approved a state constitutional amendment giving the legislature the power to overrule the courts and restrict marriage to heterosexual couples. Then the Hawaii Supreme Court threw out the Circuit Court judgment in *Baehr*, ending that state's brief flirtation with same-sex marriage.

At this point, the battle shifted to Vermont. In late 1999, the Vermont Supreme Court unanimously ruled in the case of *Baker v. State* that the state had unlawfully denied three same-sex couples the rights afforded heterosexual couples, and instructed the state legislature to remedy the situation. Their response was something legally different than same-sex marriage: a new institution called "civil union," which had the effect of extending the benefits of marriage to gay couples without altering existing marriage laws. It applied only to couples living in Vermont, so other states would not have to grapple with whether to recognize the law as they would have had Vermont legalized same-sex marriages. Governor Howard Dean signed it into law in April 2000, and nine months later, legislation was introduced in the Vermont House of Representatives in an unsuccessful effort to repeal it.[15]

In 2004, the Massachusetts Supreme Court ruled as the Hawaii Supreme Court had six years earlier, finding nothing in the state Constitution to prohibit gay marriage and giving the legislature six months to rewrite marriage laws to permit it. The Massachusetts ruling produced another wave of protests from gay marriage opponents like former President Bush, culminating in the overwhelming approval in the 2004 election of measures banning gay marriage by voters in eleven states. At the same time, San Francisco responded in solidarity with the Massachusetts ruling by briefly issuing marriage licenses to gay couples. The remainder of the decade witnessed ballot, legislative and court initiatives in states across the country on both sides of the issue: either codifying heterosexual marriage or extending greater rights to gay couples. Culturally conservative states like Texas, Alabama, South Carolina and Idaho passed constitutional amendments restricting marriage to one man and one woman. Culturally liberal states like New Jersey, Washington and Oregon extended domestic partnership rights to same-sex couples. Connecticut, Vermont, Iowa, New Hampshire, and for a brief time California, legalized gay marriage.

Deeply held cultural values about marriage, sexuality, justice, and equality lie behind the intense feelings many people have about same-sex marriage. Positions on same-sex marriage are strongly value-driven and can defy one's sexual orientation. Same-sex marriage is opposed by some conservative gays who see it as a threat to bedrock cultural values and by some on the far left who see marriage itself as a patriarchal institution to be rejected.[16] This is the same breakdown of opinion we find among heterosexuals.

• *Arguments in Support*

Supporters and opponents of same-sex marriage make value-based arguments to support their positions. Supporters would argue that:

- It's about discrimination. Denying same-sex couples the rights and privileges stemming from marriage subjects them to differential treatment because of their sexual orientation.
- It's about personal liberty. Sexual orientation is a personal matter, not a public

issue. Anyone who wishes to get married should have the freedom to do so regardless of his or her sexual orientation.

- Marriage is defined by relationships. It is about the bonds that hold two people together. Same-sex couples regularly engage in such relationships, but without the legal benefits and protections accorded heterosexual couples that share similar bonds.
- Marriage is good for society. It promotes social stability and provides a suitable environment for raising children, so any couple that marries—regardless of sexual orientation—advances family values.

Arguments Against

Opponents of same-sex marriage invoke a different set of values than supporters to explain their position. They might say:

- Discrimination isn't an issue. Rejecting a behavior one considers morally wrong is not discriminatory, and engaging in it is qualitatively different from being a member of a racial or ethnic group.
- Liberty isn't an issue. Advocates of same-sex marriage want public benefits and

public recognition for same-sex couples, placing their efforts in the policy arena—not in the private realm of personal freedoms. Granting those benefits and privileges would amount to publicly sanctioning homosexuality.

- Marriage is defined by the law. Advocates of same-sex marriage seek legal recognition, rendering irrelevant the fact that relationships are involved. On this matter, the law is clear and uniform: Marriage is defined as the union of a husband and a wife.
- Same-sex marriage is bad for society. It undermines core values centered on heterosexual marriage, procreation, and traditional family structures.

My Opinion

When considering your opinion on same-sex marriage, think about the history of the issue and the arguments supporting and opposing it. In particular, ask yourself if same-sex marriage:

- Is or is not about discrimination.
- Is or is not about personal liberty.
- Is about relationships or laws.
- Is good or bad for society.

the form of domestic and foreign policy and laws regarding individual rights and liberties.

Chapter Review

The judiciary resolves disputes arising from other branches of government, but it does so without the formal powers of the other branches and has to rely on the executive branch to enforce its rulings. This initially placed the United States Supreme Court in a weak position, which was strengthened enormously with the establishment of the Court's power of judicial review in the 1803 case *Marbury v.*

Madison. Other rulings of the Marshall Court helped establish the supremacy of the federal government over the states.

The federal court system is a three-tiered structure with trial courts, circuit courts of appeals, and the Supreme Court. Most cases work their way up this system through an appellate process, although the Supreme Court has original jurisdiction over cases involving the federal government, states, and foreign officials as detailed in the Constitution. State court systems follow this three-tiered structure and have jurisdiction over state criminal and civil law. Cases can only be appealed from a state court to the U.S. Supreme Court if they raise a point of constitutional law.

Courts have a lot of latitude in the cases they select for review, although interest groups try to influence case selection. Deciding cases is a complicated process that starts with oral arguments in court, proceeds with closed conferences, and continues with a period of writing decisions, during which justices attempt to influence each others' opinions and may even change their votes.

Judicial nominations can cause contentious battles between the president and Congress because the direction of the judiciary depends on the philosophy and ideology of the people the president appoints. Historically, presidents get most of the appointments they want, but the Senate takes its consent function seriously and has blocked nominations considered controversial. Presidents will also defer to senatorial courtesy and avoid appointing justices and judges who are not acceptable to their home-state senators.

Although the vast majority of Supreme Court appointees have been white Protestant men, today's Supreme Court reflects more religious, ethnic, and gender diversity. This is less evident on lower federal courts, where President Clinton is alone among his immediate predecessors in the diversity of his appointments.

In order to turn its relatively weak political position to advantage, the Court plays on its mystique to bolster its legitimacy with the public, making it difficult for political officials to defy Court rulings. It also pays attention to public opinion, often taking pains not to get ahead of what the public will accept. So, when Franklin D. Roosevelt attempted to pack the Court with sympathetic justices, the public recoiled at his efforts to play politics with a revered institution, and the scheme failed. However, a justice who had been holding up Roosevelt's New Deal legislation acknowledged its broad public support and began changing his vote, which brought the Court in line with public sentiment.

Justices put a lot of stock in the doctrine of *stare decisis*, making dramatic reversals unusual. But as public opinion changes the Court may become willing to revisit past rulings. The Court may overturn some of its earlier bad judgments, the way *Plessy v.* *Ferguson* (1896) was reversed by *Brown v. Board of Education* (1954). Events may conspire to reverse the Court, as when the decision affirming slavery in *Dred Scott v. Sanford* (1857) was overturned by constitutional amendment following the Civil War.

Justices differ in judicial philosophy. Judicial activists believe the Court should be a forum for correcting social wrongs. Justices advocating judicial restraint feel the Court should defer to the actions of Congress and the president unless they are blatantly unconstitutional.

Key Terms

amicus curiae Briefs filed by interested parties to a case, whose opinions are offered in an effort to shape the Court's discussion and judgment.

appellate jurisdiction The authority of a high court to hear cases only after the cases originate in and are appealed from a lower court.

Brown v. Board of Education The landmark 1954 Supreme Court case that declared racial segregation unconstitutional, overturning the Court's ruling in Plessy v. Ferguson.

Bush v. Gore The controversial 2000 Supreme Court case in which a sharply divided Court ended manual ballot recounts in Florida, following which George W. Bush became president.

concurring opinion A statement issued by a justice who agrees with a vote of the Court but differs on the legal or constitutional rationale for the majority decision.

constructionists Those who hold to the judicial philosophy that the Constitution should be interpreted strictly and literally, and in the context in which it was written.

dissenting opinion A statement issued by a justice who disagrees with a vote of the Court, offering a legal or constitutional rationale for that disagreement.

docket The list of cases pending before a court.

Dred Scott v. Sanford The 1857 Supreme Court case that legalized slavery nationwide, while holding that people of color had no rights or protection under the Constitution. The ruling hastened the Civil War; it was subsequently overturned by constitutional amendment.

Gibbons v. Ogden The Supreme Court case, heard by the Marshall Court in 1824, that established the federal government's primacy in regulating interstate commerce, saying that the state of New York could not grant an exclusive license to a steamboat company operating between New York and New Jersey

judicial activism The philosophy that the Court should take an aggressive posture toward politics and the law, striking down presidential and congressional actions whenever it is deemed necessary and instituting far-reaching remedies to social wrongs.

judicial restraint The philosophy that the Court should defer to the other branches of government and only overturn legislation when it is clearly unconstitutional.

judicial review The authority of the Supreme Court to overrule actions of Congress or the president by declaring them to be unconstitutional.

judiciary The federal and state court systems charged with resolving legal and personal disputes and interpreting the law.

Judiciary Act of 1789 The act of Congress that established the federal court system. It initially called for a six-person Supreme Court and three circuit courts, each to be administered by two Supreme Court justices and one district court judge.

jurisdiction The authority of a court to hear a case.

legal system The web of institutions and individuals involved in bringing legal and personal disputes to the attention of the courts.

Marbury v. Madison The Supreme Court case, heard by the Marshall Court in 1803, that established judicial review.

McCulloch v. Maryland The 1819 Supreme Court case that established federal supremacy over the state governments.

New Jersey Plan A proposal for the new Constitution, supported by small states, that would have provided for equal representation of large and small states in the national legislature, while limiting the power of the national government over the states.

original jurisdiction The authority of the U.S. Supreme Court to be the first court to hear a case, precluding the need for an appeal from a lower court. The Constitution grants original jurisdiction to cases involving a dispute between the United States and a state; two or more states; citizens of different states; a state and a citizen of another state; and foreign ambassadors.

Plessy v. Ferguson The 1896 Supreme Court case that upheld racial segregation. It was reversed in 1954 in the case of Brown v. Board of Education.

Roe v. Wade The 1973 Supreme Court case that found a constitutional right to privacy applied to reproductive issues, striking down all state laws that prohibited abortions during the first trimester of pregnancy.

senatorial courtesy The custom that presidents will defer to the wishes of senators from a judicial nominee's home state before making a court appointment.

solicitor general The White House official responsible for arguing on behalf of the United States in Supreme Court cases where the United States is a party.

stare decisis Literally, "let the decision stand," it is a guiding principle of judicial interpretation that places a premium on letting previous judicial rulings guide current rulings.

United States v. Nixon The 1974 case in which a unanimous Supreme Court ruled that President Nixon could not use executive privilege to protect the secrecy of incriminating tapes documenting his involvement in the cover-up of the Watergate break-in.

Virginia Plan   A proposal for the new Constitution, supported by large states, that would have based representation on population and provided for a centralized national government that could overrule the states.

writ of certiorari   An order issued by the Supreme Court demanding a lower court turn over all records of a case that the Supreme Court has decided to hear on appeal.

writ of mandamus   A court order commanding a public official to perform an official act.

Resources

You might be interested in examining some of what the following authors have said about the topics we've been discussing:

Abraham, Henry J. *Justices, Presidents and Senators: A History of the U.S. Supreme Court Appointments from Washington to Bush II, 5th ed.* Lanham, MD: Rowman & Littlefield, 2007. A colorful account of the nominating process and the Supreme Court through history.

Baum, Lawrence. *The Supreme Court,* 10th ed. Washington, DC: CQ Press, 2009. Baum offers a thorough exploration of the extent to which the Supreme Court operates as a political institution despite appearances to the contrary.

Carp, Robert A., and Ronald Stidham. *The Federal Courts*, 4th ed. Washington, DC: CQ Press, 2001. A detailed overview of the federal court system.

Epstein, Lee, and Jack Knight. *The Choices Justices Make.* Washington, DC: CQ Press, 1998. The authors offer a rational approach to the way Supreme Court justices reach decisions, which should appeal to anyone interested in strategic decision-making.

Epstein, Lee, Jeffrey A. Segal, Harold J. Spaeth, and Thomas G. Walker. *The Supreme Court Compendium: Data, Decisions, and Development,* 4th ed. Washington, DC: CQ Press, 2006. If you have a factual question about the Supreme Court, chances are you can find the answer here. It's everything you've ever wanted to know about the Supreme Court.

O'Brien, David M. *Storm Center: The Supreme Court in American Politics*, 8th ed. New York: W. W. Norton, 2008. An accessible account of the Supreme Court that emphasizes how the Court functions as a political branch of government.

Toobin, Jeffrey. The Nine*: Inside the Secret World of the Supreme Court.* New York: Doubleday, 2008. Toobin pulls back the veil of secrecy on the Supreme Court to reveal a world that's heavily influenced by personalities and politics.

You may also be interested in looking at the Supreme Court's website, at http://www.supremecourt.gov. You can browse the Court's docket, read about the rules and history of the Court, and even plan a visit if you're going to be in Washington, DC.

Notes

1. Herbert Jacob, *Law and Politics in the United States*, 2d ed. (New York: HarperCollins, 1995), 6–18.
2. You can take a virtual tour of the Supreme Court, and even virtually visit a Justice's chambers, by going to oyez.org at http://www.oyez.org/tour.
3. Lawrence Baum, *The Supreme Court*, 7th ed. (Washington, DC: CQ Press, 2001), 2–4.
4. Alexander Hamilton, *The Federalist*, No. 78. See http://www.constitution.org/fed/federa78.htm.
5. Robert A. Carp and Ronald Stidham, *The Federal Courts,* 4th ed. (Washington, DC: CQ Press, 2001), 4.
6. David M. O'Brien, *Storm Center*: *The Supreme Court in American Politics*, 6th ed. (New York: WW. Norton, 2003), 105.
7. Ibid., 106.
8. Carp and Stidham, *The Federal Courts*, 6.
9. Ibid, 6-7.
10. Ibid.
11. Baum, *The Supreme Court*, 23–24.
12. Carp and Stidham, *The Federal Courts*, 7–8.

13. Ibid., 71. Jackson may not have actually spoken these words, but there's little doubt that they expressed how he felt about Marshall's Federalist tendencies.
14. Ibid., 16–17.
15. O'Brien, *Storm Center*, 105.
16. Carp and Stidham, *The Federal Courts*, 46–47.
17. Ibid., 248.
18. Ibid., 255.
19. Ibid., 257–267.
20. Lee Epstein and Jack Knight, *The Choices Justices Make* (Washington, DC: CQ Press, 1998), 1–21.
21. O'Brien, *Storm Center*, 267–296.
22. Carp and Stidham, *The Federal Courts*, 32–34.
23. O'Brien, *Storm Center*, 164–182.
24. U.S. Courts: The Federal Judiciary, at: http://www.uscourts.gov. See also Supreme Court of the United States, at http://www.supremecourt.gov/faq.aspx#faqgi9.
25. If you're curious about the types of cases pending before the Supreme Court right now, you can access the Court's docket at http://www.supremecourt.gov/docket/docket.aspx. At the search bar, type in an area that interests you, like "environment," "transportation," or "tax." The website will return all pending and recently decided cases pertaining to that area. If you're a budding lawyer, you can click on the docket number of a case and you'll find the path the case has taken to reach the Supreme Court, and the action taken (or lack thereof), expressed in language only a lawyer could love.
26. You can read more about the solicitor general online at http://www.justice.gov/osg/.
27. O'Brien, *Storm Center*, 222–225.
28. Ibid., 225.
29. See http://www.whitehouse.gov/the_press_office/Background-on-Judge-Sonia-Sotomayor.
30. Lee Epstein and others, *The Supreme Court Compendium: Data, Decisions, and Development*, 2d ed. (Washington, DC: CQ Press, 1996), 329.
31. Abraham, *Justices, Presidents and Senators*, 18–19
32. Ibid., 19.
33. Ibid., 21–28.
34. Ibid., 46–47.
35. Federal Judicial Center, at http://www.fjc.gov/.
36. Carp and Stidham, *The Federal Courts*, 69–78.
37. Ibid., 78.
38. Abraham, *Justices, Presidents and Senators*, 191–192.
39. Ibid., 191–194.
40. O'Brien, *Storm Center*, 87.
41. Ibid., 56.
42. Ibid.
43. Yes, that's really what it was called.
44. O'Brien, *Storm Center*, 58.
45. Jacob, *Law and Politics*, 79–80.
46. When you're looking at the transcript, note the reference to Mark Felt, who is described by Haldeman as "ambitious." Those familiar with the Watergate case may recognize Felt as the secret source, dubbed "Deep Throat," who helped Washington Post reporter Bob Woodward crack the Watergate case, and whose identity had remained a mystery for thirty years.
47. O'Brien, *Storm Center*, 87.
48. Ibid., 251.
49. Ibid., 88 and 96.
50. Ibid., 343.
51. Baum, *The Supreme Court*, 143.
52. O'Brien, *Storm Center*, 29.
53. Ibid., 115.
54. A summary of the case may be found at http://www.oyez.org/cases/1851-1900/1895/1895_210/, while the full text of the ruling may be found at http://supreme.justia.com/us/163/537/case.html.
55. O'Brien, *Storm Center*, 115.
56. The full text of the ruling may be found at http://supreme.justia.com/us/347/483/case.html.
57. O'Brien, *Storm Center*, 195–197.
58. Lee Epstein and Thomas G. Walker, *Constitutional Law for a Changing America: A Short Course* (Washington, DC: CQ Press, 1996), 39–41.
59. See, for instance, Segal, Daniel, and Maya Nayak, "High Court's End-of-Term Opinions Erode Precedent and Stare Decisis." *The Legal Intelligencer* (August 7, 2007); and Linda Greenhouse, "Precedents Begin Falling for Roberts Court," *New York Times*, June 21, 2007.
60. Abraham, *Justices, Presidents and Senators*, 271.
61. O'Brien, *Storm Center*, 14–15.

Table, Figure and Box Notes

T1 Image of Supreme Court is in the Public Domain and is the property of the U.S. Federal Government. Courtesy Steve Petteway, Collection of the Supreme Court of the United States.

T2 Robert Carp and Ronald Stidham, *The Federal Courts*, 4th ed. (Washington, D.C. CQ Press, 2001) 3–4.

T3 Henry J. Abraham, *Presidents and Senators: A History of the U.S. Supreme Court Appointments from Washington to Clinton*. Lanham, MD: Rowman and Littlefield, 1999.

T4 David M. O'Brien, *Storm Center: The Supreme Court in American Politics*, 6th ed. (New York: W. W. Norton, 2002), 172 (table).

T5 The images of the Supreme Court justices are in the Public Domain and are the property of the U.S. Federal Government.

T6 Audio available through the National Archives and Records Administration. Photo is courtesy of the Nixon Library.

T7 Herbert Jacob, *Law and Politics in the United States*, 2nd edition (New York: Harper Collins College Publishers, 1995): 232–233.

T8 Lee Epstein and Joseph F. Kobylka, *The Supreme Court and Legal Challenge: Abortion and the Death Penalty* (Chapel Hill, University of North Central Press, 1992): 244–245.

T9 Ibid, 203–298.

T10 David M. O'Brien, *Storm Center: The Supreme Court in American Politics*, 6th edition (New York: W. W. Norton, 2003).

T11 Reprinted in Robert M. Baird and Stuart E. Rosenbaum (eds.), *Same-Sex Marriage: The Moral and Legal Debate* (Amherst, NY: Prometheus Books, 1997), 37–41.

T12 William R. Eskridge, Jr., *Equality Practice: Civil Unions and the Future of Cay Rights* (New York: Routledge, 2002), xi.

T13 Ibid., 1–3.

T14 Baird and Rosenbaum, *Same Sex Marriage*, 9–10.

T15 Eskridge, *Equality Practice*, 6–82.

T16 Baird and Rosenbaum, *Same Sex Marriage*, 10–11.

Judicial Review

By Isaac Balbus

The debate over judicial review is as old as the debate over the American constitution itself. Although the power of the Supreme Court to nullify legislative acts by declaring them unconstitutional is nowhere explicitly granted in that constitution, Federalists supporting ratification such as Alexander Hamilton hoped, and anti-Federalist opponents of ratification such as Robert Yates feared, that Article 3, section 2, which declares that "The judicial power shall extend to all cases in law and equity arising under this constitution, the laws of the United States, and treaties made, or which shall be made, under their authority," would be invoked by the Court to justify overturning acts of Congress that were deemed to be inconsistent with other provisions of that constitution. In fact this is exactly what happened, for the first time, in 1803 in *Marbury* v. *Madison* when Chief Justice John Marshall, writing for the Court, declared section 13 of the Judiciary Act of 1789 unconstitutional. Ever since then judicial review has been one of the defining, yet still controversial, features of the American system of government. The controversy boils down to the question of whether, or the extent to which, the nullification of laws passed by elected representatives of the people, by judges who are not elected by the people, is consistent with the republican principle of popular sovereignty, or, more simply, whether or the extent to which judicial review is consistent with democracy.

This was the issue joined by Hamilton in *Federalist* 78 and Yates in his "Letters of Brutus." Yates argues that judicial review implies the supremacy of the judicial over the legislative branch of government and that it is therefore inconsistent with republican, or representative democratic, government. Hamilton tries to rebut this argument and to demonstrate that judicial review is an essential "bulwark against the legislative encroachments" that, as we have seen, so worried his colleague James Madison. I will begin with a summary of Yates's position, since his "Letters" were in fact published a few months before Hamilton's *Federalist* 78, which is an explicit rejoinder to some of the arguments in those letters. (I will not focus on Yates's characteristically anti-Federalist preoccupation with the supposed way in which federal judicial review, like other provisions of the proposed constitution, would weaken and ultimately destroy the power of the individual state governments, but rather concentrate exclusively on his claim that judicial review is incompatible with popular sovereignty whether exercised at the state or national level, since that is the issue that is joined by Hamilton in *Federalist 78*.)

Yates's argument, in a nutshell, is that the judicial review (that he believes is) authorized by Article 3, section 2, would entail an unaccountable and therefore illegitimate exercise of tremendous power. On the one hand, and against those who, like Hamilton in *Federalist 78*, would claim that the judiciary, including the Supreme Court, would be confined to the "steady, upright and impartial administration of the laws,"[1] Yates argues in Letter XV that "this court will be authorized to decide on the meaning of the constitution, and that, not only according to the natural and obvious meaning of the words, but also according to the spirit and intention of it."[2] In other words, what we now call "strict constructionism" is effectively impossible, because (as Yates argues in Letter XI) judges "will not confine themselves to fixed or established rules, but will determine, according to what appears to them, the reason and spirit of the constitution":[3] judicial interpretation necessarily requires an interpretation of not merely the letter but also the "spirit" of the laws, and interpretation of the spirit of the laws necessarily leaves room for a great deal of judicial discretion and thus judicial power. Thus there is no way to ensure that judges will not inject their personal or political preferences in the course of determining whether a given law is or is not consistent with the meaning of the constitution.

On the other hand, under the proposed constitution there would be absolutely no check on this inescapable exercise of judicial power. Because (Supreme Court) justices would be appointed for life (contingent on "good behavior"):

> there is no power above them, to controul any of their decisions. There is no authority that can remove them, and they cannot be controuled by the laws of the legislature. In short they are independent of the people, of the legislature, and of every power under heaven.[4]

Thus Yates questions whether there was ever "a court of justice with such immense powers, and yet placed in a situation so little responsible," and concludes that "in the exercise of this power [of deciding upon the meaning of the constitution] they will not be subordinate to, but above the legislature."[5] Hence judicial review is inconsistent with popular sovereignty or republican government.

Although Yates rejects judicial review as a remedy for legislative abuses, he is by no means insensitive to the need to correct those abuses. But he believes that the only way to correct them that is consistent with republican principles is to rely on the people themselves: if the people's elected representatives "determine contrary to the understanding of the people, an appeal will lie to the people at the period when the rulers are to be elected."[6] In short, the people can vote abusive legislators out of office. When, in contrast, the power to remedy the evil "is lodged in the hands of men independent of the people," that is, in the hands of judges "who are not accountable [to the people] for their opinions, no way is left to controul them but *with a high hand and an outstretched arm*"[7] in other words by forcible measures. Thus judicial review is not only undemocratic, it is also a recipe for political instability.

Hamilton in *Federalist 78* attempts to rebut Yates's case against judicial review in at least two different—and not necessarily compatible—ways. First, he argues, famously, that "the judiciary is beyond comparison the weakest of the three departments of power . . . it may truly be said to have neither Force nor Will, but merely judgment."[8] The claim that the judiciary lacks force clearly refers to the fact that the judiciary is entirely dependent on the executive branch to enforce its decisions. But the claim that the judiciary lacks *will* is less clear and is I think harder to sustain. Presumably Hamilton means that the judiciary is reactive rather than proactive: it responds to cases that are brought before it rather than initiates action of its own. But the mere fact that the judiciary decides cases that are brought before it on the initiation of others in no way guarantees that the will of the judges will not be exercised in the course of deciding those cases. In fact Hamilton acknowledges that judges might "substitute their own pleasure [for] the constitutional intentions of the legislature," but argues that this fact in no way counts against judicial review, since the risk that judges might be "disposed to exercise will instead of judgment" is present not only in constitutional interpretation but in ordinary, non-constitutional types of judicial decision making as well: "the observation, if it proved anything, would prove that there ought to be no judges distinct from that [legislative] body"[9] In other words, he attempts to undermine the force of Yates's objection that Supreme Court judges will exercise unaccountable power in interpreting the constitution by arguing that, since this danger is inherent in any type of judicial decision making, Yates's objection logically leads to the (absurd) conclusion that a judiciary independent of the legislature should not exist at all. But surely the consequences of the "substitution of the pleasure [of judges] to that of the legislative body" are far more serious when it comes to the interpretation of the constitution than to ordinary adjudication, so Yates has good reason to be more far more worried about the former than the latter exercise of judicial power. And, to the extent that Hamilton grants that there is a permanent possibility that any judge who "must declare the sense of the law" might be "disposed to exercise will instead of judgment," he undermines his own claim that the judiciary "may truly be said to have neither Force nor Will, but merely judgment." Indeed, it can be argued that judgment—since it presupposes discretion—*always requires* an exercise of will, and that the opposition that Hamilton attempts to establish between "will" and "judgment" necessarily breaks down.

Indeed, Hamilton's other main argument against Yates implies as much. Yates, you will recall, argued that a judicial nullification of a law passed by the representatives of the people would be an exercise of power that was contrary to the will of the people, and thus would be inconsistent with popular sovereignty. Hamilton cleverly parries this objection by arguing, to the contrary, that in upholding the constitution against the legislature the court would be representing the will of the people in opposition to the will of their (supposed) representatives: "where the will of the legislature declared in its statutes, stands in opposition to that of the people declared in the constitution, the judges ought to be governed by the latter, rather than by the former." But this conclusion, according to Hamilton, does not "by any means suppose a superiority of the judicial to the legislative power. It only supposes that the power of the people is superior to both."[10] Thus Hamilton, by equating the court with the constitution and the constitution with the will of the people, is able to argue that an unelected court is actually more responsive to the will of the people—*more democratic*—than the legislatures the people elect.

But this argument is unpersuasive, because Hamilton arbitrarily assumes that any law overturned by the court would be an expression not of the will of the people but rather of their (supposedly unresponsive) representatives. Rather than independently ascertaining the will of the people, he effectively equates the will of the people with the will of the court whenever it acts against the will of the legislature. But one could with as much or even more reason equate the will of people with the will of their elected representatives—which is exactly what Yates does—and thus conclude that when the court overturns a law passed by the representatives of the people the court is contravening the will of the people, and thus undermining democracy. Thus Hamilton's effort to reconcile judicial review with democracy or popular sovereignty is ultimately unsuccessful.

Consequently it has fallen to subsequent legal scholars to wrestle with this problem. In recent years—especially since the 1960s period of so-called "judicial activism"—a number of different approaches to this problem have emerged, only two of which I have space to discuss in this chapter. The first—associated above all with the writings of Judge Robert Bork—is usually referred to as "originalism," which, as the name implies, argues that judges' interpretation of the constitution should be guided exclusively by their understanding of the intent of the original framers of the constitution. Thus, according to this approach, the only legitimate reason for declaring a law unconstitutional would be the incompatibility between that law and "the principles [the framers] enacted, the values they sought to protect."[11] Worried about "activist judges"—for him, Liberal judges—who (supposedly) read their own personal or political preferences into the meaning of the constitution, Bork prescribes deference to the intentions of the framers as the only way to prevent this kind of judicial license and thus to reconcile judicial review with constitutional democracy. Only if judges confine themselves to the meaning of the constitution as it was understood by the framers of the constitution can the power of judicial review be reconciled with the principles of representative democracy, because in this case judges would be guided exclusively by the (popular) intentions that authorized representative democracy in the first place. In the words of Bork, "no other method of constitutional adjudication [than originalism] can confine courts to a defined sphere of authority and thus prevent them from assuming powers whose exercise alters ... the design of the American republic."[12]

But Bork's argument that the intentions—understood as the principles and values—of the framers should be determinative in judicial review suffers from a number of serious—I think ultimately fatal—defects.[13] To begin with, there is no unambiguous way to identify the "principles and values" enshrined by the framers in the words of the constitution. At the time of the founding, the American public was in fact deeply divided over the meaning of such values as freedom and equality. Thus there was no consensus on what the "public at that time would have understood the words [of the constitution] to mean"[14] and thus the appeal to a supposedly original understanding cannot suffice to determine the particular interpretation of the "principle and values" that judges should apply in deciding contemporary cases. Second, some of the principles and values that *were* widely accepted are clearly repugnant to modern sensibilities: the constitution legitimated slavery by specifying that, for purposes of legislative apportionment, slaves should count as three-fifths of a person, and all women were excluded from citizenship because it was assumed that they were intellectually inferior to men. Originalist jurisprudence, it would seem, would require that current commitments to human equality and dignity be trumped by long since repudiated commitments to racial and sexual inequality. And it is not clear how an originalist such as Bork could resist this conclusion without drawing distinctions between acceptable and unacceptable

original "principles and values," a distinction that itself could not be legitimated by an appeal to origins. Finally, and relatedly, originalists such as Bork never convincingly explain why the interpretations of past generations—in this case the founding generation—should be binding on present generations, who, after all, have the benefit of more than two hundred years of political hindsight that was not available to the founding generation itself.

John Hart Ely attempts to avoid these difficulties of originalism—its problematical assumption of an original consensus as to the meaning of the constitution, its apparent endorsement of relationships of domination and subordination, and its arbitrary assumption of the superior wisdom of past generations—by justifying judicial review as a means of protecting and enhancing democratic participation. Unelected judges can serve democracy—judicial review is consistent with popular sovereignty—when they strike down laws that "impede the democratic process,"[15] that limit citizens' political participation. For example, Ely argues that judges may legitimately overturn laws that discriminate against so-called "minorities," that place unreasonable limits on popular assembly, or that make it unnecessarily burdensome for people to vote.[16] In all these cases judges would be acting to open up closed channels of popular participation and making it more likely that the will of the people will prevail. Thus insofar as judicial review is confined to the defense of procedural or "participational" values there is, according to Ely, no inconsistency between judicial review and the fundamental principle of republican government, namely that people should be governed only by laws that (through their elected representatives) they impose on themselves.

The problem, however, is that Ely is able to reconcile judicial review and popular sovereignty only at the cost of an overly narrow scope of judicial review. The constitution guarantees any number of rights that are not (directly or obviously) participational—the right not to testify against oneself, the right not to be subject to unreasonable search and seizure, the right freely to exercise ones religion, perhaps the right to privacy, etc.—and Ely's participational defense of judicial review would appear to prevent judges from striking down laws that violate these non-participational rights, thus leaving them unprotected from the tyranny of an unprincipled majority. It is of course possible to respond to this danger with the argument that the rights to which I have just referred, as well as others, are ultimately essential for political participation—that they are, in effect, "participational" in an extended sense of that term—and should therefore be protected through judicial review. But the difficulty here is that, since virtually any right could be considered participational, we would be left with no effective way to delimit or justify the scope of judicial review. Moreover, in the name of "participation" more rights could be read into the constitution than are actually set forth in that document. For example, because gross economic inequality obviously impedes equal political participation, a court that was committed to enhancing participation could well conclude that laws permitting the unequal acquisition of wealth, e.g., laws that protect private property in the means of production, were unconstitutional. Equalizing the distribution of wealth might indeed be a desirable political outcome, but if we believe in democracy presumably we believe that this outcome should be produced by elected representatives of the people rather than by unelected judges.

The general point I am making is this: if we construe the meaning of "participation" strictly, then the scope of judicial review in the name of participation would be much too narrow, but if we construe it broadly then in the name of participation a court could claim an entirely unlimited scope for judicial review and effectively assume the role of policy-makers, that is, usurp the legislative function that ought properly be left to the people and or their elected representatives. Thus it seems to me Ely's "participationalism" is no more successful in reconciling judicial review with popular sovereignty than is Bork's originalism.

What Bork's and Ely's positions have in common—despite the obvious differences between them—is what Ingram calls a "backward-looking"[17] concept of democratic legitimation. That is, they both assume that the decision of the court is final and that a prior justification for its finality must be found. Bork finds this source to be the (publicly articulated) intentions of the framers: judicial review

is legitimate only if it is consistent with those intentions. Ely defines this source as democratic procedure: judicial review is legitimate only if it protects popular participation. It may be that if we think of democratic legitimation in this way there is no effective way to legitimate judicial review. If we assume that the decisions of the Court are final—a case of the will of unelected judges trumping the will of elected representatives—then we will inevitably conclude that these decisions are in tension with democracy, and will look for ways to reduce that tension by limiting the scope of judicial review. But limiting the scope of judicial review means limiting the ability of judges to protect *and* expand our rights in a way that reflects our developing moral sensibilities.

In contrast, what Ingram calls a "forward-looking"[18] concept of democratic legitimation might offer a more promising approach. If we think of the outcome of a judicial review as not a final, definitive result but rather a contribution to an ongoing democratic dialogue among judges, legislators, judicial scholars, the press, and the general public, then the legitimacy of the judicial outcome cannot be evaluated independently of the evaluation of this multifaceted democratic dialogue to which the judicial opinion is only one important contribution. This assumption of a dialogue between judges and other political actors implies, of course, that there is space for legislative and other democratic responses to the decisions of those judges, including amending the constitution, changing the composition of the court by the election of a President who is committed to that goal, publishing critiques of majority judicial opinions that give voice to the opinion of dissenting justices, demonstrating in front of the Supreme Court, etc. To the extent that this space exists and is occupied by people who listen to and perhaps even learn from each other, to the extent that judicial review helps to engender a robust and respectful conversation about how a society should be organized, judicial review can be considered to be consistent with, indeed to be an important contribution to, the democratic process. But this conclusion presupposes that we think of democracy as a process of society-wide *deliberation* rather than as a mere method of making decisions based on majority rule or the counting of votes. These conflicting conceptions of democracy are the subject of the next chapter.

Reframing Federalism

The Affordable Care Act (and Broccoli) in the Supreme Court

By Wendy K. Mariner, Leonard H. Glantz, and George J. Annas

The U.S. Supreme Court decision to uphold most of the Affordable Care Act (ACA), including the insurance-coverage requirement, allows historic reforms in the health care system to move forward.[12] Because the justices were split four to four on whether the ACA was constitutional, Chief Justice John Roberts was able to write the lead opinion that commanded five votes for whatever outcome he determined was constitutional. The chief justice's leadership in upholding almost all of the ACA was unanticipated, as was much of his legal reasoning. It was widely assumed that the interpretation of the Commerce Clause by the Court would determine whether the Constitution authorized Congress to require individuals to purchase a product from private companies, something Congress had never done before and, therefore, something the Court had never considered.[34] It was not surprising that the chief justice found no Commerce Clause authority for the individual mandate. The surprise was that he saved the individual mandate by determining that it was a constitutional tax. The chief justice received support for each of these conclusions from two different four-justice groups, sometimes referred to as the liberal and conservative wings of the Court. Perhaps most unexpected, seven justices voted to limit the power of the federal government to impose conditions on federal funding allocated to the states.

Direct Federal Regulation Under the Commerce Clause

The chief justice began his opinion by describing our federal system, underlining that the federal government possesses only limited powers—those listed or enumerated in the Constitution. Powers not granted to the federal government in the Constitution are retained by the states. In this case, the question was whether either the federal power to regulate commerce or the power to tax authorized specific provisions of the ACA.

The Commerce Clause has historically been interpreted as granting the federal government broad power to regulate matters of interstate commerce and activities that affect such commerce.[5] Examples include the regulation of drugs,[6] consumer products,[7] air and water pollution,[8] workplace safety,[9] and discrimination in employment.[10] Nonetheless, the chief justice concluded that the Commerce Clause did not include the power to impose a mandate on individuals to buy health insurance from a private company. Justices Antonin

Scalia, Anthony Kennedy, Clarence Thomas, and Samuel Alito, in a jointly written dissent, agreed with the chief justice regarding the limitations of the Commerce Clause.

In the majority view on this issue, the power of the federal government to require or regulate behavior applies only to people who are actively engaged in commerce. As the chief justice put it, "The Framers gave Congress the power to *regulate* commerce, not to *compel* it. ..."[1] (italics in original). These justices accepted the argument that individuals who are not currently seeking care or under the care of physicians or other health professionals "are not currently engaged in any commercial activity involving health care." They rejected the argument by the government that the fact that virtually everyone is or will at some point be in the health care market empowers Congress to regulate how they pay for their care. Instead, the chief justice distinguished the health insurance market from the health care market, concluding that they "involve different transactions, entered into at different times, with different providers."[1] He concluded, "The individual mandate forces individuals into commerce precisely because they elected to refrain from commercial activity. Such a law cannot be sustained under a clause authorizing Congress to regulate Commerce.'"[1]

The decisive issue for these five justices was their view of federalism, specifically how to distinguish federal authority to regulate commerce from the inherent authority of the state ("police power") to directly regulate individuals, such as by requiring immunizations and school attendance. If the Commerce Clause allowed the federal government to regulate people who are not engaged in commerce, they worried, then the federal government would have the same power that states have to regulate individual behavior, because almost anything that anyone does or does not do can affect the national economy. Congress can regulate a great deal of what people do, but these five justices drew the line at inactivity, lest the Commerce Clause "give Congress the same license to regulate what we do not do, fundamentally changing the relation between the citizen and the Federal Government. ... That is not the country the Framers of our Constitution envisioned."[1] In the chief justice's words, "Every day individuals do not do an infinite number of things. ... Any police power to regulate individuals as such, as opposed to their activities, remains vested in the states."[1]

Justice Ruth Bader Ginsburg dissented from the Commerce Clause ruling. The Ginsburg opinion was joined by Justices Sonia Sotomayor, Stephen Breyer, and Elena Kagan, together comprising the remaining four justices on the Court. They accepted the argument of the government that health insurance is simply a method of paying for health care, along with self-payment (or self-insurance) and reliance on charity.[11] Virtually everyone in the country uses health care,[12] so they are necessarily health care consumers. More than 86% of national personal health care expenditures are paid through insurance.[13] Thus, Justice Ginsburg concluded, the mandate regulates people who are or will inevitably be active in the health care market and Congress can regulate the terms on which they pay for their care: "Persons subject to the mandate must now pay for medical care in advance (instead of at the point of service) and through insurance (instead of out of pocket)."[1] The Ginsburg opinion characterized the uninsured as getting a "free ride,"[1] a term often used as a major justification for the individual mandate.[14]

Justice Ginsburg concluded that health care and its financing were unique and therefore found that Commerce Clause authority for the individual mandate would not result in an unrestrained expansion of federal power. She specifically rejected the conclusion that finding the individual mandate valid under the Commerce Clause would mean that the federal government could require people to purchase healthy vegetables, including broccoli, which she characterized as "the broccoli horrible."[1] She argued that broccoli purchases could be easily distinguished and that the claim that broccoli or vegetable purchases would have a substantial effect on health care costs required a "chain of inferences" that previous Commerce Clause cases had rejected.[15]

Federal Power to Tax

Chief Justice Roberts saved the individual mandate by finding that the payment for noncompliance is a tax, not a penalty, that Congress has authority to impose under the Taxing Power, an enumerated power distinct from the Commerce Clause.[16] With the Ginsburg opinion, the chief justice had a five-to-four majority for this conclusion.

The ACA calls the payment a "penalty" for not having health insurance, but the Court is not bound by this label. The chief justice reasoned that the penalty functions like a tax. The ACA does not prescribe any punishment for failing to have coverage. Instead, the Internal Revenue Service (IRS) collects the payment with federal income taxes. The IRS is authorized to withhold the payment from any refund due the taxpayer, but it is barred from imposing criminal prosecution or additional penalties for nonpayment. Moreover, the payment amount is a small percentage of taxable income and is capped at a relatively low-level health insurance premium.[17] Thus, the failure to have coverage is not unlawful; it is simply taxable.

The joint dissent argued that the Court should take Congress at its word in calling the payment a "penalty," asserting that upholding the mandate as a tax amounted to rewriting, rather than interpreting, the statute.[1]

Indirect Federal Regulation Through Conditional Federal Spending

The ACA amends the Medicaid statute by adding a new category of eligible recipients: persons younger than 65 years of age with incomes below 133% of the federal poverty level ($14,170 for an individual and $23,050 for a family of four).[18] Existing categories were narrower and more specific, such as families with children, pregnant women, and Supplemental Security Income recipients, with varied income ceilings for different groups. The federal government will pay 100% of the cost of the newly eligible beneficiaries through 2016 and 90% after 2020, instead of the 50% to 83% that it now pays

for currently eligible categories. One of the possible sanctions for a state that does not comply with the new Medicaid eligibility rules is forfeiture of federal funding for the entire Medicaid program in the state.

In the most unexpected result, seven justices concluded that the new category of eligibility for Medicaid in the ACA could not be imposed on the states as a condition of continuing to receive federal Medicaid funds for existing state Medicaid programs. The Spending Power of Congress is an important source of power in areas in which the federal government does not have direct authority.[16] For example, although Congress has no constitutional authority to set a national minimum drinking age (or to require states to enact state laws), it has restricted eligibility for full federal highway funding to states that have laws that set the minimum drinking age at 21 years.[19] Because states are free to accept or reject federal funds and the conditions that come with them, the Court has never found that a condition on federal funding is an impingement on state sovereignty.

The Court, nonetheless, agreed with the argument of the 26 states that challenged this provision of the ACA, that, in practice, the states have no choice but to accept the "new," expanded eligibility category and amend state Medicaid laws accordingly. The Court reasoned that if a state refused to accept this "new" Medicaid expansion, the federal government could "penalize" the state by terminating its participation in — and all federal funding for — the "old" Medicaid program. The Court found that this "penalty" made the offer of new federal funding "coercive," such that the federal government was "forcing" the states to accept it. In the opinion of the Court, federal coercion of states violated the core principle of federalism.

The chief justice also emphasized that the Medicaid expansion was intended to complete the construction of an overarching federal program: "It is no longer a program to care for the neediest among us, but rather an element of a comprehensive national plan to provide universal health insurance coverage."[1] Medicare covers persons 65 years of age or older, and the ACA will allow all those younger than 65 years of age to buy federally regulated health insurance through a federally regulated exchange, with federal subsidies for those with incomes between 100% and 400% of the federal poverty level. The Medicaid expansion, if adopted by all states, would bring almost everyone into a federally regulated system, something that both the chief justice and joint-dissent justices appear to consider objectionable.

Federalism

The three opinions present strikingly different views of the authority of the federal government in relation to individuals and to the states. The chief justice and the joint dissent emphasized that the Constitution grants Congress only specifically enumerated powers, leaving all other sovereign powers to the states. They focused on how the Framers might have understood "commerce," and the joint dissent quoted definitions from 18th-century dictionaries.[1] The joint dissent argued that if Congress could regulate people who do nothing other than "breathe in and out," then it becomes, in the words of Alexander Hamilton in The Federalist, No. 33, "the hideous monster whose devouring jaws … spare neither sex nor age, nor high nor low, nor sacred nor profane."[1] Their language suggests alarm at the prospect of an all-powerful national government — alarm that they believe the Framers shared.

In contrast, the Ginsburg opinion viewed the federal government as one designed to craft solutions to national problems that the states cannot solve by themselves. The joint dissent disparaged this view as treating "the Constitution as though it is an enumeration of those problems that the Federal Government can address,"[1] rather than as a document that grants the federal government only specific, enumerated powers. The Ginsburg opinion replied that their views "bear a disquieting resemblance to those long-overruled decisions" of the Court that struck down federal legislation from the early 20th century requiring minimum wages and maximum hours for employees.[120] The different perspectives are reminiscent of disagreements over New Deal legislation. This seems to be why the Ginsburg opinion compared the ACA to the Social Security Act, noting that although Social Security

was unprecedented when first enacted, the Court found it to be a permissible exercise of the power of Congress to tax and spend for the general welfare.[21] They also expressed a disagreement over the nature of health care, which Justice Ginsburg argued is unique and critical to life and which the majority of justices saw as just another market good.

Questions The Court Did Not Answer

By limiting the power of Congress to directly regulate individuals under the Commerce Clause, while allowing Congress to indirectly regulate individuals by taxation, the Court permits the federal government to influence individuals by taxing them for not having health insurance. This is now a constitutional way to regulate people who are doing nothing. It is also precisely the type of expansion of federal power that the chief justice said would redefine the relationship of the federal government to individuals. Yet nothing in the opinions appears to limit the use of this power. Given the number of things that "people do not do," the taxing power is now remarkably broad. The chief justice even suggested that a $50 tax on homeowners without energy-efficient windows would be a permissible tax.[1] He did not address whether a $15,000 tax on the uninsured would be permissible or would be an unjustified penalty. Future questions may include whether a federal tax on failing to use public transportation or failing to maintain a normal body-mass index would be constitutional. As for the "broccoli horrible" hypothetical, this opinion arguably supports congressional power to tax people for not buying broccoli.

The most unsettling aspect of the Court decision is the novel limit on the authority of the federal government to impose conditions on how its money is used. The Court had never before found a federal spending program to be coercive, and most scholars believed coercion to be an illusory standard that the Court would not apply. It is remarkable that the Court could conclude that states have no choice but to accept the new Medicaid conditions with their Medicaid funding. Although federal funding provides an incentive for states to participate in a federal program, it is hardly a "gun to the head," as the chief justice called it.[1] The ACA made the new Medicaid funding generous in order to entice the states to participate, and Congress expected all states to do so. However, that expectation was based on the fact that the offer was so generous that no rational decision maker would refuse it, not because it was coercive.

Because the coercion rationale seems so weak, it is perhaps not surprising that the opinions fail to explain what counts as coercion. The leading case on the Spending Power, *South Dakota v. Dole*, held that it was not coercive for the federal government to withhold 5% of federal highway funds from states that failed to enact a state law raising the minimum age for drinking alcohol to 21 years.[19] In the ACA case, the Court found that it was coercive to withhold 100% of federal Medicaid funds. However, the Court did not attempt to draw any principled line between coercive and noncoercive payments, so it is unclear whether withholding anything between 5% and 100% of funding could qualify as unconstitutionally forcing states to accept a federal program.

Moreover, although the Court found that it is coercive to make the funding of an old program conditional on the adoption of a new program, it did not provide a meaningful standard for determining when a statutory amendment might be considered a "new" federal funding program, rather than an "amendment" of a previous program. The chief justice said that "a shift in kind, not merely degree" creates a new program.[1] The expansion of Medicaid in the ACA altered both the categories of individuals and the income level that qualified for eligibility. Is a change in both required to constitute a new program, or does only one suffice? Federal programs, including Medicaid, are often altered as experience suggests needed improvements.[22] At this point, no one can confidently predict how to distinguish a new program from an amendment. Because so many federally funded health, education, and housing programs depend on the use of the conditional spending power, this ruling may encourage opponents of these programs to challenge new conditions in court.

Implications

Remarkably, given all the commentary about the importance of this case to the future authority of the federal government, none of the opinions made any attempt to limit the currently broad power to regulate interstate commerce that the federal government currently possesses. Rather, the Court seems to have expanded federal power to tax people for "doing nothing," the primary fear that brought this case to court. It is hard to believe that this power is as expansive as the chief justice suggested, but his opinion did not discuss limitations. The current taxing power certainly would permit an increased income or payroll tax to expand Medicare or create a new federal substitute for Medicaid. However, the limits of the taxing power probably will not be tested soon. It is the power that Congress is least likely to exercise in an era of widespread antipathy to tax increases.

The lack of health care for the poor is a national problem that the federal government was trying to fix and one that only the federal government can fix. States cannot solve national problems. With health insurance exchanges open to all legal residents and Medicare providing coverage for elderly adults, the addition of all low-income, nonelderly adults to Medicaid by the ACA would give virtually the entire population access to affordable health insurance. The decision of the Court to allow the states to reject the Medicaid expansion, however, creates a substantial gap in the comprehensive-coverage design of the ACA. States such as Florida and Texas, whose governors have already pledged to reject the Medicaid expansion, have large uninsured populations.[23] Such states may leave their uninsured populations doubly burdened. They will deny impoverished citizens the coverage that the federal government was willing to finance and also leave many (who are above the tax-filing threshold) subject to the new tax on the uninsured. The ACA does not provide tax subsidies to those below 100% of the poverty level, because they were expected to be covered by Medicaid. Their impoverished legal residents must continue to rely on the charity of safety-net providers, which is the very problem that the ACA was designed to solve.

The broad significance of this case can be found in the justices' views of the proper roles of the state and federal governments and not just in what they ruled about the ACA itself. The immediate effect is to return the constitutionally blessed ACA to the political realm. It is now up to Congress, the individual states, and especially the next president to determine the fate of the ACA. Because the case was decided by the vote of a single justice, however, the future of federal involvement in health care may also depend on the views of the next justice appointed to the Court.

CHAPTER 8

Civil Liberties

Chapter 8 Vignette

By Jennifer Byrne

In March 2006, seven Westboro Baptist Church members traveled more than 1,000 miles to protest at the funeral of 20-year-old Lance Corporal, Matthew Snyder, who was killed while serving in Iraq. They carried signs that said things like, "You're going to hell," "Thank God for dead soldiers," and "Thank God for 9/11." What later ensued was a 4-year legal battle waged by Albert Snyder, the father of Matthew Snyder, to recover monetary damages for the harm that the Kansas-based group had inflicted through their actions. The Westboro Baptist Church stages protests at military funerals to deliver the message that God is angry with America because of its tolerance of homosexuality. But, were their actions also considered speech, and therefore protected under the 1st Amendment of the U.S. Constitution? Snyder argued that, though he was suing for millions of dollars, his main goal was to silence the group. Is this constitutional?

Snyder argued that he became very depressed after the funeral and that it would have been better if the Westboro protestors had taken a gun and shot him, because at least the wound would heal over time. Their words, however, were always with him.[1] A lower district court jury awarded Snyder 5 million dollars, but this was overturned upon appeal. The final decision was up the U.S. Supreme Court, who in an eight to one decision ruled against Snyder, and in favor of the members of the Westboro Baptist Church. According to the Supreme Court, the 1st Amendment protects the members from torts of the infliction of emotional distress, even offensive and hurtful speech … but why? Part of the decision rests on whether the disputed speech is of a public or private concern. Signs displayed at the protest that carried messages about God being angry with America because of its political and moral character highlight issues of public concern and also bring attention to broad issues, such as homosexuality in the military. While some of the signs were specifically directed at Matthew Snyder, Justice Roberts, who was writing for the majority, argued that the majority of the signs centered on broader issues, and thus, the totality of the protest was characterized as one of "public concern." Roberts did not, however, suggest that there was a specific number or percentage of the signs that must focus on broader issues to make the "dominant thrust" of the speech one of public concern. The lone dissenting justice, Samuel Alito, found it troubling that there were no clear guidelines established and that the signs that were considered defamatory should not have been protected just because they were amongst signs that were protected.

The other issue in this case was that of the captive audience, arguing that since Snyder had to attend his son's funeral and it was too late to move it, that he had no choice but to attend the funeral and, therefore, the protest. Where there is a captive audience, speech is less likely to be protected. The Court has ruled in the past that for this reason, it is constitutional to restrict protests in front of private residences. But in this instance, the majority of the justices found that because the protest took place on a public street, with the signs displayed on private lands, it could be considered constitutional. The members of the Westboro Baptist Church also made sure to stay more than 1,000 feet away from the funeral, which is a typical distance mandated in many states for protestors to keep from a person or event. In fact, Snyder only saw the tops of the signs while driving to the funeral, and only learned of their content later that evening from a news broadcast. However, he was clearly affected by this knowledge, suffering from depression and lack of concentration. Snyder argued that it would be common sense to make a free-speech exception for funerals, but in the end, the Supreme Court disagreed. Snyder's response was one of disbelief and disgust, contending that Westboro members could now do whatever they pleased, and there was not a damn thing anyone could do about it. Two of the leaders of the church, sisters Margie and Shirley Phelps (Margie was actually the attorney for the Church in the legal battles) had a response full of gloat, promising to quadruple their protests and taking it is a sign that the destruction of the country was fast approaching. In spite of this, the justices suggested that even speech that we may not like, that we find offensive or even hurtful, may be protected.[2]

Endnotes

1. http://yalelawjournal.org/the-yale-law-journal-pocket-part/supreme-court/snyder-v.-phelps,-the-supreme-court's-speech%11tort-jurisprudence,-and-normative-considerations/, last accessed on November 14, 2013.
2. http://www.youtube.com/watch?v=JV2bHTVcNcw, last accessed on November 14, 2013.

Protecting Civil Liberties

By Matthew Kerbel

Introduction

Some of the most important and controversial questions debated in our political system involve matters of personal liberty. Although few of us question the need to protect individual freedom, actually doing so sometimes requires holding our noses and permitting behaviors we find distasteful or reprehensible. It's not easy to stand by and allow someone to make hostile statements aimed directly at our religious or ethnic group, for instance, much less stand up for their right to do so. You might even say it goes against human nature to defend those who attack us. That's why many people object to the specific liberties people are allowed, even if we agree in the abstract on the importance of maintaining them.

At the most fundamental level, there is little debate about the value of protecting **civil liberties**. The Constitution very clearly restricts government from denying us the liberty to express ourselves, congregate, worship, and protest, affording us the freedom to speak out against the government if we so desire. Remember, the authors of the Constitution were concerned that government be strong enough to protect the weakest among us but not so strong as to overwhelm personal liberty. That's why civil liberties are expressed in the Constitution as actions denied to government.

Most of these liberties were added to the Constitution in the **Bill of Rights**. Toward the end of the Philadelphia convention, George Mason of Virginia moved to include a Bill of Rights in the original document, offering to write one in short order. The delegates were fatigued, however, and in the case of some southerners, concerned that a written declaration of human liberty would conflict with their position on slavery. So, they opted to rely on the protections already included in state constitutions and not include a Bill of Rights in the final document.[1]

The new Constitution was rapidly amended to include a Bill of Rights as a political maneuver to win support for ratification. Table 14.1 is summarizing the contents of the Bill of Rights. Before we move on, take a minute and review the table as a refresher on the range of liberties that are protected from government interference by the Bill of Rights.

Table 14.1. The Bill of Rights

First Amendment	The First Amendment prevents government from interfering with several key personal freedoms, including the freedom to worship, speak, and assemble peacefully. It also prevents the government from restricting freedom of the press and the freedom to petition government.
Second Amendment	The Second Amendment protects the right to bear arms.
Third and Fourth Amendments	The Third and Fourth Amendments provide a right to privacy from government interference. The Third Amendment prevents government from forcing citizens to house soldiers during peacetime—addressing one of the complaints the colonists had against the British. The Fourth Amendment protects against unreasonable searches and seizures of property or personal effects.
Fifth through Eighth Amendments	The Fifth through Eighth Amendments establish a host of protections for individuals accused of a crime. These include the right not to be tried twice for the same crime, the right to be indicted by a grand jury before being tried for a capital crime, the right not to be forced to testify against yourself, the right to due process of law, and the right not to have property confiscated by government without compensation (all in the Fifth Amendment); and the right to a speedy and impartial trial, the right to be informed of charges against you, the right to call and confront witnesses, and the right to a lawyer (all in the Sixth Amendment); and the right to a jury in civil trials (Seventh Amendment); the right to be free from excessive bail and from the infliction of cruel and unusual punishments (Eighth Amendment).
Ninth and Tenth Amendments	The Ninth Amendment is a safety net establishing that any rights not specifically mentioned in the first eight amendments are not necessarily denied. The Tenth Amendment establishes that any powers not granted to the federal government or prohibited to the states are reserved for the states.

Due Process

The full range of civil liberties provided constitutional protection includes the important right to **due process**, or protection against arbitrary actions of the government. The Fifth Amendment states that no person shall "be deprived of life, liberty, or property, without due process of law." The Fourteenth Amendment echoes this language and applies it to the states. The presumption behind due process is that conflict between individuals and the government is inevitable and should be resolved through a defined set of legal procedures, where the rules are written to protect the individual from government power.[2]

Some of these requirements are set down in the Constitution itself, while others appear in the Bill of Rights or have been established by the Supreme Court and applied to the states through interpretation of the due process clause of the Fourteenth Amendment. They are outlined in Table 14.2.

You can think of due process as establishing the groundwork for resolving conflicts and protecting civil liberties, based on the presumption that individuals accused of a crime are innocent until proven guilty by the state. The theory is that by following clearly defined and evenly applied procedures, guilt can be assessed while the power of the state is held in check. Of course, this means that in some cases, guilty individuals will be set free because their rights were (purposely or inadvertently) violated at or before trial. This is the consequence of a fundamental choice made by the Constitution's authors: that it is better to let the guilty occasionally go free in the interest of protecting personal liberties than to inadvertently—or purposely—condemn the innocent.

In practice, the constitutionally defined system for a timely, impartial jury trial where defendants have a clear and full set of rights contrasts with the way justice is handled in many courtrooms. Because due process is slow, and courtrooms across the country are overburdened with cases, court officers with nominally adversarial roles will conspire in ways that move defendants through the system without time-consuming trials. Pressure to process a heavy caseload motivates judges to look for shortcuts. Prosecuting attorneys are evaluated for the cases they win and often jump at the chance to avoid the uncertainty of a trial. Defense attorneys, particularly those

Table 14.2. Due Process

Item	Key Term	Constitutional Origin	What This Means
Right to a writ *of habeas corpus*	**writ of *habeas corpus*:** From the Latin for "you have the body," *habeas corpus* puts the burden on the courts to demonstrate that a defendant's rights have not been violated prior to sentencing. People who believe they have been imprisoned against their constitutional rights have the privilege to petition for their release.	Article 1, Section 9	Before you can be sent to prison, the government has the burden of assuring that your rights were not violated during trial. *Habeas corpus* gives you the right to petition the court if you believe you have been wrongfully imprisoned. It may only be suspended in extreme cases of domestic rebellion or foreign invasion.
Freedom from bills of attainder	**bills of attainder:** Declarations of guilt by legislative decree without benefit of a trial.	Article 1, Section 9	Congress or other legislatures cannot find you guilty of a crime by passing legislation that convicts you.
Freedom from ex *post facto laws*	*ex post facto* **laws:** From the Latin for "after the fact," legislation that makes something a crime that was legal when it occurred.	Article 1, Section 9	If the drinking age was 18 before it was raised to 21, anyone who purchased alcohol legally at age 18 cannot subsequently, through legislation, be found guilty of a crime.
Protection against unreasonable searches and seizures		Fourth Amendment	You cannot be arrested or your person or possessions searched without a court warrant. Note the *unreasonable* qualifier: courts have determined it is *reasonable* for airport guards to frisk you at security checkpoints or for state troopers to search your car for drugs if you're pulled over for speeding.
Protection in the form of the exclusionary rule	**exclusionary rule:** To protect against unreasonable searches and seizures, the Supreme Court has established that evidence obtained illegally is not admissible in court.	Judicial Interpretation	To reinforce the protection against unreasonable searches and seizures, the Supreme Court ruled that evidence acquired in violation of Fourth Amendment protections is inadmissible in court.
Grand jury indictments for capital crimes		Fifth Amendment	The protection from being charged with a capital or "infamous" crime without an indictment from a grand jury is a way of dispersing the power to prosecute. It places the ability to charge someone with a serious crime in the hands of a jury of citizens.
Protection against double jeopardy	**double jeopardy:** Protection against the state using its power to repeatedly prosecute someone until the person is convicted. Double jeopardy precludes the prosecution of someone for the same crime in the same jurisdiction more than once.	Fifth Amendment	No one may be tried twice in the same jurisdiction for the same crime. However, someone who commits a crime that violates federal and state law can be tried in both jurisdictions, and someone who violates criminal and civil law can be tried in criminal and civil courts.
Protection against self-incrimination		Fifth Amendment	No one may be compelled to take the witness stand in a trial and testify against oneself, or confess to a crime involuntarily.

Miranda rights	Miranda Rights: The Court requirement, following a judgment in the case *Miranda v. Arizona* (1966), that apprehended individuals know and understand that they have a right against self-incrimination and a right to be represented by an attorney.	Judicial Interpretation	Before questioning may begin, arresting officers must inform suspects that they have the right to remain silent; that if they speak, anything they say may be used against them in court; and that they have a right to have a lawyer present during interrogation.
Right to a speedy public jury trial		Sixth Amendment	You have the right to a speedy and public trial in criminal cases by an impartial jury in the place where the crime was committed. This keeps a prosecutor or judge from convicting someone unilaterally.
Right to be informed of a charge against you		Sixth Amendment	This includes the right to confront your accuser and to present witnesses in your defense.
Right to an attorney	*Gideon v. Wainwright*: The 1963 Supreme Court case that established the right to have an attorney appointed at no charge by the court to defendants unable to afford representation. It was brought by Clarence Earl Gideon, who was sentenced to five years in prison for breaking into a pool hall. From prison, Gideon filed a *habeas corpus* petition, claiming his right to an attorney was violated because he was forced by poverty to represent himself at his trial.	Sixth Amendment	Originally, the Constitution simply gave defendants the right to counsel, but it was of little practical use to the vast majority who could not afford to hire a lawyer. Following the 1963 case *Gideon v. Wainwright*, the Supreme Court ruled that an attorney must be provided to anyone who cannot afford one.
Protection against excessive bail		Eighth Amendment	This precludes incarceration prior to conviction and allows the accused the freedom to prepare a defense.
Protection against cruel and unusual punishment		Eighth Amendment	Although the Constitution does not specify what makes a punishment cruel and unusual, the Court has interpreted it to mean arbitrary punishment, punishment disproportionate to the crime committed, or torture.

appointed by the court, tend to be overburdened and wish to avoid the work of a trial. Both can advance their professional interests by striking a plea bargain with the defendant. Demystifying Government: How the Justice System Often Works discusses plea bargaining, which requires that a defendant waive his or her due process rights.

Due Process and Capital Punishment

The death penalty is one place where the protection against cruel and unusual punishment has been controversial. Although the Court has established the constitutionality of capital punishment, the issue continues to divide Americans as much today as it did early in our history.

Some opponents contend that it is an inhumane violation of fundamental civil liberties for the state to take a life under any circumstances. They bolster their argument by pointing to economic and racial disparities in who is sentenced to death, claiming

DEMYSTIFYING GOVERNMENT

HOW THE JUSTICE SYSTEM OFTEN WORKS

In a **plea bargain**, defendants plead guilty to a lesser crime than the one for which they have been charged and accept a lesser sentence than what they might have expected had they been convicted on the original charge. Instead of a trial, everyone moves right to sentencing. Plea bargains are the result of negotiations where, typically, each attorney tells his or her version of the story, with prosecutors pointing out the most serious facts of the case and defense attorneys minimizing the incident. Sometimes, judges enter the negotiations and explicitly state the sentence they intend to impose. A compromise is hammered out, and if the defendant accepts it, the deed is done. Most felony and misdemeanor cases end in guilty pleas, many of which are the direct result of negotiation.[T1]

Plea bargains serve the interests of the court officers, but we can ask how well they serve the interests of defendants and society as a whole. Because defendants waive their due process rights in accepting a plea bargain, there is no impartial finding of guilt or innocence. In a sense, plea bargaining turns the assumptions behind due process upside-down, presuming guilt on the part of defendants and foregoing the opportunity to permit them to wage a defense. It's possible to imagine innocent people being pressured into accepting a guilty plea by busy defense attorneys who convince them not to take their chances at trial. Maybe it's easier to imagine guilty parties getting a lighter sentence than they would face if they had been convicted in a trial. Does either outcome seem just to you?

most death-row inmates are poor individuals lacking in funds to pay expensive lawyers who could have effectively saved their lives through more capable representation. Most of these individuals are African American. The American Civil Liberties Union counts, between 1973 and 2002, 178 African Americans put to death for killing a white person and 12 whites put to death for killing an African American person.[3]

Opponents also argue that the death penalty is carried out in a capricious way that depends largely on the state where you were convicted.

Nonetheless, the death penalty continues to receive strong popular support, either because it is viewed as just or as a deterrent to crime, or both. Take a few minutes to read about the history and background of capital punishment Issue: Capital Punishment, and consider the arguments made by supporters and opponents.

Religious Freedom

Americans are a religious people. A 2007 study by the Pew Forum on Religion and Public Life found that 83% of Americans claim a religious identity, and a comparable percentage feel religion plays an important role in their lives. Slightly more than half attend religious services at least once a month[4] The United States also boasts a great deal of religious diversity, with Americans claiming to follow over a dozen religions and over twenty-five denominations.[5] Such a wide range of affiliations can cause trouble when religious practices and customs come into conflict with each other and, at times, with nonreligious social values. Constitutional assurances of free religious worship, widely believed to be absolute, have at times been curtailed by the Court to provide for the rights of those opposed to public displays of religious expression or to uphold conflicting social standards.

The First Amendment makes twin statements about religious freedom, which offer two distinct constitutional protections: "Congress shall make no law respecting an establishment of religion, or prohibiting the free exercise thereof." The first of these, the **establishment clause**, is the basis for the widely discussed separation between church and state. The second, typically called the **free exercise clause**, restricts government from interfering with private religious practices. Both of these clauses have been open to interpretation and therefore have been a source of controversy.

No Establishment of Religion

In the most fundamental sense, the establishment clause precludes the government from sanctioning a national religion, although it is often taken to mean much more. Thomas Jefferson wrote that the establishment clause built "a wall of separation between church and State." In *Everson v. Board of Education* (1947), Justice Hugo Black elaborated in great detail:

> The "establishment of religion" clause of the First Amendment means at least

ISSUE

CAPITAL PUNISHMENT

In January 2003, as one of his final official acts, Illinois Governor George Ryan commuted the death sentences of all 167 inmates on death row to life in prison, saying the system by which people are sentenced to death was "arbitrary and capricious—and therefore immoral."[T3] The sweeping move—unprecedented in its scope—followed an exhaustive study of Illinois death row cases that revealed, among other things, that people had been sentenced to death on the basis of questionable evidence, and that African Americans were far more likely to receive the death penalty than whites. Capital punishment opponents were overjoyed. Victims' rights groups were shocked and appalled.[T4]

Governor Ryan's action was one of the more recent turns in America's conflicted history with capital punishment. Through the nineteenth and twentieth centuries, as western countries like England, West Germany, Italy, Switzerland, Norway, Sweden, and Denmark abolished the death penalty, many American states vacillated between abolishing it and reinstating it. The number of executions in the United States plummeted in the 1960s,

as the American public, strongly supportive of the death penalty for much of the twentieth century, became less sympathetic. Then, in the 1972 case *Furman v. Georgia,* a fragmented Supreme Court (nine separate opinions were issued) ruled all existing death penalty laws to be unconstitutional, saying they were instituted arbitrarily and capriciously.[T5]

The ruling came at a time when public opinion was beginning to swing back toward support of the death penalty, and it caused a backlash. Many states moved quickly to enact new capital punishment statutes. Within four years of the *Furman* verdict, a more conservative Supreme Court reinstated the death penalty in the case of *Gregg v. Georgia* (1976), ruling that capital punishment does not violate the Eighth Amendment's ban on cruel and unusual punishment and that statutory corrections made by Georgia and other states satisfactorily addressed the inequities that the Court had expressed concern about in its earlier ruling.[T6] But *Gregg* didn't put an end to questions about how equitably the death penalty was imposed. In fact, inequities in meting out capital punishment were the reason Governor

Ryan commuted all Illinois death sentences twenty-seven years later.

In the wake of the *Gregg* decision, the number of inmates on death row has grown steadily, and although the number of executions carried out has been relatively modest in comparison, they grew from one in 1977 to ninety-eight in 1999.[17]

However, subsequent rulings have placed restric tions on how the death penalty may be implemented. *Coker v. Georgia* (1977) banned capital punishment for people convicted of rape. More recently, *Atkins v. Virginia* (2002) did the same for mentally retarded criminals.[18]

Throughout America's uneasy history with the death penalty, the positions taken by opponents and advocates have remained remarkably consistent. Opponents point to what they see as a double standard in the application of the death penalty to rich and poor, white and nonwhite; and despite the opinion of the Court in *Gregg v. Georgia,* consider it cruel and unusual punishment. Supporters regard it as an appropriate penalty for the most violent crimes, a form of justice for crime victims, and a deterrent to violence.

Arguments in Support

Death penalty supporters make the following arguments:

- It deters crime. If people know they face execution, they are less likely to engage in violence.
- It's justice. The death penalty is a punishment of last resort and used only where the most horrendous crimes have been committed. In these cases, it is appropriate for guilty parties to pay with their lives.
- It's equitable. Any past inequities in the implementation of the death penalty have been sorted out, according to the Supreme Court in *Gregg v. Georgia*.

- Victims have rights. People on death row have committed the most gruesome crimes imaginable. The death penalty permits closure for the victims they left behind.

Arguments Against

Opponents of the death penalty contend:

- It's not a deterrent to violent crime. There is no clear-cut evidence that people will think about the repercussions of committing a capital offense.
- It's vengeance. Murdering someone who has committed even the most horrendous crime does not bring the victim back to life or set right the wrong that has been committed.
- It's inequitable. There is a far greater likelihood of being put to death if you're poor, nonwhite, or live in Texas.
- Everyone has rights. The beauty of the American system of justice is that it protects the rights of people who have done unjustifiable things. For the state to put someone to death, regardless of the circumstances, is the ultimate denial of individual rights.

My Opinion

When considering your opinion on the death penalty, think the history of the issue and the arguments supporting and opposing it. In particular, ask yourself if you believe the death penalty:

- Does or does not deter crime.
- Is justice or vengeance.
- Is equitably or inequitably imposed.
- Justly accounts for the rights of victims or unjustly denies the rights of the accused

this: Neither a state nor the Federal Government can set up a church. Neither can pass laws which aid one religion, aid all religions, or prefer one religion over another. Neither can force nor influence a person to go to or to remain away from church against his will or force him to profess a belief or disbelief in any religion. ... No tax in any amount, large or small, can be levied to support any religious activities or institutions, whatever they may be called, or whatever form they may adopt to teach or practice religion. Neither a state nor the Federal Government can, openly or secretly, participate in the affairs of any religious organizations or groups, and vice versa.[6]

At the same time, the phrase "In God We Trust" appears on the quarter you have in your pocket. A chaplain offers a prayer to start congressional sessions. In fact, the *Everson* decision, in which Justice Black reaffirms Jefferson's "wall of separation," upheld the right of the State of New Jersey to provide public bus service to students of a Catholic school, saying the First Amendment intended government to be neutral—not adversarial— in matters of religion. These are places where religion mixes with government that fall short of establishment. Depending on how thick you feel the wall of separation should be, they may also be points of controversy.

No doubt, the place where the barrier between church and state is put to the greatest test is over the issue of whether prayer should be permitted in public school. It's an emotional concern that moves people on both sides of the question. After reading about the history and background of school prayer in Issue: School Prayer, consider the arguments made by supporters and opponents and decide whether you believe religious freedom is the freedom to permit prayer in school or the freedom from prayer in school.

Free Exercise of Religion

The idea behind the free exercise clause is that the practice of individual worship should be free from government interference. This is fairly easy to do when religious worship doesn't violate other social values, but since that's not always the case, free exercise has been a matter of dispute over the years, as the Court has held that the free exercise of religion is not absolute.

An early battle of great significance took place between federal authorities and the Mormon Church over the practice of polygamy in the Utah territory. The conflict dated to an 1852 pronouncement by Brigham Young, prophet of the Church of Jesus Christ of Latter-Day Saints, that Mormons would practice polygamy or plural marriage as a part of their religious beliefs. This position enraged official Washington, which found the whole idea of polygamy to be an abomination and criminalized it. The dispute ended up in the Supreme Court in 1878, in the case of *Reynolds v. United States.*[7]

The Mormon Church expected the Court to uphold its right to free exercise of religion as expressed in the Constitution. They were wrong. The Court contended that the Constitution did not define the term "religion," and proceeded to offer its own explanation of the concept, distinguishing between principles and actions. Under this interpretation, the First Amendment protected religious beliefs but not behaviors taken in the name of religion that violated the law. Writing for the Court, Chief Justice Waite asked rhetorically,

Suppose one believed that human sacrifices were a necessary part of religious worship, would it be seriously contended that the civil government under which he lived could not interfere to prevent a sacrifice? Or if a wife religiously believed it was her duty to burn herself upon the funeral pile of her dead husband, would it be beyond the power of the civil government to prevent her carrying her belief into practice?[8]

ISSUE

SCHOOL PRAYER

In June 1998, the House of Representatives voted 224–203 to approve a "Religious Freedom Amendment" to the Constitution, permitting prayer in the nation's public schools. The amendment reads in part: "Neither the United States nor any State shall I establish any official religion, but the people's right to pray and to recognize their religious beliefs, heritage, or traditions on public property, including schools, shall not be infringed. Neither the United States nor any State shall require any person to join in prayer or other religious activity, prescribe school prayers, discriminate against religion, or deny equal access to a benefit on account of religion."

Because a constitutional amendment requires the approval of two-thirds of each house of Congress before it can go to the states for ratification, the amendment died. Buoyed by having won a simple majority, though, and bolstered by support from some organized religious groups, Oklahoma Republican Representative Ernest Istook reintroduced the measure the following year.[T10] It takes a lotto amend the Constitution, and the issue of school prayer is emotionally charged, but its advocates persevere.

Does religious freedom mean having the right to pray in public schools? Or does having religious freedom protect us from public school prayer? The way you answer this question is partly a matter of what you value, and partly a matter of how you interpret the constitutional separation of church and state.

Some view religion as something the government should nurture and support on an even-handed basis, without establishing a national religion or requiring people to participate in prayer. They see this as a tolerant interpretation of religious freedom consistent with the original intent of the First Amendment.[T11] Others view religion as a private matter and understand the establishment clause in the First Amendment to be a statement of every individual's private right to worship or not to worship as he or she pleases. From this perspective, if a teacher leads a class in prayer, social and institutional pressures make it difficult for students who object to express their unwillingness to participate, effectively forcing them to pray against their First Amendment rights.[T12]

In recent years, the Supreme Court has sided with the latter interpretation of the First Amendment. In the 1962 case *Engle v. Vitale,* the Court ruled that the New York State Board of Regents could not give public school teachers the option of leading classes in a voluntary, nondenominational prayer, which read, "Almighty God, we acknowledge our dependence upon Thee, and we beg Thy blessings upon us, our parents, our teachers and our country."[T13] In the Court's opinion, any prayer, no matter how neutral, is a religious activity and violates the First Amendment.

The next year, the Court issued a pair of rulings that, together with *Engle v. Vitale,* established the legal framework for school prayer. The Court struck down a Pennsylvania law in *Abington Township School District v. Schempp* (1963) that required the school day to start with Bible readings and the recital of the Lord's Prayer. In the companion case *Murray v. Curlett* (1963), the Court struck down a similar Maryland law that required unison prayer and Bible reading in public school.[T14]

However, none of these cases made mention of voluntary private personal prayer in public schools, which remained constitutional, and in *the Schempp* decision the Court recognized the importance of teaching about religion in the context of history as part of a well-rounded public school education.

More recent Court decisions have interpreted religious freedom the same way. In 1985, the Court struck down an Alabama law in *Wallace v. Jaffree* that required the school day to begin with a moment of silent meditation or voluntary prayer, on the grounds that prayer, even if voluntary, has a religious purpose. In *Lee v. Weisman* (1992), the Court struck down the recital of a prayer at public school graduation ceremonies as a form of coerced religious participation.[T15]

Blocked by the Court for decades, school prayer advocates turned to the constitutional amendment process as a way of overturning what has become established law. Its promoters seek to establish protection for what they regard as the majority of Americans who wish to have their faith expressed in schools. They believe the Court's interpretation of the First Amendment violates the wishes of that majority in the name of freedom. Students who object to classroom prayer would still have the right to sit quietly or leave the room, as they may now if they oppose the recital of the nonreligious Pledge of Allegiance, but they wouldn't have the right to silence those who wish to pray.[T16]

Opponents say a constitutional amendment is unnecessary because the law already protects an individual's right to private prayer on school property. In that regard, students who wish to pray in school are not being silenced. Instead, opponents express concern for minority rights, which they believe the amendment would violate. They believe the law needs to protect those individuals, especially impressionable schoolchildren, who would be harmed by having to tolerate the publicly sanctioned expression of ideas they do not share.[T17]

Arguments in Support

Several arguments are typically offered in support of a constitutional amendment permitting school prayer. Proponents say:

- It will put a stop to religious tyranny. Without the liberty to worship in schools, we do not have true religious freedom in America. Religious dissenters should not be compelled to silence those who wish to pray.
- It's what the Constitution intended. Religious freedom means having the right to pray in public schools. This is entirely different from the establishment of a state-sanctioned religion, which is what the First Amendment was designed to prevent.
- It's pro-family. Prayer will reinforce traditional values and the lessons that so many parents try to teach at home, including tolerance of those who desire an outlet for religious expression at school by those who would otherwise stop them.
- It's necessary to instill values. Students learn values at school, and the religious and spiritual values expressed by prayer are among the most important for individuals and society to uphold.
- It's voluntary. Students who don't want to participate can remain silent.
- It's harmless. Permitting prayer in school is entirely different than permitting government to decide what individuals can and cannot believe or how they should worship.

Arguments Against

Opponents of a constitutional amendment permitting school prayer argue:

- It's tyrannical. Sanctioned, organized prayer is a threat to the liberty of nonbelievers and those who believe differently than the majority. The law must protect the rights of minorities, no matter how unpopular that may be.
- It violates the intent of the Constitution. The Court has repeatedly affirmed that having religious freedom protects us from prayer in public school.
- It's intolerant. Those who wish to pray in school should do so without subjecting

atheists, non-believers, and those of minority faiths to a profoundly disturbing experience.

- It infringes on personal rights. School administrators would be free to impose a religious perspective on those who disagreed.
- It's coercive. Dissenters will have no protection from something they do not believe in. Private, personal prayer, which is permitted by the courts, does not pose this problem.
- It's dangerous. Any step that undermines the separation of church and state is a step in the direction of giving the government the power to sanction religion.

My Opinion

When thinking about whether we should approve a constitutional amendment permitting school prayer, consider the history of the issue and the arguments supporting and opposing it. In particular, ask yourself if prayer in school:

- Will stop religious tyranny or is a form of religious tyranny.
- Conforms to or violates the intent of constitutionally protected religious freedom.
- Is pro-family or intolerant.
- Instills values or infringes on personal rights.
- Is voluntary or coercive.
- Is harmless or dangerous.

The logic of the decision makes practical sense if the objective is to maintain the superiority of the law over personal religious practices, or to prohibit behaviors carried out in the name of worship that the broader society finds abhorrent. However, if the goal is to protect one's religious beliefs from government interference, the Court's distinction between beliefs and behaviors may appear a bit academic, for how does one hold a belief if it is not practiced? That dilemma runs through the body of law on the free exercise doctrine.

Other, more recent rulings have limited free exercise of religion when it clashes with deeply held social values. In Employment Division, Department of Human Resources of *Oregon v. Smith* (1990), the Supreme Court ruled that two Native Americans could be fired from their jobs at a drug rehabilitation organization and denied unemployment benefits for using peyote, a controlled substance with important religious significance that could be used legally on Native American reservations but not off those reservations in the state of Oregon, where the pair worked. Writing for the majority, Justice Antonin Scalia contended that the free exercise of religion can be limited as the incidental result of a law

whose primary purpose is to set legal boundaries for everyone.[9] In other words, Oregon did not make peyote illegal in order to limit Native American worship, but if it has that effect, the rights of a religious minority must take a back seat to broader social interests.

Civil rights issues clashed with religious practices in the 1983 case *Bob Jones University v. United States*. Bob Jones University is a conservative Christian university that forbade interracial dating on religious grounds. Because of this policy, the Internal Revenue Service refused the school tax-exempt status on the basis of federal civil rights laws prohibiting tax exemptions for institutions that practiced discriminatory policies. Bob Jones University sued, claiming that its interracial dating policy was a matter of free exercise of religion, not racial discrimination. The Court disagreed, saying the government's overriding interest in ending discrimination outweighed the school's religious position.[10]

However, when the issue has been something narrower than polygamy, drug policies, and civil rights, the Court has sided with religious groups. In *Cantwell v. Connecticut* (1940), the Court held that states couldn't require religious groups to get a special permit to solicit for religious purposes, even if the group's message is unpleasant to those who hear it. In *Wisconsin v. Yoder* (1972), Amish children were granted the right to be taken out of public school after eighth grade in order to comply with religious teachings. The interest of the state in universal education was in this case considered secondary to Amish religious values. As in many cases involving the free exercise clause, the outcome often depends on how sharply religious practices clash with broader social norms.

Freedom of Expression

No liberty is more central to an open society than freedom of expression. Even though the First Amendment is unequivocal in stating that "Congress shall make no law ... abridging the freedom of speech," the issue in practice—like freedom of worship—has many variations. Justice Oliver Wendell Holmes may have penned the most famous line about the margins of free expression when he wrote, "Even the most stringent protection of free speech would not protect a man in falsely shouting fire in a crowded theatre and causing a panic."[11]

Dangerous and Unpopular Speech

Holmes was writing in the 1919 case *Schenck v. United States,* which arose out of the prosecution of Charles Schenck, a Socialist leader who had printed pamphlets urging young men to resist the draft during World War I. Schenck's actions violated provisions of the Espionage Act of 1917, which made it a crime to call for draft resistance or utter disloyal statements about the United States.

Schenck petitioned the Court to have the Espionage Act declared in violation of the First Amendment, but his efforts were unsuccessful. Nonetheless, in upholding the constitutionality of the Espionage Act as a measure the government was permitted to take during wartime, Holmes set out a specific rule for determining when government

could limit free expression: the standard of **clear and present danger.**[12] Government could stifle dissent, Holmes argued, when words "are used in such circumstances and are of such a nature as to create a clear and present danger that they will bring about the substantive evils that Congress has a right to prevent. It is a question of proximity and degree."[13] Wartime created such a circumstance, Holmes argued, when unpopular speech became dangerous. Even if Schenck's pleas to avoid the draft were unsuccessful, the fact that he made them was in the Court's view sufficient to present a public danger.

Not surprisingly, people with unpopular ideas are typically the ones caught in the middle of court cases testing free expression. The same year as the Schenck decision, Eugene Debs, the Socialist Party presidential candidate, criticized American involvement in World War I and spoke out publicly against the draft. At a 1918 speech in Canton, Ohio, Debs urged his audience to oppose the war. Drawing distinctions between leaders who declare war and workers who die in war, he said (to a blue-collar audience), "You have your lives to lose; you certainly ought to have the right to declare war if you consider a war necessary."[14]

Debs was arrested under the terms of the Espionage Act and charged with inciting disloyalty, insubordination, and mutiny against the armed forces of the United States. He admitted to the statements he had made in the speech, was convicted, and was sentenced to ten years in prison. The Supreme Court upheld the conviction, using the clear and present danger standard established in Schenck, noting that the First Amendment protected the general socialist message in the speech but not the call to resist the draft.

Debs continued his 1920 presidential campaign from prison. He received 2.4 million votes.

Eight years after the *Schenck* decision, Justice Louis Brandeis elaborated on and in the process altered the clear and present danger standard. Brandeis contended that unpopular speech is critical to maintaining democratic freedom, and that for people to feel secure about democratic participation, they have to be assured that unpopular speech will not be punished. To this end, he said an idea has to be dangerous and not just disliked to pose a threat to society, and that if there is time to engage in a full discussion of an idea—which is always the case unless the country faces an immediate crisis—it can never pose a clear and present danger. To Brandeis, the way to defuse the danger posed by most threatening ideas is through more discussion, not suppression of speech.[15]

Brandeis' movement toward greater acceptance of free speech set the stage for Court decisions in the 1960s and 1970s that increased First Amendment protection for unpopular speech. The 1969 case *Brandenberg v. Ohio* established the strict standard that speech had to incite "imminent lawless action" in order for government to have the ability to suppress it. Otherwise, First Amendment protections apply, even to speech that advocates violence (but does not actually instigate violence).[16]

Unpopular Speech in a Difficult Time

During periods of national tension, though, strict protections on speech have been hard to maintain. The close of World War II found the United States settling into a protracted period of uneasy coexistence with the Soviet Union that would last forty-five years. The start of the cold war brought a hysterical reaction to Communism that was exacerbated and exploited by Republican Senator Joseph McCarthy of Wisconsin, who crusaded against Communists in government and the private sector.

McCarthy made baseless accusations without evidence, but with the backing of the FBI and congressional investigators, he wielded immense power. Employers fired people who were tainted by McCarthy's charges, leaving them blacklisted and unable to get work. People were encouraged to turn in their friends and associates to demonstrate their loyalty to America—and to save their own skin. Moderate voices were silenced by the fear that questioning McCarthy's charges would brand them Communist sympathizers, and that McCarthy would next turn his inquisition on them.[17] The publisher of this book would have placed itself at risk for printing this paragraph. For a period of time, our system failed its most basic test, as an intense minority was able to use the mechanisms of government

to tyrannize the majority, quashing criticism of the government.

During this period, it was particularly dangerous to be directly affiliated with the American Communist Party. In 1940, Congress passed the Smith Act (technically the Alien Registration Act), which made it a crime to advocate the violent overthrow of the government—the position taken by the American Communist Party leadership during the time of McCarthy's Red Scare. In this climate, party leaders were prosecuted under the Smith Act, and the Court—in a momentary departure from the trend toward protecting unpopular speech—upheld the constitutionality of the Smith Act and the convictions of the Communist Party leadership. This happened despite the fact that the American Communist Party was small and ineffectual, making it highly unlikely that its advocacy would turn to action.

In dissent, Justice William O. Douglas anticipated the turn the court would take in the next decade, stating, "Free speech has occupied an exalted position because of the high service it has given our society. Its protection is essential to the very existence of a democracy. The airing of ideas releases pressures which otherwise might become destructive."[18] This was a difficult argument to accept in the icy climate of 1951.

As we move deeper into a time when the fear of terrorism is making inroads into our national psyche, and when free expression facilitates the planning and execution of terrorist plots, we might ask ourselves whether we can embrace Douglas' rationale for the benefits of free expression, or whether we will react as our grandparents' generation did to a different but equally penetrating threat. The flashpoint for this discussion has been the USA Patriot Act (which stands for Uniting and Strengthening America by Providing Appropriate Tools Required to Intercept and Obstruct Terrorism), which was passed in haste following the September 11, 2001, terrorist attacks. In the name of fighting terrorism, the USA Patriot Act gives law enforcement officials sweeping powers to conduct surveillance operations, including the power to secretly trace telephone numbers and email addresses. Supporters say the government needs to retain such authority in order to stay in front of covert terrorist groups. Opponents feel the Patriot Act gives too much coercive power to law enforcement officials, which can be used to undermine civil liberties, and worry that it could have a chilling effect on free expression akin to what the United States experienced during the McCarthy era.

Symbolic Expression

Protesters through the ages have resorted to the use of images to make strong, emotional statements. Designed to be hard to take and often disrespectful, symbolic expression can be a potent and effective way to lash out at policies and policy makers that people find objectionable. Maybe you've seen footage—there's lots of it—of crowds in foreign cities protesting American policy by burning an effigy of the president. During the Vietnam War, hippies grew their hair long in defiance of the buttoned-down values of their parents' generation—the group that most strongly supported the war. A few desecrated national symbols like the flag as a way of expressing their opposition to the actions of political elites.

How much symbolic expression should be permissible under the First Amendment? The most emotional debate revolves around the question of whether flag burning should be condoned. The Court has narrowly upheld flag burning as a constitutionally permissible form of expression, but opponents have mounted a spirited counterattack by trying to win approval of a constitutional amendment that would overrule the Court. Take a few minutes to explore the positions people have staked out on flag burning in Issue: Flag Burning, then make your judgment on whether you believe flag burning should be permitted or prohibited.

Political Correctness and Speech Codes

What do you do when someone wants to exhibit a strong attachment to a flag that is reviled by other citizens rather than universally beloved? Some southerners have as deep a connection to the Confederate flag as they do to the American flag,

but the Confederate flag is widely regarded as an offensive emblem to African Americans, who see it as an endorsement of white supremacy and a symbol of a racist political regime. So, when a fourteen-year-old white Georgia boy arrived at school wearing a T-shirt bearing the Confederate flag, he was suspended for a day for violating a school ban on displaying the controversial symbol. The boy objected, using language that echoes the words of those who support a constitutional amendment against desecrating the American flag, saying, "My Confederate ancestors, they died for this flag."

White parents flooded the school district with complaints about the suspension, accusing the district of imposing "politically correct" values on their children. They contended that not permitting their kids to display the Confederate flag simply because it might offend some people was a form of censorship. In so doing, they employed an argument identical to what *opponents* of the flag burning amendment have said, asserting the Constitution does not protect people from being offended, and that their right to free expression should be untouchable. The American Civil Liberties Union agreed, siding with those who seek free expression over those who would restrict it.[19]

Unpopular expression is the hardest to defend. Perhaps you or your friends have been involved in or heard about free expression debates on your campus, which invoked the "politically correct" label that surfaced in the Georgia Confederate flag flap. "Political correctness" can be an emotional topic because it touches on sensitive and important personal matters, like what we get to learn and how we're allowed to act.

Those on the left who are associated with "political correctness" once used the term self-mockingly to deflate their own ideas. However, as advocates of a "politically correct" agenda became prominent in academia, their opponents started using it disparagingly. The debate has enveloped numerous elements of campus intellectual life, and it has at times been shrill, but the most tangible manifestation of political correctness in academia has been in the implementation of multicultural curricula and personal codes of conduct.

ISSUE

FLAG BURNING

Few symbols move Americans like the flag. To many it is a special icon: an emblem that represents the living nation, which should be accorded the utmost respect. Consequently, few acts of civil disobedience gall Americans like burning the American flag. It's an action that has happened rarely in our history—about two hundred times in over 225 years[T18]—but in the 1960s it became the most powerful symbol of anger and protest against the Vietnam War. During that time, many who supported the war felt American values were under attack by a militant counterculture for which flag burning became a potent form of protest. In some important respects, the social wounds opened by that conflict have yet to heal, and the sense of permissiveness and diminished respect for authority, which some people see as stemming from that time, still rubs raw. The intensity surrounding the flag-burning debate may be understood in this context.[T19]

In 1989, the Supreme Court issued a 5–4 decision in the case of *Texas v. Johnson* upholding the right of a protester to burn the American flag at the 1984 Republican National Convention in Dallas, overturning a Texas law that had made flag burning a crime punishable by a $2,000 fine and a year in prison. The Court held that flag burning is a constitutionally protected form of political expression, and Texas could not prosecute Johnson for burning the flag without violating his First Amendment rights.[T20]

Congress responded immediately by passing the Flag Protection Act of 1989, which cleared both houses by a lopsided margin and was signed into law by President Bush (senior). The next year, the Court struck down the Flag Protection Act as unconstitutional by the same one-vote margin. That set in motion an organized lobbying campaign determined to overturn the

Johnson decision with a constitutional amendment. Since 1994, an organization called the Citizens Flag Alliance has been waging a grassroots campaign in conjunction with a coalition of 120 other interests groups to recruit local and national legislative candidates who would support a flag protection amendment permitting federal, state, and local authorities to make it a crime to desecrate the flag.[T21]

Members of the Citizens Flag Alliance have been effective, but they have fallen short of their goal. Bolstered by surveys that show large majorities of Americans support their position, they were successful in winning House approval for the amendment in 1995 by a vote of 312–120, far surpassing the two-thirds majority required for passage. The amendment failed in the Senate, but only by three votes. Since then, it has fallen short several more times, with the number of House votes in favor dropping from 312 to 310 (in 1997) to 305 (in 1999) to 298 (in 2001). Each time, it failed in the Senate. Then, when Democrats regained control of Congress in 2006, it faded from the legislative agenda. The American Civil Liberties Union, which opposes the amendment as an infringement on First Amendment freedoms, connects the steady decline in congressional support to vocal opposition to the amendment by prominent Americans like former Secretary of State Colin Powell and former senator and astronaut John Glenn.[T22]

Supporters of protecting the flag believe it has a special status as a national icon, something former Chief Justice Rehnquist said is regarded by millions with "an almost mystical reverence," and that it can be protected from harm without violating First Amendment freedoms. They argue that burning the flag is a behavior, not an exercise of speech of the sort expressly mentioned in the First Amendment, and that the court erred by regarding the behavior of flag burning as an expression analogous to speech. They also point to opinion polls that repeatedly show overwhelming majorities of Americans stand behind this position.

In turn, opponents argue that the First Amendment was designed to protect noxious behavior in the face of strong popular sentiment against it. To them, the fact that most people support an amendment to protect the flag is all the more reason why we *shouldn't* have one. They contend that conduct is a form of expression long protected by the Court. They feel the greater danger to society is posed by undermining the basic rights for which the flag stands, and that protecting the object at the expense of the rights of the individual tears at a foundational principle of democratic self-rule.[T23]

Arguments in Support

Supporters of a constitutional amendment to prohibit flag burning say:

- Nothing could be more American. The flag is a singular icon for America and is entitled to be accorded special protection as a revered symbol of our democracy.
- It's honorable. People die for the American flag and what it represents. It dishonors them to permit the flag to be desecrated.
- It's popular. The will of the people is to protect the flag from destruction.
- It won't violate the First Amendment. Flag burning is an action, not a form of speech. The First Amendment does not specifically protect actions.
- The flag deserves special status. Even if you disagree that flag burning can be outlawed without harming First Amendment rights, the flag still deserves special protection because of its iconic value and the deep attachments Americans have toward it.

Arguments Against

Opponents of a constitutional amendment to prohibit flag burning believe:

- Nothing could be more un-American. Imprisoning people for expressing political opposition is something we'd expect in the former Soviet Union, not here.
- It's intolerant. If we are to be faithful to our core values, we cannot restrict flag burning, no matter how much we may dislike it.
- Democracy is not a popularity contest. The fact that most Americans find flag burning noxious and want to prohibit it is a strong reason for protecting it, because having individual liberty means having the ability to express unpopular sentiments.
- It violates the First Amendment. The Court has consistently upheld political protest as a form of protected expression.
- The First Amendment deserves special status. We dishonor the flag and all it stands for by unraveling the Constitution. Millions have died defending principles that would be destroyed if flag burning were outlawed.

My Opinion

Should there be a constitutional amendment to prohibit flag burning? Ask yourself if making it illegal to burn the flag:

- Reflects values that are distinctly American—or un-American.
- Is honorable or intolerant.
- Should happen because it's popular, or should not happen because it's popular.
- Does or does not violate the spirit of the First Amendment.
- Appropriately accords special status to the flag, or inappropriately denies special status to the First Amendment.

As a curricular matter, proponents of multiculturalism have advocated—successfully in many places—revamping curricula to emphasize cultural diversity among the writers and thinkers represented in core texts. They contend that to do otherwise is to offer an education that is homogeneous and exclusionary in its emphasis on white male European writers. Critics contend that multiculturalists and feminists have hijacked the curriculum and thrown out valuable contributions simply because they were written by white male Europeans, then justified their actions on the grounds that the writings they discard are inherently racist and sexist. In other words, they equate political correctness with censorship.

The same applies to codes of personal conduct. Some universities implemented speech codes that mandated taking disciplinary action against students who used racist or sexist epithets, broadening the umbrella of harassment to include language that critics contended was commonplace and previously regarded as a minor matter.[20] Proponents of speech codes said the fact that so many people considered offensive language to be insignificant was part of the problem, as it spoke to the level of hostility directed against people with diverse backgrounds and viewpoints. Critics spoke widely of a "thought police" attempting to regulate free expression, and speech codes did not fair well when challenged in the courts.[21]

Ironically, some of the strongest criticism of political correctness came from liberals who felt it undermines free expression. A former president of the Los Angeles chapter of the National Organization for Women (NOW) described political correctness as indulging the "culture of victimhood" and compared it to the reign of terror in George Orwell's novel 1984, under the guise of trying to promote social equality.[22] A self-described "bleeding heart liberal" undergraduate at a prominent university endorsed an anti-political-correctness student group called Foundation for Academic Standards and Tradition because of her concern that political correctness sacrificed individual freedom.[23]

One way to understand political correctness is to see it in the context of what's been dubbed the "culture wars" that date to the rise of the counterculture of the 1960s. Political correctness took hold on campuses as conservatives were successfully mobilizing voters—especially white male voters—behind an entirely different set of values that advocates of political correctness regarded as directly threatening to multiculturalism. The real dilemma raised by critics of political correctness, and the thing that makes it so controversial, is whether its advocates, in an effort to create an environment supportive of difference, impose a kind of cultural uniformity that stifles free speech and ironically makes it difficult to embrace a different or opposing perspective.

Freedom of the Press

The press carries a key constitutional responsibility as the source of the information we need to stay informed and make responsible public choices. Even though we questioned how effectively the press performs this function when we discussed the mass media in Chapter 5, the obligation to keep readers and viewers informed is so critical to democracy that news organizations are the only private, for-profit institutions afforded constitutional protection.

Prior Restraint

Press freedom stems from protection against a practice called **prior restraint**, or censorship of the news by government officials before it is printed or broadcast. The practice dates back to the seventeenth century, when the English King could censor the news before it was published. The rationale behind protecting the press against prior restraint is that the executive, legislature, or courts wield too much power if they are allowed to prevent ideas from entering circulation. Once circulated, however, the press is responsible for the consequences of its actions and can be held accountable for any misstatements of fact.[24] Protection from prior restraint was confirmed in the case of *Near v. Minnesota* (1931), when the Supreme Court struck down a Minnesota law that had been used to stop publication of embarrassing information about local political figures in a tabloid called the *Saturday Press.* In issuing the order, Chief Justice Hughes made it clear that even "miscreant purveyors of scandal" have the constitutional right to publish without government interference.[25] Prior restraint could only be imposed where the public interest was clearly jeopardized by publication, such as in the case of information that would create a major national security breach if released.

The Court has set the national security bar very high. Perhaps the most serious call for prior restraint on national security grounds occurred during the Nixon administration, which tried to block the *New York Times* and the *Washington Post* from publishing a scathing, classified study of the decisions that contributed to American involvement in Vietnam. The Pentagon Papers, as the study was known, showed how a series of presidential administrations had knowingly misled the public about the war. Daniel Ellsberg, a disillusioned senior Defense Department employee who was one of the report's authors, leaked it to the *New York Times* in 1971, and the Nixon administration—which was still prosecuting the Vietnam War—immediately moved to have a series of stories about it suppressed. The Court refused in a 6–3 decision that reaffirmed the need for an urgent national security breach to be threatened before prior restraint could be imposed.[26]

Libel

Of course, granting the press freedom from prior restraint puts a great responsibility in the hands of publishers, and gives them the power to inflict harm if that power is mishandled. The remedy available to individuals who feel they have been harmed by press coverage lies in **libel** laws, which we discussed in Chapter 5. As we noted, though, libel is difficult to prove—particularly for public figures, who have to show that false statements were published with malice.

In rare situations where sloppy reporting leads to damaging misstatements, the press can get hit hard. For instance, in 1990 the *Philadelphia Inquirer* was ordered to pay $6 million to a Pennsylvania Supreme Court judge for incorrectly accusing him of influence peddling. A year later, a Dallas television

station lost a libel suit to a Texas district attorney for falsely reporting he had taken bribes. The station was ordered to pay $58 million.[27] Such judgments, though, are unusual.

Publishing on the Internet

The advent of the Internet as a device for publishing and communicating has added new wrinkles to traditional notions of press freedom. As neither a print nor an electronic medium, the Internet cuts across previous legal distinctions as it permits us to be our own publishers, sending our ideas across national boundaries where laws on press freedom vary widely.[28] From the standpoint of libel, early indications are that self-publishers can claim to be public figures, requiring those who might sue to restrict cyber content to demonstrate the presence of malice as if they were suing a newspaper or television station.[29]

The Internet is also home to a wide variety of distasteful, troubling, and hateful websites. This can prove to be a difficult test of our tolerance, or of Justice Douglas' remedy to allow expression of offensive ideas, because much of this speech is constitutionally protected.[30] A range of material published on the Internet might be considered obscene by some observers, although traditional law is vague and confusing when it comes to identifying obscenity, and Internet postings simply confound the situation. The First Amendment does not protect obscene communication, but there's little agreement over what obscene communication is or the standards that should be used to identify it. Those who have attempted to classify material as obscene can agree on little more than the standard that was penned by Justice Potter Stewart, who wrote in a frustrated effort to define pornography: "I know it when I see it."[31]

Other justices have hardly done better. The Supreme Court has used language like "prurient,"[32] "patently offensive," and "utterly without redeeming social value"[33] as a test of whether something is obscene, leaving it to "the average person, applying contemporary community standards"[34] to determine if something fits this definition. It's problematic how this test applies to the Internet, where in addition to defining obscenity, you have to define the community.

Consider the discussion in Issue: Obscenity on the Internet, which details a specific example of an Internet posting considered obscene by some, art by others. As you do, see if you can decide where and how you would set the standard for posting potentially obscene material online.

ISSUE

OBSCENITY ON THE INTERNET

Barbara Nitke is on the faculty of the School of Visual Arts in New York. She is president of the historic Camera Club of New York, a prestigious 120-year-old institution. Her photography has been critically acclaimed as sensitive in its depiction of sometimes graphic or disturbing subjects. She has been using the camera to reveal the trust and love exhibited by couples engaged in sadomasochistic sex. And she wants to post her images on the Internet.[T24]

She knows that doing so will raise legal issues about whether her work is considered obscene because the law permits obscenity to be determined by local community standards—the same criterion applied to other media. But what are local community standards on the Internet? Nitke decided to raise that question in court, with the help of the National Coalition for Sexual Freedom, an organization that bills itself as dedicated to equal rights for "consenting adults who practice forms of alternative sexual expression."[T25]

There are a number of ways you could conceivably understand local standards on the Internet. Perhaps the entire Internet is a community. That would be the most general interpretation of the law and would allow virtually anything to be posted. Maybe local community standards are the ones in effect in New York, where she would post her material, or maybe the individuals who self-select to view her work constitute a community. Any of these interpretations would permit Nitke to post her work online for anyone in the world to see. Would these criteria be too permissive, affording constitutional protection to work that some people would definitely find objectionable?

Instead, what if "community" were defined as any place in the world where someone could access her pictures? That would be the most restrictive interpretation of the law because surely there are places were her work would be considered obscene, resulting in her having to remove it from the web. Would imposing that standard constitute censorship?

It's a difficult question because the Internet is so different from any communications medium to come before it. You can enter chat rooms and communicate with people you've never met who could be anywhere in the world. Maybe you have a Facebook page displaying pictures and some of your favorite links that anyone on earth could access. Or perhaps you instant-message your friends from your computer—maybe you're doing it right now as a diversion if you're reading this book online. With unlimited access and reach, the Internet makes location and distance irrelevant to how we communicate, even if the law continues to use pre-information-age constructs for determining obscenity. This raises profound questions about what, if anything, we should be forbidden to communicate, and what should be protected as free expression.

It was inevitable once the Internet became a form of mass communication that lawmakers and the courts would be faced with questions of what constitutes indecent and obscene communication online. The first attempt to regulate Internet communication came in the form of the **Communications Decency Act of 1996**, which prohibited the posting of "patently offensive" or "indecent" material on the web. The language it employs is similar to that applied to broadcast media like radio and television to determine what constitutes offensive material.

Of course, the Internet does not function like a television network, where content is broadcast to receivers for any viewer to watch. Instead, people seek out websites, more in the manner of a pay-per-view television movie. Chat rooms and weblogs take the form of a public gathering place, an electronic public park where freedom of speech is protected. People who post material on the web could be considered publishers, with their freedom of expression guaranteed.[T26]

These distinctions were not lost on the Supreme Court, which didn't take long to throw out most provisions of the Communications Decency Act on the grounds that it was an unconstitutional attempt to limit free expression. By a vote of 7–2, the Court ruled in the case of *Reno v. ACLU* (1997) that Internet communication was entitled to the same strict constitutional protection as print media because of its decentralized structure with many contributors and no strict gatekeepers.[T27]

However, the Court left in place the section of the law that permitted "local community standards" to determine if something was obscene, without clarifying the issue of what constitutes a community online. Hence Barbara Nitke's dilemma: Should the Internet be viewed as a global or self-selecting community where expression should be tolerated even if some communities with access to the web would find it obscene? Or should any community with access to the web have the right to veto a posting it considers obscene?

Arguments in Support

Those who advocate broad standards for determining what material is permissible to post online make the following arguments:

- The Internet is not an invasive medium. To find something you might consider offensive, you have to look for it.
- The minority should not censor the majority. A parochial interpretation of community standards creates a lowest-common-denominator yardstick for what others can say or post, permitting one small community to veto something it doesn't like or perhaps doesn't understand.
- Society must encourage artistic expression. Sometimes art is designed to offend, and the right to do so must be protected. If people don't like it, they don't have to look at it.
- There is no constitutional morality protection. The First Amendment does not permit one group to impose its ideas about morality on any other group or on the entire nation.

Arguments Against

Those supporting narrow standards for defining online obscenity might say:

- The Internet makes everything available. You can stumble across offensive material by accident or through unclear or deceptive links.
- It's not censorship. Not every place is as permissive as New York City. Individuals should have the right to be protected from material that would be considered offensive in their immediate community.
- It's not art. It's filth. And it shouldn't be online where anyone can come across it.
- There is legislative protection against distributing obscene materials. Even though the law does not provide uniform standards of obscenity, it does not

prohibit Congress from restricting the interstate transmission of items it deems obscene or offensive.

My Opinion

When considering whether there should be a broad or narrow standard for posting material on the internet that some would find obscene, ask yourself if:

- You have to seek out potentially obscene material on the Internet, or if just the act of going online puts it in proximity to you.

- Narrowly interpreting obscenity constitutes or does not constitute minority censorship of the majority.
- Artistic expression should be encouraged even if some consider it obscene, or obscenity should be discouraged even if some consider it art.
- The value of restricting any group from imposing its morals on another group is more or less important than the value of prohibiting the distribution of what some would find offensive.

Freedom of Assembly and Association

In August 2009, tens of thousands of demonstrators gathered in Washington to protest the Obama Administration's efforts to expand government involvement in health care. In February 2003, tens of thousands rallied against the looming war with Iraq in protests held in cities across the country. In both instances, protesters were protected from government retribution by the First Amendment guarantee of "the right of the people to peaceably assemble, and to petition the government for redress of grievances." This may be something we take for granted, but the authors of the Constitution certainly did not. In seventeenth-century England, you could be put in prison for peacefully assembling to advocate ideas that were opposed by the crown.

The Supreme Court has affirmed that the First Amendment protects assembly for the purpose of the lawful exchange of ideas, no matter how unpopular the assembled group may be. This provision has been used to permit meetings of the Communist Party[35] and to enable African Americans to peaceably assemble in southern states during the Civil Rights movement.[36] It has also extended rights to unions, allowing them to form picket lines during labor disputes, provided they do so in an orderly manner.[37]

The right to assemble also covers the right to protest peacefully without repercussions, even if the protest is repugnant to the general public. This is probably the most controversial application of the freedom of assembly, because it can require tolerance of visible displays of vile and hateful expression. When the American Nazi Party chose Skokie, Illinois, as the location for a march in support of fascism in 1977, they knew they were going to evoke a hostile reaction from the residents of the heavily Jewish Chicago suburb, some of whom were Holocaust survivors. Village residents were predictably outraged and went to court to block the march, but the Supreme Court upheld the constitutional rights of the Nazis to stage a public demonstration.[38]

The freedom to associate is closely related to the freedom to assemble. We devoted a lot of attention in Part 3 to group membership in political parties and interest groups, and we talked a little about how Americans like to join organizations. All of this is made possible by the freedom to associate.

While not explicitly stated in the First Amendment, freedom of association has been protected by the Court as an implied right, on the grounds that in order to petition government, people first need the freedom to gather in groups with like-minded citizens. Underlying this logic is the belief that groups of private citizens are necessary to advocate political positions and are valuable mechanisms for checking the power of government.[39]

Right to Bear Arms

The Second Amendment is one sentence long. It states, "A well-regulated militia, being necessary to the security of a free state, the right of the people to keep and bear arms, shall not be infringed." Those twenty-six simple words have been the basis for some of the most intense political battles in our recent history. The way you interpret them determines where you stand on gun ownership and probably says a lot about how you see the world.

Some people regard the Second Amendment as an unequivocal grant of freedom to possess firearms for everything from hunting to self-defense. They interpret gun ownership as a personal right. Others contend that the amendment's authors had only public defense in mind. They interpret gun ownership as a collective right, one that permits states to form militias—and nothing else.

A recent ABCNews.com poll indicates that three in four Americans take the position that the Second Amendment protects individual gun ownership. At the same time, a majority supports stricter controls on guns.

Right to Privacy

The Constitution never mentions a **right to privacy**. Neither does the Bill of Rights. Over time, though, the Court has determined that there is an implied right to privacy that may be found in several constitutional passages, and from this construction, it has secured rights ranging from legal contraceptive use to legalized abortion.

The road to this destination was uneven and bumpy. In 1902, a man living in Cambridge, Massachusetts, refused to participate in a smallpox vaccination program that was administered by city officials who feared an outbreak of the disease. He was tried, convicted, fined five dollars, and told that he would have to get a shot. The case reached the Supreme Court, where a judgment was rendered in

favor of Massachusetts on the grounds that when any individual refuses to be vaccinated against a contagious disease, he or she passes the risks of vaccination to neighbors but assumes the benefits of immunity by living in an area where an outbreak is unlikely. The Court regarded the situation as a social contract issue, where individuals have to surrender some of their freedom in order for society to function effectively.[40]

However, the Court also recognized that not every situation fits this pattern, and in so doing, established that citizens have the constitutionally guaranteed freedom to be left alone by government, which comes into play when it is not outweighed by prevailing social concerns (like making sure a city is vaccinated against a deadly disease). This was the first step to establishing a right to privacy, which was articulated sixty-three years later in *Griswold v. Connecticut*.[41]

Privacy and Birth Control

In the early 1960s, Estelle Griswold, the Executive Director of the Planned Parenthood League of Connecticut, was convicted along with a Yale University medical professor of violating a Connecticut law against advising others in the use of contraceptive devices when they counseled and prescribed birth control for a married couple at the Planned Parenthood offices. They petitioned the Supreme Court to overturn the conviction on the grounds that the Connecticut law violated their civil liberties.

The Court agreed. Writing for the majority, Justice Douglas acknowledged that the right to marital privacy is not mentioned in the Constitution, but—as we've seen—neither is the right to associate, even though the First Amendment has been interpreted to include that right. Furthermore, Douglas argued that there are places in the Constitution where "Various guarantees create zones of privacy," including:

- The right of association implied by the First Amendment

- The Third Amendment prohibition against being forced by the government to house soldiers during peacetime
- The Fourth Amendment guarantee against unreasonable searches and seizures
- The Fifth Amendment protection against self-incrimination
- The Ninth Amendment assurance that personal rights should not be construed to be limited to those enumerated in the Constitution[42]

Douglas concluded that the evidence pointed to a Constitutional right to marital privacy, which, while not expressed in the Constitution, is in keeping with the intent of its authors. "We deal," he wrote, "with a right of privacy older than the Bill of Rights."[43]

The immediate effect of the Griswold decision was to legalize the use of contraceptives among married couples. This right was soon extended to unmarried persons.[44]

Privacy and Abortion Rights

As we saw in Section 12.9, "Consistency and Legitimacy?," the right to privacy was also the basis for legalizing abortion. In the controversial case *Roe v. Wade,* Justice Blackmun established that the right to privacy was "broad enough to encompass a woman's decision whether or not to terminate her pregnancy."[45]

This line of reasoning has become a fault line in the abortion controversy, because it has generated passionate debate about when or whether a fetus should be considered part of a woman's body, permitting abortion to be a private decision. The Court addressed this issue by assigning different conditions to each of pregnancy's trimesters. An unfettered right to privacy was applied to the first trimester, when the abortion decision may be left to a woman in private consultation with her physician. In the second trimester, the state may intervene in the decision for reasons involving the health of the mother. The state can prohibit abortion in the final trimester.[46]

The rationale behind this decision is that at some point the fetus becomes viable, and the choice to have an abortion is no longer without consequences for the developing child. In the absence of a definitive medical determination about when life begins, the Court acted to protect the privacy rights of the mother without making those rights absolute. The problem this generated is that many people have strong beliefs about when life begins despite the absence of medical proof, and those who believe it begins at conception reject as immoral the application of a right to privacy over abortion decisions at any term. Those who subscribe to the Court's logic argue passionately about the immorality of permitting the state to make intimate decisions about a woman's body when a pregnancy is not viable.[47]

Whether the Constitution may be interpreted to include a right to privacy was a major point of contention during the 2005 and 2006 confirmation hearings for Chief Justice John Roberts and Justice Samuel Alito. With the ideological balance of the Supreme Court at stake, abortion opponents pressed for justices who might question the right to privacy as a basis for reversing *Roe v. Wade.* Abortion supporters worried that President Bush's nominees might not agree that there is an implied right to privacy in the Constitution, threatening the *Roe* decision and perhaps *Criswold* as well.

Privacy and Physician-Assisted Suicide

The right to privacy is also a factor in the controversy over whether critically ill individuals should have the right to end their lives. The debate about physician-assisted suicide raises questions arising at the end of life that echo the issues raised in the abortion debate about the start of life: Is it a form of murder or a personal decision without repercussions for anyone but the individual involved? Take a few minutes to read about the history of physician-assisted suicide in the next Issue box before deciding for yourself whether you believe it should be a personal right.

ISSUE

PHYSICIAN-ASSISTED SUICIDE

The last days and weeks of life can be an excruciating ordeal for individuals with terminal illnesses. Even with hospital or hospice care, it's not always possible to manage extreme pain or comfort intense suffering. People confronted with a painful death and no hope of recovery may wish to end their lives by choice; physician-assisted suicide gives them this option. It involves doctors giving terminally ill patients the means for death, usually in the form of a prescription drug. Physician-assisted suicide is not euthanasia, because the doctor does not actively participate in the patient's death. (Perhaps you've heard or read about Dr. Jack Kevorkian, the Michigan physician nicknamed "Dr. Death" for his high-profile participation in euthanasia cases dating back to 1990. This is not physician-assisted suicide.) With physician-assisted suicide, the patient must be of sound mind and make a rational decision to approach a doctor for a medical means to suicide, which the patient then applies without assistance.

In a culture that celebrates life and tends not to talk about issues surrounding death, it's not surprising that physician-assisted suicide is controversial. It flies against widely held religious beliefs about the sanctity of life and appears to invert the role of the doctor to do everything possible to save lives, although advocates contend that it is consistent with the physician's obligation to end suffering and that it is a compassionate choice for terminally ill patients in unbearable pain. Opponents worry that it will be abused, with patients who lack access to good medical treatment being forced into it, and patients suffering from depression rather than pain being most interested in it. This gives assisted suicide a complex moral and ethical dimension.

Although assisted suicide became a salient item on the national agenda in the last several years, it isn't new to American politics, and in fact, the issue dates back thousands of years. The ancient Greeks employed physician-assisted suicide (and euthanasia, for that matter) over two thousand years ago for a wide range of ailments for which there was no cure. In the United States, it was debated in the nineteenth century under the terms "patient rights" and "death with dignity"—the same language used by proponents today. However, it never took hold in this country, and disappeared from active discussion with the development of penicillin and other life-sustaining medical advances in the early twentieth century.[T28] When it reemerged at the end of the century, it again faced stiff opposition.

Like gun control, the Supreme Court has been reluctant to get involved in the issue of assisted suicide. However, in 1997 the Court heard a pair of cases on the matter. In *Washington v. Clucksberg* and *Vacco v. Quill,* the Court upheld, respectively, a Washington State and a New York State ban on physician-assisted suicide, saying the Constitution does not guarantee terminally ill individuals a right to hasten their deaths.[T29] The ruling left it to the states to determine whether they wanted to legalize physician-assisted suicide.

The first two states to consider the question turned it down. An initiative to legalize physician-assisted suicide was rejected by Washington state voters in 1991 and by California voters in 1992.

Then the Hemlock Society, an organization advocating the right to die, secured a spot for a similar initiative on the 1994 Oregon ballot. Oregonians were given the opportunity to pass judgment on whether to legalize suicide for terminally ill individuals who have "voluntarily expressed" a wish to die. Lobbying on both sides of the measure was intense, with groups as diverse as estate lawyers and the Catholic Church in opposition.

In the end, voters divided closely on the issue, opting to approve it by a slender 51–49 margin. Opponents went to court to block implementation, but their case was dismissed by the U.S. Circuit Court. Opponents then tried to overturn the law with a referendum of their own, but that measure failed by a wide margin, and Oregon became the first state in the union to legalize assisted suicide.[T30] The law went into effect in 1997. Ten months later, only eight people had taken advantage of it, suggesting that the Oregon experiment with physician-assisted suicide had not turned the state into a destination for large numbers of people looking for a final alternative to painful terminal illness.[T31]

When the Bush administration took office, the Justice Department moved to overturn the Oregon law. However, the lower courts repeatedly kept the law in place. Finally, the Supreme Court agreed to decide the matter. In 2006, the Court ruled in favor of physician-assisted suicide in *Gonzales v. State of Oregon,* and the Oregon law was allowed to remain on the books.[T32]

Arguments in Support

Several arguments are typically offered in support of physician-assisted suicide, such as:

- It's compassionate. When suffering is unbearable, the kind and moral thing to do is to give individuals with no hope for survival the opportunity to end their lives.
- It's medically ethical. Doctors have an obligation to do everything to keep patients from suffering.
- It's just. When treatment options have been exhausted and simply refusing care means a slow and painful death, it is right for patients to be able to choose suicide as their only viable option.

- It's a personal matter. The timing and circumstances surrounding one's death should be a matter of private choice, not public policy. It is important to respect the liberty of an individual over matters of personal choice.

Arguments Against

Opponents of physician-assisted suicide policies claim:

- It's immoral. The sanctity of life is absolute, even when someone is in great pain. Regardless of the circumstances, suicide is morally wrong.
- It violates medical ethics. A doctor's foremost obligation is to save lives.
- It's unjust. There is no way to guarantee that only patients in great pain will take advantage of assisted suicide, and it would be unjust if individuals who lack good medical care or who are a financial burden on their families were pushed toward suicide as a convenient option.
- It's a social matter. Death may be personal but suicide is a legal issue, and society, not individuals, should have the final say in the matter. The issue is whether to grant legal permission to take a life, something we do not permit individuals to do under any other circumstances.

My Opinion

When registering your opinion on physician-assisted suicide, consider the history of the issue and the arguments supporting and opposing it. In particular, ask yourself if physician-assisted suicide:

- Is compassionate or immoral.
- Conforms to or violates medical ethics.
- Is just or unjust.
- Is a personal or social matter.

Chapter Review

Civil liberties are constitutional and legal protections against government infringement on personal freedoms. Many civil liberties are protected by the Bill of Rights, although some are found in the Constitution and others were established through judicial precedent. Due process, or protection against the arbitrary actions of government, is central to our civil liberties. Due process guarantees fixed and equitable procedures for being charged with and prosecuted for a crime, including the right to a swift jury trial, and protection against double jeopardy, unreasonable searches and seizures, and self-incrimination. Due process also carries constitutional guarantees against cruel and unusual punishment. Opponents of capital punishment have argued that it should be classified as cruel and unusual, although the Court has disagreed.

The First Amendment guarantees a host of personal liberties: religious freedom, freedom of speech, freedom of the press, and freedom of assembly. The First Amendment's establishment clause is the basis for the separation of church and state. This is accepted to mean that the federal government cannot establish a church or force people to attend or not attend a church, but there is disagreement about the height of the barrier between church and state. For instance, advocates of school prayer understand religious freedom to be the freedom to permit prayer in school; opponents of school prayer understand it to mean protection from prayer in school. The First Amendment's free exercise clause restricts government from interfering with religious practices, but this right is not absolute.

Similarly, free expression is constitutionally protected—but not in all instances. The government can limit speech that poses a clear and present danger to others, and in the 1960s, the Court tightened that standard to speech that incited "imminent lawless action." The Court has also affirmed that constitutional safeguards apply to symbolic speech, like flag burning, although the Court was divided over the matter. Efforts to pass a constitutional amendment banning flag burning have come close to passage on several recent occasions. Unpopular expression may be the most difficult to deal with. Speech codes established at some universities in a "politically correct" effort to contend with offensive expression have met opposition in the courts because of the restrictions they placed on free expression.

The press is the only for-profit private business granted constitutional protection, because its obligations to keep people informed and to provide a check on government power are of central importance to democracy. The First Amendment protects the press from prior restraint, or government censorship. Publishing on the Internet adds a new dimension to free expression, especially when it entails hateful material or material some may deem obscene. The Communications Decency Act of 1996 attempted to set guidelines, but the Internet's global reach confounds the traditional legal test of applying contemporary community standards to determine if public communication is protected speech.

The First Amendment also protects freedom of assembly and the right to petition the government, provided that it occurs peacefully. The Court has extended the First Amendment to protect the freedom to form associations, like interest groups and political parties.

The Second Amendment right to bear arms has been understood in different ways over the years, either as an individual grant of freedom to possess firearms or as a collective right to form state militias. The Court has been reluctant to weigh in on the matter, and the controversy over gun control has played out largely in the legislative arena.

One place where the Court has been quite proactive is in establishing a right to privacy, which is not addressed specifically in the Constitution. The right to privacy has been applied to the legalization of contraceptive devices, and was the foundation for the *Roe v. Wade* decision that legalized abortion.

Key Terms

Bill of Rights The first ten amendments to the Constitution, which limit government from denying us a range of personal liberties.

bills of attainder Declarations of guilt by legislative decree without benefit of a trial.

civil liberties Constitutional and legal protections against government infringement on a host of personal freedoms.

clear and present danger The standard established by Justice Oliver Wendell Holmes for determining when the government could limit speech.

Communications Decency Act of 1996 A legislative attempt to regulate the transmission of "offensive" or "indecent" material over the Internet. The Supreme Court overturned most of the provisions of the Communications Decency Act.

double jeopardy Protection against the state using its power to repeatedly prosecute someone until the person is convicted. Double jeopardy precludes the prosecution of someone for the same crime in the same jurisdiction more than once.

due process The protection of individual liberty from the arbitrary or capricious actions of government through a defined set of legal procedures designed to protect the rights of the accused.

establishment clause The language in the First Amendment that serves as the basis for the constitutional separation of church and state.

ex post facto laws From the Latin for "after the fact," legislation that makes something a crime that was legal when it occurred.

exclusionary rule To protect against unreasonable searches and seizures, the Supreme Court has established that evidence obtained illegally is not admissible in court.

free exercise clause The language in the First Amendment that limits government interference in private religious beliefs and practices.

Gideon v. Wainwright The 1963 Supreme Court case that established the right to have an attorney appointed at no charge by the court to defendants unable to afford representation. It was brought by Clarence Earl Gideon, who was sentenced to five years in prison for breaking into a pool hall. From prison, Gideon filed a habeas corpus petition, claiming his right to an attorney was violated because he was forced by poverty to represent himself at his trial.

libel The legal restriction against the malicious publication of material that knowingly damages an individual's reputation.

Miranda rights The Court requirement, following a judgment in the case Miranda v. Arizona (1966), that apprehended individuals know and understand that they have a right against self-incrimination and a right to be represented by an attorney.

plea bargain A compromise between a defendant, defense attorney, and prosecutor, whereby the defendant foregoes due process and agrees to plead guilty without a trial to a lesser charge in exchange for a more lenient punishment.

prior restraint Censorship of the news by government officials before it is published or broadcast.

right to privacy The protection against government interference in private matters, which is not specifically guaranteed by the Constitution but which has been established by the Court and used to legalize contraception and abortion.

writ* of *habeas corpus From the Latin for "you have the body," habeas corpus puts the burden on the courts to demonstrate that a defendant's rights have not been violated prior to sentencing. People who believe they have been imprisoned against their constitutional rights have the privilege to petition for their release.

Resources

You might be interested in examining some of what the following authors have said about the topics we've been discussing:

On Capital Punishment
Epstein, Lee, and Joseph F. Kobylka. *The Supreme Court and Legal Change: Abortion and the Death Penalty.*

Chapel Hill, NC: University of North Carolina Press, 1992.

On School Prayer

Alley, Robert S. *Without a Prayer: Religious Expression in Public Schools.* Amherst, NY: Prometheus Books, 1996.

On Flag Burning

Goldstein, Robert Justin. *Flag Burning and Free Speech: The Case of Texas v. Johnson.* Lawrence, KS: University Press of Kansas, 2000.

On Hate Speech and Political Correctness

Heumann, Milton, and Thomas W. Church, eds. *Hate Speech on Campus.* Boston: Northeastern University Press, 1997.

On Gun Control

Vizzard, William J. *Shots in the Dark: The Policy, Politics, and Symbolism of Gun Control.* Lanham, MD: Rowman & Littlefield Publishers, 2000.

On Physician-Assisted Suicide

Urofsky, Melvin I. *Lethal Judgments: Assisted Suicide and American Law.* Lawrence, KS: University Press of Kansas, 2000.

Notes

1. Howard N. Meyer, *The Amendment That Refused to Die: Equality and Justice Deferred: The History of the Fourteenth Amendment* (Lantham, MD: Madison Books, 2000), 4–5.
2. J. Roland Pennock and John W. Chapman, eds., *Due Process* (New York: New York University Press, 1977), 3–4.
3. American Civil Liberties Union website, at http://www.aclu.org/capital-pßunishment.
4. 1998 General Social Survey, at http://www.thearda.com/Archive/Files/Descriptions/GSS1998.asp.
5. Ibid.
6. *Everson v. Board of Education of the Township of Ewing,* 330 US 1 (1947).
7. Sarah Barringer Gordon, "The Mormon Question: Polygamy and Constitutional Conflict in Nineteenth Century America," *Penn Law Journal,* Spring 2002.
8. *Reynolds v. United States,* 98 US 145 (1878).
9. *Employment Division, Oregon Department of Human Resources v. Smith,* 494 US 872 (1990).
10. *Bob Jones University v. United States,* 461 US 574 (1983).
11. *Schenck v. United States,* 249 US 27 (1919).
12. Nicholas Capaldi, *Clear and Present Danger: The Free Speech Controversy* (New York: Pegasus, 1969), 71–75.
13. *Schenck v. United States,* 249 US 27 (1919).
14. *Debbs v. United States,* 249 US 211 (1919).
15. *Whitney v. California,* 274 US 357 (1927).
16. *Brandenberg v. Ohio,* 395 US 444 (1969).
17. Ellen Schrecker, *The Age of McCarthyism* (Boston: Bedford Books, 1994), 92–94.
18. *Dennis v. United States,* 341 US 494 (1951).
19. "Confederate T-Shirts Spark Debate," *Associated Press,* April 6, 2001.
20. Typical of such codes was one adopted in 1988 at the University of Michigan prohibiting "any behavior, verbal or physical, that stigmatizes or victimizes an individual on the basis of race, ethnicity, religion, national origin, sexual orientation, creed, ancestry, age, marital status, handicap, or Vietnam-veteran status." It was struck down as unconstitutional on First Amendment grounds in Federal District Court in 1989. See Milton Heumann and Thomas W. Church, eds., *Hate Speech on Campus* (Boston: Northeastern University Press, 1997), 3, 130–148.
21. Marilyn Friedman and Jan Narveson, *Political Correctness: For and Against* (Lanham, MD: Rowman & Littlefield, 1995).
22. Ibid.
23. Foundation for Academic Standards and Tradition.
24. Jerome A. Barron and C. Thomas Dienes, *First Amendment Law in a Nutshell* (St. Paul, MN: West Publishing Company, 1993), 47–48.
25. Ibid., 48.
26. Ibid., 52–54.
27. Steven Pressman, "Libel Law in the United States," Department of State International Information Programs at http://usa.usembassy.de/etexts/media/unfetter/press08.htm.
28. Jeremy Harris Lipschultz, *Free Expression in the Age of the Internet: Social and Legal Boundaries* (Boulder, CO: Westview Press, 2000), 10–11. See also 277–304.

29. Mike Godwin, *Cyber Rights: Defending Free Speech in the Digital Age* (New York: Times Books, 1998), 73–100.

30. Ibid., 101–132.

31. Barron and Dienes, *First Amendment Law,* 88.

32. *Roth v. United States,* 354 US 476 (1957).

33. *A Book Named "John Cleland's Memoirs of a Woman of Pleasure" v. Attorney-General,* 383 US 413 (1966). See also *Miller v. California,* 413 US 15 (1973).

34. Ibid.

35. *De Jonge v. Oregon,* 299 US 353 (1937).

36. *Edwards v. South Carolina,* 372 US 229 (1963).

37. *Thornhill v. Alabama,* 310 US 88 (1940).

38. *National Socialist Party of America v. Skokie,* 432 US 43 (1977).

39. Barron and Dienes, *First Amendment Law,* 238–239.

40. *Jacobson v. Commonwealth of Massachusetts,* 197 US 11 (1905).

41. James E. Leahy, *Liberty, Justice and Equality: How These Constitutional Guarantees Have Been Shaped by United States Supreme Court Decisions Since 1789* Qefferson, NC: McFarland & Co., 1992), 19.

42. *Griswold v. Connecticut,* 381 US 479 (1965).

43. Quoted in Leahy, *Liberty, Justice and Equality,* 20.

44. *Eisenstadt v. Baird,* 405 US 438 (1972).

45. Quoted in Leahy, *Liberty, Justice and Equality,* 22.

46. Ibid., 23.

47. L. J. Macfarlane, *The Theory and Practice of Human Rights* (New York: St. Martin's Press, 1985), 22–23.

Table, Figure and Box Notes

T1. Herbert Jacob, *Law and Politics in the United States,* 2nd ed. (New York: HarperCollins College Publishers, 1995), 163–175.

T2. Data from http://people.smu.edu/rhalperi/summary.html.

T3. Robert E. Pierre and Kari Lyderson, "Illinois Death Row Emptied," *Washington Post,* January 12, 2003, sec. A.

T4. Ibid.

T5. Lee Epstein and Joseph F. Kobylka. *The Supreme Court and Legal Change: Abortion and the Death Penalty* (Chapel Hill: University of North Carolina Press, 1992), 34–82.

T6. Ibid.

T7. American Civil Liberties website at www.aclu.org/DeathPenalty.

T8. *Coker v Georgia,* 433 U.S. 584 (1977); *Atkins v. Virginia,* 536 U.S. 304 (2002).

T9. Gurney image is in the public domain in the United States because it is a work of the United States Federal Government under the terms of Title 17, Chapter 1, Section 105 of the US Code.

T10. See House Judiciary Committee transcript at http://judiciary.house.gov/Legacy/2106.htm.

T11. Center for Religious Freedom, Questions and Answers about the "Religious Freedom Amendment, at http://crf.hudson.org/index.cfm?fuseaction=about_detail."

T12. United States Department of State, Facts about America.

T13. William K. Muir, Jr., *Prayer in the Public Schools* (Chicago: University of Chicago Press, 1967), 15.

T14. *Abington Township School District v. Schempp,* 374 U.S. 203 (1963).

T15. Robert S. Alley, *Without a Prayer: Religious Expression in Public Schools* (Amherst, NY: Prometheus Books, 1996), 128–138.

T16. Center for Religious Freedom, Questions and Answers about the "Religious Freedom Amendment, at http://crf.hudson.org/index.cfm?fuseaction=about_detail."

T17. See, for instance, the American Civil Liberties Union, at http://www.aclu.org/religion-belief.

T18. American Civil Liberties Union, at http://www.aclu.org/free-speech/flag-desecration.

T19. Robert Justin Goldstein, *Flag Burning and Free Speech: The Case of Texas vs. Johnson* (Lawrence, KS: University Press of Kansas, 2000) xiixiv.

T20. Ibid., xi.

T21. Citizens Flag Alliance, at http://www.cfa-inc.org/about.

T22. American Civil Liberties Union, at http://www.aclu.org/free-speech/flag-desecration.

T23. Goldstein, Flag Burning and Free Speech, xixvii.

T24. Dean Schabner, "Love or Obscenity?: S/M Photographer Challenges Internet Decency Standards," ABCNews.com, June 29, 2002.

T25. The National Coalition for Sexual Freedom website at www.ncsfreedom.org/.

T26. Yousuf Dhamee, "Obscenity and the Internet: The Communications Decency Act," at http://www.cyberartsweb.org/cpace/politics/decency.html.

T27. See the Center for Democracy and Technology, at http://cdt.org/.

T28. Ezekiel Emanuel, "Whose Right to Die?," *Atlantic,* March 1997.

T29. Melvin I. Uroofsky, *Lethal Judgments: Asssisted Suicide and American Law* (Lawrence, KS, University Press of Kansas, 2000), 130–133.

T30. Ibid., 101–104.

T31. Ibid., 158–159.

T32. *Gonzales v. State of Oregon*, 546 U.S. 243 (2006)

"Green" for All

By Michelle J. Nealy

Enter into the Washington, D.C., headquarters of the environmental protection agency and encounter something never seen in its history until now, a photo of the first African-American to serve as the agency's administrator.

Born in Philadelphia and raised in New Orleans, Lisa Perez Jackson is the new face of the EPA, and, just like the president who appointed her, Jackson represents change.

Only seven months into the job, Jackson has dived into a number of important issues largely ignored by the previous administration. Under Jackson's leadership, the EPA has prompted the Obama administration to pursue legislation that cuts carbon emissions, limits green house gases and addresses climate change.

And while Jackson tackles what are, perhaps, some of the most difficult environmental challenges in a generation, her toughest assignment could be something less obvious—recruiting more minorities into the green movement.

"I am looking to open up the environmental movement to more people of color. As an African-American, I think there are still, sadly, people who see the environmental movement as belonging to White Americans and clearly the history of it is that way," Jackson says.

"Everywhere I go, I see communities that are concerned about environmental issues. Those are communities of color. We need to make sure that they see themselves here [in the EPA] and that they feel comfortable knowing that the EPA is here to address issues of concern for people of color," adds Jackson.

Prior to assuming her current post, Jackson, a chemical engineer, was just weeks into her new position as chief of staff for New Jersey Gov. Jon Corzine. Before that, Jackson headed New Jersey's Department of Environmental Protection after having already served at the EPA for 16 years.

Jackson insists that she is not daunted by any of the challenges before her. She is, instead, driven by them, particularly the mandate to diversify.

"The president's election, my nomination and the first lady's obvious concern for the environment have literally changed the face of environmentalism almost overnight," says Jackson, referring to a garden first lady Michelle Obama planted on the south lawn of the White House.

"Now, what we have to do is make sure that is not just symbolic change," Jackson explains. "We have to be effective advocates and effective workers for all of our communities. The future economy is going to be a green economy. If our communities are not a part of that economy, we are going to be left out."

An Exclusive Culture

Data show that minority environmentalists are struggling to make their way in. The Minority Environmental Leadership Development Initiative found that of 158 environmental institutions, 33 percent of mainstream environmental organizations and 22 percent of government agencies had no people of color on staff.

Part of the problem, says Dr. Robert D. Bullard, director of the Environmental Justice Resource Center at Clark Atlanta University, is the paucity of minority college graduates for these organizations to recruit, particularly at the graduate level.

In 2003, in natural resources and conservation related sciences, 2,334 White students graduated compared to 219 students of color. At the doctoral level, 458 White students graduated with doctoral degrees in agricultural sciences compared to 75 students of color, according to data collected by researchers at the Multicultural Environmental Leadership Development Institute at the University of Michigan.

That same year, 143 White students received doctoral degrees in natural resources and conservation programs compared to 13 students of color.

"There is a breakdown early on, before we even start talking about getting people of color into environmental organizations and federal agencies. The problem is that we are not getting enough young people graduating from high school and continuing their studies in the science disciplines during their undergraduate years," Bullard says. "In order for one to move up the ladder professionally it takes more than one degree. With budget cuts and financial aid dwindling, we're seeing an impact on students of color completing degrees." The shortage of minorities on the professional environmentalist career-track is not due, completely, for lack of interest in environmental issues or holes in the pipeline. Some minority environmental justice advocates suggest that the mainstream environmental movement is an "unintentionally exclusive culture" that caters to tree-hugging, White middle-class *suburbanites instead of low-income* communities of color that carve out green spaces in urban enclaves, plant community gardens and use, more than any other group, public transportation.

"The historical roots [of the environmental movement] emerged probably about the same time that the civil rights movement was going strong," says Dr. Henry Neal Williams, director of the Environmental Sciences Institute at Florida A&M University. "Minorities were focused on lots of other issues connected to equality and justice about the same time the environmental movement began gaining impetus. It took a while to switch gears. Now we are at a time where the civil rights movement has an environmental justice component."

While there may be a small recruitment pool for minority environmentalists, environmental organizations are also culpable. "Many of the so-called green groups have been slow to diversify their ranks in terms of their staff, their board of directors and their agenda," Bullard says.

After earning a master's in environmental policy from Tufts University, Marcelo Bonta, a Filipino American, began working for a prominent wildlife conservation organization. After a short period of time, he quit. Bonta was the only person of color on the staff.

"Environmental organizations focus their efforts on minority recruitment, but most of the people of color, do not stay. The culture of these organizations is not inclusive or open to diverse cultures and creativity," Bonta says.

After leaving the wildlife conservation group, Bonta, like other advocates of color, started his own organization, the Center for Diversity & the Environment

"No one is intentionally excluding others but, when a homogeneous culture flourishes in organizations, which is common in environmental organizations, there is an expectation for others to conform to this dominant mindset in order to succeed," Bonta says. "When everyone looks, thinks, and acts the same, then you create policies, programs, and practices that benefit others that look, think, and act the same and exclude others that look, think, and act differently."

On the Frontline

Despite the dearth of minority environmentalists, minority communities have consistently shown an interest in environmental issues. "Polls and surveys are showing, increasingly, that communities of color are as engaged or in some cases more engaged in environmental issues than Whites," Bonta says.

For decades ordinary citizens of color have fought against the development of oil refineries, toxic waste dumps, solid waste sites and hazardous landfills in their communities. On the frontlines of these movements have been minority environmentalists Alan Hipólito, adjunct professor at the Northwestern School of Law at Lewis & Clark College and executive director of Verde, a nonprofit organization; Majora Carter, the former director of the nonprofit Sustainable South Bronx; and Charles Sams, director of Trust for Public Land's Tribal & Native Lands Program.

In 1982, residents of Warren County, N.C., which was predominantly Black, protested the construction of a hazardous waste landfill. After the district courts ruled in favor of the landfill supporters, a large demonstration erupted. More than 500 people were arrested, including Walter Fauntroy, a former member of the U.S. House of Representatives.

Later, the incident would compel the United Church of Christ Commission for Racial Justice to produce its landmark "Toxic Wastes and Race" report, the first national study to correlate hazardous waste sites and demographic characteristics. It found that race was the most significant factor in locating the waste facilities.

It took 20 years for Warren County residents to get the landfill site detoxified by the state and federal government.

"The Warren County landfill protest proved to be a most important event for the environmental justice movement in that it became the catalyst that galvanized people of color around this country in the fight for environmental justice," says Dr. Beverly Wright, director of the Deep South Center for Environmental Justice at Dillard University.

There are other examples: In 1988, a Hispanic grassroots organization Mothers of East L.A. defeated the construction of a huge toxic waste incinerator in their Los Angeles community. The same year, in Dilkon, Ariz., a small group of Navajo community activists spearheaded a successful effort to block the construction of a $40 million toxic waste incinerator.

Diversifying the Movement

At stake for minorities is not just the protection of their communities, but access to the burgeoning green economy.

"To date, most of the jobs in the green sector have gone to people with advanced degrees such as engineers, architects and landscape architects," says Hipólito, executive director of the Oregon-based Verde. "More recently, weatherization and storm-water management projects have produced jobs for low-wage workers. The pay scale for these jobs varies."

The Obama administration's economic stimulus package contains more than $20 billion for investment in a cleaner, greener economy, including $500 million for green job training. Whether this "green collar" economy will usher in a new era of socioleconomic mobility for low-income citizens or strengthen the existing middle class has yet to be determined, Hipólito says.

'What is a green job? How do I get one?' That is what people want to know, Hipólito says. "The term 'green job' has yet to be formally defined," he adds.

Verde, an environmental justice organization, connects low-income people of color to the benefits of the green job economy by creating new job, training, and business development opportunities such as the Verde Native Plant Nursery.

Success, Hipólito says, will be dependent on whether there will be meaningful pathways and training programs that make green jobs accessible to minorities at every rung of the green job ladder.

Researchers, in a report co-sponsored by the Center for Diversity & the Environment and the Conservation Fund and titled "Diversifying the Environmental Movement," argue environmental organizations must focus on cultural inclusivity, recruitment, retention, outreach and collaboration to integrate the movement.

The most obvious places for the EPA to begin partnership-building is with minority-serving institutions, says Williams of FAMU. In 2008, the university's Environmental Sciences Institute celebrated the graduation of its 50th graduate student.

"If the government or private organizations are serious about addressing environmental issues for all communities, if they are serious about diversifying the work force, then they have to look to and invest in HBCUs [historically Black colleges and universities]," Williams says. "HBCUs can make an immediate impact both in training the next generation of environmental professionals and increasing awareness about environmental issues in minority communities."

Jackson agrees. "Historically Black institutions and Hispanic-serving institutions are churning out young, talented people who are technically trained, who are interested in environmental sciences, biological sciences and chemistry," she says. "We are going to make sure that we are recruiting them, so that we change our entry-level work force and make sure they are represented there. Students at universities are the catalyst for change at their own schools. Howard University, here in the District, we will soon be working with them on a greening effort on their campus."

Williams is encouraged by the appointment of Jackson to the EPA. He believes that her presence will make a difference in the psyches of minority children who lack environmental role models.

"One of the biggest problems that we have is recruiting students to become majors, particularly at the undergraduate level. Kids need to know that there are champions like Lisa Jackson and that the field has value. There is a tremendous value in being able to protect your community," Williams says.

CHAPTER 9

Civil Rights

Chapter 9 Vignette

By Jennifer Byrne

Affirmative action in university admissions was established by Lyndon Johnson through an executive order in 1970. The idea behind the program was to allow for an equality of opportunity, though not necessarily equality of outcome, to women and racial minorities that for many years, lived under a separate system of law. Not only were minorities prohibited from full participation in the political process, but legal frameworks such as Jim Crow laws also prevented equal access to employment and education. Affirmative action programs allow employers and admissions committees to take into account the race and gender of the applicant in evaluating their fitness for the position, as well as other characteristics that might enhance diversity. However, the implementation of affirmative action has changed substantially from the model in the 1970s, where reserving seats for applicants on the basis of race or gender was the norm; a practice that has since been deemed in violation of the 14th Amendment's equal protection guarantee in the Constitution. Currently, affirmative action is used as a tool to enhance diversity, particularly on college campuses, and focuses on a number of characteristics of potential applicants beyond race and gender; however, this model is now under criticism and is being reviewed by the U.S. Supreme Court. Let's take a brief look at some of the key cases in order to understand how affirmative action works today in college admissions.

In the early 1970s, some universities used quota systems to ensure minority admissions. For example, at the University of California Davis School of Medicine, 16 of 100 seats for new students were reserved for minorities. A white applicant challenged this model of affirmative action claiming that his GPA and test scores were higher than those of the minority applicants that were admitted, and argued that if those 16 seats had been open and available to all applicants, he would have been granted admission to the school. The majority of the Supreme Court agreed that while the concept of affirmative action was constitutional, the way that the program was implemented by the University of Davis was unconstitutional because it made the race of the applicant the sole factor for admission or denial. The justices pointed to a program that was being used by Harvard University that gave applicants points for desirable characteristics; for many decades these "point" systems were very popular at universities and awarded points not only for race, but also alumni status, geographical location, and ranking of the high school that the applicant attended. This system was

385

challenged in 2001 by an applicant to the University of Michigan, who argued that minorities were given too many points in the admissions process, relative to other characteristics. While 100 points were necessary to ensure admission, 20 points could be awarded for race or athletic ability (although the applicant could only use one of these categories if they fell into more than one). The Supreme Court argued that this was tantamount to a quota, as the points one could be granted for their race were so substantial, that the race of an individual could be enough to put him or her over the admissions ceiling. In other words, the points awarded for race were disproportionately higher than points awarded for other categories that were considered by the Michigan admissions department. The Court did once again allow for diversity, but reiterated that race could not be the determining factor used in admissions. They also allowed schools to use affirmative action to gain a critical mass of minority students, but, the battle did not end there ...

In 2013, Abigail Noel Fischer, challenged the system at the University of Texas at Austin, which granted automatic admission for students in the top 10 percent of their graduating class, but race is considered as one of many factors in the decision to admit roughly 25 percent of the applicants that do not qualify for automatic admission. Fischer finished in the top 12 percent of her class with an 1180 SAT score, and was denied admission, after which she filed suit claiming that her constitutional rights had been violated. An appeals court sided with the university, but upon review, the U.S. Supreme Court said that the lower court did not apply the correct standard. The appeals court assumed that the school acted in good faith, an assumption that puts the burden of proof on the petitioner. Yet, the Supreme Court has consistently held that a strict scrutiny test, which places the burden of proof on the government, in this case the university, to show why its actions are constitutional. Amid speculation that Chief Justice John Roberts may want his crowning achievement on the Court to be a stricter approach to affirmative action, or perhaps to abandon the program altogether, the case was sent back to the lower court. Justice Anthony Kennedy, who authored the majority opinion, stated that, "a standard

of strict scrutiny does not permit a court to accept a school's assertion that its admission process uses race in a permissible way without closely examining how the process works in practice."[1] The school must show that race is not the predominant factor for admission, and all applicants must be evaluated as individuals. What this means is that the Court, for now, has continued in its current interpretation of the 14th Amendment, which permits universities to consider race as one factor to contribute to the diversity of its student body; however, race must not be the predominant or determining factor for admission.

Some states, however, have taken matters into their own hands. In 2006, Michigan passed a statewide referendum to prohibit race and sex-based discrimination, or preferential treatment in public university admissions. The ban has been included in the state's Constitution, and now, the Supreme Court must decide whether the state of Michigan's constitution is in conflict with the U.S. Constitution. The justices appear to have interpreted the 14th Amendment to permit certain types of preferential treatment on the basis of race and gender but has not said that such considerations are required by the Constitution. The lower federal courts have said that such a policy violates the Equal Protection Clause, but supporters of the ban liken affirmative action policies to the "new Jim Crow laws." The ban was passed with support from 68 percent of the voters—which also raises concerns about judicial activism—with nine unelected justices overturning a provision in a state constitution with support from a clear majority of the voters. It is expected that the Court may split along ideological lines, with Anthony Kennedy providing the decisive vote. Some justices, such as Clarence Thomas, believe that affirmative action programs violate the 14th Amendment. Other justices, such as Sonya Sotomayor, have expressed skepticism at proposed race-neutral programs to facilitate diversity, and voted in the University of Texas at Austin case to allow race and gender-based admissions to continue under the Court standards. It becomes a question of whether the 14th Amendment requires preferential treatment for disadvantaged groups, allows for such treatment, or prohibits these programs. Or, is the 14th

Amendment silent? In this case, what resources should we use to help us decide on the continued use of affirmative action?

Below, you will find one political cartoon in support of the use of affirmative action in university admissions programs, and one against. What arguments are implicit in these cartoons? What points are the authors aiming to make with their satirical drawings, and what does this mean for the interpretation of the 14th Amendment?

Endnotes

1. Fisher v. United States, 570 U.S. __, 2013.

Establishing Civil Rights

By Matthew Kerbel

Introduction

Some people feel passionately about the kind of country they want the United States to be. Others are content to sit on the sidelines as decisions are made about who gets what. For some people, social concerns are of great importance. For others, the stuff of daily experience is enough to keep them occupied, even if that experience is shaped in part by political choices that don't interest them.

Which kind of person are you? Do you think a lot about the kind of society you're living in? Do you think about ways you'd like to maintain it or change it? Do you engage in political action to try to bring it about?

Or do you find questions like these to be uninteresting? Maybe you feel government is too distant from your everyday life to matter much. Do you think that even if you got involved on behalf of what you believe, it wouldn't make much of a difference?

Questions like these are really about values. If you believe we should be a society where we spend heavily on the military, that's a value. If you believe we should be a society where abortions are available to women who want them, that's also a value. If you believe capital punishment is a deterrent to crime, you probably value

the death penalty. If you believe traditionally disadvantaged groups should be given extra consideration in college admission decisions, you probably value affirmative action.

It's easy to see how values can conflict with one another because those who want to spend less tax money on the military will clash with those who want to spend more, those who believe abortion is morally wrong will clash with those who feel it is a matter of personal choice, and so on.

People who feel strongly about some of these things and see their positions as moral absolutes might object to having them defined as values. This complicates the battles that ensue when people with different visions of society clash in the political process because it's not unusual for people on *both sides* of an issue to believe that they are simply right. In one regard, the safeguards to the system that we talked about in the first part of the book put a drag on the most aggressive advocates of a political position and deter factions from imposing their will on others. But that doesn't stop the political debate from being intense and ferocious—even if you're personally not involved in it.

Regardless of your personal involvement in politics, all of us live with the results of those who get the political system to successfully respond to their values and their view of society. Politics creates winners and losers. In your parents' generation, advocates of government as a vehicle for bringing about social justice won a lot of battles. Your generation has witnessed the success of those who felt that approach was ineffective or misguided. Even if you didn't participate, if you hold a position on any of the wide range of things government touches, you are a winner or a loser, too.

We're going to explore four arenas where the fury of policy debate determines whose values receive official acknowledgment. It's a fluid process, where winners at one moment could turn into losers at another, and where winners in one area could be losers in another. So, as we look at policies affecting civil rights, civil liberties, domestic affairs and international relations, consider the kind of country you would like to live in, and see how it compares with the kind of country we choose to be. Along the way, think about the things you value, and whether there is any way that you can imagine your voice contributing to the debate over any of the issues we will discuss.

We'll start with issues of civil rights.

Civil Rights

The Declaration of Independence says, "all men are created equal." **Civil rights** policies are about making sure this is enforced as a matter of law: that the law treats everyone equally, regardless of differences in race, gender, ethnic background, sexual preference, or anything people might be inclined to discriminate against. Because equal treatment does not naturally materialize, ensuring civil rights can be a challenge. Even among people who agree with the principle of equal treatment under the law, there can be strong disagreements over the means to that end. Some would treat everyone the same in order to treat them equally, whereas others would make exceptions for those who have long been the object of discriminatory treatment. This can be the cause of fierce policy disputes.

There are different ways to define equality and because they are not entirely compatible with one another, advocates of different conceptions of equality readily clash. Some of the early civil rights struggles were about affording disadvantaged groups the same political rights as others, such as African Americans, who for years were kept out of the political process through legal and violent means, and women, who struggled for decades to win the right to vote. These groups sought **political equality**, which you may recall is a form of **equality of opportunity** because it creates a level playing field for all participants. Although struggles by these groups were ferocious and met with intense resistance by those whites or men who felt threatened by opening the political process to blacks and women, subsequent generations have largely embraced the political gains they made. That's because Americans tend to support equality of opportunity, and widely value the evenhanded application of political rights.

Some of the more recent civil rights battles, however, have been fought over outcomes, which we know to be problematic for many Americans. These battles have sparked enormous controversy because by attempting to advance **equality of outcome**, disadvantaged groups have run headlong into the widely held American preference for not using government to produce **economic equality** or **social equality**. So, people who argue for policies like affirmative action, meant to compensate for past and present discrimination in hiring or college admissions, meet defiance from those who see it as a misguided attempt to mandate economic equality. Women face similar resistance when they argue for comparable worth legislation, mandating equal pay for jobs predominantly performed by women that require similar skill levels and training as other jobs predominantly performed by men.

Compounding matters is the issue of who qualifies as a disadvantaged group. In recent years, Native Americans, Latinos, Asian Americans, gays, people with disabilities, and seniors have prominently organized to demand consideration for past and present discrimination. To some, having so many groups claiming redress for discriminatory practices makes a mockery of civil rights by creating a culture of victimization, whereby anyone with a grievance about how others treat them can turn to the government to rectify it. Their resistance is fueled by the fact that many of these civil rights agendas raise controversial questions about social equality: Should Spanish be used in schools with large Latino populations in order to treat Spanish-speaking children equally, or are Spanish-speaking children treated equally when schools require they learn English? Should monogamous homosexual relationships be treated the same as monogamous heterosexual relationships, with gays being allowed to marry? Should seniors be protected from discrimination by employers who may prefer to hire younger people?

In theory, most Americans would agree that everyone should have equal rights before the law and that all people should be treated with equal dignity. In practice, civil rights struggles are always controversial. People do not always accept the legitimacy of a group's grievances, and the aggrieved group's demands for a change in the economic or social order can be perceived to cut against widely held beliefs about equality of outcome. This serves to make civil rights issues among the most heated—and important—controversies that government has to address.

Equal Protection

The key to civil rights in the United States is laid out in Part 1 of the Fourteenth Amendment, which says "No state shall ... deny to any person within its jurisdiction the equal protection of the laws." The intent of this **equal protection clause** is that all laws should be applied evenly and without prejudice to all citizens. Note that it is not a mandate for equality of outcomes: The Constitution is silent on the matter of equal results. Rather, the Fourteenth Amendment makes a statement about equal treatment, that everyone is equal in the eyes of the law. This approach is consistent with the long-standing American value of equal opportunity, which is secured in part by equal application of the law.

Groups that have experienced discrimination have used the equal protection clause to rectify inequities. Most prominently, it has been used by African Americans to fight legalized segregation. The Fourteenth Amendment established full citizenship for former slaves while guaranteeing them equal protection of the law. It is one of a trio of post-Civil War amendments designed to give African Americans a legal basis for equal rights. The Thirteenth Amendment abolished slavery in the United States, and the Fifteenth Amendment gave African American males the right to vote.

Slaves prior to the Civil War were treated as property, and how the Supreme Court had affirmed the institution of slavery in the case of **Dred Scott v. Sanford** in 1857, just four years before the South seceded from the Union, and just five years before President Lincoln issued the Emancipation Proclamation of 1862, granting freedom to all slaves living in the states of the Confederacy. With the passage of the Thirteenth Amendment in 1865, a revolution in the legal status of African Americans had transpired over the course of eight wrenching years.

Note also how the Fourteenth Amendment says that no state shall deny equal protection of the laws to any of its citizens. Not trusting the states of the Confederacy to grant equal protection to freed slaves, the federal government retained the ability to impose the conditions of all three post-Civil War amendments on the states. This language, along with the Union victory in the Civil War, constituted a turning point in a key matter of **federalism** by settling the question of federal supremacy that had been one of the country's hottest political issues since the ratification of the Constitution.

Civil Rights and African Americans

For many African Americans, who make up 13% of the U.S. population, the story of contemporary citizenship has deep roots in an enduring struggle for civil rights that was shaped by the way southern states treated emancipated slaves. The authors of the post-Civil War amendments were wise to distrust southern states to implement laws that defied the political culture of the region. Immediately following the Civil War, when Union troops occupied the South, they could impose terms for **Reconstruction** of the Union. Officials of the former Confederacy were initially barred from exercising political power, and could only sit by and watch as the first African Americans were elected to Congress as Republicans from such states as South Carolina, Mississippi, and Louisiana.

Southern whites did their best to strike back. In 1865, the **Ku Klux Klan** was established in Tennessee as a secret white supremacist organization that regarded freedom for African Americans as a threat to whites. For decades, white-hooded Klansmen would terrorize, torture, and kill blacks, sometimes freely, sometimes despite tepid federal efforts to stop the violence.[1] The Klan disbanded in 1871, only to reemerge in 1915.[2]

Also in 1865, a number of southern states implemented "**Black Codes**" designed to restrict the civil rights of emancipated slaves. Although the details varied, Black Codes attempted to reinstate the social order that had existed before the Civil War by regulating where African Americans could work, live, and travel, and by preventing them from owning or renting land or from working as anything but laborers.[3] Federal civil rights laws struck down the Black Codes in 1866,[4] but this did not change the fact that millions of newly freed men and women still lived in a white-dominated society that continued to regard them as property, and required their cheap, previously free labor to prop up a devastated economy.

When Abraham Lincoln sought a second term as president in 1864, he looked ahead to the conclusion of the Civil War and the need to reconstruct a unified nation. With this in mind, Lincoln—a Republican—selected as his running mate Andrew Johnson, a southern Democrat who believed in states' rights. Johnson represented Tennessee in the Senate even after his state seceded, making him something of a hero to northerners. Even so, Lincoln's move was significant because Democrats at the time were regarded as the party of the South and secession, and Republicans viewed Democrats as the enemy in war.

In one of the great ironies of American history, when Lincoln was assassinated in 1865, Johnson became president of the United States, and the job of reconstructing the Union fell to this southern Democrat. Whatever sympathies he felt toward his home region came through in his approach to reconstruction, or at least were apparent to a

Congress dominated by radical Republicans who objected to Johnson's offer of pardons to southerners willing to swear allegiance to the United States, and implementation of a reconstruction program while Congress was out of session.

Congress saw the rise of Black Codes across the South and the return of southern prewar political leaders as clear indications that Johnson's program would undermine efforts to extend civil rights to former slaves. They quickly fought back, with civil rights legislation banning Black Codes, by refusing to seat any member of Congress who had joined the Confederacy, and by strengthening the Union's military presence in the South.

Radical Republicans so dominated Congress that they were able to impose their plan over Johnson's veto, the first time in history that Congress overrode the president on a consequential matter.

They went further, attempting to hamstring Johnson by placing restrictions on his office that were of questionable constitutionality. When Johnson violated one of these restrictions by firing the secretary of war—a member of Johnson's cabinet—without congressional authorization, he was impeached by the House—another first—and tried in the Senate, where he was acquitted by one vote in 1868.[5] His anguished tenure in office ended shortly thereafter. Republicans regained the White House with the election of President Ulysses S. Grant, and did not relinquish it until 1885.

In 1876, the disputed election between Democrat Samuel Tilden and Republican Rutherford B. Hayes appeared to have put a Democrat in the White House for the first time since the start of Reconstruction. Tilden claimed an Electoral College majority, but results from several slates were challenged by Republicans. With the election in doubt, a compromise was hammered out in which Hayes would be given the presidency in exchange for the withdrawal of Union troops from the South. This marked the end of Reconstruction, and the start of a long period in which African Americans saw their civil rights taken away. As Reconstruction ended, the plight of African Americans faded as a political issue in the North. African American representation in Congress began to tail off.[6] Southern blacks were left with few viable avenues for the protection of their civil rights despite

Table13.1 Life under Jim Crow Laws[T2]

Subject	Restriction
Nurses	No person or corporation shall require any white female nurse to nurse in wards or rooms in hospitals, either public or private, in which Negro men are placed (Alabama)
Pool and billiard rooms	It shall be unlawful for a Negro and a white person to play together or in company with each other at any game of pool or billiards (Alabama)
Barbers	No colored barber shall serve as a barber (to) white women or girls (Georgia)
Amateur baseball	It shall be unlawful for any amateur white baseball team to play baseball on any vacant lot or baseball diamond within two blocks of a playground devoted to the Negro race, and it shall be unlawful for any amateur colored baseball team to play baseball on any vacant lot or baseball diamond within two blocks of a playground devoted to the white race (Georgia)
Burial	The officer in charge shall not bury, or allow to be buried, any colored persons upon ground set aside for the burial of white persons (Georgia)
Textbooks	Books shall not be interchangeable between the white and colored schools, but shall continue to be used by the race first using them (North Carolina)
Child custody	It shall be unlawful for any parent, relative, or other white person in this State, having the control or custody of any white child, by right of guardianship, natural or required, or otherwise, to dispose of, give or surrender such white child permanently into the custody, control, maintenance, or support of a Negro (South Carolina)
Buses	All passenger stations in this state operated by any motor transportation company shall have separate waiting rooms or space and separate ticket windows for the white and colored races (Alabama)
Intermarriage	The marriage of a person of Caucasian blood with a Negro, Mongolian, Malay, or Hindu shall be null and void (Arizona)
Parks	It shall be unlawful for colored people to frequent any park owned or maintained by the city for the benefit, use and enjoyment of white persons...and unlawful for any white person to frequent any park owned or maintained by the city for use and benefit of colored persons (Georgia)
Housing	Any person...who shall rent any part of any such building to a Negro person or a Negro family when such a building is already in whole or in part in occupancy by a white person or white family, or vice versa when the building is in occupancy by a Negro person or Negro family, shall be guilty of a misdemeanor and on conviction thereof shall be punished by a fine of not less than twenty-five ($25.00) nor more than one hundred ($100.00) dollars or be imprisoned not less that 10, or more than 60 days, or both such fine and imprisonment in the discretion of the court (Louisiana)
Telephone booths	The Corporation Commission is hereby vested with power and authority to require telephone companies ... to maintain separate booths for white and colored patrons when there is demand for such separate booths. That the Corporation Commission shall determine the necessity for said separate booths only upon complaint of the people in the town and vicinity to be served after due hearing as now provided by law in other complaints filed with the Corporation Commission (Oklahoma)
Promotion of equality	Any person ... who shall be guilty of printing, publishing or circulating printed, typewritten or written matter urging or presenting for public acceptance, or general information, arguments or suggestions in favor social equality or of intermarriage between whites and Negroes, shall be guilty of a misdemeanor and subject to a fine not exceeding five hundred ($500.00) dollars or imprisonment not exceeding (6) months or both (Mississippi)

the constitutional protections that had been granted a decade earlier.

From this point on, African Americans in the South faced decades of disenfranchisement and institutionalized segregation at the hands of whites who never accepted the terms of Reconstruction. With the Union army and northern Republicans out of the way, repressive measures took hold. Institutionalized segregation in the form of **Jim Crow laws** made discrimination a way of life in the South.

Jim Crow was a character from minstrel shows, performed by white entertainers who covered their faces in burnt cork and acted out demeaning stereotypes of African Americans, depicting them as childish and incompetent. By the Civil War, the Jim Crow character was an established part of American popular culture. The exact connection between the racist minstrel show character and the racist laws of the same name is a matter of historical dispute.[7]

Because you likely never experienced it, you may have trouble imagining just how total and repressive the Jim Crow laws were. Everything from the simplest everyday experiences like going to the park or using a public telephone, everything from birth to schooling to marriage to death was legally segregated. Table 17.1 should give you a sense of how this segregation permeated society and denied African Americans their basic civil rights. As you read the table, try to imagine being an African American subjected to Jim Crow laws. Ask yourself what your life would have been like and how you would have felt about yourself if you acquiesced to these laws. There would have been enormous pressures on you to conform, sometimes life-threatening pressures—and a tremendous loss of dignity for doing so. Can you even imagine how you might have behaved?

By the start of the twentieth century, legal segregation so pervaded the South that separate public facilities from rest rooms to drinking fountains to public transportation waiting rooms were marked with "Colored Only" signs. As we know from Chapter 12, the Supreme Court had upheld this type of segregation in the 1896 case **Plessy v. Ferguson**. In some southern states, African Americans traveling by train were forced to sit in a separate "Jim Crow car." Interracial marriage was criminalized. Voting rights were taken away through high poll taxes, impossible literacy tests, and laws prohibiting grandchildren of slaves from voting. As a result of these barriers, the number of African Americans casting ballots in South Carolina and Georgia fell by half between 1880 and 1888.[8] Whatever thoughts African Americans may have had about standing up to these racist provisions were dispelled on the one hand through the debilitating effects of widespread illiteracy and poverty, and on the other hand by terrorist acts committed by white lynch mobs.[9]

Although it wasn't as institutionalized, overt, or brutal, color barriers existed nationwide. As industrialization transformed the country in the early twentieth century, manufacturing jobs prompted a mass migration of African Americans from the South to the North and Midwest. There, blacks met with a more subtle form of discrimination. They remained for the most part low-wage earners, confined to live in urban ghettos, often in poor or run-down housing. Job opportunities that held the promise of a better life were not forthcoming. Social attitudes in many cities were not much different than they had been in the South.

The Civil Rights Movement

The Supreme Court ruling in *Brown v. Board of Education* (1954) declaring segregated schools unconstitutional foreshadowed one and a half decades of activism on behalf of African American civil rights. It would culminate in the elimination of Jim Crow laws, the triumph of federal over state power, and full implementation of the Fourteenth Amendment one hundred years after its passage. As with any wrenching social change, the human cost was great, both in lives of civil rights activists lost to assassins and lives shattered by riots that decimated African American neighborhoods from Harlem in New York to Watts in Los Angeles.

It started innocuously enough. One year after the *Brown* decision, a forty-two-year-old seamstress named Rosa Parks boarded a bus in Montgomery, Alabama, and sat in the first row of what was called the "Colored" section at the back of the bus. Montgomery's law required that blacks pay their fare at the front of the bus, then leave the bus, reboard in the rear, and sit in the back. If a white patron boarded when the "White" section was full, black passengers seated in the front of the "Colored" section were required to give up their seats and move further back. This happened to Rosa Parks: When a white passenger boarded the crowded bus, the white bus driver insisted that she relinquish her seat as required by law. She refused, and was arrested.

Rosa Parks had been locally active in the National Association for the Advancement of Colored Persons (NAACP), and knew the organization was looking for an opportunity to challenge Montgomery's segregation laws. She presented the organization with an ideal political symbol for the challenge: soft-spoken, demure, gainfully employed, happily married—in short, an utterly sympathetic figure to contrast the brutality of segregation. When

Table 17.2. Civil Rights Timeline[T4]

1954: School segregation ruled unconstitutional in *Brown v. Board* of Education m Supreme Court decision.

1955: Dr. Martin Luther King, Jr. (below) leads boycotts against segregated 1 transportation facilities after Rosa Parks (right) defies Montgomery, Alabama law 1 requiring African Americans to sit at the back of public buses; bu s desegregation 1 is eventually declared unconstitutional.

1957: President Eisenhower sends federal troops to Little Rock, Arkansas, after 1 Governor Orval Faubus orders the Arkansas National Guard to block nine black 1 students from integrating Central High School.

1960: African American students begin staging "sit-ins" at southern lunch counters that refuse to serve blacks.

1962: President Kennedy sends federal troops to the University of Mississippi to stop riots so that the first black students can attend; all military reserve units are integrated.

1963: Dr. Martin Luther King, Jr. delivers "I have a dream" speech to hundreds B°f thousands of civil rights protesters who have converged on Washington, D.C.

1964: Congress passes Civil Rights Act following a 75-day long filibuster by Hsouthern senators; race riots erupt in Philadelphia and New York.

1965: Civil rights protesters march from Selma to Montgomery, Alabama, to 1 demand voting rights; Congress passes the Voting Rights Act, race riots erupt in Los Angeles.

1968: Dr. Martin Luther King, Jr. is assassinated in Memphis, Tennessee.

Parks agreed to challenge the law, the NAACP immediately organized a boycott by African Americans of Montgomery buses, led by the minister of a local Baptist church, the Reverend Dr. Martin Luther King Jr. The boycott lasted for more than a year, until the Supreme Court ruled bus segregation unconstitutional in December 1956.[10] With that victory, the **civil rights movement** was born. A brief timeline emphasizing key events in the civil rights movement may be found in Table 17.2.

The actions undertaken by Dr. King and other prominent leaders on behalf of civil rights were nonviolent forms of **civil disobedience**, along the lines of Rosa Parks disobeying what she believed to be an illegitimate law. College students were heavily involved. The **Student Nonviolent Coordinating Committee (SNCC)** formed in 1960 and organized "**sit-ins**" at "Whites Only" lunch counters, where black students would simply sit down in seats reserved for whites, to focus national attention on segregated facilities. African Americans and sympathetic whites engaged in "**freedom rides**" throughout the South in 1961, where whites would take the seats at the back of the bus and use "Colored Only" facilities at highway rest stops, while African Americans sat up front and used "Whites Only" facilities.

These activities proved dangerous. Angry mobs attacked the demonstrators, often causing serious harm. Local authorities, sympathetic to the mobs, looked the other way, while local judicial officers sent protesters to prison. The actions of the demonstrators might have gone unnoticed if not for the fact that television, now a decade old and with national reach, was there to record the cruelty of segregation, broadcast it to the country, and help put pressure on the national government to act. Small victories began to pile up, like a 1961 order by the Kennedy Justice Department that outlawed discrimination on interstate buses that was issued in direct response to the treatment of the freedom riders.

As the stakes built, violence escalated. In 1963, civil rights leader Medgar Evers was assassinated. Dr. King organized peaceful demonstrations in Birmingham, Alabama, which were met with violence from angry white mobs. Four black girls attending Sunday School were murdered in the bombing of a Birmingham church. The first of many race riots began in African American sections of major cities, leaving urban centers in ruin for decades to come.

In 1964, SNCC, in conjunction with the NAACP and the largely white-run Congress of Racial Equality (CORE), organized "Freedom Summer," which centered on a voter registration drive in Mississippi to undermine the laws that prevented blacks from voting. White college students from the North were recruited to join southern blacks in a state where less than 7 percent of African Americans were registered to vote, the lowest percentage in the country. It drew an enormous amount of media attention, in part because the students were met with a violent response that resulted in over one thousand arrests, at least eighty beatings at the hands of white mobs or police officers, and three murders.[11]

Just as the civil rights movement was generating national sympathy, it was also beginning to fray. The political success of "Freedom Summer" masked racial tensions between black and white activists, as black workers were angered by what they felt was an attitude of superiority among white workers.[12] A radical faction of SNCC, angered at the violence they endured and what they felt was a slow rate of progress, rejected civil disobedience practices in exchange for confronting violence with violence. As the 1960s progressed, violence began to overtake peaceful resistance as a means for change. In 1968, the most visible advocate of peaceful social change, Dr. King, was assassinated in Memphis.

Legislative Success

Through it all, the civil rights movement realized stunning successes in the legislative arena that effectively ended segregation and stopped voting rights violations. Congress had considered—and failed to pass—civil rights legislation every year from 1945 to 1956. Then in 1957, in reaction to the changing climate of public opinion brought about by the civil rights movement, Congress passed the first civil rights bill in eighty years.

The Civil Rights Act of 1957 was narrow in scope, establishing a federal Civil Rights Commission to hear complaints about voting irregularities. It was bolstered three years later by the Civil Rights Act of 1960, which prohibited states from destroying voter registration records.[13] In reality, complaints about voting irregularities took years to process and did not affect practices that disenfranchised African Americans, but these federal acts were valuable for what they presaged.

By 1964, political pressure largely generated by media coverage of the violent response to tactics of

peaceful resistance served to bolster public support for legislation that only several years earlier would have been impossible to imagine moving through Congress. The fact that many Americans are naturally sympathetic to the notion of political equality was working to the long-term benefit of the protesters. A coalition of Republicans and non-southern Democrats fought an epic battle in the House and Senate on behalf of this legislation, culminating in a cloture vote that ended a two-month long Senate filibuster. The result was the landmark **Civil Rights Act of 1964**, which:

- Outlawed discrimination in restaurants, hotels, motels, and all public accommodations involved in interstate commerce.
- Outlawed discrimination in hiring by businesses employing more than twenty-five people (serving as the basis for the affirmative action policies we'll talk about soon).
- Established the Equal Employment Opportunity Commission (EEOC) to hear complaints about workplace discrimination.
- Undermined practices designed to disenfranchise African Americans by mandating the equal application of voter registration requirements.
- Authorized withdrawing federal funds from institutions that practiced discriminatory policies.
- Authorized the Attorney General to file suit when necessary to desegregate public schools.[14]

Although the law was not all encompassing—for instance, it still permitted discrimination in private clubs—it was sweeping in scope and represented a profound political transformation in the area of civil rights. For the first time since Reconstruction, the federal government took an active role against discriminatory policies aimed at African Americans. A sympathetic Supreme Court upheld the legislation. Jim Crow could be heard in the distance, gasping for air.

The following year, when Congress passed the **Voting Rights Act of 1965**, Jim Crow was effectively dead. By providing for direct federal intervention in state voting and registration procedures, the Voting Rights Act put an end to requirements that disenfranchised African Americans. Specifically, the law empowered the attorney general to send inspectors to supervise voter registration in states that required literacy tests and where less than 50 percent of qualified residents had registered or voted in 1964. By authorizing inspections instead of permitting voters with a complaint to file suit, as had been the case in previous civil rights legislation, the effects were immediate and dramatic.[15]

As with the Civil Rights Act of 1964, the success of the Voting Rights Act could be measured in the rapid changes it brought about. African American voter registration increased markedly. For the first time since Reconstruction, African Americans were returning to Congress and being elected to other offices, in the South and elsewhere. In 1966, Edward Brooke of Massachusetts became the first African American senator in eighty-five years. In 1967, Carl Stokes of Cleveland became the first African American mayor of a major U.S. city; six years later, when Maynard Jackson became the mayor of Atlanta, he became the first African American to lead a southern city.[16] In 1971, there were enough African Americans in the House of Representatives to establish the Congressional Black Caucus, which coordinates the legislative strategy of black members.[17] The first African American governor, Douglas Wilder, was elected in 1989 in Virginia, the state that once housed the capital of the Confederacy.[18] Nineteen years later, Barack Obama would carry

the state of Virginia along with North Carolina and Florida on his way to the White House.

Affirmative Action

Although Jim Crow laws have been buried for so long that you may not have been familiar with the term before encountering it in school, today's civil rights advocates charge that the legacy of Jim Crow lingers in unequal access by African Americans to high-quality education, high-paying jobs, and affordable housing. From this perspective, although the turbulence of the 1950s and 1960s is long behind us, Dr. King's dream of a color-blind America remains beyond our grasp. As unequal treatment of African Americans became less blatant than it was during the time of Jim Crow, and as the black civil rights agenda turned from advancing equality of opportunity to equality of outcome, American public opinion began to divide over the remedies to present-day injustices, making contemporary solutions to discriminatory practices highly controversial.

Perhaps no civil rights policy is more controversial than affirmative action, which attempts to remedy inequities produced by long-term patterns of discrimination. In Issue: Affirmative Action, you'll have an opportunity to read about affirmative action policies, and see what supporters and opponents say about them.

ISSUE

AFFIRMATIVE ACTION

Consider two brief stories:

The first is about a man named Anthony Romero, director of the Ford Foundation's Human Rights and International Cooperation Program, where he is responsible for administering millions of dollars of grant money. His position is light-years removed from his childhood home in a crime-ridden Bronx neighborhood, where an entire family was murdered in the next apartment, his parents would not permit him to play outside out of fear for his safety, and winter nights were spent

wearing a hat and gloves because his family's apartment lacked heat and hot water.

By the time he reached high school, Romero's family had scraped together enough money to move to a working-class New Jersey community, trading in a life of crime and poverty for a life of rejection by their white neighbors. Romero responded to feelings of marginalization by throwing himself into his studies, proving his ability to himself and to anyone who cared to notice—including, it turned out, some of the most exclusive universities in the country. He never could have afforded to attend any of them on his family's income, but because he identified himself as "Puerto Rican" on the PSAT application, he was eligible for financial aid and heavily recruited by Ivy League institutions. That's how he was able to attend Princeton and take the first step toward his position at the Ford Foundation.[15]

The second story is about a manager, whom we'll call Alvin, at a utility company. As in many companies, most managers and 85 percent of the employees are white. Alvin has been employed at the company for fifteen years and has an excellent record. In fact, five years ago he received the best performance review in the company. But he's lost out for a promotion he had been expecting to someone who got weaker reviews from his subordinates, despite getting a better review from his superiors—a fact Alvin freely admits. But when he looks at the whole performance picture, Alvin wonders if there isn't something disturbing going on. The person who received the promotion is white. Alvin is African American. He feels the company is racist.[16]

The first story argues for the benefits of affirmative action. The second illustrates what critics say is the psychology of affirmative action gone awry.

Affirmative action is a policy requiring employers to address racial, ethnic, or gender inequalities by ensuring equal opportunities for employment and advancement.[17] It has been a matter of law since passage of the Civil Rights Act of 1964, which allowed the judiciary to battle discrimination by i ordering "such affirmative action as may be appropriate." The following year, President Lyndon Johnson vastly expanded that mandate with an executive order requiring all employers who do business with the federal government to apply affirmative action principles.[18]

Originally designed to address past discrimination against racial minority groups, affirmative action has been expanded over the years to include women, people with disabilities, gays, and Vietnam veterans. As affirmative action policies have grown to include more individuals, so have the methods of implementing them. Affirmative action law forbids artificial barriers to the hiring and advancement of people in the targeted groups, and if employers underutilize group members they have to take steps to remedy the situation. Affirmative action policies range from relatively uncontroversial activities like minority recruitment to more explosive approaches like preferential hiring of underrepresented group members and targeted hiring of minority individuals.[T9]

All of these methods aim to address the same objective—correcting past discriminatory practices—but they cover the spectrum from offering equality of opportunity to historically disadvantaged groups (through recruitment procedures, for instance) to compensating for past inequalities with the promise of equal outcomes (preferential hiring). That's where affirmative action is most controversial— when group characteristics are placed ahead of individual talent and ability—because it conflicts with the long-standing American preference for favoring opportunity over outcomes.

The Supreme Court took up the controversy in the 1978 case *Regents of the University of California v. Bakke*. The University of California at Davis medical school denied admission to a white applicant while accepting less well qualified minority applicants under a program that set aside a specific number of slots for members of traditionally disadvantaged groups. Bakke, the white student, claimed the policy itself was discriminatory and the Court agreed, backing away from unqualified support of affirmative action policies while upholding the constitutionality of using race as a factor (just not the factor) in college admissions.[T10]

Since the Bakke decision, the debate over affirmative action has simply grown more heated. In 2003, the Supreme Court revisited the issue in twin cases involving admissions procedures at the University of Michigan. In *Cratz v. Bollinger*, two white applicants rejected by the University of Michigan despite having been deemed qualified for admission sued the school, claiming its use of racial preferences in making admissions decisions violated the Fourteenth Amendment's equal protection clause.[T11] In *Gruffer v. Bollinger*, a white applicant rejected by the University of Michigan law school filed a similar claim to the one made in the Cratz case, asserting that she had been turned aside because of an application process that treated race as a "predominant" factor in admissions.[112]

The Court narrowly reaffirmed that race can be used as a criterion in admissions decisions in the interest of achieving diversity on campus. By a 5-4 vote, it upheld the flexible procedures used by the University of Michigan law school, which considered race as one of a number of "soft" criteria for admission. However, it overturned the approach used by the university to admit undergraduates, which consisted of assigning a fixed number of points to minority group applicants. The Court in essence said that the government has an interest in assuring that universities achieve racial diversity, but only if race is considered in a way that's narrowly structured to achieve diversity.

Divisions in the Court reflect divisions in society. Although opponents of affirmative action may still claim a commitment to redressing racist and sexist policies of the past, that's not how it's always viewed by supporters. While supporters may argue that affirmative action is not about favoritism or quotas, that's not how opponents always see it.

Arguments in Support

A lot of arguments have been offered in support of affirmative action policies. Some of the more prevalent ones are:

- It's fair. Americans chafe against inequity, and affirmative action policies correct a long history of discrimination.
- It works. Affirmative action policies have brought people from historically disadvantaged groups into the workforce and have made a difference in countless lives.
- It's needed. All the civil rights advances of the late twentieth century have failed to end discrimination.
- It's inclusive. Affirmative action promotes a cultural pluralism that's long been the American antidote to discrimination.
- It promotes opportunity. Without affirmative action, many qualified individuals would still face employment barriers.

- It's comprehensive. Affirmative action addresses a wide range of discrimination against a host of minority groups.

Arguments Against

There are probably as many arguments against affirmative action policies as there are arguments in support of them. Some of the more prevalent ones are:

- It's unfair. Even though people have long been | discriminated against because of group membership, correcting the situation with policies based on group membership is equally discriminatory.
- It stigmatizes. People who get jobs via affirmative action have to live with the fact that ability alone did not get them where they are.
- It's misguided. You cannot pretend to pursue the goals of a color-blind society with policies that use skin color or gender as a litmus test for opportunity.
- It's divisive. Keying hiring practices to group membership perpetuates differential treatment and resentment.
- It rewards mediocrity. Invariably, the pursuit of diversity will result in the advancement of some number of less qualified individuals.
- It's arbitrary. The issue of who is deserving of affirmative action and even who is a member of a disadvantaged group is open to debate.

My Opinion

When considering your opinion on affirmative action, consider the history of the issue and the arguments supporting and opposing it. In particular, ask yourself if affirmative action:

- Is fair or unfair.
- Works effectively or stigmatizes people.
- Is needed or misguided.
- Is inclusive or divisive.
- Promotes opportunity or rewards mediocrity.
- Is comprehensive or arbitrary.

Civil Rights and Native Americans

If the civil rights situation of African Americans is distinctive because they were the only immigrant group brought to North America involuntarily, the civil rights situation of Native Americans is unique because of their presence in North America prior to its colonization by European settlers. Before there were states or colonies, there were Native American tribes operating on their own governing principles with a well-established system of rights. When western political structures were superimposed on the territories inhabited by Native Americans, conflict erupted between two sets of values.

For centuries, the flashpoint for hostility and tension has been the lack of respect and recognition accorded the rights of Native Americans by the federal government. The most basic right that was abridged was tribal sovereignty, or the right of Native American tribes to self-government. Colonial settlers sharply limited tribal sovereignty so that it applied only to internal matters, subjugating tribal autonomy over land rights and affairs with other nations to the will of the colonists and later to the federal government. In many cases, settlers acquired land through treaties that left only hunting and fishing rights to native tribes, in exchange for a promise of protection by settlers that ultimately left once-autonomous Native American nations as wards of the United States. Today, some members of existing tribes practice self-rule on lands set aside by the federal government, and at the same time are subject to the laws and practices of the United States as American citizens.[19] That arrangement was generations in the making.

Early Policies: Containment and Relocation

The original policy of the American government toward native tribes was to contain them on undeveloped land. It was often implemented violently. In 1830, Congress passed the controversial **Indian Removal Act**, which called for relocating Native American tribes situated east of the Mississippi so that American expansion could continue unabated into that territory. Under the terms of the act, any

Native Americans remaining on their land would be forced to leave their tribal nation to become citizens of the state in which they resided. Some moved willingly and some assimilated, although Native Americans who decided to remain sometimes found themselves cheated out of their land by white settlers.

Others resisted and were forced to move or go to war with the United States. Three Seminole wars were fought between 1817 and 1858 over the issue of relocation (fugitive slaves who had been given refuge by the Seminoles fought alongside them in the first two). Ultimately, the Seminoles were killed, driven out, or paid to leave.[20]

In 1836, the Cherokee were given two years to leave their homes in Georgia or face forced relocation. The Supreme Court, in the case of *Worcester v. Georgia* (1832), actually recognized the Cherokee as a sovereign nation, but President Jackson had no regard for the decision and negotiated a removal treaty with a small faction of Cherokee, then used it as the legal basis for evicting the entire tribe.

The 17,000 Cherokee who wished to remain in their homeland were compelled to leave at gunpoint by American troops as whites looted their belongings. On their forced march west, four thousand Cherokee men, women, and children died of illness and exposure along what became known to Native Americans as the "**Trail of Tears.**"[21]

Many whites in the early nineteenth century felt that relocation would resolve territorial issues with Native Americans because they believed the United States would never expand beyond the Mississippi River. Once it did, the idea of separate nations was no longer viable, and national policy embraced reclaiming or dividing up reserved lands in the West and doing battle with Native American tribes.

Later Policies: "Civilizing" and Assimilating

In the 1890s, the government initiated an effort to "civilize" Native Americans as a means of incorporating them into white Christian society. Children were forced to attend boarding schools where their hair was cut short, they were given Anglo-American clothes, and they were required to speak English. This approach culminated in passage of the **Citizenship Act of 1924**, which made all Native Americans born on American soil citizens of the United States. Passage of the Citizenship Act gave Native Americans rights they lacked before, like the right to vote (a western concept, which not every state honored), but it was really a means of forcing assimilation, viewed by some Native Americans as another step toward undermining the sovereignty of native peoples.[22]

These efforts at assimilation largely failed. Generations of exploitation had left many Native Americans with deplorable living conditions. Poverty, malnourishment, and disease were rampant on reserved lands. In 1934, Congress tried to address this with the passage of the Indian Reorganization Act, which aimed at restoring traditional languages and practices in an effort to reverse the deleterious effects of forced relocation and forced assimilation.

1960s and 1970s Activism

By the late 1960s, a growing social awareness of civil rights issues gave rise to the "Red Power" movement: waves of activism designed to call attention to discrimination against Native Americans. In 1969, protesters landed on Alcatraz Island in San Francisco Bay and occupied it for nineteen months in a symbolic reclamation of lost native lands. In the decade that followed, activists occupied scores of other federal facilities, including a sit-in at Mount Rushmore, to bring attention to the political and social plight of Native Americans.[23] In 1973, armed members of the American Indian movement staged a seventy-one-day siege at Wounded Knee, South Dakota, the scene of a Sioux massacre eighty-three years earlier.

Native American civil rights activists successfully trained public attention on the long history of discriminatory practices that many white Americans would like to ignore because it is so uncomfortable to acknowledge. In some respects, their work brought about improvements in the status of Native American rights. For instance, while remaining subject to the jurisdiction of the United States

government, the Indian Civil Rights Act of 1968 extended to tribal governing bodies the protections granted in the Bill of Rights. Courts upheld the continued legal force of century-old treaties, interpreting ambiguities in a way that favored Native American interests. In 1992, Colorado elected the first Native American to the U.S. Senate: Ben Nighthorse Campbell, who is also a Chief of the northern Cheyenne tribe.[24]

During this period, the courts also began to recognize tribal sovereignty and the right of self-government on reserved lands,[25] including freedom from some state hunting and fishing regulations and special water rights.[26] Exemptions from state gaming regulations have in recent years provided an important (albeit controversial) source of revenue for over two hundred Native American tribes operating casinos and gambling ventures on reserved lands.[27]

Gambling has been an economic windfall for increasing numbers of Native American tribes, although it can hardly be considered a panacea for centuries of civil rights abuses. Poverty, unemployment, and alcoholism are still huge problems in many Native American communities, which bear little resemblance to the stable and thriving civilizations that Europeans encountered when they arrived in North America. Also, notwithstanding protests like Alcatraz and Wounded Knee that attract the national press, the concerns of Native Americans remain relatively low on the national civil rights agenda.

Civil Rights and Hispanic Americans

Hispanic Americans, or Latinos, are the largest minority group in the United States. Hailing from places as diverse as Mexico, Cuba, Puerto Rico, the Caribbean, and Central America, Hispanic Americans share a Spanish-speaking heritage even though the paths that brought them to the United States are quite varied. Mexican Americans, for instance, are most likely to have moved to the Southwest, notably California and Texas, and are likely to have come to the United States seeking economic opportunity. Cuban Americans are concentrated in southern Florida, where many arrived seeking political freedom following Fidel Castro's rise to power during the Cuban communist revolution of 1959. Large Puerto Rican communities may be found in the big cities of the Northeast, notably New York. Puerto Ricans hold U.S. citizenship because Puerto Rico is a self-governing commonwealth (it has an elected governor and legislature and its residents participate in federal programs like Social Security and welfare, but it is not represented in Congress or the Electoral College).

Latinos are also a diverse group economically and politically. Cuban Americans are more likely to be better educated and better off financially, and are more likely than other Hispanic groups to be Republicans. Many Mexican Americans are agricultural workers and, along with Puerto Ricans, experience a higher rate of poverty than the population as a whole.

Political Struggles and Victories

Although these differences point to a diversity of experiences among Latino groups, discrimination against Hispanic Americans has been a widespread phenomenon. Many Hispanics are Caucasian, but dark skin, Spanish surnames, and a language difference have through the years been a source of discrimination in educational and work opportunities. Widespread illegal immigration by Mexican Americans is an ongoing source of harassment and discrimination toward Latino citizens by resentful Anglos living in areas with large Hispanic American populations, particularly in states bordering Mexico. Parents of Latino schoolchildren have been confronted with demands for proof of U.S. citizenship by school officials, a form of discrimination that can dissuade them from enrolling their children in school.[28]

The general public first became aware of these abuses during the civil rights movements of the 1960s, when Hispanic Americans organized for political action. The National Council of La Raza was established in 1968 as an advocacy group to reduce poverty and end discrimination against Latino groups.[29]

Agribusiness is vital to California's economy, and for years vegetable and grape growers relied heavily on itinerant Mexican American labor, paying them dirt wages and forcing them to live in deplorable conditions. In 1965, typical Latino farm workers were paid ninety cents an hour and charged by their employers to live in shacks with no plumbing or cooking facilities. Child labor was commonplace. Dangerous conditions led to injury and death. The average life expectancy of a Latino farm laborer was forty-nine years.[30] Despite laws against these conditions, the plight of Hispanic agricultural workers did not register on the national political agenda.

This changed because of the work of Cesar Chavez, a former itinerant worker who painstakingly organized the first union for Hispanic American laborers, the United Farm Workers (UFW). Inspired by the success of the African American civil rights movement, Chavez used nonviolent techniques like hunger strikes and boycotts to focus media attention on the working conditions of Mexican American agricultural workers and to put economic pressure on the businesses that exploited their labor. From the union's inception in 1962 until his death in 1993, Chavez effected social change by successfully raising levels of public awareness about how Latinos were being treated in order to force employers to enter into labor agreements with the union. At the height of the UFWs success between 1973 and 1975, millions of Americans participated in a boycott against Gallo wine for its continued use of nonunion labor.

Workplace discrimination against Latinos continues to be an issue, however. In 2003, the Mexican American Legal Defense and Education Fund and the Equal Employment Opportunity Commission filed suit against a Texas ductworks factory for segregating Mexican American workers into a department where the wages were less and the working conditions far more dangerous than in other departments. When the workers tried to strike, the company moved against them and attempted to have them fired, only to back off in the face of political pressure.

Latinos have made advances in the political arena in recent years, and this offers the promise of helping to address ongoing discrimination. Republicans and Democrats recognize that by virtue of their rapidly growing numbers, Latinos could one day soon be a decisive political force. In 2008, the Latino vote was instrumental in helping Barack Obama comfortably win states that had previously been reluctant to support a Democrat, including Colorado, Nevada and New Mexico.

Recent years have brought some political milestones, notably the confirmation of Sonia Sotomayor to the Supreme Court. In 2002, both major parties nominated Latino gubernatorial candidates in New Mexico, with the Democrat, former Clinton Energy Secretary Bill Richardson, defeating state representative John Sanchez. Six years later, Richardson was a candidate for the Democratic presidential nomination. In Texas, businessman Tony Sanchez received the active backing of the Democratic Party in his primary campaign for governor because of the expectation that he could mobilize Hispanic voters in a Republican-leaning state. Sanchez lost to incumbent Republican Governor Rick Perry, but political commentators widely regarded the support he got from establishment Democrats as a harbinger of things to come.

Bilingual Education

Because language skills are critical to educational achievement, Hispanic Americans have faced roadblocks to advancement in cases where they speak little or no English. One approach to the language barrier is bilingual education, where classroom learning is conducted in English and Spanish. The rationale for bilingual education is that students who do not comprehend the language of instruction will quickly fall behind in the development of academic skills and are more likely to drop out of school, keeping them trapped in poverty or retarding the economic advancement that education makes possible.

Legally, bilingual education is a permissible alternative when English is a second language because the courts have determined that the circumstances fall under the equal protection umbrella. In the Supreme Court case *Lau v. Nichols* (1974), school districts were ordered to accommodate the needs of non-English speaking students in order to assure equal access to educational opportunities. This permitted bilingual teaching, but it did not mandate it.[31]

Bilingual education is a controversial solution, even among Latinos. Some oppose it because they fear it will have the opposite effect to what advocates contend: that students schooled in Spanish and English will simply not learn English the way they would in an all-English environment. Some Anglos oppose it for the same reason, although often in the belief that Hispanic Americans should learn the dominant language of the United States on their own and without what seems like special consideration. This gives the debate over bilingual education a sharp edge because it plays on the emotional issues of assimilation and cultural heritage.

Civil Rights and Asian Americans

Asian Americans are the fastest growing minority group in the United States. Particularly in the states of the Pacific Rim, the number of Americans of Japanese, Chinese, Vietnamese, and Filipino heritage, among others, has been growing in large numbers. In 2000, 10.9 percent of California's population was of Asian origin, as was 5.5 percent of the population of Washington state (in Hawaii, which as a chain of Pacific islands has always had a large population of Asian Americans, the figure was 41.5 percent).[32] Asian Americans, many well off and politically active, have been able to exercise influence in these regions. When Gary Locke was elected governor of the state of Washington in 1996 he became the first Chinese American governor and the only governor of Asian descent in the United States.

Still, Asian Americans have faced a long history of discrimination in housing, employment, and education at the hands of Caucasians. The most notorious incident was the forced internment of Americans of Japanese descent into "relocation camps" around the country during World War II. The official rationale for rounding up American citizens who showed no loyalty to Japan was to defend against Japanese spying, which was widely feared by American military leaders and ordinary citizens. To Asian Americans, forced relocation was a racist policy. The United States was also at war with Germany and Italy, but American citizens with these European origins were not targeted for removal.

The action appeared to violate the equal protection of Japanese Americans because it was based on a racial classification. In fact, the Supreme Court has been fairly consistent about striking down laws based on group categories as violations of the civil rights of the group singled out for differential treatment. This case was the exception, however. In *Korematsu v. United States* (1944), the Court held that the "military urgency" of the situation justified permitting Congress and the president to use their war powers to justify the relocation.[33] Essentially because the nation was at war, security arguments bested equal protection arguments. Today, many Americans look back at the government's policy toward Japanese Americans during World War II and regard it as one of the more shameful moments in the nation's history. In 1993, President Clinton formally apologized and offered reparations to internment victims.

Gender Issues

Imagine that you didn't have the right to vote. You owned some property, but once you got married, control over that property shifted to your husband. If you were fortunate enough to hold a job and earn a salary, chances are it was at a fraction of the pay that a man would earn, and your husband would control that income, too. The larger society believed that you did not have the capability or the right to engage in meaningful work outside the home, and that the proper (or divinely directed) order of things required that you have the protection and guidance of a man, who in turn controlled every significant aspect of your life.

Woman faced these circumstances well into the nineteenth century. Although women were afforded more rights and social standing than slaves, there were enough parallels between the relationship of slave to master and woman to man that it may not

be surprising that the original women's rights movement was born of the antislavery movement. When the Civil War ended and the Fifteenth Amendment extended voting rights to freed slaves but not to women, a separate women's rights movement emerged. Through writing, speaking, petitioning, and tireless organizational work, Susan B. Anthony was instrumental in convincing New York State to extend property rights to married women in 1860. In 1869, abolitionists Elizabeth Cady Stanton and Lucretia Mott formed the National Woman Suffrage Association. The right to vote, however, was not extended to women nationwide until the Nineteenth Amendment was adopted in 1920.

The Equal Rights Amendment

Securing voting rights did not translate into equal rights for women, who faced social and legal obstacles to full equality under the law. Women's rights advocates turned their attention to full constitutional protection for women's civil rights by attempting to win passage of an **Equal Rights Amendment (ERA)**. In so doing, women's rights advocates shifted their agenda from political to social and economic equality, introducing a new degree of controversy as their objectives moved from equal opportunity to equal outcomes.

First introduced in Congress in 1923, the ERA was reintroduced every year since, until it was finally approved during the period of civil rights activism in 1972.[34] The Equal Rights Amendment reads: "Equality of rights under the law shall not be denied or abridged by the United States or by any state on account of sex." This is simple enough language, but it generated remarkably stiff opposition from both men and women and therefore took decades to attract mainstream support. Would divorced women lose their right to alimony? Would women be sent into military combat?

Opponents said yes, and contended that the amendment was unnecessary because women's rights were being protected by favorable court decisions. They tapped into widely held fears that the ERA would undermine family structures, a position advocated by traditional religious organizations.[35] They were opposed by a women's rights movement that was revitalized after a half century of dormancy following passage of women's suffrage. In 1963, Betty Friedan published *The Feminine Mystique*, an account of emptiness and dissatisfaction some women of her generation felt as a result of being emotionally and financially dependent on men. The book caused an about-face in mainstream thinking about traditional values and women's roles at a time when civil rights activism was on the rise. In 1966, the **National Organization for Women (NOW)** was formed to advocate for women's equality, and became an influential force for passage of the Equal Rights Amendment.

Congress gave the ERA a seven-year window for ratification, and extended it in 1979 by three years. During that period, the political climate changed dramatically. Ronald Reagan was elected president on a platform that opposed the ERA, and opposition lobbying efforts had taken hold in the few states that had not ratified the amendment, many of which were in the culturally traditional South. When 1982 ended, the ERA was three states short of the three-quarters necessary for ratification. Proponents have tried to keep it alive by introducing it in states that failed to ratify, prepared to challenge the time limit imposed by Congress should three of them sign on, but they have faced an uphill battle in a conservative political climate.

That said, NOW has a long record of successful activism. It has been behind legal changes protecting women from sexual harassment and discrimination, encouraged unprecedented numbers of female candidates to seek public office, strived to improve conditions for women in the workplace, and promoted equal opportunity for women and men in campus athletics and education (see Demystifying Government: Universities and Title IX).

DEMYSTIFYING GOVERNMENT

UNIVERSITIES AND TITLE IX

The federal government has taken action in matters of sex discrimination on campus. Title IX of the Education Amendments of 1972 (commonly referred to simply as "Title IX") prohibits gender discrimination in education programs receiving federal assistance. Because most colleges and universities receive federal assistance, the language of Title IX effectively makes sexual harassment on campus a federal matter. The same is true of most public school districts. Title IX requires that school officials take action when sexual harassment is severe or ongoing.

Perhaps the most publicized influence of Title IX has been on women's college athletics because it requires colleges and school districts accepting federal funds to provide equal opportunities in sports. The Department of Education has interpreted this provision to mean that the percentage of female athletes at colleges and universities should reflect the percentage of female undergraduates, and that male and female athletics should receive equal funding.[T17]

This interpretation has been controversial and difficult for some universities to implement. Football programs are expensive to run and often provide schools that support them with a large share of the income generated by athletics. With no female counterpart to football, college administrators with football programs face a dilemma of how to control the costs of a profitable venture in order to equalize expenditures with women's athletics. At the same time, Title IX has improved the situation of female student athletes while helping to put some women's sports programs on the map. The growing popularity of women's basketball and gymnastics, for instance, can be attributed in part to decisions universities made to invest in these programs as a result of Title IX regulations.

Sexual Violence and Harassment

One NOW-affiliated activity with which you may be familiar is the Take Back the Night march. These rallies are held periodically across the country and on many college campuses to draw attention to the issue of violence against women.[36] The issue has also been the subject of legislative action. The 1994 Violence Against Women Act provides for federal penalties for sex crimes and for federal assistance to reduce violent crimes against women and to curb domestic violence.

The political system has also responded to long-standing complaints by women about sexual harassment in the workplace. The U.S. Supreme Court has determined workplace harassment to be a form of discrimination and, as such, it is prohibited by the Civil Rights Act of 1964. It has established that a "hostile and abusive" work environment should be the standard for determining whether sexual harassment exists. Although this standard is to be applied with reason, so that any sensible observer would perceive that a hostile environment exists, determining the presence of sexual harassment in the workplace has been a complex matter subject at times to widely varying perceptions of what qualifies as abusive. This has caused the issue to be hotly debated, and has precipitated an ongoing and evolving public dialogue about how coworkers and subordinates should be treated in the workplace.

Workplace Rights

Harassment on the job is one of a cluster of work-related women's rights issues to occupy a central place on the recent political agenda. Although the 1964 Civil Rights Act forbids gender discrimination in hiring, firing, and promoting workers, practical barriers to this objective still exist. Under the law, companies have to demonstrate a compelling business reason for providing disparate treatment to men and women. This means pregnancy, childbirth, and marital status are not supposed to be reasons for making employment or promotion decisions.[37]

In practice, obstacles to women's employment and advancement abound. It's not uncommon for women to feel they have to trade-off career opportunities if they want to have a family, or for female employees to comment to each other that their company has an unspoken "mommy track" with fewer opportunities for advancement flowing to women who choose family before career. Companies with a preponderance of men in high-level managerial positions are evidence for those who feel there is an organizational "glass ceiling" above which few women can rise. Typically, conditions such as these exist informally, as part of an amorphous "corporate culture" that favors the advancement of men. In such an atmosphere, unequal treatment may be apparent to those who feel disadvantaged by it, but difficult to rectify through the legal system.

Family and medical leave is one place where legislative advances have worked to protect the employment concerns of women who need to devote attention to seriously ill loved ones or who need time away from work after a pregnancy. Under the Family and Medical Leave Act of 1993, eligible employees at companies with more than fifty people have the right to up to twelve weeks of unpaid leave in any calendar year to care for a newborn child, or a spouse, child, or parent with a serious medical condition. Under the terms of the act, a woman who leaves her job for three months after giving birth is assured that her job will still be there when she comes back.[38] In 2009, it was expanded to provide leave for relatives of military personnel caring for loved ones who were injured while on active duty.

Laws requiring equal pay for equal work have been on the books since the Equal Pay Act of 1963, but intervening factors like differences in seniority between a male and female employee can confound attempts to demonstrate that two circumstances are comparable. Despite the law, women continue to earn on average less than men, although the gap is narrowing. In 1980, women earned roughly 60 percent of what men earned; by 2010, the difference had fallen to about 83 percent.[39] The disparity is commonly attributed to key circumstantial factors: that women as a whole have less education and have been more likely to drop out of the workforce for long stretches to raise a family.

In 2009, President Obama signed the Lilly Ledbetter Fair Pay Act, which makes it easier for women to file pay discrimination suits. The act is named after a former supervisor at the Goodyear Tire Company who had won a pay discrimination verdict against the company only to have it overturned by the Supreme Court because the statute of limitations for filing the suit had expired.[40] Under the terms of the law, every new discriminatory paycheck is regarded as a separate act of discrimination, and a 180-day window for filing suit is permitted from the time of the last paycheck.

Related to the issue of equal pay is the politically charged matter of comparable worth, which deals with matters of pay equity for comparable labor performed by men and women in different but comparable jobs. See what you think about comparable worth after reading about it in Issue: Comparable Worth, and register your opinion on whether you believe it's a policy the government should pursue.

Women and Public Office

Electoral politics is one place where women have made clear and visible gains. In 1984, when Democratic presidential candidate Walter Mondale selected Representative Geraldine Ferraro as his vice presidential running mate in a losing cause against President Reagan, his choice was considered bold and visionary. Never before had a woman held a place on the national ticket of a major party. When John McCain tapped Alaska Governor Sarah Palin for the same spot twenty-four years later, in the wake of a nearly successful presidential run by Senator Hillary Clinton, the prospect that a woman could hold a major national office was no longer as remote.

In the generation separating Ferraro and Palin, women have taken their place alongside men in positions of power. Although the number of women in high office still falls far short of the percentage of women in the population, it is no longer uncommon to see someone like Hillary Clinton, or before her Condoleezza Rice or Madeleine Albright represent the foreign policy interests of the United States as Secretary of State.

The year 1992 was a benchmark for women in electoral politics. Dubbed the "Year of the Woman" by women's groups and political reporters, a record twenty-four new women were elected to the House and five to the senate, including both senators from California, the first state to be represented by two women. Seventeen years later, there were seventeen women in the senate with three states—California, Maine, and Washington—represented by two women. In 1994, ten women won major party gubernatorial nominations, but none of them were elected. By 2002, with voters primed to accept women in executive positions, ten women again won gubernatorial primaries, and were elected in states as diverse as Michigan, Kansas, Arizona, and Hawaii.[41]

One reason why women have achieved growing electoral success is simply that more women are running for office—and one reason for that is women are now taken seriously as political candidates. Before the "Year of the Woman," female candidates were widely regarded as long-shots or jokes, and were often recruited to run against entrenched male officeholders who were assured reelection. Women serving in Congress were likely to have been appointed to their seats upon the death of their husbands. The recent electoral record of female candidates suggests those days are over.

ISSUE

COMPARABLE WORTH

Although it's been illegal to pay men and women different wages for doing the same work since the passage of the Equal Pay Act of 1963, and illegal to hire or fire someone on the basis of gender since the passage of the Civil Rights Act of 1964, comparable worth, or pay equity, is a more recent issue in our political debate. It addresses wage disparities between men and women who hold comparable jobs. This shouldn't be confused with equal pay for performing the same job. Instead, comparable worth deals with disparities between jobs held mostly by women that pay less than jobs held mostly by men, despite the fact that the two jobs require comparable skills and training. This makes it a civil rights issue.[T18]

In Washington state, for instance, the job of legal secretary is considered to require a comparable level of skill and training to the job of heavy equipment operator. Legal secretaries are overwhelmingly female. Heavy equipment operators are overwhelmingly male. If legal secretaries earn less than heavy equipment operators, there's an issue of comparable worth.[T19]

Jobs performed mostly by women include clerical workers, nurses, maids, secondary school teachers, secretaries, social workers, real estate agents, and electronics assembly-line workers. Jobs performed mostly by men include outdoor laborers, doctors, carpenters, electricians, lawyers, upper-level managers, plumbers, and manufacturing assembly-line workers. The "female" jobs require different skill sets from the "male" jobs, but jobs requiring high levels of training and education are neither exclusively "female" nor "male." Electrical engineers (mostly male) average the same number of years of education as librarians (mostly female).[T20] Pay equity supporters contend they should be paid comparably.

As a matter of legislation, comparable-worth measures have an uneven history. Congress considered including a pay-equity provision in the Equal Pay Act of 1963 but found the issue of determining comparable jobs to be too complex. In the 1980s, twenty states considered comparable worth legislation, but only Minnesota and Washington put laws on the books, and these only covered state workers. In the last few years, comparable worth legislation has been proposed in Congress and in more than half the states, backed by the resources of powerful groups like the AFL-CIO.[T21]

The controversy over comparable worth derives partly from differences in how people interpret the evidence of pay disparities, and partly from value differences. Comparable worth advocates point to persistent gaps in the pay of "female" and "male" occupations.[T22] Opponents cite data that suggest negligible or nonexistent differences between pay in "female" and "male" jobs by considering intervening factors, like the fact that men average more hours annually on the job than women.[T23] The question of how to determine comparability remains open for debate.

As a matter of values, opponents of comparable worth tend to have more faith in the ability of the free market to set wages than in the ability of government to do so. Proponents of comparable worth laws believe rectifying inequities by imposing pay standards is an appropriate role for government and something only government can do. Some supporters contend that women still suffer the effects of a cultural predisposition toward women remaining in the home and performing domestic tasks, pointing to data showing women are promoted less quickly than equally qualified men and may hit a "glass ceiling" beyond which they cannot advance in their organizations. Opponents point to salary and employment advances achieved by women in recent years and decry comparable worth initiatives as feeding a culture of victimization that they claim, in the long run, only serves to hold women back.

Arguments in Support

Several arguments are typically offered in support of comparable worth policies. Proponents might say:

- It's important. Although gender discrimination is illegal, it persists in the form of a pay differential where occupations employing mostly women pay less than occupations employing mostly men.
- The market is not a solution. The alternative to pay equity laws is to permit the free market to establish wages, but the market fails women, as evidenced by wage inequities between men and women and "glass ceiling" barriers to workplace advancement.
- It benefits women. No one questions that if gender pay disparities exist in the workforce and can be identified, pay equity laws would ' eliminate them.
- It's fair. Gender should not be a criterion for I determining what someone earns.

Arguments Against

Opponents of comparable worth policies might argue:

- It's not an issue. Proponents of pay equity use incorrect, inappropriate, or misleading statistics to argue that there's a large gender pay gap when in fact inequities between women and men are small.
- It violates market principles. Rectifying pay differences between men and women allows government bureaucracy rather than the free market to establish wages.
- It hurts women. Mandating pay increases for women will simply make employers less likely to hire women.
- It's arbitrary. Trying to classify a multitude of different jobs in order to create comparability standards produces inexact and therefore unfair results.

My Opinion

When registering your opinion on comparable worth, consider the history of the issue and the arguments supporting and opposing it. In particular, ask yourself if comparable worth:

- Is important or not an issue.
- Cannot be addressed by the free market or violates free-market principles.
- Benefits or hurts women.
- Is fair or arbitrary.

People with Disabilities

Try for a moment to envision what a staircase looks like to someone in a wheelchair, or what a telephone sounds like to someone who is hearing impaired. For years, most of us were unaware of the obstacles posed by ordinary objects to people with disabilities, and were largely oblivious to the discriminatory treatment that impaired individuals faced in the workplace or in navigating public and private buildings. In fact, the Civil Rights Act of 1964 did not cover people with disabilities.

Over time, lobbying efforts on behalf of disabled individuals helped to bring the circumstances faced by people with disabilities to the forefront of the national agenda, and in 1990 Congress passed the landmark Americans with Disabilities Act. The key provisions of the act:

- Provide civil rights protection to persons with disabilities on a par with existing protections against discrimination on the basis of race, color, religion, national origin, and gender.

- Prohibit job discrimination against persons with disabilities, including discrimination in hiring, firing, compensating, and promoting disabled individuals who can perform essential job functions. Employers are required to make "reasonable accommodations" to the work environment to accommodate the needs of disabled individuals, provided that such changes do not impose "undue hardship" on the employer's business.
- Mandate all state and local government agencies provide disabled individuals with equal access to programs and activities, and make public buildings readily accessible to disabled individuals.
- Require equal access to public accommodations, such as restaurants, hotels, theaters, stores, doctor's offices, parks, and private schools. Individuals operating such facilities are instructed to modify them for use by disabled individuals, provided that making such modifications does not present the owner with an "undue burden."[42]

The Americans with Disabilities Act is sweeping in scope, covering a wide range of physical and psychological conditions. These conditions include people with impairments that limit major life activities, such as walking, hearing, seeing, and breathing, as well as ailments such as epilepsy, HIV infection, and AIDS. Cancer survivors are protected against discrimination resulting from their medical history, as are people with a history of mental illness. People with learning disabilities are covered by the act, as are recovering alcoholics. Close relatives of people with disabilities are included, so that the spouse of someone with a disability could not be denied employment out of the concern that they might have to spend large quantities of their time caring for their partner instead of working.[43]

If the Americans with Disabilities Act is sweeping, so is it vague, and this has made it controversial. Although the act specifically excludes protection to people with short-term ailments like the flu or a broken leg, there's a large gray area

between people who obviously are disabled and people who obviously are not, and this has generated controversy about how broadly to implement the act.

Controversy can be particularly acute when it comes to people with psychological conditions. Should the law cover people with Attention Deficit Disorder (ADD), for instance, who have trouble focusing on their job? The law is broad enough to cover this condition. Supporters say this is appropriate, and that psychological conditions should be afforded the same protection as physical conditions. Opponents contend that conditions like ADD are too frequently diagnosed, and that covering them dilutes the purpose of extending equal protection to people who in their view are obviously disabled.

The Americans with Disabilities Act is equally vague about remedies. At what point does a retail store begin to realize an "undue burden" as it attempts to accommodate people with disabilities? Might an employer have to permit flexible work schedules, modify office equipment, or hire an interpreter to protect disabled employees against workplace discrimination? The Act says yes: Any of these could be an appropriate remedy to discrimination and is considered to be a "reasonable accommodation." Employers who have to pay the bill may experience it differently.

Gay and Lesbian Rights

The issue of homosexuality is emotionally charged for many Americans. Homophobia is widespread in our culture, leading some people to fear or despise gay men and women. Some believe homosexuality is an abomination against God, while others see it as an abnormality of nature. Sometimes these attitudes provide the basis for discrimination against gays, who face covert and direct obstacles in every walk of life.

At the very least, the hostile climate of public opinion has kept gays and lesbians from realizing the same level of civil rights protections that have been won by other groups that face discrimination. About one-quarter of the states have laws criminalizing sexual activities between persons of the same sex. Some local governments, colleges, and universities have acted to prevent gay and lesbian groups from organizing, holding public events, or educating others about homosexuality.[44]

At the same time, even conservative estimates suggest that homosexuality is fairly prevalent in our society, and is not bounded by socioeconomic status, race, religion, or gender. The exact percentage of gay Americans is impossible to know because many keep their sexual orientation a secret to protect against discrimination and social reprisals. Others, however, have mobilized and organized, in an effort to generate public attention that can translate into political action.

Their work has moved the issue of gay and lesbian rights to the forefront of the policy agenda. One of the most salient examples is the 1993 "Don't Ask, Don't Tell" policy forbidding the Pentagon from asking servicemen to reveal their sexual orientation. In keeping with the emotionally charged nature of the issue, this policy was born of great controversy and protest. The product of a compromise between President Clinton and military leaders, it represented a step back from the president's original intent to end discrimination based on sexual orientation in a military culture where feelings about homosexuality were strong and hostile. Essentially, the policy said that gay servicemen who kept their homosexuality private would not be asked about it or discharged because of it by their commanding officers. But, "Don't Ask, Don't Tell" fell short of the equal rights standard. President Obama promised to sign legislation to end the policy during the 2008 campaign, permitting gays to serve openly, which he did in late 2010.

Equally emotional is the issue of gay and lesbian marriage. This, too, is a place where gay rights activists have directed considerable energy and, after years of frustration, have recently experienced some success—and generated a lot of controversy.

Senior Citizen Rights

Ronald Reagan was elected president in 1980 at the age of sixty-nine. John McCain was the Republican presidential nominee at the age of seventy-two. John Glenn, the first American to orbit the earth in 1962, joined the crew of the Space Shuttle Discovery thirty-six years later—at age seventy-seven. Americans are living longer—demographically, people over eighty are the fastest growing group—and as "Baby Boomers" begin to get on in years, the generation weaned on the civil rights movement could be expected to turn its attention and political clout to the rights of seniors.

Age discrimination in its most widespread form occurs in the workplace, where employers are sometimes reluctant to hire older people. This type of discrimination has been illegal since the passage of the **Age Discrimination in Employment Act of 1967**, which makes it a crime to discriminate against people over forty in hiring, firing, and promotion decisions. Additionally, job notices cannot specify age limits or preferences, and benefits cannot legally be withheld from older employees.[45] Originally, these protections were extended to workers until they reached retirement at age sixty-five. As longevity increased, the mandatory retirement age was raised to seventy in 1978, and eliminated entirely in 1986.

It's not too difficult to expect that as people continue to live and work longer, civil rights for seniors will continue to emerge as an important political issue. In a time that has witnessed an expansion of the personal rights agenda, with groups not previously recognized as disadvantaged speaking out for equal rights, it is easy to imagine a growing, energetic movement supporting the rights of senior citizens.

Chapter Review

Civil rights policies are designed to ensure that the law treats everyone equally, regardless of differences in race, gender, ethnic background, or anything people might be inclined to discriminate against. The key to civil rights in the United States is the equal protection clause of the Fourteenth Amendment, which says "No state shall ... deny to any person within its jurisdiction the equal protection of the laws." The intent of the equal protection clause is that all laws should be applied evenly and without prejudice to all citizens.

When African Americans were granted citizenship following the Civil War, southern states used Black Codes and physical intimidation to deny former slaves their civil rights, even as those states were being reconstructed into the union. Until the 1950s, Jim Crow laws made segregation a way of life in the South. Then the civil rights movement drew national attention to segregation's abuses. A long period of civil disobedience, which was often met with violence, culminated in landmark federal civil rights legislation, notably the Civil Rights Act of 1964 and the Voting Rights Act of 1965.

Since the 1960s, affirmative action programs have been the primary way to address inequalities left from the long history of discriminatory practices against African Americans and other historically disadvantaged minority groups. Under the law, affirmative action requires that there be no artificial barriers to the hiring and advancement of people in groups that have been targets of past discrimination, and that if employers underutilize group members, they have to take steps to remedy the situation. In practice, affirmative action policies can range from minority recruitment to preferential hiring of underrepresented group members and targeted hiring of minority individuals.

Native Americans have suffered discriminatory treatment since the arrival of European settlers in North America. Colonists sharply limited Native American tribal sovereignty so that it applied only to internal matters, subjugating tribal autonomy over land rights and affairs with other nations to the will of the settlers and later to the federal government. For centuries, the federal government tried to subdue Native Americans by alternately containing them on reservations, relocating them to land that settlers hadn't developed, and westernizing them in an effort to get them to assimilate into American culture.

Latino groups have also faced discrimination, notably in education and the workplace. Mexican American farm laborers faced deplorable conditions, leading to the rise of the United Farm Workers Union under Cesar Chavez. Additionally, widespread illegal immigration by Mexican Americans is an ongoing source of harassment and discrimination toward Latino citizens by resentful Anglos living in areas with large Hispanic American populations. Parents of Latino schoolchildren have been confronted with demands for proof of U.S. citizenship by school officials, a form of discrimination that can dissuade them from enrolling their children in school.

At the dawn of the republic, women faced a male-dominated society that felt they were not capable of making decisions for themselves—an attitude manifested in laws restricting married women from owning property or managing finances. These restrictions began to come down in the mid-nineteenth century because of the work of activists like Susan B. Anthony and Elizabeth Cady Stanton. By 1920, women won the right to vote. A second wave of activism in the 1960s led to the establishment of the National Organization for Women, which works to end sexual violence and harassment, promote gender equality in the workplace and on campus, and advance the cause of women in politics.

A number of other minority groups face or have faced violations of equal protection. Japanese Americans were moved to detention centers during World War II without evidence that they posed a national security risk. Disabled individuals face discrimination in the workplace, although the Americans with Disabilities Act makes such discrimination illegal and attempts to eliminate barriers to navigating public accommodations. Widespread homophobia is the source of discrimination against gays and lesbians, who face housing and workplace discrimination. Senior citizens may face employers who do not want to hire them because of their age, an act that is illegal under the Age Discrimination in Employment Act, which makes it a crime to discriminate against people over forty in hiring, firing, and promotion decisions.

Key Terms

affirmative action Federal policies requiring employers to address inequities in hiring and advancement if they appear to unfairly treat disadvantaged groups on the basis of race, religion, gender, national origin, sexual preference, physical disabilities, or Vietnam veteran status.

Age Discrimination in Employment Act The 1967 law that made it illegal for employers to discriminate against people over age forty in hiring, firing, and promotion decisions.

Americans with Disabilities Act The landmark 1990 legislation extending equal protection in the workplace and in public accommodations to people with physical and mental disabilities.

Black Codes An effort by white southerners immediately following the Civil War to restrict the civil rights of emancipated slaves. The codes were overturned by federal civil rights laws, only to become standard practice in the South following Reconstruction.

Citizenship Act of 1924 An effort to assimilate Native Americans into white culture and society through the granting of American citizenship.

civil disobedience A peaceful means of protest whereby individuals draw attention to laws they consider unjust by disobeying them and being arrested for their actions.

Civil Rights Act of 1964 Landmark legislation arising from the civil rights movement that made racial discrimination a federal crime in the workplace and in public accommodations, while giving the federal government greater power to strengthen voting rights and desegregate public schools.

civil rights movement The organized, largely nonviolent, and widely successful efforts of the 1950s and 1960s to bring about social change on behalf of African Americans in the South, whose civil rights were denied by a century-old system of Jim Crow laws.

comparable worth A manner of determining pay equity by equalizing pay between jobs held mostly by women that demand comparable training and labor to jobs held mostly by men.

Dred Scott v. Sanford The 1857 Supreme Court case that legalized slavery nationwide, while holding that people of color had no rights or protection under the Constitution. The ruling hastened the Civil War; it was subsequently overturned by constitutional amendment.

economic equality A form of equality of outcome that values using government policy to minimize the economic disparities found in society

equal protection clause The constitutional restriction against state laws that discriminate, as stated in the Fourteenth Amendment. The equal protection clause served as the legal basis for eliminating laws that permitted racial discrimination.

Equal Rights Amendment (ERA) A proposed constitutional amendment assuring equal rights for women that was first introduced in Congress in 1923, approved by Congress in 1972, and fell three states short of ratification in 1982.

equality of opportunity One of several ways of understanding equality, this way values giving people comparable advantages for succeeding in life, regardless of the unequal outcomes that may result.

equality of outcome One of several ways of understanding equality, this way values leveling the social and economic inequities among people, rather than attempting to give people comparable advantages for succeeding in life.

Family and Medical Leave Act of 1993 Legislation designed to permit women working in medium or large companies up to twelve weeks of unpaid leave following childbirth. It also permits employees to take unpaid leave time to care for an ailing relative.

federalism The division of power between a sovereign federal government and sovereign state governments, which provides that some functions will be performed by the national government, some by the state governments, and some by both the national and state governments. As a feature designed to limit the strength of government, federalism works to decentralize power by creating dual levels of authority.

freedom rides A type of civil disobedience popular with civil rights protesters, where mixed-race groups of bus passengers would ride through the South and disobey laws on racially segregated travel, often at the expense of submitting to mob violence.

Indian Removal Act Legislation passed in 1830 that led to the forced and sometimes violent transfer of Native American nations to areas west of the Mississippi River.

Jim Crow laws Laws in place in the South through the middle portion of the twentieth century that legalized segregation in virtually every facet of life.

Ku Klux Klan The secret white supremacist society that terrorized and killed African Americans for decades following the Civil War.

National Organization for Women (NOW) The largest women's rights organization in the United States, which has been an active force for advancing social and economic equality for women.

Plessy v. Ferguson The 1896 Supreme Court case that upheld racial segregation. It was reversed in 1954 in the case of Brown v. Board of Education.

political equality Establishing political and legal rights on the basis of the individual, so that everyone has the same right to vote and is equal under the law. An alternative would be to grant political rights to elite individuals based on wealth or social standing.

Reconstruction The period following the Civil War, from 1865 to 1877, during which Union troops occupied the South as states of the Confederacy were readmitted to the Union under conditions established in Washington.

Regents of the University of California v. Bakke The 1978 Supreme Court case that marked a reversal in unlimited support for affirmative action policies by backing the claim of discrimination by a white University of California medical school applicant who was denied admission in favor of less well qualified minority applicants.

sit-ins A type of civil disobedience popular with civil rights protesters that involved African Americans peacefully sitting at "Whites Only" lunch counters, to focus attention on the injustice of segregation policies.

social equality A form of equality of outcome that values using government policy to minimize social class distinctions found in society.

Student Nonviolent Coordinating Committee (SNCC) The organization that involved college students in acts of civil disobedience to advance the cause of civil rights for African Americans.

"Trail of Tears" A one-thousand-mile forced march of Cherokee men, women, and children carried out in 1838 to satisfy a federal relocation policy.

Voting Rights Act of 1965 Landmark legislation arising from the civil rights movement that gave federal officials the power to oversee election practices in southern states where Jim Crow laws disenfranchised African American voters.

Resources

You might be interested in examining some of what the following authors have said about the topics we've been discussing:

On Affirmative Action

Lawrence, Charles R. III, and Mari J. Matsuda. *We Won't Go Back: Making the Case for Affirmative Action*. Boston, MA: Houghton Mifflin, 1997.

Thomasson, Richard R, Faye J. Crosby, and Sharon D. Herzberger. *Affirmative Action: The Pros and Cons of Policy and Practice*. Lanham, MD: Rowman and Littlefield, 2001.

On Comparable Worth

England, Paula. *Comparable Worth: Theories and Evidence*. New York: Aldine de Gruyter, 1992.

On Same-Sex Marriage

Baird, Robert M., and Stuart E. Rosenbaum, eds. *Same-Sex Marriage: The Moral and Legal Debate*. Amherst, NY: Prometheus Books, 2004.

Eskridge, William R., Jr. *Equality Practice: Civil Unions and the Future of Gay Rights*. New York: Routledge, 2002.

Notes

1. For more details, see http://afroamhistory.about. com/library/ weekly/aa121900a.htm.

2. See CNN Interactive, "The Civil Rights Movement," at http://www.cnn.eom/EVENTS/1997/mlk/links. html.

3. See http://afroamhistory.about.com/library/ weekly/ aa121900a.htm.

4. For a full timeline of the major events of Reconstruction, see http://www.pbs.org/wgbh/ amex/reconstruction/ states/sfji meline.htm l.

5. See a full account of the Johnson biography at the White House website, http://www.whitehouse.gov/ about/ presidents/andrewjohnson.

6. See http://www.africana.com/research/encarta/ tt_333.asp.

7. For a history of Jim Crow, see http://www.pbs.org/ wnet/jimcrow/.

8. Ibid.

9. Ibid.

10. You can read more about Rosa Park's story at Time.com: http://www.time.com/time/specials/packages/arti- cle/0,28804,2029774_2029776_2031835,00. html.

11. See the Congress of Racial Equality website, at http://www.core-online.org/History/freedom_sum- mer.htm. The murders were later the subject of the film Mississippi Burning.

12. Ibid.

13. See CongressLink at http://www.congresslink.Org/ print_teaching_glossary.htm#cR57.

14. See CongressLink at http://www.congresslink.org/ print_basics_histmats_civilrights64text.htm.

15. See CongressLink at http://www.congresslink.org/ print_basics_histmats_votingrights_contents.htm.

16. CNN Interactive, "The Civil Rights Movement," at http://www.cnn.com/EVENTS/1997/mlk/links. html.

17. See LawHelpMN.org, Indian Tribal Sovereignty at http://www.lawhelpmn.org/MN/ StateChannelResults. cfm/County/%20/ demoMode/%3 D%201/Language/1/State/MN/ TextOnly/N/ZipCode/%20/LoggedIn/0/iSub- TopicID/1/iProblemCodeID/1920600/sTopicImage/ feather.gif/iTopicID/272/bAllState/0/ichannelid/3

18. CNN Interactive, "The Civil Rights Movement," at http://www.cnn.com/EVENTS/1997/mlk/links. html.

19. See http://www.tribal-institute.org/lists/nations. htm.

20. See http://www.seminolewars.us/history.html.

21. North Georgia history, at http://ngeorgia.com/his- tory/nghisttt.html.

22. For an overview, see http://www.nebraskastudies. Org/0700/frameset_reset.htmRhttp://www.nebras- kastudies. org/0700/stories/0701 _0146. htm l.

23. See http://www.nps.gov/archive/alcatraz/indian2. html.

24. See http://bioguide.congress.gov/scripts/biodis- play.pl?index=C000077.

25. See, for instance, *United States v. Wheeler* (1978).

26. See http://www.usbr.gov/native/naao/water/index. html.

27. See http://www.indiangaming.org/info/about.shtml. One prominent example is the Foxwoods Casino in Connecticut, operated by the Mashantucket Pequot nation. The story of the nation that operates it may be found at http://www.mptn-nsn.gov//.

28. See the NCLR website at http://www.nclr.org/index. php/issues_and_programs/education/.

29. You can get information on La Raza at http://www. nclr.org.

30. See the United Farm Workers website at http:// www.ufw.org/_page.php?menu=about&inc=about_vi- sion.html.

31. See the National Association for Bilingual Education website at http://www.nabe.org/.

32. Figures are from the 2000 U.S. Census, at http:// factfinder.census.gov.

33. *Korematsu v. United States*, 321 US 760 (1944).

34. See the Equal Rights Amendment website, at http:// www.equalrightsamendment.org/era.htm.

35. Ibid.

36. See the National Organization for Women website, at http://www.now.org/history/history.html.

37. See http://www.archives.gov/education/lessons/ civil-rights-act/.

38. The U.S. Department of Labor, at http://www.dol. gov/whd/fmla/index.htm.

39. Dennis Cauchon, "Gender Pay Gap is Smallest on Record," *USA Today,* September 14, 2010.

40. *Ledbetter v. Goodyear Tire & Rubber Co.*, 550 U.S. 618 (2007).

41. Thomas Hargrove, "Female Candidates Look to Make Electoral Ground." Scripps Howard News Service, October 23, 2002.

42. U.S. Equal Employment Opportunity Commission, "Americans with Disabilities Act Questions and Answers," http://www.ada. gov/q&aeng02. htm.

43. Ibid.

44. American Civil Liberties Union statement on gay and lesbian rights, at http://www.aclu.org/lgbt-rights/lgbt-discrimination.

45. Equal Employment Opportunity Commission, "Facts about Age Discrimination," at http://www.eeoc.gov/facts/age. htm I.

Table, Figure and Box Notes

T1. U.S. Census Bureau 2009 Population Estimates, at http://quickfacts.census.gov/qfd/states/00000.html.

T2. Adapted from http://afroamhistory.about.com/gi/o.htm?zi=1/XJ&zTi=1 &sdn=afroamhistory&cdn=education &tm=8&f=00&tt=14&bt=0&bts=1 &zu=http%3A//www.ferris.edu/jimcrow/what.htm.

T3. Image is a work of an employee of the United States Farm Security Administration or Office of War Information domestic photographic units, created during the course of the person's official duties. As a work of the U.S. federal government, the image is in the public domain.

T4. Adapted from CNN.com at http://www.cnn.eom/EVENTS/1997/mlk/links.html. Rosa Parks image: This work was obtained from the now defunct United States Information Agency. In 1999 the agency was merged into the Bureau of Public Affairs which is the part of the United States Department of State. This work is in the public domain in the United States because it is a work of the United States Federal Government under the terms of 17 U.S.C. § 105. Martin Luther King, Jr. image:

Source: Library of Congress. New York World-Telegram & Sun Collection, http://hdl.loc.gov/loc.pnp/cph.3c26559; author: Dick DeMarsico, World Telegram staff photographer. No copyright restriction known. Staff photographer reproduction rights transferred to Library of Congress through Instrument of Gift.

T5. Charles R. Lawrence III and Mari J. Matsuda, *We Won't Co Back, Making the Case for Affirmative Action*, New York: Houghton Mifflin Company, 1997.

T6. Richard F. Thomasson, Faye J. Corsby and Sharon D. Hertberger, *Affirmative Action: The Pros and Cons of Policy and Practice* (Washington, DC: American University Press, 1996), 5–6. The first story in this section is true, the second story is fictional.

T7. Ibid., 11–12.

T8. Ibid., 12.

T9. Ibid., 12–15 and 135–136.

T10. Ibid., 18–19.

T11. *Gratz v. Bollinger*, 539 US 244 (2003).

T12. *Gratz v. Bollinger*, 539 US 306 (2003).

T13. U.S. Census Bureau 2009 Population Estimates, at http://quickfacts.census.gov/qfd/states/00000.htrnl.

T14. Ibid.

T15. Data from U.S. Census Bureau, 2000 Census.

T16. U.S. Census Bureau 2009 Population Estimates, at http://quickfacts.census.gov/qfd/states/00000.htrnl.

T17. U.S. Department of Education, Office for Civil Rights, at http://www2.ed.gov/policy/rights/reg/ocr/edlite-34cfr106.html.

T18. Paula England, *Compatible Worth: Theories and Evidence* (New York: Aldine de Gruyter, 1992) 1–2, 23–24.

T19. Ibid.

T20. Ibid.,14.

T21. "What is Comparable Worth?," Employment Policy Foundation paper.

T22. England, Comparable Worth, 125.

T23. "What is Comparable Worth?"

Macro-Level Policies—
Affirmative Action

By Margaret M. Zamudio, Caskey Russell, and Francisco A. Rios

Few topics in the last several decades have been more divisive and controversial than the debate surrounding affirmative action; particularly the use of affirmative action in higher education. As the previous chapter explained, access to higher education can have a significant impact on the quality of one's life. For a person from an impoverished or even a modest background, access to higher education can be the key which opens the door to financial security, upper social mobility, self-actualization, community development and uplift, and entrance into America's power structure. For those already at the top of the nation's social hierarchy, access to higher education, particularly the most elite schools, helps ensure one maintains one's place.

If one defines affirmative action as its opponents do as a preference or privilege given in a particular situation to an individual because of that person's group membership, then the history of affirmative action in America is a long one. Until the changes brought by the Civil Rights Movement—and even to a certain extent after such changes—a strong preference (if not blatant set-asides) for the best jobs, the highest quality education, and the best places to live has been given to whites, particularly white males (Katznelson 2005).

From its inception, the American education system has privileged white, protestant, males from wealthy families. Consider that for much of our history some schools only allowed white, male students to attend. Others, which allowed students other than white males, used quotas to put a cap on the number of Jews, minorities, or women a particular school might admit thereby assuring that white, male, protestant students would dominate (Anderson 2004; Moore 2005). Such privileging on the basis of race persists into the present day.

Despite the preferences granted to white males for centuries, the current controversy surrounding affirmative action is not centered on unearned privileges given to whites based on group membership. Such privileges, when acknowledged, are rarely viewed as a type of affirmative action. Instead the controversy over affirmative action surrounds the more recent phenomenon of expanding opportunities to previously excluded groups like women and minorities. This controversy stems from the myth of meritocracy and the deployment of colorblindness to roll back gains made by the Civil Rights Movement. They myth of meritocracy and the advocacy of colorblindness underlie the two main arguments in opposition to affirmative action.

Opponents of affirmative action informed by the myth of meritocracy assert that affirmative action confers unearned and undeserved privileges to its beneficiaries because affirmative action allows candidates entrance to institutions of higher education for which such candidates are not qualified. The rhetoric of colorblindness underlying the second oppositional argument equates invidious discrimination and historical race-based subordinating practices such as Jim Crow segregation with benign, race conscious, programs such as affirmative action. In an ironic twist, programs which help ameliorate and remedy disadvantages resulting from hundreds of years of inequality, subordination and discrimination are attacked on the basis of being discriminatory. Equating ameliorative and remedial programs with discrimination allows opponents arguing from a colorblind perspective to assert that all considerations of race are per se suspect and that affirmative action in particular should be outlawed (Haney Lopez 2007).

In the spring of 2003 the United States Supreme Court decided two affirmative action cases in the context of education. In what came to be known as the "Michigan Cases," the Supreme Court agreed to look squarely at the controversial issue of affirmative action in education for the first time since 1978.

The first case, *Gratz v. Bollinger*, 539 U.S. 244 (2003) involved the University of Michigan's use of racial preferences in the school's undergraduate admissions process. The second, *Grutter v. Bollinger*, 539 U.S. 306 (2003) involved the use of race preferences in the admission process at the University of Michigan law school. In each case, white plaintiffs asserted that the school's admission policies denied them equal protection of the laws guaranteed by the Fourteenth Amendment to the United States Constitution and that the respective school policies subjected them to racial discrimination.

In evaluating the plaintiffs' claims, the Supreme Court adopted the colorblind approach described above in deciding that any consideration of race is inherently suspect and thus subject to the highest level of review—strict scrutiny. Under this level of review, a government policy or program like affirmative action may only be found constitutional if it is narrowly tailored to achieve a compelling state interest. (Because the University of Michigan is a public state school it is considered a government entity.) In the case of the undergraduate admissions program, a majority of the court found that the program did not meet the exacting standard of strict scrutiny because its policy of automatically assigning a specified number of points needed for admission to members of underrepresented minority groups did not provide enough individualized consideration of each applicant. In contrast, the court found the law school's admission process, whereby race was just one of several factors taken into consideration when evaluating an individual and where the weight given race was not automatic or specified, did withstand strict scrutiny and was therefore constitutional.

While many of the proponents of affirmative action heralded the Grutter decision as a victory that would allow the continued use of affirmative action to address disparities in educational opportunities, subsequent events—particularly the passage of Michigan's Proposal 2—have called that seeming victory into question. Similar to California's more famous Proposition 209, Michigan's Proposal 2 amended Michigan's constitution to prohibit public educators from using race as admission criteria (Rose 2008). Although the Michigan constitutional amendment is too new for its effects to be realized, many assume that it will have the same effect in Michigan that Prop 209 had in California: a significant reduction in the number of underrepresented minorities admitted into the nation's institutions of higher education ("Transcription" 2008). As other states, like Nebraska, follow the lead of California and Michigan in constitutionally prohibiting affirmative action, it is questionable how much longer affirmative action will be available as a tool to combat documented education inequalities.

Brief Historical Context

We hold these truths to be self-evident that all men are created equal, that they are endowed by their Creator with certain unalienable rights, that among these are life, liberty and the pursuit of happiness. That to secure these rights, governments are instituted among men, deriving their just powers from the consent of the governed. (Declaration of Independence, July 4, 1776)

It may seem odd to begin a brief discussion of the history of affirmative action with these often quoted words, but it is an appropriate place to start because the current controversy surrounding affirmative action is rooted in the denial of these basic rights to millions of Americans for hundreds of years. Affirmative action—particularly the type with which we are concerned whereby race and/or gender is a plus factor in school admissions-developed in the context of the Civil Rights Movement's attempt to combat hundreds of years of denied educational opportunities to minorities.

While a comprehensive history of the development of affirmative action is beyond the scope of this book, affirmative action as currently understood was created as a tool to insure that schools and businesses complied with equal opportunity laws instituted as a result of the Civil Rights Movement. First, even when previously closed opportunities were legally opened by executive order, court decision, or legislative act, women and minorities continued to be excluded. In many instances, this was because employers and institutions either actively or passively discriminated despite changes in the law. Additionally, regardless of potential, the lack of opportunity to acquire the knowledge and skills made some women and minorities less competitive. At the same time, even when minorities and women were qualified and highly competitive, studies in cognitive and social psychology over the last several decades have shown that inherent and often unconscious bias has resulted in a denial of opportunities for even qualified women and minorities. (See Bridgeman 2008 for a review of this literature in connection with selection procedures.)

Consequently, it became clear that if the United States were to move closer to achieving true equality, affirmative steps would have to be taken. Affirmative steps meant more than simply opening

the door of opportunity; it meant actively going out and recruiting people to pass through that door. For example, a school might actively search out capable minority candidates rather than just passively wait for them to apply for a program through traditional channels. Once identified, that same school might develop a pre-education program geared specifically towards helping minority recruits with the goal of assuring greater likelihood of the candidates' academic success (Anderson 2004).

Despite rhetoric to the contrary, the history of the development of affirmative action shows that it was not at any time intended to give unqualified minorities access to unearned opportunities at the expense of whites. Instead, affirmative action developed as a strategy to provide meaningful opportunities and a full measure of equality to those American citizens who had historically been discriminated against. When in the wake of the Civil Rights Movement and the passage of laws intended to provide equal opportunity schools still refused to admit qualified minorities, regardless of merit, it became clear that affirmative steps would have to be taken to break down barriers erected by hundreds of years of racial preference given to whites. It also became clear that affirmative steps were necessary to combat the blatant denial of opportunities and equality to non-whites. Affirmative action was meant to be a tool to help break down these barriers and assure a truly level playing field for all.

Underlying Premises

As explained in the introduction to Part II, when looking at any specific policy, Gillborn (2005) prompts us to ask what is driving that particular education policy, who benefits (or doesn't) as a result of a particular policy, and what are the policy's effects. As just mentioned, the driving forces behind affirmative action as a policy can be directly linked to the Civil Rights Movement and in particular the push to desegregate America and to provide equal opportunity for all. In 1896 the United States Supreme Court decided the case of Plessy v. Ferguson, whereby it declared that separate facilities, including schools, for whites and blacks were constitutional as long as they were equal. This decision helped cement de facto and de jure segregation across the country which was to remain intact for more than half a century. While the Supreme Court in Plessy did indicate that separate facilities were legal provided they were equal, the reality was that segregation in education resulted in unequal treatment, blatant discrimination, and denial of opportunities on the basis of race. As a consequence then, the meaning of equality came to be seen as the absence of discrimination. In other words, equality would be achieved when segregation ended and opportunities were no longer denied to people on the basis of race.

The problem, unfortunately, was that ending segregation by court decree did not result in an end to segregation. As discussed, the opening of opportunities through presidential orders, court decisions, and civil rights acts did not mean that those who suffered the legacy of centuries of racial oppression could easily and immediately take advantage of such opportunities regardless of worth or merit of the particular individual. Thus, affirmative action was instituted to try to deliver on the promise of equality. In the field of education affirmative action was used to provide access to educational opportunities previously closed to minorities and women.

Minorities, but most especially women (see chapter 6 of this volume), have certainly benefitted from affirmative action. While affirmative action has opened up opportunities for many, the current backlash against affirmative action—including the assertion that such programs are reverse discrimination or unlawful racial preferences—has resulted in the dismantling of many affirmative action programs. Accordingly, affirmative action, originally designed to address a history of discrimination, subordination, and oppression, may not be available much longer. This is true despite the fact that nearly every indicator of equality shows that the United States still has a long way to go before it is truly a country of equals. Critical race theory helps explain the backlash against affirmative action and why affirmative action has not been more successful in achieving equality.

Connection with CRT Principles

In using a CRT framework for analysis regarding affirmative action, it is best to start with a brief outline regarding some of the arguments against the use of affirmative action. It is against this backdrop that much of the CRT analysis becomes clear and makes sense.

Much opposition to affirmative action is based on two important foundational assumptions. One assumption holds that America is a meritocracy where one's life chances and access to various important and necessary societal resources—like quality education—are equally open to all and equally accessible to all those who possess sufficient merit. Merit is often defined as the necessary aptitude and knowledge, which can be adequately measured by such instruments as standardized test scores and a person's past school performance (usually as measured by grade point average). A second assumption is that a key component of equality (or, at the very least, the absence of discrimination) is a belief that any public program should be colorblind. Proponents of this view assert that no public program, including affirmative action, should take race into account. Connected to this belief in colorblindness is the belief that any consideration of race is by definition improper. Any such consideration presumably violates the principle of colorblindness because it gives an illegal preference based on race. Thus, to consider race as is done in the context of affirmative action, the argument goes, is illegal and contrary to principles of equality (Cohen and Sterba 2003).

In sum, then, the basic opposition argument is that affirmative action is discrimination in that it unfairly takes account of race in violation of meritocratic and colorblind principles. This is, of course, a simplified version of the argument opposing affirmative action. Other arguments assert that affirmative action is detrimental to those it benefits since it raises questions in the beneficiaries' minds about the value of their qualifications. Another argument asserts that the minorities who have most benefitted from affirmative action (i.e., upper- or middle-class people of color) were not deserving because they were the least in need of the help it provided (Graglia 1996). However, such seemingly more sophisticated arguments still have their roots in the same meritocracy and colorblind assumptions articulated above.

A CRT analysis of affirmative action begins by understanding affirmative action within a historical context. Such analyses note from the outset that many of the arguments made in opposition to affirmative action are made with little to no regard for American history. Thus, many CRT scholars use a historical discussion to point out that education in this country is marked by a legacy of blatant racism and unequal opportunity. From the earliest days of the nation—when blacks were forbidden to read and write—up to the present where students of color are relegated to segregated, underfunded, inferior schools, America has a long history of unequal education based on race.

A CRT historical analysis, however, does not just focus solely on the unequal treatment of people of color within the education system. Focusing solely on the educational oppression of people of color masks the way in which privileges were, and continue to be, provided to whites on the basis of race (Mcintosh 1989). Recognizing such privileges is as important, if not more so, as recognizing discrimination. The failure to recognize and acknowledge privilege received solely on the basis of one's race leaves intact the false notion that the education system—with the exception of a few isolated incidents in the past—is generally race-neutral and fair. As CRT scholars have explained, the seemingly meritocratic system of education has had advantages for certain groups at the expense of other groups.

If one of the primary criticisms of affirmative action is that it provides privileges and opportunities that are unearned on the basis of irrelevant criteria such as race, then the system is rife with unacknowledged affirmative action. The student of a wealthy family that gives substantial money to a school has a much greater chance of admission on that basis as compared to anyone given any kind of preference based on race (Moore 2005; Schmidt 2007). Thus, one of the major contributions of CRT to the affirmative action discussion is highlighting the otherwise largely invisible system of privilege,

based primarily on race, which continues to unfairly disadvantage minorities and to perpetuate unequal outcomes.

A discussion of affirmative action based in CRT principles and viewed within a historical context allows an evaluation of the claim by opponents of affirmative action that all decisions should be colorblind and that to make any decision based on race is a form of discrimination. As Gotanda (2000) has pointed out, the belief that race is a neutral category—that a person's qualifications and merit are of the same value and meaning regardless of that person's race—is a fallacy. It is a fallacy that only holds up when one ignores the long history of racial subordination in this country.

Consider the argument that the outright denial of admission historically of a minority to an educational institution based solely on that person's race is the same thing as the denial of admission contemporarily of a white person under a system of affirmative action where race is just one of several criteria that can be considered. First of all, the white person is not being denied admission because he or she is white. Unlike historical cases where every qualified black student was refused admission to institutions of higher education solely because s/he was black and deemed inferior (see the following court cases, for example: Missouri ex rel. *Gaines v. Canada,* 305 U.S. 337 [1938]; *McLaurin v. Oklahoma,* 339 U.S. 637 [1950]; and *Sweatt v. Painter,* 339 U.S. 629 [1950]), the few whites who may not have been chosen for admission to a university have not lost an opportunity due to their perceived inferiority or undesirability. Second, in regard to the person of color who may have earned admission, under no circumstances was the person chosen for admission solely because of race. Even when "quotas" were used, where a certain number of slots were set aside for minorities, race was still one of several criteria considered in the overall admissions process. Thus, to say that both are equal instances of denial of opportunity is disingenuous and a misrepresentation.

Moreover, as Ian Haney Lopez (2007) explains at length in his article '"A Nation of Minorities': Race, Ethnicity, and Reactionary Colorblindness," equating invidious discrimination and racial subordination with affirmative action under the guise of colorblindness represents a return to the formalistic views of race which undergirded the Supreme Court's decision in *Plessy v. Ferguson:*

> ...[A]n abstract, empty conception of race insulates patterns of racial exclusion while linking Jim Crow and affirmative action. If race reduces to morphologies entirely disconnected from history and social position, group mistreatment on any basis but one explicitly tied to skin color cannot be racism, for axiomatically race is divorced from all other social practices. Colorblindness by this logic protects and validates as "not-racism" the actions of intentional discriminators who exercise the smallest modicum of caution as well as, much more significantly, the inertial persistence of entrenched patterns of racial hierarchy. Simultaneously, no justification can exist for the government's use of racial classifications, since by definitional fiat race lacks all social relevance. Thus reactionary colorblindness condemns as "racism" race-conscious efforts at social reconstruction, (p. 1062)

The push for colorblindness based on an ahistorical view, which equates affirmative action and invidious discrimination and racial subordination, has resulted in the passage of such measures as Prop 209 in California and Prop 2 in Michigan, mentioned above. Such measures prohibit state governments from discriminating or granting preferences on the basis of race with respect to public education. Thus, these prohibitions mandate a colorblind approach to admission decisions whereby those making such decisions cannot take race into account when deciding whom to admit. Yet, as scholars Devon Carbado and Cheryl Harris (2008) adeptly point out, such colorblind requirements assume that not considering race, in a country such as ours where race is a salient social construct, an embedded aspect of our institutions, and woven throughout our social fabric, is a near impossibility.

Using compelling hypotheticals, such as what President Obama's personal statement in his law school application might look like if he could not mention his race, Carbado and Harris (2008) illustrate the ways in which race likely informs and impacts admission decisions even in a regime mandating colorblindness. As the authors illustrate, not only does such a mandate not result in an admission process free from the taint of racial considerations, where personal statements are part of the admission process as they continue to be,

> ... prohibiting explicit references to race in the context of admissions does not make admissions processes race neutral. On the contrary, this racial prohibition installs what we call a "new racial preference." ... This racial preference benefits applicants who (a) view their racial identity as irrelevant or inessential and (b) make no express mention of it in the application process. These applicants are advantaged vis-a-vis applicants for whom race is a fundamental part of their sense of self. ... The new racial preference rewards a particular way of relating to and expressing one's racial identity. More specifically, the preference gives a priority or advantage to applicants who choose (or are perceived) to suppress their racial identity over those who do not (or are not perceived to) so choose. ... One might think of this preference as a kind of racial viewpoint discrimination— analogous to the viewpoint distinction or preference that the First Amendment prohibits. Race is the "content" and colorblindness and racial consciousness are competing "viewpoints." Just as the government's regulation of speech must be content neutral and cannot be based upon the viewpoint expressed, a university's regulation of admissions should be content neutral and should not burden or prefer applicants based upon the racial viewpoint their personal statements express, (pp. 1147–1150)

In addition to the call for colorblindness, oppositional arguments to affirmative action also come from those who assert key principles of liberalism, most especially the focus on the individual (and not her or his social group) as informed by the myth of meritocracy. The myth of meritocracy in this instance is accompanied by the belief in individual white innocence in the face of a racist nation's history. Specifically, liberalism and the myth of meritocracy assert the ahistorical belief that equality means treating everyone the same without consideration of a history of inequality that has already advantaged one group over another. As the assertion goes, affirmative action is illegitimate and should not be allowed because it gives an individual special rights and privileges based on that person's membership in a certain group rather than that person's individual merit. In other words, these opponents argue that affirmative action should be outlawed because it is a form of reverse discrimination against whites.

Preferences have been and continue to be provided for certain social groups. As Delgado (1998) has aptly illustrated, an assertion of reverse discrimination could be likened to a "… motorist cruising a large, crowded parking lot (who sees) the handful of parking spaces reserved for the disabled, certain that if it had not been for those reserved slots, (he or she) would be safely parked by now" (p. 136). Consider how preferences for admission are provided for those students with less than stellar academic records but whose parents attended the university, have political connections, or have donated significant sums of money to the university. How can reverse discrimination arguments hold merit when even today a clear majority of those accepted for admission at most universities are white candidates and, until recently, whites were the exclusive recipients of admissions decisions?

A CRT analysis highlights the way in which white privilege allows university admission of whites, sometimes regardless of actual merit, to be seen as normal, acceptable, and unquestionable. It explains also how allowing minorities access to the same set of privileges, even when it is reserved for a very small number of qualified potential applicants, is seen as suspect and illegitimate.

At the same time, the liberal meritocratic argument asserts that affirmative action disadvantages members of the dominant group who, as individuals, are devoid of responsibility for past racism. From this perspective, affirmative action disadvantages innocent members of the dominant group. Minorities, meanwhile, are perceived as being unfairly and unworthily advantaged. In each instance, the argument claims, a person is not being judged as an individual as principles of liberalism would demand, but is instead granted or denied a perceived privilege based on group membership.

Once again, a CRT perspective helps bring clarity to this argument. Recall that CRT recognizes the pervasive and entrenched racial bias that permeates all aspects of American society. Given this, CRT helps us see that despite the lip service given to liberal individualistic principles, throughout American history the granting and denying of privileges has been based on group membership—particularly racial group membership. Racial minorities were not and are not denied educational opportunities based on their status as individuals; they were, and are, denied because of their group membership. It was not only a few individual blacks who were denied opportunities, but all blacks. It was not a few individual whites who were granted privileges of competing for access to all universities because of their race, it was all whites. In fact, as scholars have pointed out, it has been the privilege conferred by one's membership in a social group that has helped white elites form solidarity with poor, working class whites even when such solidarity has not necessarily been in the latter's best interest (Bell 2004; Woodward 1974). Accordingly, the problem of educational inequality which affirmative action seeks to address has been and remains a group-based problem which requires, at least in part, a group-based solution.

Discussion of affirmative action from a CRT perspective also highlights the importance of counterstories. As mentioned, the master narrative asserts that affirmative action allows unqualified people access to privileges based on criteria other than individual merit. This argument is particularly prevalent when arguing against the consideration of race in evaluating student applications for college admissions. Affirmative action opponents have sought to eliminate all race-based college admissions considerations in favor of a quantitative marker weighing grade point average and standardized test scores. This argument assumes that quantitative measures, particularly test scores, indicate a measure of merit. Statistics have shown that, on average, minorities, at least blacks and Latinos, perform below their white counterparts on these standardized exams. In the master narrative, standardized tests are an objective and accurate measure of what a person knows and is capable of accomplishing. Given this, the use of an "objective" measure such as test scores is superior to any other criteria. However, CRT provides a counter to this majoritarian narrative. The counter narrative takes a look at the origins of standardized testing and recognizes that such tests were not meant to be an objective and neutral evaluation. Instead, they were originally designed by an unabashed white supremacist, Carl Brigham, for the purpose of proving white superiority (Delgado 1998; see chapter 6 of this volume for a more detailed history of Brigham and the development of standardized testing). Imagine whether whites would consider a test "objective" if it had been designed by a black or Latino meant to prove black or Latino superiority.

Not only do the counterstories provided by CRT prompt us to question our taken-for-granted assumptions about standardized tests, they also ask us to question the significance and meaning of merit. As CRT scholars have shown, merit can be assessed and evaluated in a variety of ways and what counts as meritorious is often subjective, context-specific, and racially biased rather than fixed, objective, and neutral (Guinier and Sturm 2001).

Affirmative action as currently understood and implemented bumps up against the unquestioned myth of meritocracy—the belief that the system is colorblind or that individuals are disconnected from the larger historical structures in society that determine group membership advantages and disadvantages. Leaving this ideology intact and unquestioned means that the unequal effects created under this ideology remain unacknowledged and that inequality is inevitable and not subject to change. Thus, this ideology prevents us from looking for alternatives, from considering alternatives as legitimate and just, and from making meaningful changes in the system, which might truly lead to bona fide equality. The result is that even with affirmative action our education system still remains racially biased and unequal—with significant change toward greater racial equality unlikely in the foreseeable future.

Justice, Equality, and Democracy's Promise

The Civil Rights Act of 1964 and the Voting Rights Act of 1965

Dennis W. Johnson

It can be said of the Civil Rights Act of 1964 that, short of a declaration of war, no other act of Congress had a more violent background—a background of confrontation, official violence, injury, and murder that has few parallels in American history.

Robert D. Loevy (1997)

I want you to write me the god-damndest, toughest voting rights act that you can devise.

Lyndon Johnson to Attorney
General Nicholas Katzenbach
(1965)

In July 1948, despondent and gloomy delegates to the Democratic Party's presidential nominating convention gathered in Philadelphia. The party was about to break apart; few thought President Harry Truman stood a chance against the Republican candidate, the popular New York governor Thomas E. Dewey, and his even more popular running mate, California governor Earl Warren. Making matters worse, the delegates were stuck in an un-air-conditioned auditorium, in the stifling summer heat, baking under the hot television lights, wiping their brows, cranky, irritated, and dejected.

On the final evening of the convention, one of the party's rising stars, thirty-seven-year old mayor of Minneapolis, Hubert H. Humphrey, approached the podium. Now a candidate for the U.S. Senate, Humphrey was risking his entire political future by insisting that the Democratic Party stand firm for civil rights reform. Truman earlier had presented a strong ten-point civil rights policy, but, once it got to the party's platform committee, its key provisions were compromised. Humphrey and his fellow liberals would not back down: the platform committee had eviscerated Truman's plan and they would not stand for it.

Humphrey, with his nerves frayed and little sleep from the night before, spoke for just eight minutes, but in that time he ignited the delegates, praised Truman for his stand on civil rights, and made that rarest of gestures, a plea for no compromise and a stand on high moral principles.

> Friends, delegates, I do not believe
> that there can be any compromise
> of the guarantees of civil rights.
> ... There will be no hedging, and
> there will be no watering down ...
> of the instruments and the prin-
> ciples of the civil rights program.

My friends, to those who say that we are rushing this issue of civil rights, I say to them, we are one hundred seventy-two years late!

Then in his most memorable moment, Humphrey soared,

To those who say that this civil rights program is an infringement on states' rights, I say this, that the time has arrived in America for the Democratic Party to get out of the shadows of states' rights and walk forthrightly into the bright sunshine of human rights.[1]

For the approximately seventy million Americans who heard Humphrey's speech on the radio and the new medium of television, this was an extraordinary moment. U.S. Senate candidate Paul Douglas, sitting as a delegate from Illinois, called the speech "the greatest political oration in the history of the country, with the possible exception of William Jennings Bryan's 'Gross of Gold' speech."[2]

Humphrey's pro-civil rights substitute prevailed in a roll call of the states, a stunning victory for Humphrey personally, for the liberal wing of the Democratic Party, and a humiliating loss for southerners. But the southern delegations would have none of it. Amid the noise and celebration, Eugene (Bull) Connor shouted out that the Alabama delegation was going to walk out; half of them did. Mississippi's entire delegation joined them in protest, waving Confederate battle flags as they left.[3] They were met with a rolling wave of boos from other delegates, along with scattered cheers.

Truman, sitting in the White House, watching Humphrey on television, characterized him and his liberal allies as "crackpots," who were just spoiling to have the southerners bolt from the convention.[4] Now the president would have to make his way to Philadelphia, the convention hall, and a sea of discontent and turmoil. Truman, his family, and his entourage boarded the special presidential train at Union Station in Washington and arrived in Philadelphia around 9:15 p.m. He finally was nominated for president at 12:42 the next morning,

receiving 948 votes, while Richard Russell, the senator from Georgia, received 263 votes from those southerners who remained at the convention. At two in the morning, the president finally mounted the podium and, to everyone's surprise, ignited the exhausted, dispirited delegates with a fiery indictment of the Republican-dominated Congress. Republicans professed to be for all kinds of reforms, including civil rights, Truman charged, but they haven't done anything. He called them the "Do-Nothing Congress," and then dropped the bombshell: he was ordering the Eightieth Congress back into session on July 26 to complete its work.[5] Of course, it was pure political hyperbole and theater, but the feisty candidate, with his back to the wall, energized the delegates and blamed the Republicans for all the nation's troubles.

Meantime, the break-away southern delegates were getting ready to strike back. Governor Fielding S. Wright of Mississippi encouraged delegates to meet in Birmingham on Saturday to make a stand for states' rights. Six thousand boisterous convention-goers met in Birmingham that weekend and lustily cheered; South Carolina governor J. Strom Thurmond was unanimously chosen as the presidential candidate of the States Rights Democrats, as they called themselves, and Wright balanced out the ticket as his running mate.[6]

States Rights Democrats was the official name, but a newspaper reporter gave them the name that stuck, the Dixiecrats. Thurmond charged that federal anti-lynching legislation was simply "bait for minority votes and to arouse prejudice and to influence public opinion." If Truman got his way with his desegregation ideas, Thurmond charged, "lawlessness will be rampant. Chaos will prevail. Our streets will be unsafe" and there would be a "virtual revolution" in the southern states. As for the integration of the races, Thurmond was adamant: "All the laws of Washington and all the bayonets of the Army cannot force the Negro into our homes, our schools, and our churches."[7]

In November, Truman surprised nearly everyone, defeating Dewey, carrying twenty-eight states, receiving 308 electoral votes, and 49.6 percent of the vote. Thurmond carried only the Deep South of Mississippi, Louisiana, Alabama, and South

Carolina. Yet while Arkansas, Texas, Georgia, Florida, Virginia, and Tennessee remained loyal to the national Democratic Party, deep fissures were growing between southern and national Democrats. At the core of it all were the vexing, contentious issues of race, civil rights, and the role of the federal government.

Humphrey would win the 1948 Senate seat, but found in his first years in Washington that his celebrated stand on civil rights was something of a "political albatross" around his neck. Because of the southern domination of Congress, Humphrey observed that "the odor of magnolia was much stronger in Washington than it was in Montgomery or Richmond."[8]

Background

From the vantage point of the early twenty-first century, it is perhaps difficult to comprehend the depth and pervasiveness of racial discrimination in America during most of its years. In the land of equal opportunity where all men are created equal, the discrimination was widespread, knowing no geographic bounds, sometimes blatant, at times subtle, legal and extra-legal, enforced by law, custom, and community will. Over the decades, ethnic and racial discrimination affected many, including Native Americans, the Irish, eastern European immigrants, Asians, Hispanics and others. This chapter, however, focuses on the most pernicious form of discrimination, the laws and actions meted out against African-Americans in the South. It was the legacy of slavery and subjugation, rigid social hierarchy, regional values and mores, reinforced by the law and the whip. This is also a study of how southern lawmakers, acting on behalf of the majority of white constituents, fought tooth and nail to prevent federal law from righting these wrongs and how non-southern lawmakers, Democrats and Republicans alike, finally banded together to enact federal protections and to eliminate, once and for all, some of the most grievous state segregation laws and practices.

After the Civil War, the federal government enacted comprehensive civil rights protections, only to have those laws negated by court rulings, the re-emergence of the southern white power structure, and the loss of national political will. In 1870, the Constitution enfranchised African-American men and their numbers swelled on voting lists. Yet, by the end of the nineteenth century, southern state legislatures had created barriers and hurdles specifically aimed at stripping African-Americans of their right to vote. Jim Crow laws[9] were widespread and, in 1896, the U.S. Supreme Court validated the legal fiction of "separate but equal," giving state and local governments permission to continue segregating public conveyances and public schools, providing, of course, that they were "equal" (which they hardly ever were).

The domination of whites over blacks was comprehensive and pervasive.[10] First was economic domination. African-Americans were consigned to non-skilled, low-paying, menial, and often dangerous or dirty jobs: cooks, maids, janitors, non-union machine operators, or common laborers. "Help wanted" ads in newspapers typically were in columns "Jobs for Whites" and 'Jobs for Coloreds." In a typical southern city, 50 percent of all African-American women in the workforce were domestic workers, while less than 1 percent of white women were so employed. In the rural South, with many African-Americans relying on farming, sharecropping beame a pervasive form of economic exploitation that tied African-Americans to the land.

The second form of domination was political oppression, through intimidation, barriers to voting and political participation, poll taxes, and the domination of a white power structure. The pillars of democratic life—the fundamental right to speak out, to vote freely for candidates of one's choice, to do so without fear of physical reprisal or losing one's livelihood—all these were denied to or severely limited African-Americans.

The third form of domination was the denial of personal freedoms and dignity. There was an intimacy between blacks and whites: blacks cooking meals for white employers, changing their diapers and bed pans, caring for their children, tending to their needs. But this was not an intimacy of equals. In the public sphere, African-Americans were denied access to white-only hotels, restaurants, drinking fountains, and swimming pools. They were separated by race on railroads and buses. Prohibitions were explicit by the posting of signs that said "colored only"; more commonly, however, no signage was needed for African-Americans to understand that they were not welcome and their presence would not be tolerated. Jim Crow laws popped up everywhere. Black and white babies were born in separate hospitals, black and white children were taught in separate schools, black and white adults were segregated in all manner of public places, and black and white old folks were buried in separate cemeteries. Sometimes the laws bordered on the absurd: Alabama forbade African-Americans from playing checkers with whites; Mississippi insisted on separate taxicabs; New Orleans segregated its prostitutes; Florida and North Carolina made sure that no textbook touched by an African-American would later be used by a white child.[11]

Some gains were made by African-Americans in the 1930s and 1940s, but they mostly came from the federal court system, not the Congress or the executive branch. World War II, probably more than anything else, opened up economic prospects for African-Americans. Halting steps were taken during the Roosevelt administration to include blacks in federal employment and the armed services.[12] Perhaps more important was the growing understanding by many white citizens that overt, blatant racial discrimination did not square with the ideals of democracy. In a series of legal challenges beginning in 1933, some of which culminated in Supreme Court decisions, the National Association for the Advancement of Colored People (NAACP) attacked racial segregation on higher education. Then the focus shifted to public school education and five consolidated cases that culminated in the 1954 and 1955 Supreme Court decisions of Brown v. Board of Education.[13]

The federal government began to take civil rights concerns seriously during the Truman administration, lead by the president himself. Truman, a son of Missouri, held fairly conventional border-state views about race relations, but he also could count votes and knew that his political fortunes depended on northern black support. Truman was worried that African-American voters might be drifting back to the Republican Party and worried about growing racial tension, increased Ku Klux Klan activity, and heightened racial violence during and following World War II. In December 1946, he appointed a distinguished panel of citizens to look into the growing racial divide in the United States.

On June 29, 1947, Truman made an extraordinarily blunt speech at the annual meeting of the NAACP, speaking in front of the Lincoln Memorial to a crowd of ten thousand and before a worldwide radio audience: "We must make the federal government a friendly, vigilant defender of the rights and equalities of all Americans. And again I mean all Americans." Turning to NAACP president Walter White, Truman concluded "We cannot wait another decade or another generation to remedy these evils. We must work, as never before, to cure them now."[14]

The civil rights panel report, a book-length study entitled To Secure These Rights, was released in October 1947. The recommendations were blunt, comprehensive, and, to many, startling: end poll taxes, create federal legislation against local police brutality, legislation to make lynching a federal crime, protection against racial discrimination in federal elections, home rule for the District of Columbia, and the elimination of racial segregation. The recommendations probably went beyond what Truman had anticipated; nevertheless, he endorsed them.[15]

Truman's standing with southern whites was becoming increasingly uncertain. The president wanted, indeed needed, the political support of the South, but he refused to back away on civil rights reform. He even refused to appear before segregated audiences in the South.[16]

In his 1948 State of the Union address, Truman outlined five "great goals" for the United States, the first being the securing of essential human rights. One month later, he expanded on that theme. In a special message to Congress on civil rights, Truman forthrightly stated that the protection of civil rights was "the duty of every government," not just the national government, but state and local governments as well. He charged Congress to enact "modern, comprehensive civil rights laws," many of which were outlined in the recommendations of the civil rights panel.[17]

Southerners were not pleased. Pollster George Gallup found that white southerners were "overwhelmingly opposed" to Truman's civil rights program; southern politicians reacted with equal ire. Senator Harry F. Byrd (Democrat-Virginia) compared Truman's actions with those of Hitler and Stalin, charging that the president's civil rights proposals "could very conceivably lead to dictatorship." Democratic leaders throughout the South, including some of Truman's close friends, began seriously thinking about rejecting him as their presidential nominee.[18] The party split, but Truman, in the end prevailed.

Brown and Its Impact

One of the most vexing civil rights issues was the segregation of public schools. Throughout the South and the border states, together with Indiana, Illinois, and Kansas, legalized segregation of the races was required in public elementary and secondary schools. Eighteen states in all required segregations and another six permitted local school board discretion.[19] The legal and constitutional basis for this separation rested on the 1896 decision of *Plessy* v. *Ferguson,* and its sanctioning of "separate but equal" facilities. The NAACP's deliberate and careful legal assault on separate education bore fruit in its first significant victories when the U.S. Supreme Court overturned Oklahoma and Texas practices of denying legal and general graduate education to African-Americans at the states' "white" law and graduate schools.[20]

The bigger challenge, of course, was public school education segregation, and that is where the NAACP turned to, gathering together five cases, from Delaware, Virginia, South Carolina, Kansas, and the District of Columbia. In all, there were over 200 plaintiffs seeking relief from racial segregation in their public schools. The cases had come before the Supreme Court in 1952, but now the court wanted them retried, giving special attention to the question of whether the Fourteenth Amendment banned racial segregation in public schools. One of the most famous Supreme Court litigants, John W. Davis, together with a battery of lawyers, argued on behalf of the states; while Thurgood Marshall of the NAACP Legal Defense and Education Fund and his team argued on behalf of the school children.

On May 17, 1954, the U.S. Supreme Court handed down one of the most important decisions in its history. In *Brown et al.* v. *Board of Education of Topeka et al.,*[21] the Court, under Chief Justice Earl Warren, unanimously ruled that the doctrine of separate but equal had no place in public education. "We cannot turn the clock back to 1868," when the Fourteenth Amendment was first ratified, said Warren, as he read from the eleven-page decision, nor could the Court go back to 1896 when it crafted the "separate but equal" doctrine. The Court looked beyond the questions of congressional intent and focused instead on the sociological impact of segregation. It was harmful to Negro students, and it "generates a feeling of inferiority as to their status in the community that may affect their hearts and minds in a way unlikely ever to be undone." The reliance on social science quickly became a sore point for critics of the decision. Constitutional historian Alpheus T. Mason, for example, curtly remarked, that "instead of relying on solid legal arguments, Chief justice Warren had based his opinion on the quicksand of social psychology."[22]

Nevertheless, the Court had ruled and thus came to an end the legal basis for maintaining racially separated public schools throughout the country. In a short companion case, the Court decided that the federal government could not maintain separate schools in the District of Columbia.[23] Many black leaders were joyful, optimistic, and eager to begin the historic process of dismantling segregated public education. Others were cautious, skeptical of any progress in this thorny area of life, and well aware that many white southerners weren't going to concede without a fight.

The Court did not set a timetable for implementation of its ruling. Rather it set aside time in the fall term for the attorneys general from the southern states and others to present re-argument. The Court was taking the highly unusual move of delaying for a full year the implementation of the children's right to education in non-segregated schools. But it was also giving the country some breathing room. By waiting a year for the implementation decision, the Court surely was hoping to avoid social turmoil in the South. On the last day in May, 1955, the Supreme Court ruled on implementation in *Brown II:* the cases would be sent back to the federal courts, which would enter the appropriate decrees to desegregate, and do so "with all deliberate speed." No timetables, no specific direction, rather the "curiously contradictory" phrase asking for both speed and deliberation. Historian James T. Patterson observed, "there is probably no Supreme Court language so hotly disputed as 'all deliberate speed.'"[24]

The decade of the 1950s was a period of increased visibility, friction, and turmoil in race relations. In 1955, the nation was shocked by the murder of fourteen-year-old Emmet Till, a black teenager from Chicago, who went to Tallahatchie County, Mississippi, to visit relatives and was killed by white vigilantes. On December 1, 1955, a seamstress named Rosa Parks refused to give her seat up to a white person on a city bus, was arrested, and helped to spark a 382-day boycott in Montgomery, Alabama, led by Martin Luther King, Jr., that gathered world-wide attention.

And now came the battle over school desegregation. The *Brown* decisions led to southern backlash and defiance. Many southerners blamed Eisenhower for appointing Earl Warren as chief justice. State governors and other politicians in the South loudly brayed their defiance of *Brown*. Senator Byrd of Virginia called for "massive resistance" to the Supreme Court decisions. Southern legislators dusted off the doctrine of "interposition," first used in 1798 against the Alien and Sedition Acts, but dormant since then, declaring *Brown* "null and void" and "of no effect" in their states.[25] In the spring of 1956, a "Southern Manifesto" was signed by seventy-seven (out of 105) congressmen and nineteen (out of twenty-two) senators from the Old Confederacy. Among other things, this "Declaration of Constitutional Principles" charged that the Warren court had no "legal basis for its action," and that overturning the separate-but-equal doctrine was a "clear abuse of judicial power," by justices who had "substituted their personal and social ideas for

the law of the land." They pledged to employ "all lawful means" to reverse this decision which was "contrary to the Constitution."[26]

A 1956 federal court order required the University of Alabama to admit graduate student Autherine Lucy; another order required the desegregation of a public high school in Mansfield, Texas. Those judicial orders were defied; and President Eisenhower did nothing.[27]

Then, in 1957, Arkansas governor Orval E. Faubus, looking to gain support for a third term in office and not shy about whipping up racial animosity, proclaimed that desegregation of Little Rock's all-white Central High School would certainly lead to violence. Against the wishes of city officials, Faubus called out the Arkansas National Guard to prevent violence, block the desegregation order and defy federal orders. When a federal judge intervened, Faubus withdrew the guardsmen, leaving the school children under the care of local police, who were no help to them.

"Keep away from our school, you burr head," one of the white protesters shouted at fifteen-year-old Terrence Roberts. The boy later admitted to a reporter that he was scared, but said, "I think the students would like me okay once I got in and they got to know me." But the growing crowds of whites were in no mood for tolerance and understanding. Some spit on the black students, pushed them around, swore racial epithets. A white woman, Grace Lorch, tried to comfort one of the black children. "Nigger lover!" came the cry. "Why don't you calm down," Mrs. Lorch said. "I'm not here to fight with you. Six months from now you'll be ashamed at what you're doing."

After nearly three weeks of tense standoff, President Eisenhower was forced to send in U.S. Army troops, bayonets at the ready, and federalized Arkansas guardsmen. In announcing his action to the Nation, Eisenhower declared that "under the leadership of demagogic extremists, disorderly mobs have deliberately prevented the carrying out of proper orders from a federal court." Eisenhower, ever the moderate on issues of race, had been forced to act, and became the first president since Reconstruction to use armed forces to protect African-Americans in pursuit of their constitutional rights. With a force of 1,000 soldiers as their protectors, the nine black school children were finally admitted to Central High. But administrative delays, the shutting down of all four Little Rock high schools, protests and foot-dragging meant that the desegregation in the autumn of 1957 was but a hollow victory.[28]

That same year, 1957, Eisenhower urged caution to those assembled at the black National Newspaper Publishers' Association: "No one is more anxious than I am to see Negroes receive first-class citizenship in this country ... but you must be patient." The NAACP's Roy Wilkins, looking at the slow progress during the Eisenhower years, observed: "President Eisenhower was a fine general and a good, decent man, but if he had fought World War II the way he fought for civil rights, we would all be speaking German today."[29]

White Citizens Councils, the somewhat more respectable cousins of the Ku Klux Klan, began sprouting up in the Deep South, vowing to protect the white race against forced integration. Mississippi went even further. The state legislature in May 1956 created the Mississippi State Sovereignty Commission, an executive agency which became that state's segregation watchdog. In its heyday in the early 1960s, it sent over 100 volunteer speakers and distributed 200,000 pamphlets to other parts of the country touting the rosy race relations in Mississippi and warning other states of the dangers of federal encroachment. More ominously, the Sovereignty Commission, chaired by the governor, also acted as a mini-KGB, employing informants, enemies lists, and surveillance to root out the activities of the NAACP and other civil rights groups.[30]

The protests, the angry white mobs, the boycotts, and the simple justice asked of black citizens—all this was making an indelible impression on the national consciousness. The Supreme Court had boldly declared segregation unconstitutional; the federal courts tried to enforce the law. Eyes now turned to Washington, to the Congress, which had not passed a single piece of civil rights legislation since Reconstruction and its aftermath.

The Southern Domination of Congress

When the Democratic Party regained control during the Eighty-Fourth Congress (1955–1956), William S. White, the Washington bureau chief of the *New York Times*, observed that "the southern Democrat ... has returned to a place of unsurpassed power in the life of the United States. He bestrides the new Democratic Congress as so often, minority man though he is in his party, he bestrode Democratic Congresses of the past." This southern Democrat could not win a presidential contest, White noted, nor could he win Congress, but "when the dust and the smoke have cleared away, who is sitting at the top of Congress? The southern Democrat."[31] In the mid-1950s, southern Democrats constituted the most important part of the national Democratic Party, with sixteen southern and border states providing more Democrats than all other regions of the country combined. In 1956, for example, there were 235 Democrats in the House, and 134 of them were southerners.[32]

Throughout the 1940s and 1950s, southerners were able to keep civil rights legislation bottled up. In the deliberations, strategy and tactics of civil rights policymaking, four southerners mattered the most. *Richard B. Russell,* Jr., the senior senator from Georgia, who had been first elected to the Senate in 1932, led the southern forces in the Senate against civil rights legislation during the 1950s and 1960s. He was co-author of the Southern Manifesto, the "declaration of constitutional principles" signed by nearly all of the southern law makers protesting *Brown* and the threat of federal civil rights legislation. Russell became the principal strategist in the months-long filibuster against the 1964 Civil Rights Act. Clarence Mitchell, the director of the Washington office of the NAACP, unhesitatingly called Russell the ablest and most effective opponent of civil rights legislation.[33]

James O. Eastland, senior senator from Mississippi, began his senate career in 1943 and served until 1978. In 1955, when Democrats regained the majority in the Senate, the new majority leader, Lyndon B. Johnson, was instrumental in getting Eastland appointed chairman of the powerful Judiciary Committee, the committee of jurisdiction over civil rights legislation. Another signer of the

Southern Manifesto, Eastland did not hide his contempt for African-Americans. Speaking in reaction to the Supreme Court decision in *Brown (I)*, Eastland delivered on the floor of the Senate this apologia for the southern way of life:

> Segregation is not discrimination. Segregation is not a badge of racial inferiority, and that it is not is recognized by both races in the southern states. In fact, segregation is desired and supported by the vast majority of the members of both races in the South, who dwell side by side under harmonious conditions.[34]

In the House of Representatives, one southerner stood out because of his crucial position as chairman of the Rules Committee. *Howard W. Smith* of Virginia, first elected to Congress in 1931, assumed the chairmanship of the Rules Committee in 1955. He played a vital role in blocking and delaying civil rights legislation by bottling it up in his all-important committee. From the floor of the House of Representatives, he castigated the 1964 civil rights legislation: "Already the second invasion of carpetbaggers and the Southland has begun. Hordes of beatniks, misfits, and agitators from the North with the admitted aid of the Communists, are streaming into the Southland on mischief bent, backed and defended by other hordes of federal marshals, federal agents, and federal power."[35]

Lyndon B. Johnson was first elected to the Senate in 1948 and in 1955 became the youngest majority leader in history. Ambitious and cunning, Johnson forged alliances both with his natural southern brethren and with liberal leaders like Humphrey and Paul Douglas. With his presidential ambitions, Johnson knew that no southerner could win the White House by adamantly sticking to civil rights resistance. He used all his persuasive skills to broker the watered-down 1957 and 1960 civil rights acts. As president, as we shall see, he was the driving force behind the two landmark pieces of legislation.[36]

In the legislative fights in Congress during the late 1940s, 1950s, and up through the early 1960s, the southern wing of the Democratic Party could count on several institutional and political weapons at its disposal: seniority, deference to committees, the conservative southern Democratic-conservative Midwest Republican coalition, and above all, the filibuster in the Senate. Following its long-standing tradition, Congress honored the seniority system, giving the most senior member of a committee the chairmanship; those chairs were disproportionately filled by southerners.[37] In the one-party South, Democrats were elected to Congress young and stayed in office for decades, inevitably rising to leadership positions.

In the Senate there was the filibuster, "the most effective parliamentary delaying tactic a legislative minority ever had," wrote Richard W. Boiling (Democrat—Missouri), a long-time liberal and advocate for congressional reform.[38] Southern Democrats would threaten to talk a bill to death with around-the-clock filibustering if necessary. The majority could attempt to invoke cloture and halt the filibuster, but it took an extraordinary two-thirds vote to do so.[39] It was a tough hurdle to overcome. J. Strom Thurmond, elected by an unprecedented write-in vote to the Senate in 1954, held the record for the longest individual filibuster on civil rights issues. During the deliberation of the 1957 civil rights bill, Thurmond spoke for twenty-four hours and eighteen minutes.[40] If the entire southern delegation worked together, coordinating the filibuster, it would be nearly impossible to stop.

In May 1956, Eisenhower's attorney general Herbert Brownell, Jr., and the Justice Department crafted a four-part civil rights bill for Congress to consider.[41] If passed, it would have become the first federal civil rights legislation since the late nineteenth century. It created a U.S. Commission on Civil Rights, gave more authority to a Civil Rights Division of the Justice Department, and increased the Justice Department's power to seek injunctions to protect the right to vote. The most controversial section permitted certain violations of the law to be tried in a court without the benefit of a jury trial. Liberals were in favor of this provision, arguing that southern white juries would be very reluctant to convict a white person accused of violating a federal civil rights law. But in the end, jury trials were included in the Act. In the end, southerners rightly concluded that the proposed legislation had little teeth and presented little threat to them.[42] Thus, the 1957 Civil Rights Act, with little other than symbolic meaning, was signed into law.

In 1959, Congress considered civil rights legislation in both houses, only to have the bills stopped cold. The chairman of the House Judiciary Committee, stalwart New Deal liberal Emmanuel Celler (Democrat–New York), reported a bill out of his committee, but then it was blocked in Howard Smith's Rules Committee. The Senate version of the civil rights bill went nowhere once it got into the jurisdiction of the Judiciary Committee, headed by Eastland.

In 1960, Senate Majority Leader Lyndon Johnson had southerners crying "foul" when he tacked civil rights legislation onto a bill dealing with the leasing of Army land to a school in Missouri. Johnson did this so that he could avoid sending civil rights legislation to Eastland's committee, where it was sure to die. The Senate had no rule requiring that an amendment be germane; and certainly this civil rights amendment was not. Southern senators struck back by filibustering the bill on the floor, and proponents could not muster up enough support to invoke cloture.[43]

On the House side, civil rights legislation was frozen in the Rules Committee, and northern Democratic leaders were determined to wrest it away from Smith. They could do so by having a majority of House members, 218, sign a discharge petition. In January 1960, 145 Democrats and just 30 Republicans had signed the petition. Soon the list of petitioners was published in the *New York Times,* and some Republicans, embarrassed that so few in their party had affixed their names, clamored to sign on. The Republican leader in the House, Charles A. Halleck (Indiana), did not want northern Democrats to get all the credit for advancing civil rights, and encouraged his colleagues to sign the petition. Howard Smith, seeing this momentum and not wanting to lose control of the legislation, finally decided to hold hearings.[44]

Eventually, civil rights legislation was passed in both the House and the Senate, and President Eisenhower signed the Civil Rights Act of 1960 into law. But it was legislation watered down with

significant compromises. At the signing ceremony, Eisenhower hailed the legislation as "an historic step forward in the field of civil rights"; however, NAACP lawyer Thurgood Marshall, like many others, complained that the law was "not worth the paper it's written on."[45]

The Kennedy Years

In November 1960, Senator John F. Kennedy defeated Vice-President Richard M. Nixon in the closest of presidential contests. Martin Luther King, Jr., was not particularly impressed with Kennedy's Senate record on civil rights and had little enthusiasm for his presidential bid. King's opinion changed somewhat after the two had a private breakfast, and Kennedy assured King that he, as president, would be a civil rights leader.[46] But King, James Forman of the Student Nonviolent Coordinating Committee (SNCC), Bayard Rustin of the Congress of Racial Equality (CORE), and other black leaders remained skeptical. During Kennedy's first six months in office, he had sent no civil rights legislation to Congress nor had he signed an executive order desegregating federally financed housing as he had promised during the campaign.[47]

With the election of 1960, Democrats not only won the presidency but also enjoyed an eighty-nine seat margin (262–173) in the House of Representatives. But this number was deceiving. Of those Democrats, 101 were from the South. What had not changed was the southern hold on key committees, particularly the Rules Committee, chaired by Howard Smith. Often characterized as the "traffic cop" of the House, the Rules Committee could block, delay, and even kill legislation that had come from a committee of jurisdiction before it went to the House floor. For civil rights legislation, the committee of jurisdiction was the Judiciary Committee, headed by Celler.[48]

At the beginning of 1960, the Rules Committee had twelve members, with two southern Democrats, Smith and William M. Colmer (Democrat–Mississippi), often joining the four Republicans to effectively block progressive legislation.[49] Speaker Sam Rayburn (Democrat–Texas) and the Democratic leadership were determined to break the conservative stranglehold on the Rules Committee; he even threatened to purge Colmer from the committee. Then the House, in a bruising, bitter skirmish, voted to temporarily enlarge the committee from twelve to fifteen members for the new Eighty-Seventh Congress (1961–1962).[50] Two years later, the expansion was made permanent.

During the early 1960s, student activists and others continued the lunch counter sit-in demonstrations that began in Greensboro, North Carolina, and then spread to other forms of nonviolent protest. The reactions of many southern whites to such demonstrations, however, were anything but nonviolent. In 1960, the Supreme Court ruled that segregation within interstate travel was illegal, including segregation in bus terminals, waiting rooms, restrooms and restaurants. Student activists in the spring of 1961 tested that ruling by riding in two buses from Washington, D.C., deep into the South. They were called the Freedom Riders. While they were stopped and arrested in Virginia, the students did not meet up with violence until they disembarked at Rock Hill, South Carolina. John Lewis and another rider were severely beaten and arrested when they used a whites-only restroom. When they arrived in Anniston, Alabama, the bus driver stopped and yelled to the waiting, angry mob, "well, boys, here they are. I brought you some niggers and nigger-lovers." Local officials gave the Ku Klux Klan permission to deal with the students. One bus was firebombed, and the students were beaten by the mob. In Birmingham, police commissioner Bull Connor offered no protection. A second group of freedom riders, arriving from Nashville, were arrested by Connor; the riders had no protection and were severely beaten. Finally, the Kennedy administration announced that the Interstate Commerce Commission would ban segregation in all interstate facilities; still, the rides continued, and jails, particularly in Mississippi, filled with protesters.[51]

Moments after John F. Kennedy was sworn into office on January 20, 1961, a young black man, James Meredith, inspired by the new president, decided to enroll at the all-white University of Mississippi. Once they found out that he was black, university officials set about a strategy of "delay, diversion, and duplicity" to postpone Meredith's admission for another twenty months. There were

federal and state court orders, two trials, a ruling by the U.S. Supreme Court, and finally federal marshals and 16,000 federal troops sent to maintain order. Governor Ross Barnett, defiant to the end, told a state-wide television audience, "No school will be integrated in Mississippi while I am governor." Barnett saw federal enforcement as the "greatest crisis since the War between the States. ... We must either submit to the unlawful dictates of the federal government or stand up like men and tell them *NEVER!* We will not drink from the cup of genocide." Meredith was ultimately enrolled, but blood flowed, and lives were lost. In the rioting instigated by white protestors, two men were killed, 160 marshals and 40 soldiers were injured, and 200 individuals were arrested.[52]

The year 1963 brought several dramatic and tragic events to the nation's conscience. In May, Birmingham, Alabama, burst into conflict, with Bull Connor's police using fire hoses, electric cattle prods, and police dogs to intimidate African-American protestors who were demanding that public facilities be opened. Over 700 African-Americans, including many children, were arrested, forcing Kennedy to send in 3,000 troops to Birmingham to keep the peace. Throughout the South during the next ten weeks, in seventy-five cities, there were some 758 demonstrations, with 13,786 arrests.[53]

On a hot, sticky June 11, Alabama governor George C. Wallace stood before the entrance to Foster Auditorium, where University of Alabama students were to be officially registered for classes. At stake was the registration of two black students, Vivian Malone and James Hood. Wallace was determined to prevent their registration, and Nicholas Katzenbach, U.S. assistant attorney general, was equally determined to ensure their right to enter the public university. Wallace and Katzenbach nervously eyed each other, each reading from their prepared notes, and following a tentatively choreographed script. In the end, the Alabama National Guard was federalized, Wallace backed down, and the two black students were admitted. Wallace, with the last word, put his best spin on the episode: "Alabama is winning this fight against federal interference because we are awakening the people to the trend toward military dictatorship in this country."[54]

Buoyed by the news from Tuscaloosa, Kennedy was determined to give a nationwide speech that evening. Hastily prepared, with no rehearsal, the president informed the nation that he would soon deliver a major civil rights bill to Congress. Kennedy told the television audience that the nation was confronted by a "moral issue" that was "as old as the scriptures and is as clear as the American Constitution."[55]

It was time for Congress to act, Kennedy urged.

Making the Law: The Civil Rights Act of 1964

Kennedy's civil rights legislation was sent to Congress on June 19, 1963. The legislation was long-anticipated, and was accompanied by a 5,500-word message, in which the president urged Congress to "join with the executive and judicial branches in making it clear to all that race has no place in American life or law."[56]

Its prospects for passage, however, were not good and would require an all-out lobbying effort.[57] At the heart of the president's proposal was the controversial Title II, prohibiting racial discrimination in public accommodations: in restaurants, hotels, amusement parks, movie theaters, and retail establishments in interstate commerce. His bill also would strengthen the attorney general's authority to start school desegregation suits when requested to do so by someone unable to sue, and other provisions.

Predictably, southern lawmakers rushed to the microphone to condemn Kennedy's proposal. Strom Thurmond said it reminded him of the terrible days of Reconstruction, castigating the president's bill as "unconstitutional, unnecessary, unwise and beyond the realm of reason." James Eastland saw this as a "complete blueprint for the totalitarian state. ... [E]very hamburger stand, every barber shop, every beauty parlor, every rooming house up to every bank and insurance company in America" would come under federal control. John C. Stennis (Democrat–Mississippi) feared that the attorney general would trample over the rights of

white people: "Bobby Kennedy could ultimately have federal marshals and troops at every crossroads" and could "become the private attorney general of every member of the NAACP, CORE, and other pressure groups and agitators."[58]

The very night that Kennedy addressed the nation, Medgar Evers, a long-time local Mississippi official of the NAACP, was gunned down in his driveway as he was about to enter his home. His murderer, fertilizer salesman Byron de la Beckwith, later told a group of fellow Klansmen that "killing that nigger gave me no more inner discomfort than our wives endure when they give birth to our children. We ask them to do that for us. We should do just as much."[59] Two all-white all-male jury trials ended in mistrial in 1964 (thirty years later, in 1994, de la Beckwith was found guilty of murder, and, in 2001, died in prison).

On that same day, Martin Luther King, Jr., announced that there would be a massive march on Washington. On August 28, over 200,000, by conservative official estimates, gathered before the Lincoln Memorial, participating in the March on Washington. It was televised worldwide on the new Telsat satellite system. Kennedy had tried to dissuade civil rights leaders from coming to Washington for this mass gathering, but, as it gathered momentum, he came out in support. This was A. Philip Randolph's defining event. In 1941, Randolph, the president of the Brotherhood of Sleeping Car Porters, had planned a march on Washington, and now it was coming to fruition. John Lewis, representing SNCC, about to give a strong, controversial speech, in the end acceded to Randolph's plea to tone it down. The final speaker was Martin Luther King, Jr., who gave his iconic "I have a Dream" speech. Journalist Murray Kempton described it as "the largest religious pilgrimage of Americans that any of us is ever likely to see."[60]

Kennedy was in a difficult position. King and other black leaders publicly were chiding him for being too timid; liberal Democrats were clamoring for tough, punitive measures; and southern Democrats, already vehemently opposed to him on civil rights threatened to take out their anger on other pending administration-backed legislation. Kennedy and his backers in Congress had to cobble together a coalition of northern Democrats and moderate Republicans to come up with strong but, inevitably, compromised language.

One of the sticking points for many Republicans was the fact that Title II, the public accommodations section, was based on the commerce clause of the Constitution rather than the ostensibly more compelling Fourteenth Amendment equal protection clause. The administration reasoned that racially segregated public accommodations impeded the free flow of interstate commerce. Republicans saw this argument as specious and open-ended: did that really mean, like Eastland said, that every local barber shop and every hamburger stand would come under federal jurisdiction? Republicans also would have preferred using the Fourteenth Amendment; after all, they could point with pride that it was the Republican-controlled Civil War Congress that crafted its protections.

The decision to anchor the anti-discrimination measures in the commerce clause, in the end, may have been rooted in the politics of the Senate. By basing the authority on the commerce clause, the civil rights bill would be routed to the Senate Commerce Committee, chaired by Warren Magnuson (Democrat–Washington), a friend of the administration. But if the bill were based on the Fourteenth Amendment, it would have to begin its journey in the Senate Judiciary Committee, headed by the implacable Eastland.[61]

The Senate, no matter the committee of first jurisdiction, would be the thorniest problem, particularly with the threat of a southern filibuster. The administration decided to approach the House of Representatives first, where its chances, despite Smith and the Rules Committee, looked more promising.

On June 19, 1963, the administration's bill went to Subcommittee No. 5 of the Judiciary Committee. The subcommittee was the only one where northern Democrats dominated, and Emmanuel Celler was chair of both the subcommittee and the full Judiciary Committee. The ranking Republican was William McCulloch, a low-profile conservative representing a rural Ohio district. Deputy Attorney General Nicholas Katzenbach and his colleague Burke Marshall worked particularly with McCulloch to fashion a bi-partisan compromise bill.[62] The bill hammered out by Katzenbach and McCulloch weakened the voting rights title of the Kennedy draft. However, liberal Democrats felt blindsided by this compromise, since they hadn't been included in its deliberations. Soon, a tough, bold substitute bill appeared from the Democrats, which added a new fair employment practices section.

McCulloch saw this as nothing more than a raw power move, with Democrats trying to embarrass the Republicans. Neither House Minority Leader Charles Halleck (Indiana), minority whip Gerald R. Ford (Michigan), or McCulloch were going to stand there and take it while Democrats accused them of being weak on civil rights. The Republicans and conservative Democrats threatened to have the liberal bill go directly to the floor and be cut to pieces; McGulloch vowed that he wouldn't lift a finger to help.[63]

Then came two extraordinary events. On September 15, 1963, a bomb exploded under the steps of the Sixteenth Street Baptist Church in Birmingham, Alabama, killing four African-American girls, aged eleven to fourteen. It was "Youth Day" Sunday at the church. The bombing, one of many racially motivated incidents that had occurred in Birmingham over the past two decades, attracted worldwide outrage. Martin Luther King, Jr., in his eulogy, said that the girls' death had "something to say to every minister of the gospel who has remained silent behind the safe security of stained-glass windows." It also said something to "every politician who has fed his constituents with the stale bread of hatred and the spoiled meat of racism" and to "a federal government that has compromised with the undemocratic practices of southern Dixiecrats and the blatant hypocrisy of right-wing northern Republicans." It was not just the murderers that citizens should be concerned with, but "the system, the way of life, the philosophy which produced the murderers."[64]

After Birmingham, civil rights legislation seemed all the more urgent. On November 20, the full Judiciary Committee finally reported its bill. There had been tremendous amounts of bickering, accusations, the breakup of tenuous coalitions, tensions over who could claim credit, and whom to blame. What finally emerged was a bill that was stronger than Kennedy's original bill and still acceptable to most Republicans. The compromise legislation added a measure first pushed by Republicans, a Title VII, which forbade discrimination in employment. Another key change was the strengthening of Title VI, prohibiting discrimination in federally funded programs.[65]

Then came the second shock, the assassination of John F. Kennedy in Dallas, Texas, two days later. With his death, the political landscape had now profoundly changed. The day after Kennedy was buried, President Lyndon Johnson, whose views on civil rights were suspect by many, addressed a joint session of Congress. So unlike Kennedy's mannerisms and speech, Johnson's cadence was slow, his voice laced with a Texas twang; lawmakers and dignitaries in the packed House chamber listened intently to his every word. Halfway through his speech, Johnson said:

> No memorial oration or eulogy could more eloquently honor President Kennedy's memory than the earliest possible passage of the civil rights bill for equal rights. We have talked for one hundred years or more. It is now time to write the next chapter—and to write it in the books of law.[66]

It was one of Lyndon Johnson's finest moments. Two days later, he summoned African-American civil rights leaders to the White House, one at a time, for lengthy, frank discussions. Johnson reached out to New Deal liberals, to assure them that they were in harmony with one another. While southern lawmakers were uncomfortable with his speech, they did not appear to be alarmed or shocked. This was, after all, a Texan, a southerner; in the end, they thought, one of their own. Privately, however, Johnson said to his beloved mentor, Richard Russell, "if you get in my way" on this civil rights bill, "I'm going to run you down. I want you to know that, because I care about you."[67]

The civil rights bill had not gone to the full House of Representatives, but was now bottled up in Howard

Smith's Rules Committee. Then on December 9, Celler filed the inevitable discharge petition to force the bill out of Rules, hoping to get the necessary 218 signatures, so that the bill could be sent to the full House and passed before the holiday recess. But only 150 lawmakers signed on, and the discharge petition failed. But over the Christmas holiday, northern members of the House heard loud and clear from their constituents who were demanding that lawmakers support the civil rights legislation. As soon as Congress reconvened in early January 1964, many other lawmakers indicated that they were ready to sign on. Furthermore, there were rumblings in the Rules Committee itself, and by January committee members were just two votes short of having a majority ready to force the bill from Smith's hand.

On January 8, in his first State of the Union address, Lyndon Johnson implored Congress: "Let this session of Congress be known as the session which did more for civil rights than the last hundred sessions combined."[68]

The next day, Howard Smith finally relented, and began hearings on the civil rights legislation. "I know the facts of life around here," he said. He held nine days' worth of hearings, during which time twenty-eight House members from the South were witnesses against the bill, while just five members were in favor. Then, on January 30, the civil rights bill finally left the Rules Committee and was now ready for general debate by the full House.[69]

Then out of the blue, Smith introduced an amendment on the House floor, on February 8, calling for the insertion of the word "sex" into the proposed Title VII, thus prohibiting employment discrimination on the basis of gender as well as race, and national origin. Many thought he was joking or more seriously, trying to throw a monkey wrench into the provision. No, assured Smith, the insertion of the word "sex" "will help an important minority." "This bill is so imperfect," Smith said, "what harm will this little amendment do?"

Every woman in the House, except for one, agreed to support Smith's amendment, no matter the motivation. Katherine St. George (Republican–New York) lectured her male colleagues: "We outlast you. We outlive you. We nag you to death. So why should we want special privileges? We want this crumb of equality." Members laughed, but not Martha W. Griffiths (Democrat–Michigan), the formidable member of the House Ways and Means Committee. In a long and impassioned plea, Griffiths made the most forceful argument, warning that if the word "sex" were not included, then "white women will be the last at the hiring gate."

Edith S. Green (Democrat–Oregon) was the only woman to oppose the amendment, arguing that, for every discriminatory action against a woman, blacks had suffered tenfold the number. She said the Smith amendment would "help destroy" this section of the bill. Emanuel Celler, no friend of the Equal Rights Amendment which he had bottled up in the Judiciary Committee for a total of twenty years, likewise pleaded that the language be dropped, saying Smith's amendment was "illogical." What were women worried about, Celler wondered: in his own house, women were not in the minority, and furthermore, he was always able to get in the two last words, "Yes, dear." Again, there were knowing guffaws from his male colleagues. Opposition also came from the Johnson administration; it did not want the Smith amendment to gum up the works.[70] But after two hours of debate, Smith's amendment passed, 168 to 133. Some observers had to be muttering about strange bedfellows as most of the old guard southern conservatives were voting to protect women and many liberal northerners were voting against the amendment.

The House heard over 120 amendments on February 10, agreed to 28 of them, mostly on technical language, and finally, after all had been dispensed with, it voted overwhelmingly to adopt the civil rights bill, 290 to 110. It was a truly bipartisan victory, with 138 Republicans joining 152 Democrats. Indeed, it was the South against everybody else: of the 110 in opposition, ninety-six came from the old Dixie.[71]

The legislation was now off to the Senate, where civil rights forces would over the course of the next four months marshal superior organization and leadership. When the House bill was walked over to the Senate, Majority Leader Mike Mansfield (Democrat–Montana) was there to intercept it at the door. If he had not, the civil rights bill automatically

would have been referred to the committee of jurisdiction, the Judiciary Committee, chaired by James Eastland. Mansfield's interception was the same tactic Lyndon Johnson used in 1956, against the same committee and the same chairman. The only way around Eastland was for the Senate to act as a committee of the whole, and consider the legislation directly on the floor. Mansfield employed another tactic: he would keep the wily Richard Russell from tying up the Senate with endless parliamentary maneuvers and quorum calls. Mansfield would make sure that there was a quorum of fifty senators on the floor at all times, and only allow the Appropriations Committee to hold its regular committee session. All other Senate business would be suspended. Francis R. Valeo, Mansfield's assistant recalled, "Russell was taken aback by this. He was quite surprised. ... Mansfield was stealing his thunder in effect."[72]

Russell warned that the embattled southern senators would resist: "We shall enter into the battle next week with the earnest hope and prayer that we may find the means and strength to bring the facts of the issue to the people of this self-governing republic before it is too late."[73] During past civil rights filibusters, the southerners formed a platoon system, where three platoons of six senators each, would take turns talking the offending legislation to death. As they had successfully done before, southern senators would talk this bill to death, water it down, or hope that the sponsors would eventually abandon it.

Johnson asked Mansfield to designate Hubert Humphrey (Democrat–Minnesota) as the floor leader; Humphrey eagerly accepted this task. Working closely with Humphrey was liberal Republican Thomas H. Kuchel of California, who was responsible for rounding up fifteen Republican senators for quorum calls.[74] Johnson wasted no time: he called Humphrey, goading him about the challenge ahead: "You have got this opportunity now, Hubert, but you liberals will never deliver. You don't know the rules of the Senate, and your liberals will be off making speeches when they ought to be present in the Senate. I know you've got a great opportunity here, but I'm afraid it's going to fall between the boards." But Humphrey swears that he knew exactly what the goading and cajoling Johnson was doing: "One thing I liked about Johnson [was that] even when he conned me I knew what was happening to me."[75]

The central strategic question was this: could the pro-civil rights Senators come up with a coalition of northern Democrats and moderate Republicans sizeable enough to invoke cloture when the inevitable southern filibuster occurred? It would take sixty-seven votes to override. The task was complicated because some senators, like the eighty-seven-year-old Carl Hayden (Democrat–Arizona), were opposed to cloture on principle, no matter what the subject. Moderate and conservative Republicans would have to be won over, despite some provisions they found objectionable in Title VII, such as the Equal Employment Opportunity Commission and provisions that cut off federal funds for noncompliance.

Everett M. Dirksen (Republican–Illinois) was key. As minority leader in the Senate, he could persuade moderate Republicans to join the Democrats, but certainly he would extract a price. But not even his aides knew where Dirksen stood on civil rights. He said he had an open mind and hadn't made any commitments or assumptions. His apparent indecision made him all the more valuable. Dirksen was a master of Senate tactics who played politics as good as any on the Hill. He was also vain, loved being the center of attention, and enjoyed the sound of his mellifluous baritone voice. Humphrey and Lyndon Johnson both worked on Dirksen, stroking his ego, giving him credit, letting him take center stage. Humphrey recalled Johnson saying to him: "You've got to play to Ev Dirksen. You've got to let him have a piece of the action. He's got to look good all the time."[76]

Thomas Kuchel would have to round up four out of every five Republican senators. Certainly northeast liberal Republicans like Kenneth Keating and Jacob Javits of New York and Clifford Case of New Jersey would be on board, and so would some progressive Midwesterners. But six of Dirksen's colleagues, all from the prairie or mountain states, were dead set against a cloture override; the most prominent opponent was Barry Goldwater of Arizona, who was vying for the Republican Party's 1964 presidential nomination.[77] Indeed, Goldwater

in early September also would vote against that year's version of Medicare-Medicaid legislation.

The Republican votes would have to come from other Midwest or mountain state Republicans, such as Len B.Jordan (Montana), Karl E. Mundt (South Dakota), Carl T. Curtis (Nebraska), or Roman Hruska (Nebraska). One key senator on the fence was conservative Bourke B. Hickenlooper of Iowa. Mansfield aide Francis Valeo recalled how Hickenlooper, and other fence-sitting Republicans, were fussed over. Hickenlooper was ushered into a meeting in Mansfield's back office in the Capitol, with Burke Marshall and Nicholas Katzenbach from the Justice Department and Mike Manatos from the White House. Mansfield told Valeo: "Go in there and talk to those lawyers … and tell them I'm going to bring Hickenlooper in there and they're to make any changes in the bill he wants." The senator from Iowa suggested a few minor changes, then said, "well, that's a hell of a lot better bill that it was."[78] Hickenlooper did not promise his vote, caused some heartburn later in the deliberations, but finally came through with his vote to override the veto, and brought a few of his Midwest colleagues with him.

The southern filibuster began on the procedural question: should the just-passed House bill be referred to the Eastland Judiciary Committee or go directly on the Senate calendar? Southerners filibustered for fifteen days, March 9 through March 26. Dirksen, a stickler for parliamentary procedure, sided with the southerners; surprisingly, so did Wayne L. Morse (Oregon), the fiercely independent liberal Democrat. But Humphrey reminded his colleagues of Eastland's track record: 120 out of 121 civil rights bills over the past decade had died in his committee. Thomas J. Dodd (Democrat–Connecticut) said enough was enough, that the civil rights bill had already gone through eighty-three days of testimony and 280 witnesses; it was time for the whole Senate to take up the matter.[79]

The pro-civil rights senators were impressively organized, under the leadership of Humphrey and Kuchel. Each morning, Humphrey, Kuchel, and their floor captains huddled with Justice Department officials, usually Nicholas Katzenbach, and often joined by Clarence Mitchell of the NAACP and Joseph Rauh of the Leadership Conference on Civil Rights. They published a daily bipartisan newsletter, parceling out floor responsibilities, summarizing procedures, and giving talking points on controversial issues. Further they stymied the southern strategy of insisting on repeated quorum calls, by having enough senators ready and available at all times.[80]

After three weeks of filibustering on the procedural issue, the Senate finally got down to the substance of the legislation. The longest filibuster in Senate history soon began, starting on March 30 and finally ending on June 10. For the southerners, it was a risky gamble. It was an all-or-none strategy, with no alternative southern proposal, and one that historians have viewed as fatefully flawed. Hubert Humphrey couldn't understand the southerners' tactics: "I never could quite understand why they didn't let us vote more often. If they had done so, they could have insisted that the legislative process, after all, was working because amendments were being voted on. But they didn't do that. Instead they just kept talking and talking. It seemed that they had lost their sense of direction and had little or no real plan."[81]

Russell, tired and fighting against the ravages of emphysema, knew he couldn't win over the Senate; all he could do was delay, fight for time, and hope that Johnson and the non-southerners in the Senate would give up in frustration. Russell vowed to fight "to the last ditch." Along with him were eighteen southern Democrats and one lone Republican, John G. Tower of Texas. Russell could count on the diehards and flame-throwers, like Eastland, Thurmond, Allen J. Ellender (Louisiana), and Stennis, but some of the other southerners, like J. William Fulbright (Arkansas), Russell B. Long (Louisiana), and George A. Smathers (Florida), were not blind to the merits of the civil rights legislation, or at least understood that African-Americans soon would be a constituency to be reckoned with, if not at least courted.[82]

Still, these southerners had to participate in the filibuster and vote against civil rights reforms; it would have been political suicide to do otherwise. In a telephone conversation with President Johnson, Fulbright confessed: "Christ, I'm really over a barrel on this thing. I wish to hell I could vote with you. You know that." Johnson: "I know that, I know it."

Fulbright: "I hope to hell I can get this thing out of the way, but I feel like a traitor, you know."[83]

The southerners droned on and on, day after legislative day. Despite the high stakes, the bitterness of the policy fight, there still was a measure of comity and civility among the lawmakers. Humphrey remembered Willis Robertson (Democrat–Virginia), seventy-seven years old in 1964 and filibustering against civil rights, was always good for an hour's speech, but the strain was showing. To make it a little easier on Robertson, Humphrey would interrupt and ask him a long, convoluted question. Robertson "would smile and respond," Humphrey wrote, "acknowledging without words my gesture. Afterward, we might share his Virginia sour-mash whiskey." Robertson, in turn, would help Humphrey out by coming to the Senate floor when Humphrey needed an extra body for a quorum call.[84]

One thing Russell and other southerners hoped for was that George Wallace's 1964 bid for the presidency would stir up grassroots support and demonstrate to the nation that his message resonated not just in the South but with Americans throughout the country. That support came in Wisconsin, which held its 1964 presidential primary on April 7. On that day in Milwaukee's Schroeder Hotel, a jubilant George Wallace, donning a feathered Winnebago war bonnet and joyously dancing a victory war dance, whooped, "We won without winning!" Governor John Reynolds, running as a favorite-son stand-in for Lyndon Johnson won the primary, but Wallace, with 34 percent of the vote, was the talk of politics nationwide the next day. "All Mississippi is thrilled," said a telegram from that state's governor Paul Johnson. Wallace, who entered the Wisconsin primary, his first ever in the North, had found his audience: blue-collar ethnic workers particularly in southside Milwaukee who were fed up with crime, were fearful of blacks in adjoining neighborhoods, and saw in Wallace a man who understood them. At his biggest rally at Serb Hall on Milwaukee, three thousand Polish immigrants belted out the first stanza of "Dixie" in their Old World tongue, much to Wallace's delight.[85]

Wallace went on to the Indiana primary where he won 24 percent of the vote. In Maryland, on May 20, the Alabama governor almost won the presidential primary on the strength of blue-collar Baltimore and rural white voters on the civil rights-scarred Eastern Shore. Those blue-collar workers in Baltimore had heavily backed John Kennedy in 1960, now were nearly unanimous for Wallace. But African-American voters came out in droves, and Wallace blamed them for his defeat. "If it hadn't been for the nigger bloc vote," he said, "we'd have won it all."[86]

Johnson was worried that Wallace's success in tapping into traditional Democratic northern blue-collar voters would only encourage the southerners in the Senate to continue their all-out effort to kill the civil rights legislation. While a number of northern Democratic senators dismissed the Wallace threat and its implications, Abraham Ribicoff of Connecticut did not. Wallace "has proved something. He has proved that there are many Americans in the North as well as the South who do not believe in civil rights." Ribicoff predicted that "the next twenty years will be years of strife and turmoil in the field of civil rights," with the troubles "not just in the South, but primarily in the North."[87]

While Wallace was making headlines in the northern primaries, and the filibuster continued on the floor of the Senate, minority leader Everett Dirksen began his legislative horse-trading. Hoping to get reluctant Republicans to join him, Dirksen proposed over one hundred amendments to the civil rights bill. The amendments ranged from the trivial to a "complete evisceration" of the major titles. No one knew for sure if Dirksen was serious about the amendments, whether he was trying to gain a better bargaining position, or if, ultimately, he just wanted to have his name on the bill.[88] Ultimately, Dirksen then reduced the number of amendments to ten, all of them related to the fair employment title.

The horse-trading continued, with Dirksen and the Democratic leadership walking a fine line: rounding up moderate-conservative Republicans, not irritating the increasingly impatient civil rights leaders, not upsetting the House Republicans, and not destroying the fragile balance in the Senate. On May 13, Attorney General Robert Kennedy, senators Humphrey, Dirksen, and others crafted a "clean bill," to be introduced as a substitute. Some seventy changes were made, mostly technical, and, in the end, the Humphrey–Dirksen substitute, as it was called, was even stronger than the original bill that had come over from the House.

On June 1, senators Mansfield and Dirksen finally announced their decision to file a cloture petition; it would be filed on Saturday, June 6, with the vote taking place on Monday, June 9. The floor leaders wanted to wait until after the California primary on June 2, where Barry Goldwater, who had already informed his Republican colleagues that he'd vote against a cloture petition, was running against New York governor Nelson Rockefeller. Dirksen didn't want to upset Goldwater backers in the Senate by pressing the issue. But Dirksen also wanted the civil rights issue settled by the time Republicans met in San Francisco for their presidential nominating convention in July 13.[89]

In his closing speech, Richard Russell lamented the work done by religious leaders in pressing for the civil rights legislation: "I have observed with profound sorrow the role that many religious leaders have played in urging the passage of the bill."[90] Russell, adept at the art of politics and persuasion, could not see that, for many, civil rights was a profoundly moral issue. Indeed, through their activities on Capitol Hill and grassroots measures, particularly in the Midwest, progressive church leaders and activists were deeply committed to ending racial discrimination. In a sense, it was a re-emergence of the early twentieth-century Social Gospel, and at the center was the National Council of Churches.[91] Under the leadership of the Rev. Eugene Carson Blake, the National Council, and many faith-based organizations became energetic civil rights activists.[92] Humphrey noted the important role played by the Leadership Conference on civil rights, various civil rights organizations, labor organizations, business leaders, and church organizations. "Without the clergy, we could never have passed the bill."[93]

On June 10, by a vote of 71 to 29, for the first time in its history, the Senate shut down debate on a civil rights filibuster. Twenty-seven Republicans joined forty-four Democrats, including the terminally ill Glair Engel from California; the back of southern resistance in the Senate had been broken. "This," said Strom Thurmond, who was about to switch over to Barry Goldwater and the Republican Party, "is

KEY PROVISIONS OF THE 1964 CIVIL RIGHTS ACT

The act had eleven separate titles, dealing with voting rights, the extension of the Civil Rights Commission, and other provisions. The most important sections, however, were these:

- Title II, which barred discrimination on the basis of race, color, religion or national origin in any public accommodation, such as restaurants, lunch counters, movie theaters, sports arenas, and other public accommodations if they affected interstate commerce.
- Title III authorized the U.S. attorney general to pursue legal proceedings on behalf of individuals who might not have the funds or feel that bringing a suit would jeopardize their personal safety or jobs.
- Title IV called for active pursuit of desegregation in public schools and called on the attorney general to file suits to enforce the act.
- Title VI declared that any government agency receiving federal funds could lose those funds it it engaged in unlawful discrimination.
- Title VII declared it unlawful for employers, employment agencies, labor unions or training programs to discriminate on the basis of race, color, religion, sex, or national origin in hiring, discharging, and terms of conditions of employment.

a sad day for America." Liberal Republican Jacob Javits retorted, "This was one of the Senate's finest hours."[94]

The following week the Senate, by 73 to 27, passed the civil rights bill. Among those voting against the civil rights bill was Barry Goldwater, who said he was personally opposed to segregation of the races, but nevertheless labeled the bill unconstitutional. Goldwater, ignoring the political advice of his Republican colleagues who were fearful that his stand would rip apart the upcoming Republican convention, stood firm. He acknowledged getting his constitutional advice from a young Arizona lawyer, William H. Rehnquist, and a young Yale law professor, Robert Bork.[95] On July 2, the Senate's version of the bill was passed by the House by an overwhelming 289 to 126.

At last, basic guarantees of freedom and equality would now become the law of the land. At the overflowing signing ceremony, on July 2, 1964, Lyndon Johnson stated that millions of Americans had been denied essential freedoms, but no longer. "Our Constitution, the foundation of our Republic, forbids it. The principles of our freedom forbid it.

Morality forbids it. And the law I sign tonight forbids it."[96]

Ceremonial signing pens, seventy-five in all, were handed out, to Dirksen and Humphrey, Celler, William McGulloch, Robert Kennedy, and a wide variety of civil rights leaders.

Just before the Republican convention in July, an informant helped the FBI locate the bodies of three civil rights workers, Andrew Goodman, Michael (Mickey) Schwerner, and James Ghaney. While nearly a thousand civil rights workers, part of the Freedom Summer voting rights program, had been arrested by Mississippi lawmen that summer, Neshoba County deputy sheriff Cecil Price released the three deep in the woods into the hands of white vigilantes. Mississippi politicians dismissed reports that they had been murdered. Eastland told Lyndon Johnson that it had to be a "publicity stunt." "Who is it that would harm 'em?" Eastland asked, "There's no white organizations in that area of Mississippi. Who could possibly harm 'em?"[97]

Most Republicans in Congress supported civil rights legislation, and, without their support, the Civil Rights Act of 1964 would not have been possible. Yet their political and symbolic leader, the man running for the presidency, had voted against the civil rights legislation. Barry Goldwater, no racist himself, was widely admired and supported in the Deep South. He won the electoral votes of his home state of Arizona and five Deep South states, but was otherwise crushed in the November presidential election.

Making the Law: The Voting Rights Act of 1965

Following the *Brown* decisions, several southern states cracked down on African-American voting. In Mississippi, by the end of 1955, there were no black voters registered in fourteen counties. Louisiana officials distributed "how-to-discriminate" pamphlets to local officials, showing how to remove blacks from the voting rolls. While in Tennessee and North Carolina, black voter registration increased, in the Deep South, the numbers of registered blacks shrunk.[98]

KEY INDIVIDUALS IN THE CIVIL RIGHTS LEGISLATION

Civil rights leaders, like Martin Luther King, Jr., John Lewis, Roy Wilkins, labor, civic and church leaders, Fannie Lou Hamer, James Meredith, and thousands of courageous ordinary citizens fill the roster of those responsible for the two civil rights laws. If they did not push, agitate, and fight, sometimes at great risk to their lives, the 1960s civil rights laws would not have been possible.

In Washington, the Civil Rights Act and Voting Rights Act were two of the most contentious and bitterly fought legislative fights in American history. Three individuals were key to their success.

Lyndon B. Johnson (1908–1973) had never supported civil rights legislation during his first twenty years in Congress. But with looming national ambitions, he made an "abrupt and total reversal" and used all his power and guile to win support of the first civil rights law in the twentieth century.[99] While he maintained a low profile in the debates and proceedings for both the 1964 and 1965 laws, he was indeed the driving force behind the scenes. The historian Robert Caro has stated that "Lyndon Johnson was the greatest champion in the halls of government that black Americans, and indeed all Americans of color, had during the 20th Century. And indeed … with the single exception of Abraham Lincoln, he was the greatest champion with white skin that they had in the history of the republic."[100]

Hubert H. Humphrey (1911–1978) was elected to the U.S. Senate in 1948; in 1965, he became vice-president of the United States from 1965 to 1969. Humphrey ran for president in 1968 and was narrowly beaten by Richard M. Nixon. He also was an unsuccessful candidate for his party's nomination for president in 1960 and 1972. Humphrey returned to the Senate in 1971, serving until 1978. Known as the "happy warrior" for his upbeat attitude and sunny disposition, he was well admired and respected by colleagues and staff in both the House and the Senate. His strategic leadership in the Senate was central to passage of the 1964 law.

Everett M. Dirksen (1896–1969) served in the House of Representatives from 1933 through 1948, then was elected to the Senate in 1950, was chosen minority leader in 1959, and served until 1969. On most issues, Dirksen was a stout conservative, hawkish on the Vietnam war, cautious on economic and social policy. Lyndon Johnson knew that Dirksen was in a tight spot politically in supporting civil rights legislation, but, in the end, could be depended upon.

By 1964, there had been some progress in registering African-Americans in parts of the South. Tennessee had enfranchised 69 percent of its adult blacks, Florida 64 percent, and Texas 58 percent. But Mississippi was by far the worst state; it had registered just 28,500 out of 422,000 eligible black voters, a mere 6.7 percent. Historian Neil R. McMillen pointed out that there were fewer blacks eligible to vote in Mississippi for Lyndon Johnson in 1964 than for William McKinley in 1896.[101]

For many blacks in Mississippi, it wasn't a question of intimidation or pressure against them not to vote; many simply did not know that the vote was available to them. Fannie Lou Hamer remembered going to a voter registration meeting in 1962, and commenting: "until then … I didn't know that a Negro could register and vote. … I guess if I'd had any sense I'd a-been a little scared, but what was the point of being scared? The only thing they could do to me was kill me and it seemed like they'd been trying to do that a little bit at a time ever since I could remember."[102]

Hamer, with a sixth-grade education, worked in the fields and as a time keeper in a plantation, had joined SNCC in 1962, to register African-Americans in Mississippi. Earlier, she had lost her job because of civil rights activities and then SNCC hired her as a field secretary. In June 1963 in Winona, Mississippi, she was thrown into jail for disorderly conduct; her offense was attempting to enter a "whites only" restaurant. In the adjoining jail cells, she heard cries and screams from other prisoners. In Hamer's words:

> The state highway patrolmen came and carried me out of the cell into another cell where there were two Negro prisoners. The patrolman gave the first Negro a long blackjack that was heavy. It was loaded with something and they had me lay down on the bunk with my face down, and I was beat. I was beat by the first Negro till he gave out. Then the patrolman ordered the other man to take the blackjack and he began to beat … ,[103]

Hamer was ordered to sign a statement saying that she had not been mistreated and was later released. She refused medical treatment and her injuries were so severe that she became partially blind and permanently disabled.[104]

In 1964, Hamer helped organize the Mississippi Freedom Democratic Party (MFDP) as an alternative to the all-white state Democratic Party. At the Democratic National Convention that year, she testified before the credentials committee about the abuse and torture she and other African-Americans had suffered when attempting to vote. She was bitterly disappointed when the Democratic delegates failed to unseat the regular Democrats from Mississippi and gave the MFDP just two at-large seats. Nonetheless, her presence and cause made a lasting impression on the delegates and the nation.

Hamer and three others from the MFDP held a mock election against incumbent Mississippi congressmen in the November 1964 elections.[105] When the new Eighty-Ninth Congress convened on January 4, 1965, Hamer and the other women challenged the election results and tried to enter the House chamber to be sworn in. William Fitts Ryan (Democrat–New York) objected to the swearing in of the four veteran Mississippi Democrats and the freshman Republican, but then Speaker of the House Carl Albert (Democrat–Oklahoma) moved that the Mississippians be seated. On a procedural vote, Hamer and the protestors lost, but were heartened to know that 148 lawmakers had voted against the Mississippians and, by extension, against the exclusion of African-Americans from the voting booth.[106]

From the November 1964 elections, the Democrats gained thirty-five seats in the House of Representatives, giving them 295 seats to 140 for the Republicans. It was such an historic, overwhelming majority that some of them had to spill over to the Republican side of the aisle so they could all be accommodated. Yet while Democrats dominated, and while the Mississippi challenge went on, Republicans did pick up support in the South. Five new Republican congressmen were elected from Alabama, and one each from Georgia and Mississippi. It was the beginning of an historic, tectonic shift of white voters, going from a solid South of Democrats to a near solid South of Republicans in the following decades.

Martin Luther King, Jr., returning from a European trip where he received the Nobel Prize for Peace, met with Johnson in mid-December 1964. At the meeting, King pressed Johnson for a voting rights bill but Johnson was hesitant. It had been just six months since the end of the bruising fight for the 1964 Civil Rights Act, and Johnson needed southern votes for a host of other Great Society legislation. Yes, a voting rights bill was important and the time would eventually come, he told King, but it could not be in 1965.[107] What the president probably did not tell King was that he had ordered Nicholas Katzenbach to begin crafting the next civil rights bill, legislation that would provide "once and for, equal voting rights."[108]

King was exhausted, physically and psychologically. He been constantly traveling, pulled in all directions and haunted by the suspicions, then the reality, that the FBI had wiretapped and recorded his activities and were threatening to reveal damaging personal information.[109] But there was work to be done: most pressing work was voter registration, particularly in Selma, Alabama. There was a solid reason for targeting this sleepy city on Highway 80 west of Montgomery. There were 15,000 African-Americans of voting age, but just 355 were registered; white registrars were determined to stop any more blacks from voting. In addition, King knew that a protest in Selma would be just as incendiary as the protests in Birmingham the year before. Sheriff Jim Clark of Dallas County (Selma) would overreact just like Bull Connor did in Birmingham.[110] Heads might crack, but the wider world would be witness.

The Eighty-Ninth Congress began its new, boisterous session. House Republican young turks, including Donald H. Rumsfeld (Illinois), persuaded Gerald R. Ford to challenge Charles A. Halleck for the senior minority leadership position. Halleck was considered as someone who drank too much, lacked initiative, and "was deemed too old, too forbidding, too irascible"[111] to be an effective leader. Ford, just as conservative as Halleck but far more likeable and reliable, became the new Republican leader in the House and was less

willing to sustain the southern Democratic-conservative Republican partnership.

EIGHTY-NINTH CONGRESS, 1ST SESSION

(January 4–October 23, 1965)

Senate: 68 Democrats; 32 Republicans

House: 295 Democrats; 140 Republicans

President: Lyndon B. Johnson

In the Senate, the biggest change was that Hubert Humphrey, who had a central role in the 1964 civil rights fight, now was vice-president. The Democrats now held a 68–32 majority, the largest such majority since 1940, and southern Democrats seemed to have lost some of the taste for the fight. Their leader, Richard Russell, was recuperating in Georgia from a long, difficult battle with emphysema. The next senior southern senator, Allen Ellender from Louisiana, seventy-five years old, adopted the same, unimaginative and inevitably defeating defensive strategy.[112]

The 1957, 1960, and 1964 Civil Rights Acts addressed part of the problem of voter discrimination, but these laws proved to be weak and piecemeal, and enforcement through litigation was exasperatingly long and discouraging. Individual states could continue creating voting standards and restrictions, the U.S. Department of Justice would then investigate and perhaps litigate, but the Justice Department often faced federal district courts unsympathetic to the government's case.[113]

Now, by the beginning of the year, Johnson was ready to unveil his voting rights legislation. The president met several times in early 1965 with King, Randolph, Roy Wilkins, Whitney Young, Jr., and

Clarence Mitchell. On January 15, Johnson, in a telephone conversation with King, said: "The greatest achievement of my administration … I said to a group yesterday, was the passage of the 1964 Civil Rights Act. But I think this will be bigger, because it'll do things that even the '64 act couldn't do."[114] In his State of the Union speech, Johnson pledged to send Congress a voting rights bill, and, in early February, Senate Majority Leader Mansfield, the new attorney general Katzenbach, and Senator Dirksen began the arduous process of crafting a tough, sweeping bill with severe penalties. Mansfield, rarely an angry man, gave his staff instructions to draft the simplest and harshest of bills, no more than one page long. "I want a bill," he told his staff, "that a man with a first grade-education, colored or white, can understand."[115] It took weeks of careful deliberation, but events soon overtook the legislative negotiations. In March, Selma exploded.

The Selma March

In early February, King and approximately three thousand demonstrators had been arrested in a voting drive in Selma, Alabama. Then on March 6, Governor Wallace banned a march planned from Selma to the state capital Montgomery, calling it a danger to public safety. King was not with the marchers, but at home in Atlanta; his life had once again been threatened and he reluctantly decided to stay away. On the evening of the March 7, the civil rights leaders were to begin their fifty-four-mile march. They came down Broad Street, then reached the Edmund Pettus bridge as it crossed the Alabama River. Sheriff Jim Clark, backed by his mounted posse, ordered them to turn around and go home. The marchers refused. Clark yelled out, "Get those god-damned niggers! And get those god-damned *white* niggers."[116]

Leading the march were John Lewis and Hosea Williams. Lewis recalls what came next: "The troopers and posse men swept forward as one, like a human wave, a blur of blue shirts and billy clubs and bullwhips. We had no chance to turn and retreat. There were six hundred people behind us, bridge

railings to either side and the river below." Lewis continued:

> I remember how vivid the sounds were as the troopers rushed toward us—the clunk of the troopers' heavy boots, the whoops of rebel yells from the white onlookers, the clip-clop of horses' hooves hitting the hard asphalt of the highway, the voice of a woman shouting, "Get 'em! *Get* the niggers!"[117]

More than fifty men and women had been severely injured. That evening, ABC television interrupted its Sunday night feature movie, *The Judgment at Nuremberg,* to show a fifteen-minute clip of the raw footage from Selma; 48 million viewers witnessed the brutality. It is not known if George Wallace was complicit in the clubbings and beatings, but he never issued a single word of criticism of the police or sympathy for the protestors.[118] There was a further national outcry when, on March 11, a Boston-based thirty-eight-year-old white Unitarian minister, the Rev. James Reeb, was severely beaten in Selma and died.[119]

After the bloody events in Selma, several hundred civil rights picketers, most of whom were white, camped outside the White House. Impatient with the president's failure to act quickly on the voting rights law, the protestors shouted their dismay. One sign said: "Johnson is Goldwater in disguise."

Almost on impulse, a Wallace aide suggested that the governor meet with President Johnson; this might divert attention away from Selma and give Wallace a chance to talk about the dangers posed by the civil rights agitators. Wallace agreed immediately, but later regretted his hasty decision. On Saturday, March 13, Governor Wallace met with Johnson in the Oval Office for three hours. Lyndon Johnson recalled: "I kept my eyes directly on the governor's face the entire time. I saw a nervous, aggressive man; a rough shrewd politician who had managed to touch the deepest chords of pride as well as prejudice among his people."[120] Johnson, "like some Texas python, had almost wrapped himself around the governor," pressed Wallace: governor, you can do more to desegregate the schools and increase voter registration. Wallace said he had no such power, that authority belonged to the local officials. "Don't you shit me, George Wallace!"[121] Then Johnson shoved in the rhetorical knife, "You had the power to keep the president of the United States off the [Alabama] ballot [in 1964]. Surely you have the power to tell a few poor county registrars what to do."[122] Indeed, it was not the conversation that Wallace had expected; he put on a brave face when he and the president met with reporters, then headed back to Alabama to regain his defiant composure.

On Monday, March 15, Johnson went before a joint session of Congress and gave the most memorable speech of his public life. In his slow southern drawl, he spoke in sweeping terms: "I speak tonight for the dignity of man and the destiny of democracy. I urge every member of both parties, Americans of all religions and of all colors, from every section of the country, to join me in that cause."[123] In two days, he would send a bill to Congress to eliminate illegal barriers to voting, demanding that Congress act. Millions were watching on television. During his forty-five-minute speech, the president was interrupted thirty-six times by applause and two standing ovations. The television audience could also see Senator Sam Ervin (Democrat–North Carolina) sitting with his arms folded, in "massive disapproval" and Senator Ellender "slumped gloomily" in his chair; the Virginia and Mississippi delegations, and some other southerners, boycotted the speech altogether.[124]

Voting obstacles in Virginia, South Carolina, Georgia, Alabama, Louisiana, and Mississippi would be suspended by the proposed legislation. But if those states couldn't abide having federal intervention, the course of action was simple, Johnson said: "Open your polling places to all your people. Allow men and women to register and vote whatever the color of their skin. Extend the rights of citizenship to every citizen of this land."

This was not just a southern problem nor is it a problem solely about African-Americans, Johnson said: "There is no Negro problem. There is no southern problem or northern problem. There is only an American problem." There could be no hesitation and no delay, for "the time for waiting is gone."

Then, in his most memorable line, Johnson echoed the determination and goal of the civil rights movement: "It is not just Negroes, but really it is all of us, who must overcome the crippling legacy of bigotry and injustice. And … we. … shall … overcome." After a moment of stunned silence, the lawmakers jumped to their feet and burst into sustained, emotional applause and shouts of approval.

Former baseball great Jackie Robinson, now a columnist for the Chicago *Defender,* remarked that the president's words "lifted a weight of what seemed like a thousand pounds crushing in on the heart." Johnson biographer Robert Dallek characterized it as "Johnson's greatest speech and one of the most moving and memorable presidential addresses in the country's history."[125]

On March 17, federal district court judge Frank M. Johnson, Jr., ruled that the Selma civil rights forces had a right, guaranteed under the Constitution, to march from Selma to Montgomery, the state capital. Having watched the television news footage of "Bloody Sunday," Judge Johnson concluded that the enormity of the wrong suffered by African-Americans outweighed concerns for unobstructed highways and sidewalks. For his courageous application of the law, Frank Johnson was ostracized by the Alabama elite, had his life threatened repeatedly, and his mother's house was burned.[126]

Governor Wallace would not guarantee police protection for the demonstrators, but Lyndon Johnson would. He swiftly mobilized nearly 4,000 troops from the "Dixie" Division of the Alabama National Guard and a nearby U.S. Army base. For Johnson, having Alabama citizens defend the marchers was key: "They were not intruders forcing their way in; they were citizens of Alabama. That made all the difference in the world."[127]

The march to Montgomery, starting out with approximately 4,000 participants, lasted five days, and by the time they reached the capital, their numbers had swelled to 22,000. It was a peaceful march, but, in its aftermath, Viola Liuzzo, a Detroit civil rights volunteer, was gunned down as she helped shuttle marchers back and forth.[128]

Emmanuel Celler immediately began hearings and, on May 12, the voting rights bill was reported

KEY PROVISIONS OF THE VOTING RIGHTS ACT OF 1965

Section 2 of the act closely followed the language of the Fifteenth Amendment, prohibiting on a nationwide basis the denial or abridgment of the right to vote based on literacy tests.

Section 5 was the most significant feature. It targeted states or their political subdivisions which had voting tests (such as literacy, good character, knowledge of the state's constitution, or others) as of November 1, 1964 and less than 50 percent of those of voting age participating in the 1964 presidential election. When those conditions existed, then the voting tests were voided and the states could not implement new changes without pre-clearance from the U.S. attorney general or the U.S. District Court in the District of Columbia. Federal examiners would be used to assist qualified voters to register and to vote, and federal observers could monitor the activities in a jurisdiction's polling place.

out of his committee and then sent to Smith's Rules Committee. Defiant to the end, Smith delayed the bill by three weeks, then, when it finally went to the full House, he delayed its passage by another five weeks of parliamentary maneuvering. On July 9, the House overwhelmingly approved its version, 333–85.

In the Senate, the bill was also introduced right after Johnson's speech. Sixty-six senators signed on as co-sponsors, assuring that the bill would quickly pass and would be impervious to a last-minute filibuster. The Senate version passed on May 26, by an equally overwhelming vote of 77–19.

There were some differences in the House and Senate versions, especially the inclusion of a poll-tax ban in the House, which was eventually dropped in the conference committee. Then on August 3 the House overwhelmingly adopted the voting rights legislation and the next day the Senate followed. Two southern senators, Democrats Ralph W. Yarborough of Texas and George A. Smathers of Florida, broke ranks and voted for the legislation.[129]

On August 6, 1965, Lyndon Johnson signed the Voting Rights Act into law. For this momentous occasion, he chose the ornate President's Room in the Capitol, becoming the first chief executive since Herbert Hoover to use this historic room to sign important legislation. More than one hundred lawmakers, cabinet officials, and civil rights leaders crowded into the room. In a televised ceremony, Johnson declared that "today we strike away the last major shackle of those fierce and ancient bonds" of oppression, and recalled how he and Congress quickly acted after the "outrage of Selma." He signed the law, sitting at the desk he had used to guide through the 1957 and 1960 civil rights legislation. This was also the room where Abraham Lincoln, 104 years ago to the day, had affixed his signature to legislation freeing slaves pressed into duty by the Confederacy.[130]

The ceremony then moved to the Capitol Rotunda, where Johnson said that "today is a triumph for freedom as huge as any victory that's ever been won on any battlefield." This law, he said, is righting a wrong which "no American in his heart can justify." He called the signing "a victory for the freedom of the American Negro, but it is also a victory for the freedom of the American nation." Johnson then implored to every African-American in the United States: "you must register; you must vote; you must learn so your choices advance your interests and the interests of our beloved nation. Your future and your children's future depend upon it and I don't believe you're going to let them down."[131]

There was much work to be done. Immediately the attorney general proclaimed that the Voting Rights provisions would apply to South Carolina, Georgia, Alabama, Louisiana, Mississippi, Virginia, twenty-six counties in North Carolina, and a few other jurisdictions.[132] In the six southern states which were the primary target of the law, just 1.1

million African-Americans had registered to vote, while twice that number had not registered. Right after Johnson signed the law, forty-five federal examiners, each one a volunteer and a southerner, from the Civil Service Commission offices in Dallas and Atlanta were dispatched to the affected counties armed with bundles of voter registration forms. They had been in Washington, undergoing an intensive three-day registration training seminar, even before the bill became law.[133]

The next day, Attorney General Katzenbach filed suit against the poll tax in Mississippi, federal law suits to follow challenging poll taxes in Alabama, Texas, and Virginia. The first voting suits had been filed in Mississippi in July 1961; by election time 1964, twenty-three additional suits had been filed. By the time the Voting Rights Act had been signed into law, federal lawsuits were pending in sixty of Mississippi's eighty-two counties. Martin Luther King announced, following an hour-long meeting with President Johnson, that he would now press for voting rights for African-Americans in northern cities and states.[134]

This legislative triumph, however, was soon overshadowed by the combustion of urban unrest. Just five days after President Johnson signed the historic legislation, a major race riot broke out in the Watts section of Los Angeles. This was triggered by a minor incident, an arrest of a black man on the suspicion of drunk driving. By the time the violence had ended, five days later, thousands had been arrested, thirty-four persons were killed, and property damage was more than $40 million.[135]

Aftermath

Well before the 1964 legislation was passed, the Department of Justice and the president himself were busy persuading southern business leaders to comply with the new law. On October 30, 1964, just days before the presidential election, the federal Community Relations Service published a survey of fifty-three southern and border-state cities with populations of 50,000 or more, showing "widespread compliance" with the law. In announcing the results, Lyndon Johnson thanked the many civic and labor leaders, clergy and educators, but then singled out those who deserved "special note:" the members of Congress who had opposed the civil rights bill "with all their strength and eloquence" but, now that it is enacted, are urging their constituents to comply with the "law of the land."[136]

TIMELINE FOR CIVIL RIGHTS AND VOTING RIGHTS

1948 Split in Democratic Party; emergence of Dixiecrat protest party; Humphrey and strong civil rights plank.
1954 *Brown* v. *Board of Education* (I); *Brown (II)* in 1955.
1957 Civil Rights Act of 1957 enacted; a weak law, but first since the 1870s.
1960 Civil Rights Act of 1960 enacted; another weak measure.
1963 Civil rights unrest in Birmingham, march on Washington, Kennedy introduces civil rights legislation.

1964 Prolonged Senate filibuster; enactment of Civil Rights Act of 1964.
1965 Beatings at Selma; enactment of Voting Rights Act of 1965.
1970s Voting Rights Act reauthorized and extended in 1970, reinforced and extended in 1975; significant increase in black registration; opposing tactics shift to voter dilution.
1982 Extension of Voting Rights Act for twenty-five years.
2006 Another extension of Voting Rights Act for twenty-five years.

Both the 1964 Civil Rights Act and the 1965 Voting Act were immediately challenged in court, and both were upheld in unanimous opinions of the U.S. Supreme Court. Less than six months after its passage, the Supreme Court upheld Title II, the public accommodations section, of the Civil Rights Act in two companion cases. In the first, the *Heart of Atlanta Motel* v. *United States,* the Court ruled that Congress had "ample power" to protect against racial discrimination in motels and hotels serving interstate commerce. In a second case, *Katzenbach* v. *McClung,* the Court ruled that even a local establishment, Ollie's Barbecue, serving only local white folks, came under the jurisdiction of Title II because it drew a substantial portion of its food supplies from out of state.[137] Senator Eastland's fears were becoming reality.

The state of South Carolina challenged the Voting Rights Act, arguing that the Congress had exceeded its authority in trying to enforce the Fifteenth Amendment, that, by singling out certain states for special treatment, Congress had violated the principle of equality of the states, and, by not allowing judicial review of the administrative procedures, it had violated the concept of bill of attainder. The Court in *South Carolina* v. *Katzenbach* upheld the Voting Rights Act in a near-unanimous opinion, rejecting out of hand the arguments of South Carolina and the states that had joined it as friends of the court. The Court also upheld a portion of the law which had outlawed New York's state English literacy requirement, and then ruled that state poll taxes posed an "invidious discrimination" that violated the equal protection clause of the Fourteenth Amendment.[138]

But soon after Johnson's solemn declaration that "we shall overcome," the civil rights revolution began to fall apart. Urban riots were symptomatic of more profound discontentment and disillusionment of African-Americans, there was a growing backlash of blue-collar white Americans who cheered on George Wallace as he again ran for president in 1968 and 1972. Martin Luther King, SNCC, and other civil rights organizations turned against Johnson and the quagmire of the Vietnam war. King's assassination and the ensuing urban riots only heightened the disappointment, frustration, and rage, from both whites and blacks. Americans

were now telling pollsters that national policy was moving too fast on civil rights reform, and the rhetoric of "law and order," "welfare cheats," and "neighborhood schools" was resonating with voters as they looked to Richard Nixon and George Wallace as alternatives to the Great Society and its excesses.[139]

Nixon focused on a "southern strategy," trying to woo disaffected white southerners away from their historic home with the Democratic Party. Nixon, he assured southerners, knew them, knew their concerns, and castigated liberals as elitists who were out of touch with the concerns of average (white) Americans. In his first State of the Union address in 1969, Nixon said, "It is time for those who make massive demands on society to make minimal demands on themselves."[140] Court-ordered school busing, the eradication of housing discrimination, advancement in employment and education, central notions of justice and fairness would take a back seat in the Nixon administration.

Despite the setbacks and the obstacles, the Civil Rights Act of 1964 has been a major accomplishment. Title II, the public accommodations section, once reinforced by the Supreme Court, became, relatively speaking, the easiest part of the Civil Rights Act to enforce. It eradicated "whites only" and "colored only" drinking fountains, restaurants, or swimming pools. In a sense, many of these were peculiarities of the old South, not problems endemic to the entire country. They were problems that were fairly straightforward, and not fraught with baggage like school desegregation, affirmative action, or employment discrimination.[141] In many ways, it just became good business for restaurants, bars, and hotels to open to a broader clientele, and certainly many national chains and franchises probably welcomed the legislation.

Civil rights and education scholar Gary Orfield argues that the law extends far beyond education and "few measures in American history have ever had so profound an effect on our schools."[142] The law has gone beyond its original purpose by developing civil rights policies to protect Hispanic children in public schools and to provide bilingual education. For Orfield, the biggest problem with enforcement of Title II protections is the continued resistance of state and local officials and the unwillingness "in the four GOP Administrations since 1964 to employ the ultimate sanctions under the law."[143]

Title VII enforcement has been most effective in cases dealing with sex discrimination. Once it became operational, the Equal Employment Opportunity Commission (EEOC) at first brushed off sex discrimination cases, but, during the first two years of enforcement, 4,000 sex discrimination complaints were filed, roughly one-quarter of the commission's case load. Ten years later, in 1975, Title VII was being characterized as "the most comprehensive and important of all federal and state laws prohibiting employment discrimination."[144]

African-American voting registration had begun in earnest before the passage of the 1965 Voting Rights Act. The Southern Christian Leadership Conference's Voter Education Project, begun in 1962 and finishing in 1964, gave funds and coordinated the activities of the NAACP, the SCLC, SNCC, CORE, and the National Urban League. The Voter Education Project was successful in many southern states, but was a failure in Mississippi.[145] Likewise, the Department of Justice had filed seventy-one suits, together with broad-based litigation against Alabama, Mississippi, and Louisiana during the eight years before passage of the Voting Rights Act.[146]

The number of African-American voters in the South increased dramatically, thanks to the Voter Education Project and, especially in areas of greatest resistance, to Voting Rights Act enforcement. With only 1.1 million African-Americans registered in 1964, the number had risen to 3.1 million in 1969, with nearly 500 African-Americans holding elective office that year in the lower South.[147]

Discrimination and voting irregularities still persisted, but the focus was now shifting from outright denial of the vote to vote dilution. By 1988, the gap between black and white registration rates had narrowed considerably.[148] The gap of 49.9 percent in Alabama in 1965 had shrunk to just 6.6 percent in 1988; in Mississippi the 63.2 percent gap closed to 6.3 percent; and in Louisiana a 48.9 percent gap in 1965 became a 2.0 gap in favor of black voters in 1988.

The more ominous problem for African-Americans and Hispanics was voter dilution. Multi-member districts, at-large elections, appointing rather than electing officials, and gerrymandering were adopted in cities throughout the South in order to dilute the strength of black neighborhoods. In 1969, a Supreme Court decision looked at such practices in Mississippi and Virginia, and ruled that any such changes were subject to the pre-clearance provisions found in section 5 of the Voting Rights Act.[149] Up until this time, the pre-clearance section was relatively unused, but now the floodgates opened. During its first five years (1965–1969), there were just 323 section 5 changes submitted to the Attorney General; during the next five years, there were 4,153 changes requested. But, in the 1980s and 1990s, the number exploded, and in 2000–2002, there were almost 50,000 such requests made.[150]

In 1970, Congress extended the Voting Rights Act for another five years. In 1975, there were extensive hearings held, and an important provision was added to assist minorities whose primary language was not English. There was a conclusive record of exclusion of voting rights to Spanish-speaking citizens, and the 1975 Voting Rights Extension required oral or written bilingual assistance for voters in jurisdictions that have significant minority voters. The pre-clearance provisions of Section 5 were extended to areas of Texas where there was considerable discrimination against citizens of Hispanic origin.

If voter dilution was now the new concern, just what constituted dilution? The Supreme Court ruled in 1980 in *City of Mobile* v. *Bolden* that any constitutional claim of minority voter dilution must include proof that there was a racially discriminatory purpose.[151] This could present a very difficult hurdle to overcome in claiming voter discrimination. The *Bolden* standard, however, was to have a short life.

In May 1981, as extension renewal deadlines approached, Congress held eighteen separate hearings in Washington, Alabama, and Texas, with a total of 122 witnesses. Don Edwards (Democrat–California), chair of the House Judiciary Subcommittee on Civil Rights, later wrote about the continued discrimination, blatant and subtle, they found: "What we learned in those eighteen days of hearings was shocking—and sad. All seven members of the subcommittee, Republicans and Democrats alike, were dismayed." The most serious abuses were suffered by Hispanics in Texas who were not protected by the Voting Rights Act until 1975.[152]

Ronald Reagan and some Republicans argued for a nationwide voting standard, but that idea was rebuffed, and the VRA extension easily passed in the House. The two Republican senators from North Carolina, Jesse Helms and John P. East, complained that there was no reward for states which had improved their voting rights enforcement since being put on the list. In the end, Robert Dole (Republican–Kansas) brokered the language which now concentrated on the results of voter dilution rather than the intent of such dilution.[153] There was a lot of infighting and back scenes maneuvering, but eventually Congress renewed section 5 of the Voting Rights Act for another twenty-five years, and decided that Section 2 should be amended to prohibit vote dilution. Even old segregationist J. Strom Thurmond and Jamie L. Whitten (Democrat–Mississippi) voted to pass the extension of the original 1965 Act.[154]

As African-Americans gained political strength, they found that even the archest of arch-segregationists had changed their tune, if for no other reason than they needed to attract these new voters. James O. Eastland, in his last run for office, courted African-American political leaders; so too, did Strom Thurmond, who in his latter years voted for the Martin Luther King, Jr., national holiday and drew a good 20 percent of African-American voters in South Carolina. Thurmond's conversion, however, didn't impress former U.S. Civil Rights commissioner Morris Abram: "The day the blacks got the vote in South Carolina you saw Strom Thurmond referring to them no longer as 'niggers' but as 'our beloved brethren.'"[155] George Wallace, permanently crippled by an assassin's bullet and nearing the end of his life, apologized to African-Americans, meeting with leaders individually, for his views and actions of the past. As his biographer Dan Carter observed, "Black Alabamians wanted Wallace to be forgiven."[156]

Still, complaints about voting rights enforcement kept mounting. The American Civil Liberties Voting Rights Project had brought 293 cases in thirty-one states since June 1982 challenging alleged discriminatory practices and failure of states or localities to comply with the law. Nearly half (145) of those cases came in Georgia, with thirty-eight coming from South Carolina. The Department of Justice, under Section 5 of the Voting Rights Act, had issued over 1,000 objections to discriminatory voting changes since 1982.[157] In 1993, the Supreme Court ruled on another dimension of race and voting, in *Shaw* v. *Reno*,[158] where it held that the redrawn congressional districts in North Carolina amounted to racial gerrymandering. The Court required that redistricting must meet both the requirements of the Voting Rights Act and the strict scrutiny standard it established for interpreting the Fourteenth Amendment. The "bizarre" results of redistricting, which led to a black-majority congressional district 160 miles long and at times no wider than a four-lane highway, could not be justified.

At the beginning of the contentious new 104th Congress, in January 1995, the Republicans had taken over the House of Representatives for the first time since 1955. Gerald Solomon (Republican–New York), the new chairman of the Rules Committee, ordered that the portrait of former committee chairman Howard Smith be hung in the committee room. John Lewis (Democrat–Georgia), who was elected to Congress in 1987, and eight of his colleagues from the Congressional Black Caucus would have none of it. Lewis, a hero of the civil rights movement, argued that Smith was "a man who represents our dark past" and that his portrait "deeply saddened and troubled" many people. Solomon averred that he did not know of Smith's segregationist views and said that Smith had always been good to committee Republicans. The portrait came down.[159]

The Voting Rights Act, amended in 1982, would be in force until 2007, unless Congress authorized its renewal. As the deadline approached, there were rumors floating around particularly on black-oriented radio stations, newspapers, and websites that President George W. Bush and the Republican-controlled Congress had no interest in extending the legislation. There were criticisms that the Justice Department, over objections from its own civil rights lawyers, had approved Republican-backed voting programs in Texas and Georgia, to the detriment of minorities.[160]

Indeed, relations between Bush and African-Americans were tense. The president had made a point to skip the annual meeting of the NAACP for five straight years, being the only chief executive since Warren G. Harding not to have made the important gesture of attending the annual gathering. But in July 2006, on the very day that the Senate unanimously voted to extend the Voting Rights Act, Bush for the first time addressed the annual NAACP convention held in Washington. Bush, and through him the Republican Party, extended its hand to the NAACP.

Using Ronald Reagan's words, Bush called the Voting Rights Act the "crown jewel" and vowed to sign its renewal. At the same time, he acknowledged the shortcomings of the position taken by the Republican Party: "I consider it a tragedy that the party of Abraham Lincoln let go of its historic ties with the African-American community. For too long, my party wrote off the African-American vote, and many African-Americans wrote off the Republican Party." Bush continued: "I understand that many African-Americans distrust my political party." This comment provoked some of the loudest cheering during the president's speech.[161]

During the summer of 2006, in the House of Representatives, the Republican leadership had to work hard to stave off a revolt from conservative southern Republican lawmakers. The Voting Rights Act extension, named in honor of Fannie Lou Hamer, Rosa Parks, and Goretta Scott King, would maintain the Justice Department's authority to review ballot changes in the states first targeted in the original 1965 legislation.[162] The extension, like the one adopted in 1982, would be in effect for twenty-five years, until 2031.

Many of the conservative complaints centered on Section 5, the pre-clearance provisions. In the forty-year history of voting rights enforcement, just eleven Virginia counties had managed to meet federal standards and became exempt from federal jurisdiction. Lynn A. Westmoreland

(Republican–Georgia) led the conservative revolt, charging that the provisions, written so long ago, did not take into account the progress made in the sixteen impacted states. "It makes no sense," Westmoreland argued, "to extend this bill as is for twenty-five years and keep Georgia in the penalty box for sixty-six years based on the results of the 1964 election." Georgia indeed had made progress: in 1965, there were just three African-American election officials; in 2006, there were more than 800. Yet, the Department of Justice had found, over the course of those forty-one years, that there were 200 incidents where Georgia state and local officials tried to dilute black voting strength.[163]

K. Michael (Mike) Conaway (Republican–Texas) argued that, by continuing to have Texas on the pre-clearance list, the extension failed to understand that the problems had been corrected. "It labels Texas as a racist state, and that's not true," implored Conway. Steve King (Republican–Iowa) led a group of eighty fellow conservatives who argued against a requirement for bilingual ballots in districts where some of the voters had limited English skills. In the end, however, the Voting Rights Act extension passed the House of Representative, 390–33, after seven hours of impassioned debate, according to one reporter, "punctuated by several shouting matches between white Republicans and black Democrats from Georgia, who accused each other of hypocrisy and distorting the facts."[164] On July 27, 2006, President Bush signed into law the twenty-five year extension.

In late 2006, the U.S. Department of Justice filed a first-of-a-kind suit under the Voting Rights Act: a suit brought in eastern Mississippi accusing blacks of suppressing the voting rights of whites. The focus was on African-American Ike Brown, the chairman of the Noxubee County Democratic Executive Committee, and, according to the *New York Times*, its "undisputed political boss." Brown was accused of "relentless voting-related racial discrimination" against whites, who are outnumbered in the rural county by more than three to one. Brown was accused of taking cues from segregationist policies of the past and applying them today to maximize black voting and power. In June 2007, a U.S. District Court judge ruled that there was ample evidence that Brown's actions violated the Voting Rights Act.[165]

The Civil Rights Act of 1964 and the Voting Rights Act of 1965 were extraordinary legislative achievements. Public accommodations quickly desegregated, barriers to voting were removed and millions of African-American registered to vote. But the promise of school integration and a healthy balance between black and white students in public education became elusive. Over the decades, federal and state policymakers, civil rights activists, and community organizations have fought bruising battles over the use of busing to achieve racial integration, affirmative action, and job creation, and dilution of voting strength.

What remain are the more intractable issues of educational and economic opportunity, social justice, and social responsibility. Further there is the new reality of the demographics of American society and the workforce. The old dynamic of African-Americans, the South, and the legacy of servitude are facing a new dynamic of immigrants, legal and otherwise, especially from Latin America, who now count as the largest minority population.[166]

CHAPTER 10

Voting Behavior

Chapter 10 Vignette

By Jennifer Byrne

Campaigns and Elections

Have you ever heard of Nate Silver? He is not a movie star or even a politician, but he has recently stepped into the spotlight. He is a statistician and writer who, in 2010, was licensed for publication of a blog, "FiveThirtyEight: Nate Silver's Political Calculus," in the *New York Times*. Though initially a successful sports statistician, Silver began to gain acclaim for his political predictions in 2008. He predicted a presidential win for Barack Obama, correctly predicting the voting patterns of 49 of the 50 states. He also correctly predicted the winner of all 35 senate races that year, and was named one of Time Magazines Most Influential People in 2009. He continued his accurate predictions with the 2012 elections. He correctly predicted Barack Obama's reelection in all 50 states and the District of Columbia, and called 31 of the 33 Senate races. On the morning of Election Day, November 6, 2012, Silver's model gave President Obama a 90.9 percent chance of being re-elected. Silver faced stark criticism from the media and the Republican Party for being an "ideologue" who adjusted his models to tip the balance in favor of his preferred candidate, Barack Obama. Silver characterizes his political views as somewhere in between a liberal and libertarian; this self-identification and his refusal to publicize his models led to some skepticism regarding his results. However, in the aftermath of the election, Silver's 100% accurate electoral map even correctly predicted the winner of nine key swing states, while traditional polling entities such as Rasmussen only predicted six out of the nine.

Silver was also criticized for an overtly quantitative approach and for being an outsider to politics. A Huffington Post columnist lambasted Silver as a pundit that "has never organized a precinct in his real life, much less walked one, pontificating about the dynamics in an electoral process as if he actually understood them." Silver's own probabilities were said to have exceeded the expectations of even the Obama campaign itself, particularly in an environment characterized by uncertain conclusions to the wars in Iraq and Afghanistan as well as the economic collapse. Despite his detractors, Silver has gone on to win many awards and accolades from publications such as *Newsweek*, *Rolling Stone*, and *Forbes*.

So, what is Nate Silver up to now? Though controversial, Silver has predicted that Republicans may take the Senate in 2016. This is based off the fact that incumbents Lindsey Graham of South Carolina and Mitch McConnell of Kentucky were considered "safe seats," and that the likelihood of victory was essentially a foregone conclusion. However, in the wake of a government shutdown, challengers from the Tea Party have emerged, and they might give these incumbents a run for their money in the primaries. If this is the case, then these Republican seats may be up for grabs in the general election and Silver's conclusion may not be as accurate for this election cycle. Why might American citizens suspect that there will significant challenges for these senators in the primaries? The word primary has become a verb—"primarying" means that a strong incumbent is challenged on the grounds that they are not sufficiently partisan enough; this has been a trend in the past few election cycles. Moreover, according to the Daily Beast, extreme conservatives may have a better chance of winning the upcoming Republican primaries. Recent polls show that more than 50 percent of Republican voters believe that their party isn't conservative enough, and that more than 30 percent believe that the leadership has been too compromising in its dealings with President Obama and the Democrats. It remains to be seen if Silver will continue with his current predictions for the Senate, and whether or not these will be accurate in light of this new

phenomenon of "primarying," and the divide between mainstream Republicans and the Tea party members that has come to light in the aftermath of the government shutdown in October of 2013.

Silver also has some predictions for the Democrats in 2016. He says that Hillary Clinton is in the strongest position to run for the Democratic nomination, and she is the "strongest non-incumbent ever." He claims that the Party will be looking to her to decide if she wants to run, but she should decide early enough to clear the field of potential competitors for the nomination, or to allow candidates with less experience and political connectedness a chance to build their campaigns should she choose to not run. Depending on the poll, Clinton is the Party favorite at the moment, with 60–70 percent of Democrats favoring her for the nomination. This is the first time in history that a non-incumbent, primary candidate has enjoyed backing this strong. It remains to be seen what she will decide, and what Silver's final predictions for the 2016 Presidential primaries and general election will be.

Video—Nate Silver's projections for 2016:
- http://www.youtube.com/watch?feature =player_embedded&v=nVNEzOW-Ud4

Campaigns and Elections

Vehicles for Democratic Expression

By Matthew Kerbel

Introduction

Imagine that you got up at 5:30 this morning, and you won't get to bed until after 1:00 tonight. You eat bad food whenever you have a second to grab some, which is rarely, because from the time you wake up until the time you go to sleep, you're constantly on the move, flying in and out of places so fast you lose track of where you are. In between, you go to meeting halls and auditoriums, where you're either talking to ten yawning people at a time or, if you're lucky, you're swamped by crowds and overwhelmed by reporters, leaving you no time to think for yourself. Either way, you find yourself repeating the same speech over and over until it feels like a stale, meaningless mantra. And when you're done speaking, you ask everyone you can find for money—people you know, people you don't know, it doesn't matter. You just keep asking for money—and lots of it.

Now imagine doing this every day for two years—more if you're not particularly well known. Think you can handle it?

Good. You're ready to run for president.

The process of running for president doesn't ensure that we'll send the brightest or most experienced candidates to the White House, but it does guarantee that they'll be durable. Running for president means making the sacrifice of personal time and family life for several years in the long-shot gamble that you'll be the last one standing on Election Day. "Running" for president is an appropriate term because the system in place for attaining the office is a marathon that can devour the weak.

We'll find that the Electoral College, an arcane and often misunderstood structure that usually has the last word on who is elected president, invariably drives general election strategies. Later in the chapter, we'll try to make sense of it.

As we proceed, we'll try to assess whether the process by which we select people for high office adequately provides us with a real and significant opportunity to have input to policy decisions, as we would expect if political parties are to function as effective linkages between citizens and officials. The point is not so much to determine if you would want to try your hand at running for president as it is to see if campaigns can engage you in politics in a meaningful way.

Our discussion of campaigns will focus on presidential races because they're by far the most complex, encompassing a two-step process of winning a party nomination and engaging a candidate of the other major party in the general election. This

459

two-phase process is typical of campaigns for other offices as well, but only the presidential campaign lasts years and is always hotly contested. Many congressional seats, in contrast, are uncontested because the incumbent has successfully scared off possible challengers by raising large sums of money (something that congressional incumbents have an easier time doing than challengers who do not hold power), or because congressional district lines have been drawn to protect incumbents by including a disproportionate number of Democratic or Republican partisans within their boundaries. Both parties attempt to draw district lines in this fashion, creating as many "safe seats" as possible.

Decisions, Part I: The Selection Process

There are two stages in the marathon process of choosing a president: the selection stage, which takes place within the political party, and the election stage, in which party candidates are pitted against each other. We'll look at them in that order, illustrating how the process unfolds, the strategies candidates use to advance their campaigns, and the importance of money and media to winning the race.

The Ground Rules

The end point of the selection process occurs when one candidate receives the **nomination** of a political party, formally making that candidate the official choice of the party. The race for the presidential nomination is really fifty-one individual contests (counting the District of Columbia). To win the presidential nomination of a major political party, a candidate needs to compete in these contests, called primaries or caucuses, which are held in every state to select delegates to the party's national convention, held the summer before the presidential election. The candidate who receives a majority of the votes of the delegates at the convention wins the nomination of the party.

Because of the influence of federalism, election laws are state laws, leaving each state to determine its own rules for how its delegates will be chosen. Most states select their convention delegates in a **primary,** which is an election open to party identifiers for the purpose of selecting among candidates for an office. In states that hold primaries, Republicans and Democrats hold separate contests. In presidential primaries, voters select delegates pledged to support a candidate at the national convention. For lower offices, voters select the candidate directly; in most instances, the plurality winner receives the party's nomination.

A **caucus** works quite differently from a primary. It's a series of open meetings, starting at the local level and progressing over a period of time to meetings covering larger jurisdictions, like counties or congressional districts. At each stage of the process, party members select representatives pledged to a variety of candidates to attend the next caucus stage. At the last stage of the process, representatives are selected to attend a state convention, where delegates are chosen to attend the national convention. Unlike a primary, which is a secret ballot, caucus participants make their preferences public.[1] Picture the first stage of a caucus as being small groups of people meeting simultaneously in school buildings, lodges, and social halls across a state, discussing or even debating their presidential preferences with one another. It's a lot different than going to a voting booth and making your choice in private.

The number of states holding primaries has grown steadily in your lifetime, to the point where primaries are now by far the preferred method of delegate selection. In 2008, forty-one states held Republican primaries and thirty-nine scheduled Democratic primaries.[2] In 1968, only fifteen states held primaries, and the Democratic nominee, Vice President Hubert Humphrey, didn't enter any of them.[3]

In 2008, without an incumbent president on the ballot, many states clamored to schedule their primaries and caucuses as early as possible in order to maximize their influence over the selection process. A brief look at the 2008 primary calendar in Table 20.1 shows how many states pressed to

Table 20.1. The Early 2008 Primary and Caucus Calendar

Date	Primary/Caucus
January 3	Iowa caucus
January 5	Wyoming primary (Republican)
January 8	New Hampshire primary
January 15	Michigan primary
January 19	Nevada caucus; South Carolina primary (Republican)
January 26	South Carolina primary (Democratic)
January 29	Florida primary
February 1	Maine primary (Republican)
February 5	Primaries: Alabama; Alaska; Arizona; Arkansas; California; Colorado; Connecticut; Delaware; Georgia; Illinois; Massachusetts; Minnesota; Missouri; New Jersey; New Mexico (Democratic); New York; North Dakota; Oklahoma; Tennessee; Utah. Caucuses: Idaho (Democratic); Kansas (Democratic); Montana (Republican)

get into the action during the first month of the primary season. Take special note of what happened on February 5!

A cluster of states held their contests following the first events—the Iowa caucus, held in early January, and the traditional first primary in New Hampshire, held five days later. In a brief, month-long stretch culminating in the "Super Tuesday" marathon of February 5, enough primaries and caucuses were held to assure that John McCain would be the Republican nominee. On the Democratic side, Senator Barack Obama and Senator Hillary Clinton locked in an epic battle that wasn't resolved until the primary calendar had entirely played out—four months after Super Tuesday, during the first week of June. We'll come back to this point in a little while.

If you think it's silly to select a presidential nominee by compressing the primary schedule into a few hectic weeks, you're not alone. Politicians and pundits regularly second-guess the primary system, and party leaders have been tinkering with the rules for over thirty-five years. During this period, dramatic changes have occurred in the way we select presidential nominees, many of them occurring in the name of reform.

Reforming the Ground Rules

In Chapter 6, we said that presidential candidates in the first party system were selected by a caucus of the members of their party in government. This system allowed a small, tightly controlled congressional elite to determine presidential nominees. As Jacksonian democracy came into vogue with the second party system, the congressional caucus fell out of favor and was replaced by the more open system of selecting nominees at national party conventions. So, ever since the 1830s, parties have been holding nominating conventions, but the way convention delegates are selected has changed over the years.

For much of the nineteenth century, state conventions, state party committees, or even state governors chose delegates. Initially, this reform permitted states to have a hand in the selection process, but the system remained elite-based, permitting state party bosses to exercise a heavy hand over which delegates were chosen. By the turn of the twentieth century, reformers complained that rank-and-file voters should have more say over the nomination process.

Enter the presidential primary. By 1916, more than half the states held them, but in the ensuing years, their popularity waned as party leaders objected to them, candidates ignored them, voters didn't turn out for them, and states didn't want

Fairness	All rules must be open and posted.
Elimination of the "unit rule" and institution of proportional representation	A state delegation cannot vote by majority rule to cast all its votes as a bloc. The final delegation should reflect choices made at the district levels.
Decreasing the role of the party "regulars"	The number of delegates the party committees of each state can send is limited, and elected officials do not receive automatic slots in the state delegation.
Individual delegate rights	No delegate can be compelled to cast a vote that was not the delegate's choice when selected.
Representation of women and minorities	Delegations from the states should reflect the racial and gender makeup of the state.

Figure 20.1. Major Reforms of the McGovern-Fraser Commission

to pay for them.[4] This permitted party bosses to continue to exercise leverage over the process and explains how Hubert Humphrey could enter the 1968 convention with the support of the Democratic Party elite and win the nomination without having contested any primaries.

The 1968 Democratic Convention was no ordinary gathering, though. Fighting in Vietnam was at a crescendo—the result of the policies of President Lyndon Johnson, a Democrat. An antiwar faction composed mostly of young activists planned to protest what was expected to be Johnson's renomination in Chicago that August. Even though Johnson dropped out of the race months before the convention, the antiwar faction of the Democratic Party marched in protest through the streets of Chicago, putting them at odds with the law-and-order Democratic Party boss, Chicago Mayor Richard Daley.

While the convention nominated Vice President Humphrey, the choice of party insiders, over the vocal protests of antiwar delegates, demonstrators clashed with police outside the hall. Scenes of mayhem and violence—of tear gas, arrests, and police beatings—appeared on television screens nationwide, portraying a deeply divided and torn Democratic Party. Humphrey's candidacy failed, and the cry went out to change the nomination system in a way that would shift control to rank-and-file Democrats from the party elites that had supported Humphrey.[5]

The reforms that changed the way party nominees are selected came between 1969 and 1971 from the Democratic Party Commission on Party Structure and Delegate Selection, commonly called the **McGovern-Fraser Commission** after its chairs, Senator George McGovern of South Dakota and, later, Representative Donald Fraser of Minnesota. The commission made the delegate selection process more open, egalitarian, and mass-based, making it harder for party elites to control the nomination. Major reforms of the McGovern-Fraser Commission are shown in Figure 20.1.

Like so many well-intentioned efforts, there were unexpected consequences to the McGovern-Fraser reforms. Although the Commission didn't expressly advocate the expansion of primaries, many states found that moving to a primary system was the easiest way to implement the letter if not the spirit of the reforms. Because these changes were being made on a state-by-state basis, the Republican Party soon followed suit. This shifted the arena for candidate selection in both parties to the primaries and away from the national conventions, which became vehicles for ratifying the victorious primary candidate, rather than deliberative forums for selecting the candidate.[6] Since 1968, there has not been a national convention that convened with the identity of the party's presidential nominee in doubt, and conventions have become staged **media events** showcasing the victorious nominee to the nation.

This not only resulted in control over the selection process passing from party elites to rank-and-file voters, it changed the entire nominating process from one centered in the party to one centered in

Table 20.2. Changes Made to McGovern-Fraser Reforms

Commission	Year	Objective	Major Change	Result
Mikulski	1972	No McGoverns	Delegates better represent voter preferences	Carter elected
Winograd	1978	Reelect Carter	Bind delegates on first ballot	Carter defeated
Hunt	1982	No Carters	Elite "super delegates"	Mondale defeated
"Fairness"	1986	No Mondales	No "winner-take-all" primaries	Dukakis defeated

the individual campaigns, with unprecedented emphasis on the personality and communication skills of the candidate. Successful candidates no longer had to be champions of party insiders if they could compete successfully in primary races by appealing directly to voters. After 1968, the nominating process became a long string of individual statewide campaigns, in which candidates appealed through television to primary voters in order to pile up enough delegates to win the nomination outright at the convention. Perhaps no one understood this better than the man who wrote the rules—George McGovern—a liberal who lacked the backing of the party's deal makers but who parlayed his appreciation of the new system into the 1972 Democratic presidential nomination.

The McGovern candidacy was a general election disaster, though, carrying only one state and the District of Columbia in the most lopsided Electoral College defeat to date. The new rules had opened up the system as intended, but they had produced a candidate without the elite backing that in past years had been helpful in winning a general election. So, the Democrats continued to tinker. For four straight presidential elections following McGovern's defeat, Democrats convened commissions to revise the rules. Each commission reacted to the perceived flaws of the one that came before, as all but one led to electoral failure.

The outcome of these commissions, and the political results they produced, are summarized in Table 20.2. The Mikulski Commission attempted to avoid a repeat of the McGovern debacle by ensuring that delegates more accurately represented the preferences of primary voters. This opened the process to a little-known, one-term ex-governor of Georgia, Jimmy Carter, who never would have had a chance at the presidential nomination under the old

rules and who might have been locked out under the McGovern procedures.

When Carter took hold of the Democratic Party apparatus as president, he attempted through the Winograd Commission to solidify his position through changes making it harder to challenge his re-nomination, such as by binding delegates to support the candidate they were selected to represent. Carter survived a nomination challenge by Massachusetts Senator Edward Kennedy but was denied a second term. Party insiders blamed Carter's defeat and the shortcomings of his administration on the fact that he had been an inexperienced outsider, and a movement began to return elite control to the selection process. The Hunt Commission introduced "super delegates"—state and local party leaders, members of Congress, and other elected officials—who would represent 14 percent of convention delegates and serve to throw the nomination to an experienced candidate acceptable to the party elite if needed. And in 1984, the Democrats nominated a candidate with a long resume—former Vice President Walter Mondale—who promptly took his party to its second forty-nine-state loss in twelve years.

Candidates who had lost to Mondale in the 1984 primaries, like the less established Colorado Senator Gary Hart, argued for reforms that would make it easier for challengers to compete in the primaries. Democrats responded with the "Fairness" Commission, which instituted proportional representation methods designed to make this happen. The result was as planned: In 1988, Democrats nominated Massachusetts Governor Michael Dukakis, who was not one of his party's better known national figures. He had marginally more success than Mondale, but his inexperience showed in the national campaign he waged, and the Democrats once again lost the general election.[7]

The experiment with formal commissions ended in 1986, but changes in the selection process continued to evolve. During the past few years, one of the most notable changes has been the compression of the primary schedule that we mentioned earlier. In 1976, Carter didn't secure the nomination until primaries were held in California, Ohio, and New Jersey on June 8, four months after the Iowa caucuses. In 2004, a hotly contested Democratic nomination battle ended within a matter of weeks after the Iowa caucuses because so many states—particularly delegate-rich large states—had moved their primaries up to the early stage of the selection process. The 2008 Republican contest continued this trend; only the 2008 Democratic primary season departed from form to produce the Obama-Clinton marathon–a contest so close that even the frontloading of primaries on Super Tuesday couldn't resolve it.

The reason for this movement has to do with the political advantages of going early. Not all primaries and caucuses carry the same importance, and a state's position on the calendar is more important in the scheme of things than its population or diversity. By custom, Iowa holds the nation's first caucus, typically in late January, and New Hampshire follows with the nation's first primary roughly one week later. Throughout all the years of reform, this custom remains untouched. Both are small, sparsely populated states without urban centers, demographically atypical of much of the country. But they receive a disproportionate share of media attention over all other primaries and caucuses because they're first. Horserace-centered reporters, hungry for real voters to make real decisions, magnify the results of these first contests disproportionately.

In the primary-centered selection process that the McGovern-Fraser Commission set into motion, candidates get a critical boost coming out of Iowa and New Hampshire, and larger states began to realize that the closer they could schedule their primaries to the early contests, the more influence they would have over the outcome. Conversely, the closer they were to the end of the primary calendar, the greater the risk of being cut out entirely, as

challengers dropped out and the eventual nominee became clear.

California, the largest state, traditionally held its primary in June, but in every election since 1976, the nominee was essentially decided by then. So, in 2004, California moved its primary date to March. So did New York.[8] The effect: an earlier, accelerated, and more expensive primary race, as candidates now have little time to catch their breath while expending resources to compete in populous states where buying television time is very expensive.

Jockeying among states for favorable primary calendar positions continued after the 2004 election. Representatives from western states like Colorado and Nevada said there should be at least one early western primary, perhaps even before Iowa and New Hampshire, and factions inside the Democratic Party battled over the question of whether to deny New Hampshire its traditional leadoff role. In 2008, the Democratic Party agreed to hold one early contest from every region of the country, and Nevada was elevated to January status.

As for those of us who would wish to influence the presidential selection process, geography is destiny. If you live in a state that held its 2008 Republican primary or caucus after February 5, the choice was already made before you had a chance to vote. Even if you were a Democrat living in a state that voted after Super Tuesday, you faced a more limited choice than Democrats in Iowa, New Hampshire, Nevada and South Carolina, as unsuccessful candidates like North Carolina Senator John Edwards, Delaware Senator Joe Biden, New Mexico Governor Bill Richardson, and Connecticut Senator Christopher Dodd fell by the wayside quickly after early losses. Even though it is the product of reforms designed to democratize the selection process, the system in place through 2008 offers disproportionate influence to voters in the states that go first.

Money

As campaigns became primary-centered, they also became incredibly expensive to wage. One of the greatest costs in a primary campaign is television

Table 20.3. Annual Federal Campaign Contribution Limits, 2009–2010[T4]

	To a Candidate (Per Election)	To a National Party Committee	To State, District, Or Local Party Committees	To Any Other Political Committee
Individuals	$2,400	$30,400	$10,000 (total)	$5,000
PACs	$5,000	$15,000	$5,000 (total)	$5,000

advertising, and as political parties have lost control of the nominating process to individual candidates, it is arguably the most critical resource for a campaign to have. To win primary votes, candidates have to reach those rank-and-file voters that reformers wanted to bring into the process. That means advertising and lots of it—which of course means raising a lot of money.

The rules that govern how money can be collected in a presidential campaign have gone through two significant changes during the period since the McGovern-Fraser reforms and have had as much influence on how campaigns operate as changes in the delegate selection rules. Both were campaign finance reform laws. The first was instituted in 1974, the second in 2002.

As a consequence of illegal contributions to President Nixon's reelection campaign brought to light during the Watergate scandal, Congress turned its attention to reforming the way candidates solicit money. The result was the **Federal Election Campaign Act,** passed in 1971 and revised and strengthened several times during the following eight years. It set limits on campaign contributions, set practices for public disclosure of campaign contributions, established a method of partial public funding of presidential campaigns, and created the **Federal Election Commission (FEC)** to oversee the process. In an attempt to keep the FEC nonpartisan, its six commissioners are equally divided between Republicans and Democrats. Under the law, limits were placed on how much individuals and **political action committees** or **PACs** could contribute to candidates and party organizations. Demystifying Government: Political Action Committees discusses PACs in more detail.

Individuals could contribute no more than $1,000 to a candidate for federal office, and PACs could contribute no more than $5,000. The limits

were applied to each election, with primaries and general election campaigns regarded as separate contests. Also, there were restrictions on contributions that could be made to party organizations and annual limits on individual giving. These limits were modified in 2002, then subsequently adjusted for inflation, resulting in the funding limits shown in Table 20.3.

In presidential campaigns, a system of matching public funds was first administered in 1976 to place voluntary limits on spending, while tightening the bonds to the political system for those of us interested in participating through contributing money. The idea was to give ordinary voters who might not think to make political contributions a convenient way to participate in the political process, while democratizing fund-raising at the margins by limiting the amount of big-dollar contributions in the system.

Here's how it works: The government retains a Presidential Election Campaign Fund financed by those of us who check a box on our tax return authorizing $3 of our tax payment to go to the fund (checking the box simply allocates the money—it doesn't increase the tax payment). Money from the fund can go to candidates who demonstrate broad-based support by raising $5,000 in small contributions in each of twenty states. Once a candidate qualifies, the government matches up to $250 in contributions made by individuals; PAC contributions are not matched. In turn, the candidate agrees to a spending limit, which in 2008 was $42.05 million for the primaries and $84.1 million for the general election. During the primaries, there are also spending limits candidates must adhere to within individual states.[9]

If a candidate doesn't accept matching funds, he or she is still bound by the campaign contribution limits in Table 20.3, but not by the spending

DEMYSTIFYING GOVERNMENT

POLITICAL ACTION COMMITTEES

PACs are organizations formed by special interest groups of the sort we will be discussing in Chapter 8 for the purpose of contributing money to political candidates. Most PACs represent labor unions, business groups, or organizations with an ideological agenda—all of which have an interest in affecting the public agenda. Because PACs get their money directly from group members rather than from the organization's funds, they were technically legal before the implementation of the 1974 Federal Election Campaign Act because the language of the law prohibited contributions directly from unions and businesses.

The first PAC was formed in 1944 by the Congress of Industrial Organizations (CIO) for the purpose of collecting voluntary contributions

from union members to support the re-election of Franklin D. Roosevelt. After 1974, PACs became officially sanctioned, and limits were placed on how much they could contribute. From that point, the number of PACs (and PAC dollars) grew astronomically. According to the nonpartisan Center for Responsive Politics, in 1974, 608 PACs were registered with the Federal Election Commission, and they had contributed a combined $15 million to presidential and congressional candidates. In 1998, 3,798 registered PACs had contributed $220 million.[13]

In Chapter 8, we'll take a closer look at who organizes and contributes to PACs, and how much they influence the decisions of victorious politicians.

limits. A candidate able to raise large numbers of small contributions or rely on a personal fortune would find spending limits burdensome. But, for many years, most candidates did not fall into either category, and matching funds were originally a great windfall for campaigns that lacked the means to raise equivalent amounts of money on their own. So, most candidates were willing to adhere to voluntary spending limits in return for a great infusion of cash. Between 1976 and 1996, only two independently wealthy candidates declined matching funds—former Texas Governor John Connelly, in an unsuccessful attempt to win the 1980 Republican presidential nomination, and businessman Steve Forbes, in an unsuccessful attempt to win the 1996 Republican nomination. Forbes tried to self-finance his way to the White House again in 2000, but his efforts were equally ineffective.

However, starting in 2000, a greater number of candidates and—importantly—several successful candidates began opting out of the public financing

system. George W. Bush in 2000 and 2004 assembled a remarkably proficient fund-raising organization that shattered all fund-raising records to date to fuel two successful Republican nomination bids. His opposite number in 2004, Democrat John Kerry, secured his party's presidential nomination without public money. For the first time, spending limits were regarded as a hindrance to effective campaigning, rather than a jackpot that candidates could not refuse.

And that was before the Internet became the effective fundraising medium that it is today. Former Vermont Governor Howard Dean in 2003 set fundraising records for a Democrat and propelled a long-shot effort to credibility by relying on the Internet—a previously untapped source—before his campaign deteriorated in early 2004.[10] By 2008, the Internet had matured to the point where Barack Obama could raise three-quarters of a billion dollars for his presidential bid, an unprecedented sum bolstered by a tsunami of small online contributions from individual supporters. According to the Washington Post, the Obama primary and general election campaigns combined to raise over $500 million from 6.5 million online contributions, six-million of which were $100 or less.[11]

When Obama announced his candidacy in 2007, he was a professed proponent of public financing. But that was before his campaign realized the bonanza available to them in online contributions that would give them a disproportionate fundraising advantage over their Republican challenger John McCain, who—like most other 2008 candidates—did not have an online base of support as broad or as motivated as Obama's. McCain faced an opponent who could blast through the campaign finance ceiling, leaving him at a distinct disadvantage in the fall campaign. The original idea of voluntary public funding, designed as a reform that would limit the amount of money spent on presidential campaigns, was no longer recognizable.

In fact, the intent of public financing was undermined long before Obama discovered the Internet. Candidates had been trying to work around the

public financing system from the beginning. Despite the best intentions of the reformers, there were loopholes in the system that could be exploited even by candidates who accepted matching funds, and given the pressure candidates felt to spend money on media (and travel and consultants), it wasn't long before spending dramatically increased. Campaigns were becoming expensive prior to the establishment of the FEC, but take a look in Figure 20.2 at how spending shot up after public financing went into effect in 1974.

What went wrong? Campaign finance limits restricted what's often called **hard money**—contributions made directly to candidates. They did not cover **soft-money** contributions, or money donated to state and local party committees or to the national parties' nonfederal accounts. The Federal Election Campaign Act left soft-money contributions unregulated, on the assumption that funds from these accounts would be used for state elections, voter registration, get-out-the-vote drives, and other "grassroots" activities.

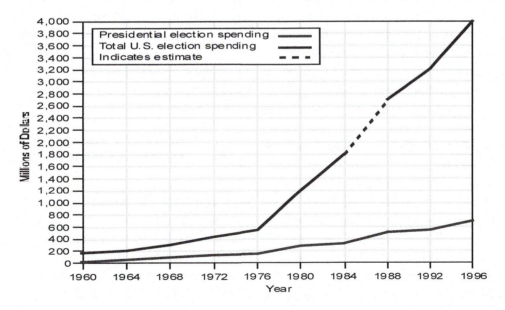

Figure 20.2. Campaign Spending Before and After Campaign Finance Reform[T5]. The amount of money spent on the presidential election campaigns more than doubled between 1964 and 1972, fueling finance campaign reform efforts. However, these reform efforts were not effective; by 1996 spending on presidential elections was 5 times what it had been in 1972. A similar rate of growth was evident in all political spending before the 1974 reforms. But after campaign finance laws went into effect, total election spending flew off the charts. Remember, the figures shown are in millions of dollars.

This, in turn, provided parties and contributors with a loophole for circumventing campaign finance limits. With a little creativity, it's easy to see how the parties could spend soft money on, say, campaign overhead, permitting candidates to spend more of their hard money on campaign commercials and other political functions. One of the more popular uses of soft money is for what are euphemistically called "issue ads" by political professionals. These are commercials produced on behalf of a candidate, which appear to advocate the candidate's election (or the defeat of his or her opponent) by spotlighting an aspect of the candidate's record (typically by putting an opponent's record in a negative context). As long as these ads do not expressly advocate the election or defeat of a candidate, they are considered educational and can be paid for with unlimited soft money.[12]

In recent years, Congress has wrestled with changing the campaign finance structure to make contributing to presidential campaigns more democratic, but it's been a hard sell. Incumbent members of Congress of both parties have been reluctant to change a system that brought them to power, and although finance reform is a widely popular issue, it's not the sort of thing that gets most people out of their homes on Election Day. Finally, in 2002, the political climate worked in favor of reform. By a narrow margin, both houses of Congress passed a version of campaign finance reform advocated by Republican Senator John McCain and Democratic Senator Russell Feingold, and a reluctant President Bush signed it into law.

The major feature of the Bipartisan Campaign Reform Act of 2002, commonly called the **McCain-Feingold Act**, is a prohibition of the use of soft money in federal elections, including a ban on "issue ads" funded with soft money. In exchange, after the 2002 elections, the annual limit that individuals can contribute in hard-money contributions to candidates and party organizations doubled—to $2,000 and $10,000, respectively.

Even after passage, McCain-Feingold met with resistance. Although ardent reform activists felt it was little more than a Band-Aid over a gaping wound, just about everyone directly influenced by the changes resisted them. Both major parties immediately searched for ways to circumvent the soft-money restrictions, while some PACs argued it went too far, challenging soft-money limitations as restrictions on free expression.

Detractors included four of the six FEC commissioners who were in office at the time the law went into effect. Because they were responsible for interpreting and enforcing the law, they were able to weaken some of the law's reforms, restoring large portions of the soft-money loophole that McCain-Feingold was designed to fill and providing exceptions under which federal candidates could still collect soft-money contributions. That led to a fight with Senator McCain, who vowed to undo the FEC action. The law got a boost in December 2002, when a divided Supreme Court upheld the soft-money ban, but McCain-Feingold was unable to prevent massive soft-money expenditures in the 2004 contest.[13]

Then, in the landmark 2010 case *Citizens United v. Federal Election Commission,* a more conservative Supreme Court effectively gutted the McCain-Feingold Act, ruling that corporations were entitled to First Amendment rights similar to those held by individuals. In the Court's view, money is a form of expression and cannot be restricted by Congress. The ruling permitted corporations to spend unlimited sums on elections, which they promptly did in 2010.

Off to the Races: Money, Media, and Momentum

Perhaps the most accurate way to characterize the presidential selection season is to say it's a marathon leading up to the primaries, then a fast sprint to the nomination (followed by another marathon to the fall election for the primary winners). The strategy followed by candidates is dictated partly by the realities of the calendar and partly by the resources at their disposal.

Every potential president starts out with advantages and disadvantages, but not in equal amounts. As the 2008 Democratic presidential contest began to take shape, potential candidates like Hillary Rodham Clinton, the former First Lady and Senator from New York, and John Edwards, the 2004 Democratic nominee for vice president, held one obvious advantage over, say, Tom Vilsack.

Who's Tom Vilsack? That's the point. If you live in Iowa, you probably know that he was recently your governor. But for the millions of Americans who do not live in Iowa (and who do not pay close attention to American governors), he had a lot of catching up to do when it came to **name recognition** because, as chief executive of a relatively small Midwestern state, he was not exactly a household name.

Name recognition gives candidates credibility; no one is going to question whether Clinton or Edwards could mount a viable presidential campaign the way one might raise that question about, say, Mike Gravel.[14] (Look at the endnote if you don't know who Mike Gravel is.) With credibility comes the ability to attract resources. It's easier to raise money if you look like you can mount a serious campaign. You'll attract seasoned campaign advisors. The media will pay more attention to you.[15]

By far, the greatest benefit of name recognition is the advantage it gives a candidate in attracting donors. Long before a single primary vote is counted in New Hampshire, well in advance of the snowy Iowa caucuses, the primary race takes shape as prospective candidates travel the country looking for financial support. This preprimary phase, which could legitimately be called the "money primary," can stretch out for a year or two for candidates with name recognition, even more for candidates who are less well known. Considering the cost of buying television commercials in large states that now hold their primaries early in the process, raising large amounts of money is essential to any candidate who hopes to have a serious chance of making the race.

Running for president has become so expensive that, in 1999, a few fairly well-known contenders dropped out before the primaries began because they were unable to raise enough money. By June 30, 1999, more than half a year before the first primary and caucus votes were cast, George W. Bush had raised a staggering (at that time) $37.2 million for his campaign. In stark contrast, former Vice President Dan Quayle and former Labor Secretary Elizabeth Dole had "only" been able to raise $3.5

million each, while former Tennessee Governor Lamar Alexander, who had essentially never stopped running after his unsuccessful presidential bid four years earlier, had raised one million less than that.[16] All three would call it quits by October 1999, recognizing that they simply did not have a realistic chance of attracting the kind of dollars they would need to compete.

In 1999, Bush was aided by his connections to the oil industry, which is a key source of Republican money. Democrats, for their part, traditionally tap big Hollywood contributors. For Democratic primary hopefuls, 90210 isn't just an old TV show—it's the zip code identifying one of the most lucrative sources of Democratic money (Beverly Hills, California)—a zip code that Bill Clinton frequently visited in 1992 and 1996.

The fact remains that once money is committed to a candidate, it's out of play, and with the frontloading of expensive contests, money raised early counts the most. In the days following the McGovern-Fraser reforms, candidates could expect to be able to raise money during the long primary season if they experienced early success. Today's compressed primary calendar makes that impossible. If big money doesn't flow early, a campaign is doomed.

As with a primary schedule that awards political influence unevenly, depending on where you live, there's a big irony in the way campaign finance reforms have restricted political competition. The reforms that produced today's primary system were intended to democratize the selection process, giving voice to the wishes of the party's rank-and-file voters. As candidates drop out before the voting starts because of inability to raise the huge sums necessary to run a primary campaign, candidate selection shifts from people willing to go to the ballot box to people willing—and able—to open their checkbooks.

Similarly, viable campaigns will strengthen their position by attracting a team of advisors with proven track records. Any successful campaign needs organization, and potential staff members will want to place their professional futures in the hands of candidates who seem to be going somewhere. That's why candidates with name recognition are in a better position to attract the people who make a campaign run: fund-raisers, pollsters, speechwriters, and political consultants who can organize a national strategy, an advance staff to organize events, and grassroots political teams in key primary and caucus states who can get out the vote.[17] The emergence of Internet campaigning hasn't changed these realities, although it has provided savvy campaigns with new options for motivating voters, as you can see in the Demystifying Government box, Obama: Doing It Differently.

The more a candidate demonstrates the ability to amass resources in the year or so before the primaries begin, the more seriously political reporters and pundits will regard the candidate. Achieving a high level of notice from the press is as critical as raising money because a campaign that depends on reaching voters on a state-by-state basis cannot survive without media attention. Press coverage then begets press coverage in a kind of self-fulfilling cycle: A candidate who gets press coverage is taken seriously by reporters, who react by bestowing even more press coverage on the candidate. Of course, this attention just works to help the candidate raise more money and build a better organization. It can work in reverse as well, with struggling candidates facing longer odds as the press ignores them.

But with the benefits of an effective early-stage campaign come the pressures of high **expectations**. Horserace coverage comes early to a campaign marked by a long march to raise money and establish credibility, and reporters will handicap the odds against each contender well before primary voters have their say.[18] When reporters see that candidates with name recognition like George W. Bush in 1999 are succeeding at fund-raising and attracting a professional staff, they will treat them as serious contenders who are expected to perform well once the voters actually have their say. Likewise, reporters will express doubts about a candidate like Connecticut Senator Joseph Lieberman, who entered the 2004 Democratic presidential primary with higher name recognition than his opponents but failed to best them at fund-raising in the year before the primaries.

As the candidate with the most early money, endorsements and name recognition, Hillary Clinton began the 2008 Democratic primary contest as the perceived **front-runner**—the candidate reporters said everyone had to beat. Accordingly, she began the race with the burden of having the highest expectations. If she stumbled—as she did in the Iowa caucus, finishing in third place—the failure to live up to expectations could threaten her front-runner status. In contrast, reporters handicapped senators Barack Obama and John Edwards as main challengers to Clinton, by virtue of their high level of name recognition and, in Edwards' case, his position on the 2004 Democratic presidential ticket. As serious challengers, reporters expected less of them than of Clinton; not until Obama bested Clinton in Iowa, then played her to a draw during Super Tuesday, did he become a co-frontrunner. A candidate like New Mexico Governor Bill Richardson, whose limited fund-raising and organizational success put him in a **long-shot** position, could afford to run behind the leaders in the months leading to the Iowa caucus without suffering negative press coverage.

The press reliably assigns these labels every four years. In the 2004 Democratic race, the early leader of the "money primary" was John Kerry, who was stripped by reporters of his front-runner status and replaced by Howard Dean following the latter's Internet fund-raising success, only to reclaim the front-runner designation after winning the Iowa caucuses and New Hampshire primary. When Dean faltered, Senator John Edwards of North Carolina emerged as the main challenger to Kerry in the February and March contests, before Kerry secured the nomination

Whether you're a front-runner, main challenger, or long shot, your strategy is largely dictated by your position in the race and the media-generated expectations that follow from it. When the primaries begin, a campaign generates **momentum** by meeting or exceeding expectations. This puts the greatest pressure on the front-runner to win early and often, while long shots simply need to do better than expected. In fact, a long shot who surprises reporters by finishing close to the top of the pack in the Iowa caucuses or New Hampshire primary can receive a goldmine of media coverage—even if he or she doesn't finish first. In that case, a candidate can win in the media without winning with the voters.

DEMYSTIFYING GOVERNMENT

OBAMA: DOING IT DIFFERENTLY

At the end of Chapter 5, we noted how long-shot presidential candidate Howard Dean became a serious contender in the summer of 2003 by drawing supporters to his Internet site and raising money—much of it online—in small amounts. Because campaign finance law matches the first $250 contributed, the Dean campaign had the opportunity to stretch its resources further by qualifying for matching funds for a large proportion of the contributions that flooded his coffers via his website, before he raised so much money that he opted to reject matching funds and spending limits entirely. This method of fund-raising will not work for everyone; other candidates have tried to leverage support from the Internet but were unable to do so. It is, however, another indication of how changing technology may make it possible to counter some of the undemocratic forces in the electoral process. Without an active Internet presence, the Dean fund-raising effort could not have kept pace with rival campaigns, and it is likely that his campaign would not have survived, no less become competitive.

Four years later, Barack Obama applied the lessons from Dean's effort to a larger, more sophisticated Internet and found a way to overcome his underdog status. As a high-profile African American senator from a large state who had made a political splash with a rousing keynote address at the 2004 Democratic National Convention, Obama was better known when he began his presidential run than Dean had been at the start of his. But Obama was facing one of the best-known figures in the country. Hillary Clinton began the 2008 contest with more name recognition, more money, more high-profile endorsements, and the expectation among journalists that she would win.

Facing such a formidable opponent, Obama needed to run a different kind of campaign in order to have any chance at victory. The Internet supplied him with the money and manpower typically denied to an underdog candidate. But the Internet was available to everyone—only the Obama campaign figured out how to turn it into a difference-maker.

Like Howard Dean before him, Obama spoke the inclusive language of "we" and the empowering language of "you" rather than the self-centered language of "I" that candidates often use when they tell audiences what they would do for them if elected. Stylistically, this worked well on the Internet, a medium that engages people and incites them to action. As his supporters grew in number, traffic on his Internet site mushroomed, the online equivalent to the enormous crowds he was drawing for his campaign events. Once online, Obama supporters found a website filled with social networking tools they could customize and use to organize events and generate support for the candidate. And his presence penetrated deep into cyberspace, with Obama pages on Facebook, MySpace, and websites geared toward African American, Latino and Asian American voters.[16] Structurally and functionally, the Obama campaign was designed to engage the maximum number of people in campaign activity, dramatically amplifying the organizational force of his campaign operation just like Internet donations dramatically multiplied his campaign funds. No one else had previously used the Internet to such stunning effect, and it is difficult to see how he would have won his party's nomination and been elected president without it.

However, when long shots beat their expectations, they're no longer long shots, and reporters will require that they begin to win, and win soon. Failure to meet newly elevated expectations can stall momentum just as surely as a front-runner that underperforms runs the risk of being tossed from the race. Momentum has tangible rewards because resources follow winners, and if you're presented as a winner in the press, the money and organization you'll attract might just be enough to validate what reporters are saying about your campaign. Figure 20.3 illustrates how momentum shaped the 2008 Republican presidential primary field.

After a long buildup to the first caucus and primary decisions, selection contests run under contemporary rules always sort themselves out fast. The 2008 Republican nomination was effectively decided when the primary season was only one month old, after about a year of preliminaries. The Democratic nomination that year was an exception, lasting as it did until the calendar had run its course, but, even here, the first few contests winnowed the field to Obama and Clinton.

The logic of horserace coverage places so much weight on Iowa and New Hampshire that candidates must exceed expectations in these early contests if they hope to survive. As Mike Huckabee demonstrated in the 2008 Republican contest, winning Iowa does not sew up the nomination. But doing better than expected can give a campaign momentum at a critical time, creating an opportunity for the campaign to demonstrate to the press that it's worthy of the higher expectations that come with success. When Hillary Clinton bounced back after a disappointing showing in Iowa to claim the New Hampshire Primary, the momentum she generated was enough to keep her in the contest until the end. When Bill Clinton was struggling with bad press and falling in the polls in his quest for the presidency 16 years earlier, a second place showing in New Hampshire was sufficient to give his campaign some breathing room and new life.

Of course, candidates can be propelled all the way to victory by winning contests they're "expected" to lose. John Kerry came out of nowhere to beat Howard Dean in Iowa in 2004; when he finished first the following week in New Hampshire,

his campaign got such a media boost that Kerry was able to ride the momentum it generated to the Democratic nomination.

The strategic importance of the early races means that all candidates need to invest a disproportionate amount of money, time, and organizational resources into Iowa and New Hampshire, while trying to save sufficient resources to carry them through the next steps. Consequently, no other states come close to commanding the kind of attention from candidates and reporters that Iowa and New Hampshire receive, even though they are small states that could hardly be considered representative of American population demographics. Since 1972, no candidate has won a nomination after finishing below third place in either state.[19] Rudy Guiliani learned the hard way that if you skip over Iowa and New Hampshire because your prospects look brighter in subsequent states, you take yourself off stage during the critical first weeks of the primary season when voters—and reporters—are sorting out winners and losers. Guiliani's defeat in Florida and his rapid demise as a candidate thereafter was rooted in his decision to effectively sit out the voting in Iowa and New Hampshire.

While campaigning in these and other primary and caucus states, candidates fashion a message that can define their campaigns. Along with investing resources in the early contests, developing an effective message is a key part of attaining viability because it's not enough to tell people you're running for president simply because you want to be president. Candidates need to give people a reason to vote for them.

Typically, candidates need to do two things. They need to distinguish themselves from their rivals, which is sometimes difficult to do in a selection contest where your rivals come from within your party and probably agree with you more than they disagree. They also need to appeal to the people who are likely to turn out to vote.

One way candidates can draw distinctions with their opponents is by positioning themselves to the "right" or "left" of the opposition. For instance, in 2004, Howard Dean took a stand against the Iraq War, positioning himself as a more liberal candidate

These are the major candidates in the crowded 2008 Republican primary field several months before the voting began in Iowa and New Hampshire. Left to right: In the lead is former New York City Mayor **Rudy Guiliani**, who built a national reputation following his actions in the wake of the September 11, 2001 terrorist attacks on New York. His main challengers were Arizona Senator **John McCain**, former Tennessee Senator **Fred Thompson**, whose political career intertwined with an acting career that included a stint on the television show "Law and Order," and former Massachusetts Governor **Mitt Romney**. Because no incumbent was running in 2008, the field was especially crowded, and there were a number of long-shot challengers: **Mike Huckabee**, the socially conservative telegenic former governor of Arkansas; Congressman **Ron Paul**, whose libertarian views earned him a small but devoted following; and a list of deep long-shots (not pictured here) that included a pair of congressmen (California's **Duncan Hunter** and Colorado's **Tom Trancredo**), a pair of governors (Virginia's **Jim Gillmore** and Wisconsin's **Tommy Thompson**), Senator **Sam Brownback** of Kansas, and former ambassador and columnist **Alan Keyes**.

DECEMBER 2007

On the eve of the Iowa caucus the frontrunner is being challenged by a cluster of contenders that now includes Mike Huckabee, who has pulled into a surprisingly strong position during the last few months as the candidates have debated each other, raised money, and campaigned hard in the early states of Iowa and New Hampshire. It looks to be a five-way contest, and right now it's anyone's bet who will win. Not surprisingly, four of the long-shots are finding it impossible to raise money in such a crowded field, and they're already out of the race. Gillmore and Thompson exited over the summer, Brownback in the fall, and Tancredo by year's end.

JANUARY 2008 WEEK 1

Off to Iowa—and as actual people cast their votes for the first time in what is already a long race, onetime long-shot Mike Huckabee is the winner, with Mitt Romney a distant second, and John McCain and Fred Thompson tied for third. Ron Paul, still a long-shot, is on McCain and Thompson's tail—so the race remains bunched up in the front. And Guiliani, still considered the frontrunner, makes a risky strategic decision not to compete in the New Hampshire primary and wait it out until the big states come around in a few weeks—a very unorthodox strategy.

JANUARY 2008 WEEK 2

As the New Hampshire results start coming in it becomes clear that John McCain is the big winner, having made a comeback from his disappointing Iowa showing. On the strength of his convincing New Hampshire win, reporters tentatively start calling him the new frontrunner, although Guiliani is still waiting for the right moment to make his move. Mitt Romney finishes second again, as the Iowa winner—Mike Huckabee—drops to third. And Fred Thompson appears to be in serious trouble, finishing dead last in a tie with Duncan Hunter.

JANUARY 2008 WEEK 3

The new frontrunner comes through in South Carolina, beating Mike Huckabee in this conservative state and giving his campaign a real boost. Romney appears to have sputtered, and everyone is still waiting for Guiliani to compete. The big loser is Fred Thompson, whose candidacy looked promising on paper but never made traction with voters. He leaves the race, along with long-shot Duncan Hunter.

JANUARY 2008 WEEK 4

The race moves to Florida, where Guiliani finally takes center stage, figuring to make a strong move in a state with a lot of transplanted New Yorkers. But too much time has passed without his presence, and his strategy of not competing early fails spectacularly. Guiliani finishes behind John McCain and Mitt Romney, and promptly leaves the field, realizing that his funding and support would instantly dry up after staking everything on a win in Florida and falling short. His departure could clear the field for McCain—if he can maintain his lead through Super Tuesday.

FEBRUARY 2008 WEEK 1

With Guiliani out of the race and Huckabee unable to repeat his early Iowa success, it's up to McCain to beat out Mitt Romney on Super Tuesday and claim the prize. And he does—taking several large states and positioning Romney as an also-ran. Romney would drop out shortly, and even though Huckabee would continue to contest more primaries, it was clear after Super Tuesday that the only McCain had the strength to compete nationally. It wouldn't become official until one month later, but McCain had emerged from the shadows of a close contest and would be the 2008 Republican presidential nominee.

Figure 20.3. Money, Media and Momentum in the 2008 Republican Primary Race

than John Kerry, even though Kerry had a more liberal record. George W. Bush used the term "compassionate conservatism" to portray a conservative philosophy with a moderate temperament that suggested unity and inclusiveness.

Even as Bush sought the middle ground, it was the middle ground within his party. Primary voters are more likely than general election voters to be closer to the poles of public opinion. Republicans are likely to be more conservative than the general population; Democrats are likely to be more liberal. Candidates need to reach these voters in order to be selected as the nominee of the party, so it's not uncommon for Republican hopefuls to sound more conservative during the primary race and for Democrats to sound more liberal.

Once the nomination is secure and the nominees start running against each other, they typically shift their campaign rhetoric toward the center of public opinion where most voters lie, and where general elections are won and lost.

Decisions, Part II: The Election Process

When a roll call of the delegates at the national convention ratifies the primary victor, the candidate becomes the official party nominee, and the general election campaign begins. Typically held in late summer before the November election, conventions are a four-day gathering that in recent years has been a protracted "infomercial" for the party nominee.

Stage-managed by the victorious campaign, conventions produce made-for-television balloon-and-streamer-filled pictures that candidates love. Celebrities join political figures to speak at the convention podium in order to maximize press interest. Everything is designed to play well on television and to maximize positive exposure for the candidate, who may have been in politics for years but who is "introducing" himself to the American public as a future president. It's typical for each newly minted nominee to get a "bounce" in the polls from favorable reaction to four days of positive press exposure.

In 2008, Barack Obama capitalized on his ability to draw huge crowds and staged his Denver acceptance speech in a football stadium, complete with a stadium-sized stage set.[20] In 2004, John Kerry surrounded himself with veterans who had served with him in Vietnam to communicate the message that, in a time of war, he would be a strong commander-in-chief. In 2000, the Republican Convention studiously featured minority supporters, like General Colin Powell and former Oklahoma Representative J. C. Watts, in an effort to portray the party as diverse and inclusive. In 1996, Elizabeth Dole, in the role of the nominee's spouse, walked through the Republican convention floor with a handheld microphone, talking about her husband in a made-for-television act that evoked a talk show.

The stagecraft has become too much for the major television networks. Wall-to-wall convention coverage, the norm a generation ago, has been reduced to four prime time hours over four days. Although the growth of cable news is one reason for diminished network interest (you can still get around-the-clock convention coverage on cable), journalists have come to doubt the newsworthiness of the conventions. In 2000, ABC News reporter Ted Koppel left the Republican Convention early and refused to go to the Democratic Convention at all. Insisting that there was no longer any news made at the conventions, Koppel refused to give his blessing to the media events they had become. In a reflection of the love-hate relationship between reporters and politicians, Koppel felt the convention event had become too manipulative. His reaction was to regain some control by walking away, essentially removing the convention from the news agenda.

Behind the scenes, delegates perform serious work in the form of writing the **platform** on which the nominee will run. The platform is a long document listing the principles that the party stands for under the leadership of its presidential nominee. Because an early resolution of the primary battle guarantees that the winning candidate will be able to stock the convention with his or her delegates, most recent platforms have been written by supporters of the victorious candidate to reflect that candidate's views. So, if you were to read the party platforms, you'd get a pretty good sense of the philosophical differences among the candidates and probably have a good sense of how they would govern. Of course, few of us even think to do this, but that doesn't diminish the value of the platform as a blueprint for the next administration's priorities.

Because the party activists who become convention delegates and help shape the platform are generally more ideological than rank-and-file party adherents, it shouldn't be surprising that the Democratic and Republican platforms reveal differences in priorities and in approaches to problems. Perhaps no place is the difference between the two parties more clearly defined than in these documents.

In Table 20.4, take a look at a few "planks" from the 2008 Democratic and Republican platforms and see if you can spot some of these differences.

Platform writing generally happens out of view of television cameras, and with the victorious candidate in control of the process, it typically generates little suspense. In 1996, a minority of pro-choice Republicans talked about challenging the language of the platform's antiabortion plank, threatening to create a newsworthy spectacle. Nothing came of it, though: A revolt was avoided, and the platform was constructed in private and with no excitement.

In fact, because conventions are no longer the scene of suspenseful balloting or factional jockeying, the only real surprise to emerge from most conventions is the identity of the nominee's vice presidential running mate (who is selected by the

Table 20.4. Party Differences

2008 Platform Planks	
Democratic Party	**Republican Party**
"We will provide an immediate energy rebate to American families struggling with the record price of gasoline and the skyrocketing cost of other necessities. We will devote $50 billion to jump starting the economy, helping economic growth, and preventing another 1 million jobs from being lost."	"Economic freedom expands the prosperity pie: government can only divide it up. That is why we advocate lower taxes, reasonable regulation, and smaller, smarter government. That agenda translates to more opportunity for more people."
"To renew American leadership in the world, we must first bring the Iraq war to a responsible end. Our Soldiers, Sailors, Airmen and Marines have performed admirably while sacrificing immeasurably. Our civilian leaders have failed them. Iraq was a diversion from the fight against the terrorists who struck us on 9-11, and incompetent prosecution of the war by civilian leaders compounded the strategic blunder of choosing to wage it in the first place."	"We uphold the right of individual Americans to own firearms, a right which antedated the Constitution and was solemnly confirmed by the Second Amendment."
"In countries wracked by poverty and conflict, citizens long to enjoy freedom from want. Because extremely poor societies and weak states provide optimal breeding grounds for terrorism, disease, and conflict, the United States has a direct national security interest in dramatically reducing global poverty and joining with our allies in sharing more of our riches to help those most in need."	"Because our children's future is best preserved within the traditional understanding of marriage, we call for a constitutional amendment that fully protects marriage as a union of a man and a woman, so that judges cannot make other arrangements equivalent to it."
"We strongly and unequivocally support *Roe v. Wade* and a woman's right to choose a safe and legal abortion, regardless of ability to pay, and we oppose any and all efforts to weaken or undermine that right."	"Faithful to the first guarantee of the Declaration of Independence, we assert the inherent dignity and sanctity of all human life and affirm that the unborn child has a fundamental individual right to life which cannot be infringed. We support a human life amendment to the Constitution, and we endorse legislation to make clear that the Fourteenth Amendment's protections apply to unborn children."

nominee and ratified by the convention delegates). Some nominees have even drained the convention of this small element of suspense by revealing the running mates' identity before the convention starts in order to generate excitement among the delegates and extra press coverage. John McCain did this in 2004, announcing his selection of Alaska Governor Sarah Palin hours after the close of the Democratic Convention —days before he was officially nominated—to deflect attention from Barack Obama's stadium acceptance speech spectacle. For his part, Obama had already sent supporters a text message announcing his choice of Delaware Senator Joseph Biden before Democrats convened to nominate him.

Nominees typically select as running mates people who promise to balance them on such factors as ideology, experience, or geography. McCain's choice of Palin was aimed at reaching out to social conservatives who might not have perceived McCain as one of their own, and perhaps women who were disappointed by Hillary Clinton's failure to secure the Democratic nomination. Obama's choice of Biden gave the relatively inexperienced Illinois senator a veteran running-mate with strong foreign policy credentials. Nominees who survived a bruising primary fight might invite their vanquished rival to run with them in a play for party unity, as Ronald Reagan did in 1980 with his selection of primary opponent George Bush (senior). Strategically selecting running mates from large, electoral-rich states is an attractive proposition for nominees, although in 2008 this did not figure into the calculations of either John McCain or Barack Obama.

Nominees facing an uphill fall battle may go against conventional wisdom to generate excitement with their pick, as John McCain did by selecting a young, female governor who was largely unknown outside her native Alaska. Bill Clinton defied expectations by running with a political twin: Al Gore, a fellow southern Baby Boomer from a neighboring state. In 2000, Al Gore's selection of Senator Lieberman produced the first Jewish nominee on a major party ticket. Sixteen years earlier, Walter Mondale generated a buzz with his selection of New York Representative Geraldine Ferraro to be the first national female nominee of a major party.

Still, as far as excitement goes at party conventions, that's about it. The primary victor's name is placed in nomination. The delegates vote. They vote for the nominee's vice presidential selection. The nominee makes a big speech and tries to stir excitement among the party faithful. Balloons and streamers drop from the rafters. Then the other major party does the same thing. And the general election campaign begins.

Organization, Media, Information and Endurance

It's tempting to begin this section with a disclaimer because here we are talking about how political parties form a link between us and our elected officials—we've already witnessed places where that link is problematic, from the primary calendar to campaign fund-raising—and what you are about to read may at times seem coldly calculated to manipulate our voting patterns more than to engage us in spirited political discourse. What you're going to read about is, frankly, an example of why many people are turned off by politics. So, if you can, try to keep an open mind, and remember that running for president is an intense ordeal, where the biggest political prize on earth hangs in the balance.

From the convention to Election Day, party nominees have roughly seventy-five days to bring their case for election to the American people. It's hard work—and it's big business, requiring a more extensive campaign structure than the candidate had during the primary season, careful attention to paid and free media, an effective information-gathering apparatus, and, as always, the ability to remain sharp with little sleep.

Today's campaigns are an amalgam of professionals brought in to manage different components of the effort, meaning the candidate becomes a client to a series of political "hired guns" responsible for plotting and executing campaign strategy.

In addition to a campaign manager to handle the daily responsibilities of the effort, the campaigns hire media consultants, pollsters, fundraisers, press officials, and staff members in much larger numbers than they had during the primary campaign. Their work entails designing, planning, and executing campaign events; testing themes for and developing television ads (media consultants); gauging and responding to public reaction to the candidate (pollsters); raising money (fund-raisers); and working to get reporters to cover the candidate's message (press secretary).

Much of this effort revolves around maximizing results from the **paid media**. In successful campaigns, the messages communicated in ads and in the press work together, are simple, and target groups of voters that the campaign needs to be victorious. As they did during the primaries, successful presidential candidates will go around the country giving essentially the same speech several times a day, hitting the same themes and staying "on message" in the hope that news stories that evening will reflect the theme crafted by the campaign. Only now, they will come under even greater press scrutiny.

In a savvy campaign, the same themes will appear in the candidate's paid advertising, allowing for a potentially powerful reinforcement tool because political professionals believe that if people hear a consistent message they're more likely to absorb it. We know from Chapter 5 that reporters often rebel against this kind of message control by retaining the last word in framing news stories. Nonetheless, when a campaign can sustain a coordinated message in paid and free media, it can typically wage the election on its terms.

In order to determine which groups of voters the candidate needs to win over and what messages will reach them, professional pollsters conduct public opinion surveys throughout the campaign. Initial polls reveal a wealth of information that can be used to plot strategy, especially information about how voters view the candidates' strengths and weaknesses. By looking closely at survey results, pollsters can identify groups that strongly support the candidate, strongly support his opponent, and all-important "swing" groups that are within the candidate's reach and that could determine the outcome of the election.

Typically, campaigns will gather more information on how targeted groups of voters are reacting to the candidate by conducting **focus groups**, which bring together a small number of people sharing a targeted demographic, like suburban women or southern white men, to "talk" about the candidate. Unlike opinion polls, which you may recall consist of random samples in which theoretically anyone can be contacted, focus groups are nonrandom and nonscientific. They can quickly and inexpensively produce a wealth of useful details for the campaign about how the selected group feels about the candidate that can help them fine-tune their strategy.

For instance, in his 1988 acceptance speech, George Bush (senior) referred to Americans as being "like a thousand points of light in a broad and peaceful sky." During the general election campaign, Bush kept using the phrase "a thousand points of light," often to refer to American volunteerism—until a focus group revealed that most people had no idea what he was talking about.[21]

Getting out the message requires travel—and lots of it. In the early days of the republic, it was customary for presidential candidates to stay home and say nothing; anything more was considered undignified. Nothing could be farther from the description of today's general election campaigns, which feature nonstop travel by the candidate and his entourage, who crisscross the country at jet speeds in a test of endurance that taxes all but the strongest constitutions. Candidates watch the country go by in a blur as they are chauffeured about in what some describe as a "bubble" of advisors, advance people (who arrange the events), reporters, and the electronic gear of twenty-first-century politics: television cameras, microphones, wires, and the like.

Strategy Again

With an infinite number of possible events to attend and a finite amount of time, campaign strategists need to set the candidate's agenda for maximum political benefit. This is accomplished by identifying where the candidate needs to shore up strength among voters.

Presidential elections are decided on a state-by-state basis. Each state is accorded electoral votes, awarded as a bloc to the candidate who carries the state, and a candidate must win a majority of electoral votes (270) to be elected. This fact drives fundamental strategic decisions. Where the candidate visits and where he or she purchases commercial airtime is determined by the states that campaign operatives believe they need to carry to win the election.

Each campaign's fundamental strategic decisions are based on dividing the map into three groups: states the campaign feels it will lose no matter what it does (where there's no realistic chance to win electoral votes); states the campaign feels it will win no matter what it does (where it feels assured of winning electoral votes); and competitive states, which get the most attention. Many of these can be determined by recent voting patterns. For instance, in 2008, the McCain campaign knew that most states in the deep South and in the Rocky Mountain West reliably support Republican candidates. Likewise, the Obama campaign knew it could count on California, New York, and the New England states. So, there was no point for either campaign to devote resources to Utah, Alabama, Rhode Island, or Massachusetts.

The remaining states make up the campaign battleground. These are "swing" states that have a history of supporting either Democrats or Republicans in recent elections, and which both candidates feel could break in either direction. The more populous of these become key to the strategies of both campaigns. In reality, the national campaign for president isn't a national campaign at all; it plays out mostly in these swing states. If you live in places like Ohio, Missouri, Michigan, Pennsylvania, and Florida, you are showered with candidate visits and campaign promises and commercials, as both campaigns advance a strategy that will move them toward Electoral College victory. If you live in a state that's reliably in one column or the other, you're more of a bystander to a contest being played out elsewhere (see Demystifying Government: Vote Swapping).

Once target states have been identified, the campaign's pollsters go into action to assess the strength of the candidate and his or her opponent. The result of this assessment determines how resources are allocated. Campaigns will start with the electoral votes of their "base"—the states they can count on—and subtract that number from 270 to arrive at the number of electoral votes they need to win the election. They can identify where these votes might come from by looking at the number of electoral votes in the states that are up for grabs. From the survey data, they can determine which of the battleground states are likely to be the most competitive and devote the most resources to them.

Pollsters constantly take the temperature of the race in battleground states, and campaigns use the data to modify where they allocate resources. If the campaign's polls indicate that a state is starting to tip one way or another, resources can be pulled from that state and reallocated to a more competitive state.

In the closing weeks of the 2008 contest, when McCain's polling indicated that he was trailing in too many states to win the Electoral College, the campaign made the decision to shift advertising funds from Michigan, essentially conceding this key battleground to Obama, in order to make a last stand in Pennsylvania, where McCain was also trailing but where he felt he had a better chance of making a comeback. McCain's strategic situation was bleak. He trailed slightly in the key battleground swing states of Florida and Ohio, and was behind or locked in a pitched contest in Virginia, Missouri, North Carolina and Indiana. McCain would need to win all of them and claim a state where Obama was strongly ahead, which was the thinking behind his Pennsylvania strategy. Pennsylvania could be decisive if he could sweep all the close contests—a long shot, for sure, but perhaps the best option available to him. Ultimately, Pennsylvania did not turn out to be critical, as Obama won it by a double-digit margin, and McCain succeeded in winning only Missouri among the swing state contests.

This result did not surprise McCain's strategists. As Election Day nears, pollsters can generally predict with great accuracy how the election will turn out, making it possible to fine-tune the campaign in its final hours if it's going to be close. Sometimes, that's not necessary. In 1992, Bill Clinton's pollsters

DEMYSTIFYING GOVERNMENT

VOTE SWAPPING

Candidates aren't the only ones who can engage in election-year strategy. In 2000, when consumer advocate Ralph Nader was the presidential candidate of the Green Party, some Nader voters living in battleground states faced a dilemma: They were concerned that if they voted for Nader (their first choice) instead of Gore (their second choice), the loss of a vote for Gore would boost the prospects of Bush (their third choice). In a close race, they were concerned that a vote for Nader would be a vote for Bush.

The solution: Trade votes with Gore voters in states where the outcome wasn't in doubt. In an example of spontaneous, grassroots political involvement, Internet sites emerged that allowed Nader voters in battleground states to find Gore voters in states where one candidate or the other was sure to win so they could agree to "swap votes." The Nader voter in the battleground state would agree to cast a vote for Gore, believing that a Gore voter in a state where the race wasn't close would cast a vote on their behalf for Nader. Of course, these "agreements" were unenforceable, and neither voter would ever know if the other carried out the agreement. Still, it demonstrates that it's not just the professionals who can be sophisticated strategists in a presidential election and that, given the opportunity to reach others via the Internet, it's possible for ordinary people to play with the electoral rules in order to maximize their political expression in presidential campaigns.

told him several days before any votes were cast that he was going to be the next president of the United States.

Other times, it can be very helpful. In 2004, after months of strategic calculations based on the electoral map, the Bush and Kerry campaigns both knew that their tight contest would be determined in Ohio, Pennsylvania, and Florida. All three states were close, and based on the electoral vote totals both campaigns believed they could count on elsewhere in the country, the only way either could reach 270 electoral votes was by carrying two of the three. Whichever candidate carried two of the three would be president. (Bush, in fact, won by carrying Florida and Ohio.) Both campaigns had reached the same conclusion from their polling, so both campaigns focused intently on these three states in the campaign's final hours.

Going Negative

It's always tempting for campaigns to use television commercials to define their opponent's character or record in negative terms through the use of negative ads (euphemistically called "comparative ads" by campaign professionals because they aim to highlight the positive qualities of the candidate by dragging down the candidate's opponent). The reason is simple: Advertising specialists believe they work. They permit the candidate to focus attention on the weaknesses of the opponent that the candidate's polling indicates will matter to undecided voters. If an opponent is relatively unknown, negative advertising can define the opponent in the most critical light to viewers who have no basis for challenging the assessment. In 2004, negative ads about John Kerry portrayed him as an unprincipled "flip-flopper" and questioned his heroism in Vietnam.

The environment produced by pervasive negative advertising can drive people away from politics, depressing turnout and increasing cynicism. However, political consultants bent on winning an election for their client will not be concerned with these serious systemic effects, and the fact is negative advertising exists because it's effective. People tend to remember negative messages, especially if they are repeated enough or left unchallenged. Even if they are challenged, the response from the opposing candidate can make him look defensive. Some campaigns actually anticipate negative ads and answer the charges before they're made in order to avoid looking defensive and "inoculate" the public against a charge they believe is coming.

Because people are repelled by negative messages even as they internalize negative allegations, negative ads can be risky to use. They can backfire by making the candidate who runs them appear mean-spirited. For this reason, negative ads will typically be shown first to focus groups to get a sense of how people from targeted demographic categories react to them. When they run, pollsters monitor public reaction closely, and campaigns will quickly pull negative ads at the slightest hint that they are hurting the campaign.[22]

Negative ads are not new to American politics, although in recent years the threshold for what we seem to be willing to accept has gone up. For a good sense of how we've become more open to negative campaigning, consider the infamous "Daisy Commercial" run on behalf of Lyndon Johnson. It's still one of the most controversial in our history, even though it ran back in 1964. President Johnson's opponent, Republican Senator Barry

Goldwater, generated concerns among many people that he might be trigger-happy and too willing to use nuclear weapons. To reinforce those concerns, the Johnson ad portrays a little girl pulling petals from a daisy while counting backwards, fading into audio of a launch countdown, followed by an image of a nuclear explosion. Although that sounds heavy-handed, consider that Goldwater is never mentioned by name, and his policies are never discussed.

Almost fifty years later, it's still powerful. When the "Daisy Ad" ran, the Goldwater campaign cried foul, saying it unfairly implied that its candidate was a threat to world peace. Johnson agreed, and the ad never ran a second time. In today's charged political environment, unless the ad began to backfire politically, it's hard to imagine a campaign responding the same way.

Televised Debates

Since 1976, televised presidential debates have been a part of every fall campaign. Although they date back to 1960, as you will see when you read Demystifying Government: The First Debate, debates do not have a long history in presidential politics and they regularly form a point of contention between the candidates, who struggle over the strategic advantages and disadvantages of debating. Before the 1960 showdown between John F. Kennedy and Richard M. Nixon, there were no presidential debates at all.

It's rare that the strategic interests of both candidates will lead them into a high-stakes confrontation with each other on the same stage in front of a huge national audience. Typically, one candidate will have more to gain by participating, leading an opponent to believe it is in his or her best interest to opt out.

That's why, after 1960, it took sixteen years before presidential debates resumed. In 1964, President Johnson was so far ahead in opinion polls that he could simply refuse to debate Barry Goldwater. With Nixon on the ballot again in 1968 and 1972, there was probably no way that debates were going to happen, considering his bad experience in 1960.

It wasn't until 1976, when imperiled incumbent Gerald Ford was locked in a tight race with Jimmy Carter, that both sides felt it was in their interest to debate. Ford, whom Nixon appointed to the vice presidency after Spiro Agnew resigned in scandal, was elevated to the Oval Office following Nixon's resignation, making him the only president ever to serve without winning a national election. Two years into his brief term, Ford was still trying to convince Americans that he was up to the job, and his campaign operatives felt a televised debate would

DEMYSTIFYING GOVERNMENT

THE FIRST DEBATE

The first televised debates between Kennedy and Nixon occurred in part because both candidates stood to benefit from them. The race was close when Kennedy issued his debate challenge to Nixon, so neither candidate had the luxury of avoiding a direct confrontation by sitting on a large lead. Kennedy was knowledgeable and quick on his feet, and believed he could use the debate forum to dispel the idea that his youth was a liability in a contest against an incumbent vice president. Nixon knew that he wasn't the most trusted politician and believed that a strong performance could give him an opportunity to erase that impression. Besides, he had a record as a good debater, and to refuse Kennedy's invitation would make it appear that he was running scared.

Nixon's debating skills turned out to be of limited value, though. He failed to grasp what Kennedy's media consultants understood:

that the debates would be about television. Kennedy's advisors knew that people are more likely to look at the pictures than listen to the words. They were savvy about the use of makeup to present a healthy image, and the inviting impression made by a blue shirt on a black-and-white television screen. They could coach their candidate to look into the camera and talk to the voters, not to his opponent on stage. In short, they knew how to make Kennedy appear "telegenic," and in so doing, to invite a positive emotional reaction to the candidate.

That Nixon was recovering from an illness, looked pale, needed to shave, and perspired too much simply served to underscore the different impressions made by the two candidates. Perhaps the most valuable lesson of the Kennedy-Nixon debates was what the debates taught about the power of pictures more than words to communicate a message on television.

give him that opportunity. For his part, Carter was relatively unknown, and his campaign handlers felt a debate would give him positive exposure and a chance to show off his command of details.

Four years later, the political dynamics again favored a debate. This time, Carter was the imperiled incumbent, and Ronald Reagan was the challenger who needed a way to reassure Cold War voters that he would not act like a cowboy with America's nuclear arsenal.

Both debates worked to the advantage of the challenger, who received a boost by appearing on stage with the president. In 1984, with Reagan far ahead in opinion polls, his campaign calculated that it would make the president look magnanimous if he debated his opponent. This established the expectation that after three consecutive presidential

elections with candidate debates, future campaigns would be expected to engage in debates as well. By 1988, debates had become the norm, and reluctant candidates found that the cost of looking like they were ducking their opponent had become too high for them to resist debating.

If you're on the debate team at school or if you know someone who is, you may be surprised at how little actual debating takes place at presidential debates. They tend to be more like joint press conferences, where both candidates repeat the same messages they've been talking about at campaign events. This can create a disconnected feeling, where candidates talk past each other or avoid questions in order to jump to their campaign talking points. In 2004, the Bush campaign went so far as to insist on guidelines that precluded the candidates from addressing each other directly. The name of the media game is to control the message by staying "on message," and that's how political advisors instruct candidates to approach televised debates.

They also instruct candidates to speak to the camera and try to relax. Because we react to what we see more than to what we hear, candidates who are unable to come across naturally in televised debates can find themselves at a disadvantage. In the 2000 debates, Al Gore was eager to show off his detailed policy knowledge, believing that it would show him to be more presidential than his less worldly opponent, George W. Bush. This turned out to be an incorrect assumption. Opinion polls conducted by both campaigns revealed that Gore turned off many undecided voters by coming across as somewhere between a bully and the smartest kid in the class. Gore may have won most of the debating points, but Bush appeared at ease and more likeable. Impressions like these can linger and factor into how people vote.

The Electoral College: Is This Any Way to Elect a President?

It's safe to say that no institution like the Electoral College has ever been created anywhere. It's been with us since the Constitutional Convention of 1787, modified once to account for political party competition, and has been the object of numerous reform proposals over the centuries, all of which have failed to materialize. It's complex, often misunderstood, and difficult to explain. Yet, it is almost always the final arbiter of who will enter the White House. First, let's make sure we understand how it works—see Demystifying Government: The Electoral College.

Who Would Create a System Like This?

Although it may seem like the Constitution's framers created the Electoral College to make life miserable for government students, in truth, it was a compromise that solved a couple of key dilemmas. The framers wanted an elite to identify the most qualified presidential candidates, but they didn't want presidents to be beholden to the elite that selected them. Also, they didn't want to undermine separation of powers by simply having Congress select the president. In the Electoral College, the framers created a mechanism for assembling an elite that would go out of business as soon as its work was done, meaning it wouldn't be in a position to ask anything of the new president. As complex as it is, the Electoral College is consistent with federalism by giving the states a key role in presidential selection, and separation of powers, by putting the choice of the president in the hands of Congress as a matter of last resort.

In its original incarnation, the Electoral College was really established as a mechanism that would perform the selection function that soon became the province of political parties. Electors were to identify the worthiest candidates in their respective states, and if a majority could not agree on a single best choice, the House of Representatives would settle the matter. By 1800, the selection process was already being performed through party nominations, and the mechanics of the Electoral College had to be changed.

In its original form, electors cast two votes, one for a candidate from another state in an effort to avoid parochial choices. The runner-up in electoral votes would become vice president. With the advent of two-party competition, it quickly became apparent that this meant the vice president could be the losing presidential candidate of the opposition party. As parties started nominating separate candidates for president and vice president, the possible outcomes became even more bizarre. In 1800, the Democratic-Republicans nominated Jefferson for president and Aaron Burr for vice president, resulting in an Electoral College tie as Democratic-Republican electors cast one vote each for Jefferson and Burr. The resulting complications led to passage of the Twelfth Amendment, providing for separate electoral tallies for president and vice president.[23]

In its time, the Electoral College was intended as a deliberative body, but as candidate selection

DEMYSTIFYING GOVERNMENT

THE ELECTORAL COLLEGE

The president and the vice-president are chosen by the Electoral College consisting of electors allocated to each state and (by virtue of the 23rd Amendment) the District of Columbia, which gets three electors. Electors are allocated by adding the number of senators (two) to the number of representatives in each state. Since the least populous states have one representative, the smallest number of electors a state can have is three.

In total, there are 538 electors in the Electoral College. Each gets one vote. The map below shows how many electors are allocated to each state. When you vote for a president and a vice president, you're really selecting the electors pledged to vote for the candidates you selected.

Electors are real people, chosen by the state party leaders in numbers equal to the electoral vote of each state. So, since Illinois has twenty-one electoral votes, the Illinois Republican Party selects twenty-one people loyal Republicans to act as electors, and the Illinois Democratic Party selects twenty-one loyal Democrats to act as electors.

Independents and third parties that qualify to be on the ballot also get to field a slate of electors. We determine which slate of electors represents our state when we go to the polls to vote for the president. Our votes for the president are called the **popular vote**. The party of the candidate receiving **plurality** of popular votes for its slate of electors wins all the electors in the state.

In 2000, Al Gore won 366 more popular votes than George W. Bush in New Mexico, out of a total of 598,605 votes cast. It was less than a majority, but Gore's slim plurality was enough to give him all five of the state's electoral votes.

Maine and Nebraska have the only exceptions in the winner-take-all rule. In those states, two electors are awarded to the plurality winner of the popular vote, and the rest are awarded to the plurality winner of the popular vote within each of the state's congressional districts. So, it possible for these states to send a combined slate of Republican and Democratic electors to the Electoral College.

On the Monday following the second Wednesday in December, the winning slate of electors gathers in the state capital to cast their votes for president and vice president. In some states, election law requires the electors to vote for the state's popular-vote winner. Other states do not have this restriction, making it possible for a **faithless elector** to vote for a different candidate. Because electors are strong partisans and devoted a lot of time and energy to their party, few ever deviate from supporting their party's candidate.

The electoral votes are sent from the states to Washington, D.C., whereon January 6, the vice-president, acting in his constitutional capacity as president of the Senate, records the votes. The presidential and vice-presidential candidates receiving an outright majority of electoral votes—270—are elected. If no candidate receives 270 electoral votes, which could happen if there were a third party candidate in the mix, the House of Representatives selects the president from the top three electoral-vote recipients. The senate selects the vice president from the top two electoral vote recipients.

The House votes for the president by state delegation, with representatives from each state together getting one vote. The candidate who receives a majority of the fifty state delegations is elected. In the Senate, each senator casts one vote for the vice president. The candidate who wins the majority is elected.

shifted to the congressional caucus, then party conventions, then primaries, the functions of the Electoral College became much more automatic. Today, network anchors talk about electoral votes as if they were coupons you clipped from a newspaper. On election night, they sit in front of big maps, rapidly assigning electoral votes to one candidate or another as soon as the popular vote from a state is determined. As the map fills in—red states for the Republican nominee, blue states for the Democrat—it becomes a race to 270, no more than a mathematical exercise.

Changing the Electoral College

The automatic quality that the Electoral College has assumed encourages reformers to question the wisdom of retaining a system that could produce a president who finished second in the popular vote. After all, every office but the highest one is determined by simple plurality vote. It's unlikely, but mathematically possible, for the electoral vote winner to be different from the popular vote winner. This has happened three times in our history; a fourth disputed election involved the House bypassing the Electoral Vote winner:

- 1824: In a disputed election that wound up in the House of Representatives, John Quincy Adams was chosen president, despite the fact that Andrew Jackson had won more electoral votes.
- 1876: In another disputed election involving questions about the accuracy of the vote in three southern states, Rutherford B. Hayes was elected president, despite having lost the popular vote to Samuel Tilden by three percentage points.
- 1888: In an undisputed election, Grover Cleveland won a majority of popular votes but lost the electoral count to Benjamin Harrison.
- 2000: In the closest election of our time, George W. Bush narrowly prevailed in the Electoral College on the basis of a contested victory in Florida, despite finishing second in the national popular vote count (See: Demys-

tifying Government: The 2000 Election: What Happened?).

Not surprisingly, every time the popular vote and the electoral vote go in different directions, there's renewed call for Electoral College reform. However, if history is a guide, the odds aren't very good. Electoral College reform is a highly charged, big-stakes partisan issue; changing the rules will inevitably favor one side or the other and, quite possibly, could introduce unintended effects that everyone would be reluctant to face. The Twelfth Amendment is the only successful alteration to the process in over two hundred years and more than one thousand attempts.[24]

Also, consider that even if these aberrant outcomes produced challenges to the legitimacy of the eventual winner, they didn't create a legitimacy crisis for the system. There was even something of a self-correction involving the first three disputed winners: Each served only one term, in two cases (1824 and 1888) to be followed in office by the candidate they had "defeated" four years earlier.

Leading or Following?

As a linkage to the candidates who will become our public officials, political parties should be a vehicle for channeling our preferences to those who wish to lead us. The most important function they perform in this capacity is contesting elections. Whether parties carry out this function effectively in the electoral arena is a matter of some discussion. On one hand, through careful attention to public opinion polls and focus groups, candidates are acutely sensitive to political currents. But to what end? Is it leadership to listen to what people want and give it to them? Or does this amount to campaigning without principle?

Harry S Truman, who was president in an age before professional political consultants dominated campaigning, mused that he "wondered how far Moses would have gone if he had taken a poll in Egypt." The former president saw polls as interfering with the judgments politicians are hired to make, distinguishing *popular* decisions from *good*

DEMYSTIFYING GOVERNMENT

THE 2000 ELECTION: WHAT HAPPENED?

During the weeks leading up to the 2000 election, public opinion polls consistently showed a narrow preference for George W. Bush over Al Gore, with a fair number of undecided voters. A lot of people simply couldn't make up their mind. On election night, it turned out that the "undecideds" got it right.

We saw in Chapter 3 how, as the television anchors at ABC, CBS, NBC, CNN, and Fox sat in front of their wall-sized maps assigning blue states to Gore and red states to Bush, something unprecedented happened. On the basis of survey results conducted as people were leaving their polling places, the major television networks predicted that Gore was the winner in Florida. And Gore remained the Florida victor—for about an hour. Then, inexplicably, every network took it back, saying that as the actual votes were being counted, it appeared that Florida was in fact too close to call. As the evening progressed, the vote tally in Florida remained breath-takingly close. It soon became clear that Florida mattered because electoral votes in the rest of the states were breaking in such a way that the entire election would hinge on the Florida outcome.

In the early morning hours, the networks finally called Florida for Bush, and the state that hours before had been posted on the map in "Gore" blue was now "Bush" red. Gore called Bush to congratulate him. The election was over, and Bush had won.

For about forty-five minutes. As he was about to leave his motorcade to address his supporters, Gore received word that the final Florida tally showed him within a few hundred votes of Bush out of almost six million cast. Gore called Bush again to retract his concession. The networks reversed themselves—again. Americans woke up to the news that the 2000 election was too close to call. There would be a recount in Florida.

What followed can best be described as high-stakes political hardball by two campaigns that had been thrown into overtime by the Electoral College. Each assembled legal teams to contest voting irregularities and public relations teams to win a heated media war that would determine how long the public would tolerate political wrangling over the outcome. The Gore team tried to build sympathy by saying that time was needed to count every vote, while the Bush team—ahead in the original balloting—created pressure to limit the scope and length of the recount with the line that the votes had been counted and counted and counted again.

The legal battle played out on several fronts. There were questions about the clarity of the ballot in Palm Beach County, a booklet with a "butterfly" design bearing candidate names on both sides of a central column. Arrows from both sides of the booklet pointed to holes in the column that the voter was supposed to punch to register his or her choice. When it was revealed that conservative Reform Party candidate Pat Buchanan—whose name appeared opposite Gore on the ballot—received a disproportionate vote in this liberal county, the Gore team tried unsuccessfully to have those Buchanan votes reconsidered.

There were questions about voting rights, as civil liberties groups charged that thousands of African Americans had been prohibited from voting as the result of having been erroneously purged from the voter registration lists in a statewide effort to delete the names of felons. Because the "purge" was supervised by Katherine Harris, the Republican secretary of state with close ties to the Bush campaign, and because 93 percent of African Americans in

Florida voted for Gore, the issue immediately assumed political overtones.

In the end, the outcome came down to which votes would be recounted and under what guidelines. The Gore campaign jumped on the fact that there had been a disproportionately high percentage of "undervotes," or ballots indicating no presidential choice, in southern Florida counties that used punch-card voting. This makes sense, considering the stylus used for removing indented squares or chads in the ballot card sometimes doesn't make it all the way through.

Because these counties also went disproportionately for Gore, a struggle ensued over the terms of the recount. What if a chad is perforated but still hanging from the card? What if it is bulging but attached on all sides? What if it is simply dimpled? The Gore camp argued for the most liberal standards for recounting, while the Bush camp argued for consistent standards—a move that helped them win public support as the nation witnessed different counties performing manual ballot recounts using different rules for what constituted a vote.

Legal and public relations wrangling dragged into December. Ultimately, the matter was decided in court. The Florida Supreme Court agreed with Gore's argument that ballots that did not indicate a clear presidential choice should be recounted, noting that Florida law gives each county the responsibility of determining the intent of the voter. But a bitterly divided U.S. Supreme Court ruled differently.

In a 5-4 decision in *Bush v. Gore,* the Court upheld the legality of the recount but determined that it should be conducted under clear and consistent guidelines, an impossible task given the limited time before members of the Electoral College were constitutionally obligated to cast their votes. In effect, their ruling halted the recount in its tracks. Gore was out of legal options; Bush would become president.[17]

It's possible to draw all sorts of conclusions from the 2000 postelection spectacle. As with the disputed elections of 1824 and 1876, the political saga was bitter, but the system continued to function. The public relations methods used by both sides illustrated the importance of a strong media campaign to set the public agenda in order to create political momentum. The often-confusing actions of well-meaning election officials who tried to decipher the "intent of the voter" demonstrated how the apparently simple act of counting ballots is not as straightforward as we might think. Americans were exposed to a range of voting irregularities that are probably very common but usually go unnoticed because few elections of this magnitude have required looking at the balloting so closely.

Finally, the Florida recount experience said something about our political divisions at the turn of the millennium. It's striking to look at the final electoral vote map (see Figure 1, below) and see the stark regional divisions between the Gore states of the coasts and upper Midwest and the Bush states of the South, plains and mountain West. New Hampshire was the only northern state won by Bush; New Mexico, the only western interior state won by Gore—and both were decided by razor-thin margins. Essentially, the country divided along regional lines between Gore's message of activist government and social liberalism, and Bush's fiscal and social conservatism

The Electoral College results told us that we had essentially produced a tie. Eight years later, Barack Obama's victory, broad as it was, could nonetheless be understood in these regional terms. Obama carried all the Gore states plus New Hampshire, made inroads in the Rocky Mountain West and the more industrialized states of the South (Virginia, North Carolina, Florida), and swept the Midwest. But the imprint of the 2000 map that left the nation deadlocked could still be found in 2008.

decisions. The natural remedy for officials who make decisions that their constituents dislike is to vote them out of office. Yet, politicians may use public opinion polls to guide their actions so as to maximize their chances of staying in office, making it harder for elections to perform a corrective function. Perhaps this is as it should be, or perhaps it comes at the cost of establishing principled links between voters and officials.

Add to this the explosion in campaign spending, and you have another potential strain on the connections parties can supply voters. Campaign finance reforms designed to strengthen the bonds between individuals and candidates by maximizing the role of small individual contributions have been undermined by the soft-money loophole. As large contributions from wealthy individuals and organizations flood the political process, it's reasonable to ask how much political influence is returned in the bargain, and to what effect. A disproportionate share of campaign money goes to incumbents who can use it to create a lopsided advantage in reelection contests. Like polls that can be used by candidates to stake out safe and popular ground, big money flowing to incumbents can drain the competition from elections.

As we noted earlier, political money is channeled through PACs that operate on behalf of organized interests. In turn, organized interests are established to represent constituencies, functioning like parties as a linkage to government. How strong and effective is this connection, and how closely do interest groups represent the wishes of people like us? Is all that PAC money advancing the agendas of people who identify with and support interest groups, or is it largely serving an elite?

Chapter Review

One of the most important functions of political parties is competing in elections. Party nominees for all elected positions are selected in primaries or caucuses, depending on the state; presidential candidates enter a series of primaries and caucuses to win delegate support at the party's nominating convention. For many years, party elites selected presidential nominees at party conventions, but following 1968, a series of reforms instituted by the Democratic Party led to the proliferation of primaries and a shift away from elite control of the nominating process. Today, would-be nominees can secure enough delegates to win the nomination by competing in primaries, provided they can acquire enough resources—money, staff, and media attention—to remain viable.

Money is particularly critical for waging successful campaigns, and candidates typically spend years raising it. The 1974 Federal Election Campaign Act attempted to regulate campaign contributions, but a loophole permitted unlimited soft-money contributions. The McCain-Feingold Act was designed to close that loophole, but parties can still find ways to raise and spend large sums, and the 2010 Supreme Court ruling in *Citizens United v. Federal Election Commission* worked to undermine it.

A candidate emerges as the nominee by raising sufficient money and maintaining momentum through the primaries by meeting or beating performance expectations generated by reporters. Nominees are introduced to the country at a national convention that has largely become a media event, and organize a professional staff of campaign aides who, with the use of opinion polls and focus groups, develop a strategy for allocating the candidate's time and money. Strategies may include running negative commercials in order to undermine support for the candidate's opponent; in recent years, nominees have faced off in televised debates. Strategy is largely shaped by the demands of the Electoral College, which makes the presidential race a state-by-state endeavor. The candidate who wins a plurality of the popular vote in enough states to win a majority of the electoral vote becomes president.

Key Terms

caucus A method of candidate selection in which party identifiers gather in a series of meetings to select delegates to the national convention.

expectations The benchmark for how well a campaign needs to perform in presidential primaries in order to receive positive horserace coverage, based on reporter assessments of the campaign's viability.

faithless elector A member of the Electoral College who does not cast a vote for the plurality winner of the popular vote in his or her state.

Federal Election Campaign Act The 1974 act aimed at limiting the influence of big-money contributions on political campaigns.

Federal Election Commission (FEC) The federal regulatory agency that administers and enforces campaign finance laws.

focus groups A small group of voters chosen by a political campaign for their demographic similarities who are brought together to gauge how the group they represent feels about the candidate.

free media The news coverage that major candidates for high office can expect to receive on a regular basis. Although free, candidates cannot control the content of this coverage or guarantee that it will be favorable.

front-runner The presidential candidate who leads the primary horserace, based on media assessments of the campaign.

hard money Funds contributed directly to candidates or national parties by individuals or PACs for the purpose of electing candidates to federal office. Federal law regulates hard-money contributions.

long shot A presidential candidate who is not expected to fare well in the primary horserace, based on media assessments of the campaign.

McCain-Feingold Act The name commonly used to describe the Bipartisan Campaign Reform Act of 2002, which prohibits the use of soft money in federal elections in an attempt to close a loophole in the 1974 Federal Election Campaign Act.

McGovern-Fraser Commission The commission organized by the Democratic Party following its 1968 convention to democratize the process of delegate selection to party conventions.

media events Activities staged by campaigns or political officials that have enough news value to draw press attention to a message the politician wants to communicate.

momentum The ability of a presidential campaign to maintain viability by meeting or exceeding press-generated expectations during the long primary period.

name recognition An informal measure of how much the public is aware of a candidate or elected official, based on how widely people are able to identify who the candidate or official is.

nomination The official endorsement of a candidate by a political party, making that candidate the one whose name will appear on the ballot next to the party label in the next general election.

paid media Radio and television ads paid for and produced by political campaigns.

platform The official document produced at the major party conventions that serves as a philosophical and policy blueprint for the party's presidential nominee.

plurality Winning the most votes in an election, or at least one more vote than the next closest candidate or party.

political action committees (PACs) Organizations formed by interest groups such as labor unions, businesses, and ideological groups for the purpose of contributing money to political candidates.

popular vote The votes individuals cast in a presidential election. Technically, these are votes for a slate of electors representing the candidate. A candidate who wins a plurality of the popular vote in a state gets all the electoral votes allocated to that state.

primary A method of candidate selection in which party identifiers vote for the candidate who will run on the party label in the general election. In presidential primaries, voters select delegates to the national convention.

soft money Funds contributed to state and local parties or to national parties for the purpose of running state elections or conducting local "grassroots" political activity.

Resources

You might be interested in examining some of what the following authors have said about the topics we've been discussing:

Cramer, Richard Ben. *What It Takes: The Way to the White House.* New York: Random House, 1992. A firsthand account of the 1988 presidential contenders, written like a novel, that explores the character and motivation of those who roll the dice to enter the high-risk, marathon presidential sweepstakes.

DeClerico, Robert E., and James W. Davis. *Choosing Our Choices: Debating the Presidential Nominating Process.* Lanham, MD: Rowman & Littlefield, 2000. The pros and cons of the way we select our presidential nominees, with suggestions for how we might do it differently.

Michael Nelson, ed. *The Elections of 2008.* Washington, DC: CQ Press, 2009. The 2008 election was one for the history books, and this book examines it from a variety of perspectives.

Polsby, Nelson W., and Aaron Wildavsky. *Presidential Elections: Strategies and Structures of American Politics,* 12th ed. Lanham, MD: Rowman and Littlefield, 2007. A comprehensive overview of campaigns and elections.

Schumaker, Paul D., and Burdett A. Loomis, eds. *Choosing a President: The Electoral College and Beyond.* New York: Chatham House Publishers, 2002. Everything you would ever want to know about the Electoral College is contained in this thoughtful volume that emphasizes proposals for reform.

You may also be interested in looking at these resource sites:

To find out more about the Electoral College, you can go to http://www.archives.gov/federal-register/electoral-college.

The Green Papers estimate voting trends for 2008: http://www.thegreenpapers.com/P08.

Notes

1. Paul R. Abramson, John H. Aldrich, and David W. Rohde, *Continuity and Change in the 1996 and 1998 Elections* (Washington, DC: CQ Press, 1999), 16.
2. Federal Election Commission 2008 Presidential Primary Filing Dates, at http://www.fec.gov/pubrec/2008pdates.pdf.
3. Robert E. DiClerico and James W. Davis, *Choosing Our Choices: Debating the Presidential Nominating Process* (Lanham, MD: Rowman & Littlefield, 2000), 22.
4. Ibid., 3–6.
5. If you'd like to read more about what happened that August week in Chicago, CNN/Time offers a summary at http://www.cnn.eom/ALLPOLITICS/1996/conventions/chicago/facts/chicago68/index.shtml.
6. DiClerico and Davis, *Choosing Our Choices,* 28–29.
7. Ibid., 14–23.
8. Nelson W. Polsby and Aaron Wildavsky, *Presidential Elections,* 10th ed. (New York: Chatham House, 2000), 110–126.
9. Federal Election Commission website at http://www.fec.gov/pages/brochures/fecfeca.shtml#anchor263917.
10. DiClerico and Davis, *Choosing Our Choices,* 16–17.
11. Jose Antonio Vargas, "Obama Raised Haifa Billion Online," washingtonpost.com at: http://voices.washing-tonpost.com/44/2008/11/20/obama_raised_half_a_bi 11 ion_on.html.
12. For a sense of who has been giving the most soft money to candidates in recent years—and how much they give—return to the Center for Responsive Politics website, at http://www.opensecrets.org/bigpicture/ softtop.php?cycle=2002.

13. Center for Responsive Politics Statement on McCain-Feingold Decision, December 10, 2003.

14. Mike Gravel is a former Alaska senator who ran for the Democratic presidential nomination in 2008.

15. Polsby and Wildavsky, *Presidential Elections,* 10th ed., 99–101.

16. Ibid., 100.

17. Ibid., 101.

18. Matthew R. Kerbel, "The Media: Old Frames in a Time of Transition," in Michael Nelson, ed., *The Elections of 2000* (Washington, DC: CQ Press, 2001), 109–132.

19. Polsby and Wildavsky, *Presidential Elections,* 10th ed., 109–110.

20. Paul S. Herrnson, "National Party Organizations at the Dawn of the Twenty-First Century," in L. Sandy Maisel, ed., *The Parties Respond,* 4th ed. (Boulder, CO: Westview Press, 2002), 19–46.

21. Ibid., 178.

22. Ibid., 190–193.

23. Donald Lutz, "The Electoral College in Historical and Philosophical Perspective," in Paul D. Schumaker and Burdett A. Loomis, eds., *Choosing a President* (New York: Chatham House Publishers, 2002), 31–51.

24. Ibid.

Table, Figure and Box Notes

T1 Opensecrets.org, at http://www.opensecrets.org/pres08/calendar.php.

T2 Photo courtesy Columbia University.

T3 Center for Responsive Politics, at http://www.opensecrets.org/.

T4 Federal Election Commission, at http://www.fec.gov/pages/brochures/contrib.shtml#Chart%23Chart.

T5 Data from Nelson W. Polsby and Aaron Wildavsky, *Presidential Elections,* 10th ed. (New York: Chatham House Publishers, 2000), 55.

T6 See Matthew R. Kerbel, *Netroots: Online Progressives and the Transformation of American Politics* (Boulder, CO: Paradigm Publishers, 2009), 137–143.

T7 *Bush v. Core,* 531 U.S. 98 (2000).

T8 Map courtesy Federal Election Commission at http://www.fec.gov/pubrec/fe2000/elecvotemap.htm.

CHAPTER 11

Public Opinion

Chapter 11 Vignette

By Jennifer Byrne

You were recently introduced to an influential figure named Nate Silver. While there is some controversy regarding Nate Silver's election forecasts, you are about to meet an even more controversial figure named Edward Joseph Snowden. While Nate Silver might have some detractors that label him as an ideologue, the reaction to Snowden is much more complex and divisive with some people labeling him a hero and a whistle blower, while others call him a dissident and at the extreme, a traitor. So, what has Snowden done to acquire such praise and such censure?

Snowden is an exiled computer specialist, former CIA employee, and National Security Agency (NSA) contractor. He was charged with espionage and theft of government property after he disclosed details of the U.S. and Britain's mass surveillance program. He first contacted journalist Glenn Greenwald at the Guardian, but then moved on to documentary filmmaker, Laura Poitras, after Greenwald refused to communicate via encrypted emails.[1] Snowden released classified information to the press about the existence of several surveillance programs, including sensitive and detailed blueprints of how the NSA operates these programs. The release of the this information violated the clearance protocol of Snowden's employment, but also stirred up tensions between the U.S. and the international community as some of his released information documented that the U.S. has spied on other countries, including its allies. Although at first anonymous, Snowden's identity was made public at his own request. He contends that he has nothing to hide and has done nothing wrong; he claims that his sole motivation for releasing the classified information was that he did not want to live in a world where everything was recorded. He claims that these programs should be illegal under Article 12 of the Universal Declaration of Human Rights, and under the 4th and 5th amendments to the U.S. Constitution. Snowden fled to Hong Kong before the stories were published, and has now been granted temporary asylum in Russia. His U.S. passport has been revoked. Snowden has described himself as a whistle-blower, has cited civil disobedience theory to justify his actions, and has called on others to be emboldened to take action in reporting wrongdoings.[2] Snowden's actions, though controversial, have raised some questions about the scope of the government's involvement in the private conversations of its own citizens and people around the world, and has caused Americans to rethink the trade-off between security concerns and civil liberties.

A recent Quinnipiac poll found a significant shift in American public opinion on the balance between civil liberties and security; 40% of Americans still believe that the government has not gone far enough to adequately protect the country. The poll also indicates that 45 percent of Americans are concerned that the government has gone too far in restricting individual civil liberties. In a 2010 poll, results showed a clear emphasis in favor of government taking the necessary measures to protect the country against terrorism, even at the expense of individual liberty with only 25 percent of Americans feeling that the government had overstepped its mandate. There may also be an ideological battle embedded in the new poll numbers, as this change of opinion was most noticeable among the Republican demographic. In 2010, 72 percent of Republicans agreed that the government had not gone far enough to adequately protect the country; this number has recently dropped to 46 percent. These numbers may suggest that Republicans are unhappy with President Obama's security policies or reflect some aspect of partisan politics; however, it may also indicate a sense of discontent due to the recent disclosure of the NSA surveillance programs. A more recent Quinnipiac poll found considerable sympathetic sentiment toward Mr. Snowden, with 55 percent of respondents describing him as a whistle-blower and only 35 percent labeling him a traitor to his country. The question only focused on Mr. Snowden's release of domestic information and not the international spying that garnered much negative attention for the U.S. in late 2013. In the aftermath of legislation such as the Patriot Act, for whatever reason, Americans are becoming more cautious of government overreach in the name of security. A Fox News poll highlights some of these trends:

Fox News Poll:

"Would you be willing to give up some of your personal freedom in order to reduce the threat of terrorism?"

Date	Yes	No	Net
August 1996	60%	30%	30
May 2001	33	40	-7
October 2001	71	20	51
June 2002	64	21	43
September 2002	61	24	37
July 2005	64	21	43
January 2006	61	27	34
May 2006	54	36	18
April 2013	43	45	-2

Below are two political cartoons that illustrate the conversation about Snowden and his actions. How do the messages of the artists reflect or contradict the opinion polls discussed here?

Endnotes

1. http://www.nytimes.com/2013/08/18/magazine/laura-poitras-snowden.html?pagewanted=all&_r=0, last accessed on November 14, 2013.
2. http://america.aljazeera.com/articles/multimedia/timeline-edward-snowden-revelations.html, last accessed on November 14, 2013.

Public Opinion

What Is It and What Does It Have to Do with Me?

By Matthew Kerbel

Introduction

D id you know that more than two in three Americans have a favorable impression of Britain's Queen Elizabeth?[1] That 16 percent of the U.S. population is actively disengaged at work?[2] That 32 percent of Americans say figure skating is their favorite Olympic sport while only 3 percent prefer luge?[3] How do we know this? *Why* do we know this? Why do we *want* to know this?

We know these and many other details about our society because we have at our disposal the means to gather information about **public opinion**—information that tells us what people think in matters relating to politics and society. We gather information about public opinion because it's of interest to lots of different groups—corporations looking for the best way to market a product, elected officials concerned with how their actions are being perceived by voters, and even political scientists who want to learn more about how government works.

We're not likely to be interested in everything there is to know about public opinion, but there's a highly attentive audience for every bit of information that's gathered. Maybe you find the high level of disengagement in the American workplace

to be little more than an interesting factoid, but it could be valuable information to a corporation looking to boost its productivity. Perhaps you could live a contented life never knowing that Americans prefer figure skating to luge, but if you're an NBC television executive looking to maximize the size of the audience for the Olympics, this small kernel of public opinion is a golden nugget.

Public opinion about politics encompasses a range of things—from what people know and understand about what's going on in Washington, D.C. or in their state capitals, to what people think government should and should not do, to how people evaluate the job elected officials are doing, and more. Public opinion in a representative democracy is a two-way street: It's the basis for officials to understand public concerns and for the public to gauge official actions.

Collecting public opinion is an **empirical** enterprise, in that it's based on systematic, scientific measurement of opinions. But the substance of public opinion has an important **normative** component. Public opinion measures the values people place on such things as the characteristics people desire in politicians or the policies people say government should pursue.

Before we look at the particulars of public opinion, there are a few things we

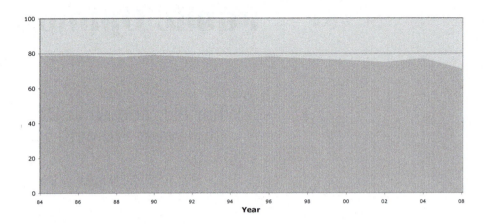

Figure 21.1. Percentage of Americans Saying Religion Is an Important Part of Life, 1984–2008[T1]

could consider about its structure. At its most basic, public opinion often has a "thumbs up" or "thumbs down" quality. We tend to think that Congress is either doing a good job or a bad job. In other words, public opinion is **directional**—it can be positive or negative. We can think of this as an expression of people's preferences—good or bad, hot or cold—about a candidate for office, the performance of the president, or a policy idea that's being batted around in Congress. When we said that 68 percent of Americans have a favorable impression of Queen Elizabeth, we were making a statement about the direction of public opinion. The simplicity of positive and negative expressions allows us to get a quick sense of where the nation stands collectively on important political matters.

Public opinion is also characterized by **intensity**, by how deeply or strongly an opinion is held. If you're capable of living a happy and satisfied existence without thinking about which Olympic sport is your favorite, we'd say you have a low intensity of feeling about the issue. You may have an opinion, of course, but it wouldn't be a deeply held one. Many issues that surface in American politics are low-intensity issues.

A good example is campaign finance reform, or whether changes should be made to the way candidates for office raise money. For many years, Americans have generally supported the idea of campaign finance reform, meaning the direction of opinion on the issue was positive. At the same time, Americans ranked it as a low-level concern,

meaning that they didn't feel strongly about it. Not coincidently, without intense public support for change, it took Congress years to seriously consider meaningful campaign reform legislation.

High-intensity issues tend to be ones that hit home for people. They can be bread-and-butter economic issues, like whether President Obama should have pursued a stimulus package in an attempt to mitigate the effects of the severe recession we were experiencing when he took office in 2009; fundamental foreign policy issues, like whether the United States should have gone to war with Iraq; or social issues with personal or moral ramifications, like whether gay couples should be allowed to marry. Beyond issues like these, Americans typically have lots of opinions, but few strong opinions.

Finally, public opinion is fluid. People change their minds about things. Circumstances change, causing people to assess situations differently, which is why it is common for public opinion on the president's job performance to fluctuate widely over the course of an administration. This speaks to the **stability** of public opinion, or changes in the direction of public support for an official, candidate, institution, or policy. When opinions are less intensely held, they are susceptible to large swings.

Let's look at two figures that contrast stable public opinion with unstable public opinion. Figure 21.1 is an example of stable public opinion. Notice that most Americans consider religion to be an important part of life at a level that's virtually unchanged

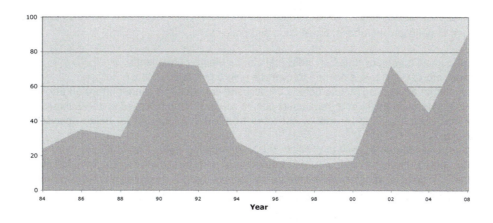

Figure 21.2. Percentage of Americans Saying the U.S. Economy is Getting Worse, 1988–2008[T2]

between 1984 and 2004, and only slightly lower in 2008.

Now look at Figure 21.2, which measures public opinion about whether the economy of the United States had gotten worse during the previous year. Look at how the figure jumps around, as economic conditions varied wildly during the past two decades. The peaks in the figure track the recessions that occurred at the start of the 1990s and the 2000s, with the largest peak coinciding with the "Great Recession" of 2008.

The direction, intensity, and stability of public opinion combine to create a barometer of where

Americans stand on political issues as time passes. An example of how these factors interact—one with real implications for politics—may be found in patterns of public approval of the job performance of the president, which invariably declines over time after the high hopes and expectations of a new president's first days. Figure 21.3 shows the decline in President Obama's job approval ratings as measured by the Gallup Poll. Immediately after Inauguration Day in 2009, the new president had the support of 68% of Americans. A few months later, after engaging in an activist agenda that would prove controversial in some quarters and

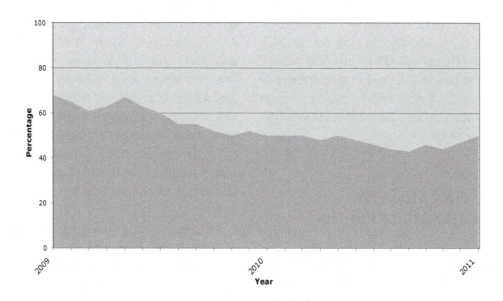

Figure 21.3. Approval of President Obama's Job Performance, 2009–2011[T3]

Table 21.1. A Quick Political Knowledge Quiz[T4]

Test your knowledge of political institutions, processes, and policies:

1. Do you happen to know how many times an individual can be elected president?
2. What percentage vote of Congress is needed to override a veto by the president?
3. True or False: A district attorney's job is to defend an accused criminal who cannot afford an attorney.
4. True or False: Every decision made by a state court can be re-viewed and reversed by the Supreme Court.
5. True or False: The Social Security tax money collected from an individual is set aside specifically for that person's retirement benefits.
6. Yes or No: Is the United States a member of NATO, the North Atlantic Treaty Organization?
7. Do you think the United States has to import oil to meet our needs, or do we produce as much oil as we need?
8. According to the U.S. census, approximately what percentage of the U.S. population is African American?

Answers:

1. Twice (percentage answering correctly in 1990: 73)
2. Two-thirds (percentage answering correctly in 1985: 63)
3. False (percentage answering correctly in 1983: 47)
4. False (percentage answering correctly in 1983: 11)
5. False (percentage answering correctly in 1981: 75)
6. Yes (percentage answering correctly in 1989: 60)
7. Has to import oil (percentage answering correctly in 1991: 51)
8. Thirteen percent (percentage answering correctly in 1990: 17)

with the unemployment rate remaining high, the new president saw his job approval ratings sag toward and then slightly below the 50% mark, where they would stay for the better part of Obama's second year in office.

Changes in opinions of President George W. Bush over the course of his eight years in office were even more dramatic, and provide a good example of how variable, shallow, and unstable opinions can be. Immediately following the September 11, 2001 terrorist attacks, President Bush had the approval of almost the entire country, topping out at 92% support in early October 2001 in the ABC News/Washington Post poll. In the days immediately prior to the election of Barack Obama to be his successor, Bush's job approval was 23 percent in the same poll, close to an all time low.

How Much Do We Know About Politics?

One component of public opinion is political knowledge—what we know about how government is structured, the policies it considers or carries out, and who serves in or is running for elected office. Let's take a quick quiz to see how your knowledge

of a few political items compares to what Americans as a whole know.

A few years ago, researchers Michael X. Delli Carpini and Scott Keeter took a comprehensive look at levels of political knowledge in America over the past fifty years. Table 21.1 on the next page shows a few of the questions they included in their study. Take a look and try to answer them to the best of your ability.

So, how did you do? If you missed some of these questions, don't feel bad. You're in good company. As you can see, some of these questions were answered correctly by large numbers of people, whereas others were correctly answered by only a few. As Delli Carpini and Keeter found, most people retain some political knowledge and some people have large reserves of political information, but many people are quite limited in what they know about politics. Some of us are totally lacking in knowledge of our political institutions and political policies.[4]

People who are capable of rattling off the names of the starting pitchers on their hometown baseball team may be at a loss to recall the names of their U.S. senators. People who can readily identify Oprah Winfrey or Elton John may go blank trying to place Ken Salazar.[5] For many of us it's a matter of priorities. Americans simply do not make politics a main concern.

This is not a new story. Low levels of political knowledge have characterized American public opinion for as long as anyone can remember. Delli Carpini and Keeter found that levels of political knowledge are essentially unchanged from what they were over a half century ago. Their findings reinforce a study of political knowledge that was conducted sixty years ago, when three researchers named Bernard Berelson, Paul Lazarsfeld, and William McPhee set out to understand how people made up their minds when they voted in the 1948 presidential election. Their study included a look at how much voters knew about the issue positions of the candidates. The answer: like today, not very much. Only about one in three voters had an accurate perception of the candidates' positions on major issues.

If you think for a second about the sources of political information we have today that didn't exist in 1948—or 1968 or 1988—the stability in our lack of political knowledge is noteworthy. We've lived through an information explosion since you were born, featuring twenty-four-hour cable news services, live television coverage of Congress, newspapers with websites, weblogs—all sorts of facts and opinions conveniently available like never before. Yet, our low levels of political knowledge remain unshaken.

One explanation is that it's simply difficult to learn new information or to be motivated to learn new information. Another explanation is that it's possible to be exposed to too much information—to find the noise and chatter of twenty-four-hour news overwhelming and to tune it out. A variation on this explanation is that it can be hard to make sense of the information we get, to put it together in a meaningful way, even to decipher what's truthful and what is not. A fairly widespread example of this phenomenon is discussed in Demystifying Government: More Information, Less Knowledge

On the face of it, having a nation of people who don't know much about politics seems at odds with the underlying assumptions of a representative democracy that the Federalists advocated during the battle over ratification of the Constitution. After all, to have an effective democratic republic, it follows that those who elect representatives should have some knowledge of what they stand for, so there can be a meaningful connection between representative and represented. It makes sense that information is an important resource for connecting our interests to the actions of our representatives, to make sure they're acting according to our wishes. As Berelson and his colleagues put it:

> The democratic citizen is supposed to be well informed about political affairs. He is supposed to know what the issues are, what their history is, what the relevant facts are, what alternatives are proposed, what the party stands for, what the likely consequences are. By such standards, the voter falls short. Even when he has the motivation, he finds it difficult to make decisions on the basis of full information when the subject is relatively simple and proximate; how can he do so when it is complex and remote?[6]

Is democracy compromised if our political knowledge is far less than what democratic theorists suggest is necessary for us to be able to make complex political decisions? Berelson and company do not believe so. No place is political knowledge more important than in the decisions Americans make in the voting booth, but people are able to make those decisions all the time without detailed knowledge of the candidates or issues. As we'll see in Chapter 4, people use all kinds of shorthand methods to figure out how to vote. While levels of political knowledge in America may fall short of what John Locke would have found desirable, the argument can be made that the political process survives just fine without highly informed citizens.

Or does it? Here's another view: Delli Carpini and Keeter say that whites, males, older people, and financially well-off individuals tend to know more about politics than blacks, women, young people, and people with low incomes. Since informed people are better able to identify what they want from the political system, people who already have economic and social advantages may

DEMYSTIFYING GOVERNMENT

MORE INFORMATION, LESS KNOWLEDGE

Berelson, Lazarsfeld, and McPhee's study of how people decide to vote found that knowledge of election issues and correct understanding of candidate positions on major issues was higher among those who paid close attention to media reports. This suggests that people who watch or read the news more often are likely to acquire more political information.

But how do we know that the information we're getting is entirely accurate?

News reports seem very authoritative when they're delivered by well-groomed anchors on television or when they appear in sharp print in the newspaper or on your screen. The problem is, in a media environment dominated by 24/7 cable news, talk radio and the Internet, misinformation can spread quickly. So, when something comes along that's misleading, it can be hard to spot, even if we know not to believe everything we see or read.

Here's an example. In 2009, the Obama administration and Congress were debating the details of overhauling the health care system. It was a huge and complex task, and a controversial one. Throughout the summer and fall of that year, news reports were filled with stories about the politics of the effort, which included discussion of various proposals for how the health care plan would operate. As is often the case in a fluid political situation, the specifics changed a lot as the president tried to put together enough votes to get some version of a health care plan through Congress. This made the health care story complicated to report and difficult to keep straight.

The situation was ideal for the spread of misinformation, and in fact opinion polls taken in mid-2009 revealed a great deal of confusion—and concern—about what Congress was doing. One of the most celebrated untruths about the plan was that it would ration care through a government board that would determine the worthiness of a patient's health care claims and deny expensive care to the very sick and the elderly. Such so-called "death panels" became a topic of widespread discussion in the summer of 2009, in part because prominent reform opponents like former Alaska Governor Sarah Palin and former House Speaker Newt Gingrich implied the claims were true.

Politifact.com, a fact-checking project of the St. Petersberg *Times,* examined the "death panel" claims and found them to be emphatically false. The foundation of the claim was that the government planned to save money by rationing care, which would be done through a panel of bureaucrats who would decide who was worthy of getting treatment. The truth behind this charge is a lot more complicated, and difficult to fit into a brief television news story, Facebook post, or tweet.

According to Politifact, the plan under consideration by Congress proposed subsidizing optional doctor visits for seniors receiving assistance from the government program Medicare to discuss living wills and other end-of-life treatments. It also proposed the creation of a government board to examine research on effective medical outcomes to improve diagnosis and treatment. And while the board could give guidance on such things as end-of-life care, it couldn't mandate or withhold it.[T5]

Politifact concluded there was no truth to Governor Palin's claim that a panel of bureaucrats would be able to determine who was worthy of receiving health care, saying it "sounds more like a science fiction movie ('Soylent Green,' anyone?) than part of an actual bill before Congress."[T6] But most people do not spend time browsing political fact-checking websites.

We can be surrounded by information and still be uninformed. If we were concerned about government getting too involved in something as personal and as important as our relationship with our doctors, we might take seriously a claim that Congress was going to interfere with that relationship, especially if the claim was discussed frequently in the press, finding ourselves with more information—but less knowledge.

be better positioned to get the political system to respond to them. From this perspective, there is an "information elite" whose control of an important resource—information—gives it political power, while the lack of political knowledge serves as a detriment to those who need it the most.

Political Attitudes: From the Heart

If political knowledge is scarce in the population, political attitudes—another component of public opinion—are commonplace. People have attitudes about all sorts of things. **Attitudes** tap how people feel about politics or how people are oriented to political figures, institutions, issues, or events. Like any feeling, attitudes are something people experience; they cannot be right or wrong in a normative sense. Maybe you have an attitude about New Age music: You hate it, love it, or just don't get it. Or maybe you couldn't care less. That's an attitude too. There's nothing inherently wrong or right about any of these positions—they're just how you feel. Political attitudes work the same way.

We have attitudes about a wide range of things. Let's look at a few and see how our attitudes compare with others in our class, and with the nation as a whole. We'll consider our attitudes toward big government, levels of trust we place in government, political efficacy, and tolerance of diversity.

Big Government

The debate over how large and strong the federal government should be continues to divide people as much now as it did two hundred years ago. Table 21.2 contains a question pertaining to the matter of government power that has appeared for many years in the National Election Studies (NES), a major survey of American public opinion. Take a minute to think about the question and decide what option best reflects your attitude.

Many people responding to the NES survey had no opinion on this matter. But among those who did, age-old concerns about a strong federal government are apparent in contemporary attitudes. More than twice as many people who had an opinion on

Table 21.2. Big Government

Some people are afraid the government in Washington is getting too powerful for the good of the country and the individual person. Others feel that the government in Washington is not getting too strong. What is your feeling?

> Government is getting too powerful
>
> Government is not too strong
>
> Don't know/no opinion

NATIONAL RESULTS

Thirty-nine percent of respondents felt that government is getting too powerful, while 17 percent answered that government is not too strong. The majority, 44 percent, did not know or had no opinion.

Source: 2000 National Election Study[T7]

the matter expressed concern that government was becoming excessively powerful.

Although the percentage of Americans voicing this sentiment has bounced between 30 and 50 percent over the past forty years, you have to go back to 1970 to find the last time a greater percentage of people had the attitude that government was not too strong. In recent times, concerns about the power of government reached their peak in the mid to late 1970s, in the aftermath of the abuses of power that characterized the Watergate scandal. This trend is displayed in Figure 21.4.

Even when unease about abuses of power began to abate in the 1980s, a large percentage of Americans continued to feel that government was too strong. This is a reflection of how concerns about government creeping too far into daily life are both deeply rooted in American history and a prominent part of how Americans experience government. Perhaps the opinions of your classmates reflect this attitude as well.

It is also the case that not all groups of Americans share the same degree of concern about the power of the federal government. Take a close look at how men and women differ in their attitudes toward government by revisiting the gender statistics in Figure

20.4. The top line tracks the percentage of men who since 1964 have expressed the opinion that government is too strong; the bottom line does the same for women. Notice how for both women and men the level of concern about government moves up and down with the overall pattern, but at every point women express less concern than men about government encroachment on their personal lives.

One way of understanding this difference is to think of it in terms of the policies government produces and the way they're received by men and women. Women as a group tend to be receptive to policies that assist the poor, minorities, and the poorly educated, while men are more likely to question whether these are appropriate things for government to be doing—or whether the fact that government involvement in policies such as these is a sign that government is doing too much.

We see an even more striking version of this when we look at racial differences. Look at the racial statistics in Figure 21.4, and notice how nonwhites are far less likely to be concerned about the power of government than whites. Again, this difference may be explained by the tendency for nonwhites as a group to be more receptive than whites to the idea of a strong central government.

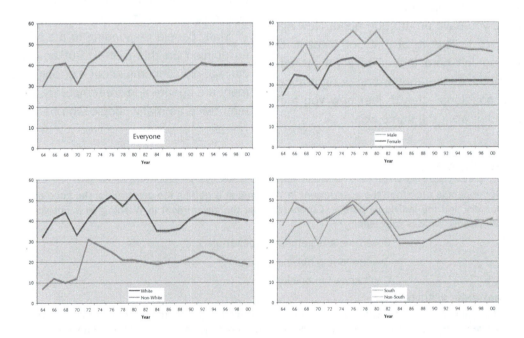

Figure 21.4. Percentage of Americans Who Feel Government Is Too Powerful, 1964–2000[T8]

When we look at regional differences, a less stable pattern of public opinion emerges. Review the regional statistics shown in Figure 20.4. You'll see two lines—one tracking opinion among southerners, the other tracking opinion among people living elsewhere in the country. Traditionally, the South has been highly sensitive to federal power. As we saw in Chapter 2, southern states were the strongest early advocates of **state-centered federalism,** seceded from the Union prior to the Civil War, and were reconstructed after the war under federal authority. More recently, in the 1950s and 1960s, the federal government was responsible for desegregating the South through policies that some white southerners regarded as excessive use of government power.

Not surprisingly, during the 1960s, southerners were more likely than others to feel that the federal government was too powerful. Then something interesting happened in the 1970s. As the era of dramatic policy changes stemming from the civil rights movement began to wind down, attitudes about government power began to change as well. By 1972, regional differences virtually disappeared. In recent years, southerners have even been incrementally less likely than others to express the opinion that the government is too powerful. As circumstances change, attitudes often follow.

Trust in Government

When your political history is infused with strong doubts about centralized authority, you might expect people to be somewhat hesitant to place their trust willingly in government. When we look at how much trust Americans place in the federal government to do what's right, we in fact find an undercurrent of doubt—not enough to bring our support for the institutions of government into question, but doubt nonetheless. Although only a tiny fraction of Americans feel their government never does the right thing, a majority feels it does the right thing only some of the time. And only 4 percent feel that government just about always gets it right.

In Table 21.3, you'll find another question from the National Election Studies, this one pertaining to the matter of trust in government.

Like opinions about government power, there has been a great deal of change over the years in this attitude as well, suggesting that Americans are not entirely predisposed to skepticism and that events can affect our disposition. Over the past several decades, the degree of trust we've placed in government has tracked very closely with the actions of prominent government officials, most notably the president. Figure 21.5 demonstrates how the amount of trust we've placed in government has taken a roller-coaster ride since 1958.

Back in the late 1950s and early 1960s, trusting government was almost a unanimous sentiment.

Table 21.3. Trust in Government

How much of the time do you think you can trust the government in Washington to do what is right—just about always, most of the time, only some of the time, or none of the time?

Just about always

Most of the time

Only some of the time

None of the time

Don't know/no opinion

NATIONAL RESULTS
Fifty-two percent of respondents felt that government could be trusted to do what was right only some of the time, while 43 percent agreed that government could be trusted to do what was right most of the time. Four percent answered that this was true just about always, while 1 percent felt it was true none of the time.

Source: 2000 National Election Study[T9]

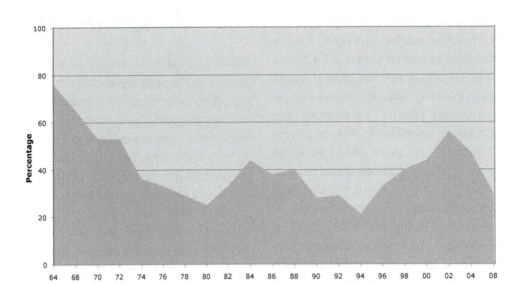

Figure 21.5. Percentage of Americans Who Always or Usually Trust Government to Do What Is Right, 1964–2008[T10]

That was a lifetime ago, before the Vietnam War and Watergate drained the well of universal trust. As the United States became deeply entrenched in Vietnam, the administration of President Lyndon Johnson purposely misrepresented the extent and likely duration of the war. His successor, Richard Nixon, assumed Johnson's misleading approach to Vietnam, then fell from office as a result of the Watergate scandal, during which he obstructed justice and concealed illegal activities. Gradually, Americans began to feel that their leaders were deceiving them as a matter of policy, and trust in government dropped accordingly—from a high of 76 percent in 1964 to only 36 percent by 1974.

And trust continued to fall. President Gerald Ford pardoned Nixon for his role in Watergate, which at the time was widely regarded as a move that sheltered Nixon from accountability. President Jimmy Carter presided over what many considered a hapless administration characterized by a sour economy and frustration overseas. By the end of Carter's term in 1980, only one-quarter of Americans felt they could trust government to generally do what is right.

Feelings of trust recovered during the Reagan administration, but hardly to the optimistic levels reached in the early 1960s, then dropped again in the wake of widespread disappointment with

President Bush (senior). In 1994, President Bill Clinton unsuccessfully attempted to make government more responsible for providing health care—after running as a moderate who downplayed the desire to create more government programs—and trust in government crashed to its modern-day low. Trust in government was buffeted again during the Clinton impeachment proceedings. During the fast economic times of the late 1990s, though, trust recovered to the modest levels of the Reagan years, peaking after the 2001 terrorist attacks then declining through the last years of the Bush administration.

The amount of confidence we have in the major institutions of government is consistent with our feelings of trust. In what may be a case of familiarity breeding a bit of contempt, the two branches of government elected by the people—Congress and the presidency—are less trusted than the Supreme Court. Between one-quarter and one-third of Americans place hardly any trust in these two branches, while only about one in six have a great deal of trust in Congress and one in five in the presidency. The figures for the Supreme Court, although more distant and unfamiliar to many people, are the mirror image of this, with about one-third of

Americans expressing trust in the Court and only 15 percent expressing distrust.

Overall, though, public trust—even in the Supreme Court—is low and ranks below nongovernmental figures like scientists and doctors (see Figure 21.6).

Another interpretation of what's happened since the early 1960s is that Americans have become more cynical about government. **Cynicism** is a pervasive feeling of mistrust or suspicion, and can be distinguished from skepticism, which is having doubts or wanting proof before believing something. Skepticism offers the possibility of acceptance when one's doubts are satisfied, but cynicism holds no such promise. Skepticism is captured in Missouri's nickname—the "Show-Me" state: Prove it to me before you ask me to believe you. Cynicism is expressed when someone rolls their eyes, looks at the sky, and says, "whatever."

The distinction is important because cynicism and skepticism can generate entirely different reactions to politics. We can be skeptical but still be engaged in the political process. It's probably fair to say that many of the framers of the Constitution were skeptical about creating a strong central government, but their reaction was to attempt to create a system that kept government under control. If they had been cynics, it's doubtful that they would even have tried.

When we're suspicious of something, we tend to withdraw from it or at least search for evidence to validate our suspicions. If we're cynical about government, we may find ourselves pointing out things we don't like about politicians or what they do, and using this as justification for feeling cynical. Or we might just withdraw from politics entirely. Of course, if we do that, we're leaving the system to others who will engage it to advance their interests.

Efficacy

The flip side of cynicism is **efficacy**, or the sense that you can get results from the political system if

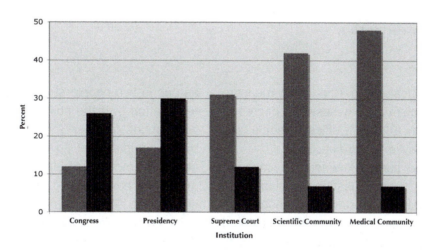

Figure 21.6. Percentage of Americans Expressing High and Low Levels of Confidence in Key Institutions, 2004[T11]. The red bars indicate the percentage of people who have a great deal of confidence in the listed institution, while the blue bars show the percentage who have hardly any confidence. The degree of confidence—or lack thereof—that have in Congress and the presidency is quite similar. About twice as many people have hardly any confidence in the two branches as have a great deal of confidence in them. The Supreme Court is the only branch of government with more supporters than doubters. In contrast, other social institutions command public confidence. Scientists generate fairly widespread feelings of confidence and only have a smattering of detractors. The medical community is comparable to the scientific community.

Table 20.4. Efficacy

Sometimes politics and government seem so complicated that a person like me can't really understand what's going on.
Agree
Disagree
Neither
Don't know/no opinion

NATIONAL RESULTS
Sixty percent of respondents agreed with this statement, 32 percent disagreed with it, and 7 percent neither agreed nor disagreed.

Public officials don't care much about what people like me think.
Agree
Disagree
Neither
Don't know/no opinion

NATIONAL RESULTS
Fifty-six percent of respondents agreed with this statement, 33 percent disagreed with it, and 10 percent neither agreed nor disagreed.

People like me don't have any say about what the government does.
Agree
Disagree
Neither
Don't know/no opinion

NATIONAL RESULTS
Forty-one percent of respondents agreed with this statement, 50 percent disagreed with it, and 9 percent neither agreed nor disagreed.

Source: 2000 National Election Study[T12]

you engage in political action. One way to measure the extent of cynicism is to assess the degree of efficacy people feel. The more efficacy people feel, the less cynical they're likely to be.

Efficacy can be hard to measure because it can be difficult for survey questions to distinguish someone who feels the system isn't responding to them from someone who feels totally alienated from government. For this reason, we'll approach efficacy from several directions by using three National Election Study questions (see Table 21.4) to determine how efficacious you feel.

As you can tell, there are limits to the degree of efficacy many people feel. Six in ten find politics to be too complicated to really understand, and only slightly fewer feel that public officials don't care much about what ordinary people think. However, these sentiments do not fully extend to attitudes about having a say over what government does,

as one in two people still feel they have some determination over the political results they get from government. In other words, many are confounded by the complexity of government and have doubts about the motives of elected officials, but not as many feel powerless to control what government does.

When we take a little closer look at this situation, something interesting pops out of the data. The degree of efficacy people feel turns out to have a lot to do with their social and economic situation, as captured by their level of education and income. You can see this by looking at how people with different levels of education and income responded to the three NES questions you just answered. See Figure 21.7.

Figure 21.7 makes it pretty clear that people with less education and income have less efficacy. There are striking attitude differences

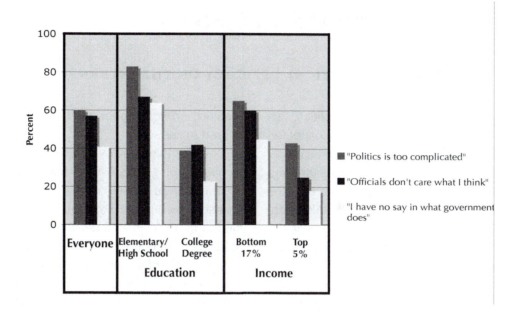

Figure 21.7. Different Perspectives on Efficacy[T13]

between the wealthiest or most educated people and the poorest or least educated people. For instance, 83 percent of people whose education falls short of a high school diploma find politics too complicated. That figure falls to 56 percent in your group—people with some college education—and drops even further to 39 percent among college graduates and people with postgraduate education. Accordingly, almost three of four high school dropouts feel they have no say in what government does, compared to less than one in four college graduates.

This suggests a relationship between having command of the kind of information and skills that come with formal education and the feelings we develop about our place in the political system. It makes sense that if something like government feels complicated because we don't understand it, we're probably not going to give it a big place in our lives. It also follows that people would feel disconnected from government if they don't understand it, and feel that elected officials don't care about them and that what they say doesn't matter. Even if formal education doesn't entail formal education about government—think of your friends who avoid taking courses in political science!—the skills that come with higher education can produce a sense

of confidence that's associated with feeling efficacious about government.

The income figures tell a similar story, possibly with an important wrinkle for who gets what, when, and how. Look at the responses people give to the question about having a say about what government does. Almost half the people in the bottom one-sixth of the income scale feel they have no say politically. Only 18 percent of the wealthiest Americans feel this way. It can make you wonder whether wealthy people feel more efficacy toward government because government really is responding to their interests with greater regularity.

Of course, if having information fuels empowerment, the Internet—which promises access to information and easy ways to link to other people—may offer a new way of building efficacy. Levels of efficacy remained low during the time when television dominated our politics, but there is some evidence that the Internet may offer an alternative to people who are interested in connecting with others through politics. Demystifying Government: Building Political Efficacy on the Internet explores this possibility by looking at two Internet-based presidential campaigns: the 2008 Obama campaign, and the unsuccessful but instructive effort by Howard Dean four years earlier.

DEMYSTIFYING GOVERNMENT

BUILDING POLITICAL EFFICACY ON THE INTERNET

When people feel cynical about politics, it's partly a consequence of feeling disconnected from a political community. It's easy to be disbelieving of political figures who seem distant and detached, and even though the United States is connected electronically through television, overall levels of cynicism have grown over the years since television became a central feature in our lives. Television has not proven to build efficacy, and may, in fact, undermine it by creating a false connection to others that does not provide the nourishment of the real thing.[T15]

Although still an adolescent medium compared to television, there is some reason to believe that the Internet may work in the opposite direction, building efficacy by building community. The first signs of this possibility appeared during the 2004 election cycle, when Democratic presidential candidate Howard Dean became the first political figure to test the potential of the Internet to bring people into the political process. Defying conventional wisdom that campaigns should be run on a top-down basis, the once-anonymous former Vermont governor built a viable political following by bringing people together online and listening to their suggestions for how to run his campaign.

Tapping into a nation that had become increasingly comfortable with the Internet, the Dean campaign created a space where supporters could interact virtually through weblogs (or "blogs") to discuss how to promote their candidate. His web page also directed supporters to a website called meetup.com, where people could sign up to attend campaign meetings in person on the first Wednesday of every month. Over the course of the year leading up to the election, tens of thousands of people joined these virtual and real communities, with the number involved in the Dean campaign growing steadily as word about what Dean was doing spread online.

Comments posted by users of Dean's official campaign blog suggested that people were reacting emotionally to the experience, expressing feelings of political efficacy that had eluded them for decades—or, for younger participants, for their entire lives. People reacted to being part of a community working together for a common goal, and they were getting out of their houses to get involved in the political process—many of them for the first time. Their comments suggested they were experiencing the full range of what politics can be—fun, exciting, purposeful and meaningful.

Dean's presidential efforts failed, but four years later Barack Obama produced a larger, more sophisticated and ultimately successful effort to organize and mobilize supporters online. The Obama campaign's web presence was like the Dean effort on steroids, or, as Dean's campaign manager Joe Trippi called it, the Apollo project compared to Dean's Wright brothers operation.[T16] The Obama website gave users a set of tools they could use to organize on behalf of the candidate, virtually and in the real world. And they responded, giving unprecedented amounts of time and money, enabling their candidate to defeat a better-known and well-funded primary opponent in Senator Hillary Clinton, then defeat Senator John McCain in the general election. Like the Dean supporters, Obama's Internet constituency believed in and were motivated by their candidate. The Internet gave voice to their efficacy, assured them they were not alone in their sentiments, and provided them with the means to take action on Obama's behalf through an outpouring of political activism noticeably at odds with the cynicism typical of the television age.

Tolerance

Following the terrorist acts of September 2001, public officials, religious leaders, and educators, among others, spoke poignantly about the need for tolerance of those who may look or act differently, particularly people of Middle East origin and of the Muslim faith. Were those messages going out to an already tolerant and accepting public?

There are as many ways to determine tolerance as there are different groups with which people identify. Table 21.5 demonstrates one with particular resonance for the 2008 election cycle: Would you vote for a woman or an African American presidential candidate? When these questions were asked in the 2000 General Social Survey (GSS), a large biennial study of trends, changes, and constants in how Americans feel, think, and act, conducted by social scientists based at the University of Chicago, it seemed unlikely that within just a few years the leading candidates for the Democratic Party presidential nomination would be a woman (Sen. Hillary Clinton) and an African American. However, the results of these questions suggested the electorate was ready to seriously consider candidates who were not male and white.

There was a time when this would have been unthinkable, as a large percentage of Americans opposed the idea of a woman or minority president. Accordingly, all of President Obama's predecessors

have been white males and all but one has been Protestant.[7] In 1984, when Democratic presidential nominee Walter Mondale chose Representative Geraldine Ferraro as his vice presidential running mate, it was considered an historic and risky choice. But, when Sen. John McCain selected Alaska Governor Sarah Palin as his running mate in 2008, in part to appeal to disappointed female supporters of Sen. Hillary Clinton, it was clear that times had changed. McCain's selection of Palin—only the second female running mate of a major party nominee—guaranteed that either an African American or female candidate would win national office in 2008. The tolerant responses related in the 2000 GSS survey may have foreshadowed this possibility several years earlier.

The interim years suggested that we may have been building to a watershed election like the one we had in 2008.[8] In 2000, former transportation secretary and American Red Cross president Elizabeth Dole ran an unsuccessful but credible campaign for the Republican presidential nomination (she later won election to the Senate from North Carolina). Former secretary of state Colin Powell, an African American, had been prominently discussed as a credible presidential candidate since his emergence as a public figure during the first Persian Gulf War. Al Gore was almost elected president in 2000, running on a ticket with Connecticut senator Joseph

Table 21.5. Tolerance

If your party nominated a woman for president, would you vote for her if she were qualified for the job?
Yes
No
Don't know/no opinion

NATIONAL RESULTS
A resounding 83 percent of respondents answered yes, while only 14 said no.

If your party nominated a black (African American) for president, would you vote for him if he were qualified for the job?
Yes
No
Don't know/no opinion

NATIONAL RESULTS
Similarly, a striking 82 percent of respondents answered yes, while 14 percent said no.

Source: 2000 General Social Survey[T14]

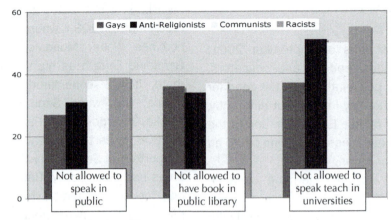

Figure 21.8. Putting Tolerance to the Test[T18]

Lieberman, the first national candidate in American history to be Jewish.

When we look beyond diversity in national candidates, though, our capacity for tolerance is more dubious. From the Boston Tea Party to Shays' Rebellion to the Revolutionary War itself, America is a nation built on protest and dissent. Nonetheless, a solid minority of the population is reluctant to accept either. We don't know their opinions of Revolutionary-War activists, but one-third of Americans responding to questions in the 1990 GSS said they are intolerant of youthful protest. They disagreed—6 percent strongly disagreed—with the statement that it was good for young people (like yourself) "to have greater freedom to protest against things they don't like and to 'do their own thing.'" Likewise, 21 percent disagreed with the statement that "it is good to treat dissenters with leniency and an open mind, since new ideas are the lifeblood of progressive change."

When people are asked to be lenient in less abstract settings, their tolerance is strained even more. Respondents to the 2000 GSS were asked if they were comfortable allowing people whose ideas or values were not mainstream to speak publicly, to have books advocating their views on the shelves of public libraries, or to teach at a college or university.

Take a look at what they said. Figure 21.8 displays the responses people gave regarding four groups whose views could be considered outside the mainstream of American public opinion: gays, anti-religionists (people who oppose all churches and religions), Communists, and racists. The figure shows that most Americans would be willing to permit each of them to speak. But a sizable minority would not, ranging from 27 percent who would object to a gay speaker publicly advocating homosexuality to 39 percent who would have a problem with a racist speaker publicly proclaiming personal views on the inferiority of African Americans. Roughly one-third of Americans have a problem with library books proclaiming positions outside the mainstream, regardless of the position at issue. When it comes to permitting members of these groups to teach in colleges or universities, Americans are at their most intolerant. Although we think of universities as being places where dissenting opinions are welcomed, accepting diverse and perhaps distasteful discourse in the classroom requires a high level of tolerance, considering the authority claimed by professors—tolerance to a degree not exhibited by many Americans.

So, are we a tolerant people? Answering this question may be like asking if the glass is half empty or half full. From one perspective, the answer would seem to be yes. Most measures of tolerance won the support of majorities of Americans, even large majorities. Some circumstances, like objecting to racist teachings, actually could be interpreted as being intolerant of an intolerant message, even though this position disregards the constitutionally protected freedom of the speaker in the effort to discard the message.

On the other hand, the numbers of people professing intolerant positions is significant. And there's always the possibility that data like these may not fully reflect the depth of intolerant attitudes. After all, it's not always easy to admit to having a position that many people would find unpopular, a topic we'll address in Demystifying Government: Saying the "Right" Thing.

Political Beliefs: From the Head

If political attitudes are plentiful and come from your heart, political **beliefs** are just as plentiful, but they're of an entirely different nature. Whereas attitudes stem from what people feel, political beliefs

DEMYSTIFYING GOVERNMENT

SAYING THE "RIGHT" THING

Some attitudes are simply easier than others to admit to, and as a result, we need to be a little careful about the face value of data on controversial attitudes like intolerance. What if you feel that gay people shouldn't be allowed to teach in universities, but you also feel that if you express this, you're going to look narrow-minded? Situations like this can give people strong motivation to cover up their antisocial attitudes and behaviors, and report positions that don't reflect what they really feel. If enough people do this, pollsters won't get an accurate reading on the extent of social intolerance. Something called a **social desirability bias** results when public opinion polls reflect what people want others to believe instead of what they really believe.

During the 2008 presidential election, with the first African American nominee of a major party on the ballot, pollsters wondered whether social desirability bias would present itself in the form of what's known as the "Bradley Effect," named for former Los Angeles mayor Tom Bradley who lost his 1982 bid to become California governor despite pre-election polls that showed him ahead. Bradley, who was African American, lost to a white candidate, and one explanation for the discrepancy between the polls and the election result was that a percentage of white voters falsely told pollsters they intended to vote for the more experienced Bradley.

The Bradley Effect did not materialize in 2008, when final aggregate polling closely matched the outcome. One possible reason why is that the political agenda had changed in the intervening years, diminishing the importance of racially charged issues like welfare and crime. Another possibility is that it was easier for people who didn't want to vote for Obama because of his race to justify their decision on other grounds—such as McCain's greater experience in politics—resulting in an accurate accounting of their vote, albeit for the wrong reason.[T19] Social desirability bias will not emerge if people have comfortable ways of rationalizing unpleasant attitudes.

Questions about voting can produce this kind of bias. Everyone knows they're *supposed* to vote, but many people do not. It's easy to imagine some nonvoters claiming they voted to avoid the social embarrassment of publicly admitting they didn't do something they felt they should have done.

Surveys of public opinion can anticipate this problem and try to mitigate it with questions worded to offset social desirability bias. For instance, questions about voting can start out with a disclaimer that many people don't vote because they lack the time or interest, suggesting that not voting is an acceptable behavior with no social consequences. In the end, of course, it's up to the individual to decide whether to admit to something that may cause them some discomfort.

are things people think to be true about politicians, politics, and policy. You might say they come from our head or mind.

We said that attitudes could never really be wrong because they're simply a reflection of how we're oriented toward political people, institutions, and events. Beliefs are more complex. People can believe things that are not true, such as that Social Security isn't a government program (it is) or that 15 percent of the federal budget goes to foreign aid (the real figure is much less). Months after Saddam Hussein was overthrown, a majority of Americans incorrectly believed that the Bush administration had found a link between Iraq and al-Qaeda.[9] Though false, people hold to beliefs like these as if they are true, muddying the political decision-making process.

Beliefs can even influence attitudes. Some people believe there was a conspiracy to assassinate President Kennedy that included members of the government. It's not hard to imagine how having a belief like this could negatively influence attitudes like efficacy and trust in government.

Similarly, people may fiercely believe that something is right or wrong when in truth their belief cannot be supported by objective facts. Some people equate legalized abortion with murder because they believe that life begins at conception. Others endorse abortion rights with as much fervor because they believe that before a fetus is viable outside the womb it is part of the mother's body, and the mother has the right to make decisions affecting her body. As a matter of scientific principle, the question of when life begins eludes clear definition. An argument can be made for both positions but neither can be proved. Of course, if you fervently hold to a belief it might be impossible to convince you that it's a belief and not a fact. It will certainly seem factual to you.

Intensely held beliefs can motivate people to political action. Recall that one dimension of public opinion is intensity, which is perhaps most clearly visible when it comes to the public expression of beliefs. Sometimes political activity stems from the actions of an intense minority of citizens whose strong beliefs lead them to make demands on government, even if most of the population

feels less strongly about the matter than they do. In cases like this, which might remind you a little of Madison's argument about the dangers of minority **factions**, the political system is supposed to diffuse the intensity of the feelings these groups express by providing them with an outlet for articulating their beliefs as part of a broader dialogue on the subject that concerns them.

Again, the abortion issue is an excellent example of this. It is prominently placed in the news, and a subject of widespread discussion, in part because of the efforts of activists on both sides of the issue. Over the years, there have been a series of legislative and judicial debates about the legal parameters of abortion. Many people view abortion as an emotional issue with complex moral dimensions.

This would suggest that abortion is a matter about which most Americans hold strong and intense beliefs. But it is not. Data from the 2000 GSS indicate that the abortion issue is one of the most important issues of the day to only 14 percent of the public. Another 14 percent say it is not at all important to them. And the rest fall somewhere in between, concerned about it perhaps but not in a deeply committed way. One-third of Americans claim to be "personally concerned" about the abortion issue, and another 44 percent claim to be somewhat concerned. They are aware of the matter and likely have beliefs about it, but the issue is not pressing enough to spur them to act. Instead, the political action we see on the issue most likely originates with the 14 percent who experience abortion as the most important issue to them.

The abortion issue also provides an excellent illustration of the complexity of beliefs. Sometimes during the course of trying to be persuasive in political debate, advocates can overly simplify an argument, even though public opinion may well be quite complicated. If pollsters were to ask people the deceptively simple question "should abortion be legal?," they might get answers, but it's unlikely that these answers would reflect the complex array of beliefs people hold on the matter.

The question "should abortion be legal?" supposes that abortion should be legal under any circumstances, a position held by four in ten Americans. Figure 21.9 demonstrates how these

Abortion should be permitted if . . .

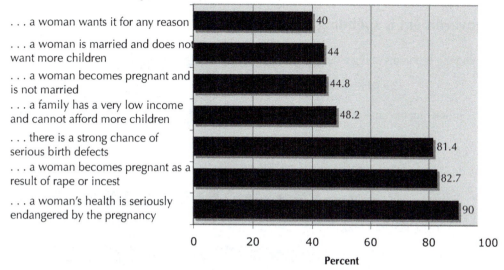

Figure 21.9. Abortion Should Be Permitted If . . .[T20]

---

figures can change dramatically when people are asked to consider different circumstances under which abortion could be permitted.

The unqualified condition that abortion should be legal under any circumstances is really a baseline for public opinion on the issue. Adding conditions to it alters what some people believe about legalizing abortion. Conditions that appear to be in the mother's control increase support for legalized abortion, but only incrementally. If a married woman doesn't want more children, if a woman is unmarried and becomes pregnant, or if a low-income family faces the prospect of an additional child, support for legalized abortion grows slightly. Conditions

that are more clearly out of the mother's control alter public opinion more dramatically. Better than eight in ten Americans support legalized abortion in the event that the child likely will have serious birth defects, or if a woman becomes pregnant as a consequence of being raped. Nine in ten support legalized abortion if the woman's health is seriously threatened by the pregnancy.

So it is with many issues: Beliefs can be more complex than any single measure indicates. This can make definitive statements about public opinion hard to come by. If you were affiliated with the Right to Life movement and wanted to make the case to legislators that there is strong

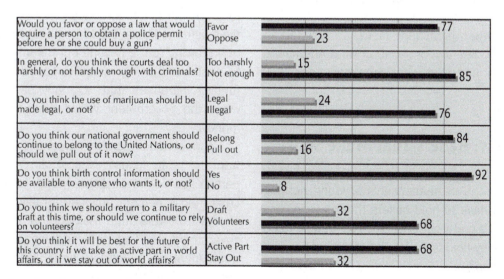

Figure 21.10. What Americans Believe[T21]

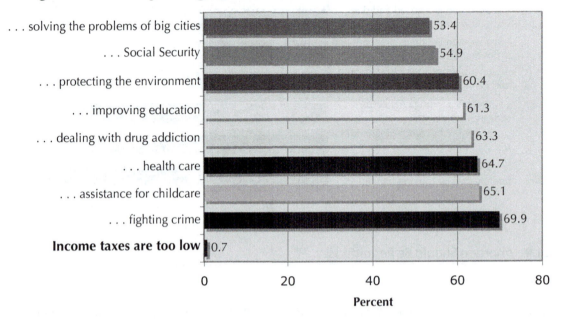

The government is spending too little on . . .

- . . . solving the problems of big cities — 53.4
- . . . Social Security — 54.9
- . . . protecting the environment — 60.4
- . . . improving education — 61.3
- . . . dealing with drug addiction — 63.3
- . . . health care — 64.7
- . . . assistance for childcare — 65.1
- . . . fighting crime — 69.9
- **Income taxes are too low** — 0.7

Percent

Figure 21.11. Consistent Beliefs?[T22]

antiabortion sentiment in America, you could point out that 60 percent believe that abortion should not be freely available under all circumstances. If you represented the abortion rights movement and wanted to make the case to legislators that most Americans are supportive of the principle of abortion, you could point to the figures on birth defects, rape, and the health of the woman. Both arguments would be accurate, at least to the degree that both arguments capture an element of public opinion on the issue.

Several other prominent issues are listed in Figure 21.10. See if your sense of what Americans believe is in line with what Americans say they believe.

Ideology: Beliefs That Make Sense

Just like opinions are neither right nor wrong, nothing says people have to hold beliefs that make collective sense. It's pretty commonplace for people to be perfectly happy holding contradictory beliefs—even without realizing it.

For instance, when people are asked if they believe government is spending too much or too little on a host of domestic social programs, large majorities repeatedly say too little. Look at Figure 21.11 to see some of the things that majorities of Americans say are underfunded.

Spending more on any of these priorities means either taking money away from other things, going into debt, or raising taxes. While it's possible to imagine a spirited debate about which priorities might be cut to make money available for the initiatives listed in Figure 21.11 or about the desirability of borrowing to live beyond our means, it's practical to assume that in order to follow through on the funding increases that so many people say they want, the government would have to raise more money.

So, does a comparable percentage of Americans want to raise taxes? Not at all. A comparable percentage—64.4 percent—wants to lower taxes. Less than 1 percent advocates raising taxes. How exactly do those large majorities of people expect government to find the additional money they want spent on education, health care, and crime prevention?

The answer is they're probably not thinking about it that way. They're not connecting the matter of tax increases with their sincere desire to have government spend more money. They simply hold contradictory beliefs: that government doesn't spend enough, and that taxes are too high.[10]

When people's beliefs fit together in a coherent way, they're considered to be ideological thinkers. We would say they have an **ideology**, or an intricately woven, complex set of beliefs that fit together in a logical manner. Many people assume their beliefs fit together in a logical manner—perhaps you do—but that alone does not make you an ideological thinker. A dispassionate observer would be able to identify an ideological individual through the lack of contradictions among the ideas he or she holds. For instance, someone might be considered an ideological thinker if he or she supported a balanced budget and higher taxes or spending cuts to make it possible.

It's difficult to pinpoint the exact percentage of Americans who think this way, but the best evidence is that it's not very high. If you go back three generations, you'll find an influential study of how Americans reason about politics in a book called *The American Voter*. Angus Campbell and his colleagues set out to understand how Americans make sense of political parties and candidates for office, and as part of their inquiry they isolated and identified ideological thinkers.[11] They found that back in 1956, less than 3 percent of the people they studied could be classified as "ideologues," in the sense that their beliefs were "functionally related" to each other. Another 13 percent could be termed "near-ideologues" for their tendencies to use ideological labels like "conservative" and "liberal" without demonstrating that they fully grasped the meaning of the terms. That meant that the remaining 85 percent of the public did not think about things ideologically.

One generation later, a different team of researchers working in a different era found that ideological thinking had increased dramatically since the late 1950s, perhaps as a consequence of the traumatic political and social events of the civil rights era and the Vietnam War. Writing in *The Changing American Voter*, Norman Nie, Sidney Verba and John Petrocik claimed that by 1972, one-third of the public could be classified as "ideologues" and about half were either "ideologues" or "near-ideologues."[12] That's a

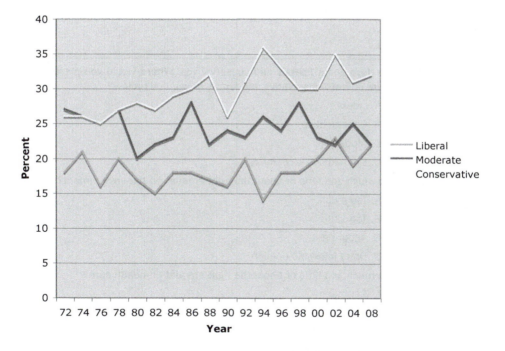

Figure 21.12. Liberal-Conservative Self-Identification, 1972–2008[T23]

huge shift upward from what *The American Voter* authors found in the 1950s, and it is possible that the relative political stability of the Eisenhower era at that time had a depressing influence on the number of ideological thinkers.[13] Given a stringent definition of ideology, though, it's probably safe to say that ideological thinking is not particularly widespread in America.

Even if by the most generous standards more than half the population falls short of ideological thinking, many people use ideological labels like "conservative" and "liberal" in everyday conversation. National Election Studies data show that over the past three decades anywhere from 40–50 percent of Americans used these labels to describe themselves, with about another one-quarter claiming to be less ideological "moderates." There's been some movement between liberals and conservatives over the years, although self-professed conservatives have outnumbered liberals throughout the period. Figure 21.12 tells the story.

Do you think of yourself as being conservative or liberal? If you do, can you come up with a clear explanation for why? Many Americans will say "yes" to the first question, then struggle with the second. If most people aren't ideological thinkers, what do these labels really mean? In Table 20.6, you'll find a list of poll questions relating to some of the issues we've been discussing—issues people have beliefs about—along with a question about whether you consider yourself a conservative or a liberal. Answer the questions and then evaluate how reliably you take liberal or conservative positions.

Liberalism in its broadest sense endorses an active role for government in addressing social and economic problems, and a more limited role for government in refereeing matters involving personal or moral values.

Liberals advocate government activism (which in a practical sense translates into spending money on government programs) for such social issues as environmental protection, health and child care, urban decay, education and drug addiction, and for such economic issues as welfare and Social Security. In this regard, liberals seek to use the power of government to assist those in need (for instance, through welfare and drug programs) and to compensate for the inequities (like unequal access to health care) or consequences (like air and water pollution) of the economic marketplace.

At the same time, liberals typically believe government should stay out of matters that they

Table 21.6. Are You Ideological?

1. We hear a lot these days about liberals and conservatives. Where would you place yourself? Would you say you are liberal, conservative, moderate, or you don't know?

      A. Liberal

      B. Conservative

      C. Moderate

      D. Don't know/no opinion

2. Are we spending too much, too little or about the right amount on the environment?

      A. Too much

      B. Too Little

      C. About right

      D. Don't know/no opinion

3. Are we spending too much, too little or about the right amount on health care?

      A. Too much

      B. Too Little

      C. About right

      D. Don't know/no opinion

(continued)

Table 20.6. (Continued)

4. Are we spending too much, too little or about the right amount on child care?

    A. Too much

    B. Too Little

    C. About right

    D. Don't know/no opinion

5. Do you favor or oppose the death penalty for persons convicted of murder?

    A. Favor

    B. Oppose

    C. Don't know/no opinion

6. Are we spending too much, too little or about the right amount on improving the nation's education system?

    A. Too much

    B. Too Little

    C. About right

    D. Don't know/no opinion

7. Would you oppose or favor a law that would require a person to obtain a police permit before he or she could buy a gun?

    A. Oppose

    B. Favor

    C. Don't know/no opinion

8. Are we spending too much, too little or about the right amount on Social Security?

    A. Too much

    B. Too Little

    C. About right

    D. Don't know/no opinion

9. Are we spending too much, too little, or about the right amount on dealing with drug addiction?

    A. Too much

    B. Too little

    C. About right

    D. Don't know/no opinion

EVALUATE YOUR ANSWERS

    The **CONSERVATIVE** answer to each question is A

    The **LIBERAL** answer to each question is B

    The **MODERATE** answer to each question is C

Do you fall most often in the liberal, conservative, or moderate category?

consider to be of a moral nature. Consequently, liberals may oppose using government power to limit abortion rights, impose the death penalty, or require prayer in public schools (however, they may be quite comfortable engaging the government to protect abortion rights and defend against school prayer). Liberals may also favor gun control laws, limits on military spending, and tax laws that benefit lower-income people.

Conservatism applies different principles to arrive at mirror-image positions. In its broadest sense, conservatism values the power of the marketplace to address economic concerns and individual initiative to confront social problems, therefore advocating a limited role for government power in economic and social matters. Contemporary conservatism for many years has accepted the reality of America's social welfare programs (although some of today's conservatives have spoken about the need to privatize or eliminate social programs), but conservatives tend to be suspicious of government programs that are not subjected to what they regard as the beneficial self-correcting forces of the marketplace, and that therefore take money out of taxpayer's pockets that could be put toward free enterprise.

Consequently, conservatives advocate less involvement in (and less money for) government programs on environmental protection, health and childcare, urban issues, education, and drug addiction. They regard welfare as a program that can undermine individual initiative, and have been successful in recent years in restructuring government welfare benefits to orient the program toward getting people to find jobs. Conservatives, like liberals, embrace Social Security, but are more likely to be interested in making it a market-oriented program.

Where conservatives seek to keep government out of economic and social matters, a hallmark of American conservatism since the Reagan administration has been an attempt to use government power to advance positions with a clear moral dimension. This, too, is a mirror image of liberalism, and it leads conservatives to seek government intervention to restrict or eliminate legal abortion, legalize the death penalty, permit prayer in public schools and forbid gay marriage. Conservatives may also oppose gun control laws, value military spending, and favor tax laws that benefit those at the top of the income scale out of the belief that it helps them produce wealth for society.

Chances are, if you call yourself a liberal or conservative, your positions on all of these issues do not align perfectly with the prescribed ideological positions advocated by the "left" (the traditional designation for "liberals") or the "right" (the designation for "conservatives"). If that's the case, you're not alone. Just like the authors of *The American Voter* discovered, most people don't hold internally consistent beliefs. That may not stop us from using the conservative or liberal labels to describe ourselves. It just means that using the labels doesn't make us ideologues.

For instance, while liberals in general favor more spending than conservatives on social and economic concerns, majorities of conservatives support the liberal position on such issues as protecting the environment, providing health care and child care, improving education and combating drug addiction. In fact, the terms are loose enough that what it means to be a liberal or a conservative has changed over time. The next Demystifying Government box explores whether former President Bush, a self-described conservative would have been considered liberal at an earlier point in American history.

Although most Americans are not ideological thinkers, and most ideological dialogue in the United States takes place between conservatives and liberals, there are other ideological positions as well. If you think of ideologies as being points on a line, with liberals on the left and conservatives on the right (remember, we said that liberals are commonly referred to as being "left" or "left-wing" and conservatives as "right" or "right-wing"), and you extend the line in both directions, you'll arrive at these other positions.

To the left of liberalism you'll find **socialism**, which applies some of the principles of liberalism to a different conclusion. American liberals place a premium on **equality of outcome**, but they strive to enhance outcomes at the margins while accepting the American preference for **equality of opportunity**. Socialists, on the other hand, strive for equality of outcome in place of equality of opportunity, and view the government rather than the free market as the vehicle for getting there. Socialists would advance what they consider a common, collective interest, and believe the creation of wealth should serve the common good instead of going to make a small number of people rich.

To the right of conservatism you'll find **fascism**, the ultra-nationalistic ideology of the far right that favors developing a strong military and police apparatus to defend the interests of the state. A militant ideology, fascism endorses the concentration of power by any and all means, and rejects liberal notions of individual rights. Following the defeat of fascism in World War II, the term became so widely discredited that it is unusual for anyone but small, militant fringe groups to use it in the United States.

DEMYSTIFYING GOVERNMENT

GEORGE W. BUSH: LIBERAL?

President Obama has advocated an aggressive role for the federal government in solving major problems. This sort of government activism would qualify the president as a liberal in today's political debate. In sharp contrast, George W. Bush regularly articulated his belief in a limited role for government and his abiding faith in individual initiative independent of government support. We've said these are all contemporary conservative beliefs. But if you think back for a second to an earlier section of Chapter 2, you may remember that we've encountered these present-day conservative beliefs before, when we were talking about John Locke and the ideas that influenced the early Federalists.

We said that in Locke's time, the idea of **limited government** was pretty radical stuff. In its day, Locke's writing was considered quite liberal since it advocated protecting the rights of the individual from encroachment by either government or the cruelty of the state of nature.

Today, Locke is regarded as a classical liberal, as someone who was a liberal in the context of the time in which he lived, and his writing is viewed as an expression of **classical liberalism**. He regarded monarchy, the strong central government of his day, as an obstacle to the advancement of individual rights and liberties.

As American government has grown in size, scope, and function, particularly in the twentieth century, liberals and conservatives have switched some of their philosophical clothes. Liberals have emerged as those who advocate using government power because they regard contemporary government social programs as a means to the traditional goals of protecting individual rights. Conservatives disagree, and have emerged as those who seek to maintain the once radical ideas of limited government advocated by classical liberals two centuries ago.

In this respect, had George W. Bush lived two centuries ago and expressed the positions he does today, there is little doubt he would have been considered a liberal.

Libertarianism is typically placed far to the right as well, but it can be harder to place on a left-right continuum. It covers a range of political and economic theories, but the basic intent of libertarians is to advance individual liberty free from government interference. In this regard, libertarians take the ideas of classical liberalism beyond where conservatives would go. For many years, conservatives have accepted the social policies and programs of twenty-first century America—even as they may work to limit them in scope and size. Libertarians would work to roll back all but the most basic functions of government, like defense and some elements of criminal justice. At the same time, some libertarians advocate social positions that are typically rejected by conservatives, like legalizing abortion, drugs, and prostitution.

Measuring Public Opinion

It puzzles a lot of people exactly how we can know what a nation of 310 million citizens believes about gun control or feels about political efficacy. You may be wondering this yourself: Where do these precise-looking figures in opinion polls come from, and how much faith should we place in their accuracy? When the Gallup Organization tried to find out about people's confidence in the work of pollsters—essentially by conducting a poll about polls—it found that despite widespread sentiment that polling produced accurate results, most people said it simply was not possible to get reliable data about a whole nation by talking to only one thousand or so people. In other words, people believe polls work even as they doubt the science that makes them work.

That's not so hard to understand, when you consider that it's not intuitive how a poll of a tiny number of people can accurately capture the beliefs and opinions of many millions. It's not an easy thing to explain either. Maybe the best way to think about it is to imagine a bowl of hot soup. If you put a spoon in the bowl, mix it around, take a spoonful to your mouth, and spit it out because it's too hot and making your tongue blister, you don't need to finish the whole bowl to know that it's boiling hot. That little sample told you everything you had to know, and you got an accurate measure as long as you mixed up the soup so you weren't taking it from a part of the bowl that might have been cooler, like the edge or the top.

Polls work pretty much the same way. The key to conducting a good poll is making sure that the "soup" is all mixed up or, to put it another way, that everyone in America has the same chance of being selected for the poll. If you only taste from the edge of the bowl where perhaps the soup is always cooler—or if you only talk to a select group of people with the same set of characteristics—you can end up misjudging the broader group. The soup you eat has to be representative of the soup in the bowl, just like the people you talk to in your survey have to be representative of the people in the country.

Early political polls ran into this problem. A magazine called the *Literary Digest* had been conducting opinion polls on how Americans were going to vote for president, and between 1916 and 1932, it had called every presidential election correctly using a method whereby millions of people were contacted and asked to fill out sample ballots. The *Literary Digest* got the names of these people from phone books and automobile registration lists, and they operated on the (flawed) assumption that the more people you contact, the more accurate the results. To continue our analogy, they wanted to finish off about one-third of the soup before deciding they had enough information to conclude that the soup was hot.

Their approach worked for many years. Then, in 1936, with Franklin Roosevelt facing reelection, the *Literary Digest* got it badly wrong, predicting a lopsided win for challenger Alf Landon, when in fact Roosevelt won in a landslide. It seems the phone books and automobile registration lists came back to haunt them. With Roosevelt's New Deal policies assisting people hurt by the Depression, the votes of those who couldn't afford phones and cars differed wildly from the votes of the wealthy and middle class that were not as affected by the Depression and were more likely to pay for than to benefit from Roosevelt's programs. This group was much less likely to support Roosevelt, and their opinions were given disproportionate weight. Without realizing it, the *Literary Digest* was sampling from only one part of the soup bowl.

That same year, the Gallup Organization predicted the election outcome correctly by talking to only a few thousand people. It was as big a win for scientific polling methods as it was for Roosevelt because it demonstrated the inherent accuracy of taking small, careful samples and discredited methods that reached out to large numbers of people. It also made a name for George Gallup, who put his reputation and a lot of money on the line by betting that his results would be more accurate than the *Literary Digest* results.[14]

What the *Literary Digest* did was comparable to what happens when we ask our friends their opinions. We'll get a response but it will only tell us about the opinions of the people we talked to—we won't be able to apply their opinions to what a larger group might say because our friends are self-selected. They just aren't representative of a larger group because we don't choose our friends at random, a factor that plays a key role in scientific polling and that's discussed in Demystifying Government: Speak to a Few, Speak for Many.

DEMYSTIFYING GOVERNMENT

SPEAK TO A FEW, SPEAK FOR MANY

Randomization is the key to being able to discern the opinions of many people by contacting only a few. A scientific surveys is based on a **random sample** of individuals, meaning that everyone contacted for an opinion poll had the exact same chance of being contacted as everyone else. The *Literary Digest* poll didn't do this because people without cars and phones had no chance of being part of their survey. You also don't do this when you ask opinions of your friends.

Professional pollsters, though, collect random samples all the time. The most cost-effective way to create a random sample is to program a computer to generate and call a random list of telephone numbers. Commonly called random-digit dialing, this method works because you can program a computer to select telephone numbers on the condition that every number has the same chance of being selected. Unlike 1936, today virtually everyone has a telephone, so you can use phone numbers as the basis for conducting a scientifically valid poll. [T24] Furthermore, selecting telephone numbers this way avoids the problem of missing unlisted numbers not published in phone directories.

If everyone has an equal chance of being selected for a poll, it turns out you don't have to talk to many people before you generate an accurate view of public opinion. This can be confusing because it seems counterintuitive, but it's what makes scientific polling possible. After only several hundred interviews with randomly selected individuals, pollsters can begin to speak with some degree of accuracy about how well the opinions they collected reflect national public opinion. Statistical models can tell them how likely it is that a survey of, say, one thousand people represents the opinions of the larger group they were sampled from.

The key word here is *likely*. Opinion polls never *definitely* say what the larger group feels or believes, but they do tell pollsters the *odds* that the figures in the poll represent national public opinion within a specified range, called a margin of error (which can be determined by statistical models). If the odds are good that the poll is accurate and the margin of error is narrow enough to be useful, they're in business.

Of course, people who use the poll still have to know how to interpret the results. Reputable surveys will claim an accuracy rate of at least 95 percent, meaning if you repeated the survey one hundred times (interviewing the same number of different, randomly selected people each time), in 95 percent of the surveys you should expect to find results that are within the margin of error of the survey you conducted.

For instance, let's say a recent Gallup Poll found that the president had a job approval rating of 55 percent (meaning 55 percent of those surveyed thought he was doing a good job as president), and the survey had a margin of error of 3 percent. We'd conclude that the president's national job approval rating was within three percentage points of 55 percent, or between 52 percent and 58 percent. We'd further conclude that we're 95 percent certain of this result because we'd expect to find a result in this range in 95 percent of the surveys we could conduct.

Of course, we could be wrong, and some surveys are indeed off base. On average, five in one hundred surveys are out of the real range of public opinion, and we can never know which ones these are. Still, the odds are with you each time you do a survey, and the overwhelming majority of them get it right, which is why random sampling is a far more accurate way of conducting opinion polls than grazing through phone books.

For all the mathematical sophistication that goes into designing and conducting public opinion polls, the degree of accuracy they return depends at least as much on the human element as scientific acumen. Both science and art go into the process of writing questions, ordering questions in a survey, and asking questions in an impartial manner. It's not always easy to anticipate how seemingly simple changes in the wording of a question can dramatically alter the answers people give, or how small voice modulations can unconsciously direct someone toward a particular response.

For instance, take a look at this question from the 2000 General Social Survey: "Are you in favor of the death penalty for persons convicted of murder?" Straightforward and simple, it generated a "yes" response of 60.3 percent. Now look at this equally straightforward variation on the question from the same survey: "Do you favor or oppose the death penalty for persons convicted of murder?" It sounds like exactly the same question, but in this form, 73.8 percent said they "favor" the death penalty, a nontrivial increase of 13.5 percentage points.

Why such a noticeable difference? One possibility lies in a subtle variation in how the two questions are constructed. The first question asks people to consider the death penalty in the affirmative, simply asking them if they favor it for persons convicted of murder. The second question asks people to make a thumbs up/thumbs down choice on the same matter, inviting them to consider whether they favor the death penalty in the context of whether they may also oppose it. It's possible that when people are invited to think about support for the death penalty in the context of opposition to the death penalty, more of them voice their support than when they're not encouraged to think about the possibility of opposing it.

At this point, you could be forgiven for wondering how pollsters can figure out how to word questions at all, if something as seemingly simple as the addition of couple of benign words can significantly alter the response to a question. In fact, a lot of attention is paid to precision in question wording because the effects can be so strong. Pollsters with a long history of conducting surveys can rely on the results they have gathered over time to fashion questions in a way that they are confident will generate accurate results. New questions are routinely tested in several forms in order to identify and weed out leading or misleading wording.

Likewise, reputable polling firms are attentive to the sequence of questions in a survey, to the fact that asking questions about one topic could unintentionally prompt people to think about subsequent topics in the context of the earlier questions. For instance, a battery of questions about the war in Afghanistan placed immediately before a question about President Obama's job performance might unintentionally lead some people to think about Obama's job performance in terms of the Afghanistan War, yielding lower performance scores during times when the war was unpopular than if the job performance question had been asked first.

Similarly, people who administer surveys over the telephone are trained in techniques for asking questions in a balanced and neutral fashion. Without careful attention to how questions are asked, the beliefs or biases of those reading the questions could influence how a respondent answers, and neither questioner nor respondent might be aware of what's going on.

For all these reasons—question wording, sequencing, and delivery—opinion polls should be regarded as imperfect mechanisms that, even in the best of cases, are susceptible to some human error. Good surveys minimize the problems, but when you add human error to the statistical error present in surveys, it should be easy to see why survey results need to be approached with some caution. Good surveys are a powerful tool and they can sketch a remarkably accurate picture of public opinion. Still, they're best approached as a snapshot of opinion that's accurate within a narrow range.

Measuring Public Opinion in Politics

Early in his campaign for reelection, Bill Clinton consulted with one of his political advisors about a weighty and critical issue: where he should take his vacation. It seems the president and those who helped him make political decisions felt it was important to use the vacation as a vehicle for sending the right image of the commander-in-chief to unde-cided voters. So, Clinton's advisors commissioned a public opinion poll. It turned out that taking the First Family to a wealthy friend's compound in the exclusive Massachusetts retreat Martha's Vineyard, as Clinton had done in the past, smacked of elitism to those swing voters who might determine the outcome of the next election. Polls showed these voters preferred camping trips.

So, the president took his family to Wyoming.

Polling has become so prevalent in politics that it's hard to find a part of the political system that polling hasn't touched. Public officials at all levels of government have come to depend on polls for a host of purposes, from figuring out what legislation to promote to crafting a public image. President Clinton relied heavily on opinion polls to decide which policies to promote, steering away from is-sues that were controversial with important voting groups while embracing issues, like welfare reform, that polls said voters wanted addressed. President Bush was careful to characterize his policy initia-tives with language that opinion polls suggested would appeal to large groups of voters, for instance, by speaking of his 2003 tax cut initiative as a "growth" and "jobs" program.

Candidates use polls for every facet of their work, from determining what issues to talk about to figuring out what slogans to use. Interest groups—which we'll discuss in Chapter 8—use polls showing public support for their positions to win the votes of legislators. The media build stories around polls, especially during election campaigns when reporters turn to them as a source of hard data for assessing likely winners and losers.

Candidates and Opinion Polls

The 1996 election, in which Bill Clinton sought a second term against Republican Senator Robert Dole, provides an excellent example of how thor-oughly polling has permeated the political world. During that election, it seemed as if no item was too small to avoid being subjected to opinion polls that would guide the two national campaigns in what they said and how they said it. For instance:

- The Clinton campaign polled four different ver-sions of a slogan before arriving at "Building a Bridge to the Twenty-First Century," which was preferred by far more people than the self-serving alternative, "Building a Bridge to a Second Term."
- The Dole campaign, looking for a way to talk about values without scaring away moderate voters, conducted an opinion poll and found that an anti-Hollywood theme would do the trick with conservative voters who worried about the movies and music their kids were exposed to.
- When polling showed that 80 percent of Americans favored a balanced budget, Clin-ton's pollsters urged him to endorse the idea, to the chagrin of some of his more principled liberal advisors who simply thought it was bad policy. (Clinton eventually sided with the pollsters.)
- Both the Dole and Clinton campaigns used polls to shape their television commercials. Ideas for ads were frequently "mall tested" by pollsters, meaning that prototype ads were shown to people in shopping malls who were then polled for their reactions.
- The Clinton campaign conducted a poll to end all polls—a "neuropersonality poll" that asked questions about every facet of people's lives in order to put together a blueprint of the electorate. From this poll, Clinton's aides were able to discern precisely which messages would appeal to the voters they needed. It played a major role in shaping the strategy that carried Clinton to a second term.[15]

There are two schools of thought about the polling phenomenon. You could argue that polling at this level is consistent with the way democra-cies are meant to function, with candidates finding out exactly what the public wants to know so they can closely align themselves with public opinion in the best model of representative democracy. You could also contend that there's something a little spineless about candidates relying on opinion polls to decide how to act and what to say. Think about whether the heavy reliance by candidates on polls seems like the ultimate expression of representatives responding to what people say they want, or whether it suggests a craven willingness for candidates to twist themselves like claymation figures into whatever shape pollsters say people want to see.

The Political Value of Misleading Polls

You may not have much familiarity with interest groups at this point (that will change soon), but the important thing to know is that they are organizations that try to get government officials to promote their views on issues they care about. Since elected officials tend to perk up when they hear that large numbers of people (read: potential voters) hold a particular viewpoint, an interest group can be persuasive if it can demonstrate widespread public support for a position it's promoting. Public opinion polls are one way for interest groups to make their case.

Remember what we said about the artistic component of polling? Scientific polls like the ones conducted by the Gallup Organization regard the nuances of question wording and question order as potential obstacles to producing accurate and reliable results. Polls commissioned by interest groups may be less inclined toward objectivity and more oriented toward demonstrating public support for the group's position—whether or not it really exists. In other words, pollsters working for interest groups may be intentionally "creative," wording questions in such a way as to generate the response that the group desires.

For instance, a group promoting widespread tax cuts might conduct a poll with questions like, "Would you support tax relief in the form of a government effort to return hard-earned money to people through a capital-gains tax cut?" It's hard to be against "tax relief" or "returning hard-earned money" to people, so questions like these could easily produce results that exaggerate the level of support for the tax cut. Where pollsters looking to accurately capture public opinion would avoid loaded phrases like these, interest groups might deliberately include them because it serves their political purposes.

Push polls are the most unethical example of using surveys to produce an outcome rather than measure opinion. With push polling, someone who sounds like they work for a professional polling firm but who really works for a political candidate calls people to ask questions that are highly biased against the candidate's opponent. The purpose is to trash the opposition by leaving people with a negative impression of them. In the 2000 election, the campaigns of George W. Bush and one of his Republican opponents, Senator John McCain, accused each other of using push polls. Not surprisingly, both campaigns denied the charge.[16]

The moral of the story is: When you're looking at poll numbers, remember the motivation of the people who commissioned the poll.

Media and Opinion Polls

Whereas candidates, elected officials, and interest groups use public opinion to try to gain political advantage, the media use public opinion as an easy and convenient way to tell political stories. Media outlets conduct polls about all sorts of social and political issues, and use results they find interesting to fashion stories for newspapers or television news programs.[17]

Media polls are most prevalent during presidential election years, when campaign news is saturated with poll results about how the race is shaping up. On television, tracking polls—which show a daily running average of support for major candidates—are a fixture in the weeks leading up to the election.

On election nights, the major television networks rely on exit polls for early predictions of the outcome. Exit polls are based on interviews with randomly selected voters as they leave the polling place. These voters are asked a small number of questions, including questions about how they voted in the day's most prominent contests. Since most respondents can accurately recollect how they voted just moments earlier, exit polls are often a highly reliable source of information. Consequently,

ISSUE

Too Much Information?

One of the bizarre twists of polling technology is that in some instances it's possible to know the outcome of an election before anyone votes. When Barack Obama hinted to a rally on Election eve that a celebration was in their near future, he wasn't being overconfident; detailed opinion polling told him he was going to win. In 1980, Jimmy Carter's chief pollster informed the president that he was not going to be reelected several days before the polls opened. In 1992, George Bush (senior) experienced the same surreal fate. Not a vote had been cast, but the outcome was assured.

From what we know about polling, it's not too hard to understand how this can happen. Obama scored an easy victory in 2008, and the 1980 and 1992 elections produced lopsided defeats for the incumbents—all well beyond the margin of error of good opinion surveys. As people put the finishing touches on their voting intentions several days before the election, pollsters captured the one-sided nature of their decisions and had a high degree of confidence in the findings.

Media outlets had access to the same information, but unlike the losing candidates (whose only use of the poll numbers was to brace themselves for what was about to happen to them), news executives confronted a serious dilemma about what to do with the information. As we'll see in Chapter 5, journalists see themselves as purveyors of information, and there are a lot of pressures on news people to report valuable information as quickly as possible. Knowing the winner of the next presidential election counts as having some of the juiciest and most coveted information a reporter can get.

Releasing that information before Election Day, though, poses a serious threat to the democratic tradition of one person–one vote because it would appear that news organizations were selecting the president on the basis of polling data. It would be reasonable for people to ask why they should go to the polls at all, especially if they intended to vote

for the eventual loser. Because news organizations want to avoid the appearance of undermining democratic processes, they studiously avoid calling the outcome of elections before people get a chance to cast their vote, despite strong pressures to quickly release important information.

But what about on Election Night itself? Television networks try to hold back on making predictions about an election until all the polls have closed, but competitive pressures to make a fast call have led to some unfortunate consequences. In lopsided presidential contests, exit poll results permit the projection of enough eastern states to make the general trend of the election clear to people living in the West. In 2008, once Barack Obama won the state of Ohio, pollsters and political reporters knew he was going to be elected president, because the states he had already won in conjunction with western states where pre-election and Election Day polls showed him comfortably ahead totaled enough Electoral Votes for victory. But, Ohio was called in the middle of the evening on the east coast, a couple of hours before polls closed out West. In an effort to avoid calling the election while people were still voting, the major television networks struggled to avoid definitive language about the outcome—and Obama himself refrained from making a victory statement—until after polls closed in California at 11 p.m. Eastern time.

They wanted to avoid a repeat of what happened in 1980, when the major networks announced that Ronald Reagan had defeated Jimmy Carter before all the polls had closed in the West, leaving some residents of California, Oregon, Washington, Alaska, and Hawaii to wonder why they should vote at all.

Considering the many other races on the ballot in those states, it's reasonable to ask if the effects of the early call could have worked their way down the ballot if some Carter voters stayed home after finding out the probable results of the presidential contest.

In 2000, the major television networks used exit polls to declare that Al Gore had won the presidential vote in the state of Florida, even though the polls were still open in a small portion of the Florida panhandle that's in the Central Time Zone. Then, in an embarrassment of unprecedented proportion, the networks one by one retracted the call as the actual votes began to indicate the exit polls might be incorrect. Late on Election Night, the networks awarded the Florida presidential vote to George W. Bush—only to retract that call when the final vote tally turned out to be too close to call. It was an ugly case of competitive pressures producing hasty judgments about what to report. We'll examine it in more detail in Chapter 7.

Still, since news people regard their job as disseminating information (and are rewarded for being first with what they know), it's difficult for them to sit still when they know something important is about to happen. It is also their constitutional right to freely express information in their control. But, at what point does the release of exit poll information interfere with the fundamental democratic act of voting? In the case of exit polls, journalistic restraint is often the best policy for democracy, but it flies against all the competitive, commercial, and professional interests of reporters. It's a rare case where polling technology can create the burden of knowing too much.

Think about whether you are more sympathetic to the journalists' perspective or the voter's perspective on the issue of how exit polls should be used on election night broadcasts.

Journalists' Perspective

- Freedom of expression is essential in a democracy.
- It is the obligation of journalists to disseminate important information.

- Journalists experience strong competitive pressures to be first with an important story.
- Journalists are professionals who can be relied on to balance value of broadcasting information in exit polls against the need for people to feel they are freely casting their vote.

Voter's Perspective

- Unencumbered voting rights are essential in a democracy, and knowing the projected winner of a presidential election before the polls close can discourage people from going to the polls.
- It is the obligation of journalists not to interfere with an election by reporting exit poll results before all polls close.
- Pressure on journalists to be first with a story should be subordinate to shielding those who have yet to vote from knowledge of the outcome of an election.
- Journalists should not be in the position of influencing election turnout.

My Opinion

In practice, do you agree more with the journalists' perspective or the voter's perspective? You should decide how to balance:

- Freedom of expression and voting rights.
- The obligation of journalists to disseminate information and the obligation of journalists not to interfere with elections.
- The competitive pressure on journalists to be first with a story and the value to voters of not knowing the outcome of an election.
- The professional judgment of journalists to decide when to report exit polls and the possibility that journalistic judgments could influence election outcomes.

networks are often able to use them to predict the outcome of races before all the votes are counted.

Survey methods have become so reliable, in fact, that in races that are not close, network television personnel sometimes know the results of an election hours or even days before anyone has voted. This has generated intense discussion among network television officials and political observers about the appropriate use of opinion polls to predict election outcomes, which we discuss in Issue: Too Much Information?

When we don't have an election going on, media organizations rely on the information in opinion polls to write stories about whether people feel the country is going in the right direction, their degree of support for highly visible policies or policy proposals debated by Congress, and how much they approve of the job the president is doing.

What Should We Make of Public Opinion?

Like any tools, opinion polls can be of value if you know how to use them. That means remembering both what they can and cannot tell us. Experienced political advisors know a great deal about the science and art of polling and can discern the currents of public opinion quite effectively.

On the other hand, journalists, who are not schooled in the ways of opinion polls, sometimes do a sloppy job of interpreting them. We know that polls present us with a good bet that public opinion reflects the numbers in the poll, but there is always a margin of error. When journalists forget to include the margin of error in their interpretation of polls—which happens frequently—they run the risk of misinterpreting what's going on. For instance, a poll with a margin of error of three points that shows one candidate three points ahead of the other is telling us that the contest is a dead heat. But it's not uncommon for journalists to inaccurately report that one candidate holds a three-point lead.

Even when polls are accurately interpreted, they still need to be handled with care. We know that Americans often do not hold strong or stable opinions about things. It's a mistake to accept poll data as a measure of deeply held or carefully considered attitudes and beliefs when in fact polls may be measuring opinion that's weak or fleeting. Polls are of limited value if the opinion they're measuring is soft or poorly developed, or if people are poorly informed about the matter in question. People will give all sorts of answers to pollsters' questions, but that doesn't automatically make their answers thoughtful or meaningful.

Even for public officials who are advised by the most sophisticated professionals, there is a difference between being responsive to public opinion and making responsible public decisions. Sometimes, simply doing what the public wants can produce policy with undesirable outcomes. Something like this happened in the 1980s. Polls showed that people wanted lower taxes. They also showed that people wanted the government to continue spending on a host of popular programs. As we saw earlier, it's not uncommon for people to hold contradictory opinions like these.

This isn't necessarily a problem unless officials follow public opinion to the letter. During the Reagan administration, the president wanted to cut taxes and spending on domestic policies; majorities in Congress wanted to maintain or increase spending on domestic programs, although a majority was also willing to go along with cutting taxes. So, the president got his way on tax cuts while Congress got its way on maintaining domestic spending. This split reflected public opinion fairly well, but it was problematic as the government soon began spending more money than it was taking in. Many years of large budget deficits followed, and while each side blamed the other for this outcome, a case can be made that the president and Congress were being more responsive than responsible.

An important component of effective leadership involves following public opinion. Another important component can be making unpopular decisions if, in the view of elected officials, public opinion is ill conceived. Governing through polls doesn't typically encourage this type of leadership.

Making decisions for a large, diverse population is a difficult proposition anyway, with or without opinion polls. From a largely homogeneous population at the turn of the eighteenth century, today's America is a multiethnic place where a rich variety of traditions support a range of sometimes incompatible approaches to how Americans should live and be governed.

Chapter Review

Public opinion is information that tells us what people think about matters relating to government, politics, and society. Because public opinion is gathered through careful scientific measurement, it is derived from empirical means. But public opinion also has an important normative component because it tells us what people value about government and politics.

There are several elements to the structure of public opinion. The direction of public opinion gives us a "thumbs up/thumbs down" reading on the degree of support people feel for a political individual, institution, or action. The intensity of public opinion tells us how strongly people hold to an opinion. The stability of public opinion tells us whether an opinion is fleeting or endures over time.

One component of public opinion is knowledge. Americans have never exhibited high levels of political knowledge, probably because politics is not a high priority for many Americans. Some argue this lack of knowledge does not prevent people from making intelligent political decisions. Others decry what they call an "information elite" of resource-rich individuals whose relatively high levels of political knowledge permit them to effectively identify what they want from government—and get it—while the poor have relatively less knowledge and therefore achieve less from government.

Another component of public opinion is attitudes, or how people feel about political figures, institutions, issues, or events. People hold attitudes on a wide range of things. For instance, many Americans say that the government is too strong, a view predominantly held by men, whites and, until the 1970s, southerners. Over the years, trust in government has declined from its pre-Vietnam highs. Cynicism has increased and efficacy has declined. However, efficacy remains generally higher among

people with higher levels of education and income, suggesting the possibility that wealthy people feel greater efficacy because government is more likely to respond to their wishes.

Beliefs address what people think is true about politics. While attitudes can never be incorrect because they reveal how people feel, it is possible to hold incorrect beliefs. Strongly held beliefs can motivate people to political action. Beliefs may also be quite complex and hard to capture with single survey questions.

When beliefs fit together in a logical order, we call it an ideology. Most people in America are not ideological thinkers. The most frequently used labels are liberal and conservative. In its broadest sense, liberalism endorses an active role for government in addressing social and economic problems, and a more limited role for government in refereeing matters involving personal or moral values. In its broadest sense, conservatism values the power of the marketplace to address economic concerns and individual initiative to confront social problems, therefore advocating a limited role for government power in economic and social matters.

There are other ideological positions as well. For instance, socialism subscribes to some of the same principles as liberalism but carries the desire for equal outcomes much further. Libertarianism subscribes to the conservative desire for freedom from government action, but also endorses moral positions conservatives would likely reject.

The most efficient way to measure the opinion of a large group like a nation is to take a random sample of the opinions of a small subset of that group, making sure that everyone in the nation had an equal chance of being selected for questioning. Opinion polls can provide an account of public opinion, if they are conducted and interpreted properly. Officials, candidates, interest groups, and the media utilize opinion polls to determine or demonstrate how Americans react to public events, although there is a difference between being responsive to public opinion and making responsible public decisions. Sometimes simply doing what the public wants can produce policy with undesirable outcomes.

Key Terms

attitudes   A component of public opinion that measures people's orientations toward politics.

beliefs   A component of public opinion that measures what people think is true about politics.

classical liberalism   A term given to the philosophy of John Locke and other seventeenth- and eighteenth-century advocates of the protection of individual rights and liberties by limiting government power.

conservatism   An ideology that advocates limits on government power to address economic and social problems, relying instead on economic markets and individual initiative to address problems like health care and education, while promoting government involvement in moral matters to, for instance, minimize or eliminate abortions or permit prayer in public schools.

cynicism   A pervasive attitude of mistrust about politics that may lead people to withdraw from political participation.

directional   An aspect of public opinion that measures whether people feel favorably or unfavorably toward a political figure, institution, or policy.

efficacy   The attitude that you can be effectual and effective in your dealings with government.

empirical   Any statement based on the assessment of data or the analysis of information, without regard to value judgments.

equality of opportunity   One of several ways of understanding equality, this way values giving people comparable advantages for succeeding in life, regardless of the unequal outcomes that may result.

equality of outcome   One of several ways of understanding equality, this way values leveling the social and economic inequities among people, rather than attempting to give people comparable advantages for succeeding in life.

faction   A group of individuals who are united by a desire that, if realized, would threaten the liberty of the larger community—in James Madison's words, individuals who are "united and actuated by some common impulse of passion, or of interest, adverse to the rights of other citizens, or to the permanent and aggregate interests of the community." A faction may be defined by size, such as when a majority of citizens threatens the liberty of the minority, or by intensity, such as when a minority of citizens with intensely held preferences threatens the liberty of a disinterested majority.

fascism   A militant, ultra-nationalistic ideology of the extreme right that rejects liberal ideas about personal rights.

ideology   A wide-ranging set of beliefs that logically fit together.

intensity   An aspect of public opinion that measures how strongly people feel toward a political figure, institution, or policy.

liberalism   An ideology that advocates the use of government power to address economic and social problems, like unemployment and environmental protection, while limiting government involvement in moral matters like abortion rights and prayer in public schools.

libertarianism   An ideology centered on the reduction of government power to advance personal liberty.

limited government   The idea that power can be denied to government and the people who serve in it, in order to restrict those in positions of authority from infringing upon individual liberty.

normative   Any statement that invokes a judgment or evaluation. Think of the word norm, which implies a standard for evaluating something.

public opinion   A collection of opinions people hold on matters relating to government, politics, and society.

push polls   Surveys that appear legitimate but in fact are a dirty campaign trick designed to generate negative opinion about an opponent in a political contest.

random sample The basis for a scientifically accurate public opinion poll, in which everyone in the community being polled has an equal chance of being selected to give their opinions to pollsters. In a poll of national opinion, everyone in the country would have to have an equal chance of being selected to participate in it.

social desirability bias A form of error in public opinion polls, whereby opinions or behaviors that could be considered undesirable are not fully reported in the data.

socialism A left-leaning ideology centered on the use of government power to advance equal outcomes.

stability An aspect of public opinion that measures how much change or variability there is in the way people feel toward a political figure, institution, or policy.

state-centered federalism One of several perspectives on federalism, which argues that the Constitution and the federal government are creations of the states and therefore can be overhauled by the states.

Resources

You might be interested in examining some of what the following authors have said about the topics we've been discussing:

Berelson, Bernard R., Paul F. Lazarsfeld, and William N. McPhee. *Voting: A Study of Opinion Formation in a Presidential Campaign.* Chicago: University of Chicago Press, 1954. A classic study of how people in the upstate New York city of Elmira decided how to vote in the 1948 elections, with important observations about political knowledge and the subject of our next chapter, political participation.

Campbell, Angus, Philip E. Converse, Warren E. Miller, and Donald E. Stokes. *The American Voter.* New York: John Wiley and Sons, 1960. A seminal study on how Americans vote, with an interesting section on ideological thinking in 1950s America.

Delli Carpini, Michael X., and Scott Keeter. *What Americans Know about Politics and Why It Matters.* New Haven: Yale University Press, 1996. A thorough account of political knowledge in America.

Nie, Norman H., Sidney Verba, and John R. Petrocik. *The Changing American Voter.* Cambridge, MA: Harvard University Press, 1979. One generation after The American Voter, this book challenges some of the assumptions about how people understood politics during the relatively sleepy 1950s.

You may also be interested in taking a current events quiz and getting a sense of the range of polling data collected by the Gallup organization, one of the nation's leading pollsters, at http://www.gallup.com/video/21538/ World-Leader-Quiz.aspx.

Notes

1. The exact figure is 68 percent, from a December 1998 Gallup Poll cited in Darren K. Carlson, "Queen Elizabeth: 50 Years of Public Opinion," Gallup Poll News Service, February 6, 2002.
2. Add to this an additional 55 percent of the population that's simply not engaged, and you have a picture of a turned-off workforce. Kenneth A. Tucker, "A Passion for Work," *Gallup Management Journal,* February 18, 2002.
3. Not too many Americans enjoy ski jumping either. The figures are from a February 2002 Gallup Poll cited in Jeffrey M. Jones, "Figure Skating Tops List of Americans' Favorite Winter Olympic Events," Gallup Poll News Service, February 8, 2002.
4. Michael X. Delli Carpini and Scott Keeter, *What Americans Know about Politics and Why It Matters* (New Haven: Yale University Press, 1996).
5. He is Secretary of the Interior.
6. Bernard R Berelson, Paul F. Lazarsfeld, and William N. McPhee, *Voting: A Study of Opinion Formation in a Presidential Campaign* (Chicago: University of Chicago Press, 1954), 308.

7. John F. Kennedy was the only Catholic president.

8. Up to a point, at least. The GSS also finds that one-third of Americans feel that most men are better suited emotionally for politics than most women.

9. Steven Kull, Americans on Iraq: WMD, Links to al-Qaeda, Reconstruction. The PIPA/Knowledge Networks Poll, July 1,2003, 4.

10. This is not a new story, either. In 1935, after two years of Franklin D. Roosevelt's New Deal policies, the Gallup Organization reported that six in ten Americans thought the federal government was spending too much money on programs designed to bring relief from the Great Depression. At the same time, nine in ten supported the Social Security program.

11. Angus Campbell, Philip E. Converse, Warren E. Miller, and Donald E. Stokes, *The American Voter* (New York: John Wiley and Sons, 1960), 216–255.

12. Norman H. Nie, Sidney Verba, and John R. Petrocik, *The Changing American Voter* (Cambridge, MA: Harvard University Press, 1979).

13. It is also possible that the authors of *The Changing American Voter* were more lenient in the standards they used to classify ideologues, inadvertently inflating the number of ideological thinkers in their study.

14. The story of early scientific polling is an interesting one that you can read about in transcripts from the PBS program, "The First Measured Century," which you can access online at http://www.pbs.org/fmc/segments/progseg7.htm.

15. Richard Stengel and Eric Pooley, "Masters of the Message: Inside the High-Tech Machine That Set Clinton and Dole Polls Apart," *Time,* November 6, 1996. You may access the full article at http://cgi.cnn.com/ALLPOLITICS/1996/elections/time.special/pollster/. It's colorful and fast moving, filled with accounts of power, personal jealousies, infighting, backstabbing, an ill-timed rendezvous with a prostitute—and enough opinion polls to make your head spin.

16. See "Push Polling," BBC News, February 22, 2000, at http://news.bbc.co.Uk/2/hi/in_depth/americas/2000/us_elections/glossary/n-p/652168.stm.

17. One way to get a sense of the wide range of topics in media polls is to check out pollster.com at the Huffington Post, http://www.huffingtonpost.com/news/pollster/.

Table, Figure and Box Notes

T1 Data from National Election Studies, at http://www.electionstudies.org/nesguide/toptable/tab1b_3.htm. The National Election Studies, Center for Political Studies, University of Michigan. Electronic resources from the NES World Wide Website (www.umich.edu/~nes). Ann Arbor, MI: University of Michigan, Center for Political Studies [producer and distributor], 1995–2010. These materials are based on work supported by the National Science Foundation under Grant Nos.: SBR-9707741, SBR-9317631, SES-9209410, SES-9009379, SES-8808361, SES-8341310, SES-8207580, and SOC77-08885. Any opinions, findings, and conclusions or recommendations expressed in these materials are those of the author(s) and do not necessarily reflect those of the National Science Foundation.

T2 Data from National Election Studies, at Ibid, http://www.electionstudies.org/nesguide/toptable/tab4e_1. htm. The National Election Studies, Center for Political Studies, University of Michigan. Electronic resources from the NES World Wide Website (www.umich.edu/~nes). Ann Arbor, MI: University of Michigan, Center for Political Studies [producer and distributor], 1995–2010. These materials are based on work supported by the National Science Foundation under Grant Nos.: SBR-9707741, SBR-9317631, SES-9209410, SES-9009379, SES-8808361, SES-8341310, SES-8207580, and SOC77-08885. Any opinions, findings, and conclusions or recommendations expressed in these materials are those of the author(s) and do not necessarily reflect those of the National Science Foundation.

T3 Source: Gallup Poll, responses to the question, "Do you approve or disapprove of the job Barack Obama is doing as president?," taken from the first monthly survey of the Gallup rolling average of 1,500 adults nationwide. See www.gallup.com.

T4 Michael X. Delli Carpini and Scott Keeter, *What Americans Know about Politics and Why It Matters* (New Haven: Yale University Press, 1996).

T5 Angie Drobnic Holan, "Palin 'Death Panel' Claim Sets Truth-O-Meter Ablaze." Politifact. com, at http://politifact.com/truth-o-meter/ar-

SES-8207580, and SOC77-08885. Any opinions, findings, and conclusions or recommendations expressed in these materials are those of the author(s) and do not necessarily reflect those of the National Science Foundation.

T14 Data from 2000 General Social Survey, http://www.icpsr.umich.edu/GSS/.

T15 For an interesting account of this phenomenon, see Roderick P. Hart, *Seducing America: How Television Charms the Modern Voter* (Sage Publications Thousand Oaks, CA 1999).

T16 Joe Antonio Vargas, "Obama's Wide Web," Washingtonpost.com, August 20, 2008.

T17 All photos in the Public Domain and all sourced from the U. S. Government with the exception of the Sarah Palin photo, which is in the Creative Commons and sourced by Therealbs2002.

T18 Data from 2000 General Social Survey, http://www.icpsr.umich.edu/GSS/.

T19 See Nate Silver, "Debunking the Bradley Effect," *Newsweek*, October 21, 2008.

T20 Data from 2000 General Social Survey, http://www.icpsr.umich.edu/GSS/.

T21 Ibid.

T22 Ibid.

T23 Data from National Election Studies, at http://www.electionstudies.org/nesguide/toptable/tab3_1.htm. The National Election Studies, Center for Political Studies, University of Michigan. Electronic resources from the NES World Wide Website (www.umich.edu/~nes). Ann Arbor, MI: University of Michigan, Center for Political Studies [producer and distributor], 1995–2010. These materials are based on work supported by the National Science Foundation under Grant Nos.: SBR-9707741, SBR-9317631, SES-9209410, SES-9009379, SES-8808361, SES-8341310, SES-8207580, and SOC77-08885. Any opinions, findings, and conclusions or recommendations expressed in these materials are those of the author(s) and do not necessarily reflect those of the National Science Foundation.

T24 Gallup estimates that about 5 percent of Americans still do not have a telephone, meaning the opinions of these people never have a chance of being included in the polling. They would still have a fair chance of being included if the pollsters information face-to-face, as they did twenty years ago, but telephone surveys are faster and more economical, so overlooking this group is a trade-off contemporary pollsters have decided to make.

Credits

CPSIA information can be obtained
at www.ICGtesting.com
Printed in the USA
LVOW03s0006011215
464736LV00005B/5/P